Reading STREET

Grade 6, Unit 4

Explorers, Pioneers, and Discoverers

PEARSON

Scott
Foresman

scottforesman.com

Editorial Offices: Glenview, Illinois • Parsippany, New Jersey • New York, New York
Sales Offices: Boston, Massachusetts • Duluth, Georgia • Glenview, Illinois
Coppell, Texas • Sacramento, California • Mesa, Arizona

We dedicate Reading Street to
Peter Jovanovich.

His wisdom, courage,
and passion for education
are an inspiration to us all.

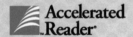
Accelerated
Reader®

Cover Dan Cosgrove

About the Cover Artist
As a kid growing up in Cincinnati, Ohio, Dan Cosgrove always liked to draw. After majoring in Graphic Design
in college, he worked for the National Park Service in Colorado and then for a design firm in Cincinnati. Now, he
works in Chicago, Illinois, drawing and designing in his studio overlooking the Chicago River, where he specializes
in both digital and traditional illustration for a variety of national clients. His work has appeared in numerous ads
and posters and on packaging.

ISBN-13: 978-0-328-24394-5

ISBN-10:   0-328-24394-9

Copyright © 2008 Pearson Education, Inc.

All Rights Reserved. Printed in the United States of America. This publication is protected by Copyright, and
permission should be obtained from the publisher prior to any prohibited reproduction, storage in a retrieval
system, or transmission in any form by any means, electronic, mechanical, photocopying, recording, or likewise.
For information regarding permission(s), write to: Permissions Department, Scott Foresman, 1900 East Lake Avenue,
Glenview, Illinois 60025.

Many of the designations used by manufacturers and sellers to distinguish their products are claimed as trademarks.
Where those designations appear in this book, and Scott Foresman was aware of a trademark claim, the
designations have been printed with initial capitals and in cases of multiple usage have also been marked with either
® or ™ where they first appear.

4 V088 10
CC:N1

Reading

STREET

Where the Love of Reading Begins

Reading Street Program Authors

Peter Afflerbach, Ph.D.
Professor, Department of
Curriculum and Instruction
University of Maryland at
College Park

Camille L.Z. Blachowicz, Ph.D.
Professor of Education
National-Louis University

Candy Dawson Boyd, Ph.D.
Professor, School of Education
Saint Mary's College of California

Wendy Cheyney, Ed.D.
Professor of Special Education
and Literacy, Florida
International University

Connie Juel, Ph.D.
Professor of Education, School of
Education, Stanford University

Edward J. Kame'enui, Ph.D.
Professor and Director, Institute for
the Development of Educational
Achievement, University of Oregon

Donald J. Leu, Ph.D.
John and Maria Neag Endowed
Chair in Literacy and Technology
University of Connecticut

Jeanne R. Paratore, Ed.D.
Associate Professor of Education
Department of Literacy
and Language Development
Boston University

P. David Pearson, Ph.D.
Professor and Dean,
Graduate School of Education
University of California, Berkeley

Sam L. Sebesta, Ed.D.
Professor Emeritus,
College of Education,
University of Washington, Seattle

Deborah Simmons, Ph.D.
Professor, College of Education
and Human Development
Texas A&M University
(Not pictured)

Sharon Vaughn, Ph.D.
H.E. Hartfelder/Southland
Corporation Regents Professor
University of Texas

Susan Watts-Taffe, Ph.D.
Independent Literacy Researcher
Cincinnati, Ohio

Karen Kring Wixson, Ph.D.
Professor of Education
University of Michigan

Components

Student Editions (1–6)

Teacher's Editions (PreK–6)

Assessment
Assessment Handbook (K–6)
Baseline Group Tests (K–6)
DIBELS™ Assessments (K–6)
ExamView® Test Generator CD-ROM (2–6)
Fresh Reads for Differentiated
Test Practice (1–6)
Online Success Tracker™ (K–6)*
Selection Tests Teacher's Manual (1–6)
Unit and End-of-Year
Benchmark Tests (K–6)

Leveled Readers
Concept Literacy Leveled Readers (K–1)
Independent Leveled Readers (K)
Kindergarten Student Readers (K)
Leveled Reader Teaching Guides (K–6)
Leveled Readers (1–6)
Listen to Me Readers (K)
Online Leveled Reader Database (K–6)*
Take-Home Leveled Readers (K–6)

Trade Books and Big Books
Big Books (PreK–2)
Read Aloud Trade Books (PreK–K)
Sing with Me Big Book (1–2)
Trade Book Library (1–6)

Decodable Readers
Decodable Readers (K–3)
Strategic Intervention
Decodable Readers (1–2)
Take-Home Decodable Readers (K–3)

Phonics and Word Study
Alphabet Cards in English and Spanish
(PreK–K)
Alphabet Chart in English and Spanish
(PreK–K)
Animal ABCs Activity Guide (K)
Finger Tracing Cards (PreK–K)
Patterns Book (PreK–K)
Phonics Activities CD-ROM (PreK–2)*
Phonics Activities Mats (K)
Phonics and Spelling Practice Book (1–3)
Phonics and Word-Building Board and Letters
(PreK–3)
Phonics Songs and Rhymes Audio CD (K–2)
Phonics Songs and Rhymes Flip Chart (K–2)
Picture Word Cards (PreK–K)
Plastic Letter Tiles (K)
Sound-Spelling Cards and Wall Charts (1–2)
Strategies for Word Analysis (4–6)
Word Study and Spelling Practice Book (4–6)

Language Arts
Daily Fix-It Transparencies (K–6)
Grammar & Writing Book and
Teacher's Annotated Edition, The (1–6)
Grammar and Writing Practice Book
and Teacher's Manual (1–6)
Grammar Transparencies (1–6)
Six-Trait Writing Posters (1–6)
Writing Kit (1–6)
Writing Rubrics and Anchor Papers (1–6)
Writing Transparencies (1–6)

Practice and Additional Resources
AlphaBuddy Bear Puppet (K)
Alphasaurus Annie Puppet (PreK)
Amazing Words Posters (K–2)
Centers Survival Kit (PreK–6)
Graphic Organizer Book (2–6)
Graphic Organizer Flip Chart (K–1)
High-Frequency Word Cards (K)
Kindergarten Review (1)
Practice Book and Teacher's Manual (K–6)
Read Aloud Anthology (PreK–2)
Readers' Theater Anthology (K–6)
Research into Practice (K–6)

Retelling Cards (K–6)
Scott Foresman Research Base (K–6)
Skill Transparencies (2–6)
Songs and Rhymes Flip Chart (PreK)
Talk with Me, Sing with Me Chart (PreK–K)
Tested Vocabulary Cards (1–6)
Vocabulary Transparencies (1–2)
Welcome to Reading Street (PreK–1)

ELL
ELL and Transition Handbook (PreK–6)
ELL Comprehensive Kit (1–6)
ELL Posters (K–6)
ELL Readers (1–6)
ELL Teaching Guides (1–6)
Ten Important Sentences (1–6)

Digital Components
AudioText CDs (PreK–6)
Background Building Audio CDs (3–6)
ExamView® Test Generator
CD-ROM (2–6)
Online Lesson Planner (K–6)
Online New Literacies Activities (1–6)*
Online Professional Development (1–6)
Online Story Sort (K–6)*
Online Student Editions (1–6)*
Online Success Tracker™ (K–6)*
Online Teacher's Editions (PreK–6)
Phonics Activities CD-ROM (PreK–2)*
Phonics Songs and Rhymes
Audio CD (K–2)
Sing with Me/Background Building
Audio CDs (PreK–2)
Songs and Rhymes Audio CD (PreK)

My Sidewalks Early Reading Intervention (K)

My Sidewalks Intensive Reading Intervention (Levels A–E)

Reading Street for the Guided Reading Teacher (1–6)

* INTERACTIVE WHITEBOARD READY

UNIT
4

Unit 4
Explorers, Pioneers, and Discoverers

Unit 5
Resources

Read It
Online
PearsonSuccessNet.com

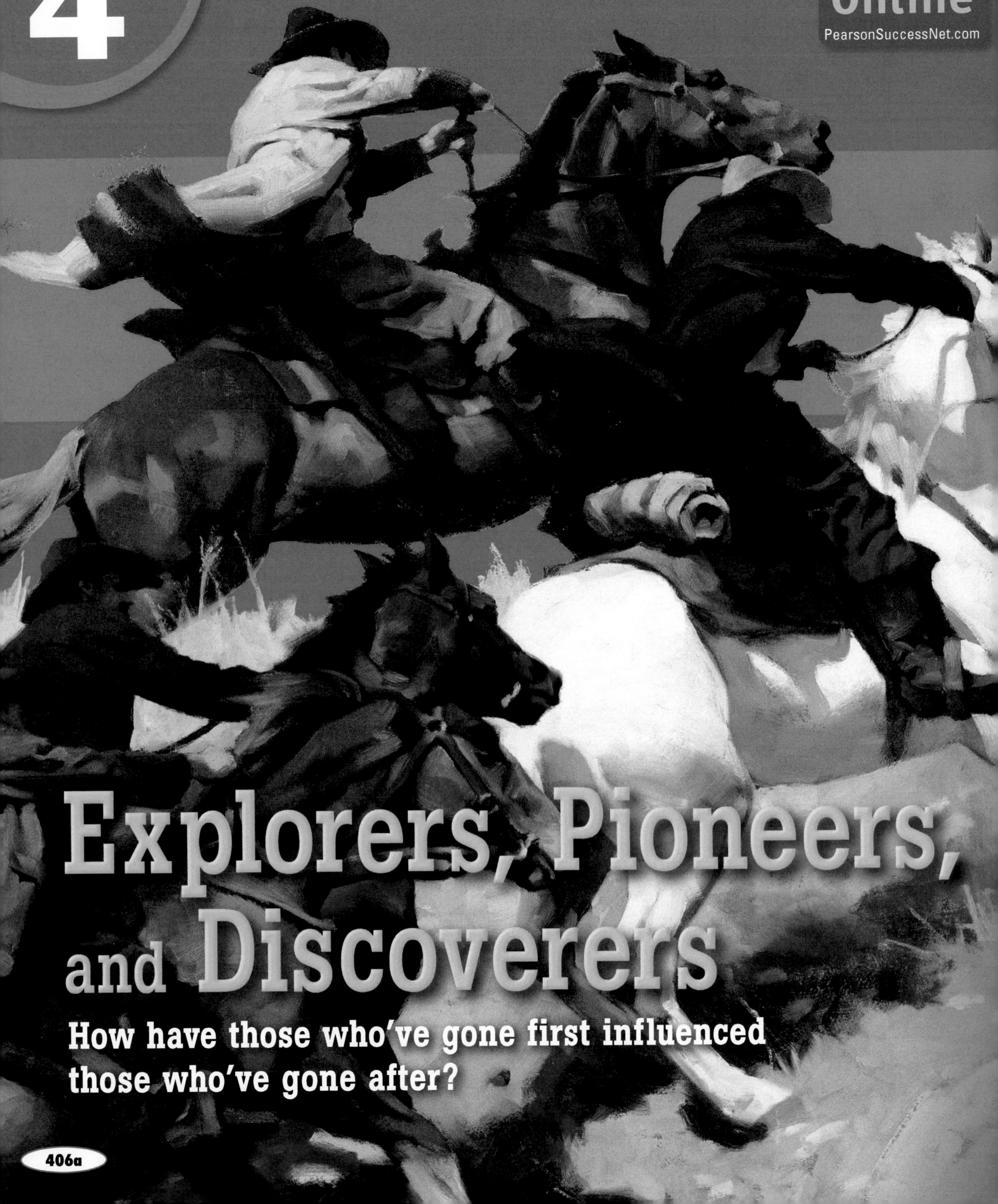

Explorers, Pioneers, and Discoverers

How have those who've gone first influenced those who've gone after?

Into the Ice

Explorers confront
harsh conditions.
NARRATIVE NONFICTION

connect to
SCIENCE

The Chimpanzees
I Love

A scientist learns about and
learns from chimpanzees.
EXPOSITORY NONFICTION

connect to
SCIENCE

Black Frontiers

African Americans move
west in the 1800s.
EXPOSITORY NONFICTION

connect to
**SOCIAL
STUDIES**

Space Cadets

A spaceship looks for
intelligent life.
DRAMA

connect to
SCIENCE

Inventing the Future

A scientist makes discoveries.
PHOTOBIOGRAPHY

connect to
SCIENCE

Unit 4
Skills Overview

412–429
Into the Ice/Polar Zones

What drives people to explore in harsh climates and dangerous places?

NARRATIVE NONFICTION

434–455
The Chimpanzees I Love/"Going Ape" Over Language

Why is it important to study animals responsibly?

EXPOSITORY NONFICTION

Reading		
Comprehension	T ⊙ **Skill** Cause and Effect ⊙ **Strategy** Summarize T REVIEW **Skill** Main Idea	T ⊙ **Skill** Author's Purpose ⊙ **Strategy** Answer Questions T REVIEW **Skill** Fact and Opinion
Vocabulary	T ⊙ **Strategy** Context Clues	T ⊙ **Strategy** Dictionary/Glossary
Fluency	Pauses	Pauses
Word Work		
Spelling and Phonics	Greek Word Parts	Prefixes *dis-, de-, out-, un-*
Oral Language		
Speaking/Listening/Viewing	Panel Discussion Analyze Media	Persuasive Speech Listen to a Speech
Language Arts		
Grammar, Usage, and Mechanics	T Subject and Object Pronouns	T Pronouns and Antecedents
Weekly Writing	News Story Writing Trait: Conventions	Story About an Animal Writing Trait: Word Choice
Unit Process Writing	Story	Story
Research and Study Skills	Diagram/Scale Drawing	Technology: Electronic Media
Integrate Science and Social Studies Standards	*Science* Ecosystems; Magnetism, Poles, and Weather	*Science* Resources, Adaptation, Animal Interaction, Animal Communication

⊙ Target Skill   T Tested Skill

 **How have those who've gone first influenced those who've gone after?**

WEEK 3	WEEK 4	WEEK 5
460–477 **Black Frontiers/ Poems by Langston Hughes** EXPOSITORY NONFICTION *What does it mean to be a pioneer?*	482–499 **Space Cadets/ Exploring Space Travel** DRAMA *How can we be open to new understandings?*	504–527 **Inventing the Future/ Garrett Augustus Morgan** BIOGRAPHY *How do inventions happen?*
T 👁 **Skill** Cause and Effect 👁 **Strategy** Prior Knowledge T REVIEW **Skill** Author's Purpose	T 👁 **Skill** Draw Conclusions 👁 **Strategy** Visualize T REVIEW **Skill** Sequence	T 👁 **Skill** Author's Purpose 👁 **Strategy** Monitor and Fix Up T REVIEW **Skill** Cause and Effect
T 👁 **Strategy** Context Clues	T 👁 **Strategy** Context Clues	T 👁 **Strategy** Word Structure
Tone of Voice	Characterization/Dialogue	Punctuation Clues
Words with *ci* and *ti*	Related Words 1	Word Endings *-ty, -ity, -tion*
Interpret Poetry Analyze Media	Newscast Listen to Media	Advertisement Analyze a Photo
T Possessive Pronouns	T Indefinite and Reflexive Pronouns	T Using *Who* and *Whom*
Describe a Setting Writing Trait: Sentences	TV Script Writing Trait: Organization/Paragraphs	Summary Writing Trait: Focus/Ideas
Story	Story	Story
Note Taking	Follow and Clarify Directions	Advertisements
SOCIAL STUDIES U.S. History, Settling the West	Science Space; Travel and Probes	Science Inventions; Technology and Society

Unit 4
Monitor Progress

Predictors of Reading Success		WEEK 1	WEEK 2	WEEK 3	WEEK 4
WCPM	**Fluency**	Pauses 130–138 WCPM	Pauses 130–138 WCPM	Tone of Voice 130–138 WCPM	Characterization/ Dialogue 130–138 WCPM
Oral Vocabulary	**Vocabulary/ Concept Development** (assessed informally)	icebergs solitary thermometer	conservationists data expedition	herd legend rugged scout	galaxy planet solar system
	Lesson Vocabulary	✿ ◉ **Strategy** Context Clues conquer destiny expedition insulated isolation navigator provisions verify	✿ ◉ **Strategy** Dictionary/ Glossary captive companionship existence ordeal primitive sanctuaries stimulating	✿ ◉ **Strategy** Context Clues bondage commissioned earthen encounter homesteaders settlement	✿ ◉ **Strategy** Context Clues aliens barge hospitable molten ore refrain universal version
Retelling	**Text Comprehension**	✿ ◉ **Skill** Cause and Effect ◉ **Strategy** Summarize	✿ ◉ **Skill** Author's Purpose ✿ ◉ **Strategy** Answer Questions	✿ ◉ **Skill** Cause and Effect ◉ **Strategy** Prior Knowledge	✿ ◉ **Skill** Draw Conclusions ◉ **Strategy** Visualize

◉ **Target Skill**   ✿ **SuccessTracker/Unit 4 Benchmark Tested Skills**

Make Data–Driven Decisions

Data Management
- Assess
- Diagnose
- Prescribe
- Disaggregate

Classroom Management
- Monitor Progress
- Group
- Differentiate Instruction
- Inform Parents

Success Tracker™

ONLINE CLASSROOM

WEEK 5

Punctuation Clues
130–138 wcpm

contemplated
invaluable
model

⭐ 🎧 **Strategy** Word
Structure

converts
devise
efficiency
generated
percentage
proclaimed
reproduce
transmitted

⭐ 🎧 **Skill** Author's
Purpose

🎧 **Strategy**
Monitor and
Fix Up

🔴 Manage Data

- Assign the Unit 4 Benchmark Test for students to take online.

- SuccessTracker records results and generates reports by school, grade, classroom, or student.

- Use reports to disaggregate and aggregate Unit 4 skills and standards data to monitor progress.

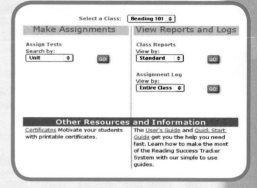

- Based on class lists created to support the categories important for AYP (gender, ethnicity, migrant education, English proficiency, disabilities, economic status), reports let you track adequate yearly progress every six weeks.

🔴 Group

- Use results from Unit 4 Benchmark Tests taken online through SuccessTracker to regroup students.

- Reports in SuccessTracker suggest appropriate groups for students based on test results.

🔴 Individualize Instruction

- Tests are correlated to Unit 4 tested skills and standards so that prescriptions for individual teaching and learning plans can be created.

- Individualized prescriptions target instruction and accelerate student progress toward learning outcome goals.

- Prescriptions include resources to reteach Unit 4 skills and standards.

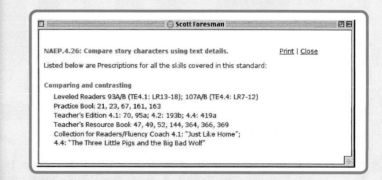

Unit 4
Grouping for AYP

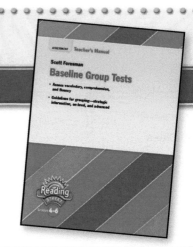

STEP 1

Diagnose and Differentiate

Diagnose
To make initial grouping decisions, use the Baseline Group Test or another initial placement test. Depending on your student's ability levels, you may have more than one of each group.

Differentiate

If... student performance is	Below-Level	**then...** use the regular instruction and the daily Strategic Intervention lessons, pp. DI·2–DI·51, throughout each selection.
If... student performance is	On-Level	**then...** use the regular instruction for On-Level learners throughout each selection.
If... student performance is	Advanced	**then...** use the regular instruction and the daily instruction for Advanced learners, pp. DI·3–DI·51.

Group Time

On-Level

- Explicit instructional routines teach core skills and strategies.
- Independent activities provide practice for core skills and extension and enrichment options.
- Leveled readers (pp. LR1–LR45) provide additional reading and practice with core skills and vocabulary.

Strategic Intervention

- Daily Strategic Intervention lessons provide more intensive instruction, more scaffolding, more practice with critical skills, and more opportunities to respond.
- Reteach lessons (pp. DI·52–DI·56) provide additional instructional opportunities with target skills.
- Leveled readers (pp, LR1–LR45) build background for the selections and practice target skills and vocabulary.

Advanced

- Daily Advanced lessons provide compacted instruction for accelerated learning, options for investigative work, and challenging reading content.
- Leveled readers (pp. LR1–LR45) provide additional reading tied to lesson concepts.

Additional opportunities to differentiate instruction:
- Reteach Lessons, pp. DI·52–DI·56
- Leveled Reader Instruction and Leveled Practice, pp. LR1–LR45
- My Sidewalks on Scott Foresman Reading Street Intensive Reading Intervention Program

4-Step Plan for Assessment

1 Diagnose and Differentiate
2 Monitor Progress
3 Assess and Regroup
4 Summative Assessment

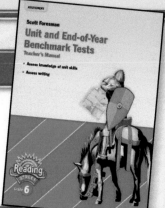

Monitor Progress

STEP 2

- **Guiding comprehension questions** and skill and strategy instruction during reading
- **Monitor Progress boxes** to check comprehension and vocabulary
- **Weekly Assessments** on Day 3 for comprehension, Day 4 for fluency, and Day 5 for vocabulary
- **Practice Book** pages at point of use
- **Weekly Selection Tests** or **Fresh Reads for Differentiated Test Practice**

Assess and Regroup

STEP 3

- **Days 3, 4, and 5 Assessments** Record results of weekly Days 3, 4, and 5 assessments in retelling, fluency, and vocabulary (pp. WA16–WA17) to track student progress.
- **Unit 4 Benchmark Test** Administer this test to check mastery of unit skills.
- Use weekly assessment information, Unit Benchmark Test performance, and the Unit 4 Assess and Regroup (p. WA18) to make regrouping decisions. See the time line below.

YOU ARE HERE
Begin Unit 4

SCOTT FORESMAN ASSESSMENT

Group Baseline Group Test → Assess → Regroup Units 1 and 2 → Regroup Unit 3 → Regroup Unit 4 (p. WA18) → Regroup Unit 5 → Assess

1 — 5 — 10 — 15 — 20 — 25 — 30 END OF YEAR

OUTSIDE ASSESSMENT

Initial placement ————————→ Outside assessment for regrouping ————————→ Outside assessment for regrouping

Outside assessments (e.g., DIBELS) may recommend regrouping at other times during the year.

Summative Assessment

STEP 4

- **Benchmark Assessment** Use to measure a student's mastery of each unit's skills.
- **End-of-Year Benchmark Assessment** Use to measure a student's mastery of program skills covered in all six units.

Unit 4
Theme Launch

Discuss the Big Idea

As a class, discuss the Big Idea question, *How have those who've gone first influenced those who've gone after?*

Point out that explorers, pioneers, and discoverers learn about the world by venturing into unknown areas or testing out new ideas. Others often benefit from the knowledge gained from their explorations and experiments.

Ask students what qualities explorers, pioneers, and discoverers have in common.

One example of a famous twentieth-century explorer is Neil Armstrong, the first person to step onto the Moon's surface. The success of this mission taught us a lot about the Moon and paved the way for others to explore space.

Theme and Concept Connections

Weekly lesson concepts help students connect the reading selections and the unit theme. Theme-related activities throughout the week provide opportunities to explore the relationships among the selections, the lesson concepts, and the unit theme.

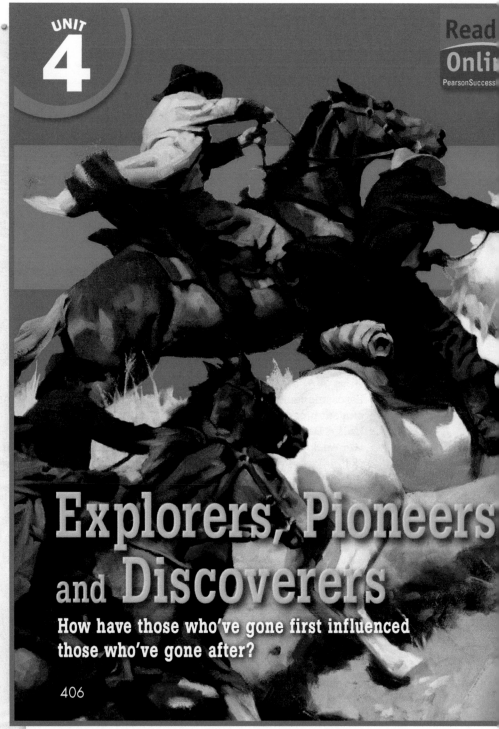

UNIT 4

Read Onlin

PearsonSuccess

Explorers, Pioneers and Discoverers

How have those who've gone first influenced those who've gone after?

406

CONNECTING CULTURES

Use the following selections to help students consider what happens when explorers make contact with other cultures.

Black Frontiers Have students discuss the cultural encounters that took place as African American pioneers moved west in the 1800s, establishing communities among white settlers and Native American tribes. Ask: *How do you think each group perceived the other groups?*

Space Cadets Have students imagine making first contact with another life form and how they would try to explain life on Earth to someone who had never been there.

Into the Ice

Explorers confront harsh conditions.

NARRATIVE NONFICTION

CONNECT TO SCIENCE

Paired Selection

Polar Zones

EXPOSITORY
NONFICTION

The Chimpanzees I Love

A scientist learns about and learns from chimpanzees.

EXPOSITORY NONFICTION

CONNECT TO SCIENCE

Paired Selection

"Going Ape" over Language

EXPOSITORY
NONFICTION

Black Frontiers

African Americans move west in the 1800s.

EXPOSITORY NONFICTION

CONNECT TO SOCIAL STUDIES

Paired Selection

Poems by Langston Hughes

POETRY

Space Cadets

A spaceship looks for intelligent life.

DRAMA

CONNECT TO SCIENCE

Paired Selection

Exploring Space Travel

ONLINE REFERENCE
SOURCES

Inventing the Future

A scientist makes discoveries.

PHOTOBIOGRAPHY

CONNECT TO SCIENCE

Paired Selection

Garrett Augustus Morgan

BIOGRAPHY

407

Unit Inquiry Project

Going First

In the unit inquiry project, students investigate the activities of a specific group of explorers, pioneers, or discoverers. They may use print or online resources as available.

The project assessment rubric can be found on p. 528a. Discuss the rubric's expectations before students begin the project. [Rubric] [4][3][2][1]

PROJECT TIMETABLE

WEEK	ACTIVITY/SKILL CONNECTION
1	**IDENTIFY QUESTIONS** Each student chooses a group of explorers, pioneers, or discoverers and browses a few Web sites or print reference materials to develop an inquiry question about this group and what it accomplished.
2	**NAVIGATE/SEARCH** Students conduct effective information searches and look for text and images that can help them answer their inquiry questions.
3	**ANALYZE** Students explore Web sites or print materials. They analyze the information they have found to determine whether or not it will be useful to them. Students print or take notes on valid information.
4	**SYNTHESIZE** Students combine relevant information they've collected from different sources to develop answers to their inquiry questions from Week 1.

ASSESSMENT OPTIONS

5	**COMMUNICATE** Students produce posters showing information about their groups and what they accomplished. Students may also create illustrated children's books and convey their research in a narrative nonfiction or historical fiction format.

Unit 4
Explorers, Pioneers, and Discoverers

CONCEPT QUESTION

How have those who've gone first influenced others who've gone after?

Week 5

Expand the Concept
How do inventions happen?

Connect the Concept

Develop Language
contemplated, invaluable, model

Teach Content
Scientific Inquiry
Phonographs and Music
Scientific Careers in Electricity
History of Traffic Signals

Writing
Summary

Internet Inquiry
Inventions

Literature

TIME FOR Science

Week 4

Expand the Concept
How can we be open to new understandings?

Connect the Concept

Develop Language
galaxy, planet, solar system

Teach Content
Light-Years
Search for Extraterrestrials
Alien Life

Writing
TV Script

Internet Inquiry
Life On Other Planets

Literature

TIME FOR Science

Week 3

Expand the Concept
What does it mean to be a pioneer?

Connect the Concept

Develop Language
herd, legend, rugged, scout

Teach Content
The Reconstruction Period
The Westward Movement
Native Americans and African Americans

Writing
Describe a Setting

Internet Inquiry
The Pioneer Experience

Literature

TIME FOR SOCIAL STUDIES

Week 1

Expand the Concept
What drives people to explore in harsh climates and dangerous places?

Connect the Concept

Develop Language
icebergs, solitary, thermometer

Teach Content
The Compass
The Polar Icecaps
Emperor Penguins

Writing
News Story

Internet Inquiry
Polar Explorers

Literature

TIME FOR Science

Week 2

Expand the Concept
Why is it important to study animals responsibly?

Connect the Concept

Develop Language
conservationists, data, expedition

Teach Content
Changes in Biodiversity
Competing for Resources
American Sign Language
Animal Communication

Writing
Story about an Animal

Internet Inquiry
Animal Research

Literature

TIME FOR Science

Read It
ONLINE
PearsonSuccessNet.com
• Student Edition
• Leveled Readers

Leveled Readers

◎ **Skill** Cause and Effect
◎ **Strategy** Summarize
Lesson Vocabulary

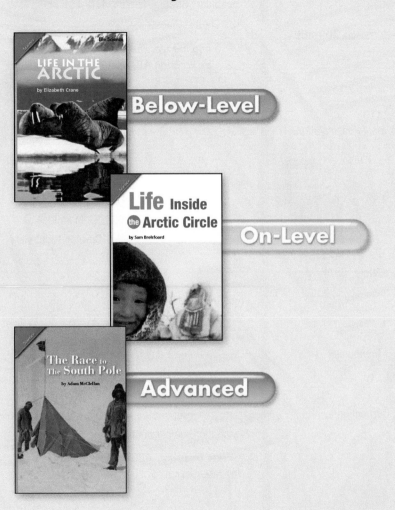

LIFE IN THE ARCTIC
by Elizabeth Crane

Below-Level

Life Inside the Arctic Circle
by Sam Brelsfoard

On-Level

The Race to The South Pole
by Adam McClellan

Advanced

Matthew Henson's Story
by Kenneth Neal Parker

ELL Reader
· Concept Vocabulary
· Text Support
· Language Enrichment

TIME FOR Science

Integrate Science Standards
• Ecosystems
• Magnetism, Poles, and Weather

✓ **Read**

Into the Ice, pp. 412–425

"Polar Zones," pp. 428–429

Leveled Readers

Below-Level
• Support Concepts

On-Level
• Develop Concepts

Advanced
• Extend Concepts
• Science Extension Activity

ELL Reader

✓ **Build**
Concept Vocabulary
Polar Exploration, pp. 408l–408m

✓ **Teach**
Science Concepts
   The Compass, p. 415
   The Polar Icecap, p. 423
   Emperor Penguins, p. 429

✓ **Explore**
Science Center
   Illustrate an Explorer, p. 408k

Weekly Plan

READING

45–90 minutes

TARGET SKILLS OF THE WEEK

- **Comprehension Skill**
  Cause and Effect

- **Comprehension Strategy**
  Summarize

- **Vocabulary Strategy**
  Context Clues

LANGUAGE ARTS

30–60 minutes

Trait of the Week

Conventions

DAY 1
PAGES 408l–410b, 429a, 429e–429k

Oral Language

QUESTION OF THE WEEK *What drives people to explore in harsh climates and dangerous places?*

Read Aloud: "20,000 Leagues Under the Sea," 408m
Build Concepts, 408l

Comprehension/Vocabulary

Comprehension Skill/Strategy Lesson, 408–409
- Cause and Effect **T**
- Summarize

Build Background, 410a

Introduce Lesson Vocabulary, 410b
conquer, destiny, expedition, insulated, isolation, navigator, provisions, verify **T**

Read Leveled Readers

Grouping Options 408f–408g

Fluency

Model Pauses, 408l–408m, 429a

Grammar, 429e
Introduce Subject and Object Pronouns **T**

Writing Workshop, 429g
Introduce News Story
Model the Trait of the Week: Conventions

Spelling, 429i
Pretest for Greek Word Parts

Internet Inquiry, 429k
Identify Questions

DAY 2
PAGES 410–421, 429a, 429e–429k

Oral Language

QUESTION OF THE DAY *What important difference led to one explorer's success and another's failure?*

Comprehension/Vocabulary

Vocabulary Strategy Lesson, 410–411
- Context Clues **T**

Read *Into the Ice: The Story of Arctic Exploration* 412–421

Grouping Options
408f–408g

- Cause and Effect **T**
- Summarize
- Context Clues **T**
- REVIEW Main Idea **T**

Develop Vocabulary

Fluency

Choral Reading, 429a

Grammar, 429e
Develop Subject and Object Pronouns **T**

Writing Workshop, 429g
Improve Writing with Answer the 5 W's and How

Spelling, 429i
Teach the Generalization

Internet Inquiry, 429k
Navigate/Search

DAILY WRITING ACTIVITIES

Day 1 Write to Read, 408

Day 2 Words to Write, 411
Strategy Response Log, 412, 421

DAILY SCIENCE CONNECTIONS

Day 1 Polar Exploration Concept Web, 408l

Day 2 Time for Science: The Compass, 415
Revisit the Polar Exploration Concept Web, 421

DAILY SUCCESS PREDICTORS
for Adequate Yearly Progress

Monitor Progress and Corrective Feedback

Vocabulary — Check Vocabulary, *408l*

RESOURCES FOR THE WEEK

- Practice Book, *pp. 151–160*
- Word Study and Spelling Practice Book, *pp. 61–64*
- Grammar and Writing Practice Book, *pp. 61–64*
- Selection Test, *pp. 61–64*
- Fresh Reads for Differentiated Test Practice, *pp. 91–96*
- The Grammar and Writing Book, *pp. 140–145*

Grouping Options for Differentiated Instruction

Turn the page for the small group lesson plan.

DAY 3
PAGES 422–427, 429a, 429e–429k

Oral Language

QUESTION OF THE DAY *What kind of person was Peary? Explain.*

Comprehension/Vocabulary

Read *Into the Ice,* 422–426

Grouping Options
408f–408g

- Cause and Effect **T**
- Summarize
- Develop Vocabulary

Reader Response
Selection Test

Fluency

Model Pauses, 429a

Grammar, 429f
Apply Subject and Object Pronouns in Writing **T**

Writing Workshop, 427, 429h
Write Now
Prewrite and Draft

Spelling, 429j
Connect Spelling to Writing

Internet Inquiry, 429k
Analyze Sources

Day 3 Strategy Response Log, 424
Look Back and Write, 426

Day 3 Time for Science: The Polar Icecap, 423
Revisit the Polar Exploration Concept
Web, 429c

DAY 4
PAGES 428–429a, 429e–429k

Oral Language

QUESTION OF THE DAY *What does it take for an animal or a person to survive in the Arctic?*

Comprehension/Vocabulary

Read "Polar Zones," 428–429

Grouping Options
408f–408g

Expository Nonfiction
Reading Across Texts
Content-Area Vocabulary

Fluency

Partner Reading, 429a

Grammar, 429f
Practice Subject and Object Pronouns for
Standardized Tests **T**

Writing Workshop, 429h
Draft, Revise, and Publish

Spelling, 429j
Provide a Strategy

Internet Inquiry, 429k
Synthesize Information

Day 4 Writing Across Texts, 429

Day 4 Time for Science: Emperor Penguins, 429

DAY 5
PAGES 429a–429l

Oral Language

QUESTION OF THE WEEK *To wrap up the week, revisit the Day 1 question.*
Build Concept Vocabulary, 429c

Fluency

Read Leveled Readers

Grouping Options 408f–408g

Assess Reading Rate, 429a

Comprehension/Vocabulary

- Reteach Cause and Effect, 429b **T**
Tone, 429b
- Review Context Clues, 429c **T**

Speaking and Viewing, 429d
Panel Discussion
Analyze Media

Grammar, 429f
Cumulative Review

Writing Workshop, 429h
Connect to Unit Writing

Spelling, 429j
Posttest for Greek Word Parts

Internet Inquiry, 429k
Communicate Results

Research/Study Skills, 429l
Diagram/Scale Drawing

Day 5 Tone, 429b

Day 5 Revisit the Polar Exploration Concept
Web, 429c

KEY = Target Skill **T** = Tested Skill

Comprehension — Check Retelling, *426*

Fluency — Check Fluency WCPM, *429a*

Vocabulary — Check Vocabulary, *429c*

SUCCESS PREDICTOR

Small Group Plan for Differentiated Instruction

Daily Plan AT A GLANCE

Reading
Whole Group
- Oral Language
- Comprehension/Vocabulary

Group Time
Differentiated Instruction

Meet with small groups to provide:
- Skill Support
- Reading Support
- Fluency Practice

Read

This week's lessons for daily group time can be found behind the Differentiated Instruction (DI) tab on pp. DI·2–DI·11.

Whole Group
- Fluency

Language Arts
- Grammar
- Writing
- Spelling
- Research/Inquiry
- Speaking/Listening/Viewing

DAY 1

On-Level	Strategic Intervention	Advanced
Teacher-Led *Page DI·3*	**Teacher-Led** *Page DI·2*	**Teacher-Led** *Page DI·3*
• Develop Concept Vocabulary • **Read** On-Level Reader *Life Inside the Arctic Circle*	• Reinforce Concepts • **Read** Below-Level Reader *Life in the Arctic*	• **Read** Advanced Reader *The Race to the South Pole* • Independent Extension Activity

(i) Independent Activities
While you meet with small groups, have the rest of the class...

- Visit the Reading/Library Center
- Listen to the Background Building Audio
- Finish Write to Read, p. 408
- Complete Practice Book pp. 153–154
- Visit Cross-Curricular Centers

DAY 2

On-Level	Strategic Intervention	Advanced
Teacher-Led *Pages 414–421*	**Teacher-Led** *Page DI·4*	**Teacher-Led** *Page DI·5*
• **Read** *Into the Ice*	• Practice Lesson Vocabulary • Read Multisyllabic Words • **Read** or Listen to *Into the Ice*	• Extend Vocabulary • **Read** *Into the Ice*

(i) Independent Activities
While you meet with small groups, have the rest of the class...

- Visit the Reading/Library Center
- Listen to the AudioText for *Into the Ice*
- Finish Words to Write, p. 411
- Complete Practice Book pp. 155–156
- Write in their Strategy Response Logs, pp. 412, 421
- Visit Cross-Curricular Centers
- Work on inquiry projects

DAY 3

On-Level	Strategic Intervention	Advanced
Teacher-Led *Pages 422–425*	**Teacher-Led** *Page DI·6*	**Teacher-Led** *Page DI·7*
• **Read** *Into the Ice*	• Practice Cause and Effect and Summarize • **Read** or Listen to *Into the Ice*	• Extend Cause and Effect and Summarize • **Read** *Into the Ice*

(i) Independent Activities
While you meet with small groups, have the rest of the class...

- Visit the Reading/Library Center
- Listen to the AudioText for *Into the Ice*
- Write in their Strategy Response Logs, p. 424
- Finish Look Back and Write, p. 426
- Complete Practice Book p. 157
- Visit Cross-Curricular Centers
- Work on inquiry projects

---

① Begin with whole class skill and strategy instruction.

② Meet with small groups to provide differentiated instruction.

③ Gather the whole class back together for fluency and language arts.

On-Level
Teacher-Led
Pages 428–429
- **Read** "Polar Zones"

Strategic Intervention
Teacher-Led
Page DI · 8
- Practice Retelling
- **Read** or Listen to "Polar Zones"

Advanced
Teacher-Led
Page DI · 9
- **Read** "Polar Zones"
- Genre Study

DAY 4

ⓘ Independent Activities

While you meet with small groups, have the rest of the class...

- Visit the Reading/Library Center
- Listen to the AudioText for "Polar Zones"
- Visit the Writing/Vocabulary Center
- Finish Writing Across Texts, p. 429
- Visit Cross-Curricular Centers
- Work on inquiry projects

On-Level
Teacher-Led
Page DI · 11
- **Reread** Leveled Reader *Life Inside the Arctic Circle*
- Retell *Life Inside the Arctic Circle*

Strategic Intervention
Teacher-Led
Page DI · 10
- **Reread** Leveled Reader *Life in the Arctic*
- Retell *Life in the Arctic*

Advanced
Teacher-Led
Page DI · 11
- **Reread** Leveled Reader *The Race to the South Pole*
- Share Extension Activity

DAY 5

ⓘ Independent Activities

While you meet with small groups, have the rest of the class...

- Visit the Reading/Library Center
- Complete Practice Book pp. 158–160
- Visit Cross-Curricular Centers
- Work on inquiry projects

Grouping Place English language learners in the groups that correspond to their reading abilities in English.

Use the appropriate Leveled Reader or other text at students' instructional level.

TIP Send home the appropriate Multilingual Summary of the main selection on Day 1.

Take It to the NET™ ONLINE
PearsonSuccessNet.com

Jeanne Paratore
For ideas on using repeated readings, see the article "Using Repeated Readings to Promote Reading Success . . . " by J. Turpie and Scott Foresman author J. Paratore.

TEACHER TALK

Fluency is the ability to read words and connected text rapidly, accurately, and smoothly. Fluency may be measured in words correct per minute.

Be sure to schedule time for students to work on the unit inquiry project "Going First." This week students research the accomplishments of a group of explorers, pioneers, or discoverers and develop an inquiry question.

Looking Ahead

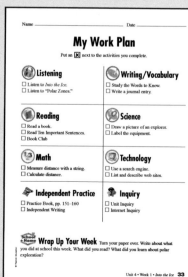

▲ **Group-Time Survival Guide**
p. 33, Weekly Contract

Customize Your Plan *by Strand*

ORAL LANGUAGE

Science

Concept Development

What drives people to explore in harsh climates and dangerous places?

CONCEPT VOCABULARY
icebergs   solitary   thermometer

BUILD

☐ **Question of the Week** Introduce and discuss the question of the week. This week students will read a variety of texts and work on projects related to the concept *polar exploration*. Post the question for students to refer to throughout the week. DAY 1 *408d*

☐ **Read Aloud** Read aloud from "20,000 Leagues Under the Sea." Then begin a web to build concepts and concept vocabulary related to this week's lesson and the unit theme, Explorers, Pioneers, and Discoverers. Introduce the concept words *icebergs, solitary,* and *thermometer* and have students place them on the web. Display the web for use throughout the week. DAY 1 *408l–408m*

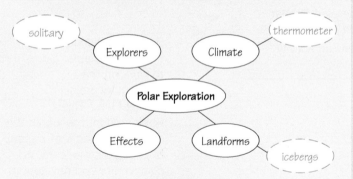

DEVELOP

☐ **Question of the Day** Use the prompts from the Weekly Plan to engage students in conversations related to this week's reading and the unit theme. **EVERY DAY** *408d–408e*

☐ **Concept Vocabulary Web** Revisit the Polar Exploration Concept Web and encourage students to add concept words from their reading and life experiences. DAY 2 *421*, DAY 3 *425*

CONNECT

☐ **Looking Back/Moving Forward** Revisit the Polar Exploration Concept Web and discuss how it relates to this week's lesson and the unit theme. Then make connections to next week's lesson. DAY 5 *429c*

CHECK

☐ **Concept Vocabulary Web** Use the Polar Exploration Concept Web to check students' understanding of the concept vocabulary words *icebergs, solitary,* and *thermometer*. DAY 1 *408l*, DAY 5 *429c*

VOCABULARY

☐ **STRATEGY CONTEXT CLUES**
Context is the words and sentences around an unknown word. When you come across an unfamiliar word as you read, you can often find clues in the context around the word. The author may give a definition, an example, a synonym or antonym, or a relationship in the context that will help you figure out the meaning of the word you don't know.

LESSON VOCABULARY
conquer   isolation
destiny   navigator
expedition   provisions
insulated   verify

TEACH

☐ **Words to Know** Give students the opportunity to tell what they already know about this week's lesson vocabulary words. Then discuss word meaning. DAY 1 *410b*

☐ **Vocabulary Strategy Lesson** Use the vocabulary strategy lesson in the Student Edition to introduce and model this week's strategy, *context clues*. DAY 2 *410–411*

Vocabulary Strategy Lesson

PRACTICE/APPLY

☐ **Leveled Text** Read the lesson vocabulary in the context of leveled text. DAY 1 *LR1–LR9*

☐ **Words in Context** Read the lesson vocabulary and apply *context clues* in the context of *Into the Ice*. DAY 2 *412–421*, DAY 3 *422–426*

☐ **Writing/Vocabulary Center** Write a journal entry as an explorer. **ANY DAY** *408k*

☐ **Homework** Practice Book pp. 154–155. DAY 1 *410b*, DAY 2 *411*

Leveled Readers

Main Selection—Nonfiction

☐ **Word Play** Have students list descriptive words and phrases from the selection, then use them to write their own descriptions of the North Pole and the polar icecap. **ANY DAY** *429c*

ASSESS

☐ **Selection Test** Use the Selection Test to determine students' understanding of the lesson vocabulary words. DAY 3

RETEACH/REVIEW

☐ **Reteach Lesson** If necessary, use this lesson to reteach and review *context clues*. DAY 5 *429c*

① Use assessment data to determine your instructional focus.

② Preview this week's instruction by strand.

③ Choose instructional activities that meet the needs of your classroom.

COMPREHENSION

◉ **SKILL CAUSE AND EFFECT** A cause is what makes something happen. An effect is something that happens as a result of a cause. Causes and effects are related to each other in a chain of events.

◉ **STRATEGY SUMMARIZE** To summarize means to briefly state important information about something. To help you understand the chain of cause and effect in a selection, make a list or graphic organizer of causes and effects as you read.

TEACH

❑ **Skill/Strategy Lesson** Use the skill/strategy lesson in the Student Edition to introduce and model *cause and effect* and *summarize*. DAY 1 *408-409*

❑ **Extend Skills** Teach tone. ANY DAY *429b*

Skill/Strategy Lesson

PRACTICE/APPLY

❑ **Leveled Text** Apply *cause and effect* and *summarize* to read leveled text. DAY 1 *LR1-LR9*

❑ **Skills and Strategies in Context** Read *Into the Ice*, using the Guiding Comprehension questions to apply *cause and effect* and *summarize*. DAY 2 *412-421*, DAY 3 *422-426*

Leveled Readers

❑ **Skills and Strategies in Context** Read " Polar Zones," guiding students as they apply *cause and effect* and *summarize*. Then have students discuss and write across texts. DAY 4 *428-429*

Main Selection—Nonfiction

❑ **Homework** Practice Book pp. 153, 157, 158. DAY 1 *409*, DAY 3 *425*, DAY 5 *429b*

❑ **Fresh Reads for Differentiated Test Practice** Have students practice *cause and effect* with a new passage. DAY 3

Paired Selection—Nonfiction

ASSESS

❑ **Selection Test** Determine students' understanding of the selection and their use of *cause and effect*. DAY 3

❑ **Retell** Have students retell *Into the Ice*. DAY 3 *426-427*

RETEACH/REVIEW

❑ **Reteach Lesson** If necessary, reteach and review *cause and effect*. DAY 5 *429b*

FLUENCY

SKILL PAUSES Pausing means to stop at appropriate places in longer, more complex sentences when you read aloud. Pausing helps listeners to follow and understand the text more easily.

TEACH

❑ **Read Aloud** Model fluent reading by rereading from "20,000 Leagues Under the Sea." Focus on this week's fluency skill, pauses. DAY 1 *408l-408m, 429a*

PRACTICE/APPLY

❑ **Choral Reading** Read aloud selected paragraphs from *Into the Ice*, having students notice how you pause during and after longer sentences. Then practice as a class by doing three choral readings of the selected paragraphs DAY 2 *429a*, DAY 3 *429a*

❑ **Partner Reading** Partners practice reading aloud, pausing at appropriate places, and offering each other feedback. As students reread, monitor their progress toward their individual fluency goals. DAY 4 *429a*

❑ **Listening Center** Have students follow along with the AudioText for this week's selections. ANY DAY *408j*

❑ **Reading/Library Center** Have students reread a selection of their choice. ANY DAY *408j*

❑ **Fluency Coach** Have students use Fluency Coach to listen to fluent readings or practice reading on their own. ANY DAY

ASSESS

❑ **Check Fluency** WCPM Do a one-minute timed reading, paying special attention to this week's skill—pauses. Provide feedback for each student. DAY 5 *429a*

☑ Customize Your Plan *by Strand*

SKILL SUBJECT AND OBJECT PRONOUNS A subject pronoun is a personal pronoun used as the subject of a sentence. Subject pronouns are *I, she, he, it, we, they,* and *you.* An object pronoun is a personal pronoun used as a direct or indirect object or an object of a preposition. Object pronouns are *me, him, her, it, us, them,* and *you.*

TEACH

❑ **Grammar Transparency 16** Use Grammar Transparency 16 to teach subject and object pronouns. DAY 1 *429e*

Grammar Transparency 16

PRACTICE/APPLY

❑ **Develop the Concept** Review the concept of subject and object pronouns and provide guided practice. DAY 2 *429e*

❑ **Apply to Writing** Have students review something they have written and apply subject and object pronouns. DAY 3 *429f*

❑ **Test Preparation** Examine common errors in using subject and object pronouns to prepare for standardized tests. DAY 4 *429f*

❑ **Homework** Grammar and Writing Practice Book pp. 61–63. DAY 2 *429e,* DAY 3 *429f,* DAY 4 *429f*

ASSESS

❑ **Cumulative Review** Use Grammar and Writing Practice Book p. 64. DAY 5 *429f*

RETEACH/REVIEW

❑ **Daily Fix-It** Have students find and correct errors in grammar, spelling, and punctuation. **EVERY DAY** *429e–429f*

❑ **The Grammar and Writing Book** Use pp. 140–143 of The Grammar and Writing Book to extend instruction for using subject and object pronouns. **ANY DAY**

The Grammar and Writing Book

Trait of the Week

CONVENTIONS Conventions are the rules for written language. They are the signals that writers use to make their meaning clear to readers. For example, sentences begin with a capital letter and end with punctuation. Paragraphs are often indented to show where a new idea begins. Grammar and spelling follow patterns.

TEACH

❑ **Writing Transparency 16A** Use the model to introduce and discuss the Trait of the Week. DAY 1 *429g*

❑ **Writing Transparency 16B** Use the transparency to show students how Answer the 5 W's and How can improve their writing. DAY 2 *429g*

Writing Transparency 16A   **Writing Transparency 16B**

PRACTICE/APPLY

❑ **Write Now** Examine the model on Student Edition p. 427. Then have students write their own news stories. DAY 3 *427, 429h,* DAY 4 *429h*

   Prompt *Into the Ice* is the story of an actual Arctic exploration. Think about one interesting event from the story. Now write a news story about that event.

Write Now p. 427

❑ **Writing/Vocabulary Center** Write a journal entry as an explorer. **ANY DAY** *408k*

ASSESS

❑ **Writing Trait Rubric** Use the rubric to evaluate students' writing. DAY 4 *429h*

RETEACH/REVIEW

❑ **The Grammar and Writing Book** Use pp. 140–145 of The Grammar and Writing Book to extend instruction for subject and object pronouns, answer the 5 W's and How, and news stories. **ANY DAY**

The Grammar and Writing Book

SPELLING

GENERALIZATION GREEK WORD PARTS The Greek word part *hydro* means "water," *onym* means "name," *archeo* means "first" or "ancient," *chronos* means "time," and *crat* means "rule." Learning the pronunciation of Greek word parts will help with the correct pronunciation of any word that contains the Greek word part.

TEACH

❑ **Pretest** Give the pretest for words with Greek word parts. Guide students in self-correcting their pretests and correcting any misspellings. DAY 1 *429i*

❑ **Think and Practice** Connect spelling to the phonics generalization for Greek word parts. DAY 2 *429i*

PRACTICE/APPLY

❑ **Connect to Writing** Have students use spelling words to write an editorial. Then review frequently misspelled words: *were, they.* DAY 3 *429j*

❑ **Homework** Phonics and Spelling Practice Book pp. 61–64. **EVERY DAY**

RETEACH/REVIEW

❑ **Review** Review spelling words to prepare for the posttest. Then provide students with a spelling strategy—dividing long words. DAY 4 *429j*

ASSESS

❑ **Posttest** Use dictation sentences to give the posttest for words with Greek word parts. DAY 5 *429j*

Spelling Words

1. hydrant
2. chronic
3. archive
4. synonym
5. antonym
6. democracy
7. hydrogen
8. aristocrat
9. dehydrated
10. chronicle
11. hydroplane
12. chronology
13. archaic
14. homonym
15. synchronize
16. hydraulic
17. archaeology
18. anarchy
19. hydroelectric
20. bureaucracy

Challenge Words

21. hydrophobia
22. chronological
23. anachronism
24. pseudonym
25. aristocracy

*Word from the selection

RESEARCH AND INQUIRY

❑ **Internet Inquiry** Have students conduct an Internet inquiry on polar explorers. **EVERY DAY** *429k*

❑ **Diagram/Scale Drawing** Review the terms *diagram* and *scale drawing*, as well as the features associated with both. Then have pairs of students make scale drawings of a geographical feature mentioned in the selection. DAY 5 *429l*

❑ **Unit Inquiry** Allow time for students to research the accomplishments of a group of explorers, pioneers, or discoverers and develop an inquiry question. **ANY DAY** *407*

SPEAKING AND VIEWING

❑ **Panel Discussion** Have students stage a panel discussion on the polar explorers featured in *Into the Ice.* DAY 5 *429d*

❑ **Analyze Media** Discuss with students any television shows or movies they have seen that focused on polar exploration. DAY 5 *429d*

Resources for Differentiated Instruction

LEVELED READERS

▶ **Comprehension**
- 🎯 **Skill** Cause and Effect
- 🎯 **Strategy** Summarize

▶ **Lesson Vocabulary**
- 🎯 **Context Clues**

conquer | destiny
expedition | insulated
isolation | navigator | provisions
verify

▶ **Science Standards**
- Ecosystems
- Magnetism, Poles, and Weather

Leveled Reader Database

ONLINE

PearsonSuccessNet.com

Use the Online Database of over 600 books to

- Download and print additional copies of this week's leveled readers.
- Listen to the readers being read online.
- Search for more titles focused on this week's skills, topic, and content.

On-Level

Life Inside the Arctic Circle
by Sam Brelsfoard

On-Level Reader

Cause and Effect

- A **cause** is why something happens. An **effect** is what happens.
- Sometimes there is more than one cause of an effect, and sometimes there are multiple effects of a cause.

Directions Skim through the following sections of *Life Inside the Arctic Circle*. For each section, write one effect or trait that is unique to the people or animals of the Arctic. Then write the element of the Arctic environment that is the cause of this effect or trait. *Possible responses given.*

The Environment

Effect:	Cause:
1. An alarm sounds so school-children know when to go home at night.	2. The sun stays in the sky all night for six months of the year.

The Arctic Tundra

Effect:	Cause:
3. Birds like the willow ptarmigan have thick, downy feathers.	4. extremely cold climate in the Arctic

Chukchi

Effect:	Cause:
5. One group herds reindeer, and the other hunts marine mammals.	6. People use the different natural resources in the areas where they live.

Science and Research

Effect:	Cause:
7. Scientists have been able to learn a lot about the Earth's history.	8. The cold has preserved the soil for thousands of years.

On-Level Practice TE p. LR5

Directions For each of the following vocabulary words, use a dictionary to find the base word and its definition. Then write the suffix of the vocabulary word. *Possible responses given.*

Check the Words You Know
- conquer
- destiny
- expedition
- insulate
- isolation
- navigator
- provisions
- verify

Vocabulary Word	Base and Definition	Suffix
1. expedition	expedite; to speed up or make easy; to send off	-tion
2. isolation	isolate; to set apart from others; place alone	-tion
3. destiny	destine; cause by fate	-y
4. navigator	navigate; to steer or direct a ship or aircraft	-or

Directions Answer the following questions based on the table above.

5. Think about the definitions of *expedition* and *isolation* and the definitions of their base words. What do you think the suffixes *-tion* or *-sion* mean?
the thing that happens when the action (base verb) takes place

6. Look at the definitions of *navigator* and its base word. What do you think the suffix *-or* means?
the person who does something

7. What do you think the word *conquerer* means?
the person who overcomes something or someone

8. What do you think the word *destination* means?
the place to which one is destined to go

9. What do you think the word *navigation* means?
the thing that happens when someone steers

10. Another spelling of the suffix *-or* is *-er*. What do you think an *expediter* is?
a person who speeds things up or makes them happen more easily

On-Level Practice TE p. LR6

Strategic Intervention

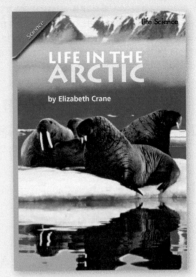

Life Science

LIFE IN THE ARCTIC
by Elizabeth Crane

Below-Level Reader

Cause and Effect

- A **cause** is why something happens. An **effect** is what happens.
- Sometimes there is more than one cause of an effect, and sometimes there are multiple effects of a cause.

Directions Several animals from *Life in the Arctic* are listed below. For each animal, elements of the Arctic environment have caused the animal to have special traits or effects. Write the effect of each cause. *Possible responses given.*

Polar Bear

Cause	Effect
1. Polar bears' white fur coat	helps disguise them in the snowy landscape, making it easier to prey on animals
2. Very cold environment	develop thick coats and a layer of blubber
3. Polar bears hunt seals and wait for them to come up for air	Polar bears wait by breathing holes waiting for seals to surface.

Arctic Fox

Cause	Effect
4. Color of its fur changes with the seasons	blends in with its surroundings so is less likely to be seen by predators
5. The ground is frozen	developed fur on bottom of feet
6. Small ears and muzzles	less skin is exposed so less heat is lost

Walruses

Cause	Effect
7. Have long, sharp tusks	helps them defend themselves
8. Filling up the air sacs in their necks	allows them to float and sleep at same time

Below-Level Practice TE p. LR2

Vocabulary

Directions Choose the word from the box that best matches each definition below. Write the word on the line.

Check the Words You Know
- conquer
- destiny
- expedition
- insulated
- isolation
- navigator
- provisions
- verify

1. a state of being alone __isolation__
2. to overcome __conquer__
3. to show that something is true __verify__
4. an adventure __expedition__
5. a guide __navigator__
6. fate __destiny__
7. kept warm __insulated__
8. supplies __provisions__

Directions For each of the following words, write your own synonym. Then use a dictionary or thesaurus to write another synonym. *Possible answers given.*

Vocabulary Word	Your Synonym	Synonym from a Dictionary or Thesaurus
verify	prove	confirm
conquer	defeat	surmount
insulated	protected	shielded

Below-Level Practice TE p. LR3

Advanced

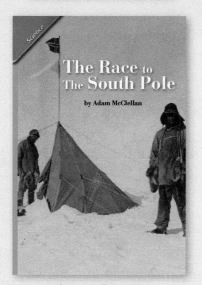

Advanced Reader

Cause and Effect

- A **cause** is why something happens. An **effect** is what happens.
- Sometimes there is more than one cause of an effect, and sometimes there are multiple effects of a cause.

Directions Use the reader *The Race to the South Pole* to answer the following questions.
Possible responses given.

1. In 1909, Ernest Shackleton attempted to reach the South Pole and came within 100 miles. What effect did his expedition have on the explorer Robert Falcon Scott?
   It made Scott even more anxious to reach the Pole himself.

2. What caused thousands of people to make offers to Robert Scott and thousands more to cheer as Scott sailed from London?
   Scott had announced that he would lead an expedition to find the South Pole.

3. What were the effects of Robert Scott's decision to spend time in Australia and New Zealand?
   Scott raised money and brought on supplies, had another festive send-off, and then ran into a fierce storm and seas thick with ice.

4. Look again at the timing of Roald Amundsen's expedition, on pages 6 and 9 of the reader. What was another effect of Robert Scott's decision to spend a long time in Australia and New Zealand?
   Amundsen was able to make up time against Scott, arriving in Antarctica only nine days after Scott.

5. What caused Roald Amundsen to leave flags at the South Pole, and letters to Scott and the King of Norway? Remember, there may be more than one cause for these actions.
   Amundsen wanted to prove he had reached the Pole first and wanted Scott to take the news to the world.

6. Look through the book again, paying close attention to the activities of the men on Scott's expedition. What factors caused Scott and four of his men to lose their lives?
   Some had been weakened by frostbite during research; the ponies had died, so they had to man haul their heavy supplies; there wasn't enough food; there were blizzards.

Advanced Practice TE p. LR8

Directions Read each of the following sentences. Select the word from the box that best completes each sentence and write it on the line.

1. When going on a ___trek___, it is important to make careful plans in advance for supplies, housing, and transportation.

2. The whistles of the boats in the harbor could be heard above the ___din___ of the crowd.

3. Antarctica is surrounded by ___turbulent___ seas, which makes approaching the continent extremely difficult.

4. The South Pole is one of the most ___remote___ locations in the world.

5. On treacherous expeditions like the one to the South Pole, it's wise not to make any ___rash___ decisions that might put people into trouble.

6. Amundsen was able to get supplies at ___depots___ on the first leg of his trip.

Check the Words You Know
- depots
- din
- expedition
- gangrene
- man hauling
- rash
- remote
- scurvy
- trek
- turbulent

Directions Write a paragraph about Robert Falcon Scott's fateful expedition to the South Pole. Use the words *gangrene, man haul, scurvy,* and *expedition* in your paragraph.

Responses will vary.

Advanced Practice TE p. LR9

ELL Reader

ELL Poster 16

Teacher's Edition Notes

ELL notes throughout this lesson support instruction and reference additional resources at point of use.

Teaching Guide pp. 106–112, 242–243
- Multilingual summaries of the main selection
- Comprehension lesson
- Vocabulary strategies and word cards
- ELL Reader 6.4.1 lesson

ELL and Transition Handbook

Ten Important Sentences
- Key ideas from every selection in the Student Edition
- Activities to build sentence power

More Reading

Readers' Theater Anthology
- Fluency practice
- Five scripts to build fluency
- Poetry for oral interpretation

Leveled Trade Books

- Extended reading tied to the unit concept
- Lessons in the Trade Book Library Teaching Guide

Homework
- Family Times Newsletter
- ELL Multilingual Selection Summaries

Take-Home Books
- Leveled Readers

Cross-Curricular Centers

Listening

Listen to the Selections

MATERIALS `SINGLES`
CD player, headphones, AudioText CD, student book

LISTEN TO LITERATURE Listen to *Into the Ice* and "Polar Zones" as you follow or read along in your book. Listen for causes and effects.

If there is anything you don't understand, you can listen again to any section.

Reading/Library

Read It Again!

MATERIALS `SINGLES` `PAIRS` `GROUPS`
Collection of books for self-selected reading, reading logs, student book

Select a book you have already read. Record the title of the book in your reading log. You may want to read with a partner.

You have the choice to read any of the following:

- Leveled Readers
- ELL Readers
- Stories Written by Classmates
- Books from the Library
- *Into the Ice*

TEN IMPORTANT SENTENCES Read the Ten Important Sentences from *Into the Ice*. Then locate the sentences in the student book.

BOOK CLUB Write a review of your chosen book. Post the review in the classroom for other students to read.

Math

Measure the Distance

MATERIALS `PAIRS` `GROUPS`
Pencil, paper, string, globe, *Student Book*

Find the number of miles Robert Peary traveled in *Into the Ice*.

1. Use the map on p. 425 of the student book to find where Peary began his journey. Tape the end of a piece of string to that same location on a classroom globe.
2. Extend the string to the end of Peary's journey. This information is given on p. 423. Measure the string.
3. The scale on the globe gives the number of miles per inch. Multiply the number of inches of the string by miles per inch in the scale. This will give you the number of miles in the journey.

EARLY FINISHERS Find the distance traveled in miles for the other explorers in *Into the Ice*.

Scott Foresman Reading Street Centers Survival Kit

Use the *Into the Ice* materials from the Reading Street Centers Survival Kit to organize this week's centers.

 **Writing/ Vocabulary**

 Science

 Technology

Write a Journal Entry

MATERIALS `SINGLES`
Writing materials

Imagine you are an explorer and write a journal entry.

1. **Choose the explorer from *Into the Ice* that interests you the most. Reread the part of the selection that tells about his expedition.**
2. **Write a journal entry that this explorer might have written. The journal entry should describe where the expedition is, the problems the men face, and what the weather conditions are like.**

EARLY FINISHERS Draw a picture that your explorer might have taken to record part of his journey.

November 4
Forty below zero today.
Bright sunshine. The lead
dog has injured his paw.
We may have to rest him
and put another dog in
his place.

Illustrate an Explorer

MATERIALS `SINGLES` `PAIRS` `GROUPS`
Art materials, writing materials

Illustrate an explorer equipped for survival in the Arctic.

1. **Draw a picture of an explorer in clothes appropriate for arctic exploration. Include needed equipment such as a compass, snowshoes, and axe.**
2. **Label the various items of clothing and equipment. Use call-out lines.**

EARLY FINISHERS List the items an explorer would be likely to include in his or her backpack.

compass

pick

snowshoes

Use a Search Engine

MATERIALS `SINGLES`
Computer with Internet access, writing materials

Use an online search engine to find out about your favorite explorer from the selection.

1. **Type an explorer's name in a student-friendly search engine.**
2. **Choose three sites. Do these sites provide interesting and useful information? Do they have photographs or maps that would interest other students?**
3. **Write down the URL for each site and describe what it has to offer.**
4. **Follow classroom rules when using the Internet.**

EARLY FINISHERS Discuss the differences between using the Internet for research and using the library. What are the advantages and disadvantages of each?

Search Engine

Peary

http://www.

 **ALL CENTERS**

OBJECTIVES

- Build vocabulary by finding words related to the lesson concept.
- Listen for causes and effects.

Concept Vocabulary

icebergs large masses of ice floating in the sea

solitary alone; by oneself

thermometer a device used to measure temperature, usually a narrow tube filled with mercury or alcohol

Monitor Progress

Check Vocabulary

If... students are unable to place words on the Web,	then... review the lesson concept. Place the words on the Web and provide additional words for practice, such as *navigator* and *isolation*.

SUCCESS PREDICTOR

DAY 1 Grouping Options

Reading

Whole Group
Introduce and discuss the Question of the Week. Then use pp. 408l–410b.

Small Group

Differentiated Instruction
Read this week's Leveled Readers. See pp. 408f–408g for the small group lesson plan.

Whole Group
Use p. 429a.

Language Arts
Use pp. 429e–429k.

Build Concepts

FLUENCY

MODEL PAUSES "20,000 Leagues Under the Sea" contains long sentences with multiple clauses. As you read, pause during the sentences at appropriate moments, rather than trying to read the longest ones in one breath. Look for punctuation marks such as commas that indicate pauses.

LISTENING COMPREHENSION

After reading "20,000 Leagues Under the Sea," use the following questions to assess listening comprehension.

1. **Why does Maury believe there are continents in the Antarctic Circle?** *(He believes that the presence of icebergs indicates a coastline; therefore, there must be a large landmass present in the Antarctic.)* ***Cause and Effect***

2. **Why does Captain Nemo say what he does in the last line of the excerpt?** *(Possible responses: He is unafraid because he knows he will not meet any enemies. Going into the unknown does not frighten him; it excites him.)* ***Cause and Effect***

BUILD CONCEPT VOCABULARY

Start a web to build concepts and vocabulary related to this week's lesson and the unit theme.

- Draw the Polar Exploration Concept Web.

- Read the sentence with the word *icebergs* again. Ask students to pronounce *icebergs* and discuss its meaning.

- Place *icebergs* in an oval attached to *Landforms*. Explain that the word *icebergs* is related to this concept. Read the sentences in which *thermometer* and *solitary* appear. Have students pronounce the words, place them on the Web, and provide reasons.

- Brainstorm additional words and categories for the Web. Keep the Web on display and add words throughout the week.

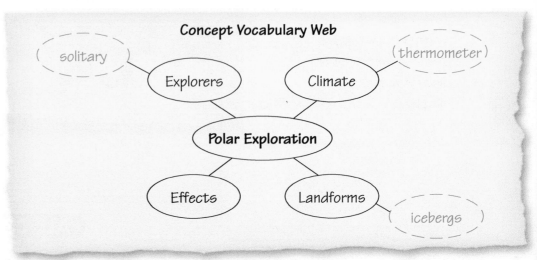

Concept Vocabulary Web

solitary — Explorers — Climate — (thermometer)

Polar Exploration

Effects — Landforms — (icebergs)

FROM

20,000 LEAGUES UNDER THE SEA

BY JULES VERNE

In the middle of the 1800s, science fiction author Jules Verne imagined what it would be like to explore the South Pole. In his novel 20,000 Leagues Under the Sea, *he tells of Captain Nemo and his miraculous submarine, the* Nautilus, *and their visit to what would later be known as Antarctica.*

I RUSHED on to the platform. Yes! the open sea, with but a few scattered pieces of ice and moving icebergs;—a long stretch of sea; a world of birds in the air, and myriads of fishes under those waters, which varied from intense blue to olive green, according to the bottom. The thermometer marked three degrees centigrade above zero. It was comparatively spring, shut up as we were behind this iceberg, whose lengthened mass was dimly seen on our northern horizon.

"Are we at the pole?" I asked the Captain, with a beating heart.

"I do not know," he replied. "At noon I will take our bearings."

"But will the sun show himself through this fog?" said I, looking at the leaden sky.

"However little it shows, it will be enough," replied the Captain.

About ten miles south, a solitary island rose to a height of one hundred and four yards. We made for it, but carefully, for the sea might be strewn with banks. One hour afterwards we had reached it, two hours later we had made the round of it. It measured four or five miles in circumference. A narrow canal separated it from a considerable stretch of land, perhaps a continent, for we could not see its limits. The existence of this land seemed to give some colour to Maury's hypothesis. The ingenious American has remarked, that between the south pole and the sixtieth parallel, the sea is covered with floating ice of enormous size, which is never met with in the North Atlantic. From this fact he has drawn the conclusion that the antarctic circle encloses considerable continents, as icebergs cannot form in open sea, but only on the coasts. According to these calculations, the mass of ice surrounding the southern pole forms a vast cap, the circumference of which must be, at least, 2500 miles. But the *Nautilus*, for fear of running aground, had stopped about three cables' length from a strand over which reared a superb heap of rocks. The boat was launched; the Captain, two of his men bearing instruments, Conseil, and myself, were in it. It was ten in the morning. A few strokes of the oar brought us to the sand, where we ran ashore. Conseil was going to jump on to the land, when I held him back.

"Sir," said I to Captain Nemo, "to you belongs the honour of first setting foot on this land."

"Yes, sir," said the Captain; "and if I do not hesitate to tread this south pole, it is because, up to this time, no human being has left a trace there."

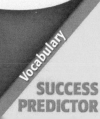

SKILLS ⟷ STRATEGIES IN CONTEXT

Cause and Effect
Summarize

INTRODUCE

Write the sentence *The cat meowed loudly* on the board. Challenge students to suggest a cause for this action and an effect of it. *(Cause: The cat was hungry. Effect: I fed the cat.)*

Have students read the information on p. 408. Explain the following:

- Causes and effects are related to each other in a chain of events. Each event causes the next one to happen. Then, that effect becomes the cause for another event. Remind students that many events have multiple causes and multiple effects.

- You can use the chain of causes and effects to help you summarize the events in a selection.

Use Skill Transparency 16 to teach cause and effect and summarizing.

Comprehension

Skill
Cause and Effect

Strategy
Summarize

Cause and Effect

- A *cause* is what makes something happen. An *effect* is something that happens as the result of a cause. To find a cause, ask yourself, "Why did this happen?" To find an effect, ask yourself, "What happened because of this?"

- Clue words such as *because, so,* and *due to* can help you spot cause-and-effect relationships.

- Sometimes there are no clue words, and a cause is not directly stated. When this is the case, think about why something happened.

Cause		Effect
what makes something happen	→	what happened

Strategy: Summarize

Good readers summarize by stating the most important information or ideas in an article or story. A good summary is only a few sentences long. It does not include minor details. As you read, you can make a list or graphic organizer of causes and effects to help you summarize. Then write a summary that includes all these important ideas.

Write to Read

1. Read "The Arctic." Make graphic organizers like the one above to note cause-effect relationships in the article.

2. Write a summary of "The Arctic." Listing important causes and effects as you read can help you.

408

Strategic Intervention

Cause and Effect Have students use a two-column chart to list causes and effects of world travel. (Causes might include *desire for adventure.* Effects might include *learned foreign language.*) Have students think about the possible causes and effects of traveling to the Arctic as they read p. 409.

ELL

Access Content

Beginning/Intermediate For a Picture It! lesson on cause and effect, see the ELL Teaching Guide, pp. 106–107.

Advanced Before reading "The Arctic," have students look at the map on p. 425 and share what they know about that area.

THE ARCTIC

Land and Water

THE ARCTIC IS located on the northernmost part of Earth. It is often considered to lie north of the "tree line," which marks where trees cannot grow because of frigid year-round temperatures. This area includes Greenland as well as parts of Alaska, Canada, Europe, and Siberia. It also includes the Arctic Ocean and, of course, the North Pole.

Ice and snow cover two-fifths of Arctic land year-round, while the rest of the land has grasses and shrubs. Ice covers more than half the Arctic Ocean all the time. This mass of jagged ice is called pack ice.

1 Strategy Stop here and summarize. What are the most important ideas you've read so far?

Arctic Temperatures

THERE ARE LARGE temperature differences throughout the Arctic. Due to Earth's tilt, the sun's rays do not even reach the northern Arctic during the winter. Yet the coldest Arctic temperatures are not at the North Pole. That's because the North Pole is located on the Arctic Ocean pack ice. Water—even as ice—slowly takes in heat during the summer. It slowly gives it off during the winter. The most extreme temperatures, then, occur on the land in northern Canada, Alaska, and Siberia.

On the pack ice, winter air is still and dry. Most of the water is already frozen. In fact, more snow falls in New York City!

2 Skill Clue words like *due to* help you spot cause-and-effect relationships. Why don't the sun's rays reach the northern Arctic in winter?

3 Skill Why aren't the coldest temperatures at the North Pole?

4 Strategy Summarize the entire article to remember its important causes and effects.

409

Available as **Skill Transparency** 16

▲ **Practice Book** p. 153

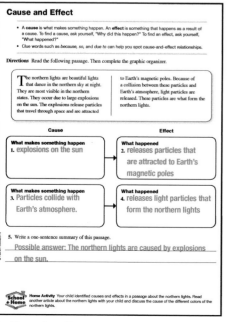

Practice Book p. 153

TEACH

1 STRATEGY Model summarizing the most important ideas and details.

Think Aloud **MODEL** These two paragraphs are about the land and water of the Arctic. To summarize the most important ideas, I would say that the Arctic, which is located on the northernmost part of Earth, is mostly covered with snow and ice.

2 SKILL Model answering the question for students.

Think Aloud **MODEL** The words "due to" tell me that Earth's tilt prevents the sun's rays from reaching the northern Arctic during the winter.

PRACTICE AND ASSESS

3 SKILL Possible response: The ice at the North Pole absorbs and gives off heat, which keeps the area warmer than areas on land.

4 STRATEGY Summary should include the main idea and key supporting details of the article.

WRITE Have students complete steps 1 and 2 of the Write to Read activity. You might use this activity as a basis for a whole-class discussion.

Monitor Progress

🔄 Cause and Effect

If... students are unable to complete **Write to Read** on p. 408,	**then...** use Practice Book p. 153 to provide additional practice.

Tech Files
ONLINE

Have students go online to learn more about the Arctic. Suggest that students use the keyword *Arctic* in a student-friendly search engine.

ELL

Build Background Use ELL Poster 16 to build background and vocabulary for the lesson concept of exploration in harsh climates and dangerous places.

▲ **ELL Poster** 16

Build Background

ACTIVATE PRIOR KNOWLEDGE

BEGIN A WORD WEB that describes the climate and geography of the North Pole.

- Have students begin word webs like the one shown. Have them write *North Pole* in the center oval of the web. The outer ovals should contain descriptive details about the Pole's geographical features, climate, and so on.
- Students can begin by filling in details they already know about the Arctic.
- Tell students that as they read, they can add details to the word web.

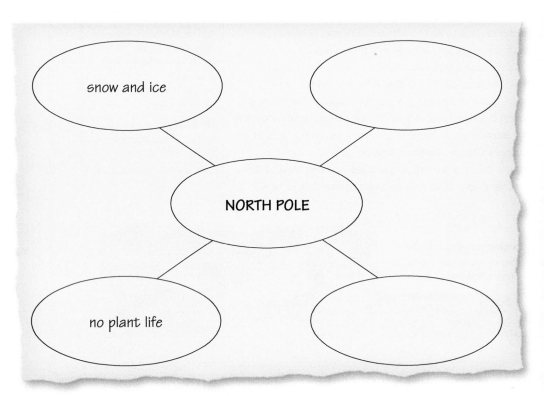

▲ **Graphic Organizer** 15

BACKGROUND BUILDING AUDIO This week's audio is an interview with Julie Hansen, who traveled to the North Pole. After students listen, discuss Hansen's experiences.

Background Building Audio

Introduce Vocabulary

VOCABULARY FRAME

Fill out a vocabulary frame for unfamiliar vocabulary words.

Word

Association or Symbol

Predicted definition: to fight

One good sentence:

George Washington and his soldiers conquered the British at Valley Forge.

Verified definition:

to take over by force

Another good sentence:

The Spaniards conquered the Inca in South America because they had

better weapons.

▲ **Graphic Organizer** 6

Read each word to students. Each student chooses a word that sounds familiar but that they are unable to define. Have students fill out the first half of the Vocabulary Frame for their chosen word based on prior knowledge. Then they can use the glossary or a dictionary to fill out the second half. **Activate Prior Knowledge**

Have students share where they may have seen some of these words. Point out that some of this week's words contain the suffix *–tion (expedition, isolation, documentation, unconventional)*. Remind students of how this suffix changes the meaning of the root word. **Suffixes**

Have students choose partners and write original sentences that use the vocabulary words. Have partners exchange lists of sentences and each partner make sure that the other has spelled and used the vocabulary words correctly each time. By the end of the week, students should be familiar with all the vocabulary words.

Use Multisyllabic Word Routine on p. DI·1 to help students read multisyllabic words.

Lesson Vocabulary

WORDS TO KNOW

T **conquer** to overcome; get the better of

T **destiny** what becomes of someone or something; one's fate or fortune

T **expedition** journey for some special purpose, such as exploration, scientific study, or military purposes

T **insulated** lined or surrounded with a material that does not conduct energy; protected from the loss of heat, electricity, or sound

T **isolation** the state of being separated from others, of being alone

T **navigator** person in charge of finding the position and course of a ship, aircraft, or expedition

T **provisions** a supply of food and drinks

T **verify** to prove to be true; confirm

MORE WORDS TO KNOW

documentation proof or support of a claim or opinion by evidence

unconventional not bound by or conforming to convention, rule, or precedent; free from conventionality

T = Tested Word

Vocabulary

Directions Choose the word from the box that best matches each definition. Write the word on the line.

conquer   1. to overcome; get the better of

verify   2. to prove to be true

destiny   3. what becomes of something or someone

navigator   4. person in charge of finding the position and course of a ship or aircraft

provisions   5. a supply of food and drinks

Check the Words You Know
___conquer
___destiny
___expedition
___insulated
___isolation
___navigator
___provisions
___verify

Directions Choose the word from the box that best matches each clue. Write the word on the line.

expedition   6. This is a journey taken for a special purpose.

insulated   7. This is done to keep something from losing heat by wrapping it with special material.

isolation   8. This is a state of being separate from the rest of the group.

verify   9. A witness is often called to do this to a person's statement in a trial.

conquer   10. This is what you try to do to your enemy in a war.

Write a Description
Imagine you have just explored the North Pole. On a separate sheet of paper, write a description of your trip there. Use as many vocabulary words as you can.
Descriptions should include words from the vocabulary list and details about the North Pole.

School + Home Home Activity Your child identified and used vocabulary words from *Into the Ice*. Write a poem together about exploring. Use the vocabulary words from the selection.

▲ **Practice Book** p. 154

Vocabulary Strategy

INTRODUCE

Discuss the strategy for context clues using the steps on p. 410.

TEACH

- Have students read "Exploring the Unknown," paying attention to how vocabulary is used.
- Model using context clues to determine the meaning of *conquer.*

MODEL The word *to* before *conquer* shows that *conquer* is a verb. The sentence says that it is something people do to unexplored places. I read on and see the word *battled.* I see that the paragraph describes how explorers battled their way to reach far away places. To *conquer* means to fight and win.

DAY 2 **Grouping Options**

Reading
Whole Group Discuss the Question of the Day. Then use pp. 410–413.

Small Group Differentiated Instruction
Read *Into the Ice.* See pp. 408f–408g for the small group lesson plan.

Whole Group Use p. 429a.

Language Arts
Use pp. 429e–429k.

Words to Know

conquer

destiny

expedition

provisions

insulated

navigator

verify

isolation

Remember

Try the strategy. Then, if you need more help, use your glossary or a dictionary.

Vocabulary Strategy
for Unfamiliar Words

Context Clues Sometimes when you are reading, you find a word that is unfamiliar. Often the author provides clues in the text that can help you figure out the meaning of the word. Look at the context, or the words and sentences around the unknown word, for clues.

1. Reread the sentence in which the unknown word appears.

2. Look for a specific clue to the word's meaning.

3. If there isn't one, think about the overall meaning of the sentence. Does that give a clue?

4. If you need more help, read the sentences near the unknown word. They may have clues or additional information that suggests the word's meaning.

5. Determine a meaning for the word based on any clues. Try your meaning in the sentence. Does it make sense?

As you read "Exploring the Unknown," use the context to help you figure out the meanings of unfamiliar words.

410

Strategic Intervention

○ **Context Clues** Have students begin by identifying the part of speech of an unfamiliar word.

Access Content Use ELL Poster 16 to preteach vocabulary. Choose from the following to meet language proficiency levels.

Beginning/Intermediate Point out the words *destiny, expedition,* and *provisions,* and explain that these words are Spanish cognates, or have related words. Let Spanish-speaking students share their knowledge of these words in Spanish.

Advanced Teach the lesson on pp. 410–411. Have students determine whether any of the tested words have cognates in their home languages.

Resources for home-language words may include parents, bilingual staff members, bilingual dictionaries, or online translation sources.

Exploring the Unknown

There have always been people determined to conquer the unexplored corners of the world. Whether they have battled their way to the top of the world, the bottom of the ocean, or the silence of the moon, explorers feel it is their destiny to be the first.

They plan, organize, and outfit their expedition. To improve their odds of surviving, they take along food, clothing, transportation, and tools. They gather everything they think they will need to protect them from the cold or the heat and the extremes of nature. However, for all their provisions and planning, they still are not insulated against the dangers of the unknown.

The navigator may be able to tell them exactly where they stand. Yet he or she can never verify that the group will make it safely there and back. Think of a little knot of people standing on Mars sometime in the future. They will have reached their goal. Nonetheless, in the cold and dark of space, they must feel keenly their isolation from all other humans.

Words to Write

What frontier would you like to explore? Write about your expedition. Use as many of the words from the Words to Know list as possible.

411

PRACTICE AND ASSESS

- Have students determine the meanings of the remaining words and explain the context clues they used.
- Remind students that a context clue will not always appear in the same sentence as the unfamiliar word. Sometimes students will have to read to the end of a paragraph to define a new word.
- If students began a vocabulary frame (p. 410b), have them check their work and revise it as needed.
- Have students complete Practice Book p. 155.

WRITE Writing should use lesson vocabulary words correctly.

Monitor Progress

Context Clues

If... students need more practice with the lesson vocabulary,	then... use Tested Vocabulary Cards.

Vocabulary · Context Clues

- When you are reading and see an unfamiliar word, use context clues, or words around the unfamiliar word, to figure out its meaning.
- Context clues include definitions, explanations, and synonyms (words that have the same or nearly the same meaning as other words).

Directions Read the following passage. Then answer the questions below.

Jared was preparing for their expedition. He was very excited about this journey. He packed their provisions: plenty of water and multigrain bars. He put their water in an insulated jug so it would stay cold. Tonight, his older brother would verify their route with their father, making sure it was the safest one possible. Tomorrow, Jared and his brother would leave early on their fishing trip. His brother would be the navigator of their fishing boat, because he knew the best fishing spots. Jared felt it was their destiny to catch enough fish for their dinner.

1. What does *expedition* mean? What clues help you to determine its meaning?
   a journey for a special purpose; The clue was the word *journey.*

2. Give examples of *provisions* mentioned in the passage. What is another example of a *provision*?
   water and multigrain bars; Possible answer: sandwiches

3. What does *verify* mean? What clues help you to determine its meaning?
   It means "to confirm, or to prove to be true"; His brother will check their route with their father.

4. What does *navigator* mean? Why is Jared's brother the *navigator?*
   The navigator is the person in charge of finding the course of a ship or expedition; He knew the best fishing spots.

5. Rewrite the sentence with the word *destiny* in it so that it contains a context clue.
   Jared felt it was their destiny, or fate, to catch enough fish for their dinner.

School + Home Home Activity Your child identified and used context clues to understand new words in a passage. Work with your child to identify unfamiliar words in an article using context clues. Have your child come up with original context clues that could be added to the article to help the reader understand the unfamiliar words.

▲ **Practice Book** p. 155

Prereading Strategies

OBJECTIVES

- Recognize cause-and-effect relationships to improve comprehension.
- Use causes and effects to summarize.

GENRE STUDY

Narrative Nonfiction

Narrative nonfiction tells a story about real people, places, and events. It is usually told in chronological order.

PREVIEW AND PREDICT

Have students preview the selection title, the question on p. 413, and the illustrations. Have them discuss what they think this selection will be about. Encourage students to use lesson vocabulary words as they discuss their ideas about the selection.

Strategy Response Log

Activate Prior Knowledge After previewing the selection, have students share what they know about the Arctic and the North Pole. Have students write down what they know about the region and what they would like to know in a KWL chart. Students will check their charts in the Strategy Response Log activity on p. 421.

Genre

Narrative nonfiction often recounts a series of events. Look for a number of related events as you read.

412

ELL

Access Content Lead a picture walk and point out illustrations of unfamiliar terms students will be reading in the selection. Notice the hot-air balloon with gondola on p. 418 and the picture of dog sledging on pp. 420–421. Ask students to also look carefully at the map on p. 425 and refer to it as they read.

Consider having students read the selection summary in English or in the students' home languages. See the Multilingual Summaries in the ELL Teaching Guide, pp. 110–112.

INTO THE ICE
The Story of Arctic Exploration

by Lynn Curlee

What kinds of obstacles would
a polar explorer encounter?

413

Pronunciation Key

Fridtjof Nansen (FREED-yuhf NAHN-suhn)

Hjalmar Johansen (YAHL-mar yoh-HAHN-suhn)

Roald Amundsen (ROO-ahld ah-MUND-suhn)

Solomon Andrée (SAH-lah-mahn an-DRAY)

Umberto Nobile (oom-BAIR-toh NOH-bee-lay)

SET PURPOSE

Read the first two paragraphs of the selection aloud to students. Have them look at what they wrote about the North Pole in their Strategy Response Logs. Students can compare their prior knowledge to what they have just learned from the selection. They can continue reading to see what else they can learn about the North Pole.

Remind students to identify and analyze causes and effects as they read.

STRATEGY RECALL

Students have now used these before-reading strategies:

- preview the selection to be aware of its genre, features, and possible content;
- activate prior knowledge about that content and what to expect of that genre;
- make predictions;
- set a purpose for reading.

Remind students to be aware of and flexibly use the during-reading strategies they have learned:

- link prior knowledge to new information;
- summarize text they have read so far;
- ask clarifying questions;
- answer questions they or others pose;
- check their predictions and either refine them or make new predictions;
- recognize the text structure the author is using, and use that knowledge to make predictions and increase comprehension;
- visualize what the author is describing;
- monitor their comprehension and use fix-up strategies.

After reading, students will use these strategies:

- summarize or retell the text;
- answer questions they or others pose;
- reflect to make new information become part of their prior knowledge.

 **AudioText**

Guiding Comprehension

414

 Cause and Effect • Inferential

Why did Nansen want to explore the Arctic and find the North Pole?

Possible answers: Nansen was bold and adventurous. He wanted to challenge himself. He wanted to explore new places in order to better understand the world around him.

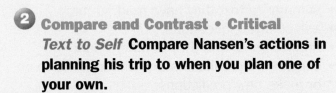
Monitor Progress
Cause and Effect

| If... students are unable to infer causes, | then... use the skill and strategy instruction on p. 415. |

2 Compare and Contrast • Critical

Text to Self **Compare Nansen's actions in planning his trip to when you plan one of your own.**

Students may say they like to plan a trip carefully.

Tech Files
ONLINE

Students can use a student-friendly search engine to find out more about Fridtjof Nansen and the *Fram* expedition on the Internet. Be sure to follow classroom rules for Internet use.

ELL

Build Background Explain that the northern lights, or *aurora borealis* are colorul lights that appear in the northern hemisphere. Encourage students to look for more information on *aurora borealis* on the Internet or in the library.

The great pioneer in the search for the North Pole was a brilliant young Norwegian scientist named Fridtjof Nansen. Also an athlete, outdoorsman, artist, and poet, Nansen wrote of the strange atmospheric effect called the *northern lights,* "The aurora borealis shakes over the vault of heaven its veil of glittering silver—changing now to yellow, now to green, now to red. . . . It shimmers in tongues of flame . . . until the whole melts away in the moonlight . . . like the sigh of a departing spirit."

In 1888, at the age of twenty-six, Nansen organized his first expedition—a trek across Greenland on skis, a feat never before accomplished. Dropped off by ship on the uninhabited east coast, Nansen and five companions had no choice but to ski westward to civilization, carrying only the provisions required for the one-way journey.

This kind of bold yet calculated risk-taking was typical of Nansen. He carefully planned every detail, even designing his own equipment. He also knew how to improvise off the land, adopting Inuit methods such as the use of dog sledges, kayaks, and snow houses.

After the Greenland trek, Nansen became interested in the idea of *polar drift.* In 1884, in the ice near Greenland, some debris was found from the *Jeannette,* a ship crushed in the ice off Siberia in 1881. There was only one possible explanation: the ice and debris had drifted around the entire Arctic Ocean. Nansen had a breathtaking proposal: he would sail a ship directly into the ice pack off Siberia, deliberately let it be frozen in, and drift with the ice across the top of the world, penetrating the heart of the Arctic.

Nansen's small ship, the *Fram* (*Onward* in Norwegian), was specially designed with a hull that would ride up over the crushing ice and living spaces insulated with cork and felt. Fully provisioned with scientific equipment and supplies for five years, the *Fram* had workshops, a smithy, and even a windmill for electricity. On June 24, 1893, the *Fram* sailed from Norway. By September 25, Nansen and his crew of twelve were frozen fast in the polar ice pack off Siberia.

Fridtjof Nansen and the Fram

415

The Compass

TIME FOR Science

A compass is a tool that determines direction. It contains a magnetic needle that always points north. The magnetic field on Earth will point the needle on the compass to where the force resides. The compass was invented in ancient China and was first used as a navigation tool in the 11th century.

SKILLS ◆▶ STRATEGIES IN CONTEXT

Cause and Effect

TEACH

- Remind students that a *cause* is what makes something happen. Something that happens as a result of a cause is called an *effect*.

- Sometimes readers have to infer the causes of certain events.

- Model inferring causes by analyzing why Nansen wanted to explore the Arctic.

Think Aloud

MODEL The selection doesn't specifically list any causes for Nansen's desire to explore the Arctic. It does tell me that Nansen was a bold outdoorsman and that he did things that hadn't been done before. Also, he was interested in the idea of polar drift, and he wanted to see if he could measure it.

PRACTICE AND ASSESS

Have students reread p. 415, paragraphs 3–4. Ask why Nansen decided to allow his ship to be frozen into the ice pack. *(He believed that the ice pack would drift toward the Pole, taking the ship with it and proving the theory of polar drift.)*

Guiding Comprehension

③ *Author's Craft • Critical*

Question the Author **How does the author make the setting come alive for the reader?**

Possible answers: The author uses sensory details to have the setting come alive for the reader. He repeats the word *ice* many times to emphasize the intense cold. He writes that the ships are completely surrounded by water, slush, and ice to give the reader a sense of the isolation and the constant dangers the explorers had to face. He also refers to the slow passage of time, which helps readers sense the monotony of an Arctic winter.

④ *Main Idea • Critical*

Why was the scientific expedition a "triumphant success"?

Students' answers should note that the purpose of the expedition, to prove the theory of polar drift, was accomplished. Also Nansen and Johansen had gone farther north than anyone before them.

Monitor Progress

(REVIEW) Main Idea

If... students have difficulty identifying the supporting details,	then... use the skill and strategy instruction on p. 417.

As they drifted slowly northward, the expedition settled into a routine of scientific observation. The ship was so comfortable that by the end of the second winter Nansen was restless and bored. Now only 360 miles from the North Pole, Nansen decided to strike out over the ice.

In the arctic dawn of mid-March 1895 Nansen set out with one companion, Hjalmar Johansen, three sledges of provisions, twenty-eight dogs, and two kayaks. As in Greenland, there could be no turning back—this time their home base was drifting. For three weeks they struggled northward, maneuvering the sledges over jumbled fields and immense ridges of broken ice. By early April they were still 225 miles from the Pole, and the drifting ice was carrying them south almost as quickly as they could push north. Provisions were also running low, so they reluctantly headed for the nearest land, three hundred miles to the south. As the weeks passed and the sun rose higher, the broken surface of the ice pack **③** became slushy, then treacherous as lanes of water called *leads* opened and

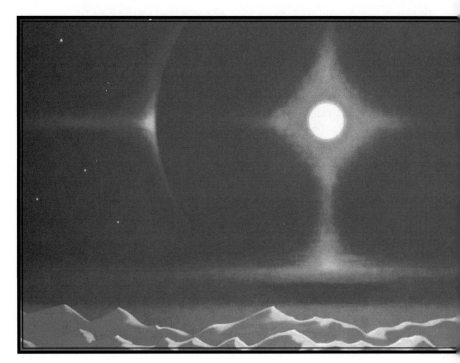

416

Extend Language Help students understand terms related to ice on pp. 416-417. *Ice pack* refers to ice that has been packed down hard. When ice melts, *leads* (lanes or long river-like areas of water) appear between *ice floes,* which are sheets of floating ice.

closed between the ice floes. It took four months to reach land. After provisions ran out, the men survived by hunting seals in the open leads and by feeding the weak dogs to the stronger ones.

Nansen and Johansen finally found a remote island. With no hope of rescue, the two men prepared for the winter, building a tiny hut and butchering walrus and bears for a supply of meat and warm furs. They survived the winter in isolation, burning greasy blubber for heat and light and growing fat on the diet of oily meat. When the ice broke up in the spring, Nansen and Johansen set out in their kayaks. On June 13, 1896—one year and four months after leaving the *Fram*—they were picked up by an English expedition. Two months later the *Fram* and its crew broke free of the ice in the ocean east of Greenland, more than a thousand miles from their starting point. The scientific expedition was a triumphant success, and Nansen and Johansen had gone farther north than anyone had before.

The Fram *drifts in the Arctic night.*

417

Main Idea REVIEW

TEACH

- Remind students that a main idea is the most important idea about the topic. Supporting details are those details that reinforce the main idea.
- Model identifying details that support the main idea that the expedition was a success.

 MODEL The text on pp. 416–417 provides details about the expedition. I can see that Nansen and Johansen faced many difficulties. But they were able to make many scientific observations accomplishing their goal with respect to polar drift, and they had traveled farther north than anyone else. So the expedition was a great success.

PRACTICE AND ASSESS

- Have students write the implied main idea of p. 416, paragraph 2. Explain that students have to read all the details and write the main idea in their own words.
- To assess, use Practice Book p. 156.

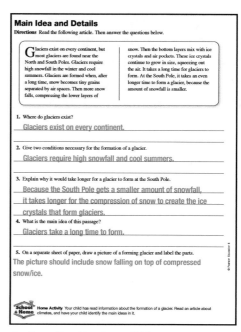

Main Idea and Details

Directions Read the following article. Then answer the questions below.

Glaciers exist on every continent, but most glaciers are found near the North and South Poles. Glaciers require high snowfall in the winter and cool summers. Glaciers are formed when, after a long time, snow becomes tiny grains separated by air spaces. Then more snow falls, compressing the lower layers of snow. Then the bottom layers mix with ice crystals and air pockets. These ice crystals continue to grow in size, squeezing out the air. It takes a long time for glaciers to form. At the South Pole, it takes an even longer time to form a glacier, because the amount of snowfall is smaller.

1. Where do glaciers exist?
   Glaciers exist on every continent.

2. Give two conditions necessary for the formation of a glacier.
   Glaciers require high snowfall and cool summers.

3. Explain why it would take longer for a glacier to form at the South Pole.
   Because the South Pole gets a smaller amount of snowfall, it takes longer for the compression of snow to create the ice crystals that form glaciers.

4. What is the main idea of this passage?
   Glaciers take a long time to form.

5. On a separate sheet of paper, draw a picture of a forming glacier and label the parts.
   The picture should include snow falling on top of compressed snow/ice.

Home Activity Your child has read information about the formation of a glacier. Read an article about climates, and have your child identify the main ideas in it.

▲ **Practice Book** p. 156

Guiding Comprehension

  Vocabulary • Context Clues

Use context clues to define the word *aeronautics* on p. 419, paragraph 1.

The clues "a flight to the pole in a balloon" and "Andrée was a Swedish engineer with experience in aeronautics" suggest that *aeronautics* means "the study or science of flight."

Monitor Progress
Context Clues

If... students have difficulty using context clues to define unfamiliar words,	then... use the vocabulary strategy instruction on p. 419.

  Cause and Effect • Inferential

Why did Andrée and his crew freeze to death?

Their balloon ran out of gas, and they landed on the ice, far from land. They wore themselves out struggling to reach an island. Once they reached land, they were unprepared to survive the winter.

418

Context Clues Use context clues to help students understand the word *aloft* on p. 419. Point out the phrases before ("the precious gas that kept them *aloft*") and after ("By the third day the *Ornen* was down on the ice"). Have students substitute words that make sense, then define *aloft* as "high in the air."

Now the race to the North Pole was on. Another daring attempt was made the very next year—a flight to the Pole in a balloon. Salomon Andrée was a Swedish engineer with experience in aeronautics and an interest in the Arctic. He had built a large hydrogen-filled balloon with a passenger gondola designed to hold three men, four months of supplies, sledges, and a small boat.

Developed more than one hundred years earlier, balloons were still the only means of flight in the 1890s. As transportation they have serious limitations: first, they cannot be steered; and second, they are sensitive to temperature changes. Andrée tried to solve the first problem with a complicated system of sails and drag lines. He completely ignored the second problem, and the result was disastrous.

In midsummer 1897 the *Ornen* (*Eagle* in Swedish) lifted off from Spitsbergen, an island north of Norway. As they sailed northward Andrée wrote in his journal, "The rattling of the drag lines in the snow and the flapping of the sails are the only sound, except for the whining of the wind." As the balloon was alternately heated by the sun and cooled by freezing fog, the precious gas that kept them aloft leaked away. By the third day the *Ornen* was down on the ice, two hundred miles from land. In the Arctic summer at the edge of the ice pack, Andrée and his two companions faced a terrifying world of slushy, grinding floes and open leads; it took them three months to struggle to the nearest island. But inexperienced and unprepared, they were unable to survive the winter. We know what happened only because thirty-three years later their frozen remains were found, along with Andrée's journal and another eerie relic—undeveloped images of the doomed expedition that were still in their camera.

PHYSICALLY THE NORTH Pole is nothing more than a theoretical point on the Earth's surface—but reaching it came to symbolize mankind's mastery of the entire planet—and a landmark human achievement. An American naval engineer desperately wanted to be the first explorer to stand on the North Pole. Robert E. Peary first entered the Arctic in 1886. For twenty years he mounted expeditions to northwest Greenland, looking for the best route north. Peary was not particularly interested in

The Ornen *comes down on the ice.*

419

VOCABULARY STRATEGY

Context Clues

TEACH

- Remind students that they can use context clues to determine the meaning of an unfamiliar word.
- Model using context clues to define the word *aeronautics* in p. 419, paragraph 1.

Think Aloud

MODEL I don't know the word *aeronautics*. Reading the whole sentence, I can see that it must have something to do with flight. But this doesn't give me enough information to define the word. When I read the whole paragraph, I can see that *aeronautics* has something to do with both flight and engineering. I think aeronautics must mean "the science of flight," but I'll look up the word in a dictionary to be sure.

PRACTICE AND ASSESS

Have students use context clues to define the word *floes* on p. 419, paragraph 3. *(The balloon lands on the ice, and the floes around it are described as "slushy and grinding." They are moving ice formations.)*

EXTEND SKILLS

Symbol

Remind students that a symbol is a person, place, or object that has a meaning in itself, but also stands for something outside itself. The first sentence in p. 419, paragraph 4, mentions the North Pole. As students continue reading, have them think about how the North Pole came to symbolize human achievement.

Guiding Comprehension

7 **Drawing Conclusions • Critical**

How do you think Peary's character contributed to his success as an explorer?

Possible answer: His arrogant personality made him run his expeditons like military campaigns, but his discipline and drive carried his crew to success.

8 **Summarize • Inferential**

Use your knowledge of the causes and effects of Peary's 1906 expedition to summarize the events of the expedition.

Peary's determination to be first caused him to pursue the goal of reaching the North Pole. The Polar Inuit people taught him many survivial skills, but Peary's expedition failed because of a blizzard. He did, however, set a new farthest-north record.

Dog sledging on the ice pack

scientific discovery or mapping. He had one goal: the glory of being first. Over the years, Peary came to believe that it was his destiny to conquer the North Pole.

Vain and arrogant, Robert Peary ran his expeditions like a military campaign. His chief lieutenant was his personal assistant, Matthew Henson, a man of African descent. This was unusual at the turn of the century, but then, Peary was unconventional in many ways. He also took his wife on some of his early expeditions. Josephine Peary was the first white woman in the High Arctic, and she gave birth to their daughter while on expedition. Inuit came from miles around to see the newborn blond "snowbaby."

As an explorer, Peary was innovative, taking ideas from everyone
7 and improving on them. But the Polar Inuit were the key to his success. Inuit women made his furs, and Inuit men used their own dogs to pull his sledges. They built his snowhouses on the trail and hunted for his

420

Understanding Idioms Help students understand the expression "full-scale assault" in the sentence, "In 1906 Peary made a full-scale assault upon the North Pole." Define *full-scale* as complete or using all resources. The term *assault* usally means attack, but here it refers to Peary using all resources available to reach the North Pole.

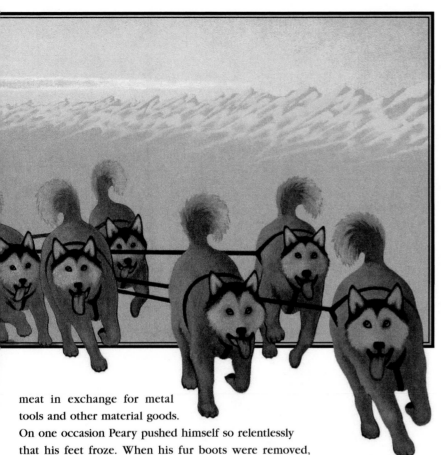

meat in exchange for metal tools and other material goods.

On one occasion Peary pushed himself so relentlessly that his feet froze. When his fur boots were removed, several of his toes snapped off. As soon as the stumps healed, he was back on the trail.

In 1906 Peary made a full-scale assault upon the North Pole. His plan was to take a ship as far north as possible, winter over in Greenland or the Canadian Islands, then strike out for the Pole in late February, before the ice pack started breaking up. The Arctic did not cooperate, however. When only a hundred miles out on the ice pack, the expedition was delayed several days by a broad lead, then a blizzard kept them camp-bound for another week. Supplies dwindled, and the disappointed Peary had to settle for a new farthest-north record, 175 miles from the Pole.

421

Develop Vocabulary

PRACTICE LESSON VOCABULARY

Students orally respond to each question and provide a reason.

1. Can an explorer reach his goal in *isolation*? *(No; he needs other people to help him on his journey.)*

2. Name one thing that can *insulate* you from the cold. *(A parka; insulate means "protect.")*

3. Can you go on an *expedition* at home? *(No; an expedition is a journey.)*

BUILD CONCEPT VOCABULARY

Review previous concept words with students. Ask if students have come across any words today in their reading or elsewhere that they would like to add to the Polar Exploration Concept Web, such as *iceberg* and *innovative*.

STRATEGY SELF-CHECK

Summarize

Ask students to summarize in one sentence of cause and effect the success of Peary's expedition. *(Possible response: Peary refused to give up in the face of difficulties, so his expedition set a new farthest-north record.)*

Students should identify specific events in the narrative that support their summaries.

SELF-CHECK

Students can ask themselves these questions to assess their ability to use the skill and strategy.

• Did I identify causes as I read about Peary's expedition?

• Did I connect the causes to their effects?

• How did this help me summarize what happened on the expedition?

Monitor Progress	
🎯 **Cause and Effect**	
If... students have difficulty using causes and effects to summarize,	**then...** revisit the skill lesson on pp. 408–409. Reteach as necessary.

Monitor Comprehension Have students compare their prior knowledge about the Arctic to what they have learned in the selection. (See p. 412.) Have them write down one thing they think they might find out as they continue reading.

If you want to teach this selection in two sessions, stop here.

Guiding Comprehension

If you are teaching the selection in two sessions, discuss cause and effect relationships so far and review the vocabulary.

 ⑨ Cause and Effect • Inferential

Why did Peary dislike Cook? What happened as a result of this?

Peary did not like Cook's attempt to draw attention to himself by publishing an article. The effect was that the two men quarreled, and Cook decided to try for the North Pole.

⑩ Summarize • Critical

Why was Peary bitter until his death, in spite of his achievements?

Peary claimed to have reached the North Pole first, but Cook said he had beaten Peary to it. Peary believed Cook lied, so Peary was bitter about the lack of credit for his achievement.

Monitor Progress

Summarize

If... students have difficulty using causes and effects to summarize,	then... use the skill and strategy instruction on p. 423.

 Grouping Options

Reading
Whole Group Discuss the Question of the Day.

Small Group *Differentiated Instruction*
Read *Into the Ice*. See pp. 408f–408g for the small group lesson plan.

Whole Group Discuss the Reader Response questions on p. 426. Then use p. 429a.

Language Arts
Use pp. 429e–429k.

422

Extend Language Help students understand the terms *claimed* and *claiming* on p. 423 by defining *to claim* as "to say very strongly that something is true."

Students can use a student-friendly search engine to find out more about Peary and Cook's rivalry. Be sure to follow classroom rules for Internet use.

After another appeal to the men who financed his expeditions, Peary sailed from New York in July 1908 in the *Roosevelt,* named for Theodore Roosevelt, then President of the United States and the explorer's most enthusiastic supporter. Peary was fifty-two years old, and he knew that this was his last expedition.

But Peary was not the only explorer in the Arctic in 1908. There was also Dr. Frederick A. Cook, a veteran of both the Arctic and the Antarctic, which was just then being explored. Cook had been the physician on one of Peary's earlier expeditions. Always jealous and overbearing, Peary had refused to allow Cook to publish an article about his experiences and they had quarreled. Now the doctor was rumored to be thinking about his own attempt on the North Pole. Peary dismissed the rumors; he considered Cook an amateur, not in the same league as himself.

On March 1, 1909, Peary stood on the frozen shore of the Arctic Ocean and faced north. With him were 23 men, 19 sledges, and 133 dogs. For the next month Matt Henson led out in front, breaking trail, while Peary rode a sledge in the rear, supervising the troops. Other sledges traveled back and forth relaying tons of supplies northward, provisions for the return trip that were stored in snowhouses strung out over almost five hundred miles of floating, shifting ice. Everything had been carefully calculated, down to the sacrificing of weak dogs to feed the strong.

For the final dash to the Pole, Peary took only Henson and three Inuit. The entry in his diary for April 6, 1909, reads, "The Pole at last!!! The prize of 3 centuries, my dream & ambition for 23 years. MINE at last."

Or was it?

PEARY CAME HOME to the stunning news that Dr. Cook had already returned, claiming to have reached the North Pole on April 21, 1908, a year before Peary. In the investigations that followed, Peary accused Cook of lying, and it was demonstrated that Cook had lied once before when he claimed to have climbed Mt. McKinley in Alaska, North America's highest peak. Lacking documentation or witnesses, except for two Inuit companions who said they were never out of sight of land, Cook's claim to have reached the Pole was officially rejected.

Peary claims the North Pole.

423

The Polar Icecap

Scientists are concerned about the effect of global warming on the polar icecap. Over the past several years, scientists have discovered a thinning of the ice in the Arctic Ocean. Glaciers around the world have begun to melt. Scientists are not certain whether this change is occurring naturally or whether it is the result of human activity. Environmental scientists continue to watch and study the situation.

Cause and Effect
Summarize

TEACH

- Explain that identifying and listing causes and effects is a useful way to summarize the events in a text.
- Model summarizing Peary's relationship with Cook.

MODEL Because Cook had traveled to the Arctic, he wanted to publish an article. Peary was jealous and overbearing, and wouldn't let Cook publish. Because Cook was angry about not being able to publish, he quarreled with Peary. Cook eventually decided to try for the North Pole on his own. I can use these causes and effects to summarize Cook and Peary's relationship as a rivalry between two ambitious men.

PRACTICE AND ASSESS

Have students identify causes and effects in paragraph 6 on p. 423. Then have them use this information to summarize the paragraph.

EXTEND SKILLS

Primary and Secondary Sources

Remind students that the author used both primary and secondary sources to write *Into the Ice.* Primary sources are direct records of events, such as journals, interviews, and official records. Secondary sources describe or interpret primary sources. They include such things as biographies, history books, and magazine articles. When writing a research paper or any product that requires citation, students should be prepared to list their sources.

Guiding Comprehension

11 🔊 Summarize • Inferential

Why did the classic era of Arctic exploration end?

Peary was finally given credit for reaching the Pole. Further exploration to Antarica and the South Pole was halted due to World War I.

12 Graphic Sources • Inferential

According to the map on p. 425, which expedition came the closest to the North Pole after Peary's?

Nansen and Johansen's expedition came the closest after Peary's.

13 Compare and Contrast • Critical

Text to World **What other human adventures do the struggles and achievements of the Arctic explorers remind you of?**

Sample response: The Arctic explorers remind me of pilots like Charles Lindbergh and Amelia Earhart. Lindbergh flew solo in a plane across the Atlantic Ocean, which no one had done before. Earhart tried to fly around the world, but her plane was lost. Like the Arctic explorers, these pioneer pilots took risks by attempting to do things other people had not done.

Strategy Response Log

Summarize When students finish reading the selection, provide this prompt: Imagine that a friend asks you what you know about Polar exploration. Summarize the various attempts to reach the Pole.

Then, incredibly, Peary was also unable to completely **verify** his own claim. The careful explorer was a sloppy **navigator**, and from his solar observations and daily journal it was impossible to say that he had stood at the Pole. Henson and the Inuit were unable to take solar readings, so it was Peary's word against Cook's. Commander Robert E. Peary was finally given the credit and made a rear-admiral, but his great prize was tarnished, and he died an embittered man. As for Cook, he vowed until his dying day that he had reached the North Pole. In recent years, historical researchers have determined that neither man actually stepped foot on the northernmost point of the globe.

11 THE CLASSIC ERA of Arctic exploration ended with Peary. Attention then shifted to the Antarctic and to the South Pole, which Roald Amundsen reached in 1911. Three years later the world was at war and most exploration was postponed. When it resumed in the 1920s the world was a different place. Balloons were no longer the only means of flight, and several attempts were made to fly to the North Pole in small airplanes.

For many years Richard E. Byrd was given credit for the first successful flight, but his claim is now disputed. In 1926 Roald Amundsen flew across the entire Arctic Ocean in an Italian dirigible piloted by its designer, Umberto Nobile. The first person to stand at the North Pole, whose claim is undisputed, is Joseph Fletcher, a United States Air Force pilot who landed there in 1952. Arctic flights are great achievements, but they are achievements of technology, somehow different from crossing nearly five hundred miles of shifting ice by dog sledge and then returning. Although many people have now stood at the North Pole, no one has ever completed

13 Peary's journey without being resupplied by plane or airlifted out.

424

ELL

Extend Language Point out that the terms *disputed* and *undisputed* on p. 424. Explain that *disputed* means that it has been argued against or is not accepted as valid. The prefix *un-* in *undisputed* changes the meaning to *not* disputed.

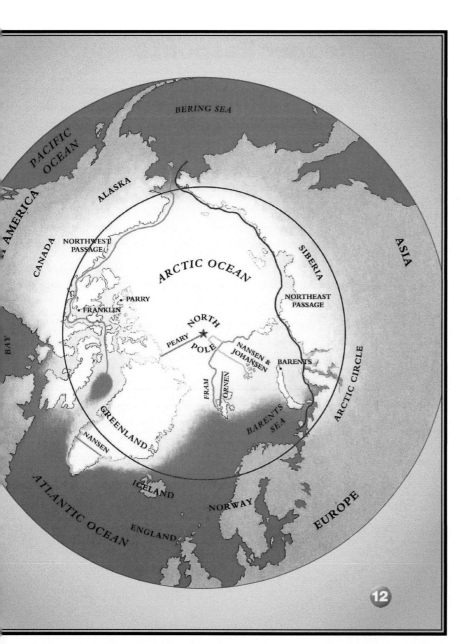

This map shows the routes of various Arctic explorers.

425

Summarize

Remind students that a cause can have more than one effect, and an effect can have more than one cause.

Ask students to try to summarize in one sentence why the classic era of Arctic exploration ended. *(It ended because Peary "won" the race to the North Pole and also because of rising interest in the South Pole, a world war, and advances in technology.)*

Have students check that their summaries include the most important causes of the end to the era. Use Practice Book p. 157.

SELF-CHECK

Students can ask themselves these questions to assess their ability to use the skill and strategy.

- Did I identify causes as I read *Into the Ice*?
- Did I identify the most important effects of these causes?
- How did this help me summarize?

Monitor Progress	
Cause and Effect	
If... students have difficulty summarizing using cause and effect,	**then...** use the Reteach lesson on p. 429b.

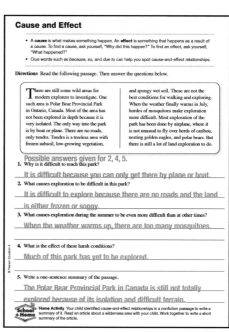

▲ **Practice Book** p. 157

Develop Vocabulary

PRACTICE LESSON VOCABULARY

Students choose the letter of the correct answer.

1. What do you do with *provisions*?
(a) eat them (b) decorate them (c) fight them *(a)*

2. What is a *navigator's* job?
(a) to sail the ship (b) to find the way (c) to record the events *(b)*

3. How can you *verify* a story?
(a) check the source (b) print the story (c) read the story *(a)*

BUILD CONCEPT VOCABULARY

Review previous concept words with students. Ask if students have come across any words that they would like to add to the Polar Exploration Concept Web, such as *solitary* and *resupplied*.

Reader Response

Reader Response

Open for Discussion **Personal Response**

 MODEL I think Andrée's flight would be an exciting scene for a movie. I think Arctic views from the balloon would be beautiful.

Comprehension Check **Critical Response**

1. The author's words help the reader know the two men. He writes that Nansen is bold but careful. *Author's Purpose*

2. Cause: The men were bored by the routine of the ship. Effect: They struck out on the ice and eventually ran out of food. *Cause and Effect*

3. After days of drifting, the balloon lost gas and landed on the ice. The explorers found land but did not survive. *Summarize*

4. Responses will vary, but should include selection vocabulary. *Vocabulary*

 Look Back and Write For test practice, assign a 10–15 minute time limit. For assessment, see the Scoring Rubric at the right.

Retell

Have students retell *Into the Ice.*

Monitor Progress

Check Retelling Rubric 4 3 2 1

If... students have difficulty retelling the selection,	then... use the Retelling Cards and the Scoring Rubric for Retelling on p. 427 to assist fluent retelling.

SUCCESS PREDICTOR

ELL

Check Retelling Have students use the illustrations to guide them in retelling the story. See the ELL and Transition Handbook.

Open for Discussion Pick from this history the best incident for a scene in a movie or TV documentary. Describe why you chose it and how it would appear.

1. This author gives you a bit of information about the personalities of two of the explorers. How does he help you get to know Nansen and Peary? Think Like an Author

2. What caused Fridtjof Nansen and Hjalmar Johansen to leave the *Fram* when they were 360 miles away from the North Pole and frozen in the polar ice? What were some of the effects of this adventure? Cause and Effect

3. Summarize Salomon Andrée's attempt to reach the North Pole in a balloon. Summarize

4. You are an explorer who is organizing a trip to Mars. Write an ad to get fellow adventurers to join you. Use words from the Words to Know list and from the selection. Vocabulary

 Look Back and Write Beyond personal fame, why would explorers have attempted to reach the North Pole? Look back at page 423 to find the author's answer. Write it in your own words. Then discuss in writing whether that reason still is important today.

Meet author **and illustrator Lynn Curlee on page 783.**

426

Scoring Rubric **Look Back and Write**

Top-Score Response A top-score response will use the information on page 423 to conclude that a sense of competition could have motivated explorers to be the first to reach the North Pole.

Example of a Top-Score Response Peary was motivated to reach the North Pole because he wanted to be the first to accomplish this feat. But he was also determined not to let Dr. Frederick A. Cook take away this title and glory. Considering Cook an amateur, Peary didn't want to lose "the prize of 3 centuries." I believe a sense of professional competition is still an important motivator for explorers today.

For additional rubrics, see p. WA10.

Write Now

News Story

Prompt

Into the Ice is the story of an actual Arctic exploration.
Think about one interesting event from the story.
Now write a news story about that event.

Writing Trait

Conventions are the rules for written language.

Student Model

Headline informs reader of main idea.

> Peary Breaks Record but Fails to Reach Pole
>
> March 1906—Innovative explorer Robert Peary has set a new record. At 175 miles from the North Pole, his expedition broke the previous record for reaching the farthest point north. However, this victory was not a true success. Peary's original goal, to reach the North Pole, was not achieved. The group set out for the Pole in late February. However, treacherous weather delayed the explorer and his crew. As supplies ran low, they had to turn back. Although he is already fifty years old, Peary plans to find supporters and funds for another expedition. "I will reach the North Pole," he promised this reporter.

Excellent control of conventions includes proper use of commas.

Writer adds variety by using a quotation.

Use the model to help you write your own news story.

Write Now

Look at the Prompt Explain that each sentence in the prompt has a purpose.

- Sentence 1 presents a topic.
- Sentence 2 suggests students think about the topic.
- Sentence 3 tells what to write—a news story.

Strategies to Develop Conventions

Have students

- read their work aloud.
- have a partner peer-edit their work.

NO: At 175 miles, from the north pole his expedishon broke previous records, for reaching farthest north.

YES: At 175 miles from the North Pole, his expedition broke previous records for reaching farthest north.

For additional suggestions and rubric, see pp. 429g–429h.

Writer's Checklist

☑ **Focus** Do sentences stick to one event?

☑ **Organization** Do words show time order?

☑ **Support** Do details give readers information about *who, what, where, when, why,* and *how?*

☑ **Conventions** Are pronoun forms correct?

427

Scoring Rubric — Expository Retelling

Rubric 4 3 2 1	4	3	2	1
Connections	Makes connections and generalizes beyond the text	Makes connections to other events, texts, or experiences	Makes a limited connection to another event, text, or experience	Makes no connection to another event, text, or experience
Author's Purpose	Elaborates on author's purpose	Tells author's purpose with some clarity	Makes some connection to author's purpose	Makes no connection to author's purpose
Topic	Describes the main topic	Identifies the main topic with some details early in retelling	Identifies the main topic	Retelling has no sense of topic
Important Ideas	Gives accurate information about events, steps, and ideas using details and key vocabulary	Gives accurate information about events, steps, and ideas with some detail and key vocabulary	Gives limited or inaccurate information about events, steps, and ideas	Gives no information about events, steps, and ideas
Conclusions	Draws conclusions and makes inferences to generalize beyond the text	Draws conclusions about the text	Is able to tell some learnings about the text	Is unable to draw conclusions or make inferences about the text

Retelling Plan

☑ **This week** assess Strategic Intervention students.

☐ **Week 2** Assess Advanced students.

☐ **Week 3** Assess Strategic Intervention students.

☐ **Week 4** Assess On-Level students.

☐ **Week 5** Assess any students you have not yet checked during this unit.

Use the Retelling Chart on p. TR17 to record retelling.

Selection Test To assess with *Into the Ice*, use Selection Tests, pp. 61–64.

Fresh Reads for Differentiated Test Practice For weekly leveled practice, use pp. 91–96.

SUCCESS PREDICTOR

Science in Reading

OBJECTIVES
- Examine features of expository nonfiction.
- Practice a test-taking strategy.
- Compare and contrast across texts.

PREVIEW/USE TEXT FEATURES

As students preview "Polar Zones," have them study the photographs and captions. Ask:

- **What do the captions and photos add to the article?** (*Captions provide facts and details about the photos, whose purpose is to visually support information in the text.*)

Link to Science

Suggest that students first research the climate of polar zones to understand their weather.

Science in Reading

Polar Zone

from *Weather* from The Nature Company Discoveries Library

Expository Nonfiction

Genre

- Expository nonfiction explains ideas through facts and information presented in written and visual forms.

- There are usually photographs with captions in expository nonfiction.

Text Features

- The author of this article includes extra information outside of the main text to keep the reader's attention on what is most important.

- The author uses words such as *severe*, *fierce*, and *extreme* to convey the harshness of the winter. As you read, think about how this article would have been different without those words.

Link to Science

The polar zones are areas with extremely cold and hazardous weather. Make a list of the kinds of clothing you would need to protect against such weather.

Climates near the North and South Poles are characterized by freezing temperatures and permanent snow and ice. Polar summers are short and cold. The extreme climate is caused by lack of heat because the sun's light is weaker and the ice reflects much of the heat from the sun back into the atmosphere. For six months of the year, the Arctic experiences winter as the North Pole is tilted away from the sun. At the same time, Antarctica, the continent around the South Pole, enjoys a brief summer. Temperatures rise to freezing, or just above, near the coast. The pack ice drifts northward and melts in the warmer waters. Winter in the Antarctic, however, is severe. Antarctica doubles in size as the sea freezes over, and pack ice extends for hundreds of miles around the continent. Frequent blizzards and fierce winds rage across the icy surface.

The Arctic is a f sea surrounding North Pole, wh Antarctic is a fr continent aroun the South Pole.

Content-Area Vocabulary — Science

atmosphere	air surrounding the Earth
camouflage	to hide, conceal, or disguise
plummet	to plunge; drop

DAY 4 — Grouping Options

Reading

Whole Group Discuss the Question of the Day.

Small Group Differentiated Instruction
Read "Polar Zones." See pp. 408f–408g for the small group lesson plan.

Whole Group Use p. 429a.

Language Arts
Use pp. 429e–429k.

COAT OF COLORS
The fur of the Arctic fox changes color during the year. In winter, it turns from smoky gray to white to camouflage the fox against the snow.

ARCTIC DWELLERS
The Inuit (Eskimos), who live in the Arctic, have adapted well to the extreme climatic conditions.

WHITE OUT
Blizzards are strong winter snowstorms. They are particularly severe in the polar zones, where they may last for weeks at a time. Snow falls on more than 150 days of the year and is swept into huge piles by the wind. Winds are equally severe and reach speeds of more than 186 miles (300 km) per hour. The average winter temperatures plummet to -76°F (-60°C). In these extreme temperatures, unprotected human skin will freeze in seconds. People need layers of warm clothing and protective shelters to survive this bitter cold.

Reading Across Texts
Referring to what you have read in *Into the Ice* and "Polar Zones," tell why you think explorers are drawn to the Arctic.

Writing Across Texts Write some reasons for which explorers are drawn to polar regions.

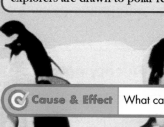 

Ⓒ Cause & Effect | What causes the extreme polar climate?

429

Emperor Penguins

TIME FOR Science

Emperor penguins are found in the Antarctic. The only source of warmth they have is their own bodies. When a female penguin lays her eggs, she leaves her mate to cover them with his body and keep them warm for several weeks while she swims away to find food. The male penguins huddle together with their eggs, using the warmth of their bodies to protect each other. When the chicks hatch from the eggs, the mother returns to feed them and shelter them for approximately two months. The father is not present during this period. He is fishing at sea for food.

EXPOSITORY NONFICTION
Use the sidebar on p. 428 to guide discussion.
- Explain that expository nonfiction explains *who, what, when, where, why,* and *how.*
- Many nonfiction articles, such as "Polar Zones," include graphic sources to make the subject come alive for the reader.
- Discuss with students the kind of information they think this article will provide.

 **AudioText**

Ⓒ Cause and Effect

The sun's light is weaker at the poles than at the equator. The polar ice reflects much of the sun's heat back into the atmosphere.

CONNECT TEXT TO TEXT

Reading Across Texts
Suggest that students scan both sections to look for reasons given there.

Writing Across Texts Students can use a graphic organizer, such as a two-column chart, to identify details from both selections to help them write at least three reasons why explorers are drawn to the polar regions.

Fluency Assessment Plan

☑ **This week assess Advanced students.**
☐ **Week 2** Assess Strategic Intervention students.
☐ **Week 3** Assess On-Level students.
☐ **Week 4** Assess Strategic Intervention students.
☐ **Week 5** Assess any students you have not yet checked during this unit.

Set individual goals for students to enable them to reach the year-end goal.
- Current Goal: 130–138 wcpm
- Year-End Goal: 150 wcpm

For English language learners, emphasize repeated readings to build fluency with enjoyable passages in English, with as much teacher guidance as feasible.

To develop fluent readers, use Fluency Coach.

DAY 5   Grouping Options

Reading
Whole Group
Revisit the Question of the Week.

Small Group
Differentiated Instruction
Reread this week's Leveled Readers. See pp. 408f–408g for the small group lesson plan.

Whole Group
Use pp. 429b–429c.

Language Arts
Use pp. 429d–429l.

PAUSES

Fluency

DAY 1

Model Reread the excerpt from *20,000 Leagues Under the Sea* on p. 408m. Explain that as you read aloud, you will pause at appropriate points in the longer, more complex sentences so that listeners can easily follow you. Model for students as you read.

DAY 2

Choral Reading Read the beginning of p. 415 aloud. Have students pay attention to the way you pause during and after sentences. Have the whole class do three choral readings of p. 415.

DAY 3

Model Read the story of the *Ornen*'s voyage on p. 419 aloud. Point out the various punctuation marks that indicate pauses. Have the class practice pauses in reading by doing three choral readings of p. 419.

DAY 4

Partner Reading Have partners practice reading p. 419 aloud, three times each. Students should read with proper pauses and offer each other feedback.

Monitor Progress   Check Fluency wcpm

As students reread, monitor their progress toward their individual fluency goals. Current Goal: 130–138 words correct per minute. End-of-Year Goal: 150 words correct per minute.

If... students cannot read fluently at a rate of 130–138 words correct per minute,
then... make sure students practice with text at their independent level. Provide additional fluency practice, pairing nonfluent readers with fluent readers.

If... students already read at 150 words correct per minute,
then... they do not need to reread three to four times.

SUCCESS PREDICTOR

DAY 5

Assessment
Individual Reading Rate Use the Fluency Assessment Plan and do a one-minute timed reading of either selection from this week to assess students in Week 1. Pay special attention to this week's skill, pauses. Provide corrective feedback for each student.

RETEACH

 # Cause and Effect

TEACH

Review the definitions of *cause* and *effect* on p. 408. Students can complete Practice Book p. 158 on their own, or you can complete it as a class. Remind students that the **effect** will be on the right-hand side of the flow chart, and the **cause** will be on the left.

ASSESS

Have partners reread p. 419 of *Into the Ice.* Have them diagram the causes and effects of Andrée's decision to travel to the Pole in a balloon. Students can use their diagrams to discuss how Andrée might have avoided disaster.

For additional instruction of cause and effect, see DI·52.

EXTEND SKILLS

Tone

TEACH

Tone is an author's attitude toward his or her subject or toward the audience.
- A author's tone is like "tone of voice" in speaking; it adds emotion to words.
- A reader can determine how the author feels about the subject of the text by recognizing tone.

Read p. 415 with the class. Have students pick out evidence of the author's tone, or attitude, toward Fridtjof Nansen and his expedition. *(great pioneer, brilliant, feat never before accomplished, bold)*

ASSESS

Reread p. 416, paragraph 2. Have students write one paragraph about an adventure they have had and a second paragraph with a different attitude toward the same adventure. Have them write one sentence explaining how changing the tone changed the paragraph.

OBJECTIVES

- Identify causes and effects.
- Identify author's tone.

Skills Trace

Cause and Effect

Introduce/Teach	TE: 6.4 408–409, 456–457; 6.5 582–583
Practice	Practice Book: 153, 157, 158, 173, 177, 178, 223, 227, 228
Reteach/Review	TE: 6.1 31; 6.3 361; 6.4 429b, 477b, 509, 519, DI•52, DI•54; 6.5 599b, 611, DI•54
Test	Selection Test: 61–64, 69–72, 89–92; Benchmark Test: Units 4, 5

ELL

Access Content Reteach the skill by reviewing the Picture It! lesson on cause and effect in the ELL Teaching Guide, pp. 106–107.

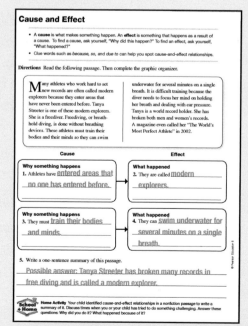

▲ **Practice Book** p. 158

Vocabulary and Word Study

VOCABULARY STRATEGY
◎ Context Clues

UNFAMILIAR WORDS Remind students that they can use context clues to determine the meaning of unfamiliar words. Have students list any unknown words they encountered as they read *Into the Ice*. They can create a chart showing the unknown word, helpful context clues, and a definition that fits the context. Students can use a dictionary or thesaurus to confirm definitions.

Words	Context Clues	Definition
provisions	"scientific equipment and supplies"	equipment; supplies
maneuvering	"the sledges"	steering

Descriptive Words

Many words in *Into the Ice* help readers picture the unique setting—the Arctic Circle. Have students list these words and phrases as they find them. Students can use these words to write their own descriptions of the North Pole and the polar icecap.

Words that Describe Setting

"As the weeks passed and the sun rose higher, the broken surface of the ice pack became slushy, then treacherous as lanes of water called leads opened and closed between the ice floes." (pp. 416–417)

BUILD CONCEPT VOCABULARY
Polar Exploration

LOOKING BACK Remind students of the question of the week: What drives people to explore in harsh climates and dangerous places? Discuss how this week's Concept Web of vocabulary words relates to the theme of polar exploration. Ask students if they have any words or categories to add. Discuss if words and categories are appropriately related to the concept.

MOVING FORWARD Preview the title of the next selection, *The Chimpanzees I Love.* Ask students which Concept Web words might apply to the new selection based on the title alone. Put a star next to these words on the Web.

Display the Concept Web and revisit the vocabulary words as you read the next selection to check predictions.

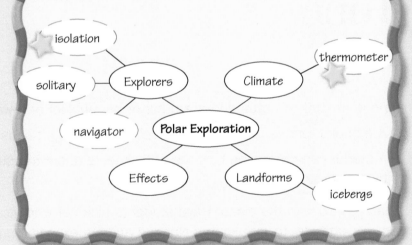

Monitor Progress
Check Vocabulary

If... students suggest words or categories that are not related to the concept,	then... review the words and categories on the Concept Web and discuss how they relate to the lesson concept.

SUCCESS PREDICTOR

Speaking and Viewing

SPEAKING

Panel Discussion

SET-UP Have students stage a panel discussion on the Polar explorers whose achievements they read about in *Into the Ice*.

ORGANIZATION Each group member should choose one explorer about whom he or she will be the "expert." Students should read more about their explorers online or in the library. They should know all the important facts about the explorers' careers.

AUDIENCE On the day of the panel discussion, the audience should come prepared with questions about the explorers. Each student can write one or two questions after they read *Into the Ice*. These questions will provide the basis for the discussion.

Rehearsal Tips
- Go into rehearsal knowing the facts about your explorer.
- Be prepared to debate the achievements of the various explorers with the other panelists.
- Listen courteously and attentively to the other panelists.

VIEWING

Analyze Media

Discuss with students any television shows or movies they have seen that focused on polar exploration. Ask questions such as the following:

1. **What do polar landscapes look like?** *(They are often shown as being all white and covered with ice and snow.)*

2. **What do the people living and working in the Arctic look like? How do they dress?** *(They dress in a way that conserves their body heat; early explorers wore furs and heavy woolen clothing, today people can wear lighter but still very warm insulating clothing.)*

3. **From what you have seen of the polar areas, would you want to go there? Why or why not?** *(Possible responses: I would not want to go there, because it is so bitterly cold. I would want to go there because scientists are still studying the poles and making new discoveries.)*

ELL

Support Vocabulary Use the following to review and extend vocabulary and to explore lesson concepts further:
- ELL Poster 16, Days 3–5 instruction
- Vocabulary Activities and Word Cards in ELL Teaching Guide, pp. 108–109

Assessment For information on assessing students' speaking, listening, and viewing, see the ELL and Transition Handbook.

Grammar   Subject and Object Pronouns

OBJECTIVES

- Identify and define subject and object pronouns.
- Use subject and object pronouns in writing.
- Use correct forms of pronouns in compounds.
- Become familiar with subject and object pronoun assessment on high-stakes tests.

Monitor Progress

Grammar

If... students have difficulty identifying subject and object pronouns,	then... provide additional instruction and practice in The Grammar and Writing Book pp. 140–143.

DAILY FIX-IT

This week use Daily Fix-It Transparency 16.

Spiral REVIEW

Support Grammar See the Grammar Transition lessons in the ELL and Transition Handbook.

▲ **The Grammar and Writing Book** For more instruction and practice, use pp. 140–143.

DAY 1   Teach and Model

DAILY FIX-IT

1. Him kept a cronicle during the exploration. *(He; chronicle)*

2. Was the crew members supposed to sinchronize their watches? *(Were; synchronize)*

READING-GRAMMAR CONNECTION

Write this sentence based on *Into the Ice* on the board:

As an explorer, Peary was innovative. He took ideas and improved on them.

Explain that *He* is a **subject pronoun** and *them* is an **object pronoun.** *He* is the subject of the second sentence, and *them* is the object of the preposition *on.*

Display Grammar Transparency 16. Read aloud the definitions and sample sentences. Work through the items.

Subject and Object Pronouns

A personal pronoun used as the subject of a sentence is called a **subject pronoun.**
  He published an article. She and I read the article.
A personal pronoun used as a direct object, indirect object, or object of a preposition is called an **object pronoun.**
  The explorer thanked them. I gave the book to Becky and him.
• Subject pronouns are *I, you, he, she, it, we,* and *they.*
• Object pronouns are *me, you, him, her, it, us,* and *them.*
• Remember to use the correct pronoun form with a compound subject or object pronoun.
• Subject pronouns replace the nouns they represent. Do not use a subject pronoun with the noun it represents.
  No: Tim he went ice fishing with his brother.
  Yes: Tim went ice fishing with his brother.

Directions Circle the pronoun in ( ) that completes each sentence correctly.

1. Tamara and (she) her) photographed the Northern Lights.
2. (Them) They) took enough supplies for five years.
3. The North Pole would be too cold for (I, me).
4. The class accompanied (they, them) to the museum.
5. Seth and (he, him) are going on the class field trip.
6. (We) Us) know what happened to the explorers who sailed on the *Ornen.*
7. Carlos and (me, I) could lose toes if they freeze.
8. Mr. Jasper wants to tell Diana and (I, me) about his trip to Greenland.
9. The scientist invited Ms. Eddings and (we, us) to view ancient relics.
10. Deidra studied hard, so there is no reason for (her, she) to worry about the test.
11. They asked if Curt and (she, her) would join the expedition.
12. The ice floe trapped the captain and (he, him).

Unit 4 *Into the Ice*   Grammar **16**

▲ **Grammar Transparency** 16

DAY 2   Develop the Concept

DAILY FIX-IT

3. Admiral Peary's team drinked plenty of fluids. Them did not get dehydrated. *(drank; They)*

4. The arkive at the library contain the journals of explorers. *(archive; contains)*

GUIDED PRACTICE

Review the concept of subject and object pronouns.

- A pronoun takes the place of one or more nouns or groups of nouns.

- A **subject pronoun** is a personal pronoun used as the subject of a sentence.

- An **object pronoun** is a personal pronoun used as a direct object, indirect object, or the object of a preposition.

HOMEWORK Grammar and Writing Practice Book p. 61. Work through the first two items with the class.

Subject and Object Pronouns

A personal pronoun used as the subject of a sentence is called a **subject pronoun.**
  She planned an archaeological dig. He and I heard the details.
A personal pronoun used as a direct object, indirect object, or object of a preposition is called an **object pronoun.**
  The sea captain took us for a ride. He told him and me stories.
• Subject pronouns are *I, you, he, she, it, we,* and *they.*
• Object pronouns are *me, you, him, her, it, us,* and *them.*
• Remember to use the correct pronoun form with a compound subject or object pronoun.
• Subject pronouns replace the nouns they represent. Do not use a subject pronoun with the noun it represents.
  No: Carrie she studied oceanography.
  Yes: Carrie studied oceanography.

Directions Circle the pronoun in ( ) that completes each sentence correctly.

1. (I, Me) am fascinated by maritime exploration.
2. (Them, They) believed the sea captain was a good navigator.
3. Robert and (he, him) read about the first people to reach the North Pole.
4. (We) Us) studied relics and artifacts.
5. Bill and (me, I) studied the habitat of the penguin.
6. David and (she, her) have always wanted to visit Alaska.
7. Mr. Douglas taught me and (her, she) about Arctic explorers.
8. The class put the fossils back in the case after students studied (they, them).
9. Teddy Roosevelt supported Admiral Peary and often wrote to (he, him).
10. She took (us, we) on a field trip.
11. I helped Sara and (they, them) with the science project.
12. My sister told you and (me, I) stories about her visit to Alaska.

Home Activity Your child learned about subject and object pronouns. Have your child show you subject and object pronouns in something he or she has written.

▲ **Grammar and Writing Practice Book** p. 61

DAY 3 — Apply to Writing

DAILY FIX-IT

5. Some Inuit people lives in snow houses on the ice *(live; ice.)*

6. Years ago, women are not permitted to participate in democrasy. *(were; democracy)*

USE PRONOUNS FOR NOUNS

Repeated words can make sentences wordy and boring. Replacing nouns and noun phrases with pronouns can make writing smoother and less wordy.

- Have students review something they have written to see if they can replace repeated nouns with pronouns.

HOMEWORK Grammar and Writing Practice Book p. 62.

Subject and Object Pronouns

Directions Write the pronoun in ( ) that completes each sentence correctly.

1. My friends and (I, me) dream about adventures. — **I**
2. A trip to the desert seems exciting to Sheila and (he, him). — **him**
3. You and (she, her) should hike in the Rocky Mountains. — **she**
4. I told Jorge and (they, them) about the whitewater raft trip. — **them**
5. A bike trip would be perfect for my parents and (I, me). — **me**
6. Leon asked Jill and (she, her) if they had been to Mexico. — **her**
7. Bob and (he, him) followed the guide up the trail. — **he**
8. Paula and (they, them) took the boat to the islands. — **they**

Directions Write a paragraph about an exploration, adventure, or discovery you would like to try with a friend. Be sure to use compound subject and object pronouns correctly.

Possible answer: Lori and I want to explore Devil's Cave. It is in the city park. My brother wants to come with us. Mom and Dad agreed to take us next weekend. We told them that we would bring everything. All they have to do is to drive us. Josh and I will pack a sack lunch, and Lori will bring a flashlight. Off we go!

Home Activity Your child learned how to use subject and object pronouns in writing. Ask your child to write about somewhere he or she went with friends. Ask your child to use at least one subject pronoun and one object pronoun.

▲ **Grammar and Writing Practice Book** p. 62

DAY 4 — Test Preparation

DAILY FIX-IT

7. Many aristochrats financed scientific exploration's. *(aristocrats; explorations)*

8. President theodore Roosevelt supported Pearys explorations. *(Theodore; Peary's)*

STANDARDIZED TEST PREP

Test Tip

Watch out for compound subject or object pronouns. If you are confused about what pronoun to use, try the sentence without the noun in the compound.

No: Jane and me read about unknown frontiers. (Me enjoy . . .)

Yes: Jane and I read about unknown frontiers. (I enjoy . . .)

No: Mother told Jane and I to do our homework. (Mother told I . . .)

Yes: Mother told Jane and me to do our homework. (Mother told me . . .)

HOMEWORK Grammar and Writing Practice Book p. 63.

Subject and Object Pronouns

Directions Mark the letter of the pronoun that correctly replaces the underlined word or words in each sentence.

1. Admiral Peary and Dr. Cook wanted to reach the North Pole first.
   A They
   B Us
   C Them
   D We

2. The Inuit called Marie Peary a blond snowbaby.
   A you
   B she
   C her
   D it

3. The sledges could glide over the ice pack.
   A him
   B it
   C they
   D them

4. Admiral Peary thanked the Inuit for their help.
   A it
   B they
   C them
   D us

5. A woman loaded furs, and then the woman prepared dinner.
   A him
   B them
   C her
   D she

6. Mother asked Pat and me to turn the volume down.
   A us
   B we
   C they
   D she

7. Robert Peary was brave. Robert Peary was also arrogant.
   A Him
   B He
   C Her
   D Her

8. Dr. Cook did not think Peary would get there before Dr. Cook.
   A she
   B they
   C he
   D him

9. The dogs were among the best dogs the Inuit had.
   A Us
   B They
   C Him
   D Her

10. The explorers longed to reach the Pole.
    A They
    B Us
    C Her
    D Them

Home Activity Your child prepared for taking tests on subject and object pronouns. With your child, read a magazine article. Have your child circle subject pronouns and underline object pronouns on one page in the article.

▲ **Grammar and Writing Practice Book** p. 63

DAY 5 — Cumulative Review

DAILY FIX-IT

9. admiral Peary was fifty-two when him made his last exploration. *(Admiral; he)*

10. Peary and me would have made a gooder team than Peary and Henson. *(I; better)*

ADDITIONAL PRACTICE

Assign pp. 140–143 in The Grammar and Writing Book.

EXTRA PRACTICE Grammar and Writing Practice Book p. 137.

TEST PREPARATION Grammar and Writing Practice Book pp. 155–156.

ASSESSMENT

CUMULATIVE REVIEW Grammar and Writing Practice Book p. 64.

Subject and Object Pronouns

Directions Circle the pronoun in each sentence. Write *SP* if it is a subject pronoun and *OP* if it is an object pronoun.

1. We felt bad that Admiral Peary's claims were disputed. — **SP**
2. The snow skis were bought for Ronny and me. — **OP**
3. Josephine Peary told them about the Arctic. — **OP**
4. He and the men hoped to reach the North Pole first. — **SP**
5. At last they spotted a ship on the horizon. — **SP**

Directions Circle the pronoun in ( ) that completes each sentence correctly.

6. Anna and (he, him) needed to do more research on Admiral Peary.
7. (They, Them) listed the obstacles an Arctic explorer might encounter.
8. (She, Her) was one of the few women who went on expeditions.
9. (We, Us) believe Admiral Peary was a great explorer.
10. Charles and (I, me) looked for a biography of Dr. Frederick A. Cook.
11. Peary quarreled with Cook and refused to allow (he, him) to publish a paper.
12. The curator gave Michael and (she, her) records on Peary's travels.
13. The compass pointed (he, him) in the right direction.
14. The tour was taken by Mr. Blades and (we, us).
15. My teacher gave Stacey and (I, me) an A on our Arctic Circle report.

Home Activity Your child reviewed subject and object pronouns. Ask your child to use subject and object pronouns in a letter he or she writes to a friend or family member.

▲ **Grammar and Writing Practice Book** p. 64

Writing Workshop News Story

OBJECTIVES

- Identify qualities of a news story.
- Write a news story answering the 5 W's and How.
- Focus on conventions.
- Use a rubric.

Genre News Story
Writer's Craft Answer the 5 W's and How
Writing Trait Conventions

ELL

Conventions Identify a particular grammar convention that presents difficulty for a student or a small group. Explicitly teach the English convention using an appropriate lesson in the ELL and Transition Handbook.

Writing Traits

FOCUS/IDEAS News story is focused and comprehensive. The 5 W's and How are all answered.

ORGANIZATION/PARAGRAPHS The writer uses journalistic organization: The lead sentence provides the basic information, and details are given in later sentences.

VOICE The writer is authoritative and engaged, though objective.

WORD CHOICE The writer uses specific words to communicate clearly.

SENTENCES Sentences are focused and clear.

CONVENTIONS There is excellent control and accuracy.

READING-WRITING CONNECTION

- The author's use of conventions makes *Into the Ice* clear and easy to understand.
- Using conventions helps keeps the reader focused on the information, such as the 5 W's and How.
- Students will accurately use writing conventions to write a **news story** that answers the 5W's and How.

MODEL CONVENTIONS Display Writing Transparency 16A. Then discuss the model and the writing trait of conventions.

Think Aloud I see that the writer of this news story uses conventions correctly. This makes the information presented in the story clear. For example, the writer uses a set of commas to indicate that Fridtjof Nansen is an appositive, or explanation, of the word scientist.

News Story

When you want to know what's happening in your community or around the world, odds are you can find out in a **news story**. A news story puts the most important information in a lead sentence. Details are provided in later sentences.

Bold Norwegian First to Ski Across Greenland

Headline gets reader's attention.

Lead sentence gives most important information.

July 20, 1888—A young Norwegian scientist, Fridtjof Nansen, became the first person ever to cross Greenland on skis yesterday. A careful planner and accomplished athlete, Nansen, 26, was dropped off with his party on the uninhabited eastern coast of the world's largest island. Taking advantage of Inuit survival methods, Nansen and his five companions used dog sledges, kayaks, and snow houses as they forged their way east toward civilization. In a bold move, Nansen's group packed only enough supplies for a one-way trip. They knew that they would either succeed or die trying. The Greenland ski trip was Nansen's first expedition. The young outdoorsman and poet says he is planning future expeditions.

Details are given in later.

Unit 4 Into the Ice   Writing Model **16A**

▲ **Writing Transparency** 16A

WRITER'S CRAFT
Answer the 5 W's and How

Display Writing Transparency 16B. Read the directions and work together to identify a news story lead that answers the 5W's and How.

Think Aloud **ANSWER THE 5 W'S AND HOW** Tomorrow we will write a news story about an event from *Into the Ice.* I will write about Perry's 1906 attempt to reach the North Pole. My news story will answer the 5W's and How. I need to inform my reader *who* was there, *what* happened, *when* and *where* it took place, and *why* it failed. I'll also give information about *how* Perry attempted the journey.

GUIDED WRITING Some students may need more help with answering the 5 W's and How. Point out facts in the selection that tell *who, what, where, when, why,* or *how.*

Answer the 5 W's and How

A news story gives key information about an event. It answers a set of questions called the **5 W's and How:** *Who? What? Where? When? Why? How?* This essential information informs readers about an event in direct, concrete, and objective sentences.

Some dogs got away the other day. (Answers only *Who* and *What* happened)

Two sled dogs escaped from Neil Olafsen's yard yesterday afternoon. Olafsen said they got out by digging under the walls of their pen. (Answers all six questions)

Directions Choose the news story lead that best answers the 5 W's and How. Explain why your choice is the best and why the other two are not.

1. Three inches of snow fell yesterday. They had trouble plowing it all, but finally it melted. There's no cause for alarm. Things were back to normal today.
   Answers only *What* and *When.* Doesn't say who "they" are.

2. A man and a woman were found stranded on a frozen Reindeer Lake yesterday, due to an ill-advised skating adventure. Marion and Geoffrey Harden of Antlerville, VT, were a little cold but not seriously injured. Best: *Who:* Marion and Geoffrey Harden; *What:* Stranded on the ice; *When:* Yesterday; *Where:* Reindeer Lake; *Why* and *How:* Ice skating where they shouldn't

3. The Prime Minister of Norway was there last Wednesday, as were several Olympic cross-country ski champions. The Oslo Banquet Hall was completely redecorated for the festivities.
   Doesn't tell *What happened*

Directions Choose one of the story leads above that was incomplete. Rewrite the lead, adding details to answer the 5 Ws and How. Possible answer: Three inches of snow fell on the residents of Bismarck, ND, yesterday. City workers had trouble plowing it all because of broken snowplows. However, sunshine melted most of the snow. Things were back to normal today.

Unit 4 Into the Ice   Writer's Craft **16B**

▲ **Writing Transparency** 16B

DAY 3 Prewrite and Draft

READ THE WRITING PROMPT
on page 427 in the Student Edition.

Into the Ice *is the story of an actual Arctic exploration.*

Think about one interesting event from the selection.

Now write a news story about that event.

Writing Test Tips

- Remember to use the past tense in your story.
- Include only the information that relates to the topic of your story. Write the facts, not opinions.
- Write a lead sentence that states the most important facts.

GETTING STARTED Students can do any of the following:

- Make a two-column chart with the 5W's and How in the left column and information in the right column.
- Research information to find exact answers.
- Look at a recent newspaper to find examples of news stories.

DAY 4 Draft and Revise

EDITING/REVISING CHECKLIST

☑ Does the story answer all 5 W's and How?

☑ Does a strong lead sentence provide the most important information?

☑ Are subject and object pronouns used correctly?

☑ Are words with Greek word parts spelled correctly?

See *The Grammar and Writing Book*, pp. 140–145.

Revising Tips

Conventions

- Consider using a phrase for a headline that grabs readers' interest.
- Make sure all sentences have the correct punctuation.
- Check capitalization, especially in your headline.

PUBLISHING Students can offer their articles for a human interest section of the school newspaper.

ASSESSMENT Use the scoring rubric to evaluate students' work.

DAY 5 Connect to Unit Writing

Story	
Week 1	News Story 429g–429h
Week 2	Story About an Animal 455g–455h
Week 3	Describe a Setting 477g–477h
Week 4	TV Script 499g–499h
Week 5	Summary 527g–527h

PREVIEW THE UNIT PROMPT

Write a story about an adventure, a discovery, or something that happened to you for the first time. Use some of these literary devices: foreshadowing, tension, suspense, conflict, humor.

APPLY

- The beginning of the story should provide answers to the 5 W's and How. The remaining sentences should add details.

Writing Trait Rubric

	4	3	2	1
Conventions	Excellent control and accuracy; very few or no errors	Solid control and accuracy; some errors	Weak control; several errors	Serious errors
	News story with conventions that make it clear and easy to read	News story generally clear; errors that do not interfere with meaning	News story confusing at times; errors that distort meaning	News story unclear; errors that obscure meaning

Spelling & Phonics Greek Word Parts

OBJECTIVE

• Spell words with Greek word parts.

Generalization

Connect to Phonics The Greek word part *hydro* means "water," *onym* means "name," *archeo* means "first" or "ancient," *chronos* means "time," and *crat* means "rule." Learning the pronunciation of Greek word parts will help with the correct pronunciation of any word that contains the Greek word part.

Spelling Words

1. hydrant	11. hydroplane
2. chronic	12. chronology
3. archive	13. archaic
4. synonym	14. homonym
5. antonym	15. synchronize
6. democracy	16. hydraulic
7. hydrogen	17. archaeology
8. aristocrat	18. anarchy
9. dehydrated	19. hydroelectric
10. chronicle	20. bureaucracy

Challenge Words

21. hydrophobia	24. pseudonym
22. chronological	25. aristocracy
23. anachronism	

ELL

Spelling/Phonics Support See the ELL and Transition Handbook for spelling support.

DAY 1 — Pretest and Sort

PRETEST

Use the Dictation Sentences from Day 5 to administer the pretest. Read the word, read the sentence, and then read the word again. Guide students in self-correcting their pretests and correcting any misspellings.

Monitor Progress

Spelling

If... students misspell more than 5 pretest words,	then... use words 1–10 for Strategic Intervention.
If... students misspell 1–5 pretest words,	then... use words 1–20 for On-Level practice.
If... students correctly spell all pretest words,	then... use words 1–25 for Advanced Learners.

HOMEWORK Spelling Practice Book, p. 61.

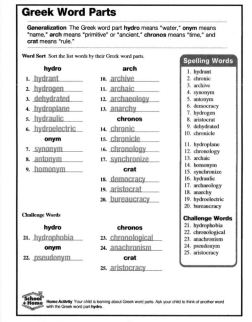

▲ **Spelling Practice Book** p. 61

DAY 2 — Think and Practice

TEACH

Many English words have Greek parts. These parts can provide clues about how to spell the word and what the word means. Write the Greek roots *hydro, onym, archeo, chronos,* and *crat* on the board. Have students take turns coming to the board to write each spelling word and underline the Greek root in each word.

ant*onym*

USE THE DICTIONARY Have pairs of students select three words they don't know the meaning of and use the dictionary to find the meanings. Then say one list word at a time and make sure each word can be defined by class members.

HOMEWORK Spelling Practice Book, p. 62

Greek Word Parts

Spelling Words

hydrant	chronic	archive	synonym	antonym
democracy	hydrogen	aristocrat	dehydrated	chronicle
hydroplane	chronology	archaic	homonym	synchronize
hydraulic	archaeology	anarchy	hydroelectric	bureaucracy

Word Meanings Write a list word that fits each definition.

1. production of electricity by water power — 1. hydroelectric
2. an arrangement in order of occurrence — 2. chronology
3. a historical account — 3. chronicle
4. a word that has the same spelling but different meaning than another word — 4. homonym
5. absence of government and law — 5. anarchy
6. to skim over the water — 6. hydroplane
7. taken water or moisture from — 7. dehydrated
8. lasting a long time — 8. chronic
9. the study of people, customs, and life of ancient times — 9. archaeology
10. no longer in general use — 10. archaic

Words in Context Write the list word that finishes each statement below.

11. Let's ___ our watches before we begin. — 11. synchronize
12. The European ___ lived in a mansion on the hill. — 12. aristocrat
13. I've been going through the family ___ to learn about my ancestors. — 13. archive
14. Water is made of molecules of oxygen and ___. — 14. hydrogen
15. Sometimes it's frustrating dealing with a ___ like the Department of Motor Vehicles. — 15. bureaucracy
16. *Almost* is a ___ for *nearly*. — 16. synonym
17. The United States government is an example of a ___. — 17. democracy
18. *Near* is an ___ for *far*. — 18. antonym
19. My new ___ shock absorbers work very well. — 19. hydraulic
20. The fireman attached their hose to the fire ___. — 20. hydrant

▲ **Spelling Practice Book** p.62

DAY 3   Connect to Writing

WRITE AN EDITORIAL

Have students write an editorial expressing their opinions on a current event. Their editorial should use at least four spelling words. Have students read their editorials aloud, or post them on the bulletin board for everyone to see.

Frequently Misspelled Words

were   they

These words are difficult for some sixth-graders to spell. Alert students to these frequently misspelled words and encourage them to think carefully before spelling them.

HOMEWORK Spelling Practice Book, p. 63.

Greek Word Parts

Proofread an Article Circle six misspelled words in the article below. Write the words correctly. Find a sentence with an incorrect verb form. Write it correctly.

Archaeology

(Archiology) is a fascinating area of science. By digging down through layers of earth, researchers can find remnants of (arkaic) civilizations ranging from bits of broken pottery to the tomb of a once mighty (aristocrat) to entire buried cities. These finds helping scientists establish the (chronology) of human development. Artifacts hidden beneath the surface provide a physical (chronocle) of the development of humankind. That's why scientists catalog and (arkive) the artifacts in museums throughout the world.

Spelling Words
hydrant
chronic
archive
synonym
antonym
democracy
hydrogen
aristocrat
dehydrated
chronicle

hydroplane
chronology
archaic
homonym
synchronize
hydraulic
archaeology
anarchy
hydroelectric
bureaucracy

1. archaeology   2. archaic
3. aristocrat   4. chronology
5. chronicle   6. archive
7. These finds help them establish the chronology of human development.

Frequently Misspelled Words
were
they

Proofread Words Circle the word that is spelled correctly. Write it on the line.

8. (hydroplane)   hidroplane   8. hydroplane
9. (chronology)   cronology   9. chronology
10. arcaic   (archaic)   10. archaic
11. homanym   (homonym)   11. homonym
12. (synchronize)   syncronize   12. synchronize
13. hidraulic   (hydraulic)   13. hydraulic
14. (archaeology)   arcaeology   14. archaeology
15. (anarchy)   anarky   15. anarchy

School + Home **Home Activity** Your child identified misspelled words. Ask your child to think of a word from the list with five syllables, spell it, and use that word in a sentence.

▲ **Spelling Practice Book** p. 63

DAY 4   Review

REVIEW GREEK WORD PARTS

Have students work in pairs to create a word search puzzle, in which each spelling word fits into a puzzle grid. Students can exchange their puzzles with other groups to solve each other's puzzles.

Spelling Strategy
DIVIDING LONG WORDS

Use syllables to make long words easier to study.

Step 1: Say the word slowly and listen for the syllables.

Step 2: Write the word and draw lines between the syllables.

Step 3: Study the word syllable by syllable.

HOMEWORK Spelling Practice Book, p. 64.

Greek Word Parts

Spelling Words

hydrant	chronic	archive	synonym	antonym
democracy	hydrogen	aristocrat	dehydrated	chronicle
hydroplane	chronology	archaic	homonym	synchronize
hydraulic	archaeology	anarchy	hydroelectric	bureaucracy

Finishing Sentences Write a list word to complete each sentence.

1. That ___ word was commonly used two hundred years ago.   1. archaic
2. I will have to see a doctor about my ___ cough.   2. chronic
3. The football player was ___ from playing under the hot sun.   3. dehydrated
4. The rainy road was so slick that the car started to ___.   4. hydroplane
5. A society without government or laws is an ___.   5. anarchy
6. I am writing a ___ of my town's history.   6. chronicle
7. I will create a ___ of the events in the order that they occurred.   7. chronology
8. A ___ power plant provides electricity for this region.   8. hydroelectric

Word Scramble Unscramble each word below to form a list word. Write the word.

9. mmoonhy   9. homonym
10. antydh   10. hydrant
11. cyracrucaub   11. bureaucracy
12. sartceroita   12. aristocrat
13. chzcnoirnys   13. synchronize
14. rcliandyh   14. hydraulic
15. myoaoccred   15. democracy
16. drgoenhy   16. hydrogen
17. taonymn   17. antonym
18. chraeiv   18. archive
19. looyearhcag   19. archaeology
20. mnyoyns   20. synonym

School + Home **Home Activity** Your child used list words to finish sentences. Ask your child to define the word "chronology."

▲ **Spelling Practice Book** p. 64

DAY 5   Posttest

DICTATION SENTENCES

1. Don't park next to a fire hydrant.
2. Her lateness is chronic.
3. The archive has many old books.
4. Do you know a synonym for kind?
5. Hot is an antonym of cold.
6. This government is a democracy.
7. She used hydrogen in the lab.
8. The duke is an aristocrat.
9. Drink water if you are dehydrated.
10. The report is a chronicle of what happened.
11. We rode a hydroplane across the lake.
12. Helen wrote a chronology of the events.
13. That is an archaic word.
14. Do you know what a homonym is?
15. Let's synchronize our watches.
16. Dad used the hydraulic lift to raise the boat.
17. He wants to study archaeology.
18. There would be anarchy if we had no rules.
19. There is the hydroelectric plant.
20. Mom thinks there is too much bureaucracy.

CHALLENGE

21. Jan's dog had hydrophobia.
22. Put the dates in chronological order.
23. A car is an anachronism in a painting of the old West.
24. She wrote under a pseudonym.
25. You are not a member of the aristocracy.

OBJECTIVES

- Formulate an inquiry question that is connected to this week's lesson focus.
- Effectively and efficiently find, evaluate, and communicate information related to an inquiry question using electronic sources.

New Literacies	
Day 1	Identify Questions
Day 2	Navigate/Search
Day 3	Analyze
Day 4	Synthesize
Day 5	Communicate

NEW LITERACIES

Internet Inquiry Activity

RESEARCH POLAR EXPLORERS

Use the following 5-day plan to help students conduct this week's Internet inquiry activity on polar exploration. Remind students to follow classroom rules when using the Internet.

DAY 1

Identify Questions Discuss the lesson focus question: *What drives people to explore harsh climates and dangerous places?* Have students work individually, in pairs, or in small groups to write an inquiry question about one of the polar explorers they studied in *Into the Ice*.

DAY 2

Navigate/Search Have students brainstorm keywords and phrases with which to search the Internet. They can note then the URLs of the sites that appear to be the most promising. They will then explore these sites on Day 3.

DAY 3

Analyze Have students explore the Web sites they identified on Day 2. Remind them to keep their inquiry questions in mind as they go through the information on the Web sites. Students should discard any information that does not specifically address the question they asked.

DAY 4

Synthesize As students synthesize the information they gathered on Day 3, have them identify the most important things they learned about the person they researched. They can use these main points to make an outline of the facts they want to present on Day 5.

DAY 5

Communicate Have students use a word-processing program to create an "Internet Guidebook" of the best Web sites to visit for information on their chosen explorer. The guidebook should give the URL of each site and a brief description of its contents.

RESEARCH/STUDY SKILLS
Diagram/Scale Drawing

OBJECTIVES
- Review the terms *diagram* and *scale drawing*.
- Make a scale drawing.

TEACH

Write the terms *diagram* and *scale drawing* on the chalkboard. Challenge students to define them. Give them help if necessary. Go over the following points:

- A **diagram** is a drawing, usually with labled parts. It shows how something is put together or it shows an action, such as a particular play in a basketball game.

- A **scale drawing** is a specific type of diagram. It is drawn in exact ratio to the object or geographical area it represents. For example, you might draw a building at a scale of $\frac{1}{4}$ inch to 1 foot.

- A **scale** is the mathematical ratio you use to make your drawing. The scale must be written somewhere on the drawing so that anyone using it for reference will know the actual size of the object or geographical area.

Have pairs of students choose among the nations, bodies of water, and geographical areas mentioned in *Into the Ice*. Students can look up maps of these areas. They can use the maps to create their own scale drawings. As they work, ask questions such as the following:

1. **Are all maps scale drawings?** *(Yes, unless there was such a thing as an actual-size map.)*

2. **Why is it important that a map be drawn to scale?** *(You use a map to find and travel to places, so you need to know the exact distances involved. You use the scale to multiply by to find out exact distances.)*

ASSESS

Make sure that students choose a scale that fits the proportions of their drawing paper, and that the scale represents distances accurately. Post finished maps in the classroom.

For more practice or to assess students, use Practice Book pp. 159–160.

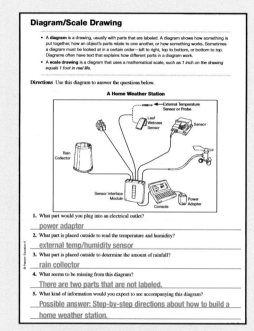

▲ **Practice Book** p. 159

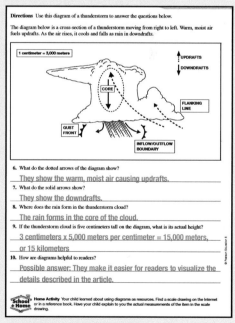

▲ **Practice Book** p. 160

Assessment Checkpoints *for the Week*

AFTER READING

Selection Assessment

Use pp. 61–64 of Selection Tests **to check:**

☑ **Selection Understanding**

☑ **Comprehension Skill** *Cause and Effect*

☑ **Selection Vocabulary**

conquer	isolation
destiny	navigator
expedition	provisions
insulated	verify

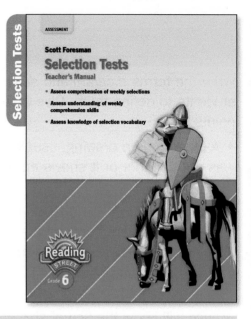

Selection Tests

ASSESSMENT

Scott Foresman

Selection Tests
Teacher's Manual

• Assess comprehension of weekly selections
• Assess understanding of weekly comprehension skills
• Assess knowledge of selection vocabulary

Reading STREET Grade 6

Leveled Assessment

On-Level

Strategic Intervention

Advanced

Use pp. 91–96 of Fresh Reads for Differentiated Test Practice **to check:**

☑ **Comprehension Skill** *Cause and Effect*

☑ **REVIEW** **Comprehension Skill** *Main Idea*

☑ **Fluency** *Words Correct Per Minute*

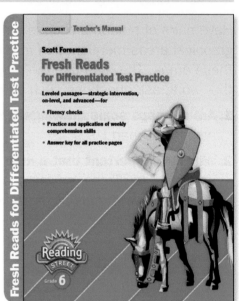

Fresh Reads for Differentiated Test Practice

ASSESSMENT   Teacher's Manual

Scott Foresman

Fresh Reads
for Differentiated Test Practice

Leveled passages—strategic intervention, on-level, and advanced—for

• Fluency checks
• Practice and application of weekly comprehension skills
• Answer key for all practice pages

Reading STREET Grade 6

Managing Assessment

Use Assessment Handbook **for:**

☑ **Observation Checklists**

☑ **Record-Keeping Forms**

☑ **Portfolio Assessment**

Assessment Handbook

ASSESSMENT

Scott Foresman

Assessment Handbook

• Suggestions for preparing students for high-stake tests
• Ideas for classroom-based assessment
• Forms in English and Spanish for students to record interests and progress
• Forms in English and Spanish for teachers to record observations of students' reading and writing abilities and progress
• Assessment and Regrouping charts reproduced from *Reading Street Teacher's Editions*

Reading STREET Grades 3–6

Read It
ONLINE
PearsonSuccessNet.com
• Student Edition
• Leveled Readers

Leveled Readers

Skill Author's Purpose
Strategy Answer Questions
Lesson Vocabulary

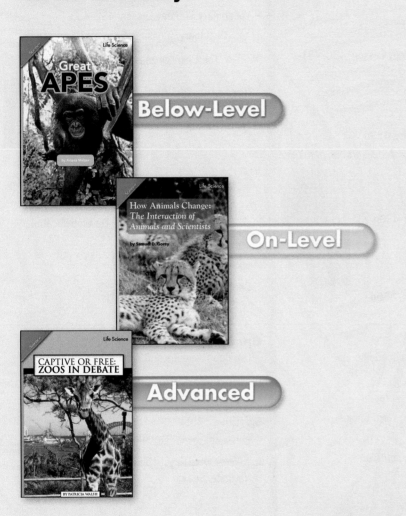

Great **APES**
Below-Level

How Animals Change: The Interaction of Animals and Scientists
by Samuel D. Gorey
On-Level

CAPTIVE OR FREE: ZOOS IN DEBATE
BY PATRICIA WALSH
Advanced

Jane Goodall
Scientist and Protector of Chimpanzees
by Asher Jonic

ELL Reader
· Concept Vocabulary
· Text Support
· Language Enrichment

TIME FOR **Science**

Integrate Science Standards
• **Resources**
• **Adaptation**
• **Animal Interaction**
• **Animal Communication**

✓ **Read**

The Chimpanzees I Love,
pp. 434–447

"'Going Ape' Over Language," pp. 450–455

Leveled Readers

Below-Level   **On-Level**   **Advanced**

• Support Concepts   • Develop Concepts   • Extend Concepts
                                     • Science Extension
                                        Activity

ELL Reader

✓ **Build Concept Vocabulary**
Animal Research,
pp. 430l–430m

✓ **Teach Science Concepts**
Biodiversity, p. 443
Resources, p. 445
American Sign Language,
p. 451
Animal Communication, p. 455

✓ **Explore Science Center**
Women in Science, p. 430k

Weekly Plan

READING

45–90 minutes

TARGET SKILLS OF THE WEEK

🔵 **Comprehension Skill**
Author's Purpose

🔵 **Comprehension Strategy**
Answer Questions

🔵 **Vocabulary Strategy**
Dictionary/Glossary

LANGUAGE ARTS

30–60 minutes

Trait of the Week

Word Choice

DAY 1
PAGES 430l–432b,
455a, 455e–455k

Oral Language

QUESTION OF THE WEEK *Why is it important to study animals responsibly?*

Read Aloud: "Something in the Elephants' Silence," 430m
Build Concepts, 430l

Comprehension/Vocabulary

Comprehension Skill/Strategy Lesson, 430–431
🔵 Author's Purpose **T**
🔵 Answer Questions
Build Background, 432a
Introduce Lesson Vocabulary, 432b
captive, companionship, existence, ordeal, primitive, sanctuaries, stimulating **T**

Read Leveled Readers

Grouping Options 430f–430g

Fluency

Model Pauses, 430l–430m, 455a

Grammar, 455e
Introduce Pronouns and Antecedents **T**

Writing Workshop, 455g
Introduce Story About an Animal
Model the Trait of the Week: Word Choice

Spelling, 455i
Pretest for Prefixes *dis-, de-, out-, un-*

Internet Inquiry, 455k
Identify Questions

DAY 2
PAGES 432–441, 455a,
455e–455k

Oral Language

QUESTION OF THE DAY *Do you think chimpanzees have feelings? Why or why not?*

Comprehension/Vocabulary

Vocabulary Strategy Lesson, 432–433
🔵 Dictionary/Glossary **T**

Read *The Chimpanzees I Love,* 434–441

Grouping Options
430f–430g

🔵 Author's Purpose **T**
🔵 Answer Questions
REVIEW Fact and Opinion **T**
Develop Vocabulary

Fluency

Choral Reading, 455a

Grammar, 455e
Develop Pronouns and Antecedents **T**

Writing Workshop, 455g
Improve Writing with Vivid Words

Spelling, 455i
Teach the Generalization

Internet Inquiry, 455k
Navigate/Search

DAILY WRITING ACTIVITIES	**Day 1** Write to Read, 430	**Day 2** Words to Write, 433 Strategy Response Log, 434, 441
DAILY SCIENCE CONNECTIONS	**Day 1** Animal Research Concept Web, 430l	**Day 2** Science Center: Research Women in Science, 430K Revisit the Animal Research Concept Web, 441

DAILY SUCCESS PREDICTORS ➤
for Adequate Yearly Progress

Monitor Progress and Corrective Feedback

Vocabulary Check Vocabulary, *430l*

RESOURCES FOR THE WEEK

- Practice Book, *pp. 161–170*
- Word Study and Spelling Practice Book, *pp. 65–68*
- Grammar and Writing Practice Book, *pp. 65–68*

- Selection Test, *pp. 65–68*
- Fresh Reads for Differentiated Test Practice, *pp. 97–102*
- The Grammar and Writing Book, *pp. 146–151*

Grouping Options for Differentiated Instruction

Turn the page for the small group lesson plan.

DAY 3 PAGES 442-449, 455a, 455e-455k

Oral Language

QUESTION OF THE DAY *How can you make a difference in the way animals are treated?*

Comprehension/Vocabulary

Read *The Chimpanzees I Love,* 442–448

Grouping Options
430f–430g

- Author's Purpose **T**
- Answer Questions
- Dictionary/Glossary **T**
- Develop Vocabulary

Reader Response

Selection Test

Fluency

Model Pauses, 455a

Grammar, 455f
Apply Pronouns and Antecedents in Writing **T**

Writing Workshop, 449, 455h
Write Now
Prewrite and Draft

Spelling, 455j
Connect Spelling to Writing

Internet Inquiry, 455k
Analyze Sources

Day 3 Strategy Response Log, 446
Look Back and Write, 448

Day 3 Time for Science: Changes in Biodiversity, 443
Competing for Resources, 445; Revisit the
Animal Research Concept Web, 447

DAY 4 PAGES 450-455a, 455e-455k

Oral Language

QUESTION OF THE DAY *What do you think humans could learn from animals?*

Comprehension/Vocabulary

Read "'Going Ape' over Language," 450–455

Grouping Options
430f–430g

- Expository Nonfiction
- Reading Across Texts
- Content-Area Vocabulary

Fluency

Partner Reading, 455a

Grammar, 455f
Practice Pronouns and Antecedents
for Standardized Tests **T**

Writing Workshop, 455h
Draft, Revise, and Publish

Spelling, 455j
Provide a Strategy

Internet Inquiry, 455k
Synthesize Information

Day 4 Writing Across Texts, 455

Day 4 Time for Science: American Sign Language,
451; Animal Communication, 455

DAY 5 PAGES 455a-455l

Oral Language

QUESTION OF THE WEEK *To wrap up the week, revisit the Day 1 question.*
Build Concept Vocabulary, 455c

Fluency

Read Leveled Readers

Grouping Options 430f–430g

Assess Reading Rate, 455a

Comprehension/Vocabulary

- Reteach Author's Purpose, 455b **T**
- Persuasive Devices, 455b
- Review Dictionary/Glossary, 455c **T**

Speaking and Listening, 455d
Persuasive Speech
Listen to a Speech

Grammar, 455f
Cumulative Review

Writing Workshop, 455h
Connect to Unit Writing

Spelling, 455j
Posttest for Prefixes *dis-, de-, out-, un-*

Internet Inquiry, 455k
Communicate Results

Research/Study Skills, 455l
Electronic Media

Day 5 Persuasive Devices, 455b

Day 5 Revisit the Animal Research Concept Web,
455c

KEY ◉ = Target Skill **T** = Tested Skill

Comprehension Check Retelling, *448*

Fluency Check Fluency WCPM, *455a*

Vocabulary Check Vocabulary, *455c*

SUCCESS PREDICTOR

Small Group Plan for Differentiated Instruction

Daily Plan
AT A GLANCE

Reading
Whole Group
- Oral Language
- Comprehension/Vocabulary

Group Time
Differentiated Instruction

Meet with small groups to provide:
- Skill Support
- Reading Support
- Fluency Practice

Read

This week's lessons for daily group time can be found behind the Differentiated Instruction (DI) tab on pp. DI·12–DI·21.

Whole Group
- Fluency

Language Arts
- Grammar
- Writing
- Spelling
- Research/Inquiry
- Speaking/Listening/Viewing

DAY 1

On-Level	Strategic Intervention	Advanced
Teacher-Led *Page DI·13*	**Teacher-Led** *Page DI·12*	**Teacher-Led** *Page DI·13*
• Develop Concept Vocabulary • Read On-Level Reader *How Animals Change*	• Reinforce Concepts • Read Below-Level Reader *Great Apes*	• Read Advanced Reader *Captive or Free* • Independent Extension Activity

(i) Independent Activities
While you meet with small groups, have the rest of the class...

- Visit the Reading/Library Center
- Listen to the Background Building Audio
- Finish Write to Read, p. 430
- Complete Practice Book pp. 163–164
- Visit Cross-Curricular Centers

DAY 2

On-Level	Strategic Intervention	Advanced
Teacher-Led *Pages 436–441*	**Teacher-Led** *Page DI·14*	**Teacher-Led** *Page DI·15*
• Read *The Chimpanzees I Love*	• Practice Lesson Vocabulary • Read Multisyllabic Words • Read or Listen to *The Chimpanzees I Love*	• Extend Vocabulary • Read *The Chimpanzees I Love*

(i) Independent Activities
While you meet with small groups, have the rest of the class...

- Visit the Reading/Library Center
- Listen to AudioText for *The Chimpanzees I Love*
- Finish Words to Write, p. 433
- Complete Practice Book pp. 165–166
- Write in their Strategy Response Logs, pp. 434, 441
- Visit Cross-Curricular Centers
- Work on inquiry projects

DAY 3

On-Level	Strategic Intervention	Advanced
Teacher-Led *Pages 442–447*	**Teacher-Led** *Page DI·16*	**Teacher-Led** *Page DI·17*
• Read *The Chimpanzees I Love*	• Practice Author's Purpose and Answer Questions • Read or Listen to *The Chimpanzees I Love*	• Extend Author's Purpose and Answer Questions • Read *The Chimpanzees I Love*

(i) Independent Activities
While you meet with small groups, have the rest of the class...

- Visit the Reading/Library Center
- Listen to the AudioText for *The Chimpanzees I Love*
- Write in their Strategy Response Logs, p. 446
- Finish Look Back and Write, p. 448
- Complete Practice Book p. 167
- Visit Cross-Curricular Centers
- Work on inquiry projects

① Begin with whole class skill and strategy instruction.

② Meet with small groups to provide differentiated instruction.

③ Gather the whole class back together for fluency and language arts.

On-Level	Strategic Intervention	Advanced
Teacher-Led *Pages 450–455*	**Teacher-Led** *Page DI · 18*	**Teacher-Led** *Page DI · 19*
• **Read** "'Going Ape' Over Language"	• Practice Retelling • **Read** or Listen to "'Going Ape' Over Language"	• **Read** "'Going Ape' Over Language" • Genre Study

ⓘ Independent Activities

While you meet with small groups, have the rest of the class...

• Visit the Reading/Library Center
• Listen to the AudioText for "'Going Ape' Over Language"
• Visit the Writing/Vocabulary Center

• Finish Writing Across Texts, p. 455
• Visit Cross-Curricular Centers
• Work on inquiry projects

On-Level	Strategic Intervention	Advanced
Teacher-Led *Page DI · 21*	**Teacher-Led** *Page DI · 20*	**Teacher-Led** *Page DI · 21*
• **Reread** Leveled Reader *How Animals Change: The Interaction of Animals and Scientists* • Retell *How Animals Change*	• **Reread** Leveled Reader *Great Apes* • Retell *Great Apes*	• **Reread** Leveled Reader *Captive or Free* • Share Extension Activity

ⓘ Independent Activities

While you meet with small groups, have the rest of the class...

• Visit the Reading/Library Center
• Complete Practice Book pp. 168–170

• Visit Cross-Curricular Centers
• Work on inquiry projects

Grouping Place English language learners in the groups that correspond to their reading abilities in English.

Use the appropriate Leveled Reader or other text at students' instructional level.

TIP Send home the appropriate Multilingual Summary of the main selection on Day 1.

Take It to the NET
ONLINE
PearsonSuccessNet.com

Sharon Vaughn
For research on intervention, see the article "Group Size and Time Allotted to Intervention" by Scott Foresman author S. Vaughn and S. Linan-Thompson.

TEACHER TALK

Text written at a student's **instructional reading level** is text in which no more than one in ten words is difficult for the student to read.

Be sure to schedule time for students to work on the unit inquiry project "Going First." This week students conduct information searches for text and images that help answer their inquiry questions about explorers, pioneers, and discoverers.

Looking Ahead

Name _____ Date _____

My Work Plan

Put an ☒ next to the activities you complete.

Listening
☐ Listen to *The Chimpanzees I Love.*
☐ Listen to "'Going Ape' Over Language."

Writing/Vocabulary
☐ Study the Words to Know.
☐ Write a letter to a friend.

Reading
☐ Read a book.
☐ Read Ten Important Sentences.
☐ Book Club

Science
☐ Research women scientists.
☐ Create a poster.

Art
☐ Design a chimp habitat.
☐ Draw a picture.

Technology
☐ Write a short summary.
☐ Use the cut-and-paste feature to edit.

Independent Practice
☐ Practice Book, pp. 161–170
☐ Independent Writing

Inquiry
☐ Unit Inquiry
☐ Internet Inquiry

Wrap Up Your Week Turn your paper over. Write about what you did at school this week. What did you read? What did you learn about animal research?

34 Unit 4 • Week 2 • *The Chimpanzees I Love*

▲ **Group-Time Survival Guide** p. 34, Weekly Contract

The Chimpanzees I Love **430g**

Customize Your Plan *by Strand*

ORAL LANGUAGE

 Science

Concept Development

Why is it important to study animals responsibly?

CONCEPT VOCABULARY

conservationists   data   expedition

BUILD

❑ **Question of the Week** Introduce and discuss the question of the week. This week students will read a variety of texts and work on projects related to the concept *animal research*. Post the question for students to refer to throughout the week. **DAY 1** *430d*

❑ **Read Aloud** Read aloud "Something in the Elephants' Silence." Then begin a web to build concepts and concept vocabulary related to this week's lesson and the unit theme, Explorers, Pioneers, and Discoverers. Introduce the concept words *conservationists*, *data*, and *expedition* and have students place them on the web. Display the web for use throughout the week. **DAY 1** *430l-430m*

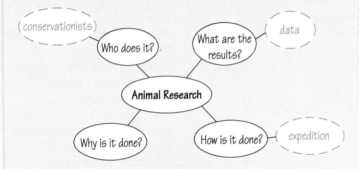

DEVELOP

❑ **Question of the Day** Use the prompts from the Weekly Plan to engage students in conversations related to this week's reading and the unit theme. **EVERY DAY** *430d-430e*

❑ **Concept Vocabulary Web** Revisit the Animal Research Concept Web and encourage students to add concept words from their reading and life experiences. **DAY 2** *441*, **DAY 3** *447*

CONNECT

❑ **Looking Back/Moving Forward** Revisit the Animal Research Concept Web and discuss how it relates to this week's lesson and the unit theme. Then make connections to next week's lesson. **DAY 5** *455c*

CHECK

❑ **Concept Vocabulary Web** Use the Animal Research Concept Web to check students' understanding of the concept vocabulary words *conservationists*, *data*, and *expedition*. **DAY 1** *430l*, **DAY 5** *455c*

VOCABULARY

⟳ **STRATEGY DICTIONARY/ GLOSSARY** A dictionary and a glossary are sources that contain alphabetical lists of words and their meanings. You can look in a dictionary or the glossary of your book to find the meaning of an unknown or unfamiliar word that you come across as you read.

LESSON VOCABULARY
captive   primitive
companionship   sanctuaries
existence   stimulating
ordeal

TEACH

❑ **Words to Know** Give students the opportunity to tell what they already know about this week's lesson vocabulary words. Then discuss word meaning. **DAY 1** *432b*

❑ **Vocabulary Strategy Lesson** Use the vocabulary strategy lesson in the Student Edition to introduce and model this week's strategy, *dictionary/glossary*. **DAY 2** *432-433*

Vocabulary Strategy Lesson

PRACTICE/APPLY

❑ **Leveled Text** Read the lesson vocabulary in the context of leveled text. **DAY 1** *LR10-LR18*

❑ **Words in Context** Read the lesson vocabulary and apply *dictionary/glossary* in the context of *The Chimpanzees I Love*. **DAY 2** *434-441*, **DAY 3** *442-448*

Leveled Readers

❑ **Writing/Vocabulary Center** Write a letter to a friend about studying chimps in Africa with Jane Goodall. **ANY DAY** *430k*

❑ **Homework** Practice Book pp. 164–165. **DAY 1** *432b*, **DAY 2** *433*

Main Selection—Nonfiction

❑ **Word Play** Discuss the category designations of the International Union for the Conservation of Nature for species in danger of extinction **ANY DAY** *455c*

ASSESS

❑ **Selection Test** Use the Selection Test to determine students' understanding of the lesson vocabulary words. **DAY 3**

RETEACH/REVIEW

❑ **Reteach Lesson** If necessary, use this lesson to reteach and review *dictionary/glossary*. **DAY 5** *455c*

COMPREHENSION

SKILL AUTHOR'S PURPOSE An author's purpose is the reason that an author writes. Authors write to persuade, inform, express ideas or feelings, or entertain. Knowing the author's purpose helps you decide how fast to read.

STRATEGY ANSWER QUESTIONS Preview a selection to predict the author's purpose. After reading, answer the question, "Did the author meet his or her purpose?"

TEACH

❑ **Skill/Strategy Lesson** Use the skill/strategy lesson in the Student Edition to introduce and model *author's purpose* and *answer questions*. DAY 1 430–431

❑ **Extend Skills** Teach persuasive devices. **ANY DAY** 455b

Skill/Strategy Lesson

PRACTICE/APPLY

❑ **Leveled Text** Apply *author's purpose* and *answer questions* to read leveled text. DAY 1 LR10–LR18

❑ **Skills and Strategies in Context** Read *The Chimpanzees I Love,* using the Guiding Comprehension questions to apply *author's purpose* and *answer questions*. DAY 2 434–441, DAY 3 442–448

Leveled Readers

❑ **Skills and Strategies in Context** Read "'Going Ape' over Language," guiding students as they apply *author's purpose* and *answer questions*. Then have students discuss and write across texts. DAY 4 450–455

Main Selection—Nonfiction

❑ **Homework** Practice Book pp. 163, 167, 168. DAY 1 431, DAY 3 447, DAY 5 455b

❑ **Fresh Reads for Differentiated Test Practice** Have students practice *author's purpose* with a new passage. DAY 3

Paired Selection—Nonfiction

ASSESS

❑ **Selection Test** Determine students' understanding of the selection and their use of *author's purpose*. DAY 3

❑ **Retell** Have students retell *The Chimpanzees I Love*. DAY 3 448–449

RETEACH/REVIEW

❑ **Reteach Lesson** If necessary, reteach and review *author's purpose*. DAY 5 455b

FLUENCY

SKILL PAUSES Pausing means to stop at appropriate places in longer, more complex sentences when you read aloud. Pausing to slow down or stop helps listeners to follow and understand the text more easily.

TEACH

❑ **Read Aloud** Model fluent reading by rereading "Something in the Elephants' Silence." Focus on this week's fluency skill, pauses. DAY 1 430l–430m, 455a

PRACTICE/APPLY

❑ **Choral Reading** Read aloud selected paragraphs from *The Chimpanzees I Love,* having students notice how you pause for commas, dashes, and periods. Then practice as a class by doing three choral readings of the selected paragraphs. DAY 2 455a, DAY 3 455a

❑ **Partner Reading** Have partners practice reading aloud, pausing at commas and periods, and offering each other feedback. As students reread, monitor their progress toward their individual fluency goals. DAY 4 455a

❑ **Listening Center** Have students follow along with the AudioText for this week's selections. **ANY DAY** 430j

❑ **Reading/Library Center** Have students reread a selection of their choice. **ANY DAY** 430j

❑ **Fluency Coach** Have students use Fluency Coach to listen to fluent readings or practice reading on their own. **ANY DAY**

ASSESS

❑ **Check Fluency** WCPM Do a one-minute timed reading, paying special attention to this week's skill—pauses. Provide feedback for each student. DAY 5 455a

☑ Customize Your Plan *by Strand*

GRAMMAR

SKILL PRONOUNS AND ANTECEDENTS A pronoun is a word that takes the place of a noun. Every pronoun has an antecedent or referent. A pronoun's antecedent is the word that it takes the place of; a referent is the word a pronoun refers back to.

TEACH

❑ **Grammar Transparency 17** Use Grammar Transparency 17 to teach pronouns and antecedents.
DAY 1 *455e*

Grammar Transparency 17

PRACTICE/APPLY

❑ **Develop the Concept** Review the concept of pronouns and antecedents and provide guided practice. DAY 2 *455e*

❑ **Apply to Writing** Have students review something they have written and apply pronouns and antecedents. DAY 3 *455f*

❑ **Test Preparation** Examine common errors in using pronouns and antecedents to prepare for standardized tests. DAY 4 *455f*

❑ **Homework** Grammar and Writing Practice Book pp. 65–67.
DAY 2 *455e*, DAY 3 *455f*, DAY 4 *455f*

ASSESS

❑ **Cumulative Review** Use Grammar and Writing Practice Book p. 68. DAY 5 *455f*

RETEACH/REVIEW

❑ **Daily Fix-It** Have students find and correct errors in grammar, spelling, and punctuation.
EVERY DAY *455e–455f*

❑ **The Grammar and Writing Book** Use pp. 146–149 of The Grammar and Writing Book to extend instruction for using pronouns and antecedents. ANY DAY

The Grammar and Writing Book

WRITING

Trait of the Week

WORD CHOICE Good writers always search for the perfect words to express an idea. For example, when you write a story about an animal, use precise, interesting nouns, verbs, and adjectives to convey your ideas effectively.

TEACH

❑ **Writing Transparency 17A** Use the model to introduce and discuss the Trait of the Week. DAY 1 *455g*

❑ **Writing Transparency 17B** Use the transparency to show students how use vivid words can improve their writing.
DAY 2 *455g*

Writing Transparency 17A **Writing Transparency 17B**

PRACTICE/APPLY

❑ **Write Now** Examine the model on Student Edition p. 449. Then have students write their own story about an animal. DAY 3 *449, 455h,* DAY 4 *455h*

> **Prompt** In *The Chimpanzees I Love,* Jane Goodall tells the story of her work with chimpanzees. Think about an animal that interests you. Now write a story about that animal, complete with a beginning, middle, and end.

Write Now p. 449

❑ **Writing/Vocabulary Center** Write a letter to a friend about studying chimps in Africa with Jane Goodall. ANY DAY *430k*

ASSESS

❑ **Writing Trait Rubric** Use the rubric to evaluate students' writing. DAY 4 *455h*

RETEACH/REVIEW

❑ **The Grammar and Writing Book** Use pp. 146–151 of The Grammar and Writing Book to extend instruction for pronouns and antecedents, using vivid words, and stories about an animal. ANY DAY

The Grammar and Writing Book

① Use assessment data to determine your instructional focus.

② Preview this week's instruction by strand.

③ Choose instructional activities that meet the needs of your classroom.

SPELLING

GENERALIZATION **PREFIXES** *dis-, de-, out-, un* The prefixes *dis-, de-, out-,* and *un-* change the meaning of the base word. They do not, however, change the spelling or pronunciation of the base word.

TEACH

❑ **Pretest** Give the pretest for words with prefixes *dis-, de-, out-, un-*. Guide students in self-correcting their pretests and correcting any misspellings. DAY 1 455i

❑ **Think and Practice** Connect spelling to the phonics generalization for prefixes *dis-, de-, out-, un-*. DAY 2 455i

PRACTICE/APPLY

❑ **Connect to Writing** Have students use spelling words to write an essay. Then review frequently misspelled words: *because, everything*. DAY 3 455j

❑ **Homework** Phonics and Spelling Practice Book pp. 65–68. **EVERY DAY**

RETEACH/REVIEW

❑ **Review** Review spelling words to prepare for the posttest. Then provide students with a spelling strategy—divide and conquer. DAY 4 455j

ASSESS

❑ **Posttest** Use dictation sentences to give the posttest for words with prefiixes *dis-, de-, out-, un-*. DAY 5 455j

Spelling Words

1. discontent	8. outstanding	15. disarray
2. decline	9. uncommon	16. unconscious
3. outward	10. outburst	17. outskirts
4. dispatch	11. outrageous	18. unfasten
5. unwavering	12. defensive	19. disenchanted
6. destruction*	13. unappetizing	20. decompose
7. disintegrate	14. disillusioned	

Challenge Words

21. unbusinesslike	23. deactivate	25. outlandish
22. disembark	24. disenfranchise	26. adolescence

*Word from the selection

RESEARCH AND INQUIRY

❑ **Internet Inquiry** Have students conduct an Internet inquiry on animal research. **EVERY DAY** 455k

❑ **Electronic Media** Review the tools used in computer and non-computer electronic media for researching. Then have pairs of students formulate questions on animal research, and discuss the questions on p. 455l. DAY 5 455l

❑ **Unit Inquiry** Allow time for students to conduct information searches for text and images that help answer their inquiry questions about explorers, pioneers, and discoverers. **ANY DAY** 407

SPEAKING AND LISTENING

❑ **Persuasive Speech** Have students prepare short persuasive speeches about their positions on the treatment of animals used in research. DAY 5 455d

❑ **Listen to a Speech** Have students take notes during their classmates' persuasive speeches, then determine positions that were well-supported with facts and valid opinions. DAY 5 455d

Resources for Differentiated Instruction

LEVELED READERS

▶ **Comprehension**
  - **Skill** Author's Purpose
  - **Strategy** Answer Questions

▶ **Lesson Vocabulary**
  - Dictionary/Glossary

captive
ordeal
companionship
existence
sanctuaries
primitive
stimulating

▶ **Science Standards**
- **Resources**
- **Adaptation**
- **Animal Interaction**
- **Animal Communication**

Leveled Reader Database ONLINE

PearsonSuccessNet.com

Use the Online Database of over 600 books to
- Download and print additional copies of this week's leveled readers.
- Listen to the readers being read online.
- Search for more titles focused on this week's skills, topic, and content.

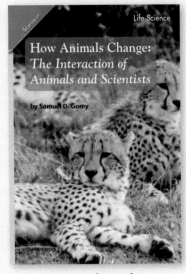

Life Science

How Animals Change: The Interaction of Animals and Scientists

by Samuel D. Gorey

On-Level Reader

Author's Purpose

An **author's purpose** is his or her reason for writing. There are four main reasons for writing: to **persuade, inform, entertain,** and **express** a mood or feeling.

Directions Answer the questions below about the author's purpose.

1. Why might the author have written this book?
   To inform people about the effects of scientific study on animals

2. What was the author's purpose for using photographs?
   To help the reader better understand what she is saying

3. In what ways did the author succeed in her purpose?
   She gave facts about how studying animals affects them.

Directions Read the following sentences from *How Animals Change: The Interaction of Animals and Scientists* and write the author's purpose.

1. Using a Global Positioning System, or GPS, the collar can pinpoint an animal's exact longitude and latitude at any time, day or night for researchers. inform

2. Worst of all, ducks could get so frightened by the dragging operation that they give up on nesting altogether. inform

3. For instance, researchers seeking an effective way of drawing cheetahs to camera traps in the wild recently stumbled across a strange fact. entertain

4. As we move into the future, we must listen to scientists' recommendations about animals and the environment. persuade

5. The main idea behind operant conditioning is that if an animal performs a behavior, and if the consequences of that behavior are pleasing to the animal, then the animal will probably repeat the behavior. inform

On-Level Practice TE p. LR14

Vocabulary

Directions Use the vocabulary words in the box to fill in the blanks in the sentences below.

Check the Words You Know
- captive
- companionship
- existence
- ordeal
- primitive
- sanctuary
- stimulating

1. There are many kinds of bears in existence today.
2. Primitive people had to hunt animals to survive.
3. Animals are happier when there are other animals around for companionship
4. Exercise is stimulating for zoo animals.
5. It is an ordeal to keep track of all the wild buffalo.
6. Captive animals are not free to roam.
7. A sanctuary keeps animals safe and protected.

Directions Write a synonym for each vocabulary word below.

1. stimulating interesting, exciting
2. existence survival, life, being
3. sanctuary haven, refuge
4. companionship friendship, company
5. captive caged, jailed
6. ordeal trial, test, problem
7. primitive ancient, prehistoric

On-Level Practice TE p. LR15

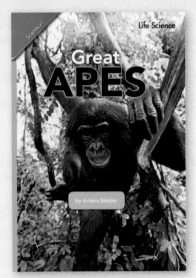

Life Science

Great APES

by Ariana Melzer

Below-Level Reader

Author's Purpose

An **author's purpose** is his or her reason for writing. There are four main reasons for writing: to **persuade, inform, entertain,** and **express** a mood or feeling.

Directions Answer the questions below about the author's purpose.

1. Why might the author have written this book?
   To inform the reader about the pros and cons of keeping animals in zoos

2. What was the author's purpose for using photographs?
   To help the reader better understand what she is saying

3. In what ways did the author succeed in her purpose?
   She helped me understand the pros and cons of keeping animals in zoos by giving facts.

Directions Write whether each statement's purpose is to persuade, inform, entertain, or express.

1. The blue water was so clear that you could almost see to the bottom of the ocean. express
2. It's up to you to save those precious birds from extinction. persuade
3. The animals finally broke free and raided the ice cream truck. entertain
4. There are over 1,000 kinds of fish in the ocean. inform
5. Anyone who donates money will get a free zoo pass. persuade
6. The kangaroo, koala bear, and wallaby are all natives of Australia. inform
7. It was quiet and still, except for the gentle breeze blowing through the trees. express
8. You must see this great movie about the wilderness! persuade
9. The elephant is the largest zoo animal, weighing about 12,000 pounds. inform
10. The man was startled by a low growl behind him. entertain

Below-Level Practice TE p. LR11

Vocabulary

Directions Write the vocabulary word that means the same as the words below.

Check the Words You Know
- captive
- companionship
- existence
- ordeals
- primitive
- sanctuaries
- stimulating

1. hardships ordeals
2. being existence
3. confined captive
4. ancient primitive
5. exciting stimulating
6. company companionship
7. refuges sanctuaries

Directions Write the vocabulary word that means the opposite as the words below.

1. alone companionship
2. boring stimulating
3. free captive
4. modern primitive
5. easy solutions ordeals
6. dangerous places sanctuaries
7. extinction existence

Directions Fill in the blanks with vocabulary words from the box.

The animal sanctuaries came into existence to give animals companionship and freedom.

Below-Level Practice TE p. LR12

Advanced

Advanced Reader

Author's Purpose

An **author's purpose** is his or her reason for writing. There are four main reasons for writing: to **persuade, inform, entertain,** and **express** a mood or feeling.

Directions Answer the questions below about the author's purpose.

1. Why might the author have written this book?
   To inform the reader about the pros and cons of keeping animals
   in zoos

2. What was the author's purpose for using photographs?
   To help the reader better understand what she is saying

3. In what ways did the author succeed in her purpose?
   She helped me understand the pros and cons of keeping
   animals in zoos by giving facts.

Directions Write whether each statement's purpose is to persuade, inform, entertain, or express.

1. The blue water was so clear that you could almost see to the bottom of the ocean. express

2. It's up to you to save those precious birds from extinction. persuade

3. The animals finally broke free and raided the ice cream truck. entertain

4. There are over 1,000 kinds of fish in the ocean. inform

5. Anyone who donates money will get a free zoo pass. persuade

6. The kangaroo, koala bear, and wallaby are all natives of Australia. inform

7. It was quiet and still, except for the gentle breeze blowing through the trees. express

8. You must see this great movie about the wilderness! persuade

9. The elephant is the largest zoo animal, weighing about 12,000 pounds. inform

10. The man was startled by a low growl behind him. entertain

Advanced Practice TE p. LR17

Vocabulary

Directions Write a definition for each vocabulary word below.

Check the Words You Know
— activists
— confinement
— controversial
— exotic
— moats
— realistic
— species
— zoolgical

1. realistic actual
2. exotic rare
3. zoological relating to animal study
4. activists advocates
5. confinement being trapped
6. moats waterways used for protection
7. species group with common properties
8. controversial debatable

Directions Fill in the blanks with vocabulary words from the box.

1. Professor Talbot consulted a zoological expert for our class project on mammals.
2. The hundreds of activists demanded that labs stop killing rabbits.
3. The Supreme Court has made some controversial rulings.
4. That movie set was very realistic.
5. It was common for kings and queens to construct palaces with moats.
6. Some new species are still being discovered.
7. Many exotic environments exist close to the equator.
8. For certain animals, confinement seems like abuse.

Directions Write a sentence below using any two vocabulary words.
Responses will vary.

Advanced Practice TE p. LR18

ELL

ELL Reader

ELL Poster 17

Teacher's Edition Notes

ELL notes throughout this lesson support instruction and reference additional resources at point of use.

Teaching Guide
pp. 113–119, 244–245
- Multilingual summaries of the main selection
- Comprehension lesson
- Vocabulary strategies and word cards
- ELL Reader 6.4.2 lesson

ELL and Transition Handbook

Ten Important Sentences
- Key ideas from every selection in the Student Edition
- Activities to build sentence power

More Reading

Readers' Theater Anthology
- Fluency practice
- Five scripts to build fluency
- Poetry for oral interpretation

Leveled Trade Books

Below-Level
On-Level
Advanced

- Extended reading tied to the unit concept
- Lessons in the Trade Book Library Teaching Guide

School + Home

Homework
- Family Times Newsletter
- ELL Multilingual Selection Summaries

Take-Home Books
- Leveled Readers

The Chimpanzees I Love

Cross-Curricular Centers

 Listening

 Reading/Library

 Art

Listen to the Selections

MATERIALS `SINGLES`
CD player, headphones, AudioText CD, student book

LISTEN TO LITERATURE Listen to *The Chimpanzees I Love* and "Going Ape Over Language" as you follow or read along in your book. As you listen, think about the authors' purposes for writing.

If there is anything you don't understand, you can listen again to any section.

Read It AGAIN!

MATERIALS `SINGLES` `PAIRS` `GROUPS`
Collection of books for self-selected reading, reading logs, student book

Select a book you have already read. Record the title of the book in your reading log. You may want to read with a partner.

You have the choice to read any of the following:

- Leveled Readers
- ELL Readers
- Stories Written by Classmates
- Books from the Library
- *The Chimpanzees I Love*

TEN IMPORTANT SENTENCES Read the Ten Important Sentences from the story. Then locate the sentences in the student book.

BOOK CLUB Write a letter to Jane Goodall and ask for more information about her work with chimps and what you can do to help save them.

Design a Chimp Habitat

MATERIALS `SINGLES`
Drawing materials, writing materials

Design a zoo habitat that will keep a group of chimps safe, stimulated, and happy.

1. Decide how many chimps will be in the zoo habitat.
2. Think of what infant and adult chimps need to be happy every day. Ask yourself: How much space will they need? What will keep them from getting bored? What will make them feel safe and comfortable? How will they stay healthy?
3. Draw a picture of your habitat.

EARLY FINISHERS Write a paragraph describing the features of your chimp habitat.

Writing/Vocabulary

Science

Technology

Write a LETTER

MATERIALS `SINGLES`
Writing materials

Imagine that you are studying chimps in Africa with Jane Goodall. Write a letter to a friend about your experience.

1. Think about what you have learned about chimp behavior from reading the selection.
2. Imagine that you've been watching and studying the chimps, and that you've had some contact with them.
3. Write a letter to a friend back home describing what you have seen and how you feel about your experience.

EARLY FINISHERS Draw a picture for your friend that illustrates something in your letter.

Dear Tom,
I am learning so much about chimps! Yesterday, one of the chimps slowly walked up to me...

Research Women in Science

MATERIALS `SINGLES`
Books on women scientists, Internet access, writing and drawing materials

Read books and use the Internet to find out about other women scientists. Then make a poster about one of them.

1. Choose a branch of science that you are interested in, such as chemistry, medicine, astronomy, or biology.
2. Choose a woman scientist who works or has worked in this field.
3. Create a poster that gives some biographical information about the scientist and some information about her work.
4. Display your poster in your classroom.

EARLY FINISHERS Make a list of other women scientists that you would like to learn more about.

 Jane Goodall

1. Born in England
2. Started a camp in Africa in 1960

Learn to Edit

MATERIALS `SINGLES`
Computer, word-processing program

Use the cut-and-paste feature to help edit your writing.

1. Write a short summary of *The Chimpanzees I Love* on the computer.
2. With your mouse, highlight one of the main ideas. Go to the Edit pull down menu and choose *Cut.* The sentence will disappear.
3. Move your cursor to where you want to place the sentence and click once.
4. Go to the Edit pull down menu again and choose *Paste.* Your sentence will reappear in its new location.
5. Follow classroom rules when using the computer.

EARLY FINISHERS Experiment with the Copy feature, which lets you copy text without erasing it and put it in another place.

ALL CENTERS

- Build vocabulary by finding words related to the lesson concept.
- Listen to determine the author's purpose.

Concept Vocabulary

conservationists people who want to preserve and protect natural resources

data facts from which conclusions can be drawn

expedition journey for some special purpose

Monitor Progress

Check Vocabulary

If... students are unable to place words on the Web,	then... review the lesson concept. Place the words on the Web and provide additional words for practice, such as *experiment* and *biologists*.

SUCCESS PREDICTOR

DAY 1   Grouping Options

Reading

Whole Group
Introduce and discuss the Question of the Week. Then use pp. 430l–432b.

Small Group

Differentiated Instruction
Read this week's Leveled Readers. See pp. 430f–430g for the small group lesson plan.

Whole Group
Use p. 455a.

Language Arts
Use pp. 455e–455k.

Build Concepts

FLUENCY

MODEL PAUSES As you read "Something in the Elephants' Silence," pause appropriately for the different types of punctuation, which include periods, commas, colons, dashes, and ellipses. For example, you might pause longer for an ellipsis than for a comma.

LISTENING COMPREHENSION

After reading "Something in the Elephants' Silence," use the following questions to assess listening comprehension.

1. **What is the author's purpose in writing this article?** *(to inform readers about elephant research and its purpose)* **Author's Purpose**

2. **Do you think the author met her purpose? Why or why not?** *(Sample response: Yes, because she explained the researchers' work in a clear and interesting way.)* **Author's Purpose**

BUILD CONCEPT VOCABULARY

Start a web to build concepts and vocabulary related to this week's lesson and the unit theme.

- Draw the Animal Research Concept Web.
- Read the sentence with the word *conservationists* again. Ask students to pronounce *conservationists* and discuss its meaning.
- Place *conservationists* in an oval attached to Who Does It? Explain that *conservationists* is related to this concept. Read the sentences in which *expedition* and *data* appear. Have students pronounce the words, place them on the Web, and provide reasons.
- Brainstorm additional words and categories for the Web. Keep the Web on display and add words throughout the week.

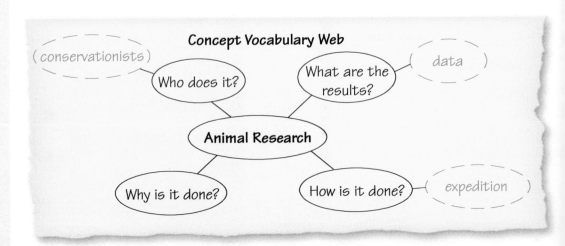

Concept Vocabulary Web

Something in the ELEPHANTS' SILENCE

by April Pulley Sayre

Deep in a rain forest in the Central African Republic, elephant expert Katy Payne writes to family and friends: "I am in Mya's and my field house. Writing by lantern light and the glow of my computer…Beyond us the night is full of insect calls—some crickety, others unfamiliar—distant frogs, an owl, and beyond that a deep peaceful silence except for every now and then an elephant rumble or roar…"

Payne has spent most of her life doing this: listening. As a child, she loved music—from folk songs to classical, especially Bach. She majored in Music in college. But instead of pursuing a traditional music career, she went on to become a scientist studying animal sound.

[In 1999] she realized that studies of elephants' calls might be helpful in counting the number of elephants. A better count of wild elephants is useful because conservationists must prove elephants are rare or decreasing in number in order to convince governments to take action to protect elephants. Payne was particularly interested in finding out how many elephants lived in the forests of central and western Africa.

Payne wanted to see if she could estimate their numbers by listening to their calls. To study this problem, she traveled to the Central African Republic with Steve Gulick, Mya Thompson, and Melissa Groo. The expedition, based at Andrea Turkalo's research site, was one of the highlights of her career.

Payne and the others began to set up their equipment on, under, and around the thatch-roofed platform that had been built by previous expeditions. From there Payne could look out over an opening in the forest. This opening was a special gathering place for forest elephants, who often visited to wade in the mud holes that formed there.

Payne's research in the Central African Republic was successful. While there, she was able to study infrasonic calls. About half of the elephant calls recorded by the computer were calls that the scientists themselves couldn't hear. By looking back over the videos of elephant behavior, Payne hopes to understand what these calls mean.

Payne's research also linked the number of calls to the number of elephants. She's still analyzing the data, but it now looks as if elephants can be counted by sounds, as has been done with whales. "This is turning out to be wonderful," Payne says. "If you listen carefully to the calls of an elephant group you can figure out how many there are, and who they are—whether there's a healthy balance of babies, adult males, and females. The calls of elephants open a window on the lives and health of hidden elephant populations." It is hoped that knowing how many elephants live in the forest and where those elephants roam will help conservationists gather support for protecting the habitat elephants need.

 SKILLS ⟷ STRATEGIES IN CONTEXT

Author's Purpose
Answer Questions

INTRODUCE

Write this summary: *This guidebook describes places to visit in Europe.* Ask what the author's purpose is. *(to inform)*

Have students read the information on p. 430. Explain the following:

- Often writers have one main purpose, but they can also have more than one. For example, the author of a humorous article may write both to entertain and to persuade.

- Answering questions about author's purpose requires you to evaluate an author's writing.

Use Skill Transparency 17 to teach author's purpose and answering questions.

Comprehension

Skill
Author's Purpose

Strategy
Answer Questions

 ## Author's Purpose

- Authors may write to persuade, inform, express ideas or feelings, or entertain.

- If you know the author's purpose, you can adjust the way you read. If the purpose is to entertain, you may choose to read faster. If the purpose is to inform, read more slowly.

- As you preview a selection, predict the author's purpose. After reading, ask if the author met the purpose.

Before Reading Preview to decide purpose. Set reading pace.
↓
During Reading Look for clues to purpose.
↓
After Reading Ask if purpose was met and how.

Strategy: Answer Questions

Good readers search for important information to answer questions completely and accurately. Often it is right in the text because the author's purpose is to inform you clearly. Some questions, though, require you to combine the information in the text with what you already know.

Write to Read

1. Read "Jane Goodall's Career." Make a graphic organizer like the one above in order to determine the author's purpose.

2. Use your graphic organizer to write complete and accurate answers to these questions: In your opinion, did the author meet her purpose? Why or why not?

430

Strategic Intervention

Author's Purpose To help students evaluate how well an author meets his or her purpose, give them these questions after reading:

- If the purpose was to persuade, were the author's arguments convincing?
- If the purpose was to inform, was the information presented clearly?
- If the purpose was to express ideas or feelings, did the ideas and feelings come across?
- If the purpose was to entertain, did I find the writing entertaining?

ELL

Access Content

Beginning/Intermediate For a Picture It! lesson on author's purpose, see the ELL Teaching Guide, pp. 113–114.

Advanced Before reading "Jane Goodall's Career," have students share what they know about chimpanzees.

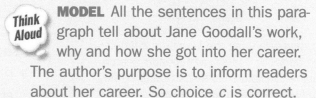

Jane Goodall's Career

JANE GOODALL is known worldwide for studying chimpanzees. As a child she became interested in how animals behaved. She left school at age 18 and eventually traveled to Africa, where in 1960 she started a camp in the Gombe Stream Game Reserve. From there she could carefully research the chimpanzees that lived in the region.

Goodall and her family lived in Gombe until 1975. Over the years Goodall discovered many surprising facts about chimpanzees. For example, she learned that chimpanzees are omnivorous. This means that they eat both plants and animals. Before her discovery most scientists believed that chimpanzees were vegetarians, or plant eaters. Goodall also discovered that chimpanzees are capable of making and using their own tools, using twigs and the like.

Goodall wrote several fascinating books about her research with chimpanzees. In 1971 she told about her first years at Gombe in the book *In the Shadow of Man*. Later, in 1986, she wrote all she had learned about chimpanzee behavior in *The Chimpanzees of Gombe*.

> **1** **Skill** What is the purpose of this paragraph?
> **(a)** to persuade you that Jane Goodall was a poor scientist
> **(b)** to express what it felt like to live in Africa
> **(c)** to inform you about Jane Goodall's career

> **2** **Strategy** If you were asked, "What did Goodall learn about chimpanzees?" you could find the answer in the text. What does that tell you about the author's purpose?

> **4** **Strategy** What makes you think the author did or did not meet her purpose?

> **3** **Skill** Do you think the author met her purpose in writing this article?

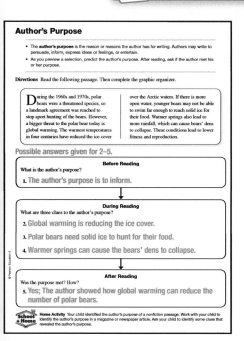

431

Available as **Skill Transparency** 17

Author's Purpose

• The **author's purpose** is the reason or reasons the author has for writing. Authors may write to persuade, inform, express ideas or feelings, or entertain.
• As you preview a selection, predict the author's purpose. After reading, ask if the author met his or her purpose.

Directions Read the following passage. Then complete the graphic organizer.

During the 1960s and 1970s, polar bears were a threatened species, so a landmark agreement was made to stop sport hunting of the bears. However, a bigger threat to the polar bear today is global warming. The warmest temperatures in four centuries have reduced the ice cover over the Arctic waters. If there is more open water, younger bears may not be able to swim far enough to reach solid ice for their food. Warmer springs also lead to more rainfall, which can cause bears' dens to collapse. These conditions lead to lower fitness and reproduction.

Possible answers given for 2–5.

Before Reading
What is the author's purpose?
1. The author's purpose is to inform.

During Reading
What are three clues to the author's purpose?
2. Global warming is reducing the ice cover.
3. Polar bears need solid ice to hunt for their food.
4. Warmer springs can cause the bears' dens to collapse.

After Reading
Was the purpose met? How?
5. Yes; The author showed how global warming can reduce the number of polar bears.

School + Home **Home Activity** Your child identified the author's purpose of a nonfiction passage. Work with your child to identify the author's purpose in a magazine or newspaper article. Ask your child to identify some clues that revealed the author's purpose.

▲ **Practice Book** p. 163

TEACH

1 **SKILL** Use the first paragraph to model how to determine the author's purpose.

Think Aloud **MODEL** All the sentences in this paragraph tell about Jane Goodall's work, why and how she got into her career. The author's purpose is to inform readers about her career. So choice *c* is correct.

2 **STRATEGY** Discuss the answer to the question about author's purpose.

Think Aloud **MODEL** The fact that I could find the answer to the question in the text tells me that the author's purpose is to inform readers about Jane Goodall.

PRACTICE AND ASSESS

3 **SKILL** Possible response: Yes; students should justify their responses.

4 **STRATEGY** Possible response: The author provides a clear, well-organized summary of Jane Goodall's career and includes the most important information.

WRITE Have students complete steps 1 and 2 of the Write to Read activity. You might consider using this as a whole class activity.

Monitor Progress	
Author's Purpose	
If... students are unable to complete **Write to Read** on p. 430,	then... use Practice Book p. 163 to provide additional practice

ONLINE

Students can use the keywords *chimpanzee behavior* in a student-friendly search engine to explore research trends in the study of chimpanzee behavior.

ELL

Build Background Use ELL Poster 17 to build background and vocabulary for the lesson concept of why it is important to study animals responsibly.

▲ **ELL Poster** 17

Build Background

ACTIVATE PRIOR KNOWLEDGE

BEGIN A KWL CHART about chimpanzees and animal research.

- Give students two to three minutes to write as many things as they can about chimpanzees and animal research. Record what students know on the KWL chart.

- Give students two minutes to write three questions that they would like to ask about chimpanzees and animal research. Record questions on the KWL chart. Add a question of your own.

- Tell students that, as they read, they should look for the answers to their questions and note any new information to add to the chart.

Topic Chimpanzees and Animal Research

K	W	L
Chimpanzees are intelligent animals. There are many chimpanzees living in captivity.	What can scientists learn by studying chimpanzees? How has captivity affected chimpanzees?	

▲ **Graphic Organizer** 4

BACKGROUND BUILDING AUDIO This week's audio explores the difference between verbal and nonverbal language. After students listen, discuss what they found out.

Background Building Audio

Introduce Vocabulary

THREE-COLUMN CHART

Have students complete a three-column chart for this week's lesson vocabulary words.

Word	Meaning	Sentence
captive		
companionship		
existence		
ordeal		
primitive		
sanctuaries		
stimulating		

▲ **Graphic Organizer** 26

Students should provide definitions for words they already know, check their definitions against the dictionary definitions for each word, and write an example sentence. **Activate Prior Knowledge**

Have students share where they may have seen some of these words. Point out that some of this week's words have multiple meanings *(captive)* and students may learn new definitions for these words. **Multiple-Meaning Words**

By the end of the week, students should know the lesson vocabulary words. Have them revise their charts as necessary.

Use Multisyllabic Word Routine on p. DI·1 to help students read multisyllabic words.

Vocabulary

Directions Choose the word from the box that best matches each definition. Write the word on the line.

primitive _____ 1. very simple

captive _____ 2. kept in confinement

ordeal _____ 3. a severe test or experience

sanctuaries _____ 4. places of refuge or protection

companionship _____ 5. friendly feeling among companions

Check the Words You Know
___captive
___companionship
___existence
___ordeal
___primitive
___sanctuaries
___stimulating

Directions Choose the word from the box that best completes each sentence. Write the word on the line shown on the left.

companionship _____ 6. Margaret really enjoyed the ___ among her friends.

existence _____ 7. Karl did not believe in the ___ of ghosts.

stimulating _____ 8. She joined the Film Club so she could meet people who liked ___ conversations about movies.

ordeal _____ 9. The class survived the ___ of taking the hardest test they had ever had.

sanctuaries _____ 10. The science class went to visit several wildlife ___.

Write a Newspaper Article
On a separate sheet of paper, write a newspaper article about a person who is trying to save an endangered animal. Use as many vocabulary words as you can.

Newspaper articles should include words from the vocabulary list and details about saving an endangered animal.

Home Activity Your child identified and used vocabulary words from *The Chimpanzees I Love*. Read a story or nonfiction article with your child. Have him or her point out unfamiliar words. Use a dictionary to look up the unfamiliar words.

▲ **Practice Book** p. 164

Vocabulary Strategy

INTRODUCE

Discuss the strategy for a dictionary or glossary using the steps on p. 432.

TEACH

- Have students read "Zoos Then and Now," paying attention to how vocabulary is used.
- Model using a dictionary to determine the meaning of the word *captive.*

Think Aloud **MODEL** *Captive* appears on the dictionary page with the guide words *capital* and *captor.* It has two definitions, one as a noun and one as an adjective. In the second sentence on page 433, the word is used as an adjective. So the correct definition is "made a prisoner."

Words to Know

- captive
- existence
- ordeal
- primitive
- stimulating
- companionship
- sanctuaries

Vocabulary Strategy
for Unfamiliar Words

Dictionary/Glossary Sometimes when you are reading, you find a word you do not know. If the sentences around the word do not give good clues to its meaning, you may need to look up the word in a dictionary or in the glossary of your book.

1. Check the back of your book to see if there is a glossary. If there is not, look in a dictionary.

2. Find the entry for the word. Words in both dictionaries and glossaries are listed in alphabetical order.

3. Read the pronunciation of the word, if one is given. You may recognize the word when you say it.

4. Read all the meanings listed in the entry.

5. Choose the meaning that makes sense in your sentence.

As you read "Zoos Then and Now," use this book's glossary or a dictionary to determine the meanings of unfamiliar words that the text does not define.

432

DAY 2 — Grouping Options

Reading
Whole Group Discuss the Question of the Week. Then use pp. 432–435.

Small Group Differentiated Instruction
Read *The Chimpanzees I Love.* See pp. 430f–430g for the small group lesson plan.

Whole Group Use p. 455a.

Language Arts
Use pp. 455e–455k.

Strategic Intervention

 Dictionary/Glossary Have students work in pairs to follow the steps on p. 432 with one of the vocabulary words.

ELL

Access Content Use ELL Poster 17 to preteach vocabulary. Choose from the following to meet language proficiency levels.

Beginning Use the Multilingual Lesson Vocabulary list in the ELL Teaching Guide and other home-language resources to provide translations of the tested words.

Intermediate After reading, students can choose one of the tested words to use to complete a vocabulary frame.

Advanced Teach the lesson on pp. 432–433. Have students find home-language terms for some of the tested words.

Resources for home-language words may include parents, bilingual staff members, bilingual dictionaries, or online translation sources.

Zoos Then and Now

The first zoos existed to entertain people, who came to see strange wild animals from around the world. Hardly anyone thought about the health and happiness of these captive animals. For the most part, they were kept in small cages. Little was known about them, so no one knew what they needed for food or homes. Zoo life was nothing like their existence in the wild. Being shut in a tiny space and looking at metal and concrete all day was surely an ordeal.

Today, zoos are very different from those early, primitive places. They try hard to make life interesting and "normal" for their animals. The best zoos provide environments like those the animals would have in the wild. They offer many stimulating objects to keep the animals from getting bored. Animals are grouped in ways that make sure they have companionship. One aim is to set up family groups so babies can be born, helping endangered species increase their numbers. Zoos have become important to the survival of many animals. They are both sanctuaries and places of learning. They offer a safe place for animals to live and opportunities for people to understand them.

Words to Write

Look at the pictures in *The Chimpanzees I Love*. Choose one to write about. Use as many words from the Words to Know list as you can.

433

PRACTICE AND ASSESS

- Have students determine the meanings of the remaining words and explain how they used a dictionary or glossary to determine meaning.
- Point out that the word *stimulating* is used as an adjective in the second paragraph on p. 433. Students would only find the verb form *stimulate* in a dictionary and would need to adapt the definition.
- If students began a word meaning chart (p. 432b), have them revise their definitions as necessary to fit the context in "Zoos Then and Now."
- Have students complete Practice Book p. 165.

WRITE Writing should include at least three of the vocabulary words listed on p. 432.

Monitor Progress

Dictionary/Glossary

If... students need more practice with the lesson vocabulary,	then... use Tested Vocabulary Cards.

Vocabulary · Dictionary/Glossary

- **Dictionaries** and **glossaries** provide alphabetical lists of words and their meanings.
- Sometimes looking at the words around an unfamiliar word can't help you figure out the word's meaning. If this happens, use a dictionary or glossary to find the meaning.

Directions Read the following passage. Then answer the questions below.

Mary found the little bird on the ground after it had fallen from its nest. It survived the ordeal of the fall, but now needed someone to take care of it. Mary took it home and made a primitive shelter out of a shoebox. She called a bird sanctuary to ask what to do. They gave her feeding instructions and told her to keep the bird captive until it was strong enough to fly on its own. Mary enjoyed the bird's companionship for the two weeks she took care of it, but it was time to release the little bird to its wild existence.

Possible answers given for 4, 5.

1. Find the word *ordeal* in a dictionary or glossary. What does it mean?
   Ordeal means "a very severe test or experience."
2. Find the word *primitive* in a dictionary or glossary. Why is a shoebox a *primitive* nest?
   The shoebox is primitive because it is a very plain and simple version of a nest.
3. Find the word *sanctuary* in a dictionary or glossary. What is the plural form of the word?
   sanctuaries
4. What does the word *captive* mean? Why would the bird experts want Mary to keep the bird captive until it could fly on its own?
   Captive means "kept in confinement"; The little bird would have to be looked after until it could take care of itself.
5. What does the word *existence* mean? What is a wild existence?
   Existence means "condition of being"; "Wild existence" means to live like a bird in the wild.

Home Activity Your child used a dictionary or glossary to understand new words in a passage. Work with your child to identify unfamiliar words of an article. Then use a dictionary to look up the meanings of these unfamiliar words.

▲ **Practice Book** p. 165

Prereading Strategies

OBJECTIVES

- Identify the author's purpose to improve comprehension.
- Answer questions to help identify the author's purpose.

GENRE STUDY

Expository Nonfiction

The Chimpanzees I Love is expository nonfiction. Explain that expository nonfiction is organized by topic and provides information about real-life events, objects, ideas, or themes.

PREVIEW AND PREDICT

Have students preview the title, subtitles, subheads, and photographs and discuss the topics or ideas they think this selection will cover. Encourage students to use selection vocabulary words as they talk about what they expect to learn.

Strategy Response Log

Ask Questions Have students write three questions about what they want to find out about chimpanzees and the author's feelings about them. Students will try to answer their questions in the Strategy Response Log activity on p. 441.

The Chimpanzees I Love

Saving Their World and Ours

by Jane Goodall

Expository nonfiction explains the nature of something. Look for explanations about the nature of chimpanzees as you read.

434

Activate Prior Knowledge Have students look through the illustrations in the selection and predict what the selection is about. Invite students to share what they already know about chimpanzees and what they would like to know more about.

Consider having students read the selection summary in English or in students' home languages. See the Multilingual Summaries in the ELL Teaching Guide, pp. 117–119.

How are chimpanzees unlike most other animals?

435

SET PURPOSE

Read the first page of the selection aloud to students. Have students consider their preview discussion and tell what they hope to find out as they read.

Remind students to think about the author's purpose as they read.

STRATEGY RECALL

Students have now used these before-reading strategies:

- preview the selection to be aware of its genre, features, and possible content;
- activate prior knowledge about that content and what to expect of that genre;
- make predictions;
- set a purpose for reading.

Remind students that, as they read, they should monitor their own comprehension. If they realize something does not make sense, they can regain their comprehension by using fix-up strategies they have learned, such as:

- use phonics and word structure to decode new words;
- use context clues or a dictionary to figure out meanings of new words;
- adjust their reading rate—slow down for difficult text, speed up for easy or familiar text, or skim and scan just for specific information;
- reread parts of the text;
- read on (continue to read for clarification);
- use text features such as headings, subheadings, charts, illustrations, and so on as visual aids to comprehension;
- make a graphic organizer or a semantic organizer to aid comprehension;
- use reference sources, such as an encyclopedia, dictionary, thesaurus, or synonym finder;
- use another person, such as a teacher, a peer, a librarian, or an outside expert, as a resource.

After reading, students will use these strategies:

- summarize or retell the text;
- answer questions they or others pose;
- reflect to make new information become part of their prior knowledge.

Audio CD **AudioText**

The Chimpanzees I Love **435**

Guiding Comprehension

1 🎯 **Author's Purpose • Critical**

Question the Author **Read paragraphs 1 and 2 on p. 436. What do you think is the author's purpose for writing this selection? Give reasons for your answer.**

In the selection, the author wishes to inform the reader about chimpanzees. Answers should include specific examples from the text on this page.

Monitor Progress

🎯 Author's Purpose

If... students are unable to determine the author's purpose,	then... use the skill and strategy instruction on p. 437.

2 **Summarize • Inferential**

Reread paragraphs 2 and 3. Summarize the paragraphs in two or three sentences.

The author states that chimpanzees have brains very similar to human brains. They can use tools to get food and water, and to clean and protect themselves. Infant chimpanzees learn how to use tools by watching adults.

Tech Files
ONLINE

Students can use a studently-friendly search engine to find out more about chimpanzees or animal intelligence. Suggest that they use *chimpanzee, chimpanzee tool use, animal intelligence,* or *Jane Goodall* as key words for their search. Be sure to follow classroom rules for Internet use.

The Mind of the Chimpanzee

ANIMALS ARE much smarter than scientists used to think. I was told at school (fifty years ago) that only human beings have personalities, can think and reason, feel pain, or have emotions. Luckily, as a child, I had spent hours learning about animal behavior from my dog, Rusty—so I knew none of that was true!

The more we have learned about chimpanzees, the clearer it is that they have brains very like ours and can, in fact, do many things that we used to think only humans could do. I've described how the Gombe chimps use grass stems and twigs to fish termites from their nests. The chimps also use long smooth sticks to catch vicious biting army ants. They use crumpled leaves to soak up water from hollows in trees that they cannot reach with their lips, then suck the homemade sponge. They wipe dirt from their bodies with leaf napkins. They use stout sticks to open up holes in trees to get at birds' nests or honey and as clubs to intimidate one another or other animals. They pick up and throw rocks as missiles. In other parts of Africa, chimps have different tool-using behaviors. For instance, in west Africa and parts of central Africa, they use two stones, a hammer and an anvil, to crack open nuts. It seems that infant chimps learn these behaviors by watching the adults, and then imitating and practicing what they have seen. So the chimps have their own primitive culture.

Many scientists are finding out more about the chimpanzee mind from tests in captive situations. For example, chimps will go and find sticks to pull in food that has been placed outside the cage, beyond their reach. They can join two short sticks together to make one long tool. They have excellent memories—after eleven years' separation, a female named Washoe recognized the two humans who had brought her up. A chimp can plan what he or she is going to do. Often I've watched a chimp wake up, scratch himself

436

Context Clues Use context clues to help students determine the meaning of *intimidate* on p. 436. Have students substitute other words in the phrase "as clubs to *intimidate* one another or other animals." Explain that *intimidate* means "to try to scare or frighten."

"How many times I have wished that I could look out onto world through the eyes, with the mind, of a chimpanzee. such minute would be worth a lifetime of research."

437

Author's Purpose

TEACH

- Remind students that there are four common reasons for authors to write: to persuade, to inform, to express ideas or feelings, and to entertain.

- Explain that, very often, an author can have more than one purpose for writing.

- Model identifying one of the author's purposes on p. 436.

 Think Aloud **MODEL** First I'll see what kinds of details the author includes. I'll ask myself: Do the details give factual information? Do they express feelings? Are they funny? Do they give strong opinions? I see that there is a lot of factual information about chimpanzees. I think that, so far, one of the reasons the author is writing is to inform the reader about chimps.

PRACTICE AND ASSESS

Have students reread p. 436. Ask them to identify another purpose of the author. (*To express her opinions; in the first paragraph she talks about how her dog taught her that animals are similar to humans in many ways. She speaks in the first person and uses expressive language.*)

Guiding Comprehension

Chimpanzees can communicate by means of calls, gestures, postures, and facial expressions.

Ai has been learning language skills at Kyoto University since 1978. Her infant Ayumu, will learn to stack blocks.

③ Compare and Contrast • Inferential

How does the author state that chimps and humans are similar? How are they different?

Similar: Both chimps and humans can learn, communicate, make tools, ride bikes, sew, paint and draw, recognize themselves in mirrors, and use computer languages. Different: Chimps cannot speak words.

④ Fact and Opinion • Critical

Reread p. 439. Is the author's statement of opinion, " . . . we have often treated chimpanzees like slaves . . . " a valid opinion? Support your answer.

Possible response: It is valid. The author is an expert and gives many examples of how chimps have been held captive and terribly abused.

Monitor Progress

REVIEW Fact and Opinion

If... students have difficulty determining if the statement is a valid opinion,	then... use the skill and strategy instruction on p. 439.

⑤ Graphic Sources • Critical

Look at the photos and captions on pp. 438–439. Why do you think they are included on these pages?

They illustrate and give more information about the characteristics of chimpanzees. They also show more similarities between humans and chimps.

slowly, gaze around in different directions, then suddenly get up, walk over to a clump of grass, carefully select a stem, trim it, and then travel quite a long way to a termite mound that was out of sight when he made his tool.

Chimpanzees can be taught to do many of the things that we do, such as riding bicycles and sewing. Some love to draw or paint. Chimps can also recognize themselves in mirrors. But they cannot learn to speak words because their vocal cords are different. Two scientists, the Hayeses, brought up a little chimp named Vicky and tried to teach her to talk. After eight years she could only say four words, and only people who knew her could understand even those.

The Gardners had another idea. They got an infant chimpanzee, named her Washoe, and began teaching her American Sign Language (ASL) as used by deaf people. Then other infant chimps were taught this language. Chimps can learn 300 signs or more. They can also invent signs. The chimp Lucy, wanting a Brazil nut but not knowing its name, used two signs she knew and asked for a "rock berry." A fizzy soda became "listen drink," a duck on a pond, "water bird," and a piece of celery, "pipe food." Washoe's adopted son learned fifty-eight signs from Washoe and three other signing chimps by the time he was eight years old. He was never taught these signs by humans. Other chimps have been taught computer "languages" and can punch out quite complicated sentences. These experiments have taught us, and continue to teach us, more and more about the chimpanzee mind.

438

Build Background Explain that American Sign Language (ASL) is a language that uses hand movements and gestures to communicate ideas and words. Encourage students to research ASL in encyclopedias or on the Internet.

e two young chimps are good friends.

Fifi is a very good mother. Here she is with offspring Ferdinand, Faustino, and Fanni. **5**

Chimpanzees in Captivity

UNFORTUNATELY chimpanzees, so like us in many ways, are often very badly treated in many captive situations. Chimpanzees were first brought to Europe from Africa in the middle of the seventeenth century. People were amazed by these humanlike creatures. They dressed them up and taught them tricks.

Since then we have often treated chimpanzees like slaves, shooting their mothers in Africa, shipping them around the world, caging them in zoos, training them to perform in movies and circuses and advertisements, selling them as pets, and imprisoning them in medical research laboratories. Some chimps become famous. J. Fred Muggs starred on TV's *Today* show for years and was known by millions of viewers. What they didn't know was that whenever J. Fred Muggs got too big and strong for the show, he was replaced by a younger one.

A young male called Ham was sent up into space. He was shot up in a Mercury Redstone rocket in January 1961, and because he survived the ordeal (he was terrified), it was decided that it was safe for the first **4** human astronauts. Ham was taught his routine by receiving an electric shock every time he pressed the wrong button. Often circus chimps

439

Fact and Opinion REVIEW

TEACH

- Remind students that statements of fact can be proved true or false. Statements of opinion are someone's judgment, belief, or way of thinking about something.
- Explain that a valid opinion is one that is well supported by facts.
- Model determining if an opinion is valid on p. 439.

Think Aloud **MODEL** First I will read the opinion and then I will try to find any supporting facts. On this page, there are many supporting facts that illustrate how chimps have been abused. Because of this, I would say that the opinion is valid.

PRACTICE AND ASSESS

- Have students determine if the author's statement of opinion, " . . . chimpanzees, so like us in many ways . . . " is valid. Have them support their answer with specific details. (*It is valid. Chimps can communicate, sew, use tools, and do many other things that humans do.*)
- To assess, use Practice Book 166.

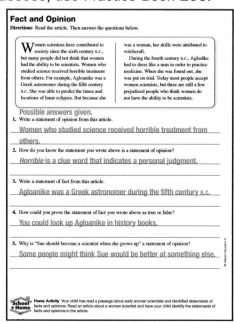

Fact and Opinion
Directions Read the article. Then answer the questions below.

Women scientists have contributed to society since the sixth century B.C., but many people did not think that women had the ability to be scientists. Women who studied science received horrible treatment from others. For example, Agloanike was a Greek astronomer during the fifth century B.C. She was able to predict the times and locations of lunar eclipses. But because she was a woman, her skills were attributed to witchcraft.

During the fourth century B.C., Aglodike had to dress like a man in order to practice medicine. When she was found out, she was put on trial. Today most people accept women scientists, but there are still a few prejudiced people who think women do not have the ability to be scientists.

Possible answers given.
1. Write a statement of opinion from this article.
   Women who studied science received horrible treatment from others.
2. How do you know the statement you wrote above is a statement of opinion?
   Horrible is a clue word that indicates a personal judgment.
3. Write a statement of fact from this article.
   Agloanike was a Greek astronomer during the fifth century B.C.
4. How could you prove the statement of fact you wrote above as true or false?
   You could look up Agloanike in history books.
5. Why is "Sue should become a scientist when she grows up" a statement of opinion?
   Some people might think Sue would be better at something else.

Home Activity Your child has read a passage about early women scientists and identified statements of facts and opinions. Read an article about a woman scientist and have your child identify the statements of facts and opinions in the article.

▲ **Practice Book** p. 166

Guiding Comprehension

6 **Compare and Contrast • Inferential**

How are infant chimps different from adult chimps?

Infant chimps are gentle and easy to handle. Adult chimps do not like discipline, will bite, and can be as strong as an adult human male.

7 **Draw Conclusions • Inferential**

Text to World **How can zoos help keep chimps and other exotic animals from being mistreated or abandoned by pet owners?**

Zoos can work with communities to educate people about the lives of these animals and how best to care for them.

8 **Answer Questions • Critical**

What is the author's purpose in writing about chimps in captivity? Support your answer with details from the text.

Jane Goodall wants to express her opinion that chimps are treated unfairly and cruelly and inform the reader about their situation and about their human-like intelligence. She uses details such as descriptions of their cement-floored laboratory cages, their learning abilities, and how their existence is threatened.

are taught, right at the start of their training, that instant obedience is the way to avoid a beating. The beatings are given when the trainer and chimp are on their own, so no one sees. It is the same for other animals—and for many of those used in movies and other forms of entertainment.

Infant chimpanzees are adorable and, for the first two or three years, are gentle and easy to handle. People buy them and treat them like human children. But as they grow older they become more and more difficult. They are, after all, chimpanzees, and they want to behave like chimpanzees. They resent discipline. They can—and do—bite. And

6 by the time they are six years old they are already as strong as a human male. What will happen to them then? Zoos don't want them, for they have not been able to learn chimpanzee social behavior and they do

7 not mix well with others of their kind. Often they end up in medical research labs.

It is because their bodies are so like ours that scientists use chimps to try to find out more about human diseases and how to cure and prevent them. Chimpanzees can be infected with almost all human diseases. Hundreds have been used (with no success) in AIDS research. The virus stays alive in their blood, but they do not show the symptoms. It is very unfair that, even though chimpanzees are being used to try to help humans, they are almost never given decent places to live.

Zoos are improving gradually, but thousands of chimpanzees around the world spend their lives in barren cement-floored cages with nothing to do.

Jou-Jou has been caged alone in a Congolese zoo. He reaches to touch me, desperate for contact.

440

Extend Language Point out the term *groomed* on p. 441 and explain that chimpanzees groom, or clean each other by picking off dirt or debris with their fingers.

Hundreds of them are shut up in 5' x 5' x 7' bare, steel-barred prisons, all alone, bored, and uncomfortable. Measure out this space and imagine having to live in it your whole life. (Many closets are much bigger!)

I shall never forget the first time I looked into the eyes of an adult male chimpanzee in one of these labs. For more than ten years he had been living in his tiny prison. The sides, floor, and ceiling were made of thick steel bars. There was a car tire on the floor. His name, I read on the door, was JoJo. He lived at the end of a row of five cages, lined up along a bare wall. Opposite were five more cages. At either end of the room was a metal door. There was no window. JoJo could not touch any of his fellow prisoners—only the ends of his fingers fitted between the bars. He had been born in an African forest, and for the first couple of years he lived in a world of greens and browns, leaves and vines, butterflies and birds. Always his mother had been close to comfort him, until the day when she was shot and he was snatched from her dead or dying body. The young chimpanzee was shipped away from his forest world to the cold, bleak existence of a North American research lab. JoJo was not angry, just grateful that I had stopped by him. He groomed my fingers, where the ridges of my cuticles showed through the surgical gloves I had to wear. Then he looked into my eyes and with one gentle finger reached to touch the tear that rolled down into my mask.

JoJo and I touch through the bars of his prison cage in a research lab.

La Vieille spent years alone in a Congolese zoo. We were able to move her to our Tchimpounga sanctuary and introduce her to other chimpanzees.

441

Develop Vocabulary

PRACTICE LESSON VOCABULARY

Students orally respond *yes* or *no* to each question and provide a reason.

1. Can *captive* chimps climb trees in the jungle? *(No; they are usually in cages or other places where they are not free to move around).*

2. Do you think circus chimps enjoy a happy *existence*? *(No; they are often treated cruelly).*

3. Do chimps have a *primitive* culture? *(Yes; they can use simple tools).*

BUILD CONCEPT VOCABULARY

Review previous concept words with students. Ask if students have come across any words today in their reading or elsewhere that they would like to add to the Animal Research Concept Web such as *data* and *sanctuary*.

STRATEGY SELF-CHECK

Answer Questions

Ask students to identify the author's purpose. Remind them to think about where they will get the information to answer that question. *(The author wants to give us some information about chimps, to express her feelings and opinions about the plight of chimps, and in a less obvious way, to persuade us to care, or even take action to help them.)*

Students can make a list of examples from the selection that illustrate the author's purpose.

SELF-CHECK

Students can ask themselves these questions to assess their ability to use the skill and strategy.

- Did I identify the author's purpose in writing *The Chimpanzees I Love*?
- Was I able to figure out where I would find the information to identify the author's purpose?
- How did this help me identify her purpose more easily?

Monitor Progress
🎯 Author's Purpose

If... students have difficulty figuring out where to find the details to determine the author's purpose,	then... revisit the skill lesson on pp. 430–431. Reteach as necessary.

Strategy Response Log

Answer Questions Have students review the questions they wrote at the beginning of this selection. (See p. 434.) Then provide the following prompt: Were your questions answered? If yes, was all the information you needed in the selection? Then have students ask another question for the rest of the selection.

If you want to teach this selection in two sessions, stop here.

Guiding Comprehension

If you are teaching the selection in two days, discuss the author's purpose(s) for writing so far and review the vocabulary.

9 🔊 **Vocabulary • Dictionary/Glossary**

Reread the first sentence on p. 443. Look up the word *surplus* in a dictionary. What part of speech is it? What does it mean in that sentence?

It's a noun. It means an amount over and above what is needed; a leftover quantity.

Monitor Progress

🎯 **Dictionary/Glossary**

If... students have difficulty explaining the meaning of *surplus*,	then... use the strategy instruction on p. 443.

---

10 Paraphrase • Inferential

Reread p. 443, paragraph 2. Write two or three sentences about what chimps need for a happy life in captivity.

Chimps need an environment with trees and sun. They need other chimp friends and fun and interesting activities to do every day.

DAY 3 **Grouping Options**

Reading
Whole Group Discuss the Question of the Day.

Small Group Differentiated Instruction
Read *The Chimpanzees I Love.* See pp. 430f–430g for the small group lesson plan.

Whole Group Discuss the Reader Response questions on p. 448. Then use p. 455a.

Language Arts
Use pp. 455e–455k.

"Chimpanzees are more like us than any other living beings."

442

ELL

Build Background Define the term *extinct* on p. 443 as no longer in existence or alive. Preview the term *endangered species* on p. 447 and explain that an animal in danger of becoming *extinct* is *endangered*. Encourage students to look for more information on *extinct* and *endangered species* in the library or on the Internet.

In the United States, several hundred chimpanzees have been declared "surplus"—they are no longer needed for medical research. Animal welfare groups are trying to raise the money to build them sanctuaries so that they can end their lives with grass and trees, sunshine and companionship. Some lucky ones—including JoJo— have already been freed from their laboratory prisons. Many others are waiting.

Zoos are getting better, but there are still many chimps in small concrete and metal cages with no soft ground and nothing to occupy them. Good zoos keep their chimpanzees in groups and provide them with all kinds of stimulating things to do, different things each day, so that they don't get bored. Many zoos now have artificial termite mounds. Chimps use sticks or straws to poke into holes for honey or other foods. These innovations make a world of difference.

Protecting the Chimpanzees

CHIMPANZEES live in the forested areas of west and central Africa. In some places, where there is a lot of rain, these are thick tropical rain forests. In other places there are strips of dense forest along the rivers, with woodland and even open grassland in between. The chimpanzees usually cross open ground in groups, traveling without stopping until they reach the safety of the trees again. Chimpanzees can survive in quite dry areas, but there they have very big home ranges, for they must travel widely to get food. Like the other African great apes, the gorillas and bonobos, they are disappearing very fast. One hundred years ago we think there were about two million chimpanzees in Africa; now there may be no more than 150,000. They are already extinct in four of the twenty-five countries where they once lived. There are more chimpanzees in the great

443

Changes in Biodiversity

Biodiversity refers to the variety of all the plants, animals, and other living organisms (such as fungi and microorganisms) that live in a given area. All these organisms compete for resources such as water, space, food, and sunlight. When the ecosystem is well balanced, there is a healthy biodiversity and organisms have enough access to resources. Sometimes, however, non-native plants or animals are introduced to an ecosystem by accident, or on purpose. The new plants or animals compete with the native species for resources. Some species will not survive the competition. This leads to a decrease in biodiversity.

VOCABULARY STRATEGY

Dictionary/ Glossary

TEACH

Read sentence 1 on p. 443. Model using a dictionary to find the meaning of the word *surplus*.

Think Aloud **MODEL** In the first sentence, I'm not sure what the word *surplus* means even if I read the words around it. When I look up *surplus* in a dictionary, I see that there is more than one definition. When I read the definitions and then read the first sentence again, I can choose the correct meaning. The phrase *they are no longer needed for medical research* helps me choose the correct definition.

PRACTICE AND ASSESS

Have students use a dictionary to find the part of speech and the meaning of the word *innovations* in the last sentence of p. 443, paragraph 2. *(Noun. Something new and different.)*

EXTEND SKILLS

Author's Perspective

The author's perspective is the way an author looks at the subject he or she is writing about. If the author is writing with a balanced perspective, he or she shows both sides of an issue. If the author is biased, he or she will favor one side of the issue over the other. Is the author of this selection biased about her subject? Are there places where she shows a balanced perspective?

Guiding Comprehension

① Main Idea • Inferential

Reread p. 444, paragraphs 1-4. Write the main idea for each.

1: Humans are destroying the chimps' forest homes. 2: Chimps get caught in wire snares set for other animals and are badly hurt or die. 3: Adult chimps are killed so dealers can steal the infants for the live animal trade. 4: Many chimps are killed and sold as food in the "bush-meat" trade.

⑫  Author's Purpose • Inferential

Does the author want to persuade the reader to feel a certain way about chimpanzees? What is her purpose in doing so?

She wants us to care about what is happening to the chimpanzees. Her purpose is to evoke sympathy and compassion in the reader in the hopes of persuading them to take some kind of action to improve the chimpanzees' situation.

Monitor Progress

Author's Purpose

If... students are unable to determine if the author wants to persuade the reader,	then... use the skill and strategy instruction on p. 445.

Congo basin than anywhere else—but that is where they are disappearing the fastest. They are disappearing for various reasons:

1 All over Africa, their forest homes are being destroyed as human populations grow and need even more land for their crops and for their homes, and even more wood for making charcoal or for firewood.

2 In many places chimpanzees are caught in snares set for bushpigs or antelopes. Snares were once made of vines, but now hunters use wire cable. Often the chimps are strong enough to break the wire, but they cannot get the noose off. Some die; others lose a hand or a foot, after months of agony.

3 There are still dealers who are trying to smuggle chimpanzees out of Africa for the live animal trade. Mothers are shot so that hunters can steal their infants for entertainment or medical research. Many individuals die in the forest (including adult males who rush to the rescue and are shot) in order for one infant to reach its destination alive. The dealers pay the hunters only a few dollars while they themselves can sell an infant chimp for $2,000 or more.

4 The greatest threat to chimpanzees in the great Congo basin is commercial hunting for food. Local tribes, like the Pygmies, have lived in harmony with the forest and its animals for hundreds of years. Now logging companies have made roads deep into the heart of the last remaining forests. Hunters ride the trucks to the end of the road and shoot everything—chimps, gorillas, bonobos, elephants, antelopes—even quite small birds. The meat is smoked or even loaded fresh onto the trucks and taken for sale in the big towns. The trouble is that so many people living there prefer the taste of meat from wild animals, and they will pay more for it than for that from domestic animals. If this trade (known as the "bush-meat" trade) cannot be stopped, there will soon be no animals left.

⑪ There are many people and organizations trying to help protect chimpanzees and their forests, but the problems are very hard to solve. Most of the people destroying the forests are very poor. They can't afford to buy food from elsewhere, so they cut down more trees for

444

ELL

Access Content Have students examine the text format on p. 444 and ask them why there are numbered paragraphs. Point out the sentence preceding the numbered text ("They are disappearing for various reasons") and explain that numbers indicate a list of reasons will follow.

"...very individual has a role to play. Every individual makes a difference. And we have a choice: What sort of difference do we want to make?"

445

SKILLS ⟷ STRATEGIES IN CONTEXT

Author's Purpose
Answer Questions

TEACH

Read pp. 443–446. Have students ask themselves where they will find information that will help them determine if the author is trying to persuade the reader.

Think Aloud **MODEL** If I want to determine if the author is trying to persuade me, I know that I will probably get that information from the words she uses. If I read pp. 443 and 445, I see that the author gives a lot of information about the plight of chimps and uses language, such as *die* and *agony*, that expresses pain and urgency. When I look at the author's quote on p. 445, I feel like she is trying to persuade me to take action.

PRACTICE AND ASSESS

Have students identify other purposes of the author and write where they found the information to make that evaluation.

TIME FOR Science

Competing for Resources

The Amazon Rain forest in Brazil comprises 2.5 million square miles (seven times the size of Texas). The rain forest has an enormous amount of resources that are used by many other countries in the world, including the United States. Resources such as lumber, oil, and gold are taken out in such a way that is very harmful to the rain forest. In fact, the world's rain forests are disappearing at a rapid rate! What this means is that the unique habitats of the plants and animals living there may be gone forever, causing the extinction of many species.

The Chimpanzees I Love **445**

Guiding Comprehension

13 **Cause and Effect • Literal**

Why are some chimps heavier when they are in captivity?

They get less exercise than when they live in the wild.

14 **Author's Purpose • Critical**

Text to Self **Has the author achieved her purpose of persuading you to care about chimps and maybe take some sort of action to help?**

Possible response: Now that I know the danger many chimps are in and what they are like, I want to learn more and maybe even find out how I can help.

15 **Graphic Sources • Inferential**

Look at the map on p. 447. In which countries do chimpanzees live?

Gambia, Guinea-Bissau, Guinea, Sierra Leone, Liberia, Ivory Coast, Ghana, Nigeria, Cameroon, Equatorial Guinea, Gabon, Congo-Brazzaville, Democratic Republic of the Congo, Uganda, Rwanda, Burundi, Tanzania.

Strategy Response Log

Summarize When students finish reading the selection, provide this prompt: In three or four sentences, summarize the ways in which chimpanzees display their intelligence.

Fanni gazes down at Fax.

their farms and shoot or snare more animals for food. Because the soil needs the shelter of the trees in the tropics, the people are soon struggling to survive in a desert-like place. So they cut down more trees. And the bushmeat trade has become a very big money-making operation, with many high-up government officials involved. We shall not give up until solutions have been found.

Chimpanzee Facts

* A fully grown male chimpanzee at Gombe is about 4 feet tall and weighs up to 115 pounds. The female is about as tall, but she is lighter, seldom weighing more than 85 pounds.
* In west and central Africa the chimpanzees are a little bigger and heavier. Often they are heavier in captivity, too, at least when they are well fed and given medicine. This is not surprising, as they have **13** much less exercise than when they live in the wild.
* Chimpanzees in the wild seldom live longer than fifty years, though some captive individuals have lived more than sixty years.
* A female chimpanzee in the wild raises two to three offspring, on average. But she may raise as many as eight or nine.

446

ELL

Extend Language Help students to understand the sentence "Chimps live in the greatest concentrations in the rain forest areas along the equator" on p. 447 by defining *greatest concentrations* as the greatest number in one area.

Chimpanzee Habitats

Chimpanzees are found in twenty-one African countries, from the west coast of the continent to as far east as western Uganda, Rwanda, Burundi, and Tanzania. Chimps live in the greatest concentrations in the rain forest areas along the equator. Due to the fast-paced destruction of these rain forests, as well as other pressures, chimpanzees are considered an endangered species.

The Gombe Stream Research Center is located on the eastern shore of Lake Tanganyika, in Tanzania.

447

Develop Vocabulary

PRACTICE LESSON VOCABULARY

Students choose the correct answer.

1. Which of the following is an *ordeal*? (a)
a) being a lab animal   b) playing in the jungle   c) using tools

2. Which of the following are *sanctuaries*? (c)
a) cages   b) circuses   c) protected wild animal parks

3. Which of the following would not provide *stimulation*? (b)
a) an interesting book   b) a nap   c) an exciting movie

BUILD CONCEPT VOCABULARY

Review previous concept words with students. Ask if students have come across any words today in their reading or elsewhere that they would like to add to the Animal Research Concept Web such as *expedition* and *destruction*.

STRATEGY SELF-CHECK

Answer Questions

Have students determine where they will find the information to identify all the author's purposes for the selection. Have them write a statement of the author's purpose and list the details, facts, and opinions that helped them to determine the author's purpose. Use Practice Book p. 167.

SELF-CHECK

Students can ask themselves these questions to assess their ability to use the strategy.

- Did I identify all the author's purposes in *The Chimpanzees I Love*?
- Was I able to determine where I would get the information to answer that question?

Monitor Progress
Author's Purpose

If... students have difficulty making a list of information and writing an author's purpose statement,	then... use the Reteach lesson on p. 455b.

Author's Purpose

- The **author's purpose** is the reason or reasons the author has for writing. Authors may write to persuade, inform, express ideas or feelings, or entertain.
- As you preview a selection, predict the author's purpose. After reading, ask if the author met his or her purpose.

Directions Read the following passage. Then answer the questions below.

> Human beings have been one of the main reasons the bald eagle was put on the endangered species list. In the first half of the twentieth century, more than a hundred thousand eagles were killed in Alaska because the salmon fishermen thought they were a threat to the salmon population. DDT, a poisonous insecticide, was also a major cause of death in bald eagles. It was sprayed on plants that were eaten by small animals that the eagles hunted. As a consequence, the eagles were poisoned. Also, as people keep expanding into the eagles' natural habitats, the eagles are losing their nesting areas.

Possible answers given for 3–5.
1. What is the author's purpose in writing this passage?
The author's purpose is to inform.
2. What is the main idea of this article?
Humans are one of the major reasons the eagle has been put on the endangered species list.
3. What is one important detail about the author's purpose?
More than a hundred thousand eagles were killed by salmon fishermen.
4. What is another detail about the author's purpose?
Eagles are losing their nesting areas because people keep expanding into their natural habitat.
5. Did the author achieve his purpose? How?
Yes, because the author gave many reasons why people have endangered the bald eagle.

School + Home Home Activity Your child identified the author's purpose in a nonfiction passage. Work with your child to identify the author's purpose in an article about an endangered species. Ask your child to identify some clues that reveal the author's purpose.

▲ **Practice Book** p. 167

Reader Response

Open for Discussion Personal Response

Think Aloud **MODEL** I'd think first of what a chimp needs in a living space, such as room to exercise and stimulating things to do.

Comprehension Check Critical Response

1. Responses will vary, but students should explain their choices. ***Author's Purpose***

2. Possible response: Her purpose was to inform readers about chimps, to persuade that animals need more respect, and to express her opinions. ***Author's Purpose***

3. Possible responses: What can we do to improve the treatment of chimpanzees? I could search the Internet or read books on the topic. ***Answer Questions***

4. Arguments must have supporting reasons and use selection vocabulary.
   Vocabulary

Look Back and Write For test practice, assign a 10–15 minute time limit. For assessment, see the Scoring Rubric at the right.

Retell

Have students retell *The Chimpanzees I Love.*

Monitor Progress
Check Retelling Rubric 4 3 2 1

If... students have difficulty retelling the selection,	then... use the Retelling Cards and the Scoring Rubric for Retelling on page 449 to assist fluent retelling.

SUCCESS PREDICTOR

ELL

Check Retelling Have students use the selection subheads to guide their retellings of the story. See the ELL and Transition Handbook.

Reader Response

Open for Discussion The author tells us that some chimpanzees in captivity live in small metal cages. Based on what you've learned, what features might you combine to create a "dream living space" for a chimp?

1. Jane Goodall tells readers a great deal about chimpanzees. Which passages or details of her story did you find most interesting, and why? **Think Like an Author**

2. Do you think the author's purpose in writing *The Chimpanzees I Love* was to inform, to persuade, to entertain, to express an idea or feeling, or a combination of these? Explain your answer. **Author's Purpose**

3. What are two questions you are left with after reading this selection? How could you find the answers? **Answer Questions**

4. Take a debate position on the value of zoos. Write an argument for your position. Use words from the Words to Know list and from the selection. **Vocabulary**

Look Back and Write Look back at page 441 to review the author's meeting with JoJo. Then rewrite the passage from JoJo's point of view. Explain what he was doing, seeing, and feeling.

Meet author Jane Goodall on page 779.

448

Scoring Rubric | Look Back and Write

Top-Score Response A top-score response will use details from page 441 to recount the meeting between Jane Goodall and JoJo from JoJo's point of view.

Example of a Top-Score Response I will never forget the first time I met Jane. I was sitting in my cold cage, separated from everyone. Then Jane came and put her hand up to the bars. I groomed her fingers, the way my mother used to groom mine. I saw she was crying. "We're friends now," I wanted to say. "Don't cry."

For additional rubrics, see p. WA10.

Write Now

Story About an Animal

Prompt

In *The Chimpanzees I Love*, Jane Goodall tells the story of her work with chimpanzees. Think about an animal that interests you. Now write a story about that animal, complete with a beginning, middle, and end.

Writing Trait

Vivid **word choice** helps readers imagine the story you are telling. Select precise and interesting words.

Student Model

Opening sets the scene of the story.

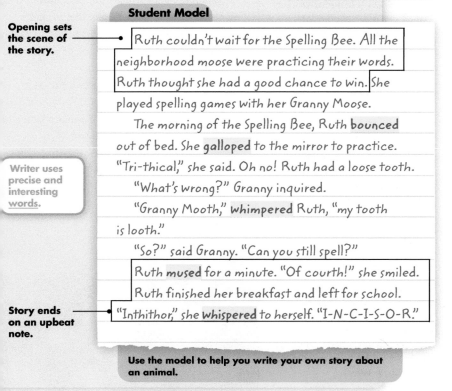

Ruth couldn't wait for the Spelling Bee. All the neighborhood moose were practicing their words. Ruth thought she had a good chance to win. She played spelling games with her Granny Moose.

The morning of the Spelling Bee, Ruth **bounced** out of bed. She **galloped** to the mirror to practice. "Tri-thical," she said. Oh no! Ruth had a loose tooth.

"What's wrong?" Granny **inquired**.

"Granny Mooth," **whimpered** Ruth, "my tooth is looth."

"So?" said Granny. "Can you still spell?"

Ruth **mused** for a minute. "Of courth!" she smiled. Ruth finished her breakfast and left for school. "Inthithor," she **whispered** to herself. "I-N-C-I-S-O-R."

Writer uses precise and interesting words.

Story ends on an upbeat note.

Use the model to help you write your own story about an animal.

449

Write Now

Look at the Prompt Have students identify and discuss key words and phrases in the prompt. *(animal, story, beginning, middle, end)*

Strategies to Develop Word Choice

Have students

- draw an illustration or storyboard of their story.
- brainstorm precise words to describe the characters' actions and emotions.
- use a thesaurus to find interesting words.

NO: Melanie got out of bed. She was tired.

YES: Melanie limped out of bed. She felt as if she had just sprinted through a marathon.

For additional suggestions and rubric, see pp. 455g–455h.

Hints for Better Writing

- Carefully read the prompt.
- Use a graphic organizer to plan your writing.
- Support your ideas with information and details.
- Use words that help readers understand.
- Proofread and edit your work.

Scoring Rubric — Expository Retelling

Rubric 4 3 2 1	4	3	2	1
Connections	Makes connections and generalizes beyond the text	Makes connections to other events, texts, or experiences	Makes a limited connection to another event, text, or experience	Makes no connection to another event, text, or experience
Author's Purpose	Elaborates on author's purpose	Tells author's purpose with some clarity	Makes some connection to author's purpose	Makes no connection to author's purpose
Topic	Describes the main topic	Identifies the main topic with some details early in retelling	Identifies the main topic	Retelling has no sense of topic
Important Ideas	Gives accurate information about events, steps, and ideas using details and key vocabulary	Gives accurate information about events, steps, and ideas with some detail and key vocabulary	Gives limited or inaccurate information about events, steps, and ideas	Gives no information about events, steps, and ideas
Conclusions	Draws conclusions and makes inferences to generalize beyond the text	Draws conclusions about the text	Is able to draw some conclusions about the text	Is unable to draw conclusions or make inferences about the text

Retelling Plan

☑ **Week 1** Assess Strategic Intervention students.

☑ **This week assess Advanced students.**

☐ **Week 3** Assess Strategic Intervention students.

☐ **Week 4** Assess On-Level students.

☐ **Week 5** Assess any students you have not yet checked during this unit.

Use the Retelling Chart on p. TR17 to record retelling.

Selection Test To assess with *The Chimpanzees I Love*, use Selection Tests, pp. 65–68.

Fresh Reads for Differentiated Test Practice For weekly leveled practice, use pp. 97–102.

Retelling

SUCCESS PREDICTOR

Science in Reading

> ## OBJECTIVES
>
> - Examine features of expository nonfiction.
> - Practice a test-taking strategy.
> - Compare and contrast across texts.

PREVIEW/USE TEXT FEATURES

As students preview "'Going Ape' Over Language," have them scan the story in the last paragraph on p. 451. After they preview, ask:

- **How can including stories about a particular subject make a nonfiction composition more interesting for the reader?** (A story can make the subject both more personal and real to a reader.)

- **Why do you think the author chose to put the words "gone ape" in the first paragraph on p. 450 in quotation marks?** (It's slang and also a play on words.)

Link to Science

To help students, suggest they think about what words children learn first and why they learn these words first.

DAY 4 Grouping Options

Reading

Whole Group Discuss the Question of the Day.

Small Group Differentiated Instruction
Read "'Going Ape' over Language." See pp. 430f–430g for the small group lesson plan.

Whole Group Use p. 455a.

Language Arts
Use pp. 455e–455k.

Science in Reading

"Going Ape over Language
by Natalie M. Rosinsky

Expository Nonfiction

Genre
- There are different kinds of nonfiction compositions.
- Expository nonfiction tells and explains facts and information.
- Sometimes it includes stories that are more typical of narrative nonfiction.

Text Features
- In this article, the author includes stories about the subjects to make the facts more relevant and interesting to the reader.
- The author uses quotation marks to mean many things, yet she never uses them for dialogue. As you come across words in quotation marks, think about what the author means by them.

Links to Science
The apes in this selection learned some basic symbols to communicate with their trainers. If you were training apes, what words do you think would be important to teach first? Why?

450

Humans Talking with Apes?

Such conversations were once found only in fables or in science fiction like *Planet of the Apes*. But, since the 1960s, scientists have "gone ape" over other methods of interspecies communication.

Great apes physically cannot produce the consonants or some vowel sounds of human speech. So, instead of spoken language, researchers are using **American Sign Language (ASL)** and technology to teach human language to other primates.

Content-Area Vocabulary	**Science**
bonobo	an ape of tropical Africa that closely resembles a chimpanzee but is smaller and more slender
canine	of or like a dog
interspecies	between different species
primates	group of mammals that have very advanced brains and hands with thumbs that can grasp things

Access Content Have students preview the selection by looking at the photographs and discussing what they think this selection will be about. Have students share their own experiences of learning a new language.

A Chimpanzee Named Washoe

In 1966, Dr. Allen Gardner and his wife, Beatrix, began teaching ASL to a year-old female chimpanzee named Washoe. They taught Washoe by "cross-fostering" her—that is, treating her like a deaf human child. Washoe had a stimulating environment filled with toys and attentive human companions who used ASL to "discuss" daily activities. In those first years, one important topic of conversation was—of course—potty training! Dr. Roger Fouts, an early companion, and his wife, Debbi, have now spent more than 30 years with "Project Washoe." In 1992, the Foutses founded the Chimpanzee and Human Communication Institute at Central Washington University, where Washoe lives with an adoptive family of four other ASL-using chimpanzees.

Washoe is the most "talkative" member of this group, with an ASL vocabulary of 240 signs. She often "translates" spoken words she understands into ASL. Washoe signs correctly even when an object is out of sight—signaling "DOG," for example, whenever she hears canine barking. She also accurately puts together short "sentences"— signing "ROGER TICKLE WASHOE" when this is what has occurred. If she does not know the sign for an item, Washoe creatively yet logically "renames" it. She called her first candy bar a "CANDY BANANA"!

Yet emotion, not just logic, has filled some of Washoe's most memorable conversations with humans. Washoe had already had two unsuccessful pregnancies when she learned that a caregiver's baby had died. The chimpanzee looked groundward, then directly into the woman's eyes, and signed "CRY" while touching the woman's cheek just below her eye. Later that day, Washoe wouldn't let her caregiver go home without further consolation, signing "PLEASE PERSON HUG."

"DOG"

"Candy Banana"

"Please Person Hug"

Author's Purpose | How do the author's section heads help?

451

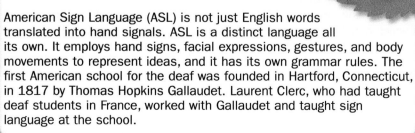

American Sign Language

American Sign Language (ASL) is not just English words translated into hand signals. ASL is a distinct language all its own. It employs hand signs, facial expressions, gestures, and body movements to represent ideas, and it has its own grammar rules. The first American school for the deaf was founded in Hartford, Connecticut, in 1817 by Thomas Hopkins Gallaudet. Laurent Clerc, who had taught deaf students in France, worked with Gallaudet and taught sign language at the school.

EXPOSITORY NONFICTION

Use the sidebar on p. 450 to guide discussion.

- Explain to students that the purpose of a non-fiction composition like this one is to communicate information about the natural or social world.

- Tell students that authors of expository nonfiction want to make their writing interesting to readers. Including stories or anecdotes is one way to do this.

- Discuss with students how they think stories make information more interesting or easier to remember. Ask students to relay their own anecdotes about communicating with their pets.

Audio CD   AudioText

Author's Purpose

Possible response: The section heads inform readers of the topic to follow.

TEST PRACTICE ✓

Strategies for Nonfiction

DRAW CONCLUSIONS Explain to students that the stories or anecdotes within a non-fiction article often make important points. Some test questions may require students to draw conclusions from such stories. Provide the following strategy.

Use the Strategy

1. Read the test question and locate the story it refers to.
2. Reread the story and think about the facts and details.
3. Use your own knowledge and common sense to decide what reasonable con-clusion can be derived from the facts.

GUIDED PRACTICE Have students discuss how they would use the strategy to answer the following question.

What conclusions might you draw about Washoe from her responses to the care-giver whose baby had died?

INDEPENDENT PRACTICE After students answer the following test question, discuss the process they used to find information.

What did Koko's answers to questions about the gorillas dying demonstrate about her understanding of death?

"Aping Their Betters"?

Linguist Noam Chomsky insists that human beings are the only primates neurologically capable of language. Some other scientists, including MIT's Dr. Steven Pinker, share this view. They conclude that "Project Washoe" and similar research prove only that apes can be trained, and that they will imitate the behavior of trainers just for rewards or approval. These critics maintain that investigators, along with animal rights activists, have misinterpreted the results of these research projects because they *want* to believe that apes can "talk."

But there are answers to these objections. The private signing done by chimpanzees is evidence that apes use language for more than rewards or approval. And the technology used to teach "Yerkish" to bonobos lessens the possibly questionable element of imitation in this and similar research. Furthermore, as Dr. Sue Savage-Rumbaugh notes, comprehension and visual cues between humans are themselves part of a broader definition of language. It may be unfair to define language for apes only in the narrowest sense. Lastly, current research into how apes communicate among themselves in the wild is reshaping our views of them. Geographically separated groups of bonobos have their own "dialects" of communicative gestures and sounds. And bonobos already may communicate symbolically among themselves, smashing plants and placing them at particular angles as "road signs."

Researchers are also excited by the chimpanzees' use of ASL among themselves. Washoe, her adoptive son Loulis, and other family members have been videotaped having ASL conversations on their own about games, food, and "housecleaning." Birthday parties and holiday celebrations are other "hot" topics of conversation. The chimpanzees have even been observed "talking to themselves," much as a human might mutter under her breath. When Loulis mischievously ran away with one of her favorite magazines, an annoyed Washoe signed "BAD, BAD, BAD" to herself.

It is Loulis's use of ASL, though, that may be most significant. In a planned experiment, researchers avoided signing in Loulis's presence during his first five years. Yet Loulis—like deaf human children—learned ASL by watching and imitating his adoptive mother and other family members! Chimpanzees, it seems, not only can learn human language, but also can transmit it to others.

"Bad, Bad, Bad"

452

ⒺⓁⓁ

Test Practice Write the Guided Practice test question on the board and have students locate and reread the story the question refers to. Create a graphic organizer on the board, listing the key facts and details. Ask which conclusions students might draw from this information.

A Gorilla Named Koko

Koko, a female lowland gorilla, began learning ASL in 1972, when she was one year old. Her teacher, Dr. Francine Patterson, provided her with a gorilla companion in 1976, when three-year-old Michael joined them at the official start of the Gorilla Foundation.

Koko has a working vocabulary of 1,000 signs and understands 2,000 spoken words. Michael—before his unexpected death in 2000—used 600 signs to communicate. Both gorillas, like Washoe, have shown creativity and logic in naming unknown objects. It was obvious to Koko that a face mask is an "EYE HAT," while Michael had no difficulty at all in titling his painting (yes, gorillas paint) of a bouquet of flowers "STINK GORILLA MORE"! Koko has even used ASL to "talk" herself out of trouble. When a teacher caught her eating a crayon, Koko signed "LIP" and pretended to be applying lipstick! Koko also likes to joke using ASL, calling herself an "ELEPHANT" after pointing to a long tube held out in front of her like that animal's trunk.

Koko has also used ASL to express sadness and some complex ideas. She mourned the death of her kitten, named All Ball, by repeatedly signing "SAD." When asked when gorillas die, Koko signed "TROUBLE OLD." When she was then asked what happens to gorillas after they die, Koko answered "COMFORTABLE HOLE." With Dr. Patterson as an interpreter, Koko has even participated in online, computerized "chats"!

"Trouble Old"

"Lip"

"Eye Hat"

"Sad"

© Author's Purpose | Why are there both funny and sad incidents here?

453

© Author's Purpose

Possible response: To show the range of Koko's behavior, emotions, and use of language; to get readers to like and identify with her.

USE TEXT FEATURES

Ask students:

- **Why does the author put the word *speaks* in quotation marks in the first sentence on p. 454?** *(She is using the word figuratively rather than literally. Kanzi cannot actually speak, but he communicates through a visual code.)*

- **Why does the author put the word *Yerkish* in quotation marks in the second sentence on p. 454?** *(It is the made-up name of a visual code.)*

- **Why does the author put the word *later* in quotation marks in the last sentence on p. 455?** *(To clarify "later" as one of the vocabulary words used by Kanzi and other bonobos.)*

Dr. Sue Savage-Rumbaugh teaches Panibasha to speak using a complex sign language called Yerki

A Bonobo Named Kanzi

Kanzi, a male bonobo born in 1980, "speaks" a different human language than Washoe and Koko. He communicates in "Yerkish," a visual code invented by researchers at Georgia State University and the Yerkes Primate Research Center. "Yerkish" is a set of several hundred geometric symbols called "lexigrams," each representing a verb, noun, or adjective. These lexigrams are placed on an adapted computer keyboard, which bonobos learn to use while learning the meanings of the lexigrams. Kanzi communicates by computer! (Outdoors, Kanzi points to lexigrams on a carry-around tagboard.)

454

Kanzi, who also understands more than 1,000 spoken English words, first learned Yerkish by watching humans train his mother. Like a silent toddler who astonishes parents by first speaking in complete sentences, two-year-old Kanzi amazed researchers on the day he first "spoke" Yerkish by using most of the lexigrams taught to his mother. By the age of six, he had a Yerkish vocabulary of 200 lexigrams. According to Dr. Sue Savage-Rumbaugh, Kanzi and other bonobos construct logical sentences in Yerkish and even use the lexigram for "later" to discuss future activities.

Dr. Savage-Rumbaugh and an assistant teach sign language to a chimp.

Reading Across Texts

After reading *The Chimpanzees I Love* and "'Going Ape' over Language," what are some amazing things you learned about what apes can do?

Writing Across Texts Write about the most amazing thing you learned about chimps from these selections.

Answer Questions | How is Kanzi different from Koko?

455

Animal Communication

It's not only human beings who communicate with gestures and sounds. Animals display a tremendous range in their ways of communicating. Birds sing songs of course—marsh wrens, for example, have hundreds of songs with different meanings. Honeybees perform "dances" to inform other honeybees about the specific location of food. Elephants can communicate across distances of up to 20 miles with low-pitched rumbles. And apes aren't the only animals to use human language. Parrots not only imitate human speech, they can also use it to communicate with people.

CONNECT TEXT TO TEXT

Reading Across Texts

Write the heading "Amazing Things Apes Can Do" on the board and make a list of students' responses. Ask students to express an opinion about what they learned. Are apes simply imitating behavior or are they truly communicating? Encourage students to justify their answers.

Writing Across Texts Direct students to write at least one paragraph in which they explain why they found the behavior they chose amazing.

Answer Questions

Kanzi is a different species, sex, and age than Koko. Kanzi lives in a different place and also uses a different language. Kanzi is a male bonobo born in 1980, while Koko is a female lowland gorilla born in 1971. Kanzi is at the Yerkes Primate Research Center, and Koko is at the Gorilla Foundation. Kanzi uses Yerkish, and Koko uses American Sign Language.

DAY 5

Fluency Assessment Plan

- ☑ **Week 1** Assess Advanced students.
- ☑ **Week 2 This week assess Strategic Intervention students.**
- ☐ **Week 3** Assess On-Level students.
- ☐ **Week 4** Assess Strategic Intervention students.
- ☐ **Week 5** Assess any students you have not yet checked during this unit.

Set individual goals for students to enable them to reach the year-end goal.
- Current Goal: 130–138 wcpm
- Year-End Goal: 150 wcpm

Read interesting sentences aloud to English language learners frequently, adding think-aloud comments to explain how cues such as letter patterns in words, phrases or other "chunks" of words, and punctuation can help you understand and read fluently.

To develop fluent readers, use Fluency Coach.

DAY 5 Grouping Options

Reading
Whole Group
Revisit the Question of the Week.

Small Group
Differentiated Instruction
Reread this week's Leveled Readers. See pp. 430f–430g for the small group lesson plan.

Whole Group
Use p. 415b–415c.

Language Arts
Use pp. 455d–455l.

PAUSES
Fluency

DAY 1

Model Reread "Something in the Elephants' Silence" on p. 430m. Explain that you will pause where the text has commas, periods, and other punctuation marks. Model for students as you read.

DAY 2

Choral Reading Read aloud the first two paragraphs on p. 436. Have students notice how you pause for commas, dashes, and periods. Have students practice as a class by doing three choral readings of the first two paragraphs on p. 436.

DAY 3

Model Read aloud the first paragraph on p. 440. Have students notice how you pause slightly longer at the ends of sentences than for internal punctuation. Practice as a class by doing three choral readings.

DAY 4

Partner Reading Partners practice reading aloud the first paragraph on p. 440 three times. Students should pause at commas and periods and offer each other feedback.

Monitor Progress | Check Fluency WCPM

As students reread, monitor their progress toward their individual fluency goals. Current Goal: 130–138 words correct per minute. End-of-Year Goal: 150 words correct per minute.

If... students cannot read fluently at a rate of 130–138 words correct per minute,
then... make sure students practice with text at their independent level. Provide additional fluency practice, pairing nonfluent readers with fluent readers.

If... students already read at 150 words correct per minute,
then... they do not need to reread three to four times.

SUCCESS PREDICTOR

DAY 5

Assessment
Individual Reading Rate Use the Fluency Assessment Plan and do a one-minute timed reading of either selection from this week to assess students in Week 2. Pay special attention to this week's skill, pauses. Provide corrective feedback for each student.

RETEACH

Author's Purpose

TEACH

Remind students of the four main purposes for writing: to persuade, to inform, to express ideas or feelings, and to entertain. After students finish reading a selection, they should think about whether the author met his or her purpose in writing and why the author was or was not successful. Students can complete Practice Book p. 168 on their own, or you can complete it as a class.

ASSESS

Have partners answer these questions about *The Chimpanzees I Love,* pp. 434–447:

1. **Do you think the author met her purpose or purposes in writing? Why or why not?**

2. **If you had the same reasons for writing as the author, how would you have written the selection?**

For additional instruction of author's purpose, see DI·53.

EXTEND SKILLS

Persuasive Devices

TEACH

In *The Chimpanzees I Love,* Goodall presents facts, expert opinion, and both logical and emotional arguments to persuade readers that people should treat chimpanzees humanely. Some persuasive writing, however, relies on devices that are less valid. The Extend Skills lesson on p. 111b discusses bandwagon, loaded words, and testimonial. Students should also be aware of these common persuasive devices:

- Vague *generality* is a statement that is intentionally broad or vague, such as "Chimpanzees are the coolest animals!"

- *Sweeping generalization* overstates a situation, such as "No one cares about chimpanzees because they're animals."

Elicit other examples of these two devices from students.

ASSESS

Have students write two sentences, demonstrating the persuasive devices of vague generality and sweeping generalization.

OBJECTIVES

- Evaluate author's purpose.
- Recognize persuasive devices.

Skills Trace	
Author's Purpose	
Introduce/Teach	TE: 6.4 430–431, 500–501; 6.6 652–653
Practice	Practice Book: 163, 167, 168, 193, 197, 198, 253, 257, 258
Reteach/Review	**TE: 6.1 125; 6.4 455b, 465, 527b, DI•53, DI•56; 6.6 733, 671b, DI•52**
Test	Selection Test: 65–68, 77–80, 101–104; Benchmark Test: Unit 4

ELL

Access Content Reteach the skill by reviewing the Picture It! lesson on author's purpose in the ELL Teaching Guide, pp. 113–114.

Author's Purpose

- The **author's purpose** is the reason or reasons the author has for writing. Authors may write to persuade, inform, express ideas or feelings, or entertain.
- As you preview a selection, predict the author's purpose. After reading, ask if the author met his or her purpose.

Directions Read the following passage. Then complete the graphic organizer.

Bats are one of the most misunderstood animals in the United States. Because they are associated with vampires in the movies and are often depicted trying to get into people's hair, most people do not like bats. But bats are very beneficial to humans. They are the only major predators of night-flying insects. One bat can eat almost 1,000 mosquitoes and other pests in just one hour. They are a natural insecticide. Unfortunately, many of the 45 species of bats in the United States are either on the endangered or threatened species list. People need to be more educated about the benefits of bats in our environment.

Possible answers given for 2–5.

Before Reading
What is the author's purpose?
1. The author is writing to inform and persuade.

↓

During Reading
What are three clues to the author's purpose?
2. Bats are misunderstood.
3. Bats are very beneficial to humans.
4. People should learn more about bats.

↓

After Reading
Was the author's purpose met? How?
5. Yes; The author gave a lot of information about bats and gave reasons why bats are beneficial.

School + Home Home Activity Your child identified the author's purpose in a passage. Read an article from the editorial page of a newspaper. Have your child identify the clues to the author's purpose.

▲ **Practice Book** p. 168

Vocabulary and Word Study

VOCABULARY STRATEGY

Dictionary/Glossary

UNFAMILIAR WORDS Give students additional practice in using a dictionary to find the meaning of unfamiliar words by having them find the definition for each word in the chart below.

Word	Definition(s)
bleak	cheerless and depressing; dismal
artificial	
innovations	
offspring	

Conservation Labels

The International Union for the Conservation of Nature (IUCN) is an international organization that maintains a list of species threatened with extinction. The Red List, as it is called, places species into different categories based on the severity of the threat.

Category	Meaning
Extinct	Last individual has died
Extinct in the wild	No longer exists in the wild
Critically endangered	Extremely high risk of extinction in the wild
Endangered	Very high risk of extinction in the wild
Vulnerable	High risk of extinction in the wild

BUILD CONCEPT VOCABULARY

Animal Research

LOOKING BACK Remind students of the question of the week: Why is it important to study animals responsibly? Discuss how this week's Concept Web of vocabulary words relates to the theme of animal research. Ask students if they have any words or categories to add. Discuss if words and categories are appropriately related to the concept.

MOVING FORWARD Preview the title of the next selection, *Black Frontiers.* Ask students which Concept Web words might apply to the new selection based on the title alone. Put a star next to these words on the Web.

Display the Concept Web and revisit the vocabulary words as you read the next selection to check predictions.

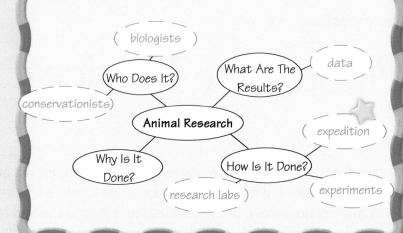

Monitor Progress

Check Vocabulary

If... students suggest words or categories that are not related to the concept,	then... review the words and categories on the Concept Web and discuss how they relate to the lesson concept.

SUCCESS PREDICTOR

Speaking and Listening

SPEAKING

Persuasive Speech

SET-UP Have students prepare short persuasive speeches on the treatment of animals used in research. Students should take a position on the issue and back up their position with facts and reasons. Students can base their speeches on what they learned from *The Chimpanzees I Love,* or they can do some additional research.

ORGANIZATION Tell students their speeches should have a clear beginning, middle, and end. Share the following with students:

- In the beginning, introduce the issue and clearly state your position.
- In the middle, give facts and reasons to support your position.
- In the end, restate your position by summarizing the facts.

AUDIENCE Point out to students the importance of knowing your audience when giving a persuasive speech. For example, students should consider how much the audience already knows about an issue. If the audience knows little, the speaker should provide more background information.

LISTENING

Listen to a Speech

Have students listen closely to their classmates' persuasive speeches. Direct them to take notes on the facts and reasons each speaker gives to support his or her opinion. You might suggest that students use a three-column chart for note-taking. After students give their speeches, have the class identify positions that were well-supported with facts and valid opinions.

Speaker's Name	Position	Facts and Reasons

▲ **Graphic Organizer** 26

Support Vocabulary Use the following to review and extend vocabulary and to explore lesson concepts further:
- ELL Poster 17, Days 3–5 instruction
- Vocabulary Activities and Word Cards in ELL Teaching Guide, pp. 115–116

Assessment For information on assessing students' speaking and listening, see the ELL and Transition Handbook.

Grammar Pronouns and Antecedents

OBJECTIVES

- Identify and define pronouns and antecedents.
- Use pronouns that agree with their antecedents.
- Use pronouns and antecedents correctly in writing.
- Become familiar with pronoun and antecedent assessment on high-stakes tests.

Monitor Progress

Grammar	
If... students have difficulty identifying pronouns and antecedents,	**then...** provide additional instruction and practice in The Grammar and Writing Book pp. 146–149.

DAILY FIX-IT

This week use Daily Fix-It Transparency 17.

Spiral REVIEW

ELL

Support Grammar See the Grammar Transition lessons in the ELL and Transition Handbook.

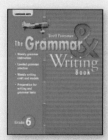

▲ **The Grammar and Writing Book**
For more instruction and practice, use pp. 146–149.

DAY 1 Teach and Model

DAILY FIX-IT

1. She thought the pare was unapetizing. *(pear; unappetizing)*

2. The zoo attendant's welcomed all the children and his parents. *(attendants; their)*

READING-GRAMMAR CONNECTION

Write this sentence on the board:

People throughout the world know Jane Goodall and respect her.

Explain that the pronoun *her* refers to the antecedent *Jane Goodall.* An antecedent is the noun to which a pronoun refers. A pronoun and its antecedent can appear in the same sentence or in separate sentences.

Display Grammar Transparency 17. Read aloud the definitions and sample sentences. Work through the items.

Pronouns and Antecedents

A **pronoun** takes the place of a noun or nouns. An **antecedent,** or referent, is the noun or nouns to which the pronoun refers. A pronoun and its antecedent must agree in number and gender.

Before you use a pronoun, ask yourself whether the antecedent is singular or plural. If the antecedent is singular, decide whether it is masculine, feminine, or neuter. Then choose a pronoun that agrees. In the following sentences, the antecedents are underlined once; the pronouns are underlined twice.

Sal and Jo bought a book about chimps, and they read it together.

Erik brought a camera to the zoo so he could take pictures.

Directions Circle the pronoun that refers to the underlined antecedent.

1. The chimpanzees gathered smooth sticks and used (them) to catch ants.
2. Jane Goodall observed chimpanzees and helped (them) survive in nature.
3. Chimpanzees have interesting ways of finding food when (they) are hungry.
4. Although Vicky learned to say four words, very few people could understand (her)
5. (We) students are eager to meet Jane Goodall when she speaks at the school.
6. Ai grabbed the doll and hugged (it)
7. In 1961, Ham was placed aboard a rocket to see whether (he) could survive the space flight.

Directions Write the correct pronoun to complete each sentence. Underline the antecedent to which the pronoun refers.

they	it	she	us	him

8. Paige and I wanted to hold the baby chimp, but the mother would not let __us__
9. Chimpanzees cannot speak because __they__ have different vocal cords than ours.
10. After Lucy grabbed a stone, __she__ used it to crack open a nut.
11. The chimpanzee saw the banana and reached for __it__
12. Bill will take pictures if you give __him__ film.

Unit 4 The Chimpanzees I Love   Grammar **17**

▲ **Grammar Transparency** 17

DAY 2 Develop the Concept

DAILY FIX-IT

3. The monkeys were difensive about territory that they thought belonged to him. *(defensive; them)*

4. Dad drived Aunt Paula and I to the zoo. *(drove; me)*

GUIDED PRACTICE

Review the concept of pronouns and antecedents.

- A **pronoun** takes the place of a nouns or nouns.
- An **antecedent,** or referent, is the noun or nouns to which the pronoun refers.
- A personal **pronoun** and its **antecedent** must agree in number and gender.

HOMEWORK Grammar and Writing Practice Book p. 65. Work through the first two items with the class.

Pronouns and Antecedents

A **pronoun** takes the place of a noun or nouns. An **antecedent,** or referent, is the noun or nouns to which the pronoun refers. A pronoun and its antecedent must agree in number and gender.

Before you use a pronoun, ask yourself whether the antecedent is singular or plural. If the antecedent is singular, decide whether it is masculine, feminine, or neuter. Then choose a pronoun that agrees. In the following sentences, the antecedents are underlined once; the pronouns are underlined twice.

Jay and I walked to the zoo, and we saw the new exhibit.

Jay called Carla to pick him up from the zoo.

Directions Circle the pronoun that refers to the underlined antecedent.

1. Infant chimps are cute and cuddly, but eventually (they) it) become more difficult.
2. Faustino's mother tried to comfort (him) them).
3. (We) They) humans must learn to respect the animal kingdom.
4. The African forest is perfect for chimps because (they) it) is full of life.
5. The chimp was caught in a snare, but (he) you) was able to break free.
6. I convinced Tim that (it) he) should come to the zoo with me.
7. Jane Goodall worked at the Gombe Stream Research Center, where (she) they) studied chimps.
8. Chimps sometimes make a tool and use (them, (it).

Directions Write the pronoun that completes each sentence. Underline the antecedent to which the pronoun refers.

you	they	him	us	it

9. Hunters kill the animals so __they__ can sell the meat in the big town.
10. The "bush-meat trade" will be hard to stop because __it__ is a big money-making operation.
11. Dr. John wanted JoJo to walk to __him__
12. Alexander and I sat next to Fix, and she played with __us__

Home Activity Your child learned about pronouns and antecedents. Have your child find examples of singular or plural antecedents in a favorite book.

▲ **Grammar and Writing Practice Book** p. 65

DAY 3 Apply to Writing

DAILY FIX-IT

5. Jane Goodall have exhibited her unwaivering devotion to chimps. (has; unwavering)

6. The apes outburst surprised she. (ape's; her)

WRITE THE CORRECT PRONOUN

Explain that if a pronoun's antecedent is confusing, the sentence should be rewritten. Sometimes it is clearer to use a noun instead of a pronoun.

Unclear: Pat and Kate went to her house.

Clear: Pat and Kate went to Pat's house.

• Have students review a recent assignment to check that pronouns have clear antecedents.

HOMEWORK Grammar and Writing Practice Book p. 66.

Pronouns and Antecedents

Directions Read each sentence. Write another sentence with a pronoun that refers to the underlined noun(s). Possible answers:

1. Africa is a lush and fertile continent.
It is home to many chimpanzees.

2. Jane Goodall visited chimps in a zoo.
She watched them play in a tree.

3. Buku is a large male gorilla.
He weighs more than 200 pounds.

4. J.J. and I are going to the circus.
We hope to see some chimps.

5. Helen and Andrew fed the chimp with a baby's bottle.
They had filled it with milk.

6. I wrote a story about Jane Goodall.
I called it "A Heart for Chimpanzees."

7. Phil and I joined an organization to help protect the chimps.
We will meet for the first time this week.

8. Mr. Blackwell is a scientist who studies monkeys.
He studies them at the Gombe Stream Research Center.

Home Activity Your child learned how to correctly use pronouns and antecedents in writing. Have your child write a letter to a relative using pronouns and antecedents correctly.

▲ **Grammar and Writing Practice Book** p. 66

DAY 4 Test Preparation

DAILY FIX-IT

7. Doug and his classmates has finished her ape projects. (have; their)

8. Do you agree that the logging companies is destroying the rain forest with their trucks. (are; trucks?)

STANDARDIZED TEST PREP

Test Tip

When writing pronouns with appositives, try omitting the noun to see which pronoun form to use.

Example: (We, Us) sixth graders use the computers daily.

We use the computers daily.

We sixth graders use the computer daily.

Since *We* is a subject pronoun for the sentence, *We* is the correct pronoun.

HOMEWORK Grammar and Writing Practice Book p. 67.

Pronouns and Antecedents

Directions Mark the letter of the pronoun that agrees with the antecedent to complete each sentence.

1. My friends wanted to see the chimps at the zoo, so I bought _____ tickets.
A you   C her
B him   (D) them

2. Kiki is a female chimp, and _____ weighs eighty-three pounds.
A her   C we
(B) she   D it

3. Gorillas and bonobos are African apes, and _____ are disappearing very fast.
(A) they   C it
B he   D you

4. You should never tease an animal, even when _____ are just playing.
A it   C us
(B) you   D them

5. We knew that the animal shelter was nearby, but we had trouble finding _____
A you   C them
B her   (D) it

6. My brother and I ran from Fanni as she chased _____
A he   C I
(B) us   D she

7. Some people used to dress chimps and teach _____ tricks.
A her   C us
(B) them   D it

8. My sister loves stuffed animals, so I bought _____ one as a gift.
A they   C he
B it   (D) her

9. I told Mom that chimps can learn sign language, but she did not believe _____
(A) me   C they
B she   D we

10. Washoe's son wanted to play with Rory and me, but _____ did not trust him.
A her   (C) we
B them   D him

Home Activity Your child prepared for taking tests on pronouns and antecedents. Write a person's name, a noun, and a compound noun such as *Mom* and *Sam* on paper. Have your child write one sentence using the correct pronoun to refer to each antecedent you wrote.

▲ **Grammar and Writing Practice Book** p. 67

DAY 5 Cumulative Review

DAILY FIX-IT

9. Before the chimps are fed they chatter in there cages. (fed,; their)

10. The crowd are listening to Dr Goodall's seminar. (is; Dr.)

ADDITIONAL PRACTICE

Assign pp. 146–149 in The Grammar and Writing Book.

EXTRA PRACTICE Grammar and Writing Practice Book p. 138.

TEST PREPARATION Grammar and Writing Practice Book pp. 155–156.

ASSESSMENT

CUMULATIVE REVIEW Grammar and Writing Practice Book p. 68.

Pronouns and Antecedents

Directions Circle the pronoun in each sentence and underline its antecedent.

1. Mrs. Taylor teaches about chimps because they are an endangered species.

2. Kent and James want to visit Africa so they can see chimps in a natural habitat.

3. The forest ranger just started working at the park, but he knows about the plants and animals.

4. Mike is driving to the wildlife shelter, and Carrie is following him.

5. Mrs. Taylor brought photos of Kenya and showed them during the presentation.

6. Scientists have tried to teach sign language to chimps, but Kaatu could not learn it.

7. One chimp tried to use a computer, but she failed.

8. Charlotte and Terry were hiding, but Tiki found them.

9. Emily was hoping Pete would go with her to the lecture.

10. Jesse and Owen's parents sat with them at the lecture.

Directions Write the pronoun that agrees with the antecedent. Underline the antecedent to which the pronoun refers.

[me   she   he   we   they]

11. Jane Goodall gave a lecture; then she answered questions.

12. As Jon listened attentively, he took notes.

13. Laurel and Mike arrived later, so they sat in the back of the hall.

14. I wanted Dr. Goodall to call on me.

15. We students were responsible for refreshments.

Home Activity Your child reviewed pronouns and antecedents. Have your child find correct pronoun and antecedent usage in an ad or a catalog.

▲ **Grammar and Writing Practice Book** p. 68

Writing Workshop
Story About an Animal

OBJECTIVES

- Identify features of a story.
- Use vivid words in a story about an animal.
- Focus on word choice.
- Use a rubric.

Genre Story
Writer's Craft Use Vivid Words
Writing Trait Word Choice

Word Choice Pair an English learner with a proficient English speaker to discuss pictures in books or magazines. Have them list descriptive words from the discussion to use in writing, such as *friendly, picnic, caterpillar, broken, snowstorm,* and *furry.*

Writing Traits

FOCUS/IDEAS Organized, vivid details build and develop the plot.

ORGANIZATION/PARAGRAPHS The story is purposefully and carefully built and easy to follow.

VOICE An honest and caring personality in the writing interacts with the reader.

WORD CHOICE The intended message and effect are conveyed with precise, interesting nouns, verbs, and adjectives.

SENTENCES The writer communicates clearly through varied but connected sentences and paragraphs.

CONVENTIONS There is excellent control and accuracy.

DAY 1 — Model the Trait

READING-WRITING CONNECTION

- In *The Chimpanzees I Love,* Jane Goodall uses precise and interesting nouns, verbs, and adjectives.
- Choosing vivid words makes writing clear and strong.
- Students will use vivid words to write a **story about an animal.**

MODEL WORD CHOICE Display Writing Transparency 17A. Then discuss the model and the writing trait of word choice.

Think Aloud I see many precise word choices in this story. For example, the writer uses specific animal names to describe the characters: *llama, alpaca,* and *spider monkey.* The writer also chooses strong verbs, such as *enticing* and *bellowed.* There are exact descriptions to help me see the *steep, cold mountains,* and hear how *the phone rang ominously.*

Story About an Animal

A **story** tells about an event or how characters solve a problem. It has a beginning, a middle, and an end. To make a story interesting, writers use devices such as suspense, conflict, dialogue, and humor.

A Llama's Laugh

Conflict and tension get the story rolling. — Lloyd, the llama, was worried. He had to improve his mountain delivery service, or he'd lose his most important customer—Monica, the spider monkey.

Lloyd hauled heavy packages across the steep, cold mountains for smaller animals. The alpacas had been enticing customers away from Lloyd's service. Just yesterday, Monica had said, "Look, Lloyd, I like you. But the alpacas are always on time, and you've been late." Lloyd knew this was his last chance.

Suspense propels the reader to the conclusion. — He was wondering where he would go for lunch when the phone rang ominously. Al, the alpaca, was calling! "I hear Monica has given you one last chance," bellowed Al. "Slip up and the monkey's business is mine!" Lloyd grunted and hung up.

Humor ends the story on an upbeat note. — "Forget lunch," Lloyd muttered. "Instead of going out, I'll pack a lunch." Suddenly, Lloyd burst into shrieks and honks of llama laughter. "Get it?" he yelled to no one in particular. "'Alpaca' lunch! I crack myself up sometimes." Now Lloyd was ready for the challenge.

Unit 4 The Chimpanzees I Love   Writing Model **17A**

▲ **Writing Transparency** 17A

DAY 2 — Improve Writing

WRITER'S CRAFT
Use Vivid Words

Display Writing Transparency 17B. Read the directions and work together to practice using vivid words.

USE VIVID WORDS
Tomorrow we will be writing a story about an animal. I am going to write about my favorite animal, the giant panda. To help create a sharp picture in the reader's mind, I need to use vivid words. Saying *the panda ate food* is not very vivid. However, saying that *the panda nibbled on bamboo shoots* paints a clear picture for my reader.

GUIDED WRITING Some students may need more help with using vivid words. Point out the author's use of vivid words that create a sharp image.

Use Vivid Words

Vivid words create a sharp picture in the reader's mind. Vague words can be boring. Use vivid adjectives, nouns, and verbs to make your writing sparkle!
Vague An animal went into the box.
Vivid The sprightly chimp scampered into the rickety cardboard box.

Directions Replace the underlined word in each sentence with a more vivid or exact word. You can also replace other words or add more vivid words. Write the new sentence.
1. We <u>went</u> to the ape exhibit.   Possible answers:

We raced eagerly to the ape exhibit.
2. Their habitat was <u>nice.</u>

Their brand-new habitat looked wonderful.
3. The keeper <u>said</u> something to her assistant.

The keeper whispered a message to her assistant.
4. We saw the <u>animals</u> eat lunch.

We watched the orangutans eat lunch.
5. They like <u>fruit.</u>

Apes love bananas, apples, pears, and other fruit.
6. One <u>ate</u> all its food.

One young ape quickly gobbled all its food.

Directions Write a description of an animal. Use vivid words to describe what the animal looks and acts like.
Possible answers: The towering elephant has thick, leathery gray skin. It lumbers across the short grasses of the savanna. It uses its powerful trunk like a drinking straw to siphon water. In the scorching heat, it cools itself by spraying dry dirt all over its wrinkled back.

Unit 4 The Chimpanzees I Love   Writer's Craft **17B**

▲ **Writing Transparency** 17B

DAY 3 · Prewrite and Draft

READ THE WRITING PROMPT
on page 449 in the Student Edition.

In The Chimpanzees I Love, *Jane Goodall tells the story of her work with chimpanzees.*

Think about an animal that interests you.

Now write a story about that animal, complete with a beginning, middle, and end.

Writing Test Tips

- Keep your story short. Write about a single event.
- Give your animal or animals character traits.
- Use vivid and exact words to make the story come alive for the reader.

GETTING STARTED Students can do any of the following:

- Make a plot outline including the beginning, middle, and end of the story.
- List vivid words that describe their animal.
- Write an opening sentence that sets the scene for the story.

DAY 4 · Draft and Revise

EDITING/REVISING CHECKLIST

- ☑ Have I used the most exact and vivid words possible?
- ☑ Do I have a beginning, middle, and end?
- ☑ Do I use pronouns and antecedents correctly?
- ☑ Are words with the prefixes *dis-, de-, out-,* and *un-* spelled correctly?

See *The Grammar and Writing Book,* pp. 146–151.

Revising Tips

Word Choice

- Support exact word choice by choosing words specific to your animal.
- Make sure nouns, verbs, and adjectives are strong.
- Avoid vague words and phrases.

PUBLISHING Students can illustrate their stories with animal photographs or drawings. Some students may wish to revise their work later.

ASSESSMENT Use the scoring rubric to evaluate students' work.

DAY 5 · Connect to Unit Writing

Story	
Week 1	News Story 429g–429h
Week 2	Story About an Animal 455g–455h
Week 3	Describe a Setting 477g–477h
Week 4	TV Script 499g–499h
Week 5	Summary 527g–527h

PREVIEW THE UNIT PROMPT

Write a story about an adventure, a discovery, or something that happened to you for the first time. Use some of these literary devices: foreshadowing, tension, suspense, conflict, humor.

APPLY

- When writing a longer story, maintain your focus and choose words that will enliven your story.

Writing Trait Rubric

	4	3	2	1
Word Choice	Precise nouns, verbs, and adjectives	Clear and interesting nouns, verbs, and adjectives	Vague or repetitive words	Dull and/or inaccurate word choices
	Story entertaining and engaging with strong word choices	Story generally entertaining and engaging	Story weakened by lack of exact language	Story weak and/or dull with ineffective language

Spelling & Phonics
Prefixes *dis-, de-, out-, un-*

- Spell words with prefixes *dis-, de-, out-, un-*.

Generalization

Connect to Phonics The prefixes *dis-, de-, out-,* and *un-* change the meaning of the base word. They do not, however, change the spelling or pronunciation of the base word.

Spelling Words

1. discontent	11. outrageous
2. decline	12. defensive
3. outward	13. unappetizing
4. dispatch	14. disillusioned
5. unwavering	15. disarray
6. destruction*	16. unconscious
7. disintegrate	17. outskirts
8. outstanding	18. unfasten
9. uncommon	19. disenchanted
10. outburst	20. decompose

Challenge Words

21. unbusinesslike	24. disenfranchise
22. disembark	25. outlandish
23. deactivate	26. adolescence

*Word from the selection

Spelling/Phonics Support See the ELL and Transition Handbook for spelling support.

DAY 1 Pretest and Sort

PRETEST

Use the Dictation Sentences from Day 5 to administer the pretest. Read the word, read the sentence, and then read the word again. Guide students in self-correcting their pretests and correcting any misspellings.

Monitor Progress
Spelling

If...	then...
If... students misspell more than 5 pretest words,	**then...** use words 1–10 for Strategic Intervention.
If... students misspell 1–5 pretest words,	**then...** use words 1–20 for On-Level practice.
If... students correctly spell all pretest words,	**then...** use words 1–26 for Advanced Learners.

HOMEWORK Spelling Practice Book, p. 65.

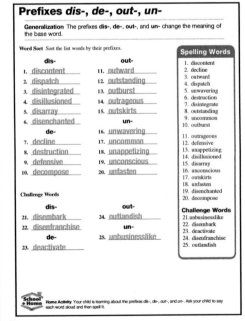

▲ **Spelling Practice Book** p. 65

DAY 2 Think and Practice

TEACH

Adding certain prefixes can change the meaning of a word. Demonstrate this by writing each spelling word on the board. Have students identify and give the meaning for each base word. Then have them identify the prefix and identify the meaning of the new word.

discontent

FIND THE PATTERN Ask students to group spelling words by the number of syllables they contain.

HOMEWORK Spelling Practice Book, p. 66

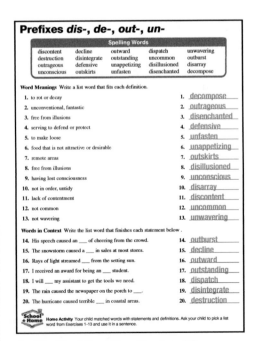

▲ **Spelling Practice Book** p.66

DAY 3 Connect to Writing

WRITE AN ESSAY

Have students write an essay about a historical event. Their essay should use at least four spelling words. Have students read their essays aloud, or post them on the bulletin board for everyone to see.

Frequently Misspelled Words

because   *everything*

These words are difficult for some sixth-graders to spell. Alert students to these frequently misspelled words and encourage them to think carefully before spelling them.

HOMEWORK Spelling Practice Book, p. 67.

Prefixes dis-, de-, out-, un-

Proofread the Story Read the story below. Circle six misspelled words in the story. Write them correctly. Find a sentence fragment. Write it correctly.

Pete's New Pet

For Pete, today was a day like no other. His parents had decided he was old enough to have a pet. They would go to the animal shelter and choose a pet.

At the shelter Pete was pleased (because) all the attendants were (unwaviring) in their kindness and knowledge. Pete wished he could take all the pets home.

Then he stopped before a cage with a tiny Chihuahua pup. When Pete (unfastined) the latch and took the little dog out of its cage, it ran around in an (outragous)(outbirst) of energy and joy. The little pup gently licked Pete's face. Pete thought this was an (outstaning) puppy.

The veterinarian examined the pup and gave it vaccinations. Then Pete's parents took him home, along with his new best friend.

Spelling Words
discontent
decline
outward
dispatch
unwavering
destruction
disintegrate
outstanding
uncommon
outburst
outrageous
defensive
unappetizing
disillusioned
disarray
unconscious
outskirts
unfasten
disenchanted
decompose

1. because   2. unwavering
3. unfastened 4. outrageous
5. outburst   6. outstanding
7. For Pete, today was a day like no other.

Proofread Words Circle the word that is spelled correctly. Write it on the line.

8. (destruction) distraction   8. destruction
9. (outskirts) outskerts   9. outskirts
10. (unappetizing) unapetizing 10. unappetizing
11. (unconscious) onconshious   11. unconscious
12. diserray (disarray)   12. disarray
13. disiluzioned (disillusioned) 13. disillusioned
14. difensive (defensive)   14. defensive
15. uncomon (uncommon)   15. uncommon

Frequently Misspelled Words
because
everything

Home Activity Your child identified misspelled words in a story. Have your child say words from the list and then spell them aloud.

▲ **Spelling Practice Book** p. 67

DAY 4 Review

REVIEW PREFIXES DIS-, DE-, OUT-, UN-

Have students work in small groups to create a matching game using the spelling words. Then have groups exchange games and solve each puzzle.

Spelling Strategy
Divide and Conquer

Step 1: Draw a line between the base words and the prefix.

Step 2: Study the word one part at a time.

Step 2: Exaggerate or change a sound in the word.

HOMEWORK Spelling Practice Book, p. 68.

Prefixes dis-, de-, out-, un-

Spelling Words				
discontent	decline	outward	dispatch	unwavering
destruction	disintegrate	outstanding	uncommon	outburst
outrageous	defensive	unappetizing	disillusioned	disarray
unconscious	outskirts	unfasten	disenchanted	decompose

Finishing Sentences Write a list word to complete each sentence.

1. Apples and tomatoes ___ quickly in the heat.
2. Your costume is truly fantastic and ___.
3. I felt ___ after learning how the magician did his tricks.
4. Every boxer needs good ___ moves to protect himself.
5. The zipper on my jacket is stuck and I can't ___ it.
6. The leftover food was ___.
7. They live far away on the ___ of the city.
8. I was completely ___ when I learned the truth of the matter.
9. She bumped her head so hard that she was ___ for a moment.
10. My mom says my room is in ___ and needs to be tidied up.
11. We watched the ___ of the old building.
12. I had to ___ the invitation to the party.

1. decompose
2. outrageous
3. disenchanted
4. defensive
5. unfasten
6. unappetizing
7. outskirts
8. disillusioned
9. unconscious
10. disarray
11. destruction
12. decline

Adding Word Parts Add a prefix to each word to make a list word. Write the list word.

13. content
14. ward
15. patch
16. wavering
17. integrate
18. standing
19. common
20. burst

13. discontent
14. outward
15. dispatch
16. unwavering
17. disintegrate
18. outstanding
19. uncommon
20. outburst

Home Activity Your child used list words to finish sentences. Ask your child to pick two list words and use each in a sentence.

▲ **Spelling Practice Book** p. 68

DAY 5 Posttest

DICTATION SENTENCES

1. She felt a lot of <u>discontent</u>.
2. There has been a <u>decline</u> in reading scores.
3. Her <u>outward</u> smile hid her anger.
4. Please <u>dispatch</u> a taxi.
5. His support was <u>unwavering</u>.
6. The storm caused great <u>destruction</u>.
7. The paper will <u>disintegrate</u>.
8. He is an <u>outstanding</u> student.
9. That is an <u>uncommon</u> bird.
10. Her <u>outburst</u> surprised us.
11. He was wearing an <u>outrageous</u> shirt.
12. He is on the <u>defensive</u> team.
13. What an <u>unappetizing</u> meal!
14. I am <u>disillusioned</u> by the answer.
15. Her room is in <u>disarray</u>.
16. He was <u>unconscious</u> after the operation.
17. We live on the <u>outskirts</u> of town.
18. Please <u>unfasten</u> the ropes.
19. He became <u>disenchanted</u> with his new coach.
20. The garbage began to <u>decompose</u> in the sun.

CHALLENGE

21. She acted in an <u>unbusinesslike</u> way.
22. The people <u>disembark</u> from the ship.
23. The spy will <u>deactivate</u> the bomb.
24. Don't <u>disenfranchise</u> anyone.
25. What an <u>outlandish</u> outfit!
26. Sixth graders are entering <u>adolescence</u>.

OBJECTIVES

- Formulate an inquiry question that is connected to this week's lesson focus.
- Effectively and efficiently find, evaluate, and communicate information related to an inquiry question using electronic sources.

New Literacies	
Day 1	**Identify Questions**
Day 2	**Navigate/Search**
Day 3	**Analyze**
Day 4	**Synthesize**
Day 5	**Communicate**

NEW LITERACIES

Internet Inquiry Activity

EXPLORE ANIMAL RESEARCH

Use the following 5-day plan to help students conduct this week's Internet inquiry activity on animal research. Remind students to follow classroom rules when using the Internet.

DAY 1

Identify Questions Discuss the lesson focus question: *How can we study animals more responsibly?* Brainstorm ideas for specific inquiry questions about animal research. For example, students might want to find out about language research with dolphins. Have students work individually, in pairs, or in small groups to write an inquiry question they would like answered.

DAY 2

Navigate/Search Have students begin an Internet search using a student-friendly search engine. Tell students to develop a list of a few helpful Web sites relevant to their inquiry questions. Ask them, if possible, to order these sites into categories, such as online references, personal Web sites, or animal research organization sites.

DAY 3

Analyze Direct students to explore the Web sites they identified on Day 2 to find information related to their inquiry questions. Advise students that they may need to do additional searching if they do not find enough information to completely answer their inquiry questions. Students should analyze information for reliability and usefulness, and either take notes or print out and highlight the relevant information.

DAY 4

Synthesize Have students synthesize information from Day 3 to develop an extended answer to their inquiry questions. Advise students on the format for documenting Internet sources. Students should identify the author's name (if available), the title of the page, the source of the page, the date the page was last updated (if available), and the URL address.

DAY 5

Communicate Have students share their inquiry results on animal research by preparing a visual presentation that includes clip art and uses different font styles and sizes for headings and text.

RESEARCH/STUDY SKILLS
Electronic Media

TEACH

Ask students what electronic media they use most often for doing research. Students will most likely answer *the Internet*. Remind students that there are two types of electronic media available for research—computer and non-computer. Tell students the same strategies apply to both printed and electronic sources, such as analyzing information, evaluating sources, asking questions and taking notes. Read the list of available electronic media options for students.

- **non-computer electronic media** include audiotapes, videotapes, DVDs, television, and radio
- **computer programs and services** include online Internet searches, online encyclopedias, CD-ROMs, Internet databases, computer programs, and e-mail

Group students in pairs and have them formulate a question on animal research. Then discuss the following questions.

1. **What are the best computer and non-computer electronic sources you can use to answer your question?** *(Answers will vary.)*

2. **How can you conduct an effective and safe Internet search?** *(Use a student-friendly search engine, and use reliable URL addresses that end in .edu, .org, and .gov.)*

ASSESS

As students conduct their search using various electronic media, make sure they are using the following strategies; analyzing information, evaluating sources, asking questions, and taking notes.

For more practice or to assess students, use Practice Book pp. 169–170.

OBJECTIVES

- Review the tools used to navigate the Internet.
- Use the Internet to answer research questions.

Electronic Media

- **Electronic media** includes online newspapers, magazines, encyclopedias, and other sources on the Internet.
- Noncomputer electronic media sources are audio tapes, videotapes, films, filmstrips, television, and radio.

Directions Use the following list of possible electronic media to answer the questions below.

- *The Rain forest Project* (Public Television documentary about saving endangered species in the Brazilian rain forest)
- A Rain Forest of Flowers (Internet site developed by a 2nd grade class about the flowers found in the rain forest)
- *Forest Voices* (CD of various rain forest animal sounds)
- "Rain Forest for the Future" (Taped interview with several rainforest experts about the future of the rain forest)
- *The Rain forest Encyclopedia* (CD-ROM with general information about the flora and fauna of the rain forest)
- Natural Habitat (Internet site about endangered primates in the Brazilian rain forest)

1. Which source would be least helpful in writing a report on endangered animals in the rain forest? Why?
   A Rain Forest of Flowers; it doesn't have any information on animals.
2. How would you find a video copy of *The Rain forest Project*?
   Contact the TV station by phone or e-mail; see if the library has a copy.
3. If you were doing an Internet search, what keywords would you type into the search engine to find the Web site Natural Habitat?
   endangered primates, Brazilian rain forest
4. Which source would be most helpful if you needed sound effects for a class presentation about the rain forest?
   Forest Voices
5. Which source would you start with if you needed to decide on a subtopic for a report on the rain forest?
   The Rain forest Encyclopedia

▲ **Practice Book** p. 169

Directions Use the following Internet search results found on a search engine to answer the questions below.

Search Results

Rain Forest Monkeys
University of Brazil's official site for rain forest monkey information. Natural habitats, eating and sleeping habits, scientific studies.

The Eroding Environment
University of Brazil Professor Winston Soela's five-year study of the effect of the disappearing habitat on the spider monkey, its population, food and water sources, social habits.

Fight for the Rain Forest
Sao Paolo Endangered Species Protection Society site. Information about endangered species, monkeys, reptiles. Updates on preservation efforts, fundraising efforts, Brazilian government decision deadlines.

The Brazilian Rain Forest
Our trip to the Brazilian rain forest was fantastic! We saw monkeys, all kinds of insects. Photos.

6. What does the information below the underlined links tell you?
   It tells you more specific information about the site.
7. What keywords might have been used to get these search results?
   Possible answer: Brazil, rain forest, monkey
8. Which sites are university sites regarding rain forest monkeys?
   Rain forest Monkeys and The Eroding Environment
9. Which site would be the least reliable if you were doing a report for school? Why?
   The Brazilian Rain Forest; It is someone's description of their vacation and not scientific, reliable information.
10. Why might the *Fight for the Rain Forest* site be valuable if you wanted to help preserve endangered species?
    Possible answer: It gives information about preservation efforts.

Home Activity Your child answered questions about electronic media. With your child, look around your house and see how many different types of electronic media you have on hand. Talk with him or her about how each of the various electronic media sources could be valuable in his or her studies.

▲ **Practice Book** p. 170

Assessment Checkpoints *for the Week*

Selection Assessment

Use pp. 65–68 of Selection Tests **to check:**

 Selection Understanding

 Comprehension Skill *Author's Purpose*

 Selection Vocabulary

captive	primitive
companionship	sanctuaries
existence	stimulating
ordeal	

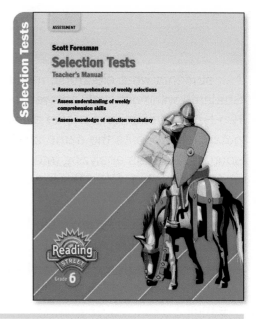

ASSESSMENT

Scott Foresman

Selection Tests
Teacher's Manual

• Assess comprehension of weekly selections
• Assess understanding of weekly comprehension skills
• Assess knowledge of selection vocabulary

Reading STREET
Grade 6

Leveled Assessment

On-Level

Strategic Intervention

Advanced

Use pp. 97–102 of Fresh Reads for Differentiated Test Practice **to check:**

 Comprehension Skill *Author's Purpose*

 REVIEW **Comprehension Skill** *Fact and Opinion*

 Fluency *Words Correct Per Minute*

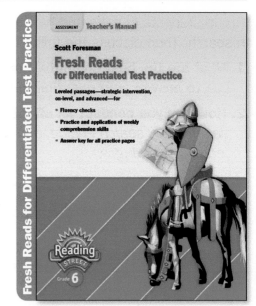

ASSESSMENT   Teacher's Manual

Scott Foresman

Fresh Reads
for Differentiated Test Practice

Leveled passages—strategic intervention, on-level, and advanced—for

• Fluency checks
• Practice and application of weekly comprehension skills
• Answer key for all practice pages

Reading STREET
Grade 6

Managing Assessment

Use Assessment Handbook **for:**

 Observation Checklists

 Record-Keeping Forms

 Portfolio Assessment

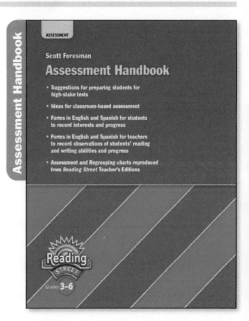

ASSESSMENT

Scott Foresman

Assessment Handbook

• Suggestions for preparing students for high-stake tests
• Ideas for classroom-based assessment
• Forms in English and Spanish for students to record interests and progress
• Forms in English and Spanish for teachers to record observations of students' reading and writing abilities and progress
• Assessment and Regrouping charts reproduced from *Reading Street Teacher's Editions*

Reading STREET
Grades 3–6

Unit 4
Explorers, Pioneers, and Discoverers

CONCEPT QUESTION
How have those who've gone first influenced others who've gone after?

Week 1
What drives people to explore harsh climates and dangerous places?

Week 2
Why is it important to study animals responsibly?

Week 3
What does it mean to be a pioneer?

Week 4
How can we be open to new understandings?

Week 5
How do inventions happen?

EXPAND THE CONCEPT
What does it mean to be a pioneer?

CONNECT THE CONCEPT

▶ **Build Background**
herd, legend, rugged, scout

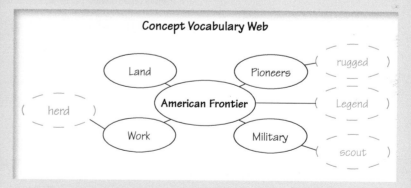

Concept Vocabulary Web

▶ **Social Studies Content**
The Reconstruction Period, The Westward Movement, Native Americans and African Americans

▶ **Writing**
Describe a Setting

▶ **Internet Inquiry**
The Pioneer Experience

Black Frontiers 456a

Preview Your Week

What does it mean to be a pioneer?

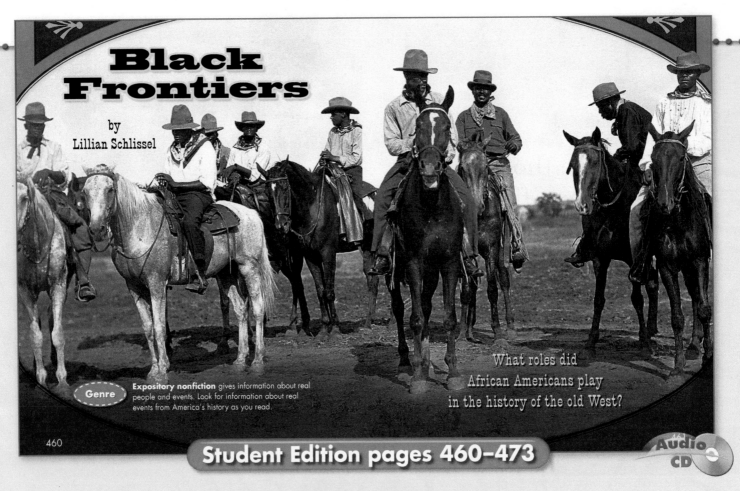

Black Frontiers
by Lillian Schlissel

460

Genre Expository nonfiction gives information about real people and events. Look for information about real events from America's history as you read.

What roles did African Americans play in the history of the old West?

Student Edition pages 460–473

Audio CD

Genre Expository Nonfiction
Vocabulary Strategy Context Clues
Comprehension Skill Cause and Effect
Comprehension Strategy Prior Knowledge

Paired Selection

Reading Across Texts
Imagine Langston Hughes' Message to Black Settlers

Genre
Poetry

Poetry

Genre
- Poems are compositions arranged in lines. The lines do not have to rhyme, but many poems have lines with a clear, regular rhythm.
- Poems have the ability to make readers feel a diverse range of emotions.
- Poets use their life experiences or views as they compose their poems.
- A poet might create new words or combinations of words to reflect the mood or image.
- Notice that a poet might write short poems in a single verse or a few short verses.

Link to Writing
Write a few lines or thoughts that you have about dreams or hopes.

Poems
by Langston Hughes

The Dream Keeper

Bring me all of your dreams,
You dreamers.
Bring me all of your
Heart melodies
That I may wrap them
In a blue cloud-cloth
Away from the too-rough fingers
Of the world.

Youth

We have tomorrow
Bright before us
Like a flame.

Yesterday
A night-gone thing,
A sun-down name.

And dawn-today
Broad arch above the
road we came.

We march!

Dreams

Hold fast to dreams
For if dreams die
Life is a broken-winged bird
That cannot fly.

Hold fast to dreams
For when dreams go
Life is a barren field
Frozen with snow.

Reading Across Texts
What message do you think the poet Langston Hughes would have for the black settlers of communities like Nicodemus and Dunlap?

Writing Across Texts Write a message of hope for frontier settlers. Use lines from the poems if you wish.

What are some causes and effects in these poems?

476

Student Edition pages 476–477

Audio CD

Read It
ONLINE
PearsonSuccessNet.com
• Student Edition
• Leveled Readers

Leveled Readers

⊙ **Skill** Cause and Effect

⊙ **Strategy** Prior Knowledge

Lesson Vocabulary

Below-Level

On-Level

Advanced

ELL Reader

· Concept Vocabulary
· Text Support
· Language Enrichment

Integrate Social Studies Standards

• U.S. History
• Settling the West

✓ Read

Black Frontiers, pp. 460–473

Poems by Langston Hughes, pp. 476–477

Leveled Readers

Below-Level On-Level Advanced

• Support Concepts • Develop Concepts • Extend Concepts

ELL Reader

✓ Build
Concept Vocabulary
American Frontier,
pp. 456l–456m

✓ Teach
Social Studies Concepts
Reconstruction, p. 463
Westward Movement, p. 465
Native and African
Americans, p. 471

✓ Explore
Social Studies Center
Make a Map, p. 456k

Weekly Plan

 *My Lesson Planner* ONLINE
PearsonSuccessNet.com

READING

45–90 minutes

TARGET SKILLS OF THE WEEK

- **Comprehension Skill**
  Cause and Effect
- **Comprehension Strategy**
  Prior Knowledge
- **Vocabulary Strategy**
  Context Clues

LANGUAGE ARTS

30–60 minutes

Trait of the Week

Sentences

DAY 1
PAGES 456l–458b, 477a, 477e–477k

Oral Language

QUESTION OF THE WEEK   *What does it mean to be a pioneer?*

Read Aloud: "Under the Coonskin Cap," 456m
Build Concepts, 456l

Comprehension/Vocabulary

Comprehension Skill/Strategy Lesson, 456–457
- Cause and Effect **T**
- Prior Knowledge

Build Background, 458a

Introduce Lesson Vocabulary, 458b
bondage, commissioned, earthen, encounter, homesteaders, settlement **T**

Read Leveled Readers

Grouping Options 456f–456g

Fluency

Model Tone of Voice, 456l–456m, 477a

Grammar, 477e
Introduce Possessive Pronouns **T**

Writing Workshop, 477g
Describe a Setting
Model the Trait of the Week: Sentences

Spelling, 477i
Pretest for Words with *ci* and *ti*

Internet Inquiry, 477k
Identify Questions

Day 1   Write to Read, 456

Day 1   American Frontier Concept Web, 456l

DAY 2
PAGES 458–467, 477a, 477e–477k

Oral Language

QUESTION OF THE DAY   *What were some things that made pioneer life difficult?*

Comprehension/Vocabulary

Vocabulary Strategy Lesson, 458–459
- Context Clues **T**

Read *Black Frontiers,* 460–467

Grouping Options
456f–456g

- Cause and Effect **T**
- Prior Knowledge
- **REVIEW** Author's Purpose **T**

Develop Vocabulary

Fluency

Choral Reading, 477a

Grammar, 477e
Develop Possessive Pronouns **T**

Writing Workshop, 477g
Improve Writing with Order

Spelling, 477i
Teach the Generalization

Internet Inquiry, 477k
Navigate/Search

Day 2   Words to Write, 459
Strategy Response Log, 460, 467

Day 2   Time for Social Studies: The Reconstruction Period, 463; The Westward Movement, 465
Revisit American Frontier Concept Web, 467

DAILY WRITING ACTIVITIES

DAILY SOCIAL STUDIES CONNECTIONS

DAILY SUCCESS PREDICTORS
for Adequate Yearly Progress

Monitor Progress and Corrective Feedback

Vocabulary   Check Vocabulary, *456l*

RESOURCES FOR THE WEEK

- Practice Book, *pp. 171–180*
- Word Study and Spelling Practice Book, *pp. 69–72*
- Grammar and Writing Practice Book, *pp. 69–72*

- Selection Test, *pp. 69–72*
- Fresh Reads for Differentiated Test Practice, *pp. 103–108*
- The Grammar and Writing Book, *pp. 152–157*

Grouping Options for Differentiated Instruction
Turn the page for the small group lesson plan.

DAY 3 PAGES 468–475, 477a, 477e–477k

Oral Language

QUESTION OF THE DAY *What are similarities in the ways black and white Americans helped in the expansion of the country?*

Comprehension/Vocabulary

Read *Black Frontiers*, 468–474

Grouping Options 456f–456g

- 🔵 Cause and Effect **T**
- 🔵 Prior Knowledge
- 🔵 Context Clues **T**
- Develop Vocabulary

Reader Response
Selection Test

Fluency

Model Tone of Voice, 477a

Grammar, 477f
Apply Possessive Pronouns in Writing **T**

Writing Workshop, 475, 477h
Write Now
Prewrite and Draft

Spelling, 477j
Connect Spelling to Writing

Internet Inquiry, 477k
Analyze Sources

Day 3 Strategy Response Log, 472
Look Back and Write, 474

Day 3 Time for Social Studies: Native Americans and African Americans, 471; Revisit the American Frontier Concept Web, 473

DAY 4 PAGES 476–477a, 477e–477k

Oral Language

QUESTION OF THE DAY *Are dreams necessary for growth and change? Explain.*

Comprehension/Vocabulary

Read Poems by Langston Hughes, 476–477

Grouping Options 456f–456g

Poetry
Genre
Reading Across Texts

Fluency

Partner Reading, 477a

Grammar, 477f
Practice Possessive Pronouns for Standardized Tests **T**

Writing Workshop, 477h
Draft, Revise, and Publish

Spelling, 477j
Provide a Strategy

Internet Inquiry, 477k
Synthesize Information

Day 4 Writing Across Texts, 477

Day 4 Social Studies Center: Make a Map, 456k,

DAY 5 PAGES 477a–477l

Oral Language

QUESTION OF THE WEEK *To wrap up the week, revisit the Day 1 question.*
Build Concept Vocabulary, 477c

Fluency

Read Leveled Readers

Grouping Options 456f–456g

Assess Reading Rate, 477a

Comprehension/Vocabulary

- 🔵 Reteach Cause and Effect, 477b **T**
- Author's Viewpoint/Bias, 477b
- 🔵 Review Context Clues, 477c **T**

Speaking and Viewing, 477d
Interpret Poetry
Analyze Media

Grammar, 477f
Cumulative Review

Writing Workshop, 477h
Connect to Unit Writing

Spelling, 477j
Posttest for Words with *ci* and *ti*

Internet Inquiry, 477k
Communicate Results

Research/Study Skills, 477l
Note Taking

Day 5 Author's Viewpoint/Bias, 477b

Day 5 Revisit the American Frontier Concept Web, 477c

KEY 🔵 = Target Skill **T** = Tested Skill

Comprehension Check Retelling, *474*

Fluency Check Fluency wcpm, *477a*

Vocabulary Check Vocabulary, *477c*

SUCCESS PREDICTOR

Small Group Plan *for Differentiated Instruction*

Daily Plan
AT A GLANCE

Reading
Whole Group
- Oral Language
- Comprehension/Vocabulary

Group Time
Differentiated Instruction

Meet with small groups to provide:
- Skill Support
- Reading Support
- Fluency Practice

Read

This week's lessons for daily group time can be found behind the Differentiated Instruction (DI) tab on pp. DI·22–DI·31.

Whole Group
- Fluency

Language Arts
- Grammar
- Writing
- Spelling
- Research/Inquiry
- Speaking/Listening/Viewing

DAY 1

On-Level	Strategic Intervention	Advanced
Teacher-Led *Page DI·23*	**Teacher-Led** *Page DI·22*	**Teacher-Led** *Page DI·23*
• Develop Concept Vocabulary	• Reinforce Concepts	• Read Advanced Reader *Grizzled Bill Turns Over a New Leaf*
• Read On-Level Reader *Homesteaders in Nebraska*	• Read Below-Level Reader *A Very Special Gift*	• Independent Extension Activity

(i) Independent Activities
While you meet with small groups, have the rest of the class...

- Visit the Reading/Library Center
- Listen to the Background Building Audio
- Finish Write to Read, p. 456
- Complete Practice Book pp. 173–174
- Visit Cross-Curricular Centers

DAY 2

On-Level	Strategic Intervention	Advanced
Teacher-Led *Pages 462–467*	**Teacher-Led** *Page DI·24*	**Teacher-Led** *Page DI·25*
• Read *Black Frontiers*	• Practice Lesson Vocabulary	• Extend Vocabulary
	• Read Multisyllabic Words	• Read *Black Frontiers*
	• Read or Listen to *Black Frontiers*	

(i) Independent Activities
While you meet with small groups, have the rest of the class...

- Visit the Reading/Library Center
- Listen to the AudioText for *Black Frontiers*
- Finish Words to Write, p. 459
- Complete Practice Book pp. 175–176
- Write in their Strategy Response Logs, pp. 460, 467
- Visit Cross-Curricular Centers
- Work on inquiry projects

DAY 3

On-Level	Strategic Intervention	Advanced
Teacher-Led *Pages 468–473*	**Teacher-Led** *Page DI·26*	**Teacher-Led** *Page DI·27*
• Read *Black Frontiers*	• Practice Cause and Effect and Prior Knowledge	• Extend Cause and Effect and Prior Knowledge
	• Read or Listen to *Black Frontiers*	• Read *Black Frontiers*

(i) Independent Activities
While you meet with small groups, have the rest of the class...

- Visit the Reading/Library Center
- Listen to the AudioText for *Black Frontiers*
- Write in their Strategy Response Logs, p. 472
- Finish Look Back and Write, p. 474
- Complete Practice Book p. 177
- Visit Cross-Curricular Centers
- Work on inquiry projects

① Begin with whole class skill and strategy instruction.

② Meet with small groups to provide differentiated instruction.

③ Gather the whole class back together for fluency and language arts.

On-Level
Teacher-Led
Pages 476–477
- **Read** "Poems by Langston Hughes"

Strategic Intervention
Teacher-Led
Page DI · 28
- **Read** or Listen to "Poems by Langston Hughes"

Advanced
Teacher-Led
Page DI · 29
- **Read** "Poems by Langston Hughes"
- Genre Study

DAY 4

ⓘ Independent Activities

While you meet with small groups, have the rest of the class...

- Visit the Reading/Library Center
- Listen to the AudioText for "Poems by Langston Hughes"
- Visit the Writing/Vocabulary Center
- Finish Writing Across Texts, p. 477
- Visit Cross-Curricular Centers
- Work on inquiry projects

On-Level
Teacher-Led
Page DI · 31
- **Reread** Leveled Reader *Homesteaders in Nebraska*
- Retell *Homesteaders in Nebraska*

Strategic Intervention
Teacher-Led
Page DI · 30
- **Reread** Leveled Reader *and A Very Special Gift*
- Retell *A Very Special Gift*

Advanced
Teacher-Led
Page DI · 31
- **Reread** Leveled Reader *Grizzled Bill Turns Over a New Leaf*
- Share Extension Activity

DAY 5

ⓘ Independent Activities

While you meet with small groups, have the rest of the class...

- Visit the Reading/Library Center
- Complete Practice Book pp. 178–180
- Visit Cross-Curricular Centers
- Work on inquiry projects

Grouping Place English language learners in the groups that correspond to their reading abilities in English.

Use the appropriate Leveled Reader or other text at students' instructional level.

TIP Send home the appropriate Multilingual Summary of the main selection on Day 1.

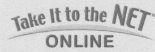
Take It to the NET™ ONLINE
PearsonSuccessNet.com

P. David Pearson
For ideas on teaching comprehension strategies, see the article "Developing Expertise in Reading Comprehension" by Scott Foresman author P. David Pearson and others.

TEACHER TALK

Differentiated instruction is instruction tailored to the needs of groups of students, such as struggling students, gifted students, or English language learners.

Be sure to schedule time for students to work on the unit inquiry project "Going First." This week students research the group of explorers, pioneers, or discoverers they have chosen and analyze the information.

Looking Ahead

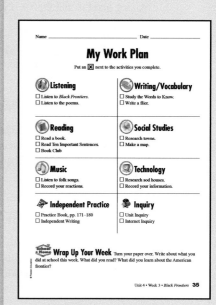

Name _____ Date _____
My Work Plan
Put an ☒ next to the activities you complete.

Listening
☐ Listen to *Black Frontiers*.
☐ Listen to the poems.

Writing/Vocabulary
☐ Study the Words to Know.
☐ Write a flier.

Reading
☐ Read a book.
☐ Read Ten Important Sentences.
☐ Book Club

Social Studies
☐ Research towns.
☐ Make a map.

Music
☐ Listen to folk songs.
☐ Record your reactions.

Technology
☐ Research sod houses.
☐ Record your information.

Independent Practice
☐ Practice Book, pp. 171–180
☐ Independent Writing

Inquiry
☐ Unit Inquiry
☐ Internet Inquiry

Wrap Up Your Week Turn your paper over. Write about what you did at school this week. What did you read? What did you learn about the American frontier?

Unit 4 • Week 3 • *Black Frontiers* **35**

▲ **Group-Time Survival Guide**
p. 35, Weekly Contract

☑ Customize Your Plan *by Strand*

ORAL LANGUAGE

 SOCIAL STUDIES

Concept Development

What does it mean to be a pioneer?

CONCEPT VOCABULARY

herd legend rugged scout

BUILD

☐ **Question of the Week** Introduce and discuss the question of the week. This week students will read a variety of texts and work on projects related to the concept *American Frontier.* Post the question for students to refer to throughout the week.
DAY 1 *456d*

☐ **Read Aloud** Read aloud " Under the Coonskin Cap." Then begin a web to build concepts and concept vocabulary related to this week's lesson and the unit theme, Explorers, Pioneers, and Discoverers. Introduce the concept words *herd, legend, rugged,* and *scout* and have students place them on the web. Display the web for use throughout the week. DAY 1 *456l–456m*

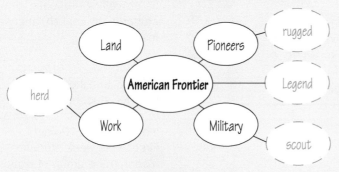

DEVELOP

☐ **Question of the Day** Use the prompts from the Weekly Plan to engage students in conversations related to this week's reading and the unit theme. **EVERY DAY** *456d–456e*

☐ **Concept Vocabulary Web** Revisit the American Frontier Concept Web and encourage students to add concept words from their reading and life experiences. DAY 2 *467*, DAY 3 *473*

CONNECT

☐ **Looking Back/Moving Forward** Revisit the American Frontier Concept Web and discuss how it relates to this week's lesson and the unit theme. Then make connections to next week's lesson. DAY 5 *477c*

CHECK

☐ **Concept Vocabulary Web** Use the American Frontier Concept Web to check students' understanding of the concept vocabulary words *herd, legend, rugged,* and *scout.*
DAY 1 *456l*, DAY 5 *477c*

VOCABULARY

STRATEGY CONTEXT CLUES
Context is the words and sentences around an unknown word. When you come across an unfamiliar word as you read, you can often find clues in the context around the word. The author may give a definition, a synonym or antonym, an example, or a relationship in the context that will help you figure out the meaning of the word you don't know.

LESSON VOCABULARY
bondage   encounter
commissioned homesteaders
earthen   settlement

TEACH

☐ **Words to Know** Give students the opportunity to tell what they already know about this week's lesson vocabulary words. Then discuss word meaning. DAY 1 *458b*

☐ **Vocabulary Strategy Lesson** Use the vocabulary strategy lesson in the Student Edition to introduce and model this week's strategy, *context clues.* DAY 2 *458–459*

Vocabulary Strategy Lesson

PRACTICE/APPLY

☐ **Leveled Text** Read the lesson vocabulary in the context of leveled text. DAY 1 *LR19–LR27*

☐ **Words in Context** Read the lesson vocabulary and apply *context clues* in the context of *Black Frontiers.*
DAY 2 *460–467*, DAY 3 *468–474*

Leveled Readers

☐ **Writing/Vocabulary Center** Write a flier for African Americans to join the troops to serve at frontier outposts.
ANY DAY *456k*

Main Selection—Nonfiction

☐ **Homework** Practice Book pp. 174–175. DAY 1 *458b*, DAY 2 *459*

☐ **Word Play** Have partners brainstorm a list of verb and noun pairs in which the noun names a person who does a particular action, and the name made by adding *-er* or *-or* to the verb, for example, write—writer. **ANY DAY** *477c*

ASSESS

☐ **Selection Test** Use the Selection Test to determine students' understanding of the lesson vocabulary words. DAY 3

RETEACH/REVIEW

☐ **Reteach Lesson** If necessary, use this lesson to reteach and review *context clues.* DAY 5 *477c*

COMPREHENSION

⚙ **SKILL CAUSE AND EFFECT** A cause is what makes something happen. An effect is something that happens as a result of a cause. Causes and effects are related to each other in a chain of events.

⚙ **STRATEGY PRIOR KNOWLEDGE** Prior knowledge is everything you already know about a subject. Connecting your prior knowledge to what you are reading helps you better understand and figure out cause and effect relationships. For example, connecting what you know about how you feel on a hot day can help you understand how a heat wave might affect a town.

TEACH

☐ **Skill/Strategy Lesson** Use the skill/strategy lesson in the Student Edition to introduce and model *cause and effect* and *prior knowledge.* DAY 1 *456–457*

☐ **Extend Skills** Teach author's viewpoint/bias. **ANY DAY** *477b.*

Skill/Strategy Lesson

PRACTICE/APPLY

☐ **Leveled Text** Apply *cause and effect* and *prior knowledge* to read leveled text. DAY 1 *LR19–LR27*

☐ **Skills and Strategies in Context** Read *Black Frontiers,* using the Guiding Comprehension questions to apply *cause and effect* and *prior knowledge.* DAY 2 *460–467,* DAY 3 *468–474*

Leveled Readers

☐ **Skills and Strategies in Context** Read the Hughes poems, guiding students as they apply *cause and effect* and *prior knowledge.* Then have students discuss and write across texts. DAY 4 *476–477*

Main Selection—Nonfiction

☐ **Homework** Practice Book pp. 173, 177, 178. DAY 1 *457,* DAY 3 *473,* DAY 5 *477b*

Paired Selection—Poetry

☐ **Fresh Reads for Differentiated Test Practice** Have students practice *cause and effect,* with a new passage. DAY 3

ASSESS

☐ **Selection Test** Determine students' understanding of the selection and their use of *cause and effect.* DAY 3

☐ **Retell** Have students retell *Black Frontiers.* DAY 3 *474–475*

RETEACH/REVIEW

☐ **Reteach Lesson** If necessary, reteach and review *cause and effect.* DAY 5 *477b*

FLUENCY

SKILL TONE OF VOICE Tone of voice is the way someone sounds when speaking with emotion. A reader uses different tones to show a character's feelings, or to emphasize interesting or important information.

TEACH

☐ **Read Aloud** Model fluent reading by rereading "Under the Coonskin Cap." Focus on this week's fluency skill, tone of voice. DAY 1 *456l–456m, 477a*

PRACTICE/APPLY

☐ **Choral Reading** Read aloud selected paragraphs from *Black Frontiers,* having students listen to your change of tone as you read. Then practice as a class by doing three choral readings of the paragraphs. DAY 2 *477a,* DAY 3 *477a*

☐ **Partner Reading** Partners practice reading aloud the first paragraph on p. 473, using a serious, convincing tone, and offering each other feedback. As students reread, monitor their progress toward their individual fluency goals. DAY 4 *477a*

☐ **Listening Center** Have students follow along with the AudioText for this week's selections. **ANY DAY** *456j*

☐ **Reading/Library Center** Have students reread a selection of their choice. **ANY DAY** *456j*

☐ **Fluency Coach** Have students use Fluency Coach to listen to fluent readings or practice reading on their own. **ANY DAY**

ASSESS

☐ **Check Fluency WCPM** Do a one-minute timed reading, paying special attention to this week's skill—tone of voice. Provide feedback for each student. DAY 5 *477a*

☑ Customize Your Plan *by Strand*

GRAMMAR

SKILL POSSESSIVE PRONOUNS Possessive pronouns are pronouns that show that something belongs to someone or something. Possessive pronouns agree with their antecedents in person and gender; that is, if the antecedent is singular and feminine, so is the possessive *(hers)*.

TEACH

❏ **Grammar Transparency 18** Use Grammar Transparency 18 to teach possessive pronouns. DAY 1 *477e*

Grammar Transparency 18

PRACTICE/APPLY

❏ **Develop the Concept** Review the concept of possessive pronouns and provide guided practice. DAY 2 *477e*

❏ **Apply to Writing** Have students review something they have written and apply possessive pronouns. DAY 3 *477f.*

❏ **Test Preparation** Examine common errors in using possessive pronouns to prepare for standardized tests. DAY 4 *477f*

❏ **Homework** Grammar and Writing Practice Book pp. 69–71. DAY 2 *477e*, DAY 3 *477f*, DAY 4 *477f*

ASSESS

❏ **Cumulative Review** Use Grammar and Writing Practice Book p. 72. DAY 5 *477f*

RETEACH/REVIEW

❏ **Daily Fix-It** Have students find and correct errors in grammar, spelling, and punctuation. **EVERY DAY** *477e–477f*

❏ **The Grammar and Writing Book** Use pp. 152–155 of The Grammar and Writing Book to extend instruction for using possessive pronouns. **ANY DAY**

The Grammar and Writing Book

WRITING

Trait of the Week

SENTENCES Good writing has a natural flow. Sentences that vary in structure and length create a readable style that communicates ideas clearly as well as sustaining the reader's interest. When writing follows the rhythms of speech, it is a pleasure to read aloud.

TEACH

❏ **Writing Transparency 18A** Use the model to introduce and discuss the Trait of the Week. DAY 1 *477g*

❏ **Writing Transparency 18B** Use the transparency to show students how order can improve their writing. DAY 2 *477g*

Writing Transparency 18A **Writing Transparency 18B**

PRACTICE/APPLY

❏ **Write Now** Examine the model on Student Edition p. 475. Then have students write their own description of a setting. DAY 3 *475, 477h,* DAY 4 *477h*

> **Prompt** The photographs in *Black Frontiers* show the setting of the story in pictures. Think about a setting from a favorite story or book. Now write a detailed description of that setting.

Write Now p. 475

❏ **Writing/Vocabulary Center** Write a flier for African Americans to join the troops to serve at frontier outposts. **ANY DAY** *456k*

ASSESS

❏ **Writing Trait Rubric** Use the rubric to evaluate students' writing. DAY 4 *477h*

RETEACH/REVIEW

❏ **The Grammar and Writing Book** Use pp. 152–157 of The Grammar and Writing Book to extend instruction for possessive pronouns, order, and descriptions of a setting. **ANY DAY**

The Grammar and Writing Book

① Use assessment data to determine your instructional focus.

② Preview this week's instruction by strand.

③ Choose instructional activities that meet the needs of your classroom.

SPELLING

GENERALIZATION **WORDS WITH** *ci* **AND** *ti*   The sounds /sh/ and /ch/ can be spelled *ci* and *ti*: espe*ci*ally, an*ci*ent, fric*ti*on, ques*ti*on.

TEACH

❑ **Pretest** Give the pretest for words with *ci* and *ti*. Guide students in self-correcting their pretests and correcting any misspellings. DAY 1 *477i*

❑ **Think and Practice** Connect spelling to the phonics generalization for words with *ci* and *ti*. DAY 2 *477i*

PRACTICE/APPLY

❑ **Connect to Writing** Have students use spelling words to write a poem. Then review frequently misspelled words: *especially, when.* DAY 3 *477j*

❑ **Homework** Phonics and Spelling Practice Book pp. 69–72. **EVERY DAY**

RETEACH/REVIEW

❑ **Review** Review spelling words to prepare for the posttest. Then provide students with a spelling strategy—problem parts. DAY 4 *477j*

ASSESS

❑ **Posttest** Use dictation sentences to give the posttest for words with *ci* and *ti*. DAY 5 *477j*

Spelling Words

1. precious	8. suggestion	15. cautious
2. commercial	9. friction	16. efficient
3. especially	10. lotion	17. sensational
4. ancient*	11. potion	18. vicious
5. gracious	12. digestion	19. official
6. position	13. artificial	20. ration*
7. question	14. glacier	

Challenge Words

21. fictitious	23. beneficial	25. emancipation
22. vaccination	24. precocious	

*Word from the selection

RESEARCH AND INQUIRY

❑ **Internet Inquiry** Have students conduct an Internet inquiry on the pioneer experience. **EVERY DAY** *477k*

❑ **Note Taking** Review taking notes to keep track of information; include a review of such terms as keywords, paraphrase, and synthesize (combine). Have students work in small groups to paraphrase and synthesize information from resource books about American history. DAY 5 *477l*

❑ **Unit Inquiry** Allow time for students to research the group they have chosen and analyze the information. **ANY DAY** *407*

SPEAKING AND VIEWING

❑ **Interpret Poetry** Have students choose one of the three poems on pp. 476–477 to interpret orally for the class. DAY 5 *477d*

❑ **Analyze Media** Discuss with students any television shows or movies they have seen about the American frontier, cowboys, or homesteading, then answer questions orally or in writing. DAY 5 *477d*

Resources for Differentiated Instruction

LEVELED READERS

▶ **Comprehension**
  - 🎯 **Skill** Cause and Effect
  - 🎯 **Strategy** Prior Knowledge

▶ **Lesson Vocabulary**
  - 🎯 **Context Clues**

bondage
commissioned
earthen
homesteaders
encounter
settlement

▶ **Social Studies Standards**
  - U.S. History
  - Settling the West

Leveled Reader Database

ONLINE

PearsonSuccessNet.com

Use the Online Database of over 600 books to

- Download and print additional copies of this week's leveled readers.
- Listen to the readers being read online.
- Search for more titles focused on this week's skills, topic, and content.

On-Level

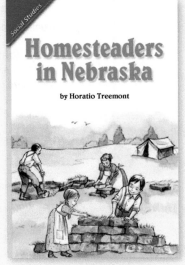

Social Studies

Homesteaders in Nebraska

by Horatio Treemont

On-Level Reader

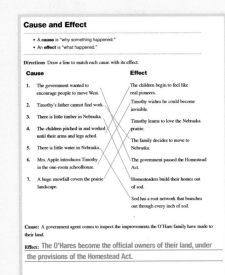

Cause and Effect

- A **cause** is "why something happened."
- An **effect** is "what happened."

Directions Draw a line to match each cause with its effect.

Cause

1. The government wanted to encourage people to move West.
2. Timothy's father cannot find work.
3. There is little timber in Nebraska.
4. The children pitched in and worked until their arms and legs ached.
5. There is little water in Nebraska.
6. Mrs. Apple introduces Timothy in the one-room schoolhouse.
7. A huge snowfall covers the prairie landscape.

Effect

The children begin to feel like real pioneers.

Timothy wishes he could become invisible.

Timothy learns to love the Nebraska prairie.

The family decides to move to Nebraska.

The government passed the Homestead Act.

Homesteaders build their homes out of sod.

Sod has a root network that branches out through every inch of soil.

Cause: A government agent comes to inspect the improvements the O'Hare family have made to their land.

Effect: The O'Hares become the official owners of their land, under the provisions of the Homestead Act.

On-Level Practice TE p. LR23

Vocabulary

Directions Write the word from the box that belongs in each group.

Check the Words You Know

___bondage ___commissioned ___earthen
___encounter ___homesteaders ___settlement

1. village, town ___settlement
2. greet, meet ___encounter
3. slavery, captivity ___bondage
4. clay, sod ___earthen
5. registered, paid ___commissioned
6. homebuilders, pioneers ___homesteaders

Directions Write a brief paragraph about *Homesteaders in Nebraska*. Use as many vocabulary words as you can.

Responses will vary.

On-Level Practice TE p. LR24

Strategic Intervention

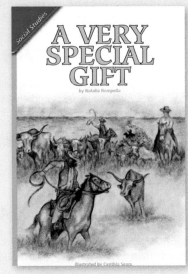

Social Studies

A VERY SPECIAL GIFT

by Natalie Rompella

Illustrated by Cynthia Sears

Below-Level Reader

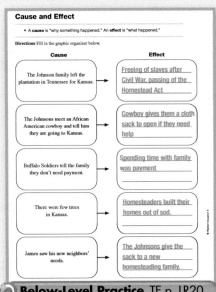

Cause and Effect

- A **cause** is "why something happened." An **effect** is "what happened."

Directions Fill in the graphic organizer below.

Cause	Effect
The Johnson family left the plantation in Tennessee for Kansas.	Freeing of slaves after Civil War, passing of the Homestead Act
The Johnsons meet an African American cowboy and tell him they are going to Kansas.	Cowboy gives them a cloth sack to open if they need help
Buffalo Soldiers tell the family they don't need payment.	Spending time with family was payment
There were few trees in Kansas.	Homesteaders built their homes out of sod.
James saw his new neighbors' needs.	The Johnsons give the sack to a new homesteading family.

Below-Level Practice TE p. LR20

Vocabulary

Directions Write the word from the box that matches each definition.

Check the Words You Know

___bondage ___commissioned ___earthen
___encounter ___homesteaders ___settlement

1. earthen — made of clay
2. homesteaders — people who work on a piece of land to improve it, so that they may eventually own it
3. settlement — a grouping of homes, a small village or town
4. encounter — meet or become acquainted with
5. bondage — slavery or captivity
6. commissioned — paid to do something

Directions Imagine you are a member of the Johnson family in *A Very Special Gift*. Write a brief journal entry from the point of view of one of the characters in the story. Use as many vocabulary words as you can.

Responses will vary.

Below-Level Practice TE p. LR21

Advanced

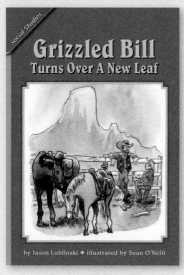

Advanced Reader

Cause and Effect

- A **cause** is "why something happened."
- An **effect** is "what happened."

Directions Read the following sentences. Write a cause or an effect on the lines below.

1. **Cause:** Sam Granite is educated, but from a poor family.

   Effect: Sam works at the Triple J, where cowboys get room and board.

2. **Cause:** Sam encounters an outlaw who asks him if he likes working for Wilkinson.

   Effect: Sam blurts out his feelings about working for Curtis Clay Wilkinson.

3. **Cause:** The outlaw tells Sam his name.

   Effect: Sam faints dead away.

4. **Cause:** Sam meets Bill in Heiferville to help him find a job.

   Effect: Grizzled Bill gets a haircut and trims his gray beard, wears nice clothes, and has cleaned his hat.

5. **Cause:** Bill admits he's robbed plenty of general stores.

   Effect: The owner of the Heiferville General Store shows them the door.

Directions On the lines below, write a brief paragraph about the effects of the events that happen, and what causes them to happen, starting with Chapter 4 of the story.

Advanced Practice TE p. LR26

Vocabulary

Directions Write the word from the box that belongs in each sentence.

Check the Words You Know

- arrogant
- profitable
- cattle barons
- suspicious
- feat
- treasury

1. Normally, not much happened to the **cattle barons** in Texas.

2. Some new ranchers moved here to build their **profitable** businesses.

3. It was as if we were to do whatever Mr. Wilkinson wanted and help him add to his **treasury**

4. That's why I was surprised, one day, when a wild-looking outlaw offered me a cool drink of water. I thought he would be **arrogant**

5. It was quite a **feat** to go from outlaw to sheriff, but Grizzled Bill did it.

6. You could have knocked me over with a feather when the sheriff asked Grizzled Bill to be his deputy; I thought for sure he would be **suspicious**

Directions On the lines below, write a brief tale about a do-good outlaw in the Wild West. Use as many of the vocabulary words as you can.

Advanced Practice TE p. LR27

ELL

ELL Reader

ELL Poster 18

Teacher's Edition Notes

ELL notes throughout this lesson support instruction and reference additional resources at point of use.

Teaching Guide pp. 120–126, 246–247

- Multilingual summaries of the main selection
- Comprehension lesson
- Vocabulary strategies and word cards
- ELL Reader 6.4.3 lesson

ELL and Transition Handbook

Ten Important Sentences

- Key ideas from every selection in the Student Edition
- Activities to build sentence power

More Reading

Readers' Theater Anthology

- Fluency practice
- Five scripts to build fluency
- Poetry for oral interpretation

Leveled Trade Books

Below-Level

On-Level

Advanced

- Extended reading tied to the unit concept
- Lessons in the Trade Book Library Teaching Guide

School + Home

Homework

- Family Times Newsletter
- ELL Multilingual Selection Summaries

Take-Home Books

- Leveled Readers

Family Times

Black Frontiers **456i**

Cross-Curricular Centers

 Listening

 Reading/Library

 **Music**

Listen to the Selections

MATERIALS `SINGLES`
CD player, headphones, AudioText CD, student book

LISTEN TO LITERATURE Listen to *Black Frontiers* by Lillian Schlissel and Poems by Langston Hughes as you follow or read along in your book. Listen for the results of what happened because African Americans dreamed of a better future.

If there is anything you don't understand, you can listen again to any section.

Read It Again!

MATERIALS `SINGLES` `PAIRS` `GROUPS`
Collection of books for self-selected reading, reading logs, student book

Select a book you have already read. Record the title of the book in your reading log. You may want to read with a partner.

You have the choice to read any of the following:

- Leveled Readers
- ELL Readers
- Stories Written by Classmates
- Books from the Library
- *Black Frontiers*

TEN IMPORTANT SENTENCES Read the Ten Important Sentences from *Black Frontiers.* Then locate the sentences in the student book.

PENPAL READING BUDDY Write a letter telling a friend about the African Americans who journeyed to the frontier.

Listen to Cowboy Songs

MATERIALS `GROUPS`
CD player, headphones, cassettes of cowboy songs or African American folk songs

Listen to some cowboy or folk songs. Then use a chart like the one below to record your reactions.

1. Write the title of the song in the first column.
2. Think about the lyrics and the music you hear.
3. In the second column, write down what the song is about.

EARLY FINISHERS Write a brief review of the songs you listened to. Tell whether or not you enjoyed listening to the songs and explain why.

Song	What the song is about
"Chisholm Trail"	a cowboy driving cattle in the rain
"The Range of the Buffalo"	shooting buffalo on the prairie

Scott Foresman Reading Street Centers Survival Kit
Use the *Black Frontiers* materials from the Reading Street
Centers Survival Kit to organize this week's centers.

Writing/Vocabulary

Write a
Flier

MATERIALS `SINGLES`
Construction paper, markers

Write a flier that could have been used to recruit African Americans to join the troops to serve at frontier outposts. Use the flier on p. 467 as a model.

1. Write an opener that grabs the reader's attention.
2. Tell who is needed and where they will be sent.
3. Provide information about how they will be paid.

EARLY FINISHERS Make a list of places to display your flier.

Social Studies

Make a
Map

MATERIALS `GROUPS`
Copies of a simple outline map of the United States showing state boundaries, Internet access, crayons or markers

Map the migration trail of African Americans from the South to Nicodemus.

1. Work with a small group.
2. Use a search engine to find the locations of Nicodemus, Kansas, and Nashville, Tennessee.
3. Mark and label the two places on your map.
4. Draw a line to show the trail between Nashville and Nicodemus.

EARLY FINISHERS Add other points of interest to your map and label them.

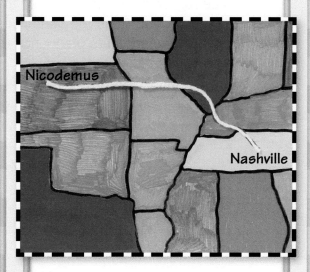

Technology

Research
Sod Houses

MATERIALS `SINGLES`
Internet access, Web graphic organizer

Use a search engine to learn more about soddies, or sod houses.

1. Access the Internet using a student-friendly search engine.
2. Type in the keywords *sod house*.
3. View more than one Web site.
4. Use a graphic organizer to record the new information that you learn.
5. Follow classroom rules when using the Internet.

EARLY FINISHERS Use what you learn to write step-by-step directions for building a soddie.

OBJECTIVES

- Build vocabulary by finding words related to the lesson concept.
- Listen for causes and effects.

Concept Vocabulary

herd to care for and drive cattle

legend a person whose achievements and deeds are a part of history

rugged rough, sturdy, hardy, and strong

scout person sent to find out what the enemy is doing

Monitor Progress

Check Vocabulary

If... students are unable to place words on the Web,	then... review the lesson concept. Place the words on the Web and provide additional words for practice, such as *courageous* and *build*.

SUCCESS PREDICTOR

DAY 1 Grouping Options

Reading

Whole Group
Introduce and discuss the Question of the Week. Then use pp. 456l–458b.

Small Group

Differentiated Instruction
Read this week's Leveled Readers. See pp. 456f–456g for the small group lesson plan.

Whole Group
Use p. 477a.

Language Arts
Use pp. 477e–477k.

Build Concepts

FLUENCY

MODEL TONE OF VOICE As you read "Under the Coonskin Cap," use the tone of your voice to model reading with expression. You can emphasize the humor in such phrases as *a grin so powerful that he could knock a pack of raccoons out of a tree just by smiling at them* and *figuring he was a few trees short of a forest.*

LISTENING COMPREHENSION

After reading "Under the Coonskin Cap," use the following questions to assess listening comprehension.

1. **What caused Davy Crockett to join the Tennessee Volunteer Militia?** *(He wanted to fight the Creek Indians because they were partly responsible for killing his grandparents.)* **Cause and Effect**

2. **What kind of character does the text present in its description of Crockett?** *(He's presented as a unique, fearless individual with a good sense of humor.)* **Character**

BUILD CONCEPT VOCABULARY

Start a web to build concepts and vocabulary related to this week's lesson and the unit theme.

- Draw the American Frontier Concept Web.

- Read the sentence with the word *rugged* again. Ask students to pronounce *rugged* and discuss its meaning.

- Place *rugged* in an oval attached to Pioneers. Explain that *rugged* is related to this concept. Read the sentences in which *legend, herd,* and *scout* appear. Have students pronounce the words, place them on the Web, and provide reasons.

- Brainstorm additional words and categories for the Web. Keep the Web on display and add words throughout the week.

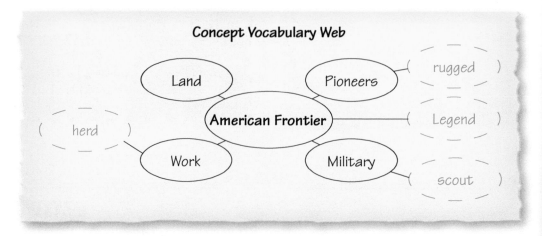

Concept Vocabulary Web

UNDER THE COONSKIN CAP

Read ALOUD

When you hear the name Davy Crockett, it probably brings to mind stories of the rugged frontiersman and his coonskin cap. Some say he was only three when he fought a grizzly bear. And some stories say he had a grin so powerful that he could knock a pack of raccoons out of a tree just by smiling at them. Well, these tall tales—many of them told by Davy himself—cloud the truth of a heroic and even humorous American legend.

Now, what we do know for sure is that Davy Crockett was born in the hills of Tennessee on August 17, 1786. After that it gets a bit sketchy. At the age of 12, his daddy hired him out to herd cattle. A year later, Davy left home again, but this time it was to escape punishment for not attending school. Davy once said there are three kinds of people in the world—those who can count and those who can't. Even though he wasn't a star student in the classroom, when it came to hunting, fishing, and surviving in nature, he was on the honor roll.

In 1813, Davy got wind of problems with the Creek Indians. He joined the Tennessee Volunteer Militia and served as a scout in the Creek War. He played a big part in getting the Creek to surrender. He stayed in the military for eight years, earning the rank of colonel before deciding to try his hand at politics.

At the age of thirty-five, Davy was elected to the State Legislature of Tennessee. At first the Ivy League politicians made fun of Davy, figuring he was a few trees short of a forest, but Davy quickly earned their respect for his humor and common sense. At the time, he was the type of politician folks needed; he was honest, hardworking, and great at telling funny stories. Davy is quoted as saying upon entering Congress, "I can whip my weight in wildcats and if any gentleman pleases, for a ten dollar bill, he can throw in a panther too."

Perhaps the most defining moment in Davy's life came at the age of fifty when he and a group of fellows from Tennessee headed for Texas to help fight for independence from Mexico. Davy said, "I have come to aid you all that I can, in your noble cause." Whether it was a noble cause or just plain crazy, the fact remains that he, along with 188 Texans, went up against thousands of Mexican soldiers on the morning of February 23, 1836. While it only took ninety minutes for the Mexicans to defeat the Texans, the lines "Remember the Alamo" became the new battle cry to eventually liberate Texas from Mexico.

While the name Davy Crockett will always be mentioned in the same breath as other legends of the frontier like Paul Bunyan and Pecos Bill, the real man under the coonskin cap should be remembered as a frontiersman, soldier, and politician.

Activate Prior Knowledge

Before students listen to the Read Aloud, ask them what they know about life on the frontier in the American West.

Set Purpose

Read aloud the title and have students predict what the selection will be about.

Have students listen for reasons why Davy Crocket is a legend in American history.

Creative Response

On the board, write three or four colorful sentences from the Read Aloud. Then have groups of three or four prepare Reader's Theater presentations. **Drama**

ELL

Access Content Before reading, explain that this selection is a brief biography of Davy Crockett, a well-known frontiersman.

School + Home

Homework Send home this week's Family Times newsletter.

SKILLS ⬌ STRATEGIES IN CONTEXT

Cause and Effect Prior Knowledge

INTRODUCE

Write this sentence on the board: *People have fought for the right to be free.* Explain that using prior knowledge can help to identify the cause *(people want to be free)* and the effect *(they have fought for their freedom).*

Have students read the information on p. 456. Explain the following:

- A cause tells what makes something happen; an effect is what happens as a result of a cause.

- Thinking about what you already know helps you find the cause-and-effect relationships.

Use Skill Transparency 18 to teach cause and effect and prior knowledge.

Comprehension

Skill
Cause and Effect

Strategy
Prior Knowledge

 # Cause and Effect

- A *cause* is what makes something happen. An *effect* is something that happens as a result of a cause. Sometimes several causes lead to one effect.

- Clue words and phrases, such as *consequently, as a result,* and *therefore,* can help you spot cause-effect relationships. Sometimes, though, there are no clue words.

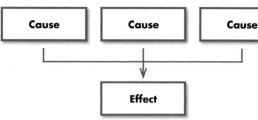

Strategy: Prior Knowledge

Prior knowledge is all of what you know about a given topic. Connecting your prior knowledge to what you are reading helps you comprehend better and is especially helpful when looking for cause-effect relationships. For example, suppose you are asked to state how a heat wave might affect a town. To answer, think about what you know about hot days and how people respond to them.

Write to Read

1. Read "Goodbye, Jim Crow." Make a graphic organizer like the one above in order to describe an overall effect and its causes.

2. Use the graphic organizer and your prior knowledge to help you write a brief paragraph about the way many black Americans might have felt in 1 when the Civil Rights Act was passed

456

Strategic Intervention

Cause and Effect Explain that a single effect can have multiple causes. To help students develop the cause-and-effect graphic organizer on p. 456, begin with the effect stated in the first sentence. *(It took many years for African Americans to receive full legal rights in the United States.)* Help students use information about the 1954 Supreme Court ruling and the acts passed in 1964 and 1965 to fill in the cause boxes.

ELL

Access Content

Beginning/Intermediate For a Picture It! lesson on cause and effect, see the ELL Teaching Guide, pp. 120–121.

Advanced Before reading "Goodbye, Jim Crow," remind students that unfamiliar terms are often defined within the text. Point out that the term *segregated* on p. 457 is followed by a synonym, *separated.*

Goodbye, Jim Crow

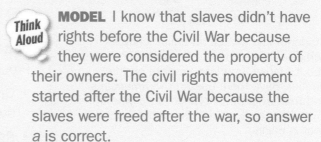

It took many years for black people to receive full legal rights in the United States. The push for fair laws began after the Civil War ended. ●

Unfair Laws Starting in 1865, a group of laws called black codes stopped blacks from having basic rights. Citizens in the northern part of the United States disagreed with these laws. This led to the Reconstruction laws, which got rid of the black codes. But soon new laws were passed that segregated, or separated, blacks from whites in many areas of life. These were called the Jim Crow laws. ●

New Laws In 1954, the United States Supreme Court ruled that it was not fair or lawful to have separate black and white schools. This helped the civil rights movement move forward with a strong, organized push to end segregation. In 1963, leaders of the movement staged a huge march in Washington, D.C. to speak out against racial discrimination. ●

President Kennedy could not get Congress to pass equal rights laws. After President Kennedy was murdered, President Johnson got Congress to pass the Civil Rights Act in 1964, which ended legal segregation. Then, in 1965, Congress passed the Voting Rights Act. ● This led to a huge increase in the number of blacks registered to vote.

(1) Strategy Use your prior knowledge to answer this question: Why did the civil rights movement start *after* the Civil War ended?
(a) Once the war ended, slaves were free.
(b) There wasn't interest on the part of black people until then.
(c) Before the war, discrimination was illegal.

(2) Skill What caused the United States to pass the Reconstruction laws? Are there clue words?

(3) Skill What was the effect of the important 1954 Supreme Court decision? Notice the pronoun *this*.

(4) Strategy Think about what you know about voting and elections. Why was it important for black citizens to have the right to vote?

457

Available as **Skill Transparency** 18

Cause and Effect

- A **cause** is what makes something happen. An **effect** is something that happens as a result of a cause. Sometimes several causes lead to one effect.
- Clue words and phrases such as *consequently, as a result,* and *therefore* can help you spot cause-and-effect relationships. Sometimes, though, there are no clue words.

Directions Read the following passage. Then complete the graphic organizer below.

The tornado destroyed everything we had: our sod house, our windmill, and our barn. Even though the tornado touched down a mile away, the ferocious winds affected all the farms in the area. Also, this wasn't your ordinary tornado. According to witnesses, two funnel clouds came together to produce one strong force of nature. Pa still believed we could have avoided such a disastrous outcome, though. He said if we had had sturdier materials to build our home with, then maybe things would've been different. Because our house and the barn were made from the resources of the earth, they didn't stand a chance against the mighty tornado.

Possible answers given.

Cause (What makes something happen)
1. tornado had ferocious winds

Cause (What makes something happen)
2. tornado was more powerful than usual

Cause (What makes something happen)
3. home and barn were made out of materials from the earth

Effect (What happened)
4. tornado destroyed the family homestead

5. What prior knowledge did you use to help you understand the passage?
I have seen on television what a tornado can do to buildings and homes.

School + Home **Home Activity** Your child identified causes and effects in a passage while using prior knowledge to better understand its contents. Together, discuss the causes and effects of natural disasters in your area.

Practice Book p. 173

TEACH

(1) STRATEGY Use paragraph 1 to model how to use prior knowledge to identify a cause.

Think Aloud **MODEL** I know that slaves didn't have rights before the Civil War because they were considered the property of their owners. The civil rights movement started after the Civil War because the slaves were freed after the war, so answer *a* is correct.

(2) SKILL Discuss the paragraph following the heading "Unfair Laws."

Think Aloud **MODEL** The text says citizens in the North didn't agree with the black codes. I think that the Reconstruction laws came about as a result of this disagreement. The words *This led* are a clue.

PRACTICE AND ASSESS

(3) SKILL Effect of the 1954 Supreme Court decision: schools were desegregated; the clue word *this* shows the connection of the Supreme Court decision to the movement forward for civil rights.

(4) STRATEGY Activating prior knowledge will lead to the conclusion that when black citizens have the right to vote, they have a voice in the laws passed by the government.

WRITE Have students complete steps 1 and 2 of the Write to Read activity. You might consider using this as a whole-class activity.

Monitor Progress
🎯 **Cause and Effect**

If... students are unable to complete **Write to Read** on p. 456,	**then...** use Practice Book p. 173 to provide additional practice.

Tech Files ONLINE

Students can search an online encyclopedia or the Internet to find out more about African American settlers on the frontier. Have them use *African Americans and frontier* or *African American cowboys* for their search, using a student-friendly search engine.

ELL

Build Background Use ELL Poster 18 to build background and vocabulary for the lesson concept of what it means to be a pioneer.

▲ ELL Poster 18

Build Background

ACTIVATE PRIOR KNOWLEDGE

BEGIN A TIME LINE of American history starting with the Emancipation Proclamation of 1863.

- Give students two to three minutes to list the important events they know surrounding the Civil War and the nation's growth in the years that followed.
- Record students' suggestions on a time line.
- Students will probably fill in only part of the chart at this point. As students read *Black Frontiers*, they will be able to add dates and examples.

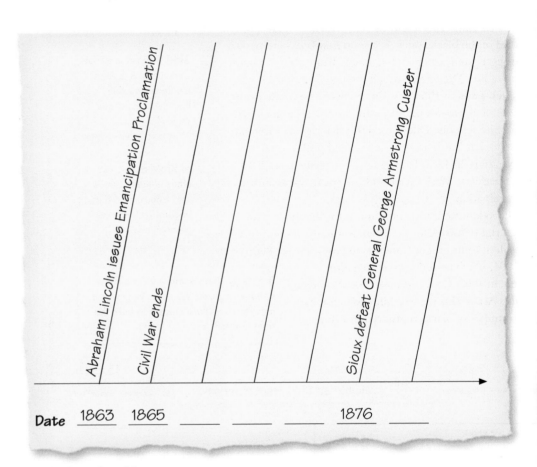

▲ Graphic Organizer 23

BACKGROUND BUILDING AUDIO This week's audio explores African American cowboys. After students listen, discuss what they learned about African Americans and the Wild West.

 **Background Building Audio**

Introduce Vocabulary

ANALOGIES

Review with students that an analogy shows a relationship between words: *pioneer* is to *frontier* as *astronaut* is to *space.* To complete an analogy, students must first understand how the first words are related and then choose a word that fits the second pair in the same way.

1. **explorers** is to **discoverers** as **settlers** is to _____
2. **liberty** is to **slavery** as **freedom** is to _____
3. **nation** is to **country** as **colony** is to _____
4. **corporal** is to **second lieutenant** as **noncommissioned officer** is to _____ **officer**
5. **fight** is to **battle** as **meet** is to _____
6. **timber** is to **wooden** as **clay** is to _____

Have students work in pairs to complete each analogy with a lesson vocabulary word. Then have them look up the meanings of the vocabulary words in the glossary to confirm or correct their analogies. ***Activate Prior Knowledge***

Have students share where they may have seen some of these words. Point out that students' knowledge of word structure can help them find the meanings of unfamiliar words. Ask them to look for base words in *bondage, earthen, homesteaders,* and *settlement. (Bond* means "something that ties or binds," *earth* means "ground or soil," *homestead* means "a house and its land," and *settle* means "to take up residence in a new place.") ***Unfamiliar Words • Word Structure***

By the end of the week, students should know the lesson vocabulary words. Have students check their analogies and revise their answers, as necessary.

Use Multisyllabic Word Routine on p. DI·1 to help students read multisyllabic words.

Lesson Vocabulary

WORDS TO KNOW

T **bondage** being held against your will under the control of another; slavery

T **commissioned** holding the rank of second lieutenant or above in the U.S. Army

T **earthen** made of ground, soil, or earth

T **encounter** meet unexpectedly; meet in a battle

T **homesteaders** persons who own and live on land granted by the U.S. government

T **settlement** a group of buildings and the people living in them

MORE WORDS TO KNOW

desolate not lived in; deserted

sharecroppers people who farm land for the owner in return for part of the crops

T = Tested Word

Vocabulary

Directions Choose the word from the box that best matches each definition. Write the word on the line.

encounter — 1. to meet unexpectedly; meet in a battle

settlement — 2. group of buildings and the people living in them

homesteaders — 3. people who own and live on land granted by the government

bondage — 4. being held against your will

earthen — 5. made of the ground or soil

Check the Words You Know
— bondage
— commissioned
— earthen
— encounter
— homesteaders
— settlement

Directions Choose the word from the box that best matches each clue. Write the word on the line.

settlement — 6. This is what a town or city of today once was.

earthen — 7. A mud house could be described as this.

commissioned — 8. This describes someone who holds the rank of second lieutenant or higher.

bondage — 9. Enslaved people experienced this condition.

encounter — 10. Two soldiers on opposite sides in a war might be involved in this.

Write a Friendly Letter
Imagine what it would be like living on the frontier. Write a friendly letter to someone back home about your experiences as a pioneer. Use as many vocabulary words as you can.

Friendly letters should include words from the vocabulary list and details about frontier life.

Home Activity Your child identified and used vocabulary words from *Black Frontiers.* With your child, write a story set back in the pioneer days. Use your family members as characters. Include as many vocabulary words from the selection as possible.

▲ **Practice Book** p. 174

Vocabulary Strategy

OBJECTIVE

⊙ Use context clues to determine the meanings of unfamiliar words.

INTRODUCE

Discuss the strategy for context clues using the steps on p. 458.

TEACH

• Have students read "Settling the West," paying attention to context clues surrounding the highlighted words.

• Model using context clues to determine the meaning of *encounter.*

Think Aloud **MODEL** The sentence says that settlers never knew when they would *encounter* Native Americans. From the sentence that follows, I can conclude that *encounter* is a synonym for *meet.*

DAY 2 Grouping Options

Reading
Whole Group Discuss the Question of the Day. Then use pp. 458–461.

Small Group Differentiated Instruction
Read *Black Frontiers.* See pp. 456f–456g for the small group lesson plan.

Whole Group Use p. 477a.

Language Arts
Use pp. 477e–477k.

Words to Know

encounter

homesteaders

earthen

settlement

commissioned

bondage

Remember
Try the strategy. Then, if you need more help, use your glossary or a dictionary.

Vocabulary Strategy
for Unfamiliar Words

Context Clues If you find a word you do not know while reading, check the context, or the words and sentences around the unknown word. Often the author provides clues that suggest the meaning of a difficult word.

1. Reread the sentence in which the unknown word appears. Look for a specific clue to the word's meaning.

2. Think about the overall meaning of the sentence.

3. If more help is needed, read the sentences near the sentence with the unknown word. They may contain enough information about the subject to suggest the meaning of the word.

4. See if your meaning makes sense in the original sentence.

As you read "Settling the West," use the context to help you figure out the meanings of unfamiliar words.

458

Strategic Intervention

⊙ **Context Clues** Have students work in pairs to follow the steps on p. 458. Suggest that they list the clues they find for unfamiliar words.

Access Content Use ELL Poster 18 to preteach vocabulary. Choose from the following to meet language proficiency levels.

Beginning Point out that the word *homesteader* in the second paragraph on p. 459 is followed by its definition.

Intermediate After reading, students can choose one of the tested words to use to complete a vocabulary frame.

Advanced Teach the lesson on pp. 458–459. Have students find home-language terms for some of the tested words.

Resources for home-language words may include parents, bilingual staff members, bilingual dictionaries, or online translation sources.

Settling the West

Settling in the American West took bravery and staying power. Men, women, and children traveled by boat or wagon, taking all their goods along. They never knew when they might encounter Native Americans. If the settlers did meet them, would these people be friendly or angry?

Once they chose a plot of land, the pioneers faced many difficulties. Homesteaders were pioneers who bought public land cheap and set up farms or ranches. In the grasslands, they often had to build makeshift earthen homes. They built with dirt or sod because wood was so scarce.

Over time, their numbers grew. In time, a settlement, or community in the wilderness, was established.

Battles between settlers and Native Americans continued in many places, as the Native Americans saw their land disappearing. There were losses on both sides. The U.S. government saw the land as their own. They commissioned officers and sent troops to battle the Native Americans. After many years of conflict and negotiation, Native Americans were mostly forced into the bondage of living on reservations. They no longer had the freedom to live as they once had.

Words to Write

Choose a picture from the selection and write a description of the picture. Use words from the Words to Know list.

459

PRACTICE AND ASSESS

- Have students determine the meanings of the remaining words and explain the context clues they used.
- Point out that context doesn't always include synonyms or definitions for unfamiliar words. Students may have to use the glossary or a dictionary to find the exact meaning of some words.
- Have students complete Practice Book p. 175.

WRITE Writing should include vocabulary words related to life or homes on the frontier.

Monitor Progress

Context Clues

| If... students need more practice with the lesson vocabulary, | then... use Tested Vocabulary Cards. |

Vocabulary · Context Clues

- When you are reading and see an unfamiliar word, you can use **context clues**, or the words around the unfamiliar word, to figure out its meaning.

Directions Read the following passage. Then answer the questions below.

Today I found out more about my family's history. I thought we had always lived in Kansas, but that wasn't the case. My ancestors were enslaved people in Alabama. When they were no longer held in bondage by white plantation owners, they decided to move as far away from the South as they could. They became homesteaders, moving to the open lands of the West that they bought from the government. My ancestors joined other African Americans who started their own settlement. Their community was a group of homes and buildings made out of earthen materials, such as sod, mud, and grass at first. I found it very strange that the towns and cities I know of today were once crude and small. I also found out that my great-great-great-uncle Thomas was a commissioned officer. I had no idea that my family's history was so interesting!

Possible answers given for 4, 5.

1. What is the definition of *bondage*? What context clue helps you figure out its meaning?
   "being held against your will": The context says that the people who experienced bondage were enslaved.

2. What context clue helps you figure out the definition of *homesteaders*?
   The information following the comma gives the definition.

3. How do you know a *settlement* is unlike the towns and cities of today?
   The settlement is described as crude and small.

4. What are some examples of *earthen* materials? What is another example not used in the passage?
   sod, mud, and grass; Clay is another example.

5. The sentence containing the word *commissioned* does not have a context clue. Rewrite the sentence so that a context clue appears. (You may write it as more than one sentence.)
   I also found out that my great-great-great-uncle Thomas ranked higher than second lieutenant—he was a commissioned officer.

Home Activity Your child identified the definitions of unfamiliar words by using context clues. Read a story or article together. Have your child underline or highlight the context clues that suggest the meanings of unfamiliar words.

▲ **Practice Book** p. 175

Prereading Strategies

OBJECTIVES

- Identify cause-and-effect relationships to improve comprehension.
- Use prior knowledge to understand cause-and-effect relationships.

GENRE STUDY

Expository Nonfiction

Black Frontiers is expository nonfiction. Explain that expository nonfiction gives information about real people and events.

PREVIEW AND PREDICT

Have students preview the selection title, subheadings, and photographs, and discuss the topics or ideas they think this selection will cover. Encourage students to use lesson vocabulary words as they talk about what they expect to learn.

Strategy Response Log

Activate Prior Knowledge Have students write what they already know about frontier life in their strategy response logs. Students will monitor their comprehension in the Strategy Response Log activity on p. 467.

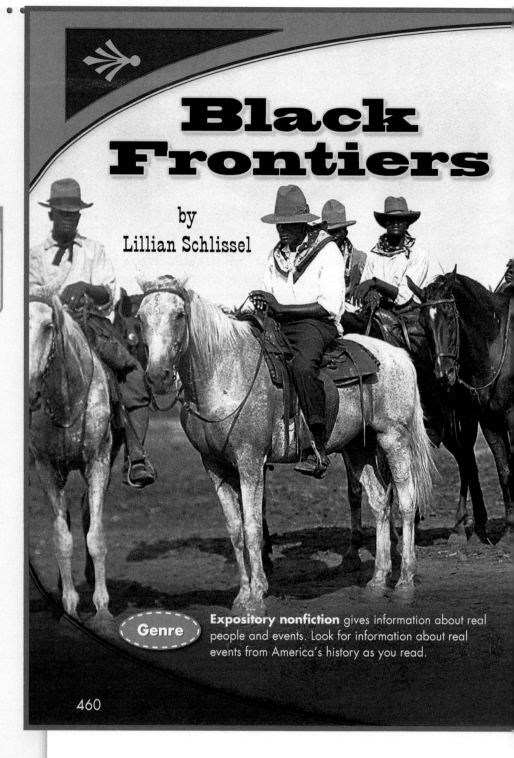

Black Frontiers

by
Lillian Schlissel

Genre

Expository nonfiction gives information about real people and events. Look for information about real events from America's history as you read.

460

ELL

Activate Prior Knowledge Lead a picture walk and have students describe what is happening in the illustrations. Invite students to share what they know about the history of the old West, as well as questions they have about it.

Consider having students read the selection summary in English or in students' home languages. See the Multilingual Summaries in the ELL Teaching Guide, pp. 124–126.

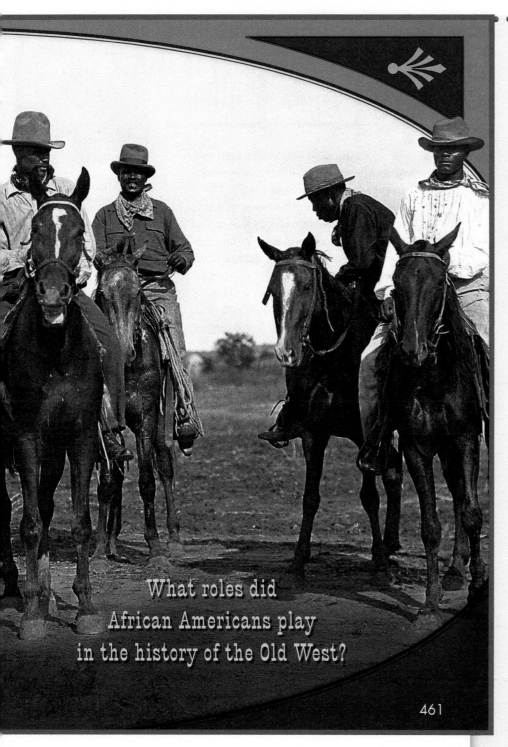

What roles did
African Americans play
in the history of the Old West?

461

SET PURPOSE

Read the first paragraph of the selection aloud to students. Have them consider their preview discussion and tell what they expect to better understand as they read about why African Americans left the South.

Remind students to look for cause-and-effect relationships as they read.

STRATEGY RECALL

Students have now used these before-reading strategies:

- preview the selection to be aware of its genre, features, and possible content;
- activate prior knowledge about that content and what to expect of that genre;
- make predictions;
- set a purpose for reading.

Remind students to be aware of and flexibly use the during-reading strategies they have learned:

- link prior knowledge to new information;
- summarize text they have read so far;
- ask clarifying questions;
- answer questions they or others pose;
- check their predictions and either refine them or make new predictions;
- recognize the text structure the author is using, and use that knowledge to make predictions and increase comprehension;
- visualize what the author is describing;
- monitor their comprehension and use fix-up strategies.

After reading, students will use these strategies:

- summarize or retell the text;
- answer questions they or others pose;
- reflect to make new information become part of their prior knowledge.

Audio CD AudioText

Guiding Comprehension

1 **Cause and Effect • Literal**

Why did sharecroppers have to give up some of their crops?

The former slaves didn't own land or have money, so they had to exchange crops for rent, food, seed to plant, plows, and mules.

Monitor Progress

Cause and Effect

If... students are unable to identify the cause and effect,	then... use the skill and strategy instruction on p. 463.

---

2 **Draw Conclusions • Critical**

What conclusions can you draw from the photograph on p. 463?

Possible responses: Some former slaves (men, women, and children) went north by boats on the Mississippi River. Some people had to wait a long time for a boat since the people in this photograph look tired and unhappy.

ONLINE

Suggest that students use a student-friendly search engine and enter the keywords *America's Reconstruction, sharecroppers after Civil War,* and *Nicodemus, Kansas,* to learn about the former slaves who traveled north in search of freedom. Be sure to follow classroom rules for Internet use.

Leaving the South

1 When the Civil War ended, men and women who had been slaves waited to see what freedom would bring. The land they farmed still belonged to the families who had once owned them, and because they had no money, former slaves were expected to pay back a share of their crops in exchange for seed, plows, and mules. They had to pay back a share of everything they raised for rent and food. These sharecroppers soon found they were perpetually in debt.

In 1879, a Louisiana sharecropper named John Lewis Solomon, his wife, and four children packed their belongings and started walking toward the Mississippi River. Along the riverbank they found other black families waiting for a chance to travel north. Some built rafts to carry them over the river's dangerous undertows and eddies. Others had money for passage, but riverboat captains would not let them on board. When a steamboat called the *Grand Tower* came close to shore, John Lewis Solomon called to the captain that he could pay his way. He said he had been a soldier in the Union Army. "I know my rights, and if you refuse to carry me on your boat, I will go to the United States Court and sue for damages." Solomon took a great risk, but the captain

462

Extend Language Explain unfamiliar terms related to rivers on p. 462. An *undertow* is a strong surface current that can pull you under or make it hard to swim. An *eddy* is water that moves in a whirling motion within the river.

agreed to let him and his family board the steamboat.

Reaching Kansas, Solomon said, "This is free ground. Then I looked on the heavens, and I said, 'That is free and beautiful heaven.' Then I looked within my heart, and I said to myself, 'I wonder why I was never free before'."

Black families waited on the banks of the Mississippi River for a chance to go north.

463

The Reconstruction Period

Time for SOCIAL STUDIES

The Reconstruction period following the Civil War was a time of rebuilding and also a time of upheaval, especially in the South. After the war, many people had no money, land, animals, or other property. As a result, some people, including many African Americans, became sharecroppers. Sharecroppers farmed land that belonged to someone else. A landowner would provide seeds, supplies, food, and shelter. In exchange, the landowner would receive a share, or part, of the crop. However, because there was often little of the crop left over, many sharecroppers and their families were poor. They began migrating north in search of better opportunities.

SKILLS ←→ STRATEGIES IN CONTEXT

Cause and Effect

TEACH

- Remind students that a cause is what makes something happen and an effect is the thing that happens as a result of the cause.
- An effect may have more than one cause.
- Sometimes there are no clue words to a cause-and-effect relationship.
- Model finding cause and effect on p. 462, paragraph 1.

Think Aloud **MODEL** The second sentence says that former slaves had to pay back a share of their crops. That is what happened, so it must be the effect. I ask myself what made it happen. I look at the first part of the sentence, and read that the slaves did not have enough money to own the land they farmed. The word *because* is a clue to the cause-and-effect relationship.

PRACTICE AND ASSESS

Have students reread the second paragraph on p. 462. Ask why former slaves had to wait so long at the Mississippi River. *(Most riverboat captains refused to let former slaves on board even when they had money to pay for the trip.)*

Guiding Comprehension

3 Author's Purpose • Inferential

Why do you think Lillian Schlissel wrote *Black Frontiers*?

Possible responses: to inform readers about the African Americans who settled on the frontier and the difficulties they encountered; to inform them of the contributions of African Americans to the growth of the country.

Monitor Progress
REVIEW Author's Purpose

If... students have difficulty identifying the author's purpose,	then... use the skill and strategy instruction on p. 465.

4 Generalize • Inferential

What generalization does the author make about the effect of the first black families choosing to homestead?

By keeping to their goal, they made it easier for those who followed in later years.

EXTEND SKILLS

Steps in a Process

Point out that the homesteaders needed to follow steps in order to plant seeds and tend the crops. They also needed to follow steps in building a shelter. For a soddie, they began by locating soil with a root system. Ask students to discuss what other steps would be part of the process. They can check Internet sites to gather additional details.

Black Homesteaders

3 Homesteading was not easy for black or white settlers. Rocks, grass, and trees had to be cleared before crops could be planted. A farmer needed a horse, a mule, and a plow. He needed seed to plant and food for his family until the crops were ready to harvest. Most of all a pioneer needed a home.

In regions where there were trees, pioneers built log cabins. But in Kansas and Nebraska, there was only tall grass, as high as a man's shoulder. Pioneers learned that tough root systems under the grass held the dirt firmly, and sod could be cut like bricks and piled, layer upon layer, until it took the shape of a house. These homesteaders were called *sod busters,* and their homes were called *soddies.*

Sod homes could be warm and comfortable. Some were two stories high, with glass windows and chimneys. But in heavy rain, smaller sod houses leaked, and some families remembered being surprised by a snake slithering through a wall.

In North and South Dakota, where the land was rocky and winter temperatures fell to 30 degrees below zero, early pioneers burrowed into the ground and covered themselves with an earthen roof. They brought their small animals into the house in the winter, while cows and goats

464

Context Clues Remind students that unfamiliar terms are often defined within the context of the selection. *Buffalo chips,* on p. 465, is followed by its definition ("the droppings of buffalo"). The term *adobe* is defined in the sentence that precedes it ("thick walls made of mud and straw").

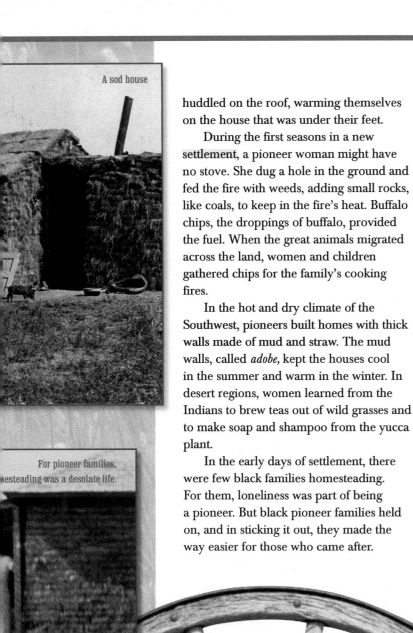

A sod house

For pioneer families, homesteading was a desolate life.

huddled on the roof, warming themselves on the house that was under their feet.

During the first seasons in a new settlement, a pioneer woman might have no stove. She dug a hole in the ground and fed the fire with weeds, adding small rocks, like coals, to keep in the fire's heat. Buffalo chips, the droppings of buffalo, provided the fuel. When the great animals migrated across the land, women and children gathered chips for the family's cooking fires.

In the hot and dry climate of the Southwest, pioneers built homes with thick walls made of mud and straw. The mud walls, called *adobe,* kept the houses cool in the summer and warm in the winter. In desert regions, women learned from the Indians to brew teas out of wild grasses and to make soap and shampoo from the yucca plant.

In the early days of settlement, there were few black families homesteading. For them, loneliness was part of being a pioneer. But black pioneer families held on, and in sticking it out, they made the way easier for those who came after. **4**

465

The Westward Movement

Time for SOCIAL STUDIES

The British government issued a proclamation in 1763 banning white settlers from areas west of the Appalachian Mountains. The situation changed after the American Revolution, when the U.S. government passed laws allowing the sale of land. Later a series of laws required only a filing fee to acquire land. The first was the Homestead Act signed by Abraham Lincoln in 1862. Under this law, anyone twenty-one years of age or older, or the head of a family, or someone who had served in the military could claim up to 160 acres after living on or cultivating the land for five years.

Author's Purpose REVIEW

TEACH

- Remind students that the author's purpose is his or her reason for writing.
- Model finding the author's purpose.

Think Aloud **MODEL** When I read the first sentence in paragraph 1, p. 464, I think the author wants to inform readers about the frontier and how homesteaders coped with difficulties, and to persuade them that a homesteader's life was difficult. The rest of the paragraph gives details about what made this way of life challenging.

PRACTICE AND ASSESS

- Have students find other evidence on pp. 464–465 that supports their statement of author's purpose. (*information about building homes from available materials and subzero winter temperatures; loneliness; women's lack of stoves*)
- To assess, use Practice Book p. 176.

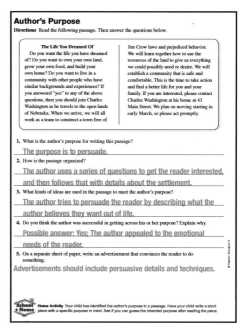

Author's Purpose
Directions Read the following passage. Then answer the questions below.

The Life You Dreamed Of
Do you want the life you have dreamed of? Do you want to own your own land, grow your own food, and build your own home? Do you want to live in a community with other people who have similar backgrounds and experiences? If you answered "yes" to any of the above questions, then you should join Charles Washington as he travels to the open lands of Nebraska. When we arrive, we will all work as a team to construct a town free of

Jim Crow laws and prejudiced behavior. We will learn together how to use the resources of the land to give us everything we could possibly need or desire. We will establish a community that is safe and comfortable. This is the time to take action and find a better life for you and your family. If you are interested, please contact Charles Washington at his home at 43 Main Street. We plan on moving starting in early March, so please act promptly.

1. What is the author's purpose for writing this passage?
   The purpose is to persuade.
2. How is the passage organized?
   The author uses a series of questions to get the reader interested, and then follows that with details about the settlement.
3. What kinds of ideas are used in the passage to meet the author's purpose?
   The author tries to persuade the reader by describing what the author believes they want out of life.
4. Do you think the author was successful in getting across his or her purpose? Explain why.
   Possible answer: Yes; The author appealed to the emotional needs of the reader.
5. On a separate sheet of paper, write an advertisement that convinces the reader to do something.
   Advertisements should include persuasive details and techniques.

School + Home **Home Activity** Your child has identified the author's purpose in a passage. Have your child write a short piece with a specific purpose in mind. See if you can guess the intended purpose after reading the piece.

▲ **Practice Book** p. 176

Guiding Comprehension

5 👁 **Prior Knowledge • Critical**

Text to Text **How does the journey of the Exodusters remind you of what you may have read about the Israelites who followed Moses to freedom?**

The Bible and other books recount the story of the journey of the Israelites, who followed Moses out of Egypt to escape slavery. The Exodusters also made a journey to gain freedom.

6 **Sequence • Inferential**

What was the sequence of events in Nicodemus and Dunlap from the years after the Civil War until 1900?

First, Benjamin Singleton visited Kansas and bought land. In 1877, he advertised for homesteaders. By 1879, black home-steaders began coming. Soon there were eight hundred, and the number grew to about eight thousand by 1900. Have stu-dents add 1879 and 1900 to the time line they started on p. 458a.

7 **Author's Viewpoint • Critical**

Question the Author **Why do you think the author wrote, "Black farmers planted their first crops and *in time they prospered*," instead of simply writing that they planted crops?**

Possible response: The author seems to believe that the early black settlers made important contributions to the growth of America. To say that it took time but they *prospered* shows that they worked hard and succeeded. It portrays them in a favorable way.

The Exodusters

5 Men and women who had been slaves read in the Bible about the ancient Israelites who were brought out of bondage and delivered into freedom. Benjamin Singleton, born a slave in Tennessee, was determined that he would bring his people to free soil if it was the last thing he ever did.

After the Civil War, Singleton visited Kansas and over a period of years, he and his friends managed to buy part of a Cherokee reservation. In 1877 they advertised for homesteaders to start an all-black community there. They hoped to attract two hundred families. Fliers promised that settlers who paid one dollar "in installments of 25 cents at a time or otherwise as may be desired" could be part of the new community. By 1879 an exodus of black families out of the Old South began, and before long, there were eight hundred homesteaders in the new Kansas communities of Dunlap and Nicodemus. Benjamin Singleton said, "My people that I carried to Kansas came on our own resources. We have tried to make a people of ourselves . . ." They were **6** known as the Exodusters.

In the early days of the town the farmers in Nicodemus owned only three horses. One man plowed with a milk cow,

Benjamin Singleton, founder of the black community of Dunlap, Kansas

466

Extend Language Point out that the term *exoduster* came from the word *exodus* ("an exodus of black families out of the Old South began"). The term *exodus* means "departure of a large group of people."

o for Kansas!

rethren, Friends, & Fellow Citizens:

I feel thankful to inform you that the

REAL ESTATE

AND

omestead Association,

Will Leave Here the

5th of April, 1878,

pursuit of Homes in the Southwestern
Lands of America, at Transportation
Rates, cheaper than ever
was known before.

For full information inquire of

nj. Singleton, better known as old Pap,
NO. 5 NORTH FRONT STREET.

eware of Speculators and Adventurers, as it is a dangerous thing
all in their hands,

ashville, Tenn., March 18, 1878.

Handbills encouraged black families to move to Kansas.
Notice the warning at the bottom of the flier.

and others broke ground with shovels and
spades. White farmers saw how hard their
new neighbors worked and lent the new
settlers a team of oxen and a plow. Black
farmers planted their first crops and in
time they prospered. By the turn of the
century there were about eight thousand
black homesteaders in Nicodemus and
Dunlap.

7

Schoolhouse in Dunlap, Kansas. Pupil in foreground carries
a sign that reads, "God Bless Our School."

467

Develop Vocabulary

PRACTICE LESSON VOCABULARY

Students orally respond to each question using a sentence.

1. Is a *settlement* a lone cabin or a community with buildings and people? *(It is a community with buildings and people.)*

2. If people are in *bondage,* are they enslaved people or free? *(They are enslaved people.)*

3. Is an *earthen* roof made of sod or of wood? *(It is made of sod.)*

BUILD CONCEPT VOCABULARY

Review previous concept words with students. Ask if students have come across any words that they would like to add to the American Frontier Concept Web such as *herd* and *cleared*.

STRATEGY SELF-CHECK

Prior Knowledge

Ask students to use their prior knowledge to explain the cause-and-effect relationship between formerly enslaved people reading the Bible and moving to Kansas. *(Possible response: Kansas was a free state. Reading in the Bible that the Israelites moved to escape bondage must have caused many formerly enslaved people to move to a state where they would find freedom.)*

Students can use cause-and-effect relationships and clue words to write a summary of the selection so far.

SELF-CHECK

Students can ask themselves questions to assess how well they used the skill and strategy.

- Did I identify causes as I read *Black Frontiers*?
- Was I able to link these causes to effects?
- How did using prior knowledge help me understand cause-and-effect relationships?

Monitor Progress	
🔄 **Cause and Effect**	
If... students have difficulty using prior knowledge to identify causes and effects,	**then...** revisit the skill lesson on pp. 456–457. Reteach as necessary.

Monitor Comprehension Provide the following prompt: What new information have you learned about frontier life? (See p. 460.) Then ask students what they expect to learn about the rest of the selection.

If you want to teach this selection in two sessions, stop here.

Guiding Comprehension

If you are teaching the selection in two sessions, discuss the causes and effects so far and review the lesson vocabulary.

8 Graphic Sources • Inferential

Compare and contrast the photographs on pp. 468 and 469. How do the graphics relate to the text?

Possible response: All of the photographs illustrate the text, which is about African American people building communities.

9 Vocabulary • Context Clues

Explain how to use the context of the last paragraph on p. 469 to determine the meaning of *designated*.

Possible response: The second sentence tells what is being done to the town as an effect of being designated a National Historical Landmark.

Monitor Progress

Context Clues

If... students have difficulty using context to determine the meaning of *designated*,	then... use vocabulary instruction on p. 469.

DAY 3 Grouping Options

Reading

Whole Group Discuss the Question of the Day.

Small Group Differentiated Instruction
Read *Black Frontiers*. See pp. 456f–456g for the small group lesson plan.

Whole Group Discuss the Reader Response questions on p. 474. Then use p. 477a.

Language Arts
Use pp. 477e–477k.

The Shores family in front of their sod house near Westville, Custer County, Nebraska, 1887. The Shores became famous as musicians.

Some black settlers moved farther west to Nebraska and Oklahoma where they built three new black communities–Taft, Langston, and Boley. George Washington Bush went all the way to Oregon Territory where he introduced the first mower and reaper into the area around Puget Sound.

Of all the black communities, however, Nicodemus and Dunlap remained the most famous. Each year they celebrated the Fourth of July, and they had their own special holiday, Emancipation Day. On July 31 and August 1, a square mile of land was set aside as a carnival fairground. There were boxing matches and baseball games. In

468

Build Background Help students locate the states mentioned in this selection (Kansas, Nebraska, Oklahoma, Texas, Louisiana, etc.) on a map of the United States. Use an atlas or Internet resources to find specific communities or towns such as Nicodemus and Dunlap in Kansas.

1907 the town formed one of the nation's first black baseball teams–the Nicodemus Blues. The Blues played black teams as far away as Texas, Nevada, and Louisiana. Satchel Paige, one of the greatest black pitchers in American baseball history, played ball in Nicodemus.

In 1976 Nicodemus was designated a National Historic Landmark. The town's history is being recorded and buildings restored. It marks the proud legacy of black homesteaders in America.

The Moses Speese family—neighbors of the Shores family—outside their sod house near Westville, Custer County, Nebraska

469

VOCABULARY STRATEGY

Context Clues

TEACH

Read the last paragraph on p. 469. Model using context clues to determine the meaning of *designated*.

MODEL I'll start by rereading the sentence in which *designated* appears. It says that Nicodemus was *designated* as a landmark. I know that a landmark is a place that is significant in history. I think that Nicodemus was named or chosen as an important place. *Designated* must mean "named" or "chosen."

PRACTICE AND ASSESS

Have students use context clues to determine the meaning of *legacy* in the last sentence on p. 469. *(something left for a future generation; a heritage)* Clues include the word *proud* and the information about the recording of history and the restoration of buildings to honor the contributions of black homesteaders.

Guiding Comprehension

 Fact and Opinion • Critical

Find a sentence in paragraph 2 on p. 470 that contains a statement of a fact and a statement of an opinion. Explain your choice.

Possible response: The second sentence. It can be proved that the Army paid African American troops thirteen dollars a month plus rations, but not everyone might agree that they served under the harshest conditions—that is an opinion.

11 **Cause and Effect • Inferential**

Why do you think African American soldiers signed up to be sent to the most dangerous and desolate outposts?

Possible responses: It was a chance to escape poverty and live a life of adventure. Thirteen dollars a month was probably a lot of money then.

Monitor Progress

Cause and Effect

If... students are unable to infer a cause-and-effect relationship,	then... use the skill and strategy instruction on p. 471.

The Buffalo Soldiers

uring the Civil War, nearly 180,000 black troops fought with the Union Army against the Confederacy, and more than 33,000 gave their lives to end slavery. After the war, General Ulysses S. Grant ordered Generals Philip Sheridan and William Tecumseh Sherman to organize regiments of black cavalry. These were designated the Ninth and Tenth Cavalry, each containing about a thousand men under the command of white commissioned officers—Colonel Edward Hatch for the Ninth and Colonel Benjamin Grierson for the Tenth. Two black regiments of infantry were organized, the Twenty-fourth and the Twenty-fifth. George Armstrong Custer refused to command black troops, but others accepted their tasks gladly.

Black troops who had been farmers, cooks, carpenters, and blacksmiths came from all parts of the country. The Army paid them thirteen dollars a month plus rations and sent them to the most desolate and dangerous frontier outposts where they served under the harshest conditions with the oldest equipment. They fought Indian tribes few soldiers wished to encounter—the Cheyenne, Comanche, Kiowa, Apache, Ute, and Sioux.

Henry Flipper, first black graduate of West Point

470

Extend Language Define unfamiliar military terms on p. 470. *Cavalry* were groups of soldiers on horseback and *infantry* were soldiers on foot. A *regiment* is a military unit made up of several smaller groups or units. A *commissioned* officer is a high ranking officer.

It was the Indians who gave the black troops the name Buffalo Soldiers because their hair resembled the shaggy coats of the buffalo. The buffalo was sacred to the Indians, and the men of the Ninth and Tenth Cavalry and the Twenty-fourth and Twenty-fifth Infantry accepted the name as a badge of honor, and the buffalo became a prominent part of their regimental crest.

Thirteen men of the Buffalo Soldiers won the highest military award of the nation, the Congressional Medal of Honor.

Serving under harsh conditions, these Buffalo Soldiers of the Tenth Cavalry camped on Diamond Creek in New Mexico.

471

Native Americans and African Americans

Time for **SOCIAL STUDIES**

At one time in history, some Native American groups kept African Americans as enslaved people. During the 1830s, Native Americans were taken from their homes and forced to move west to Oklahoma, Kansas, and Nebraska. The enslaved African Americans went with them. After the Civil War, the African Americans became free people and some of them founded African American communities in the area.

Cause and Effect Prior Knowledge

TEACH

Read p. 470, paragraph 1. Ask students to use their prior knowledge to explain why black troops may have been organized into regiments apart from white troops. *(Soldiers were segregated during the Civil War.)* Model how to apply prior knowledge to determine cause and effect.

Think Aloud

MODEL I wonder why black cavalry and black infantry regiments were organized apart from white troops. I know that people do not easily change their ideas and habits, and segregation had been in place during the Civil War. That may be why the troops were organized separately.

PRACTICE AND ASSESS

Have students work in pairs to use their prior knowledge of how an army works to determine the effects of "the harshest conditions" and "oldest equipment" on the African American troops. *(The African American troops must have had to work even harder to survive.)*

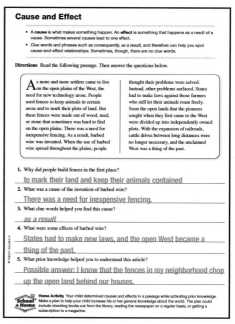

▲ **Practice Book** p. 177

Guiding Comprehension

12 🔄 **Cause and Effect • Inferential**

Why did African Americans move to the frontier?

They had dreams of freedom and independence and were willing to face hardship and danger in order to begin new lives after slavery.

13 **Main Idea • Inferential**

What is the main idea stated in the "Conclusion"?

The main idea is at the end of the last sentence: ". . . some of our bravest pioneers were African Americans who lived and worked on America's western frontiers."

14 **Summarize • Critical**

Text to World **How can we put together the information we have learned in this selection to help us understand the lives of African Americans today?**

African Americans demonstrated that they had the skills and determination to live as free citizens. Today, African Americans hold places of honor and importance in government, business, and education. Many are still working for equal rights in education and employment.

Strategy Response Log

Summarize When students finish reading the selection, provide this prompt: Imagine that a friend has asked you what *Black Frontiers* is about. In four or five sentences, explain its important points.

When all-black regiments were disbanded after World War II, almost one hundred years after they were organized, the Tenth Cavalry became the 510th Tank Battalion. But memories of frontier days were strong, and the 510th was redesignated the Tenth Cavalry in 1958 and stationed at Fort Knox, Kentucky.

A bronze statue in memory of the Ninth and Tenth Cavalry and the Twenty-fourth and Twenty-fifth Infantry was dedicated in 1992 at Fort Leavenworth, Kansas, to commemorate the courage of the Buffalo Soldiers and mark their place in American military history.

The Buffalo Soldiers helped to bring law and order to regions where ranchers fought with farmers, where Indian tribes warred with each other and with settlers, and where bandits threatened to overrun small towns. On rare occasions, settlers acknowledged their great debt to the black troops. When the Twenty-fifth was ordered to duty in the Spanish-American War, the people of Missoula, Montana, postponed Easter church services so that they could line up along the town's main street and wave goodbye to the black troops who had become their protectors and friends.

Over the years, that strange name, Buffalo Soldiers, became a prized possession of those black troops who left a legacy of courageous service in U.S. military history.

472

John Hanks Alexander, an African American graduate of West Point, class of 1887. He served among the respected Buffalo Soldiers during the Indian Wars.

ELL

Context Clues Help students use context clues to determine the meaning of the term *legacy* on p. 472. Have students read the phrases before and after it, and substitute other words that might make sense for *legacy*. Define *legacy* as something that is handed down or passed on to next generations. Ask what in their own family might be a legacy.

Conclusion

It would be wrong to suggest that the frontier was without prejudice. It had its share of violence and racial injustice. As settlements grew into cities, Jim Crow segregation laws confronted black settlers. But on those lonely, dangerous, and beautiful lands we call the frontier, black pioneers built new lives. Born into slavery, African Americans had the same dreams of freedom and independence as did all other Americans. Given the chance, they proved time and again that they possessed skills, initiative, and courage.

West of the Mississippi, between 1850 and 1900, there were some ten thousand African American exodusters, homesteaders, and sod busters. There were also four thousand miners, eight thousand wranglers and rodeo riders, and some five thousand Buffalo Soldiers. According to some historians, there were some eighty thousand African Americans doing whatever else the frontier demanded. They were trappers and mountain men, hotel keepers, and scouts. They were businessmen and women, teachers, and nurses.

And they were cowboys. From the Chisholm Trail to Hollywood, the American cowboy is a hero who walks tall. It is important to remember, then, that some of America's best cowboys and rodeo riders were black, and that some of our bravest pioneers were African Americans who lived and worked on America's western frontiers.

473

Develop Vocabulary

PRACTICE LESSON VOCABULARY

Students complete each sentence orally with this week's vocabulary words.

1. People who have been given the power to lead troops are _____ officers. *(commissioned)*

2. People who have been given land to cultivate by the U.S. government are _____. *(homesteaders)*

3. The troops had to be ready to _____ hostile Indians. *(encounter)*

BUILD CONCEPT VOCABULARY

Review previous concept words with students. Ask if students have come across any words that they would like to add to the American Frontier Concept Web, such as *ragged* and *reaper*.

STRATEGY SELF-CHECK

Prior Knowledge

Have students identify the important causes and effects under each heading in this selection. Students can compare these causes and effects to what they knew about black people in American history before reading and write a summary of the selection. Use Practice Book p. 177.

SELF-CHECK

Students can ask themselves these questions to assess understanding of the selection.

- Did I accurately identify causes and effects in the selection?
- How did my prior knowledge help me identify causes and effects?

Monitor Progress
Cause and Effect

If... students have difficulty using prior knowledge to identify causes and effects,	then... use the Reteach lesson on p. 477b.

Cause and Effect

- A **cause** is why something happens. An **effect** is something that happens. Sometimes several causes lead to one effect.
- Clue words and phrases such as *consequently*, *as a result*, and *therefore* can help you spot cause-effect relationships. Sometimes, though, there are no clue words.

Directions Read the following passage. Then answer the questions below.

As more and more settlers came to live on the open plains of the West, the need for new technology arose. People used fences to keep animals in certain areas and to mark their plots of land. But these fences were made out of wood, mud, or stone that sometimes was hard to find on the open plains. There weren't enough of these natural materials to go around. As a result, barbed wire was invented. When the use of barbed wire spread throughout the plains, people thought their problems were solved. Instead, other problems surfaced. States had to make laws against those farmers who still let their animals roam freely. Soon the open lands that the pioneers sought when they first came to the West were divided up into independently owned plots. Cattle drives between long distances began to fall out of fashion, and the unclaimed West was a thing of the past.

1. Why did people build fences in the first place?
   to mark their land and keep their animals contained
2. What was a cause of the invention of barbed wire?
   There were not enough natural materials for everyone to use.
3. What clue words helped you find this cause?
   as a result
4. What were some effects of barbed wire?
   States had to make new laws, cattle drives could not occur, and the open West became a thing of the past.
5. What prior knowledge helped you to understand this article?
   Possible answer: I know that the fences in my neighborhood chop up the open land behind our houses.

School + Home **Home Activity** Your child determined causes and effects in a passage while activating prior knowledge. Make a plan to help your child increase his or her general knowledge about the world. The plan could include checking books out from the library, reading the newspaper on a regular basis, or getting a subscription to a magazine.

▲ **Practice Book** p. 177

Black Frontiers **473**

DURING READING

Reader Response

Open for Discussion **Personal Response**

Think Aloud **MODEL** I'd start with the reasons why African Americans went West. One important reason was that they wanted to own land. To do this, they became homesteaders.

Comprehension Check **Critical Response**

1. Responses will vary but should include details about the people and the setting. *Author's Purpose*

2. Because the buffalo was sacred to the Indians, the black troops felt honored by the name. They chose to use the buffalo in their regiment's crest. *Cause and Effect*

3. Responses will vary but should relate students' prior knowledge to information in *Black Frontiers*. *Prior Knowledge*

4. Responses will vary but should include words from the selection vocabulary. *Vocabulary*

 Look Back and Write For test practice, assign a 10–15 minute time limit. For assessment, see the Scoring Rubric at the right.

Retell

Have students retell *Black Frontiers*.

Monitor Progress
Check Retelling [4][3][2][1]

If... students have difficulty retelling the selection,	then... use the Retelling Cards and the Scoring Rubric for Retelling on page 475 to assist fluent retelling.

SUCCESS PREDICTOR

Check Retelling Have students use the selection illustrations, captions, and headings to guide their retellings. Model retelling by talking about these features on pp. 462–463. See the ELL and Transition Handbook.

474 Explorers, Pioneers, and Discoverers • Week 3

Reader Response

Open for Discussion They went West. What were their reasons? What roles did they fulfill? What would you put into a collage, drama, or notebook to commemorate African Americans in the western frontier?

1. To see why this author included old photographs, select one and study it for one full minute. Then cover it and report the scene as if you were there. **Think Like an Author**

2. The author tells us that the Indians gave the black troops the name Buffalo Soldiers because of their hair. How did the troops respond to this name given to them? **Cause and Effect**

3. How did what you already know about pioneers and the Old West help you to better understand what you read in this piece? **Prior Knowledge**

4. Write a journal entry that a homesteader might have written during his or her first winter in South Dakota. Use words from the Words to Know list. **Vocabulary**

 Look Back and Write Who and where were the Exodusters? Did they succeed? Review pages 466–467 before writing your answer.

Meet author **Lillian Schlissel on page 781.**

474

Scoring Rubric **Look Back and Write**

Top-Score Response A top-score response will use details from pages 466 and 467 to explain that the "exodusters" were black families who started a community in Kansas.

Example of a Top-Score Response Exodusters were black families who followed Benjamin Singleton to Kansas. Their goal was to start an all-black homestead in the Midwest. They created the communities of Nicodemus and Dunlap. Their undertaking was successful. By the end of the 1800s, their numbers has grown to eight thousand.

For additional rubrics, see p. WA10.

Write Now

Description of a Setting

Prompt

The photographs in *Black Frontiers* show the setting of the story in pictures. Think about a setting from a favorite story or book. Now write a detailed description of that setting.

Writing Trait

Vary your **sentences** to sustain your reader's interest. Include different structures and styles.

Student Model

Setting includes both place and time.

It's the late 1800s on the uninhabited coast of Greenland. The ground is frozen, and the water is icy. The overwhelming colors are black-blue and white. The sky is not nearly as dark as the water. In the night sky, colors shine. Red! Green! Magenta! The aurora borealis performs its magic trick of color and light over the horizon.

Writer varies the style and structure of sentences and uses fragments for effect.

Four explorers take shelter in a snow house. A thin wisp of smoke escapes from a hole in the igloo. In the distance, the silhouette of their ship looms. Is it a mirage? Or will the craft ferry them to warmth as soon as the ice thaws?

Vivid details give a sense of mood.

Inside the house, scientific equipment competes for space with things to keep a person warm. There are parkas, furs, boots, mittens, and hats.

Use the model to help you write your own description of a setting.

Write Now

Look at the Prompt Explain that each sentence in the prompt has a purpose.

- Sentence 1 presents a topic.
- Sentence 2 suggests students think about the topic.
- Sentence 3 tells what to write—a description.

Strategies to Develop Sentences

Have students

- use varied sentence lengths and types.
- combine short, related sentences and vary sentence beginnings.

NO: The setting is a shaded forest. The trees hang like curtains. The sun is hidden behind the foliage.

YES: In the shaded forest, trees hang like curtains. Behind the foliage, the sun is hidden.

Writer's Checklist

☑ **Focus** Do sentences stick to the setting?

☑ **Organization** Is the description presented in spacial order or another order that makes sense?

☑ **Support** Do details help readers picture the setting?

☑ **Conventions** Are possessive pronouns spelled correctly?

For additional suggestions and rubric, see pp. 477g–477h.

475

Scoring Rubric — Expository Retelling

Rubric 4 3 2 1	4	3	2	1
Connections	Makes connections and generalizes beyond the text	Makes connections to other events, texts, or experiences	Makes a limited connection to another event, text, or experience	Makes no connection to another event, text, or experience
Author's Purpose	Elaborates on author's purpose	Tells author's purpose with some clarity	Makes some connection to author's purpose	Makes no connection to author's purpose
Topic	Describes the main topic	Identifies the main topic with some details early in retelling	Identifies the main topic	Retelling has no sense of topic
Important Ideas	Gives accurate information about events, steps, and ideas using details and key vocabulary	Gives accurate information about events, steps, and ideas with some detail and key vocabulary	Gives limited or inaccurate information about events, steps, and ideas	Gives no information about events, steps, and ideas
Conclusions	Draws conclusions and makes inferences to generalize beyond the text	Draws conclusions about the text	Is able to tell some learnings about the text	Is unable to draw conclusions or make inferences about the text

Retelling Plan

☑ **Week 1** Assess Strategic Intervention students.

☑ **Week 2** Assess Advanced students.

☑ **This week assess Strategic Intervention students.**

☐ **Week 4** Assess On-Level students.

☐ **Week 5** Assess any students you have not yet checked during this unit.

Use the Retelling Chart on p. TR17 to record retelling.

Selection Test To assess with *Black Frontiers*, use Selection Tests, pp. 69–72.

Fresh Reads for Differentiated Test Practice For weekly leveled practice, use pp.103–108.

Retelling

SUCCESS PREDICTOR

Poetry

PREVIEW

As students preview the poems by Langston Hughes, have them look at the illustrations and the three titles. After they preview, ask:

- **What do the illustrations tell you about the poems?** *(They are probably about something important and common to all people.)*

Link to Writing

Have students tell some of the ways hopes and dreams are described in these poems. Then have them list their own hopes and dreams.

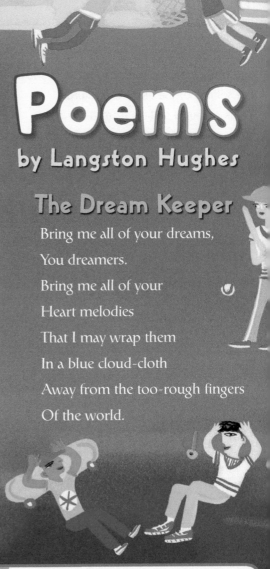

Poetry

Genre

- Poems are compositions arranged in lines. The lines do not have to rhyme, but many poems have lines with a clear, regular rhythm.
- Poems have the ability to make readers feel a diverse range of emotions.
- Poets use their life experiences or views as they compose their poems.
- A poet might create new words or combinations of words to reflect the mood or image.
- Notice that a poet might write short poems in a single verse or a few short verses.

Link to Writing

Write a few lines or thoughts that you have about dreams or hopes.

Poems
by Langston Hughes

The Dream Keeper

Bring me all of your dreams,
You dreamers.
Bring me all of your
Heart melodies
That I may wrap them
In a blue cloud-cloth
Away from the too-rough fingers
Of the world.

Cause/Effect What are some causes and effects in these poems?

476

DAY 4 **Grouping Options**

Reading

Whole Group Discuss the Question of the Day.

Small Group Differentiated Instruction
Read the poems by Langston Hughes. See pp. 456f–456g for the small group lesson plan.

Whole Group Use p. 477a.

Language Arts
Use pp. 477e–477k.

Youth

We have tomorrow
Bright before us
Like a flame.

Yesterday
A night-gone thing,
A sun-down name.

And dawn-today
Broad arch above the
    road we came.

We march!

Dreams

Hold fast to dreams
For if dreams die
Life is a broken-winged bird
That cannot fly.

Hold fast to dreams
For when dreams go
Life is a barren field
Frozen with snow.

Reading Across Texts

What message do you think the poet Langston Hughes would have for the black settlers of communities like Nicodemus and Dunlap?

Writing Across Texts Write a message of hope for frontier settlers. Use lines from the poems if you wish.

477

DURING READING

POETRY

Use the sidebar on p. 476 to guide discussion.

- Explain that poetry is the arrangement of words in lines. Many poems have a regular rhythm.
- Tell students that poetry often gives readers a new way of looking at things.
- Discuss with students how these poems are written in short lines, with each line beginning with a capital letter.

AudioText

Cause/Effect

Possible response: Because young people have the future ahead of them, they can march forward with confidence.

CONNECT TEXT TO TEXT

Reading Across Texts

Discuss the dreams of the black settlers of the frontier and help students relate them to the poet's message about dreams.

Writing Across Texts Suggest using a main idea organizer to plan the writing (Graphic Organizer 17). Students can record a main idea statement about dreams and add lines from the poems under the supporting details.

Fluency Assessment Plan

☑ **Week 1** Assess Advanced students.

☑ **Week 2** Assess Strategic Intervention students.

☑ **This week assess On-Level students.**

☐ **Week 4** Assess Strategic Intervention students.

☐ **Week 5** Assess any students you have not yet checked during this unit.

Set individual goals for students to enable them to reach the year-end goal.

• Current Goal: 130–138 wcpm

• Year-End Goal: 150 wcpm

Measuring a student's oral reading speed—words per minute—provides a low-stress informal assessment of fluency. Such an assessment should not take the place of more formal measures of words correct per minute.

To develop fluent readers, use Fluency Coach.

DAY 5 Grouping Options

Reading
Whole Group
Revisit the Question of the Week.

Small Group
Differentiated Instruction
Reread this week's Leveled Readers. See pp. 456f–456g for the small group lesson plan.

Whole Group
Use pp. 477b–477c.

Language Arts
Use pp. 477d–477l.

TONE OF VOICE
Fluency

DAY 1

Model Reread "Under the Coonskin Cap" on p. 456m. Explain that you will use tone of voice to show the humor. Students can imagine sitting around a campfire listening to a storyteller. Model for students as you read.

DAY 2

Choral Reading Read aloud from near the bottom of p. 462, beginning with "He said he had been a soldier," through p. 463. Have students listen for your softer tone as you read what Solomon says about Kansas. Have students practice as a class doing three choral readings of the passage.

DAY 3

Model Read aloud the first paragraph on p. 473. Have students notice how your voice takes on a serious tone as the writer draws a conclusion. Practice as a class by doing three choral readings.

DAY 4

Partner Reading Partners practice reading aloud the first paragraph on p. 473 three times. Students should read using a serious, convincing tone and offer each other feedback.

Monitor Progress   Check Fluency WCPM

As students reread, monitor their progress toward their individual fluency goals. Current Goal: 130–138 words correct per minute. End-of-Year Goal: 150 words correct per minute.

If... students cannot read fluently at a rate of 130–138 words correct per minute,
then... make sure students practice with text at their independent level. Provide additional fluency practice, pairing nonfluent readers with fluent readers.

If... students already read at 150 words correct per minute,
then... they do not need to reread three to four times.

SUCCESS PREDICTOR

DAY 5

Assessment
Individual Reading Rate Use the Fluency Assessment Plan and do a one-minute timed reading of either selection from this week to assess students in Week 3. Pay special attention to this week's skill, tone of voice. Provide corrective feedback for each student.

RETEACH

Cause and Effect

TEACH

Review the definitions of *cause (what makes something happen)* and *effect (what happens)* on p. 456. Students can complete Practice Book p. 178 on their own, or you can complete it as a class. Point out that this organizer is used when there are several causes leading to one effect. Sometimes a writer may use clue words to signal causes and effects, but many times readers must infer causes and effects based on the information they read.

ASSESS

Have partners read the paragraph that begins at the bottom of p. 466 and ends on p. 467. Have them identify the cause that resulted in 8,000 African American homesteaders living in Nicodemus and Dunlap. *(The first African American farmers worked hard and prospered.)*

For additional instruction of cause and effect, see DI·54.

EXTEND SKILLS

Author's Viewpoint/Bias

TEACH

Write the terms *viewpoint* and *bias* on the board and explain the difference.

• A *viewpoint* is how a person looks at the world. Every person has his or her own individual viewpoint of events, people, and ideas.

• A *bias* is a slant. If a person is biased about a topic, he or she has a slanted view of that topic. Being biased is the opposite of being objective.

Read pp. 462–463 with students and help them identify the author's point of view. Have students look for clues that might indicate the author's bias.

ASSESS

Have students write a short paragraph about a recent trip they took. Remind them to provide their viewpoint in the form of opinions when relating their experiences.

OBJECTIVES

⊙ Identify cause-and-effect relationships.

● Evaluate the author's viewpoint /bias.

Skills Trace	
⊙ **Cause and Effect**	
Introduce/Teach	TE: 6.4 408–409, 456–457; 6.5 582–583
Practice	Practice Book: 153, 157, 158, 173, 177, 178, 223, 227, 228
Reteach/Review	**TE: 6.1 31; 6.3 361; 6.4 429b, 477b, 509, 519, DI•52, DI•54; 6.5 599b, DI•54**
Test	Selection Test: 61–64, 69–72, 89–92; Benchmark Test: Units 4, 5

ELL

Access Content Reteach the skill by reviewing the Picture It! lesson on character in the ELL Teaching Guide, pp. 120–121.

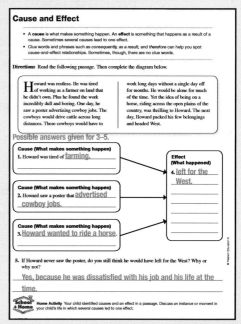

▲ **Practice Book** p. 178

Vocabulary and Word Study

VOCABULARY STRATEGY

🎯 Context Clues

UNFAMILIAR WORDS Remind students that they can use context clues to determine the meaning of unfamiliar words. Have students list any unfamiliar words they encountered while reading *Black Frontiers.* They can create a chart showing the unfamiliar word, helpful context clues, and their definition of the word based on its context. Students can confirm word meanings using a dictionary.

Word	Context Clues	Meaning
installments	paid one dollar, 25 cents at a time	parts of a sum of money to repay
colonel		
wrangler		

Nouns from Verbs

A *wrangler* is a person who *wrangles*, or tends horses or cattle. Many nouns, such as this one, name people who do a particular action. Have partners brainstorm a list of verb and noun pairs. If they have difficulty, suggest they look through some books for ideas.

Some Nouns from Verbs

Verb	Noun
pitch	pitcher
mine	miner
homestead	homesteader
edit	editor

BUILD CONCEPT VOCABULARY

American Frontier

LOOKING BACK Remind students of the question of the week: What does it mean to be a pioneer? Discuss how this week's Concept Web of vocabulary words relates to the theme of the American Frontier. Ask students if they have any words or categories to add. Discuss if words and categories are appropriately related to the concept.

MOVING FORWARD Preview the title of the next selection, *Space Cadets.* Ask students which Concept Web words might apply to the new selection based on the title alone. Put a star next to these words on the Web.

Display the Concept Web and revisit the vocabulary words as you read the next selection to check predictions

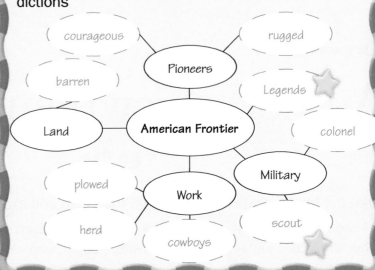

courageous, rugged, barren, Pioneers, Legends, Land, American Frontier, colonel, plowed, Work, Military, herd, cowboys, scout

Monitor Progress

Check Vocabulary

If... students suggest words or categories that are not related to the concept,	**then...** review the words and categories on the Concept Web and discuss how they relate to the lesson concept.

SUCCESS PREDICTOR

Speaking and Viewing

SPEAKING

Interpret Poetry

SET-UP Have students choose one of the three poems on pp. 476–477 to interpret orally. They can read their interpretations to the class or in groups.

REHEARSAL Point out to students that reading the poem silently several times will help them determine the feelings of the poet and how they might speak the lines to express these emotions. Also provide some time for them to prepare by practicing aloud.

ASSESSMENT Explain that students learn by assessing their own performances. Have them answer these questions after reading.

- Did I emphasize certain important words?
- Did I read to show the poem's rhythm?
- Did I pause where a comma indicated?

Listening Tips
- Show courteous, enthusiastic attention.
- Don't do other activities during the reading.
- Listen to appreciate the rhythm of the lines.
- Think about the poet's meaning.
- Connect the poet's experiences with your own.

VIEWING

Analyze Media

Discuss with students any television shows or movies they have seen about the American frontier, cowboys, or homesteading. With partners, they can answer these questions orally or in writing.

1. **What were heroes of the frontier like?** *(Possible response: They were adventurous, strong, and courageous.)*

2. **What animals were important on the frontier and why?** *(Possible responses: Horses provided transportation. Cattle provided food.)*

3. **What challenges did pioneers meet on the frontier?** *(Possible responses: It was difficult to travel and living and working conditions were harsh.)*

Support Vocabulary Use the following to review and extend vocabulary and to explore lesson concepts further:
- ELL Poster 18, Days 3–5 instruction
- Vocabulary Activities and Word Cards in ELL Teaching Guide, pp. 122–123

Assessment For information on assessing students' speaking, listening, and viewing, see the ELL and Transition Handbook.

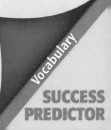
Vocabulary

SUCCESS PREDICTOR

Grammar   Possessive Pronouns

OBJECTIVES

- Identify and define possessive pronouns.
- Use pronouns to show possession.
- Use possessive pronouns correctly in writing.
- Become familiar with possessive pronoun assessment on high-stakes tests.

Monitor Progress

Grammar

If... students have difficulty identifying possessive pronouns,	then... provide additional instruction and practice in The Grammar and Writing Book pp. 152–155.

DAILY FIX-IT

This week use Daily Fix-It Transparency 18.

 Spiral REVIEW

 **ELL**

Support Grammar See the Grammar Transition lessons in the ELL and Transition Handbook.

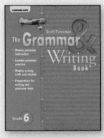

▲ **The Grammar and Writing Book**
For more instruction and practice, use pp. 152–155.

DAY 1   Teach and Model

DAILY FIX-IT

1. Having they own land was pretious to formerly enslaved African Americans. (*their; precious*)

2. In the Southwest, many people builded them homes from dried mud. (*built their*)

READING-GRAMMAR CONNECTION

Write this sentence about history on the board:

We had a new appreciation for <u>our</u> basic freedoms after we read the amendments to the Constitution.

Explain that *our* is a **possessive pronoun** that shows ownership. Ask the question "to whom does our freedom belong," and the answer is "our freedom belongs to us."

Display Grammar Transparency 18. Read aloud the definitions and sample sentences. Work through the items.

Possessive Pronouns

Pronouns that show ownership are called **possessive pronouns**. A possessive pronoun and its antecedent must agree in number and gender. Before you use a possessive pronoun, ask yourself whether the antecedent is singular or plural. If the antecedent is singular, decide whether it is masculine, feminine, or neuter. Then choose a pronoun that agrees.

Possessive Pronouns
My/mine, your/yours, his, her/hers, its, our/ours, their/theirs

- *My, your, her, our,* and *their* are always used with nouns.
  Your understanding of history is important.
- *Mine, yours, hers, ours,* and *theirs* stand alone.
  Is that history book yours?
- *His* and *its* can be used with nouns or can stand alone.
  His book report was on a biography of Satchel Paige.
  The book about Satchel Paige was his.
- Do not use an apostrophe with a possessive pronoun.

Directions Underline the possessive pronouns in the sentences.

1. Research increased my understanding of the Civil War.
2. Some homesteaders built their houses by piling layers of sod.
3. The Nicodemus Blues was one of our nation's first black baseball teams.
4. Is American history your favorite subject?
5. That Louisiana farmer was able to buy his own land.
6. The soldiers in the Union Army knew the uniforms were theirs.
7. The goat used its hooves to climb through the snow.
8. The report about African American cowboys is mine.
9. This antique sewing machine is ours, and that spinning wheel is hers.
10. My dream of freedom is the same as yours.

Directions Circle the possessive pronoun in ( ) that completes each sentence.

11. On July 31, the town of Dunlap celebrated (its, his) own holiday.
12. The pioneer woman warmed (her) home with fire fueled from buffalo chips.
13. In hot, dry climates, pioneers used adobe bricks to build (their) theirs) homes.
14. The Civil War tore apart this country of (our, ours).
15. (Your) yours) family has a long history in this community.

Unit 4 Black Frontiers   **Grammar 18**

▲ **Grammar Transparency** 18

DAY 2   Develop the Concept

DAILY FIX-IT

3. Before the civil War fricion arose between the North and the South. (*Civil; friction*)

4. In 1879 freedom will be cherished, especialy by former slaves. (*was; especially*)

GUIDED PRACTICE

Review the concept of possessive pronouns.

- Pronouns that show ownership are called **possessive pronouns**.
- *My, your, her, our,* and *their* are used with nouns.
- *Mine, yours, hers, ours,* and *theirs* stand alone.
- *His* and *its* can be used with nouns or can stand alone.

HOMEWORK Grammar and Writing Practice Book p. 69. Work through the first two items with the class.

Possessive Pronouns

Pronouns that show ownership are called **possessive pronouns**. A possessive pronoun and its antecedent must agree in number and gender. Before you use a possessive pronoun, ask yourself whether the antecedent is singular or plural. If the antecedent is singular, decide whether it is masculine, feminine, or neuter. Then choose a pronoun that agrees.

Possessive Pronouns
My/mine, your/yours, his, her/hers, its, our/ours, their/theirs

- *My, your, her, our,* and *their* are always used with nouns.
  I did my report on the Exodusters.
- *Mine, yours, hers, ours,* and *theirs* stand alone.
  Which science project is yours?
- *His* and *its* can be used with nouns or can stand alone.
  His report discussed life on the frontier.
  The report on frontier life was his.
- Do not use an apostrophe with a possessive pronoun.

Directions Underline the possessive pronoun in each sentence.

1. My history book tells the story of the Buffalo Soldiers.
2. Some black settlers moved to Nebraska and started their new lives.
3. Our country has a rich cultural heritage.
4. Does your family come from Louisiana?
5. Former slaves knew that as sharecroppers, freedom would never be theirs.
6. As an American, the right to life, liberty, and the pursuit of happiness is mine.
7. The pioneer woman gathered buffalo chips for her cooking fire.

Directions Circle the pronoun in ( ) that completes each sentence.

8. John Lewis Solomon knew (their, his) rights.
9. The dog stayed in (our, its) warm bed on the floor.
10. For early black homesteaders, loneliness was part of (their, theirs) lives.
11. The woman worked to build (hers, her) home with mud walls.

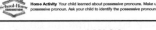 **Home Activity** Your child learned about possessive pronouns. Make up or read a sentence with a possessive pronoun. Ask your child to identify the possessive pronoun.

▲ **Grammar and Writing Practice Book** p. 69

DAY 3 — Apply to Writing

DAILY FIX-IT

5. Nearly 180,000 african Americans fighted in the Union Army. (*African; fought*)

6. Every enslaved person longed for he or she freedom? (*his or her freedom.*)

USE POSSESSIVE PRONOUNS

Possessive pronouns can make your writing easier to read if they are used correctly.

No: Are you coming to mine?

Yes: Are you coming to my recital?

• Have students check something they have written recently to see if they have used possessive pronouns correctly.

HOMEWORK Grammar and Writing Practice Book p. 70.

Possessive Pronouns

| his | her | its | your | their |

Directions Rewrite each sentence, replacing the underlined noun or noun phrase with a possessive pronoun from the box.

1. After the Civil War, former slaves stayed in the South hoping <u>the former slaves'</u> circumstances would change.
   <u>After the Civil War, former slaves stayed in the South hoping their circumstances would change.</u>

2. A sharecropper found that <u>the sharecropper's</u> debts were never paid off.
   <u>A sharecropper found that his debts were never paid off.</u>

3. A farm woman made soap and shampoo out of plants for <u>the woman's</u> family.
   <u>A farm woman made soap and shampoo out of plants for her family.</u>

4. A goat warmed <u>a goat's</u> hooves on the roof of the house.
   <u>A goat warmed its hooves on the roof of the house.</u>

Directions Write sentences about African American history. Include a possessive pronoun in each sentence. Underline the possessive pronoun.

<u>Possible answers: My brother and I love to read about great African American athletes. We visited Kansas on our vacation to see where the Exodusters settled. The Buffalo Soldiers got their nickname from their hair. You will enjoy studying the brave black regiments in your history class.</u>

 Home Activity Your child learned how to use possessive pronouns in writing. Ask your child to write several sentences about what it would have been like to live in the United States shortly after the Civil War. Ask your child to use at least three possessive pronouns and to point them out.

▲ **Grammar and Writing Practice Book** p. 70

DAY 4 — Test Preparation

DAILY FIX-IT

7. The indians nicknamed the black troops Buffalo Soldiers (*Indians; Soldiers.*)

8. The farmers pateintly waited for his crops to grow. (*patiently; their*)

STANDARDIZED TEST PREP

Test Tip

When taking a test, remember that possessive pronouns do not use apostrophes. Do not confuse possessive pronouns with contractions that combine a pronoun with a verb.

No: Find you're coat.

Yes: Find your coat.

No: The dog hurt it's paw.

Yes: The dog hurt its paw.

HOMEWORK Grammar and Writing Practice Book p. 71.

Possessive Pronouns

Directions Circle the letter of the possessive pronoun in the sentence.

1. He studied the tactics of the Tenth Cavalry in his history book.
   A he
   B tenth
   C book
   (D) his

2. Black soldiers had been farmers, blacksmiths, cooks, and carpenters in their towns before they enlisted in the cavalry.
   A black
   B they
   (C) their
   D towns

3. Each black community celebrated Emancipation Day as its own special holiday.
   A each
   (B) its
   C own
   D day

4. Our class admires the former slaves who started new lives after the Civil War.
   A them
   (B) Our
   C former
   D who

5. A pioneer woman brewed tea from wild grasses on her farm.
   A a
   B pioneer
   C she
   (D) her

6. His great-grandparents were among the pioneers who persevered under harsh conditions.
   (A) His
   B who
   C pioneers
   D harsh

7. You can learn about the strength of African Americans' spirit as you study their history.
   A You
   B African Americans'
   C the
   (D) their

8. Following the Civil War, every American could exclaim, "Freedom is mine."
   A every
   B American
   C the
   (D) mine

9. John Solomon could pay for his own transportation on the boat.
   (A) his
   B the
   C John Solomon
   D boat

10. Nicodemus and Dunlap were two of the communities of African Americans in our country.
    (A) our
    B two
    C of
    D Nicodemus and Dunlap

 Home Activity Your child prepared for taking tests on possessive pronouns. With your child, read a short article in the newspaper. Have your child circle any possessive pronoun he or she finds in the article.

▲ **Grammar and Writing Practice Book** p. 71

DAY 5 — Cumulative Review

DAILY FIX-IT

9. The riverboat Captain was cautous about giving passage to the sharecropper. (*captain; cautious*)

10. In the Winter, pioneers stayed warm under earthen rooves. (*winter; roofs*)

ADDITIONAL PRACTICE

Assign pp. 152–155 in The Grammar and Writing Book.

EXTRA PRACTICE Grammar and Writing Practice Book p. 139.

TEST PREPARATION Grammar and Writing Practice Book pp. 155–156.

ASSESSMENT

CUMULATIVE REVIEW Grammar and Writing Practice Book p. 72.

Possessive Pronouns

Directions Underline the possessive pronoun in each sentence.

1. <u>Our</u> class is studying the plight of slaves after the Civil War.
2. Slaves read about Israelites who were delivered out of <u>their</u> bondage.
3. Nicodemus marked <u>its</u> legacy by becoming a National Historic Landmark.
4. Can you remember the date of Emancipation Day from <u>your</u> study of history?
5. Exodusters were named for <u>their</u> exodus, or departure, from the South.
6. The Army paid every black man in the cavalry thirteen dollars a month for <u>his</u> service.
7. Anne claimed that the idea to make soap from the yucca plant was <u>hers</u>.
8. We should respect <u>our</u> civil rights and be willing to fight for them.
9. Mr. Singleton hoped two hundred families would settle on <u>his</u> Cherokee reservation.
10. That book about African Americans is <u>mine</u>.

Directions Replace the underlined word or words with a possessive pronoun. Write the possessive pronoun.

11. African American athletes owe a great deal of <u>African American athletes'</u> success to athletes such as Satchel Paige. _their_
12. A pioneer woman worked hard making a home for a <u>pioneer woman's</u> family. _her_
13. The Exodusters left <u>the Exodusters'</u> homes in the South. _their_
14. The small animal made <u>the small animal's</u> bed inside the home in cold weather. _its_
15. Christine was happy that the story her teacher read aloud was <u>Christine's</u>. _hers_

 Home Activity Your child reviewed possessive pronouns. Ask your child to look at a story in a magazine or newspaper and provide the correct possessive pronouns for at least three proper nouns.

▲ **Grammar and Writing Practice Book** p. 72

Writing Workshop Describe a Setting

- Identify features of setting.
- Describe a setting in a logical order.
- Focus on sentences.
- Use a rubric.

Genre Setting
Writer's Craft Order
Writing Trait Sentences

ELL

Sentences Have language learners read their sentences aloud to check rhythm, completeness, and sense. Point out opportunities to change a declarative sentence to another type of sentence, or to vary sentence beginnings.

Writing Traits

FOCUS/IDEAS Strong supporting details make the setting come alive.

ORGANIZATION/PARAGRAPHS The setting description is organized in spatial order. An important detail of the setting is revealed in the final paragraph.

VOICE The writing is engaging and lively. The writer shows knowledge of the subject.

WORD CHOICE The writer uses specific words to create vivid images of the setting (broken plowshare, solid-plank door).

SENTENCES The writer communicates clearly and creates and sustains interest through varied sentence structures.

CONVENTIONS The writer demonstrates excellent control and accuracy.

DAY 1 Model the Trait

READING-WRITING CONNECTION

- The text of *Black Frontiers* contains varied sentences.
- Arranging sentences in a particular order gives your writing emphasis.
- Students will **describe a setting** using a variety of sentences in a logical order.

MODEL SENTENCES Discuss Writing Transparency 18A. Then discuss the model and the writing trait of sentences.

Think Aloud I see varied sentence structures in this description of a setting. Some of the sentences are short and simple. "Behind the cabin is a shed." Other sentences are longer and more complex, such as the second sentence of the description. The different kinds of sentences help the description flow smoothly as I picture it in my mind.

Describe a Setting

A **setting** is the time and place in which a story occurs, such as a frontier home in the 1870s. A setting provides a background for a story and can reveal information about the characters and events.

Once Upon a Time on the Plains

Setting includes both place and time. — Our story takes place in a log cabin in the late 1800s. The cabin, built by Jedediah and Earline Whitley, sits on a low-rising hill surrounded by tall grasses and plowed land. Behind the cabin is a shed. A broken plowshare by the shed shows how hard it has been to "bust" the sod.

Vivid details give sense of mood. — As night begins to fall, a kerosene lamp shines through the cracks in the solid-plank door. The door is the only opening in the windowless cabin.

Details of setting are presented in spatial order. — On the left side of the room stands one bed for the parents and one for the two daughters. In the middle of the room is a handmade table and four chairs. On the right side of the room, a hearth with a blazing fire throws off heat.

A single framed photograph decorates the wall of the cabin. This picture shows Jed and Earline when they were much younger and still enslaved.

Unit 4 Black Frontiers Writing Model **18A**

▲ **Writing Transparency** 18A

DAY 2 Improve Writing

WRITER'S CRAFT
Order

Display Writing Transparency 18B. Read the directions and work together to identify and use different orders.

Think Aloud **ORDER** Tomorrow we will be writing a description of a setting from *Black Frontiers.* It is important that I organize my description in a logical order. If I list details randomly, my reader might get confused. Since I am describing a place, I am going to organize my details in spatial order. I'll pretend I'm looking around the army camp, for example, and describe each thing that I see.

GUIDED WRITING Some students may need more help with order. Refer back to a lesson on sequence and show how events and objects can be ordered using similar logic.

Order

Sometimes you may describe a setting, event, or character using many details. Arranging these details in an **order** can give your writing emphasis. You can list details in spatial order—left to right, front to back, up to down. You can list things in order of importance. And as you have learned, events can be written in time order, or the order in which they happen.

Spatial Order	I see a horse on the left, a cow in the middle, and a chicken on the right.
Order of Importance	Her spritely walk surprised me, and her twinkling eyes delighted me. However, her outrageous purple hat tickled me most of all.
Time Order	The bell rang, books snapped closed, and students rushed into the hall.

Directions Tell whether the items in each list are arranged in order. If they are not, put the items in order. Identify the type of order used.

1. train engine, caboose, box car
   No; engine, box car, caboose; spatial order
2. President, Vice President, Governor
   Yes; order of importance
3. summer, spring, winter, fall
   No; spring, summer, fall, winter; time order
4. head, shoulders, knees, and toes
   Yes; spatial order
5. elephants, mice, llamas   No; elephants, llamas, mice or
   mice, llamas, elephants; spatial order (size)
6. wake up, get dressed, eat breakfast, go to school
   Yes; time order

Directions Describe what you see in front of you. Write a paragraph giving details in spatial order, order of importance, or time order. **Possible answer:** Windows span the left side of the classroom, and the teacher's desk sits in front of them. The teacher is using the transparency projector. It sits on a small table in the middle of the room. The white board on the right side of the room shows a projection of a writing model.

Unit 4 Black Frontiers Writer's Craft **18B**

▲ **Writing Transparency** 18B

DAY 3 Prewrite and Draft

READ THE WRITING PROMPT
on page 475 in the Student Edition.

The photographs in Black Frontiers show the settings of the selection in pictures.

Think about a setting from a favorite story or book.

Now write a detailed description of that setting.

Writing Test Tips

- Picture your setting in your mind while writing.
- Don't forget the obvious: doors, windows, floors, ceilings.
- Vary the sentence structure to add a sense of mood.

GETTING STARTED Students can do any of the following:

- Make a list of the objects, features, and moods related to their setting.
- Choose a photograph from the selection and describe the setting in detail.
- Visualize a scene in their mind and write what they see.

DAY 4 Draft and Revise

EDITING/REVISING CHECKLIST

☑ Are my descriptions and details written in a logical order?

☑ Do I give a sense of mood as well as a complete description of the setting?

☑ Do I use possessive pronouns correctly?

☑ Are words with *ci* and *ti* spelled correctly?

See *The Grammar and Writing Book*, pp. 152–157.

Revising Tips

Sentences

- Support sentence variety by using different sentence structures.
- Vary sentence beginnings.
- Add interrogative and exclamatory sentences.

PUBLISHING Students can draw pictures of classmates' settings.

ASSESSMENT Use the scoring rubric to evaluate students' work.

DAY 5 Connect to Unit Writing

	Story
Week 1	News Story 429g–429h
Week 2	Story About an Animal 455g–455h
Week 3	Describe a Setting 477g–477h
Week 4	TV or Radio Script 499g–499h
Week 5	Summary 527g–527h

PREVIEW THE UNIT PROMPT

Write a story about an adventure, a discovery, or something that happened to you for the first time. Use some of these literary devices: foreshadowing, tension, suspense, conflict, humor.

APPLY

- A good setting description provides a complete picture of where and when your story takes place.

Writing Trait Rubric

	4	3	2	1
Sentences	Varied sentence structures	Some variety to sentence structures	Sentences lacking in variation	Run-on sentences, fragments
	Description that flows smoothly; presented in a clear and logical order	Description that generally flows smoothly; presented in order	Inconsistent flow to description; order confusing at times	Description confusing with ineffective sentences and illogical order

Spelling & Phonics Words with *ci* and *ti*

OBJECTIVE

● Spell words with *ci* and *ti*.

Generalization

Connect to Phonics The sounds /sh/ and /ch/ can be spelled *ci* and *ti*: espe*ci*ally, an*ci*ent, fric*ti*on, ques*ti*on.

Spelling Words

1. precious	11. potion
2. commercial	12. digestion
3. especially	13. artificial
4. ancient*	14. glacier
5. gracious	15. cautious
6. position	16. efficient
7. question	17. sensational
8. suggestion	18. vicious
9. friction	19. official
10. lotion	20. ration*

Challenge Words

21. fictitious	24. precocious
22. vaccination	25. emancipation
23. beneficial	

*Words from the selection

Spelling/Phonics Support See the ELL and Transition Handbook for spelling support.

DAY 1 Pretest and Sort

PRETEST

Use the Dictation Sentences from Day 5 to administer the pretest. Read the word, read the sentence, and then read the word again. Guide students in self-correcting their pretests and correcting any misspellings.

Monitor Progress

Spelling

If… students misspell more than 5 pretest words,	then… use words 1–10 for Strategic Intervention.
If… students misspell 1–5 pretest words,	then… use words 1–20 for On-Level practice.
If… students correctly spell all pretest words,	then… use words 1–25 for Advanced Learners.

HOMEWORK Spelling Practice Book, p. 69.

Words with *ci* and *ti*

Generalization The sounds /sh/ and /ch/ can be spelled *ci* and *ti*: especially, ancient, friction.

Word Sort Sort the list words by whether they contain the letter combination *ci* or *ti*.

Spelling Words
1. precious
2. commercial
3. especially
4. ancient
5. gracious
6. position
7. question
8. suggestion
9. friction
10. lotion
11. potion
12. digestion
13. artificial
14. glacier
15. cautious
16. efficient
17. sensational
18. vicious
19. official
20. ration

ci
1. precious
2. commercial
3. especially
4. ancient
5. gracious
6. artificial
7. glacier
8. efficient
9. vicious
10. official

ti
11. position
12. question
13. suggestion
14. friction
15. lotion
16. potion
17. digestion
18. cautious
19. sensational
20. ration

Challenge Words
ci
21. beneficial
22. precocious

ti
23. fictitious
24. vaccination
25. emancipation

Challenge Words
21. fictitious
22. vaccination
23. beneficial
24. precocious
25. emancipation

Home Activity Your child is learning about the sounds of the letter combinations *ci* and *ti*. Ask your child to identify five words with the /ch/ sound and spell the words.

▲ **Spelling Practice Book** p. 69

DAY 2 Think and Practice

TEACH

The sounds /sh/ and /ch/ can be spelled in different ways. Demonstrate this by writing each spelling word on the board. Have students come to the board and identify the letters that make the /sh/ or /ch/ sound in each word.

> *potion*

FIND THE PATTERN Ask students to group spelling words by the way /sh/ or /ch/ is spelled.

HOMEWORK Spelling Practice Book, p. 70.

Words with *ci* and *ti*

Spelling Words

precious	commercial	especially	ancient	gracious
position	question	suggestion	friction	lotion
potion	digestion	artificial	glacier	cautious
efficient	sensational	vicious	official	ration

Word Meanings Write a list word that fits each definition.
1. a drink or mixture of liquids — potion
2. a food allowance for one day — ration
3. the process of digesting food — digestion
4. a person who holds an office — official
5. imitation, unreal — artificial
6. dangerously aggressive — vicious
7. a large body of ice — glacier
8. unexpectedly excellent or great — sensational
9. careful — cautious
10. without wasting time — efficient

Words in Context Write the list word that finishes each statement below.
11. A diamond is a ___ stone. — precious
12. Use ___ to keep your skin soft and supple. — lotion
13. The ___ was sixty seconds long. — commercial
14. The ___ from the sandpaper makes the wood smooth. — friction
15. Your performance tonight was ___ great. — especially
16. I have a ___ for making your essay better. — suggestion
17. He enjoys learning about the history of ___ Greece. — ancient
18. May I ask you a ___? — question
19. The ___ host made his guests feel welcome. — gracious
20. My favorite ___ when playing softball is third base. — position

Home Activity Your child wrote words with *ci* and *ti*. Ask your child to pick a list word from Exercises 11-20 and define it.

▲ **Spelling Practice Book** p.70

DAY 3 — Connect to Writing

WRITE A POEM

Have students write a poem, using at least four spelling words. Have students read their poems aloud, or post them on the bulletin board for everyone to see.

Frequently Misspelled Words

especially   when

These words are difficult for some sixth-graders to spell. Alert students to these frequently misspelled words and encourage them to think carefully before spelling them. Make sure students correctly pronounce all of the syllables in *especially*.

HOMEWORK Spelling Practice Book, p. 71.

▲ **Spelling Practice Book** p. 71

DAY 4 — Review

REVIEW WORDS WITH *ci* AND *ti*

Have students work individually or in pairs to create word mazes. Each path in the maze should include words with similar spellings. Then have students exchange puzzles and try to solve them.

Spelling Strategy
Problem Parts

We all have words that are hard for us to spell.

Step 1: Ask yourself: Which part of the word gives me a problem?

Step 2: Underline your problem part.

Step 3: Picture the word. Focus on the problem part

HOMEWORK Spelling Practice Book, p. 72.

▲ **Spelling Practice Book** p. 72

DAY 5 — Posttest

DICTATION SENTENCES

1. The doll was very precious to her.
2. That is a funny commercial.
3. Dad was especially pleased with my grades.
4. We read about an ancient city.
5. The lady was very gracious.
6. He sat in a comfortable position.
7. Do you have a question?
8. She made a good suggestion.
9. Rubbing sticks together causes friction.
10. Put some lotion on the burn.
11. He had a magic potion.
12. His poor digestion was caused by illness.
13. Are those artificial flowers?
14. Icebergs break off from a glacier.
15. You must be cautious crossing the street.
16. Mom is efficient with the baby.
17. He wrote a sensational song.
18. That is a vicious dog.
19. Here is the official report.
20. He had a small ration of meat.

CHALLENGE

21. She is a fictitious character.
22. The doctor gave me a vaccination.
23. Sleep is beneficial to your health.
24. My sister is quite precocious.
25. The act of setting free from slavery is called emancipation.

Black Frontiers **477i**

OBJECTIVES

- Formulate an inquiry question that is connected to this week's lesson focus.
- Effectively and efficiently find, evaluate, and communicate information related to an inquiry question using electronic sources.

New Literacies	
Day 1	Identify Questions
Day 2	Navigate/Search
Day 3	Analyze
Day 4	Synthesize
Day 5	Communicate

NEW LITERACIES

Internet Inquiry Activity

EXPLORE THE PIONEER EXPERIENCE

Use the following 5-day plan to help students conduct this week's Internet inquiry activity on the pioneer experience. Remind students to follow classroom rules when using the Internet.

DAY 1

Identify Questions Discuss the lesson focus question: *What does it mean to be a pioneer?* Brainstorm ideas for specific inquiry questions about pioneer life and experiences. For example, students might want to find out about the trails pioneers followed or the supplies they took with them. Have students work individually, in pairs, or in small groups to write an inquiry question they would like answered.

DAY 2

Navigate/Search Have students list keywords related to their inquiry questions. For example, if students want to know about the trails pioneers followed, they might choose *trails* and *pioneers.* Point out that when the search engine locates Web sites, the keywords will be in bold-face type in the description. Caution students to read the descriptions because not all of the sites found will have information they can use. With your permission, they can bookmark sites by adding the page to a list of favorites.

DAY 3

Analyze Have students explore the Web sites they identified on Day 2. Point out that they may have to try several keywords before they find the information to answer their inquiry questions. They may even need to revise their inquiry question after analyzing the information that is available. For example, if their inquiry question is about the trails pioneers followed, they may find so much information that they will want to narrow the question focus to trails pioneers followed to California.

DAY 4

Synthesize Have students synthesize information from Day 3. Remind them that to synthesize means to take information from several sources and put it in their own words. They should always document their sources.

DAY 5

Communicate Have students share their inquiry results. They can use charts, graphs, or tables to display the data they have gathered about the pioneer experience.

RESEARCH/STUDY SKILLS

Note Taking

TEACH

Ask students how they keep track of the information they find while doing research, reading a story, or studying. Students should respond that taking notes is a good way to record their findings, as well as sort and remember information. Give them the following pointers.

- In doing research, keep **keywords** and **questions** in front of you so that you can refer to them and remember to make notes about them.

- Paraphrase, or state the information in your own words.

- Use keywords, phrases, or short sentences.

- **Synthesize**, or combine, the information to include only important details.

Give each small group of students a resource book about American history, or suggest they use the Internet. Ask the group to write a research question or keyword about the American frontier. The group can choose what information to include and write sample notes. Then, discuss these questions:

1. What question or keyword did you decide to research? *(Responses will vary but should relate to the frontier.)*

2. What information did you document for the source? *(the name of the source, the volume or chapter, the page; the complete Web site address)*

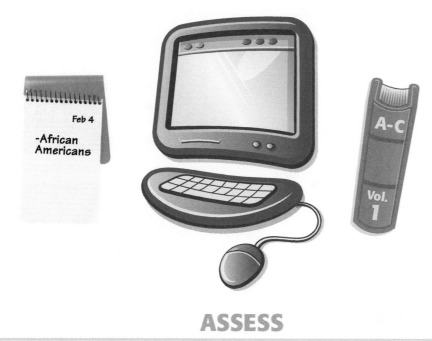

ASSESS

As students take notes, check that they paraphrase the information when they record their findings. If students are doing research, make sure they include a date, and document the source.

For more practice or to assess students, use Practice Book pp. 179–180.

Sidebar:

OBJECTIVES

- Review taking notes to keep track of information.

- Use paraphrasing and synthesizing to record findings.

Note Taking

- **Note taking** can help you when you are collecting information for a report. It can also help you keep track of information in a story and remember what you have read for a test.
- When you take notes, paraphrase, or put what you read into your own words. Synthesize, or combine, information so that you include only important details. Use keywords, phrases, or short sentences.

Directions Read the following passage. Takes notes as you read on the lines to the right.

As a kid, I believed cowboys had only existed in myths, legends, and movies. I wanted to think that people really roamed across the countryside and involved themselves in all kinds of adventures, but it just sounded like the stuff of bad novels to me. Then as I grew older, I began to do a little research into the subject, and, boy, were my eyes opened.

One of the cowboys I researched was Nat Love. Nat Love was born into slavery in 1854. He lived as an enslaved person until all such people were given their freedom in 1865. When he was 15, he decided he would try the cowboy life. He moved to Dodge City, in Kansas, where he found a job as a cowboy. Nat Love spent twenty years of his life driving cattle across the open lands of the country. He won a contest in 1876 for his cowboy skills (such as roping cattle, shooting, and riding a horse).

Eventually, Love decided to record his thoughts and stories about life as a cowboy in a book. The book was published as Love's autobiography in 1907. Books like these included the stories that I remember hearing as a child—the wild adventures of cowboys. Yet, experts believe many of Love's stories are tall tales and not very close to the truth. We may never know how exciting the cowboy life in the Old West really was, but we have the freedom of letting our imaginations run wild.

NOTES

Notes should include only important details and use keywords, phrases, or short sentences.

▲ **Practice Book** p. 179

Directions Answer the questions below using the article and your notes.
Possible answers given for 2, 4, 5, 7, 8, 10.

1. Synthesize the information in the first paragraph and write it as a single sentence.
   The author did not believe that cowboys had really existed until researching the topic.

2. Paraphrase the first sentence in the third paragraph of the article.
   Nat Love wrote a book about his cowboy life.

3. How long was Nat Love's cowboy career?
   twenty years

4. What fact about Nat Love's childhood is most important to write down?
   He was a former slave.

5. Why would writing your notes into a table or diagram help you understand the article?
   It can help you see how the ideas in the article are related.

6. What did Nat Love do in 1876 that led to his fame?
   He won a contest that proved his abilities in shooting, horseback riding, and roping animals.

7. For what purpose would you want to take notes on the author's opinions of cowboy stories?
   You would take notes if you were comparing and contrasting the ideas of this author to another.

8. Why should you only write down important ideas when taking notes?
   The important ideas are the ones you are likely to need later.

9. Is there only one way to take notes?
   No—you can take notes any way you want, as long as you understand them when you are finished.

10. Name two ways taking notes can help you study for a test.
    Taking notes helps you focus on the important ideas in a text. It also gives you something to review before a test.

Home Activity Your child learned how to take notes, synthesize, and paraphrase information. Read an article or story with your child. Help your child experiment to find a method of note-taking he or she is most comfortable with (traditional, chart, web, outline etc.).

▲ **Practice Book** p. 180

Assessment Checkpoints *for the Week*

Selection Assessment

Use pp. 69–72 of Selection Tests **to check:**

 Selection Understanding

 Comprehension Skill *Cause and Effect*

 Selection Vocabulary
bondage
commissioned
earthen
encounter
homesteaders
settlement

ASSESSMENT

Scott Foresman
Selection Tests
Teacher's Manual

• Assess comprehension of weekly selections
• Assess understanding of weekly comprehension skills
• Assess knowledge of selection vocabulary

Reading STREET
Grade 6

Leveled Assessment

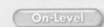
On-Level
Strategic Intervention
Advanced

Use pp. 103–108 of Fresh Reads for Differentiated Test Practice **to check:**

 Comprehension Skill *Cause and Effect*

 REVIEW **Comprehension Skill**
Author's Purpose

 Fluency *Words Correct Per Minute*

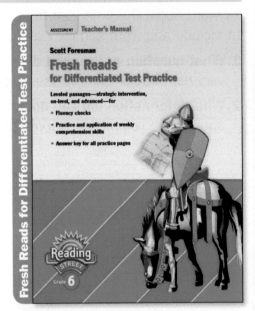

ASSESSMENT   Teacher's Manual

Scott Foresman
Fresh Reads
for Differentiated Test Practice

Leveled passages—strategic intervention, on-level, and advanced—for
• Fluency checks
• Practice and application of weekly comprehension skills
• Answer key for all practice pages

Reading STREET
Grade 6

Managing Assessment

Use Assessment Handbook **for:**

 Observation Checklists

 Record-Keeping Forms

 Portfolio Assessment

ASSESSMENT

Scott Foresman
Assessment Handbook

• Suggestions for preparing students for high-stake tests
• Ideas for classroom-based assessment
• Forms in English and Spanish for students to record interests and progress
• Forms in English and Spanish for teachers to record observations of students' reading and writing abilities and progress
• Assessment and Regrouping charts reproduced from *Reading Street* Teacher's Editions

Reading STREET
Grades 3–6

Unit 4
Explorers, Pioneers, and Discoverers

EXPAND THE CONCEPT
How can we be open to new understandings?

CONCEPT QUESTION
How have those who've gone first influenced others who've gone after?

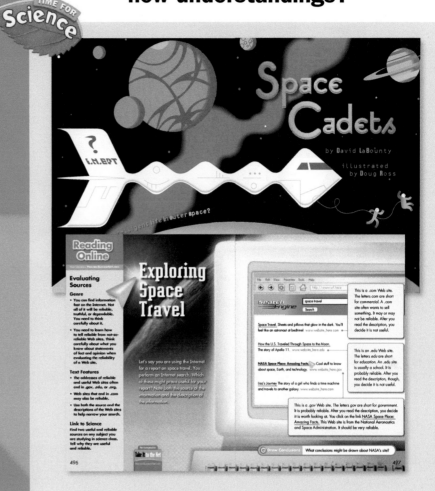

What drives people to explore harsh climates and dangerous places?

Why is it important to study animals responsibly?

What does it mean to be a pioneer?

How can we be open to new understandings?

How do inventions happen?

CONNECT THE CONCEPT

▶ **Build Background**
galaxy, planet, solar system

Concept Vocabulary Web

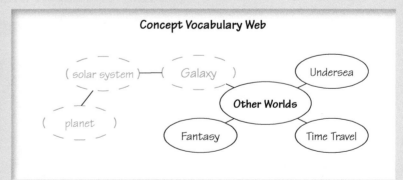

▶ **Science Content**
Light-Years, Search for Extraterrestrials, Alien Life

▶ **Writing**
TV Script

▶ **Internet Inquiry**
Life On Other Planets

Preview Your Week

How can we be open to new understandings?

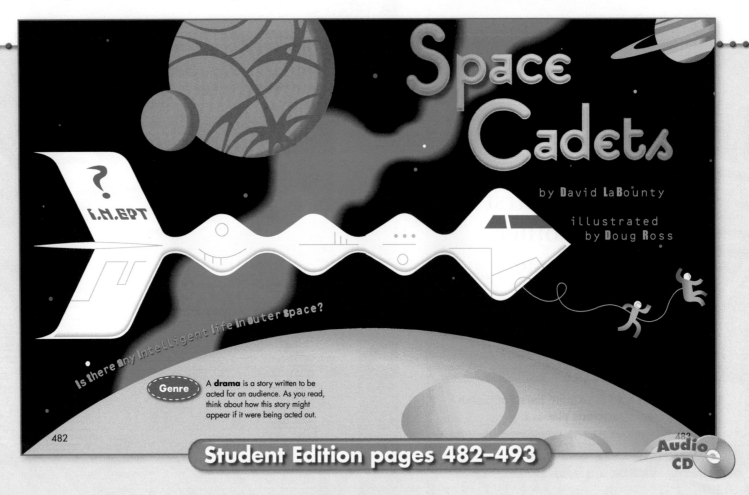

Space Cadets
by David LaBounty

illustrated by Doug Ross

I.N.EPT

Is there any intelligent life in outer space?

Genre A **drama** is a story written to be acted for an audience. As you read, think about how this story might appear if it were being acted out.

482

Student Edition pages 482–493

Audio CD

Genre Drama

Vocabulary Strategy Context Clues

Comprehension Skill Draw Conclusions

Comprehension Strategy Visualize

Paired Selection

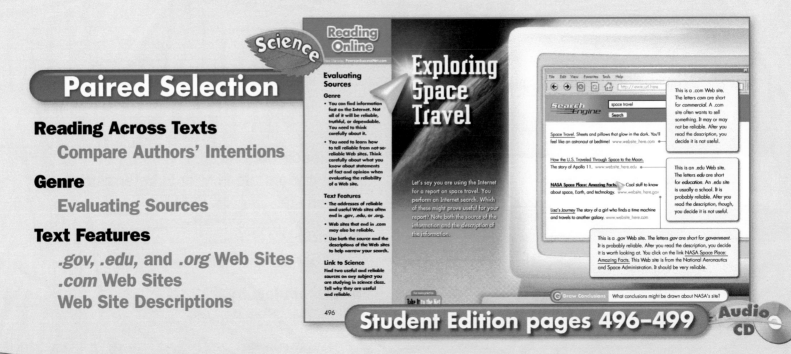

Reading Across Texts
Compare Authors' Intentions

Genre
Evaluating Sources

Text Features
.gov, .edu, and .org Web Sites
.com Web Sites
Web Site Descriptions

Student Edition pages 496–499

Audio CD

Leveled Readers

🔵 **Skill** Draw Conclusions

🔵 **Strategy** Visualize

Lesson Vocabulary

Below-Level

On-Level

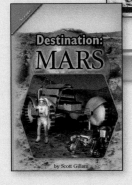

Advanced

ELL Reader

· Concept Vocabulary
· Text Support
· Language Enrichment

TIME FOR Science

Integrate Science Standards

• Space
• Travel and Probes

✓ Read

Space Cadets,
pp. 482–493

"Exploring Space Travel,"
pp. 496–499

Leveled Readers

Below-Level • Support Concepts

On-Level • Develop Concepts

Advanced
• Extend Concepts
• Science Extension Activity

ELL Reader

✓ Build
Concept Vocabulary
Other Worlds, pp. 478l–478m

✓ Teach Science Concepts
Light-Years, p. 485
Search for Extraterrestrials, p. 487
Alien Life, p. 491

✓ Explore Science Center
Think About Life Forms, p. 478k

Weekly Plan

READING

45–90 minutes

TARGET SKILLS OF THE WEEK

Comprehension Skill
Draw Conclusions

Comprehension Strategy
Visualize

Vocabulary Strategy
Context Clues

DAY 1
PAGES 478l–480b,
499a, 499e–499k

Oral Language

QUESTION OF THE WEEK *How can we be open to new understandings?*

Read Aloud: "Mush, A Dog from Space," 478m
Build Concepts, 478l

Comprehension/Vocabulary

Comprehension Skill/Strategy Lesson, 478–479
Draw Conclusions **T**
Visualize
Build Background, 480a
Introduce Lesson Vocabulary, 480b
aliens, barge, hospitable, molten, ore, refrain, universal, version **T**

Read Leveled Readers

Grouping Options 478f–478g

Fluency

Model Characterization/Dialogue, 478l–478m, 499a

DAY 2
PAGES 480–489, 499a,
499e–499k

Oral Language

QUESTION OF THE DAY *Why is* Inter Nova (I.N.) Ept *a good name for the spaceship?*

Comprehension/Vocabulary

Vocabulary Strategy Lesson, 480–481
Context Clues **T**

Read Space Cadets, 482–489

Grouping Options
478f–478g

Draw Conclusions **T**
Context Clues **T**
REVIEW Sequence **T**
Develop Vocabulary

Fluency

Echo Reading, 499a

LANGUAGE ARTS

30–60 minutes

Trait of the Week

Organization/Paragraphs

Grammar, 499e
Introduce Indefinite and Reflexive Pronouns **T**

Writing Workshop, 499g
Introduce TV Script
Model the Trait of the Week:
Organization/Paragraphs

Spelling, 499i
Pretest for Related Words 1

Internet Inquiry, 499k
Identify Questions

Grammar, 499e
Develop Indefinite and Reflexive Pronouns **T**

Writing Workshop, 499g
Improve Writing with Stage Directions

Spelling, 499i
Teach the Generalization

Internet Inquiry, 499k
Navigate/Search

DAILY WRITING ACTIVITIES

Day 1 Write to Read, 478

Day 2 Words to Write, 481
Strategy Response Log, 482, 489

DAILY SCIENCE CONNECTIONS

Day 1 Other Worlds Concept Web, 478l

Day 2 Time for Science: Light-Years, 485; Search for Extraterrestrials, 487
Revisit the Other Worlds Concept Web, 489

DAILY SUCCESS PREDICTORS
for Adequate Yearly Progress

Monitor Progress and Corrective Feedback

Vocabulary Check Vocabulary, 478l

RESOURCES FOR THE WEEK

- Practice Book, *pp. 181–190*
- Word Study and Spelling Practice Book, *pp. 73–76*
- Grammar and Writing Practice Book, *pp. 73–76*

- Selection Test, *pp. 73–76*
- Fresh Reads for Differentiated Test Practice, *pp. 109–114*
- The Grammar and Writing Book, *pp. 158–163*

Grouping Options for Differentiated Instruction

Turn the page for the small group lesson plan.

DAY 3 PAGES 490-495, 499a, 499e-499k

Oral Language

QUESTION OF THE DAY *What misunderstanding do the space cadets make about the aliens?*

Comprehension/Vocabulary

Read *Space Cadets, 490–494*

Grouping Options 478f–478g

🔘 Draw Conclusions **T**
🔘 Visualize
Develop Vocabulary

Reader Response

Selection Test

Fluency

Model Characterization/Dialogue, 499a

Grammar, 499f
Apply Indefinite and Reflexive Pronouns in Writing **T**

Writing Workshop, 495, 499h
Write Now
Prewrite and Draft

Spelling, 499j
Connect Spelling to Writing

Internet Inquiry, 499k
Analyze Sources

Day 3 Strategy Response Log, 492
Look Back and Write, 494

Day 3 Time for Science: Alien Life, 491
Revisit the Other Worlds Concept Web, 493

DAY 4 PAGES 496-499a, 499e-499k

Oral Language

QUESTION OF THE DAY *How is using the Internet for research like exploring space?*

Comprehension/Vocabulary

Read *"Exploring Space Travel," 496–499*

Grouping Options 478f–478g

Evaluating Source
Reading Across Texts

Fluency

Partner Reading, 499a

Grammar, 499f
Practice Indefinite and Reflexive Pronouns for Standardized Tests **T**

Writing Workshop, 499h
Draft, Revise, and Publish

Spelling, 499j
Provide a Strategy

Internet Inquiry, 499k
Synthesize Information

Day 4 Writing Across Texts, 499

Day 4 Science Center: Think about Life Forms, 478k

DAY 5 PAGES 499a-499l

Oral Language

QUESTION OF THE WEEK *To wrap up the week, revisit the Day 1 question.*
Build Concept Vocabulary, 499c

Fluency

Read Leveled Readers

Grouping Options 478f–478g

Assess Reading Rate, 499a

Comprehension/Vocabulary

🔘 Reteach Draw Conclusions, 499b **T**
Exaggeration, 499b
🔘 Review Context Clues, 499c **T**

Speaking and Listening, 499d
Newscast
Listen to Media

Grammar, 499f
Cumulative Review

Writing Workshop, 499h
Connect to Unit Writing

Spelling, 499j
Posttest for Related Words 1

Internet Inquiry, 499k
Communicate Results

Research/Study Skills, 499l
Follow and Clarify Directions

Day 5 Exaggeration, 499b

Day 5 Revisit the Other Worlds Concept Web, 499c

KEY 🔘 = Target Skill **T** = Tested Skill

Comprehension | Check Retelling, *494*

Fluency | Check Fluency WCPM, *499a*

Vocabulary | Check Vocabulary, *499c*

SUCCESS PREDICTOR

Small Group Plan *for Differentiated Instruction*

Daily Plan
AT A GLANCE

Reading
Whole Group
- Oral Language
- Comprehension/Vocabulary

Group Time
Differentiated Instruction

Meet with small groups to provide:
- Skill Support
- Reading Support
- Fluency Practice

Read

This week's lessons for daily group time can be found behind the Differentiated Instruction (DI) tab on pp. DI·32–DI·41.

Whole Group
- Fluency

Language Arts
- Grammar
- Writing
- Spelling
- Research/Inquiry
- Speaking/Listening/Viewing

DAY 1

On-Level	Strategic Intervention	Advanced
Teacher-Led *Page DI·33*	**Teacher-Led** *Page DI·32*	**Teacher-Led** *Page DI·33*
• Develop Concept Vocabulary	• Reinforce Concepts	• **Read** Advanced Reader *Destination: Mars*
• **Read** On-Level Reader *The United States and Russian Space Race*	• **Read** Below-Level Reader *The Solar System and Beyond*	• Independent Extension Activity

ⓘ Independent Activities
While you meet with small groups, have the rest of the class...

- Visit the Reading/Library Center
- Listen to the Background Building Audio
- Finish Write to Read, p. 478
- Complete Practice Book pp. 183–184
- Visit Cross-Curricular Centers

DAY 2

On-Level	Strategic Intervention	Advanced
Teacher-Led *Pages 484–489*	**Teacher-Led** *Page DI·34*	**Teacher-Led** *Page DI·35*
• **Read** *Space Cadets*	• Practice Lesson Vocabulary	• Extend Vocabulary
	• Read Multisyllabic Words	• **Read** *Space Cadets*
	• **Read** or Listen to *Space Cadets*	

ⓘ Independent Activities
While you meet with small groups, have the rest of the class...

- Visit the Reading/Library Center
- Listen to the AudioText for *Space Cadets*
- Finish Words to Write, p. 481
- Complete Practice Book pp. 185–186
- Write in their Strategy Response Logs, pp. 482, 489
- Visit Cross-Curricular Centers
- Work on inquiry projects

DAY 3

On-Level	Strategic Intervention	Advanced
Teacher-Led *Pages 490–493*	**Teacher-Led** *Page DI·36*	**Teacher-Led** *Page DI·37*
• **Read** *Space Cadets*	• Practice Draw Conclusions and Visualize	• Extend Draw Conclusions and Visualize
	• **Read** or Listen to *Space Cadets*	• **Read** *Space Cadets*

ⓘ Independent Activities
While you meet with small groups, have the rest of the class...

- Visit the Reading/Library Center
- Listen to the AudioText for *Space Cadets*
- Write in their Strategy Response Logs, p. 492
- Finish Look Back and Write, p. 494
- Complete Practice Book p. 187
- Visit Cross-Curricular Centers
- Work on inquiry projects

---

① Begin with whole class skill and strategy instruction.

② Meet with small groups to provide differentiated instruction.

③ Gather the whole class back together for fluency and language arts.

DAY 4

On-Level
Teacher-Led
Pages 496–499
- Read "Exploring Space Travel"

Strategic Intervention
Teacher-Led
Page DI · 38
- Read or Listen to "Exploring Space Travel"

Advanced
Teacher-Led
Page DI · 39
- Read "Exploring Space Travel"
- Genre Study

(i) Independent Activities

While you meet with small groups, have the rest of the class...

- Visit the Reading/Library Center
- Listen to the AudioText for "Exploring Space Travel"
- Visit the Writing/Vocabulary Center
- Finish Writing Across Texts, p. 499
- Visit Cross-Curricular Centers
- Work on inquiry projects

DAY 5

On-Level
Teacher-Led
Page DI · 41
- Reread Leveled Reader *The United States and Russian Space Race*
- Retell *The United States and Russian Space Race*

Strategic Intervention
Teacher-Led
Page DI · 40
- Reread Leveled Reader *The Solar System and Beyond*
- Retell *The Solar System and Beyond*

Advanced
Teacher-Led
Page DI · 41
- Reread Leveled Reader *Destination: Mars*
- Share Extension Activity

(i) Independent Activities

While you meet with small groups, have the rest of the class...

- Visit the Reading/Library Center
- Complete Practice Book pp. 188–190
- Visit Cross-Curricular Centers
- Work on inquiry projects

Grouping Place English language learners in the groups that correspond to their reading abilities in English.

Use the appropriate Leveled Reader or other text at students' instructional level.

TiP Send home the appropriate Multilingual Summary of the main selection on Day 1.

ONLINE
PearsonSuccessNet.com

Peter Afflerbach
For ideas on assessing engagement, see the article "Engaged Assessment of Engaged Readers" by Scott Foresman author Peter Afflerbach.

TEACHER TALK

Curriculum compacting
is a technique for content acceleration. Students skip work they already have mastered and complete more challenging content.

Looking Ahead

Be sure to schedule time for students to work on the unit inquiry project "Going First." This week students combine relevant information they have collected from different sources to develop answers to their inquiry questions.

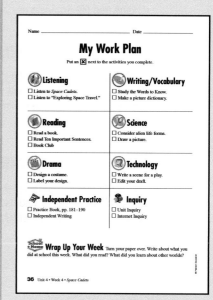

▲ **Group-Time Survival Guide**
p. 36, Weekly Contract

Customize Your Plan *by Strand*

ORAL LANGUAGE

Concept Development

How can we be open to new understandings?

CONCEPT VOCABULARY
galaxy   planet   solar system

BUILD

☐ **Question of the Week** Introduce and discuss the question of the week. This week students will read a variety of texts and work on projects related to the concept *other worlds*. Post the question for students to refer to throughout the week. DAY 1 *478d*

☐ **Read Aloud** Read aloud "Mush, A Dog from Space." Then begin a web to build concepts and concept vocabulary related to this week's lesson and the unit theme, Explorers, Pioneers, and Discoverers. Introduce the concept words *galaxy, planet,* and *solar system* and have students place them on the web. Display the web for use throughout the week. DAY 1 *478l–478m*

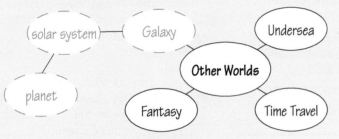

DEVELOP

☐ **Question of the Day** Use the prompts from the Weekly Plan to engage students in conversations related to this week's reading and the unit theme. **EVERY DAY** *478d–478e*

☐ **Concept Vocabulary Web** Revisit the Other Worlds Concept Web and encourage students to add concept words from their reading and life experiences. DAY 2 *489,* DAY 3 *493*

CONNECT

☐ **Looking Back/Moving Forward** Revisit the Other Worlds Concept Web and discuss how it relates to this week's lesson and the unit theme. Then make connections to next week's lesson. DAY 5 *499c*

CHECK

☐ **Concept Vocabulary Web** Use the Other Worlds Concept Web to check students' understanding of the concept vocabulary words *galaxy, planet,* and *solar system.* DAY 1 *478l,* DAY 5 *499c*

VOCABULARY

STRATEGY CONTEXT CLUES
Context is the words and sentences around an unknown word. As you read, you often come across words with more than one meaning. To help you figure out the meaning that makes sense in the context, look for clues in the sentences around the word. The author may give a definition, a synonym or antonym, an example, or a relationship in the context that will help you figure out the meaning of the word you don't know.

LESSON VOCABULARY
aliens   ore
barge   refrain
hospitable   universal
molten   version

TEACH

☐ **Words to Know** Give students the opportunity to tell what they already know about this week's lesson vocabulary words. Then discuss word meaning. DAY 1 *480b*

☐ **Vocabulary Strategy Lesson** Use the vocabulary strategy lesson in the Student Edition to introduce and model this week's strategy, *context clues.* DAY 2 *480–481*

Vocabulary Strategy Lesson

PRACTICE/APPLY

☐ **Leveled Text** Read the lesson vocabulary in the context of leveled text. DAY 1 *LR28–LR36*

☐ **Words in Context** Read the lesson vocabulary and apply *context clues* in the context of *Space Cadets.* DAY 2 *482–489,* DAY 3 *490–494*

Leveled Readers

☐ **Writing/Vocabulary Center** Use the multiple-meaning words to create a picture dictionary. **ANY DAY** *478k*

☐ **Homework** Practice Book pp. 184–185. DAY 1 *480b,* DAY 2 *481*

Main Selection—Drama

☐ **Word Play** Have students brainstorm pairs of homophones, use a dictionary to check spellings and meanings, and then make lists of homophones and their meanings. **ANY DAY** *499c*

ASSESS

☐ **Selection Test** Use the Selection Test to determine students' understanding of the lesson vocabulary words. DAY 3

RETEACH/REVIEW

☐ **Reteach Lesson** If necessary, use this lesson to reteach and review *context clues.* DAY 5 *499c*

COMPREHENSION

⊙ **SKILL DRAW CONCLUSIONS** When you draw a conclusion, you form a reasonable opinion about something you have read. A conclusion should be valid, that is, it should make sense.

⊙ **STRATEGY VISUALIZE** When you visualize, you put yourself into the story, becoming part of it. Visualizing the details that the writer has given you can help you to draw valid conclusions about the selection.

TEACH

❏ **Skill/Strategy Lesson** Use the skill/strategy lesson in the Student Edition to introduce and model *draw conclusions* and *visualize* DAY 1 478-479

❏ **Extend Skills** Teach exaggeration. **ANY DAY** 499b

Skill/Strategy Lesson

PRACTICE/APPLY

❏ **Leveled Text** Apply *draw conclusions* and *visualize* to read leveled text. DAY 1 LR28-LR36

❏ **Skills and Strategies in Context** Read *Space Cadets*, using the Guiding Comprehension questions to apply *draw conclusions* and *visualize*. DAY 2 482-489, DAY 3 490-494

❏ **Skills and Strategies in Context** Read "Exploring Space Travel," guiding students as they apply *draw conclusions* and *visualize*. Then have students discuss and write across texts. DAY 4 496-499

❏ **Homework** Practice Book pp. 183, 187, 188. DAY 1 479, DAY 3 493, DAY 5 499b

❏ **Fresh Reads for Differentiated Test Practice** Have students practice *draw conclusions* with a new passage. DAY 3

Leveled Readers

Main Selection—Drama

Paired Selection—Nonfiction

ASSESS

❏ **Selection Test** Determine students' understanding of the selection and their use of *draw conclusions*. DAY 3

❏ **Retell** Have students retell *Space Cadets*. DAY 3 494-495

RETEACH/REVIEW

❏ **Reteach Lesson** If necessary, reteach and review *draw conclusions*. DAY 5 499b

FLUENCY

SKILL CHARACTERIZATION/DIALOGUE Dialogue is the conversation between characters in a selection. Often, the writer will give you clues about the characters' personalities or feelings through dialogue.

TEACH

❏ **Read Aloud** Model fluent reading by rereading "Mush, A Dog from Space." Focus on this week's fluency skill, characterization/dialogue. DAY 1 478l-478m, 499a

PRACTICE/APPLY

❏ **Echo Reading** Read aloud the dialogue on p. 486, having students notice how the dialogue between the First Officer and the Captain reveals their characters. Then practice as a class doing three choral readings of the dialogue. DAY 2 499a, DAY 3 499a

❏ **Partner Reading** Partners practice reading p. 491 aloud naturally, keeping character in mind, and offering each other feedback. As students reread, monitor their progress toward their individual fluency goals. DAY 4 499a

❏ **Listening Center** Have students follow along with the AudioText for this week's selections. **ANY DAY** 478j

❏ **Reading/Library Center** Have students reread a selection of their choice. **ANY DAY** 478j

❏ **Fluency Coach** Have students use Fluency Coach to listen to fluent readings or practice reading on their own. **ANY DAY**

ASSESS

❏ **Check Fluency** WCPM Do a one-minute timed reading, paying special attention to this week's skill—characterization/dialogue. Provide feedback for each student. DAY 5 499a

Customize Your Plan *by Strand*

GRAMMAR

SKILL INDEFINITE AND REFLEXIVE PRONOUNS Indefinite pronouns are pronouns that may not have specific antecedents; that is, they don't refer to specific words. *Someone, anybody, each, few, several,* and *some* are indefinite pronouns. Reflexive pronouns are pronouns that refer back to another noun or pronoun in the same sentence. *Herself, himself, yourself,* and *themselves* are reflexive pronouns.

TEACH

☐ **Grammar Transparency 19** Use Grammar Transparency 19 to teach indefinite and reflexive pronouns. DAY 1 *499e*

Grammar Transparency 19

PRACTICE/APPLY

☐ **Develop the Concept** Review the concept of indefinite and reflexive pronouns and provide guided practice. DAY 2 *499e*

☐ **Apply to Writing** Have students review something they have written and apply indefinite and reflexive pronouns. DAY 3 *499f*

☐ **Test Preparation** Examine common errors in using indefinite and reflexive pronouns to prepare for standardized tests. DAY 4 *499f*

☐ **Homework** Grammar and Writing Practice Book pp. 73–75. DAY 2 *499e,* DAY 3 *499f,* DAY 4 *499f*

ASSESS

☐ **Cumulative Review** Use Grammar and Writing Practice Book p. 76. DAY 5 *499f*

RETEACH/REVIEW

☐ **Daily Fix-It** Have students find and correct errors in grammar, spelling, and punctuation. **EVERY DAY** *499e–499f*

☐ **The Grammar and Writing Book** Use pp. 158–161 of The Grammar and Writing Book to extend instruction for indefinite and reflexive pronouns. **ANY DAY**

The Grammar and Writing Book

WRITING

Trait of the Week

ORGANIZATION/PARAGRAPHS Organization is the structure, or arrangement, of your information and ideas. A careful writer tells about events and details in order. When you prepare a TV script, for example, arrange the events in sequence, and include stage directions that signal a shift in setting.

TEACH

☐ **Writing Transparency 19A** Use the model to introduce and discuss the Trait of the Week. DAY 1 *499g*

☐ **Writing Transparency 19B** Use the transparency to show students how stage directions can improve their writing. DAY 2 *499g*

Writing Transparency 19A   **Writing Transparency 19B**

PRACTICE/APPLY

☐ **Write Now** Examine the model on Student Edition p. 495. Then have students write their own TV scripts. DAY 3 *495, 499h,* DAY 4 *499h*

    Prompt *Space Cadets* is written as a drama for the stage. Think about a story that you have read recently. Now rewrite part of the story as a TV script with dialogue and stage directions.

Write Now p. 495

☐ **Writing/Vocabulary Center** Use the multiple-meaning words to create a picture dictionary. **ANY DAY** *478k*

ASSESS

☐ **Writing Trait Rubric** Use the rubric to evaluate students' writing. DAY 4 *499h*

RETEACH/REVIEW

☐ **The Grammar and Writing Book** Use pp. 158–163 of The Grammar and Writing Book to extend instruction for indefinite and reflexive pronouns, stage directions, and TV scripts. **ANY DAY**

The Grammar and Writing Book

SPELLING

GENERALIZATION **RELATED WORDS 1**   Related words often have parts that are spelled the same but pronounced differently: _poem, poetic._

TEACH

❑ **Pretest** Give the pretest with related words 1. Guide students in self-correcting their pretests and correcting any misspellings. DAY 1 _499i_

❑ **Think and Practice** Connect spelling to the phonics generalization for related words 1. DAY 2 _499i_

PRACTICE/APPLY

❑ **Connect to Writing** Have students use spelling words to write a news article. Then review frequently misspelled words: _always, myself._ DAY 3 _499j_

❑ **Homework** Phonics and Spelling Practice Book pp. 73–76. **EVERY DAY**

RETEACH/REVIEW

❑ **Review** Review spelling words to prepare for the posttest. Then provide students with a spelling strategy—related words. DAY 4 _499j_

ASSESS

❑ **Posttest** Use dictation sentences to give the posttest for related words 1. DAY 5 _499j_

Spelling Words

1. poem	8. combination	15. academy*
2. poetic	9. repeat	16. academic
3. direct	10. repetition	17. inspire
4. direction	11. critic	18. inspiration
5. origin	12. criticize	19. depart
6. original	13. history	20. departure
7. combine	14. historic	

Challenge Words

21. erode	23. maintain	25. confiscate
22. erosion	24. maintenance	26. confiscation

*Word from the selection

RESEARCH AND INQUIRY

❑ **Internet Inquiry** Have students conduct an Internet inquiry on life on other planets. **EVERY DAY** _499k_

❑ **Follow and Clarify Directions** Review terms and features of a set of directions, such as the steps, numbering, illustrations, and diagrams. Have students work in small groups to follow, then discuss, a set of directions to complete a task or make something. DAY 5 _499l_

❑ **Unit Inquiry** Allow time for students to combine relevant information to develop answers to their inquiry questions. **ANY DAY** _407_

SPEAKING AND VIEWING

❑ **Newscast** Have students use information from the news articles they wrote for the Writing Workshop to give newscasts to the class. DAY 5 _499d_

❑ **Listen to the Media** Have students listen to a television newscast in class or at home, then answer questions orally or in writing. DAY 5 _499d_

Resources for
Differentiated Instruction

LEVELED READERS

▶ **Comprehension**
- 🔊 **Skill** Draw Conclusions
- 🔊 **Strategy** Visualize

▶ **Lesson Vocabulary**
- 🔊 Context Clues

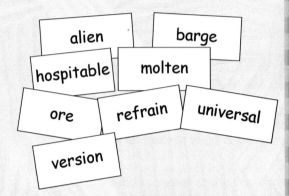

alien · barge · hospitable · molten · ore · refrain · universal · version

▶ **Science Standards**
- Space
- Travel and Probes

Leveled Reader Database ONLINE
PearsonSuccessNet.com

Use the Online Database of over 600 books to
- Download and print additional copies of this week's leveled readers.
- Listen to the readers being read online.
- Search for more titles focused on this week's skills, topic, and content.

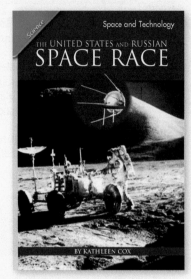

Space and Technology

THE UNITED STATES AND RUSSIAN
SPACE RACE

BY KATHLEEN COX

On-Level Reader

Draw Conclusions
- A conclusion is a sensible decision reached after thinking about details or facts.
- Drawing conclusions, or making inferences, is the process of making those decisions.
- You should always be able to back up your conclusions with information from the text.

Directions Read the paragraph below, then answer the questions that follow.

During the late 1950s, the Soviets and Americans were locked in a space race. On October 4, 1957, the Soviets launched *Sputnik*, the world's first man-made satellite. *Sputnik* traveled about 400 miles above the Earth at a speed of 18,000 miles per hour and took about 96 minutes to circle the planet. About a month later, the Soviet Union launched *Sputnik II*. This second satellite was much heavier than the original *Sputnik*. It also had a passenger: a dog named Laika, the world's first Earthling in space. After the launch of *Sputnik II*, U.S. President Dwight D. Eisenhower tried to restore the confidence of the American people in the U.S. space program. And on December 6, 1957, American scientists launched a rocket called the *Vanguard*. It carried a satellite intended to orbit the Earth. But the rocket went up four feet, then fell to the ground. People called it "kaputnik." Americans did succeed in launching a rocket in January 1958, but just three months later, the Soviets successfully launched *Sputnik III*. This third Russian satellite weighed more than a ton. It was hard to believe at the time that the Americans would beat the Russians in landing a man on the moon.

Possible responses given.

1. What conclusion can you reach about the success of the Soviet space program in the late 1950s?
   The Soviets were more successful than the Americans.

2–3. What are two facts or examples that support your conclusion?
   Soviets launched three rockets with satellites on board;
   Americans launched one successful rocket and one
   unsuccessful one.

4. What can you infer about why President Eisenhower tried to restore the confidence of the American people?
   He wanted Americans to feel that the U.S. would catch up and
   build the best space program in the world.

5. What can you infer from the last sentence in this paragraph?
   Americans will be first to land a man on the moon.

🔊 **On-Level Practice** TE p. LR32

Vocabulary
Directions Choose the word from the box that best matches each definition. Write the word on the line.

Check the Words You Know
alien · barge · hospitable · molten · ore · refrain · universal · version

1. version — one particular statement, account, or description
2. hospitable — friendly; receptive
3. molten — made liquid by heat; melted
4. alien — an imaginary creature from outer space
5. ore — rock containing metals to make mining profitable. After it is mined, it must be treated to extract the metal.
6. barge — large, strongly built vehicle or flat-bottomed boat for carrying freight
7. universal — of or belonging to all; concerning all
8. refrain — to keep yourself from doing something

Directions Write a paragraph about the space race using as many vocabulary words as possible.

   Paragraphs will vary.

On-Level Practice TE p. LR33

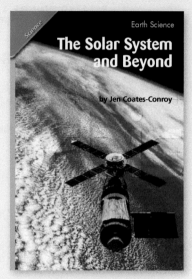

Earth Science

The Solar System and Beyond

by Jen Coates-Conroy

Below-Level Reader

Drawing Conclusions
- A **conclusion** is a sensible decision you reach after you think about facts and details in what you read.
- **Drawing conclusions** means to make sensible decisions or form reasonable opinions after thinking about those facts and details.
- A **conclusion** may be stated at the beginning or end of a passage. Or you may need to reach your own conclusion after reading.

Directions Read the following passage.

What would we be without the Sun? The Sun is the most prominent feature in our solar system. It is the largest object and contains approximately 98 percent of the total solar system mass. One hundred and nine Earths would be required to fit across the Sun's face, and its interior could hold over 1.3 million Earths. The Sun's outer visible layer is called the photosphere and has a temperature of more than 9,930 degrees Fahrenheit. This layer has a rough appearance due to the turbulent eruptions of energy at the surface. Even though Earth is about 93 million miles from the Sun, the rays that hit the planet are still very powerful. Astronomers study the Sun by using special telescopes.

Directions Use the graphic organizer below. First, find a conclusion in the passage above, or draw a conclusion on your own. Write the conclusion in the center circle labeled *Conclusion*. In the small circles around the main circle, write facts or details that helped you or the author reach that conclusion.

Supporting Facts or Details:

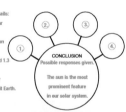

① largest object of solar system
② 109 Earths could fit on sun's face.
③ Its interior could hold 1.3 million Earths.
④ The sun creates very powerful rays that hit Earth.

CONCLUSION
Possible responses given.
The sun is the most prominent feature in our solar system.

🔊 **Below-Level Practice** TE p. LR29

Vocabulary
Directions Choose the word from the box that best matches each definition. Write the word on the line.

Check the Words You Know
alien · barge · hospitable · molten · ore · refrain · universal · version

1. version — one particular statement, account, or description
2. hospitable — friendly; receptive
3. molten — made liquid by heat; melted
4. alien — an imaginary creature from outer space
5. ore — rock containing metals extracted after mining
6. barge — large, strongly built vehicle or flat-bottomed boat for carrying freight
7. universal — of or belonging to all; concerning all
8. refrain — to keep yourself from doing something

Directions For each word below, write a meaning different from the ones above.
   Responses will vary.
9. barge

10. refrain

Below-Level Practice TE p. LR30

Advanced

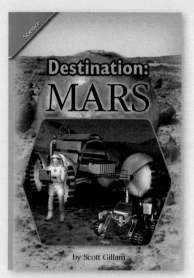

Advanced Reader

Draw Conclusions

- A conclusion is a sensible decision reached after thinking about details or facts.
- Drawing conclusions, or making inferences, is the process of making those decisions.
- You should always be able to back up your conclusions with information from the text.

Directions Read the paragraph below, then answer the questions that follow.

Recent trips to Mars have turned up how different Mars is from Earth. Mars Global Surveyor, launched in 1996, revealed a surface made up of dust at least three feet thick caused by millions of years of meteoroid impacts, and an atmosphere made up of 95 percent carbon dioxide and only about .1 percent oxygen. The elevation of Mars' polar ice cap was found to be between 6,600 and 7,900 feet higher than the surrounding terrain. MGS also found canyons and troughs as deep as 3,600 feet in the frozen water and carbon dioxide in Mars' polar ice cap. Additional explorations have found that the deepest canyon on Mars is six times deeper than the Grand Canyon and as long as the United States from the West to the East Coast. The highest mountain on Mars covers an area that is the size of the entire state of Arizona. In addition, Mars has a much thinner atmosphere than Earth and much higher radiation levels. In fact, Mars' radiation is about two to three times higher than the radiation around Earth.

Possible responses are given.

1. What conclusion can you reach about how easily humans could survive on Mars?
   Humans could not survive on Mars without special protections.

2–3. Give at least two facts or examples that support your conclusion.
   Radiation is 2-3 times higher. Mars has a thinner atmosphere,
   dust on Mars' surface is at least three feet thick.

4. What can you infer about the differences between the environments of Mars compared to Earth?
   The atmosphere on Mars has only .1 percent oxygen.

5. What can you infer about differences between the physical terrains of Mars and Earth?
   Mars' mountains and polar ice caps are much more extreme
   – larger and colder – than those on Earth.

6. What facts help you support this conclusion?
   Mars' polar ice cap is over 6,600 feet higher than the

Advanced Practice TE p. LR35

Vocabulary
Directions Choose the word from the box that best completes each sentence. Write the word on the line.

Check the Words You Know
- axis
- durable
- infrared
- interaction
- Martian
- panoramic
- robotic
- routine

1. The technicians designed the _durable_ parts to withstand extreme temperatures.
2. One of the _robotic_ arms would have to be fixed.
3. The satellite launch was planned around the _axis_ of the "red planet."
4. Astronauts are less protected from _infrared_ radiation while traveling in space.
5. Is it possible that someday we will have _interaction_ with other intelligent life forms?
6. The _Martian_ environment continues to be an interesting mystery.
7. Earth displays its natural beauty when seen from space in a _panoramic_ view.
8. Sending orbiters and rovers to other planets has become more _routine_ since the 1960s.

Directions For each word below, write a sentence that highlights its meaning.

9. axis

10. routine

Advanced Practice TE p. LR36

ELL Reader

ELL Poster 19

Teacher's Edition Notes
ELL notes throughout this lesson support instruction and reference additional resources at point of use.

**Teaching Guide
pp. 127–133, 248–249**
- Multilingual summaries of the main selection
- Comprehension lesson
- Vocabulary strategies and word cards
- ELL Reader 6.4.4 lesson

ELL and Transition Handbook

Ten Important Sentences
- Key ideas from every selection in the Student Edition
- Activities to build sentence power

More Reading

Readers' Theater Anthology
- Fluency practice
- Five scripts to build fluency
- Poetry for oral interpretation

Leveled Trade Books

Below-Level

Advanced

On-Level

- Extended reading tied to the unit concept
- Lessons in the Trade Book Library Teaching Guide

Homework
- Family Times Newsletter
- ELL Multilingual Selection Summaries

Take-Home Books
- Leveled Readers

Cross-Curricular Centers

 **Listening**

 Reading/Library

 Drama

Listen to the *Selections*

MATERIALS `SINGLES`
CD player, headphones, AudioText CD, student book

LISTEN TO LITERATURE Listen to *Space Cadets* and "Exploring Space Travel" as you follow or read along in your book. Listen to draw conclusions and make inferences based on the information in the selections.

If there is anything you don't understand, you can listen again to any section.

Read It *Again!*

MATERIALS `SINGLES` `PAIRS` `GROUPS`
Collection of books for self-selected reading, reading logs, student book

Select a book you have already read. Record the title of the book in your reading log. You may want to read with a partner.

Choose from the following:

- Leveled Readers
- ELL Readers
- Stories Written by Classmates
- Books from the Library
- *Space Cadets*

TEN IMPORTANT SENTENCES Read the Ten Important Sentences from *Space Cadets*. Then locate the sentences in the student book.

BOOK CLUB Discuss why *Space Cadets* works well as a play. Conduct a drama genre study. Read other drama selections and get together with a group to share your favorites. *Drama*

Design *Costumes*

MATERIALS `SINGLES` `PAIRS`
Art materials

Choose a scene from *Space Cadets* and design a costume described in the scene.

1. **Choose one of the scenes from *Space Cadets* and create a design for a costume worn by a character that appears in the scene.**
2. **Label the colors, fabrics, and other details included for your costume design.**

EARLY FINISHERS Write a description of the scenery you would design for the same scene.

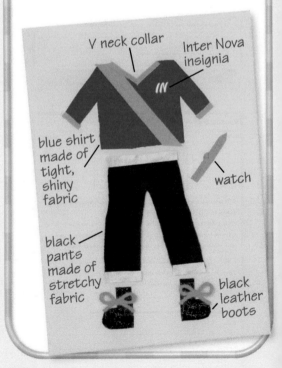

Scott Foresman Reading Street Centers Survival Kit
Use the *Space Cadets* materials from the Reading Street
Centers Survival Kit to organize this week's centers.

Writing/ Vocabulary

Science

Technology

Make a Dictionary

MATERIALS GROUPS
Writing and drawing materials

Use the multiple-meaning words from the lesson vocabulary to create a picture dictionary.

1. Determine which of the vocabulary words have more than one meaning.
2. On separate pieces of paper, write each word, along with the word's different meanings, to resemble a dictionary entry. Draw a picture on the page for one of the definitions.
3. Staple the pages together to make a picture dictionary.

EARLY FINISHERS Find other words in the selection that have multiple meanings. Choose one to add to your picture dictionary.

Think about Life Forms

MATERIALS SINGLES PAIRS GROUPS
Writing and drawing materials

Draw a picture of what you think an intelligent life form from another planet might look like.

1. Think about what a life form from another planet might look like. Would it be human-like or something entirely different?
2. Draw a picture of what you think this life form might look like. Consider the environment that the life form might be living in and how this would affect its appearance.

EARLY FINISHERS Write a brief speech that this life form might make to visitors from other planets.

Use Editing Tools

MATERIALS SINGLES
Word processing software

Use editing tools in your word processing software to edit text.

1. Log on to your computer and open your word processing software.
2. Write a draft of a first scene for a play about space exploration. Print your first draft.
3. Use the editing tools in your word processing software to edit and revise the text. Print your second draft and compare it to your first.
4. Follow classroom rules when using the computer.

EARLY FINISHERS Write a short paragraph discussing how the features of the word processing program make it easier to edit and revise your writing.

ALL CENTERS

Concept Vocabulary

galaxy a group of billions of stars forming one system

planet a large astronomical body that orbits the Sun or another star

solar system a star and all the planets, satellites, comets, etc., that revolve around it

Monitor Progress

Check Vocabulary

If... students are unable to place words on the Web,	then... review the lesson concept. Place the words on the Web and provide additional words for practice, such as *future* and *coral reef.*

SUCCESS PREDICTOR

DAY 1 Grouping Options

Reading

Whole Group
Introduce and discuss the Question of the Week. Then use pp. 478l–480b.

Small Group
Differentiated Instruction
Read this week's Leveled Readers. See pp. 478f–478g for the small group lesson plan.

Whole Group
Use p. 499a.

Language Arts
Use pp. 499e–499k.

Build Concepts

FLUENCY

MODEL CHARACTERIZATION/DIALOGUE As you read "MUSH, a Dog from Space," use characterization to model reading dialogue with expression. As the two characters talk, you can stress through your vocal delivery the highly educated, sophisticated personality of the dog Mush and the adolescent enthusiasm and curiosity of the girl Kelly.

LISTENING COMPREHENSION

After reading "MUSH, A Dog from Space," use the following questions to assess listening comprehension.

1. **What planet does Mush's family members live on?** *(They live on the planet Growf-Woof-Woof, which is where he is from.)* **Draw Conclusions**

2. **How can you tell that Mush is a highly educated dog?** *(Possible responses: He speaks very proper English; he answers questions clearly and logically.)* **Draw Conclusions**

BUILD CONCEPT VOCABULARY

Start a web to build concepts and vocabulary related to this week's lesson and the unit theme.

• Draw the Other Worlds Concept Web.

• Read the sentence with the word *galaxy* again. Ask students to pronounce *galaxy* and discuss its meaning.

• Place *galaxy* in an oval attached to Other Worlds. Explain that *galaxy* is related to this concept. Read the sentences in which *planet* and *solar system* appear. Have students pronounce the words, place them on the Web, and provide reasons.

• Brainstorm additional words and categories for the Web. Keep the Web on display and add words throughout the week.

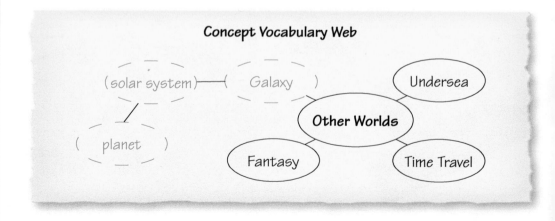

Concept Vocabulary Web

MUSH, A Dog from Space

by Daniel Pinkwater

One day a young girl named Kelly went for a walk in the woods by her home when she notices a dog watching her.

Mush looked like one of those dogs that pulls sleds in Alaska—sort of like a fat wolf.

"Are you a husky?" I asked Mush.

"I am a mushamute," Mush said. "I am certainly the only mushamute on this planet."

"How can that be?" I asked. "Your mother and father must have been mushamutes."

"That is so," said Mush.

"And you have brothers and sisters?"

"Many."

"Then how could you be the only mushamute on this planet?" I asked

"Guess," Mush said.

"Did something terrible happen to your mother and father, and all the other mushamutes?" I asked.

"No," said Mush.

"And yet, you are the only mushamute on this planet."

"That is correct," Mush said.

I thought for a while. "Are there mushamutes on some planet other than Earth?"

"Yes, there are," Mush said.

""Are you from another planet?"

"You guessed it!" Mush said. "I come from a planet known as Growf-Woof-Woof, in the solar system of Arfturus, a star similar to Canis Major in your galaxy."

"You are a dog from space?"

"Yes."

"Wow! That means you don't belong to anybody on Earth!"

"I suppose you could say that,"Mush said.

"So you could come and live with me," I said. "That is, if you would like to."

"We could give it a try," Mush said.

By this time, Mush and I were walking together through the woods in the direction of my house.

"Is that the reason you are able to talk to me—because you are a dog from another planet?" I asked.

"I am able to talk to you because I am a highly educated dog," Mush said.

We walked a little farther.

"Did you know that 'Mush!' is what sled-dog drivers say to make their dogs go?" I asked.

"Yes, I knew that," Mush said.

We walked on.

"Does it ever snow here?" Mush asked.

"Oh, yes—in the winter," I said.

"Good," Mush said.

We walked some more.

"How did you happen to come to Earth?" I asked.

"It's a long story," said Mush.

BEFORE READING

Activate Prior Knowledge

Before students listen to the Read Aloud, remind students that science fiction selections contain elements of realism and fantasy.

Set Purpose

Read aloud the title and have students predict what the selection will be about.

Have students listen for details to help them draw conclusions.

Creative Response

Have students work with partners to improvise what happens after the end of the story as Mush tells Kelly how he came to Earth. **Drama**

Access Content Before reading, share this summary: A person interviews a talking dog named Mush, who comes from another planet. Mush accepts an invitation to go live with that person.

School + Home **Homework** Send home this week's Family Times newsletter.

Vocabulary

SUCCESS PREDICTOR

SKILLS ↔ STRATEGIES IN CONTEXT

Draw Conclusions
Visualize

OBJECTIVES

◎ Draw conclusions to improve comprehension.

◎ Visualize to help draw conclusions.

Skills Trace

	Draw Conclusions
Introduce/Teach	TE: 6.3 372–373; 6.4 478–479; 6.6 724–725
Practice	Practice Book: 143, 147, 148, 183, 187, 188, 283, 287, 288
Reteach/Review	TE: 6.3 307, 399b, DI·56; 6.4 499b, DI·55; 6.6 681, 707, 715, 749b, DI·55
Test	Selection Test: 57–60, 73–76, 113–116; Benchmark Test: Unit 6

INTRODUCE

Write the sentence *Astronauts have found footprints on a distant planet.* Ask students which of the following conclusions they might draw from that statement and ask them to justify their answers: *This planet has life. This planet does not have life.* (Possible response: *This planet has life. Footprints indicate the presence of animals or people.*)

Have students read the information on p. 478. Explain the following:

• Drawing conclusions helps you better understand what you read.

• Visualizing helps you draw conclusions that the author has not stated openly.

Use Skill Transparency 19 to teach drawing conclusions and visualizing.

Comprehension

Skill
Draw Conclusions

Strategy
Visualize

Draw Conclusions

• When you draw a conclusion, you form a reasonable opinion about what you have read. Use what you know about real life to help you draw conclusions.

• Be sure that there are enough facts or information in the text to support your conclusions.

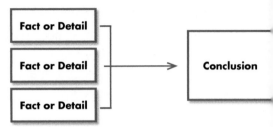

Strategy: Visualize

When you visualize, you create pictures in your mind. This strategy helps you make sense of a story. It can help you place yourself into the story, as if you were there. Visualize the details that the writer has given you. That can also help you to draw conclusions the writer has not stated.

Write to Read

1. Read the letter from Isabel. Make a graphic organizer like the one above to show how you would support the conclusion that technology in the time period the letter was written has advanced from what it is today.

2. Draw or write a detailed description of the place where Isabel now lives.

478

Strategic Intervention

Draw Conclusions To help students draw conclusions, explain that they must use their prior knowledge, as well as the information they have read, to form an opinion. In the letter from Isabel, Isabel tells her old friend Rachel about life on her new planet. Have students look closely at the illustration of Isabel at the bottom of p. 479. Have them conclude from her expression if they think she is happy in her new home or misses life on Earth.

ELL

Access Content

Beginning/Intermediate For a Picture It! lesson on drawing conclusions, see the ELL Teaching Guide, pp. 127–128.

Advanced Before reading the letter from Isabel, ask students to tell about letters they have written to or received from friends describing a new school.

Earth Date: April 12, 2099

1221 Galaxy Way
Planet Enilorac

Greetings, Rachel,

How are you, old buddy? It has been ten Earth-weeks now since we moved to this planet. This is a different place from Earth, that's for sure. The atmosphere is greenish, and we have two suns and three moons.

The entire planet is really urban. We live on a busy flyway, with lots of aircars zipping past. So much for cruising on our air scooters like we used to, huh? Remember how much we would scooter up and down and back and forth in front of my house on Earth? It is so quiet and safe there where you are.

My new school is called Albert Einstein School. Last week the telecommunicator of this one boy—his name is Santino—started smoking and almost blew up, right in the middle of our History of the Galaxy class. He got in trouble because we are supposed to switch our telecommunicators off at school.

At recess, I sort of sit on the sidelines and watch the other kids duel with their laser swords or play dodge orb. There's no one like you here. Are you doing all right? Are you still spying on Ellen and Juanita at recess like we used to? That was awesome!

Sincerely,
Isabel

1 **Strategy** Visualize this scene. What do you see in your mind? How would it make you feel?

2 **Skill** Which conclusion can you draw about Isabel's view of her new home?
(a) She feels more comfortable on Earth.
(b) She wishes it were busier.
(c) She likes her new home better than her old home.

3 **Skill** What conclusion can you draw about how Isabel is feeling?

4 **Strategy** How would you visualize Isabel on the school playground? What details must you add to the picture that aren't in the text?

479

Available as **Skill Transparency** 19

Draw Conclusions
- When you **draw conclusions**, you form reasonable opinions about what you have read. Use what you know about real life to help you draw conclusions.
- Be sure that there are enough facts or information in the text to support your conclusions.

Directions Read the following passage. Then complete the diagram.

I think in the future people will live on other planets in our solar system. They will have grown tired of the crowded cities on Earth and will manage a way to build smaller communities on other planets. Life will be slower on these planets. People won't feel like they have to compete with each other for space, jobs, and resources since the whole solar system will be opened up for their use. People will spend their days exploring the universe and learning about new life forms instead of being consumed with day-to-day details.

Possible answers given.

| Fact or Detail 1. People will build their own small communities. | Fact or Detail 2. Daily life will be at a slower pace. | Fact or Detail 3. They will spend their time exploring. |

Conclusion 4. People in the future will live a more relaxed and free life.

5. How did you visualize the future described in the passage?
I saw groups of homes set up on different planets. I saw people jetting off in space ships to discover the universe.

Home Activity Your child visualized the details in a passage to draw a conclusion about it. Look through books or magazines for a detailed illustration or photo. Have your child study the picture and draw a conclusion about what is going on in it.

Practice Book p. 183

TEACH

1 **STRATEGY** Use paragraph 2 to model how to visualize.

MODEL I close my eyes and try to picture in my mind being on an air scooter and flying. I see other scooters and people whizzing by. I feel happy and completely carefree.

2 **SKILL** Read and discuss paragraph 2.

 MODEL Isabel contrasts the urban scene on her new planet with the quiet and safety on Earth that allowed her to cruise on her air scooter without a care. I conclude that she misses Earth and that Choice *a* is the correct answer.

PRACTICE AND ASSESS

3 **SKILL** Possible response: Isabel is feeling isolated and lonely, and she misses her friends back on Earth.

4 **STRATEGY** Possible response: I visualize her sitting alone and looking sad. I would add that she is sitting with her knees drawn up, looking tense and unhappy.

WRITE Have students complete steps 1 and 2 of the Write to Read activity. You might consider using this as a whole class activity.

Monitor Progress

 Draw Conclusions

| **If...** students are unable to complete **Write to Read** on p. 478, | **then...** use Practice Book p. 183 to provide additional practice. |

Space Cadets **479**

ONLINE

Students can search an online encyclopedia or the Internet to find out more about life on other planets. Have them use *extraterrestrials* or *UFOs* as keywords for their search in a student-friendly search engine.

ELL

Build Background Use ELL Poster 19 to build background and vocabulary for the lesson concept of being open to new understandings.

▲ **ELL Poster** 19

Build Background

ACTIVATE PRIOR KNOWLEDGE

BEGIN A WEB DIAGRAM about life on other planets.

- Have students write the word "Extraterrestrials" in the center circle of the web. Prompt students to use their imagination when thinking of outer space and what might exist there.

- Give students two minutes to write as many words as they can think of to describe extraterrestrials in the web extension circles.

- Tell students that, as they read, they should see how many of their descriptions fit the extraterrestrials in the story, which words they might change, and what words they would like to add to their web diagrams.

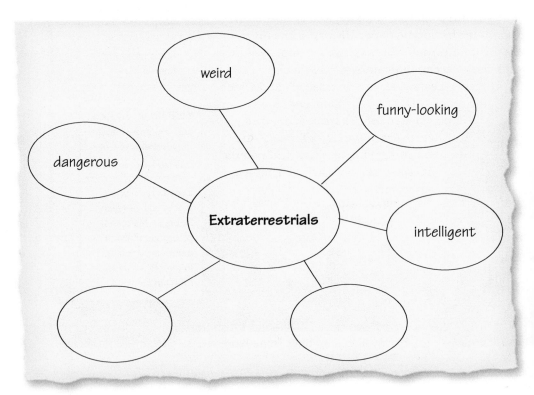

▲ **Graphic Organizer** 15

BACKGROUND BUILDING AUDIO This week's audio explores the topic of space technology. After students listen, discuss what they found out and what surprised them most about the technology found in science fiction versus what is actually possible according to NASA.

Background Building Audio

Introduce Vocabulary

WRITING DEFINITIONS

Ask students to write their own definition of a word from the list. Then have them write a sample sentence using the word and underline it. Next have them look up the word's definition in the glossary. Have them compare this definition to their own. If their definition was incorrect, have them rewrite it.

Activate Prior Knowledge

Have students share where they may have seen some of these words. Point out that some of this week's words are homophones *(ore)* or have multiple meanings *(refrain* and *barge),* and students may learn new definitions for these words. **Homophones • Multiple-Meaning Words**

Have students use these steps for reading multisyllabic words. (See the Multisyllabic Word Routine on p. DI·1.)

1. **Look for Meaningful Word Parts** (base words, endings, prefixes, suffixes, roots) Think about the meaning of each part. Use the parts to read the word. Model: I see the suffix *able* at the end of the word *hospitable.* The *able* at the end means "given to or tending to." The root of the word *hospitable* comes from the Latin word that means "a place where travelers can rest." With the suffix it means, "giving to being receptive or friendly."

2. **Chunk Words with No Recognizable Parts** Say each chunk slowly. Then say the chunks fast to make a word. Model: *ver, sion—version.*

By the end of the week, students should know the lesson vocabulary words. Have them review the sentences they wrote and revise when necessary. The sentences should reflect word meanings as they are used in the text.

Lesson Vocabulary

WORDS TO KNOW

T **aliens** imaginary creatures from outer space

T **barge** a large, strongly-built boat or ship for carrying freight or waste

T **hospitable** friendly; receptive

T **molten** made liquid by heat; melted

T **ore** rock containing enough of a metal or metals to make mining profitable

T **refrain** to keep yourself from doing something

T **universal** existing everywhere, for all purposes

T **version** a special form or variant of something

MORE WORDS TO KNOW

fortitude courage in facing pain, danger, or trouble

repulsive causing strong dislike or aversion

T = Tested Word

Vocabulary

Directions Draw a line from the words on the left to their definitions on the right.

1. barge — friendly; receptive
2. refrain — existing everywhere
3. hospitable — made liquid by heat; melted
4. universal — to keep yourself from doing something
5. molten — boat or ship carrying freight

Check the Words You Know
___aliens
___barge
___hospitable
___molten
___ore
___refrain
___universal
___version

Directions Choose the word from the box that best completes each sentence. Write the word on the line shown on the left.

ore _____ 6. They mine iron ___ here.

version _____ 7. Her ___ of the story was hilarious.

aliens _____ 8. Do you believe that ___ exist?

hospitable _____ 9. I hope they are ___ beings.

refrain _____ 10. Please ___ from exiting the space ship while in flight.

Write a Story
Write a science fiction story set in outer space. Use as many vocabulary words as you can.
Stories should include words from the vocabulary list and details concerning outer space and science fiction elements.

Home Activity Your child identified and used vocabulary words from *Space Cadets.* With your child, have a conversation about what you perceive the future to be like. Try to use the vocabulary words from the selection while conversing.

▲ **Practice Book** p. 184

Vocabulary Strategy

 Use context clues to determine the meanings of multiple-meaning words.

INTRODUCE

Discuss the strategy for context clues using the steps on p. 480.

TEACH

- Have students read "The Universe According to Hollywood," paying attention to vocabulary.

- Model using context clues to determine the meaning of *aliens*.

Think Aloud **MODEL** The third sentence talks about "no proof of life on other planets." The fourth sentence says people meet *aliens* in movies. The fifth sentence says "These beings are not always hospitable to the visiting humans." Based on these context clues, *aliens* must mean "beings from other planets."

Words to Know

molten
aliens
hospitable
refrain
universal
ore
barge
version

Remember

Try the strategy. Then, if you need more help, use your glossary or a dictionary.

Vocabulary Strategy
for Multiple-Meaning Words

Context Clues Some words have more than one meaning. You can use the words and sentences around a multiple-meaning word to figure out which meaning the author is using.

1. Read the words and sentences around the unknown word.

2. Think about the possible meanings of the word. For example, *refrain* can mean "to keep oneself back" or "a phrase repeated over and over."

3. Decide which meaning makes sense in the sentence: Everyone sang the *refrain*.

4. Reread the sentence and replace the word with the meaning you chose.

5. Does this meaning make sense? If not, try another meaning.

As you read "The Universe According to Hollywood," use the context and your knowledge to decide which meaning a multiple-meaning word has in this article. For example, does *barge* mean "a large, flat-bottomed boat" or "to enter quickly"?

480

DAY 2 Grouping Options

Reading

Whole Group Discuss the Question of the Day. Then use pp. 480–483.

Small Group **Differentiated Instruction**
Read *Space Cadets.* See pp. 478f–478g for small group lesson plan.

Whole Group Use p. 499a.

Language Arts
Use pp. 499e–499k.

 Context Clues Have students work in pairs to follow the steps on p. 480. Encourage them to also look for clues in the sentences around the word.

ELL

Access Content Use ELL Poster 19 to preteach vocabulary. Choose from the following to meet language proficiency levels.

Beginning/Intermediate Point out the words *universal* and *version*. Explain that these words have Spanish cognates, or related words: *universal* and *version*.

Advanced Teach the lesson on pp. 480–481. Have students determine whether any of the tested words have cognates in their home languages. Resources for home-language words may include parents, bilingual staff members, bilingual dictionaries, or online translation sources.

THE UNIVERSE
ACCORDING TO HOLLYWOOD

Travel to outer space is not a dream. It is part of the real world. We have had a close look at planets hot enough to turn glass to a molten pool and cold enough to put the North and South Poles to shame. So far, we have found no proof of life on other planets. However, in movies people travel to the ends of the galaxy and meet all sorts of aliens.

These beings are not always hospitable to the visiting humans. In fact, misunderstandings are always leading to trouble. It sometimes seems as though none of these beings can refrain from war and crime. It seems these ills do not belong to Earth alone. They are universal truths.

Of course, beings all over the universe also have ambition and honor. Suppose a precious ore has been discovered on Planet X. Three-eyed aliens with tentacles are just as likely as humans to be greedy. A barge loaded with valuable cargo may well be stolen by space pirates and then returned to its rightful owners by "the forces for good." In fact, the Hollywood version of life in outer space is like life at home, with special effects.

Words to Write

What do you imagine life would be like on a distant planet? Write a description, using as many words from the Words to Know list as you can.

481

BEFORE READING

PRACTICE AND ASSESS

- Have students determine the meanings of the remaining words and explain the context clues they used.
- Point out that context clues aren't given with every word. Students may have to use the glossary or a dictionary to find the exact meanings of some words.
- Have students complete Practice Book p. 185.

WRITE Writing should include vocabulary words that relate to life on other planets as well as words that are related to space travel.

Monitor Progress

Context Clues

If... students need more practice with the lesson vocabulary,	then... use the Tested Vocabulary Cards.

Vocabulary · Context Clues

- When you are reading and see a word that has more than one meaning, you can use **context clues**, or words around the multiple-meaning word, to figure out its meaning.

Directions Read the following passage. Then answer the questions below.

Before we could start on the mission, we had to obtain a permit to land on the planet Apollo. The planet had recently been added to the Dangerous Zone by the Space Council. There was evidence that the environment of Apollo was dangerous to humans. Since we were on a special mission to extract molten lava for research purposes, we were granted permission. It took a full day to gather the material into canisters and load them onto the space barge, the vehicle that would take us back to Earth. We had to refrain from bringing any other substance from Apollo onboard with us for fear of contamination. So when I noticed some planet Apollo dust on my elbow, I had to be quarantined immediately. I was not allowed to return to work until the foreign dust was contained and proven harmless.

1. What is the definition of *permit* in this passage? What is another definition of the word?
   "written order of permission"; "to let or allow"
2. How do you know *barge* does not mean "to enter quickly" in the passage?
   The passage says that they were loading canisters onto "the barge, the vehicle taking them back to Earth."
3. What is the definition of *refrain* as it is used in the passage? How do you know?
   "to keep oneself back"; The crew had to keep themselves from bringing foreign substances onto the barge.
4. What is another meaning of *elbow*?
   "to make your way by pushing"
5. Use one of the multiple-meaning words in an original sentence. Make sure to include a context clue in the sentence, so that the intended meaning of the word is clear.
   Possible answer: I had to elbow my way through the crowd in order to get to the exit.

Home Activity Your child identified the definitions of multiple-meaning words by using context clues. Make a list of words that have multiple meanings. Have your child pick a word from the list and draw an illustration of its meaning while you try to guess which word it is. Switch roles, and repeat the activity.

▲ **Practice Book** p. 185

Prereading Strategies

OBJECTIVES

- Draw conclusions to improve comprehension.
- Visualize to help draw conclusions.

GENRE STUDY

Drama

Space Cadets is a drama. Explain that a drama or play is a story meant to be acted out for an audience. It has the same story elements as other forms of literature, such as characterization, setting, plot, and theme.

PREVIEW AND PREDICT

Have students preview the title and the question posed on p. 482. Ask them to answer the question. Then have them discuss their answers and how they think the play might provide a different answer. Encourage students to use selection vocabulary words as they talk about what they expect to learn.

Strategy Response Log

Predict Have students write their predictions in their strategy response logs. Students will check their predictions in the Strategy Response Log activity on p. 489.

Is there any intelligent life in outer space?

Genre A **drama** is a story written to be acted for an audience. As you read, think about how this story might appear if it were being acted out.

482

ELL

Access Content Preview the selection with your students and review the format of a play. Remind them that a character's name is written in boldfaced type followed by his or her dialogue (no quotations are used). Any descriptions of how a dialogue should be said or stage directions are italicized and in parentheses.

Consider having students read the selection summary in English or in students' home languages. See the Multilingual Summaries in the ELL Teaching Guide, pp. 131–133.

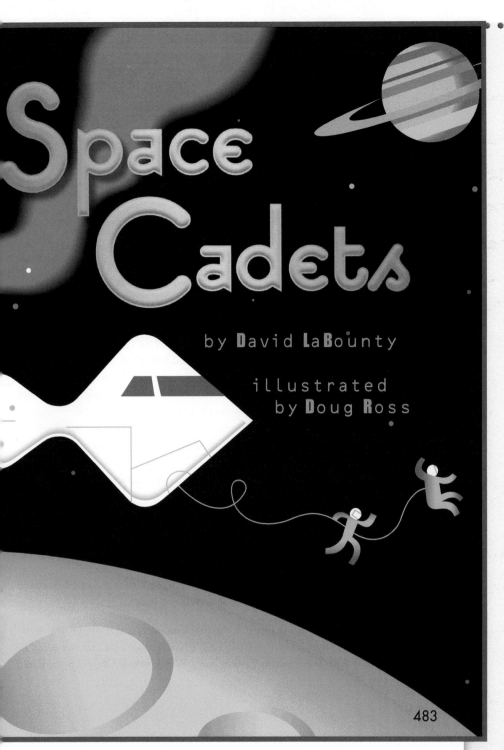

Space Cadets

by David LaBounty

illustrated by Doug Ross

483

SET PURPOSE

Read the cast of characters, as well as the time and setting, aloud to students. Have them visualize the characters based on their titles, as well as the time and setting. Based on the students' ideas, have them tell what they hope to find out as they read.

Remind students to draw conclusions about what they read.

STRATEGY RECALL

Students have now used these before-reading strategies:

- preview the selection to be aware of its genre, features, and possible content;
- activate prior knowledge about that content and what to expect of that genre;
- make predictions;
- set a purpose for reading.

Remind students that, as they read, they should monitor their own comprehension. If they realize something does not make sense, they can regain their comprehension by using fix-up strategies they have learned, such as:

- use phonics and word structure to decode new words;
- use context clues or a dictionary to figure out meanings of new words;
- adjust their reading rate—slow down for difficult text, speed up for easy or familiar text, or skim and scan just for specific information;
- reread parts of the text;
- read on (continue to read for clarification);
- use text features such as headings, subheadings, charts, illustrations, and so on as visual aids to comprehension;
- make a graphic organizer or a semantic organizer to aid comprehension;
- use reference sources, such as an encyclopedia, dictionary, thesaurus, or synonym finder;
- use another person, such as a teacher, a peer, a librarian, or an outside expert, as a resource.

After reading, students will use these strategies:

- summarize or retell the text;
- answer questions they or others pose;
- reflect to make new information become part of their prior knowledge.

Audio CD AudioText

Guiding Comprehension

1 **Draw Conclusions • Inferential**

Is the Captain telling the truth when he says he didn't forget to set his watch ahead? How do you know?

No, because the stage direction indicates that he adjusts his watch without the First Officer seeing him.

Monitor Progress

Draw Conclusions

If... students are unable to determine the correct conclusion,	**then...** use the skill and strategy instruction on p. 485.

---

2 **Dialogue • Critical**

How is the dialogue in this play different from the way it would appear in a novel or short story?

In novels and short stories, dialogue is a part of the narrative and set off with quotation marks. In a play, such as *Space Cadets*, the dialogue is the main focus of the work and is only preceded by the name of the character speaking it.

ONLINE

Have students look for information about life on other planets using a student-friendly search engine. Have them try keywords such as *extraterrestrial life* and *aliens*. Be sure to follow classroom rules for Internet use.

Characters

Captain
First Officer
Ensign
Tom [cadet]
Harold [cadet]

Space Cow
[alien]
Og [alien]
Mog [alien]

Scene 1

TIME: *The days of warp drive and phasers set to stun.*

SETTING: *The bridge of the spaceship* Inter Nova *(I. N.) E Captain's chair is center. It sits high enough above stage s he can see over control panel, placed several feet in front o*

AT RISE: CAPTAIN *is sitting on the edge of his chair, staring intently at the view screen (audience). He is wearing bright blu shirt, black pants, and boots.* FIRST OFFICER *is standing behind an the right of* CAPTAIN. *Her hands are folded behind her back. She is wearing bri red shirt, black pants, and boots. There is a curious look on her face as she exam view screen.* ENSIGN, *sitting at control panel, is wearing a bright yellow shirt, black pants, and boots. He is looking from view screen to his controls, checking to make sure they are still on course. Each crew member is wearing identical watches that serve as both timepieces and communication devices.*

Captain: Spacedate: Wednesday *(Checks watch, taps it)*—what time do you have, First Officer?

First Officer *(Consulting watch):* Nine-thirty A.M., sir.

Captain *(Looking back at watch and frowning):* Is that Earth Standard Time?

First Officer: No, sir. We crossed over into Alpha Centauri Time two days ago. Did you forget to set your watch ahead an hour?

1 **Captain** *(Testily):* I didn't forget. I was just making sure the computers were operational. *(Turns his back on* FIRST OFFICER *so she won't see him adjust his watch, which she does anyway. Turning back)* Where was I? Oh, yes Spacedate:

484

Access Content Point out that the selection is science fiction, and the characters are crew members of a space ship. Their jobs or positions are based on a military setting, with a *captain* in charge and a *first officer* as the second in command. *Ensigns* are lower-ranking positions. A *cadet* is someone still in training.

Wednesday, 9:30 A.M. We've entered a new solar system, 73 light years from Earth. Seven planets orbit this system's star, Mensa.

First Officer: Sir.

Captain: Yes?

First Officer: I don't mean to interrupt, sir. But whom are you talking to? ②

Captain *(As if this were a silly question):* The ship's log, of course.

First Officer: We don't have a ship's log, sir.

Captain: Sure we do. It's the thing that records everything I say—you know, for posterity. It turns on when I say "spacedate."

First Officer *(After slowly shaking her head):* It's a novel idea, sir, but all information about our journey is typed into the computer at the end of the day by Ensign Smith and beamed back to Star Base 12, where it is saved in triplicate with one copy returning to us, one forwarded to Earth Command, and one kept in Star Base's files.

Captain: Impressive. Wait a minute. You're telling me for the past three weeks I've been talking for no reason? Out loud?

First Officer: We thought you liked to hear the sound of your voice, sir. (ENSIGN *stifles a laugh.*)

Captain: I do, but that's not the point. *(Shakes head, turns back to view screen)* I can't believe I've been talking to myself like some crazy old man sitting on a park bench feeding breadcrumbs to Neruvian pigeons. Maybe I need a vacation, or at the very least a nap. *(Looking over at* FIRST OFFICER*)* I'm doing it again, aren't I? (FIRST OFFICER

485

Light-Years

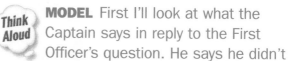

A light-year is the distance light can travel in one year. Since light travels at a speed of 186,282 miles per second (299,792 kilometers), one light-year is equal to 5.88 trillion miles (9.46 trillion km). Distances in space are so vast that the light-year is the most practical measure to use. The distance from Earth to the next nearest star beyond the Sun, Proxima Centauri, is 4.24 light-years. The Milky Way Galaxy, of which Earth is a part, is about 150,000 light-years across.

Draw Conclusions

TEACH

- Remind students that when they draw a conclusion, they make a sensible decision after thinking about the facts and details they have read.

- They should make sure the conclusion is well supported by information in the play or story.

- Model drawing the conclusion from the information on p. 484, speeches 4 and 5.

Think Aloud **MODEL** First I'll look at what the Captain says in reply to the First Officer's question. He says he didn't forget to set his watch ahead. Then I'll look at his actions, which are given as stage directions. It says he turns his back so the First Officer can't see him and adjusts his watch. This tells me that he isn't telling the truth, but doesn't want to appear foolish to the First Officer. I think this is a reasonable conclusion.

PRACTICE AND ASSESS

- Have students reread p. 485, speeches 8 and 9. Ask them to draw the best conclusion about why the Ensign gives a stifled laugh. *(Choice c)*

  a) He thinks of a funny joke.

  b) He thinks the First Officer is acting silly.

  c) He thinks the Captain is acting silly.

Guiding Comprehension

3 **Characters • Inferential**

What are two character traits that the Captain reveals in his conversation with the First Officer on pp. 486–487?

Possible response: The Captain is incompetent as a leader and is a coward who is afraid to lead an exploration of the planet.

4 (REVIEW) **Sequence • Inferential**

What does the Captain do immediately after he refuses to lead the exploration party?

He thinks for a moment and then calls for the space cadets, Tom and Harold, to report to the bridge.

Monitor Progress

(REVIEW) Sequence

If... students have difficulty determining the sequence,	then... use the skill and strategy instruction on p. 487.

5 **Compare and Contrast • Critical**

Text to World **Compare what you know about real space travel with space travel as it is depicted by the playwright. How is it similar? How is it different?**

Possible response: Similarities—The First Officer uses a computer as an astronaut would in real life. The cadets practice space walking as astronauts might in real life (page 488). Differences—Only unmanned spacecrafts have traveled to other planets. The only place in outer space where people have traveled is the moon.

---

nods. CAPTAIN *clears throat, gets out of his chair and moves to stand next to* ENSIGN.) What are the scanners telling us, Ensign?

Ensign: We're detecting seven planets: four R-class planets, two L-class, and an M-class.

Captain: M-class, you say? We should probably stay away from that one. (*To* FIRST OFFICER) M. What's that stand for? Molten? Menacing?

First Officer: Actually, Sir, M-class planets are the most hospitable for carbon-based life forms. (CAPTAIN *looks confused.*) Humans. Us. (*Checking her computer*) My computers show the atmosphere to be breathable, and I am picking up signs of several types of life forms on the planet's surface.

Captain (*Nodding*): Cool.

First Officer (*Drolly*): Yes, sir. Most excellent. (*Pause*) Sir?

Captain: Yes?

First Officer: What exactly was it you were the captain of before this assignment?

Captain: I was the captain of a space barge. We mostly transported garbage from Mars to the Sun, but sometimes we would move ore from the moon to the inner planets. (*Laughs*) Funny story—(*Notices impatient look on* FIRST OFFICER*'s face and interested smile on* ENSIGN*'s*) Yes, well. We can always save that for later. (*Claps hands and returns to chair*) As we all know, our mission is to make first contact. I can't think of a better place to make first contact than with this M-Class planet. How do we land this puppy?

First Officer: We don't. As I am sure you know, the *I. N. Ept* is a starship, suitable for long, long voyages between the stars. This puppy orbits planets; it does not land.

486

Understanding Idioms Help students understand the sentence "How do we land this puppy?" on p. 486 by explaining that the term "puppy" is an affectionate term used in reference to the spaceship.

Captain: Then we need to assemble an away team.

First Officer *(Impressed):* Excellent idea, sir. Who will be joining you?

Captain: Me? Oh, I'm not going down there. We don't know what kind of scary, freaky creatures live on that rock. Uh uh. No way. My momma didn't raise no Voloreain space slug.

First Officer: In this case, I think it is in the best interest of your *safety*— *(Aside)* and the galaxy's—that you remain on board. So whom should we send? ③

Captain *(Thinking a moment):* We need a team of intelligent, fearless, somewhat pleasing-to-look-at people. Someone with the intestinal fortitude to withstand any repulsive or violent species they may encounter while on the planet below. (ENSIGN *starts to look worried and shrinks down in his chair.*) Who knows what flesh-eating, mind-warping aliens they will find down there? We need someone who isn't afraid to lose a limb—and possibly his or her life—in order to bring peace to the galaxy. *(Touches a button on the arm of his chair)* Tom, Harold, report to the bridge, on the double. ④

First Officer: Are you sure that's wise?

Captain: Why not? They're perfect.

First Officer: They're cadets. (TOM *and* HAROLD *come "floating" on, as if trying to walk in zero gravity.*) ⑤

Captain *(Grabbing arms of chair):* Red Alert! The gravity stabilizers must be off-line.

First Officer *(Checking computer):* Actually, sir, the stabilizers are fine. *(Jumps up and down in place)* Gravity seems to be normal.

487

Sequence REVIEW

TEACH

- Remind students that sequence refers to the order of events in stories and plays.
- Keeping track of the sequence of events will help them better understand the story or play.
- Model finding the correct sequence of events on p. 487.

Think Aloud **MODEL** In the third speech on page 487, the Captain refuses to go on the expedition to explore the planet. When the First Officer asks the Captain whom they should send, the Captain responds by listing the desired characteristics of the people to be sent. Then, in a stage direction, he pushes a button and asks Tom and Harold to report to the bridge. The sequence on this page ends with Tom and Harold entering.

PRACTICE AND ASSESS

- Have students read the Captain's fourth speech on p. 486. What event in the Captain's life took place before the play began? *(He was the captain of a space barge that transported garbage.)*
- To assess, use Practice Book p. 186.

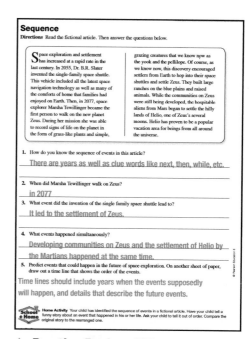

▲ **Practice Book** p. 186

TIME FOR **Science**

Search for Extraterrestrials

SETI stands for the Search for Extraterrestrial Intelligence. It began in 1959 when two American physicists published a paper on the possibility of aliens on other planets and how we might communicate with them using radio waves. A year later, astronomer Frank Drake searched two stars for alien radio signals over two weeks, but received none. In 1984, the SETI Institute was founded in California. Today SETI sponsors numerous projects to contact alien life. One of these projects is Project Phoenix, which uses radio telescopes to search star systems for life.

Guiding Comprehension

6 **Plot • Literal**

What assignment does the Captain give to Tom and Harold, the space cadets?

He tells them to beam down to the planet, seek out life forms, and make contact.

7 **Vocabulary • Context Clues**

Have students determine the meaning of *beam* on p. 488, speech 9.

In the play, *beam* means to travel through space by the transformation of matter.

Clue: The phrase "down to the planet below" follows the word *beam*, signaling it means a type of travel.

Monitor Progress	
Context Clues	
If... students have difficulty determining the meaning of *beam*,	**then...** use vocabulary strategy instruction on p. 489.

EXTEND SKILLS

Humor

Point out that humor can be conveyed in drama through dialogue and action. What a character says or does can be funny, as can the way that other characters react to him or her. Have students find examples of humorous dialogue and actions in *Space Cadets* and discuss what makes them funny.

Captain: Cancel red alert. (*Frowns at* TOM *and* HAROLD) What are you doing?

Tom: Practicing our space walking.

Captain: Why?

Harold: Section 7 paragraph 3 of the Space Cadet Training Guide states that you should always stay alert in case of a loss of gravity.

Tom (*Crashing into* HAROLD *and bouncing off wildly*): We're practicing in case of an emergency.

Captain: Not a bad idea.

First Officer: Actually, section 7 paragraph 3 of the Space Cadet Training Guide states, and I quote: "Stay away from the moss on planet Grassy T." (HAROLD *pulls small book from back pocket, thumbs to proper page, reads to himself, nods.*)

Harold: Well, I'll be. She's right. How do we practice that? (TOM *shrugs.*)

6 **7** **Captain:** We can worry about that later. Men, I have an assignment for you. I want you to beam down to the planet below, seek out the first life forms you find, and make contact.

First Officer: Again, sir, not to question your command, but do you think it is wise to send these two—cadets—on this mission? They are not exactly trained to represent Earth Command when it comes to a first contact with unknown aliens.

488

Extend Language Point out that on p. 488, Harold thinks that the guide states "You should always stay alert in case of a loss of gravity." The First Officer tells him that it really states "Stay away from the moss on Planet Grassy T." Explain that *gravity* sounds like "Grassy T" and *loss* is close to "moss."

Tom: I've been on several first-contact missions.

Captain and First Officer: Really?

Tom: Sure. Every time I ask a girl out on a date, it's my first contact with her—and it's usually my last, as well. (HAROLD *consolingly pats* TOM *on the shoulder.*)

First Officer *(Rolling her eyes):* I don't doubt it.

Captain: Sounds good to me. I know I don't understand women. Aren't they from Venus or someplace like that?

First Officer: We wish. However, I still believe these men are ill-prepared for a mission of this magnitude.

Captain *(Slowly nodding):* You may be right. That's why I want you to accompany them.

First Officer: Me?

Captain: You.

First Officer *(Obviously disappointed, but seeing no way out of it):* Yes, sir.

Tom and Harold *(Ad lib):* We won't let you down, sir. Absolutely not. (*Etc. They exit as if floating in zero gravity.* FIRST OFFICER *follows, shaking her head.*)

Ensign: This should be interesting.

Captain *(Getting out of his chair and moving to control panel):* Yes, it should. You think we could watch on this view screen thingy we've got here? (*Curtain*)

489

Develop Vocabulary

PRACTICE LESSON VOCABULARY

Students orally respond *yes* or *no* to each question and provide a reason.

1. Can you carry something on a *barge*? *(Yes; barges transport things.)*

2. Is a place that is *hospitable* somewhere you would want to go? *(Yes; a hospitable place is livable and appealing.)*

3. Do *aliens* supposedly live on other planets? *(Yes; some believe aliens inhabit other planets.)*

BUILD CONCEPT VOCABULARY

Review previous concept words with students. Ask if students have come across any words today in their reading or elsewhere that they would like to add to the Other Worlds Concept Web, such as *galaxy* or *orbit.*

VOCABULARY STRATEGY

Context Clues

DURING READING

TEACH

Read the ninth speech on p. 488. Model using context clues to determine the meaning of the word *beam,* which has multiple meanings.

Think Aloud **MODEL** I know the word *beam* can mean both a ray of light and to move through space by transforming matter. In the Captain's fourth speech, he tells the space cadets he wants them "to beam down to the planet below." I can tell from the context clues that *beam* is being used as a verb. I also know that the setting of the play is outer space. Based on these clues, I can conclude that the meaning of *beam* in this sentence is to move through space.

PRACTICE AND ASSESS

Have students use context clues to determine the multiple-meaning word *mission* in speech 10. *(an official task or goal)* Clues include *send, represent Earth Command,* and *first contact with unknown aliens.*

Strategy Response Log

Confirm Predictions Provide the following prompt: Was your prediction accurate? (See p. 482.) Revise your old prediction or make a new prediction about the rest of the selection.

If you want to teach this selection in two sessions, stop here.

Guiding Comprehension

If you are teaching the selection in two days, discuss the conclusions you have drawn so far and review the vocabulary.

8 **Visualize • Inferential**

Have students picture in their minds the "strange and exotic world" that is the setting of Scene 2. Have them write a description of what they imagine it to be.

Answers will vary according to students' experiences and thoughts.

9 **Draw Conclusions • Inferential**

Why does Harold think that they should approach the aliens with cotton?

He confuses the word "cotton" with "caution."

Monitor Progress

 Draw Conclusions

If... students are unable to determine the correct conclusion,	**then...** use the skill and strategy instruction on p. 491.

DAY 3 **Grouping Options**

Reading
Whole Group Discuss the Question of the Day.

Small Group Differentiated Instruction
Read *Space Cadets.* See pp. 478f–478g for the small group lesson plan.

Whole Group Discuss the Reader Response questions on p. 494. Then use p. 499a.

Language Arts
Use pp. 499e–499k

Scene 2

TIME: *A few minutes later.*

8 **SETTING:** *The surface of the alien planet, a strange and exotic world. May be played before curtain, if desired.*

AT RISE: SPACE COW, MOG, *and* OG *are standing left.* FIRST OFFICER, TOM, *and* HAROLD *enter right.* HAROLD *is holding a small scanner and whistling a trilling sound.*

First Officer (*To* HAROLD): What are you doing?

Harold: Scanning for life signs.

First Officer: What's with the whistling?

Harold: Sound effects.

First Officer (*Rolling her eyes*): Please refrain from making that noise.

Harold (*Disappointed*): Yes, sir.

Tom (*Consolingly*): I thought it sounded pretty cool.

Harold: Thanks. You should hear the sound I can make when I fire my phaser. (FIRST OFFICER *suddenly notices* SPACE COW *and holds up her hand.*)

First Officer: Sh-hh! Look. (TOM *and* HAROLD *look toward* SPACE COW *and take a step back.*)

Tom (*In awe*): An alien.

Harold: Do you think it's friendly?

Tom: What are we supposed to do?

Harold: Section 2 paragraph 6 of the Space Cadet Training Guide says we should approach aliens with cotton.

Tom (*Confused*): Cotton? I didn't bring any cotton. Where are we going to find some cotton?

490

Context Clues Have students use context to understand the meaning of the term *telepathic* on p. 491. Point out that the definition is in the dialogue preceding it ("Maybe it communicates with thoughts.").

First Officer *(Annoyed):* First of all, there is no section 2 paragraph 6 in the Space Cadet Training Guide. Second, the section you are probably referring to is section 6 paragraph 2, which states, and I quote, "Approach aliens with *caution*." ⑨

Tom and Harold *(Together):* Ohhhh.

Tom: That makes sense. (SPACE COW *makes a grunting noise.* TOM *takes another step back.*) What did it say?

First Officer *(Puzzled):* I do not know. Our universal translators do not seem to be functioning.

Harold *(Holding out hands to SPACE COW and taking a bold step forward):* Greetings, alien. We come in peace. (SPACE COW *makes a grunting noise.*)

Tom: Do you think it understands?

First Officer: It does not seem so.

Harold *(Speaking louder):* Greetings, alien! We come in peace!

First Officer *(Sarcastically):* Oh, yes. That should do it. Speaking louder will help it understand.

Tom: She's right. Maybe it doesn't have ears. Maybe it communicates with thoughts. *(Closes eyes and strains)*

First Officer: What are you doing?

Tom *(Eyes still closed, still straining):* Trying–to–send–it–a–telepathic–message. Ugh! *(Opens eyes and sways, almost falling)*

Harold *(Catching TOM):* What happened? Did it hear you? Did it try to melt your mind?

Tom: No. I'm O.K. All that hard thinking made me a little dizzy.

491

Alien Life

Belief in life on other planets goes back thousands of years. The modern craze for space aliens, however, began in 1877 when Italian astronomer Giovanni Schiaparelli discovered what he thought were canals on the surface of Mars. Many people thought these were artificial waterways created by a great civilization trying to survive on a dry planet. Over the years, the American public saw "Martians" as peaceful, sophisticated creatures; comic little green men; or warlike monsters that sought to dominate Earth. The theory of intelligent life on Mars persisted until the Mariner probes in the 1960s and early 1970s sent back photographs proving Mars to be a dry, desolate planet with no signs of life.

SKILLS ↔ STRATEGIES IN CONTEXT

Draw Conclusions
Visualize

TEACH

- Remind students that visualizing the details of a story or play can help you make sense of it and help you draw conclusions the writer has not stated.
- You can also use what you know about real life to help you draw conclusions.
- Model drawing a conclusion about the events described on pp. 490–491.

Think Aloud

MODEL First it's funny to hear Harold say they should approach aliens with cotton. It's even funnier to think this was in the Space Cadet Training Guide. I'll try to visualize this happening. Then I read that the First Officer tells the cadets that the training guide says to "Approach aliens with *caution*." I'm struck by the fact that *cotton* and *caution* are words that sound very similar. I come to the conclusion that Harold has confused the two words. This is easy to believe knowing that Harold is absentminded.

PRACTICE AND ASSESS

Have students reread p. 491, beginning with speech 9. Ask which of the following is the best conclusion they can draw about what the First Officer thinks of Harold's greeting to the aliens. *(Choice a)*

a) She thinks it is ridiculous.

b) She thinks it is effective.

c) She thinks it is very courageous.

Guiding Comprehension

10 **Detail • Literal**

Who is Admiral Hastings?

He is Harold's father and the Commander of Star Base One.

11 **Irony • Critical**

Question the Author **Why do you think the playwright ends his play with a dialogue between Mog and Og?**

We learn that Mog and Og are the intelligent beings on the planet, not Bessie the Space Cow (as the cadets assumed).

12 **Draw Conclusions • Critical**

Text to Text **What other story have you read about visitors from Earth exploring an alien planet? What conclusions can you draw about humans' interest in alien life based on these stories?**

Responses will reflect students' interests and prior knowledge.

Strategy Response Log

Summarize When students finish reading the selection, provide this prompt: Imagine that a friend has asked you what *Space Cadets* is about. In four or five sentences, explain its important points.

EXTEND SKILLS

Word Play

Remind students that a play on words is often based on the similarity of sound between two words with different meanings. This confusion is often used for purposes of humor. On p. 492, Tom thinks the First Officer is speaking literally when she asks how he and Howard were able to "get into" the Academy. What she really means is how he qualified to be accepted in its training program. Tom's answer is humorous. Have students find another example of word play on pp. 490–493.

First Officer: I do not doubt it.

Harold (*To* FIRST OFFICER): Do you have any ideas?

First Officer: I have been observing the two creatures behind the alien.

Tom: Those creepy-, crawly-looking things?

First Officer: Yes. Your scientific language needs some work, but those cre crawly-looking things seem to be observing us, following our movements.

Harold: Come on. They're just a couple of dogs.

First Officer: What do you mean?

Harold: Look at them. The blank looks on their faces, tongues hanging out of their mouths. They're like space dogs, or this planet's version of space dogs. Obviously the alien is taking them out for their morning walk.

Tom: Aren't they cute? (*Taking a step toward aliens with one hand outstretched*) Hey, little fella. Don't be scared. I just wanna pet you.

Harold (*Grabbing* TOM): You fool! You have no idea where that dog has been. It could have rabies, for all we know.

Tom: You're right.

First Officer (*Rubbing her forehead*): How did you two ever get into the Academy training program?

Tom: Just walked right in the front door.

First Officer: No. I mean, how did you pass the entrance exam?

Harold: I didn't have to take a test.

First Officer: Why not?

Harold: My father wrote a letter to the Dean.

First Officer: Who is your father?

492

ELL

Fluency Have students work in small groups and choose a one page passage to read in parts. Remind students to read only the dialogue and not the name of the character or stage directions. Help students with pronunciation and expression.

Harold: Admiral Hastings.

First Officer *(In disbelief)*: Your father is Admiral Hastings?

Harold *(Surprised)*: You know him?

First Officer: He is the Commander of Star Base One.

Harold *(Impressed)*: Really? *(During this conversation, SPACE COW has been slowly walking toward TOM.)*

Tom: Um, you guys, the alien is coming over here. *(SPACE COW walks up to TOM, who is frozen with fear. SPACE COW reaches out a hand, touching TOM's head.)* Um—what's it doing?

First Officer: It seems to be scanning you.

Harold: Or getting ready to suck out your brains! *(TOM yells and pushes SPACE COW's hand away. SPACE COW screams. TOM and HAROLD start running around.)*

First Officer *(Speaking hurriedly into her watch)*: First Officer to Ept. Three to beam up—and make it fast. *(TOM and HAROLD run off; FIRST OFFICER follows. There is a pause.)*

Mog: Well, Og, that was strange.

Og *(Nodding)*: Yes, definitely. Where do you think they were from?

Mog: Not from around here.

Og: Why do you suppose they kept trying to talk to Bessie?

Mog: Maybe she reminded them of someone they know.

Og *(Looking up and shaking his head)*: Like I've always said, Mog. There is no intelligent life out there. *(To SPACE COW)* Come on, Bessie, let's get you back to the barn. *(SPACE COW grunts and follows OG and MOG off. Curtain)*

The End

493

⟳ STRATEGY SELF-CHECK

Visualize

Remind students that by using stage directions to visualize what is happening in a play, they can gain information to help them reach a conclusion. Ask students to draw some general conclusions about the play and its characters based on visualizing. *(Possible responses: The Captain and the space cadets are incompetent and humorous characters. Only the First Officer knows what she's doing on this space mission, but even she misjudges the aliens.)* Use Practice Book p. 187.

SELF-CHECK

Students can ask themselves these questions to assess their ability to visualize and draw conclusions.

- Did I draw conclusions about the play that were based on information in the play?
- Was I able to visualize the setting and events to help me better understand what I was reading?

Monitor Progress
Draw Conclusions

If... students have difficulty visualizing to draw conclusions,	then... use the Reteach lesson on p. 499b.

Draw Conclusions

- When you **draw conclusions**, you form reasonable opinions about what you have read. Use what you know about real life to help you draw conclusions.
- Be sure that there are enough facts or information in the text to support your conclusions.

Directions Read the following scene. Then answer the questions.

> COMMANDER 1 I think we need to be aware that the aliens on Zolta may be dangerous. COMMANDER 2 Why do you think that? Just because they're different from us doesn't mean they are dangerous. COMMANDER 1 Do you want to take that chance? I sure don't want to risk my life because I'm afraid I may hurt some unknown being's feelings. COMMANDER 2 I am only trying to give them the benefit of the doubt. *(The two commanders prepare to leave the ship and explore. COMMANDER 1 takes a ray gun and tranquilizing devices. COMMANDER 2 packs a translator and space ice cream meant to be a gift to the aliens.)* COMMANDER 2 Let me do the talking. COMMANDER 1 Fine, but don't say I didn't warn you!

1. What conclusion can you draw about Commander 1's personality?
Commander 1 is a pessimistic person who fears the worst.
2. What details from the scene support this conclusion?
Commander 1 packs a ray gun and tranquilizer devices.
Commander 1 talks of how dangerous the aliens are.
3. What conclusion can you draw about Commander 2's personality?
Commander 2 is an optimistic person—perhaps too optimistic.
4. What details from the scene support this conclusion?
Commander 2 doesn't want to prejudge the aliens. Commander 2 packs a translator and a gift for the aliens.
5. How did you visualize this scene taking place?
I saw the commanders getting their gear on near the exit door of the space ship. I saw them talking while preparing themselves.

Home Activity Your child drew conclusions by visualizing the details in a scene. Read a story together. Have your child pretend he or she is going to make a movie out of the story. Ask your child to draw out a few of the scenes based on the details he or she visualized.

▲ **Practice Book** p. 187

Develop Vocabulary

PRACTICE LESSON VOCABULARY

As a class complete the following sentence orally. Possible responses are given.

1. When something is *molten*, it is a *(liquid)*.

2. If you *refrain* from doing something, you *(don't do it)*.

3. *Ore* comes from the *(ground)*.

BUILD CONCEPT VOCABULARY

Review previous concept words with students. Ask if students have come across any words today in their reading or elsewhere that they would like to add to the Other Worlds Concept Web, such as *fantasy* or *observing*.

Reader Response

Open for Discussion Personal Response

Think Aloud **MODEL** I'd start by saying that this is not a serious play, but a comedy.

Comprehension Check Critical Response

1. Possible response: Space Cow looks like a regular cow from Earth, but has three horns. ***Author's Purpose***

2. Possible response: The First Officer thinks they are incompetent. Her questioning of the Captain's actions in the first scene and her frustration with the two space cadets in the second scene support this opinion. ***Draw Conclusions***

3. Responses will vary, but should describe costumes and make-up that would help actors to play the parts of Mog and Og. ***Visualize***

4. Responses should be imaginative and include Words to Know. ***Vocabulary***

Look Back and Write For test practice, assign a 10–15 minute time limit. For assessment, see the Scoring Rubric at the right.

Retell

Have students retell *Space Cadets*.

Monitor Progress

Check Retelling Rubric 4 3 2 1

If... students have difficulty retelling the play,	then... use the Retelling Cards and the Scoring Rubric for Retelling on page 495 to help assist fluent retelling.

SUCCESS PREDICTOR

Check Retelling As you ask students to focus on comprehension and provide accurate information about the play, you may need to overlook mistakes in English including inconsistent verb tenses as they retell the play. See the ELL and Transition Handbook.

Reader Response

Open for Discussion Science fiction is about smart humans coping splendidly in alien space, right? Then why is *Space Cadets* so different? How does the play depart from the pattern?

1. The author did not describe the clothes and appearance of Space Cow, so an artist drew an impression. Based on Scene Two, give another description of a Space Cow. **Think Like an Author**

2. How does the First Officer feel about the other members of *Inter Nova Ept*'s crew? Support your answer with information from the play's text. **Draw Conclusions**

3. Mog and Og are supposed to be "creepy-, crawly-looking" aliens. How do you picture the actors as they play these parts? What costumes and make-up do you see them wearing to make them look like the aliens? **Visualize**

4. Draw a picture of the alien planet described as a "strange and exotic world" in this story. Include in the picture all life forms mentioned. Add labels using words from the Words to Know list and from the selection. **Vocabulary**

Look Back and Write Look at page 486. What was *Inter Nova Ept*'s mission, and did it fulfill that mission? Write your answer in the form of a message to Earth.

Meet author David LaBounty on page 786.

494

Scoring Rubric **Look Back and Write**

Top-Score Response A top-score response will use details from page 486 to explain that the *Inter Nova Ept*'s mission was to make first contact, and that it did not fulfill that mission in part.

Example of a Top-Score Response *Inter Nova Ept* to Earth. Message #445. An away team of three officers (well, two cadets and one officer) did succeed in making first contact with an alien life form today. The "space cow" with two pet dogs did not communicate and appeared hostile. Officers quickly left the scene.

For additional rubrics, see p. WA10.

Write Now

TV Script

Prompt

Space Cadets is written as a drama for the stage.

Think about a story that you have read recently.

Now rewrite part of the story as a TV script with dialogue and stage directions.

Student Model

Script begins with title, characters, and setting.

Dialogue and stage directions are presented in an <u>order</u> that makes sense.

Skit follows conventions of plays: Dialogue is not in quotes. Stage directions are in parentheses.

> *A Journey's Beginning*
>
> **CHARACTERS**: John Lewis Solomon, his wife, their four children, a riverboat captain
>
> **SETTING**: Exterior: The banks of the Mississippi River. The family is carrying all of their belongings.
>
> **SOLOMON** (<u>Shouting out to a riverboat</u>): Sir! Sir! I need passage for my family. I can pay.
>
> **CAPTAIN**: Sorry, but I'm afraid I can't. (Captain tries to steer boat away from shore.)
>
> **SOLOMON**: I was a soldier in the Union Army! If you refuse to take us, I will sue you in the United States court!
>
> **CAPTAIN**: No need for that. Prepare to board. (The boat approaches the shore.)

Use the model to help you write your own TV script.

495

Write Now

Look at the Prompt Have students identify and discuss key words and phrases in the prompt. *(drama for the stage, TV script, dialogue, stage directions)*

Strategies to Develop Organization/ Paragraphs

Have students

- read their scripts aloud. Does the scene unfold in an order that makes sense?
- trade scripts with a partner to peer-edit.
- try acting out the scene with friends. Are clearer stage direction needed?

NO: *The characters act strange. Pam is frightened.*

YES: *Max and Min walk backwards and make cooing noises. Pam cowers under the table.*

For additional suggestions and rubric, see pp. 499g–499h.

Hints for Better Writing

- Carefully read the prompt.
- Use a graphic organizer to plan your writing.
- Support your ideas with information and details.
- Use words that help readers understand.
- Proofread and edit your work.

Scoring Rubric — Narrative Retelling

Rubric 4 3 2 1	4	3	2	1
Connections	Makes connections and generalizes beyond the text	Makes connections to other events, stories, or experiences	Makes a limited connection to another event, story, or experience	Makes no connection to another event, story, or experience
Author's Purpose	Elaborates on author's purpose	Tells author's purpose with some clarity	Makes some connection to author's purpose	Makes no connection to author's purpose
Characters	Describes the main character(s) and any character development	Identifies the main character(s) and gives some information about them	Inaccurately identifies some characters or gives little information about them	Inaccurately identifies the characters or gives no information about them
Setting	Describes the time and location	Identifies the time and location	Omits details of time or location	Is unable to identify time or location
Plot	Describes the problem, goal, events, and ending using rich detail	Tells the problem, goal, events, and ending with some errors that do not affect meaning	Tells parts of the problem, goal, events, and ending with gaps that affect meaning	Retelling has no sense of story

Retelling Plan

- ☑ **Week 1** Assess Strategic Intervention students.
- ☑ **Week 2** Assess Advanced students.
- ☑ **Week 3** Assess Strategic Intervention students.
- ☑ **This week assess On-Level students.**
- ☐ **Week 5** Assess any students you have not yet checked during this unit.

Use the Retelling Chart on p. TR16 to record retelling.

Selection Test To assess with *Space Cadets*, use Selection Tests, pp. 73–76.

Fresh Reads for Differentiated Test Practice For weekly leveled practice, use pp. 109–114.

SUCCESS PREDICTOR

Reading Online

- Evaluate online sources.
- Compare and contrast across texts.

PREVIEW/USE TEXT FEATURES

Have students preview "Exploring Space Travel."
Ask:

- **Which URL, or Web address, would probably be more reliable, one ending in .gov or .com? Why?** *(The address ending in .gov because it is put out by the government; a .com Web site is commercial.)*

- **How would you access one of the links on p. 497?** *(You would click on it.)*

If students have trouble evaluating sources, use the Technology Tools Box below.

Link to Science

Have students work in pairs to find the sources on the Internet. Remind them to pay attention to the endings of the Web addresses.

DAY 4 Grouping Options

Reading

Whole Group Discuss the Question of the Day.

Small Group Differentiated Instruction
Read "Exploring Space Travel." See pp. 478f–478g for the small group lesson plan.

Whole Group Use p. 499a.

Language Arts
Use pp. 499e–499k.

Reading Online

New Literacies: PearsonSuccessNet.com

Exploring Space Travel

Evaluating Sources

Genre

- You can find information fast on the Internet. Not all of it will be reliable, truthful, or dependable. You need to think carefully about it.

- You need to learn how to tell reliable from not-so-reliable Web sites. Think carefully about what you know about statements of fact and opinion when evaluating the reliability of a Web site.

Text Features

- The addresses of reliable and useful Web sites often end in .gov, .edu, or .org.

- Web sites that end in .com may also be reliable.

- Use both the source and the descriptions of the Web sites to help narrow your search.

Link to Science

Find two useful and reliable sources on any subject you are studying in science class. Tell why they are useful and reliable.

Let's say you are using the Internet for a report on space travel. You perform an Internet search. Which of these might prove useful for your report? Note both the source of the information and the *description* of the information.

For more practice
Take It to the Net
PearsonSuccessNet.com

496

TECHNOLOGY TOOLS

Evaluating Sources

.com Web site: This kind of site is commercial. Its purpose may be to sell you something. It may or may not be reliable.

.edu Web site: This site is usually produced by an educational institution. Its purpose is to educate. It is usually reliable.

.gov Web site: This site is produced by the government or a government agency. It should have reliable information.

.org Web site: This site is produced by a not-for-profit organization. It may or may not be reliable.

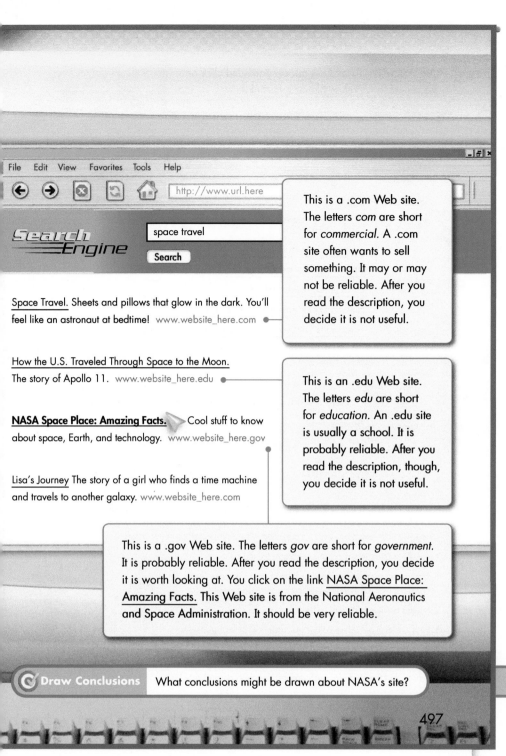

File Edit View Favorites Tools Help

http://www.url.here

Search Engine

space travel

Search

Space Travel. Sheets and pillows that glow in the dark. You'll feel like an astronaut at bedtime! www.website_here.com ●

> This is a .com Web site. The letters *com* are short for *commercial*. A .com site often wants to sell something. It may or may not be reliable. After you read the description, you decide it is not useful.

How the U.S. Traveled Through Space to the Moon. The story of Apollo 11. www.website_here.edu ●

> This is an .edu Web site. The letters *edu* are short for *education*. An .edu site is usually a school. It is probably reliable. After you read the description, though, you decide it is not useful.

NASA Space Place: Amazing Facts. Cool stuff to know about space, Earth, and technology. www.website_here.gov

Lisa's Journey The story of a girl who finds a time machine and travels to another galaxy. www.website_here.com

> This is a .gov Web site. The letters *gov* are short for *government*. It is probably reliable. After you read the description, you decide it is worth looking at. You click on the link NASA Space Place: Amazing Facts. This Web site is from the National Aeronautics and Space Administration. It should be very reliable.

Draw Conclusions What conclusions might be drawn about NASA's site?

497

WEB-IQUETTE

Evaluating Sources

Tell students that while evaluating online sources, there are certain things they should look for and rules of etiquette they should follow:

- Formal language may be one indicator of reliability in a Web site. Informal language and sloppy text (misspellings and poor grammar) may indicate an unreliable source.
- The kind of sponsors a site has may be another clue as to whether it is reliable or not.
- If a site is highly opinionated and does not support its opinions with facts, it is probably unreliable.

NEW LITERACIES: EVALUATING INTERNET RESOURCES

Use the sidebar on p. 496 to guide discussion.

- Tell students when they evaluate Internet resources, they must decide which Web sites contain reliable information and which ones contain questionable information that may be based on opinions more than fact.
- Point out that they can evaluate resources by looking critically at both the source and the description of each Web site. Here, students can use the Internet for information to create a report on space travel. Ask what kind of Web sites might be most useful for this purpose.
- Discuss with students what kinds of things they might look for when evaluating a Web site, such as the end address. Have students name kinds of sites that would have reliable and unreliable information on a topic.

 **AudioText**

Draw Conclusions

Possible response: I would conclude that NASA has reliable information and tries to make it fun and interesting for young people.

Access Content Preview the selection with students, naming and discussing such important features as the search box and URLs.

Strategies for Navigation

USE HEADINGS Explain to students that headings identify topics and subject information that will help them decide if the site has information they can use. By evaluating the headings and their usefulness, students can quickly scan the site and move on to the next one without wasting time.

Use the Strategy

1. The next time you are exploring a Web site, look for headings that identify topics or subjects that are covered in the site.

2. Look for keywords that indicate the kind of information to be found under each heading. Match this with the information you are looking for.

3. If the heading does not have the information you want, don't waste time investigating further. Go on to the next heading.

PRACTICE Think about the ways you evaluate Internet sources at home and at school.

- Make a list of topics that you could explore for information to create a report you are writing.

- The next time you go online, look for Web sites that contain information on these topics.

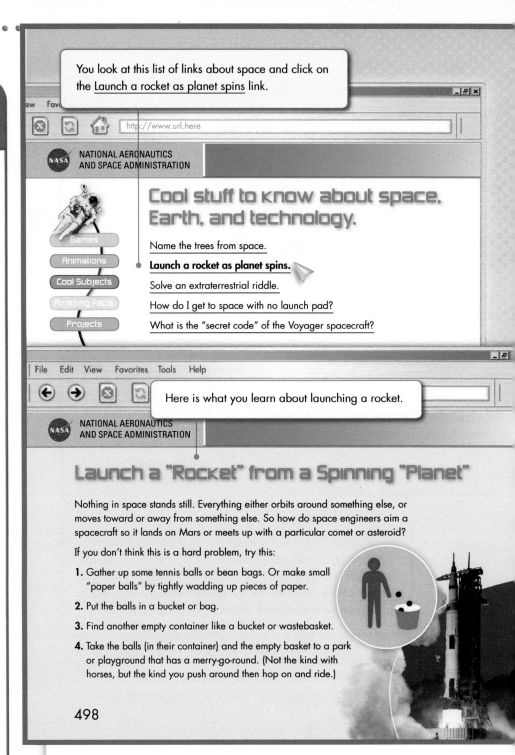

You look at this list of links about space and click on the Launch a rocket as planet spins link.

NATIONAL AERONAUTICS AND SPACE ADMINISTRATION

Cool stuff to know about space, Earth, and technology.

Games
Animations
Cool Subjects
Amazing Facts
Projects

Name the trees from space.

Launch a rocket as planet spins.

Solve an extraterrestrial riddle.

How do I get to space with no launch pad?

What is the "secret code" of the Voyager spacecraft?

File Edit View Favorites Tools Help

Here is what you learn about launching a rocket.

NATIONAL AERONAUTICS AND SPACE ADMINISTRATION

Launch a "Rocket" from a Spinning "Planet"

Nothing in space stands still. Everything either orbits around something else, or moves toward or away from something else. So how do space engineers aim a spacecraft so it lands on Mars or meets up with a particular comet or asteroid?

If you don't think this is a hard problem, try this:

1. Gather up some tennis balls or bean bags. Or make small "paper balls" by tightly wadding up pieces of paper.

2. Put the balls in a bucket or bag.

3. Find another empty container like a bucket or wastebasket.

4. Take the balls (in their container) and the empty basket to a park or playground that has a merry-go-round. (Not the kind with horses, but the kind you push around then hop on and ride.)

498

E L L

Guided Practice If time allows, have students log onto the Internet. Show them how to use headings to find information. Help students make connections between the steps they are doing and related vocabulary terms.

File   Edit   View   Favorites   Tools   Help

http://www.url.here

NATIONAL AERONAUTICS
AND SPACE ADMINISTRATION

5. Place the empty basket on the ground about 9 to 12 feet from the merry-go-round. Then, step up on the merry-go-round with your container of balls.

6. Without moving the merry-go-round, try tossing a few balls into the empty basket.

7. Leave the container of balls on the merry-go-round, hop off, push to get it going slowly. Then hop back on.

8. Try tossing the balls into the basket on the ground as you go around.

Adding the motion makes it a lot harder to hit your target, doesn't it? Now imagine the target is on another spinning merry-go-round on the other side of the playground. Even if your paper balls were real basketballs or baseballs, you'd have a lot of trouble.

The Earth moves around the sun counter-clockwise and the Earth spins around its own axis counter-clockwise. This motion can be used to give a boost to a rocket as it launches.

As you begin to learn more about space travel, you can take notes and extend your research into more areas by using online directories.

Reading Across Texts

Would you use either *Space Cadets* or "Launch a 'Rocket' from a 'Spinning Planet'" to write a report on space travel? What was the author's purpose in each of these?

Writing Across Texts Explain how the author's purpose affects what you learned in each selection.

 Visualize   Mentally picturing each of the eight steps will help you.

499

CONNECT TEXT-TO-TEXT

Reading Across Texts

Have students make a two-column chart to record the information about the similarities and differences between *Space Cadets* and "Exploring Space Travel."

Writing Across Texts Before writing, students may want to be certain they understand the author's purpose for writing each selection.

Visualize

Students should read each step carefully in order to visualize what they are reading. After reading the step, have students close their eyes and create a mental picture of what they have just read.

Fluency Assessment Plan

- ☑ **Week 1** Assess Advanced students.
- ☑ **Week 2** Assess Strategic Intervention students.
- ☑ **Week 3** Assess On-Level students.
- ☑ **This week assess Strategic Intervention students.**
- ☐ **Week 5** Assess any students you have not yet checked during this unit.

Set individual goals for students to enable them to reach the year-end goal.
- Current Goal: 130–138 wcpm
- Year-End Goal: 150 wcpm

Provide opportunities for students to read one-on-one with an aide or parent volunteer, if possible. The adult models by reading first, and the child reads and rereads the same text, with adult guidance. Allow extra repetitions for English language learners, to improve their fluency.

To develop fluent readers, use Fluency Coach.

DAY 5   Grouping Options

Reading
Whole Group
Revisit the Question of the Week.

Small Group
Differentiated Instruction
Reread this week's Leveled Readers. See pp. 478f–478g for the small group lesson plan.

Whole Group
Use pp. 499b–499c.

Language Arts
Use pp. 499d–499l.

CHARACTERIZATION/DIALOGUE
Fluency

DAY 1

Model Reread "MUSH, a Dog from Space" on p. 478m. Explain that you will use your tone of voice to express the personality of each character and the content of their dialogue as you read. Model for students as you read.

DAY 2

Echo Reading Read aloud p. 486. Have students notice how the dialogue between the First Officer and the Captain reveal their characters. Have them do three echo readings of p. 486.

DAY 3

Model Read aloud p. 491. Have students note how you change the tone of your voice for each character, using stage directions to reflect the characters' feelings. Practice as a class by doing three echo readings.

DAY 4

Partner Reading Partners practice reading aloud p. 491, three times. Students should read the dialogue naturally, keeping character in mind, and offer each other feedback.

Monitor Progress   Check Fluency WCPM

As students reread, monitor their progress toward their individual fluency goals. Current Goal: 130–138 words correct per minute. End-of-Year Goal: 150 words correct per minute.

If... students cannot read fluently at a rate of 130–138 words correct per minute,
then... make sure students practice with text at their independent level. Provide additional fluency practice, pairing nonfluent readers with fluent readers.

If... students already read at 150 words correct per minute,
then... they do not need to reread three to four times.

SUCCESS PREDICTOR

DAY 5

Assessment
Individual Reading Rate Use the Fluency Assessment Plan and do a one-minute timed reading of either selection from this week to assess students in Week 4. Pay special attention to this week's skill, characterization/dialogue. Provide corrective feedback for each student.

RETEACH

Draw Conclusions

TEACH

Review with students that a conclusion is a reasonable opinion based on what students have read and what they know about real life. Students can complete Practice Book p. 188 on their own, or you can complete it as a class. Point out that they should check their facts and details for accuracy before reaching their conclusions and placing them in their graphic organizers.

ASSESS

Have partners use pp. 490–491, to draw a conclusion about the First Officer's opinion of Space Cadet Tom *(She doesn't think very highly of his abilities).* Then ask students to identify the information in the dialogue and stage directions that led them to draw this conclusion *(Tom misinterprets what a first-contact mission is and the First Officer rolls her eyes, a sign of disbelief).*

For additional instruction of drawing conclusions, see DI·55.

EXTEND SKILLS

Exaggeration

TEACH

Exaggeration is something overstated and made greater than it actually is. An author can use exaggeration to emphasize a point for either serious or comic effect. In *Space Cadets,* exaggeration is mostly used for comedic effect.

- Exaggeration does not often signal itself. It is up to the reader to recognize it and infer its purpose.

- Understatement is the opposite of exaggeration, or hyperbole. Unlike exaggeration, it is done almost exclusively for humorous or satiric effect.

Read the fifth speech on p. 487. Help students recognize the use of exaggeration and discuss why the author uses it here.

ASSESS

Have students work in pairs to write about the exaggeration on p. 487. Ask:

1. What effect does the Captain's exaggerated speech have on the Ensign? Is this funny or serious?

2. Having read the rest of the play, why is the Captain's assessment of Tom and Harold humorous?

OBJECTIVES

- Draw conclusions.
- Recognize exaggeration.

Skills Trace

Draw Conclusions

Introduce/Teach	TE: 6.3 372–373; 6.4 478–479; 6.6 724–725
Practice	Practice Book: 143, 147, 148, 183, 187, 188, 283, 287, 288
Reteach/Review	**TE: 6.3 307, 399b, DI•56; 6.4 499b, DI•55; 6.6 681, 707, 715, 749b, DI•55**
Test	Selection Test: 57–60, 73–76, 113–116; Benchmark Test: Unit 6

ELL

Access Content Reteach the skill by reviewing the Picture It! lesson on draw conclusions in the ELL Teaching Guide, pp. 127–128.

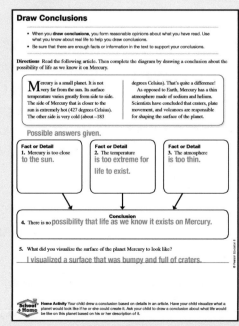

▲ **Practice Book** p. 188

Vocabulary and Word Study

VOCABULARY STRATEGY
Context Clues

MULTIPLE-MEANING WORDS Explain to students that they may come across a word that has more than one meaning when reading. In this case, students will have to look for context clues to determine the correct meaning of the word. Have students identify words with multiple meanings in *Space Cadets*. They can complete a chart like one shown to list the different meanings of the word, any useful context clues, and a definition that fits the context of the sentence. Students can check their definitions in a dictionary.

Word	Possible Meanings	Context Clues	Definition
reason	1. cause or explanation	"talking for no reason"	cause or explanation
	2. ability to think		
	3. to think logically		

Homophones

Homophones are words that are pronounced the same but have different spellings, origins, and meanings, such as "ore" and "or." Have partners brainstorm other homophones and use a dictionary to check spellings and meanings. Then have them make a list of homophones and meanings.

Some Homophones

wait to stay or stop until something happens	**weight** how heavy a thing is
eight a number one more than seven	**ate** past tense of eat
sow to scatter seed	**sew** to work with needle and thread

BUILD CONCEPT VOCABULARY
Other Worlds

LOOKING BACK Remind students of the question of the week: How can we be open to new understandings? Discuss how this week's Concept Web of vocabulary words relates to the theme of outer space. Ask students if they have any words or categories to add. Discuss if words and categories are appropriately related to the concept.

MOVING FORWARD Preview the title of the next selection, *Inventing the Future*. Ask students which Concept Web words might apply to the new selection based on the title alone. Put a star next to these words on the Web.

Display the Concept Web and revisit the vocabulary words as you read the next selection to check predictions.

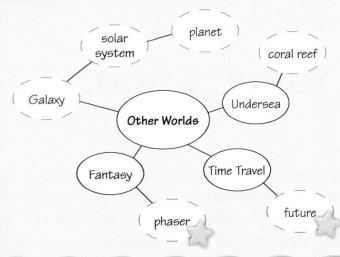

Monitor Progress	
Check Vocabulary	
If... students suggest words or categories that are not related to the concept,	then... review the words and categories on the Concept Web and discuss how they relate to the lesson concept.

SUCCESS PREDICTOR

Speaking and Listening

SPEAKING

Newscast

SET-UP Have students look for information about the search for life on other planets. They should then plan and give newscasts to the class.

VISUAL AIDS Tell students to present photos, graphs, and other visual aids that will support their main points. They should make sure all audience members can see their visual aids clearly. Students should organize all the visuals in the proper sequence so they will not be shown at the wrong time during their newscast.

ADAPTATION Advise students to stay calm and be adaptable if something unexpected happens during their newscast. Share these suggestions:

- If a bell rings or there is some other disruption during your newscast, wait for it to pass, take a deep breath, and then continue.

- If you are running out of time, don't rush. Eliminate unnecessary details and get to the conclusion.

Delivery Tips
- Speak clearly and fluently.
- Avoid long pauses and fillers such as like, you know, I mean, and um.
- Stand or sit up straight.
- Make eye contact with the audience.

LISTENING

Listen to Media

Have students listen to a television newscast in class or at home. They can answer these questions orally or in writing.

1. **What is the speaker's tone, mood, and emotion?** *(Responses will vary but should reflect an understanding of these speaking elements, noting that most newscasters are neutral in tone.)*

2. **Are the speaker's statements facts, opinions, or both? How does this affect your reaction to what he or she says?** *(Reponses will vary but should show an understanding of the difference between facts and opinions, noting that newscasters generally stick to facts, leaving opinion to the viewer.)*

3. **Do the details of the news story support its main idea?** *(Responses will vary but should reflect an understanding of main ideas and supporting details. Students should qualify their answers by describing one particular story and naming a few details.)*

ELL

Support Vocabulary Use the following to review and extend vocabulary and to explore lesson concepts further:
- ELL Poster 19, Days 3–5 instruction
- Vocabulary Activities and Word Cards in ELL Teaching Guide, pp. 129–130

Assessment For information on assessing students' speaking and listening, see the ELL and Transition Handbook.

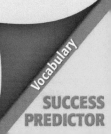

Grammar
Indefinite and Reflexive Pronouns

Monitor Progress

Grammar	
If... students have difficulty identifying indefinite and reflexive pronouns,	then... provide additional instruction and practice in The Grammar and Writing Book pp. 158-161.

DAILY FIX-IT

This week use Daily Fix-It Transparency 19.

Spiral REVIEW

ELL

Support Grammar See the Grammar Transition lessons in the ELL and Transition Handbook.

▲ **The Grammar and Writing Book**
For more instruction and practice, use pp. 158–161.

DAY 1 — Teach and Model

DAILY FIX-IT

1. Can he walk to the acadamy by hisself? *(academy; himself)*

2. The space ships deparshure time was unknown. *(ship's; departure)*

READING-GRAMMAR CONNECTION

Write these sentences about *Space Cadets* on the board:

> *Someone must bring peace to the galaxy. Maya thinks she can do it herself.*

Explain that *someone* is a singular **indefinite pronoun.** It does not refer to a specific person. *Herself* is a **reflexive pronoun.** It reflects the action of the verb *do* back upon the subject *Maya.*

Display Grammar Transparency 19. Read aloud the definitions and sample sentences. Work through the items.

Indefinite and Reflexive Pronouns

Indefinite pronouns may not refer to specific words. They do not always have definite antecedents: No one got a new uniform.
Some common indefinite pronouns are listed below:

Singular Indefinite Pronouns	Plural Indefinite Pronouns
someone, somebody, anyone, anybody, everyone, everybody, something, no one, either, each	few, several, both, others, many, all, some

- Use singular verb forms with singular indefinite pronouns and plural verb forms with plural indefinite pronouns: Everyone wants to go into space. Few will go.

Reflexive pronouns reflect the action of the verb back upon the subject.
Reflexive pronouns end in *-self* or *-selves*: The cadet imagined herself a hero.

Singular Reflexive Pronouns	Plural Reflexive Pronouns
himself, herself, myself, itself, yourself	ourselves, yourselves, themselves

- There are no such words as *hisself, theirself, theirselves,* or *ourself.*

Directions Underline the correct indefinite pronoun(s) in ( ) to complete each sentence.

1. (Few, No one) wonder where the captain is heading.
2. (Nobody, Many) of the cadets laugh during the humorous performance.
3. I struggle to understand the computer system while (anybody, others) learn it right away.
4. The captain hopes (each, both) knows the way to the space port.
5. (Everyone, Several) stands on the bridge of the spacecraft waiting for (their, his or her) orders.
6. (Some, Somebody) leaves the hatch open until (all, each) have left the spaceship.

Directions Write the correct reflexive pronoun from the box to complete each sentence.

| yourself | myself | himself | itself | themselves | ourselves |

7. The cadets give **themselves** enough time to dress every morning.
8. The officer usually does the paperwork **himself**.
9. I asked **myself** why I had become a cadet.
10. The ensign could not transmit the data, so we did it **ourselves**.
11. You will have to cook the Volorean space slugs **yourself**.
12. A spaceship can be programmed to fly **itself**.

Unit 4 Space Cadets — Grammar **19**

▲ **Grammar Transparency** 19

DAY 2 — Develop the Concept

DAILY FIX-IT

3. Capt Smith did not want to critisize the cadets. *(Capt.; criticize)*

4. Both planets rotates in the same direction. *(rotate; direction)*

GUIDED PRACTICE

Review the concept of indefinite and reflexive pronouns.

- **Indefinite pronouns**, such as *someone* and *nobody*, do not always have definite antecedents.

- **Reflexive pronouns** reflect the action of the verb back upon the subject. Reflexive pronouns end in *-self* or *-selves.*

- There are no such words as *hisself, theirself, theirselves,* or *ourself.*

HOMEWORK Grammar and Writing Practice Book p. 73. Work through the first two items with the class.

Indefinite and Reflexive Pronouns

Indefinite pronouns may not refer to specific words. They do not always have definite antecedents: Someone needs to press her uniform.
Some common indefinite pronouns are listed below:

Singular Indefinite Pronouns	Plural Indefinite Pronouns
someone, somebody, anyone, anybody, everyone, everybody, something, no one, either, each	few, several, both, others, many, all, some

- Use singular verb forms with singular indefinite pronouns and plural verb forms with plural indefinite pronouns: Everyone wants to fly a spaceship. Few do it well.

Reflexive pronouns reflect the action of the verb back upon the subject. Reflexive pronouns end in *-self* or *-selves:* The cadet wanted to see the planet himself.

Singular Reflexive Pronouns	Plural Reflexive Pronouns
himself, herself, myself, itself, yourself	ourselves, yourselves, themselves

- There are no such words as *hisself, theirself, theirselves,* or *ourself.*

Directions Underline the correct indefinite pronoun in ( ) to complete each sentence.

1. Does (few, anyone) see the horizon?
2. (Several, Everyone) believe that the planet is habitable.
3. (Many, No one) have volunteered to travel to the M-class planet.
4. If (others, somebody) pilots the spaceship, Tom will go along.

Directions Write the correct reflexive pronoun to complete each sentence.

| yourselves | myself | himself | ourselves |

5. We may have to defend **ourselves** against the alien life forms.
6. I **myself** will represent Earth Command.
7. You cannot allow **yourselves** to be captured by the aliens.
8. Tom blamed **himself** for putting the crew in danger.

Home Activity Your child learned about indefinite and reflexive pronouns. Ask your child to circle three indefinite pronouns in a newspaper article and identify whether each is singular or plural.

▲ **Grammar and Writing Practice Book** p. 73

DAY 3 — Apply to Writing

5. Neither Harry nor Candace study the originle manual. *(studies; original)*

6. I feeled sick traveling in space? *(felt; space.)*

WRITE REFLEXIVE PRONOUNS

Remind students that reflexive pronouns can be first, second, and third person, as well as singular and plural.

• Have students check their writing to see if it can be improved by adding reflexive and indefinite pronouns.

HOMEWORK Grammar and Writing Practice Book p. 74.

Indefinite and Reflexive Pronouns

Directions Write a sentence using the indefinite pronoun and the correct verb in ( ).

1. everyone (listen, listens) Possible answers:
Everyone listens to the First Officer.

2. several (learns, learn)
Several learn the aliens' language.

3. no one (understands, understand)
No one understands how the aliens communicate.

4. both (walk, walks)
Both of the aliens walk toward the spaceship.

5. somebody (is, are)
Somebody is on the planet.

6. everything (fall, falls)
On Earth, everything falls back to the ground.

Directions Write a sentence using the reflexive pronoun. Possible answers:

7. myself
I wanted to go myself, but my brother insisted on going.

8. themselves
Cary and Lil bought themselves tickets to the play.

 Home Activity Your child learned how to use indefinite and reflexive pronouns in writing. Have your child write a note to his or her teacher using two indefinite or two reflexive pronouns and tell you which is which.

▲ **Grammar and Writing Practice Book** p. 74

DAY 4 — Test Preparation

7. The Moon walk was an inspration to us all. *(moon; inspiration)*

8. Somebody lost their way while on the planet *(his or her; planet.)*

STANDARDIZED TEST PREP

Test Tip

When taking tests, watch for incorrect reflexive pronouns.

Incorrect: hisself, theirself, theirselves, or ourself

Correct: himself, themselves, or ourselves

HOMEWORK Grammar and Writing Practice Book p. 75.

Indefinite and Reflexive Pronouns

Directions Mark the letter of the pronoun(s) that complete each sentence.

1. Roger tried to fly the spaceship ____.
 A hisself
 B himself
 C yourself
 D ourselves

2. ____ is falling apart on our spaceship.
 A Others
 B Myself
 C Everything
 D Many

3. ____ have failed the training program.
 A Many
 B Somebody
 C No one
 D Yourself

4. The officers regard ____ as professional pilots.
 A anything
 B yourselves
 C herself
 D themselves

5. Claire taught ____ how to pilot a space cruiser.
 A yourself
 B herself
 C hisself
 D herselves

6. ____ enlist in the space cadet program to see the universe.
 A Ourselves
 B Both
 C Everyone
 D Somebody

7. The crew is lost because ____ knows how to set the coordinates.
 A nobody
 B many
 C themselves
 D both

8. If ____ volunteers for the spacewalk, will be rewarded.
 A everyone, they
 B anyone, he or she
 C anyone, they
 D ourselves, we

9. ____ may have to prepare ____ for combat.
 A Many, they
 B Ourselves, he
 C We, ourselves
 D We, yourself

10. ____ want to do it ____ without the captain's help.
 A We, themselves
 B He, himself
 C We, ourselves
 D We, yourself

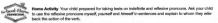 **Home Activity** Your child prepared for taking tests on indefinite and reflexive pronouns. Ask your child to use the reflexive pronoun *myself, yourself* and *himself* in sentences and explain to whom they refer back the action of the verb.

▲ **Grammar and Writing Practice Book** p. 75

DAY 5 — Cumulative Review

9. The officer's spoke to Rourke and I. *(officers; me)*

10. There knowledge of histry was evident. *(Their; history)*

ADDITIONAL PRACTICE

Assign pp. 158–161 in The Grammar and Writing Book.

EXTRA PRACTICE Grammar and Writing Practice Book pp. 140.

TEST PREPARATION Grammar and Writing Practice Book pp. 155–156.

ASSESSMENT

CUMULATIVE REVIEW Grammar and Writing Practice Book p. 76.

Indefinite and Reflexive Pronouns

Directions Underline the correct word in ( ) to complete each sentence.

1. Everyone (<u>thinks</u>, think) the captain is strange because he talks to himself.

2. Many of the space pilots (practices, <u>practice</u>) on the flight simulator.

3. Everybody (<u>studies</u>, study) the Space Cadet Training Guide.

4. The captain assures us that nothing (are, <u>is</u>) going to stop our journey.

5. Both of the boys (stumbles, <u>stumble</u>) onto the bridge.

6. (<u>Several</u>, One) of them have gone back to Earth for training.

7. The alarm is sounding because (many, <u>something</u>) is wrong!

8. (<u>Both</u>, Anyone) of the officers train to become Star Generals.

9. The aliens approach the landing party, but (few, <u>nobody</u>) panics.

10. (Everyone, <u>Both</u>) shows (their, <u>his</u>) best manners.

Directions Write the correct reflexive pronoun from the box to complete each sentence.

> yourself   myself   herself   themselves   ourselves

11. The First Officers designed the training program **themselves**

12. I am not interested in space travel **myself**

13. We introduced **ourselves** to Og and Mog.

14. Do not leave **yourself** open to an attack by the hostile aliens.

15. Molly prepares the officers' lunch **herself**

 **Home Activity** Your child reviewed indefinite and reflexive pronouns. Have your child make up a slogan for a favorite product using one indefinite pronoun or one reflexive pronoun.

▲ **Grammar and Writing Practice Book** p. 76

Writing Workshop   TV Script

OBJECTIVES

- Identify features of a TV script.
- Write a TV script with stage directions.
- Focus on organization/paragraphs.
- Use a rubric.

Genre TV Script
Writer's Craft Stage Directions
Writing Trait Organization/Paragraphs

Organization/Paragraphs Explain that transition words make order clear in writing. Write *first, next, then, after, before, also,* and *but* on index cards, one to a card, and model their meaning and use. Help language learners use these transition words in their writing.

Writing Traits

FOCUS/IDEAS Strong dialogue and stage directions support clear action.

ORGANIZATION/PARAGRAPHS Events are arranged in sequence. Stage directions signal a shift in setting.

VOICE The writing is engaging and lively. The writer shows knowledge of the subject.

WORD CHOICE The writer uses specific words to create vivid images.

SENTENCES Dialogue includes natural speech elements such as sentence fragments.

CONVENTIONS There is excellent control and accuracy.

READING-WRITING CONNECTION

- *Space Cadets* is organized as a drama for the stage.
- Stage directions make the characters' actions and emotions clear.
- Students will write a **TV script** using stage directions to organize the action.

MODEL ORGANIZATION/PARAGRAPHS

Display Writing Transparency 19A. Then discuss the model and the writing trait of organization/paragraphs.

 Think Aloud When I read this TV script, I see that it is well organized. There is a specific format. The characters and setting are listed at the top to tell me who will be speaking and where. The conversation then flows in a logical, sequential order. Stage directions help me to imagine the characters' actions and emotions.

TV Script

A TV script, or play written to be performed on television, is similar to a story. It has characters, plot, setting, and dialogue. A TV script is also similar to a play. It has stage directions.

O'Brien's Dilemma
adapted from Mother Fletcher's Gift

Script begins with title, characters, and setting. → **CHARACTERS:**
Officer O'Brien, a New York City police officer
Mother Fletcher

SETTING: Interior: A small but spotless bedroom. O'BRIEN is standing by a bed. MOTHER FLETCHER is sitting upright in the bed, looking stern.)

Dialogue reveals character traits. → **O'BRIEN** (getting out his pad): What's your name, please?
MOTHER FLETCHER: I'm Mother Fletcher. How are you going to get me an ambulance?
O'BRIEN: We can't just call an ambulance for anyone.
MOTHER FLETCHER: Look here! I am not just anyone. I am Mother Fletcher. Use that radio of yours.

Stage directions help with mood and action. → (O'BRIEN flips out his radio and calls dispatch.)
O'BRIEN: All right, Ma'am. (to radio) Dispatch, I have a 519 here at 221 145th Street, requesting an ambulance. Subject is—(to MOTHER FLETCHER) What is your age?
MOTHER FLETCHER (glaring at him): Full grown.
(Fade to black.)

Unit 4 Space Cadets   Writing Model **19A**

▲ **Writing Transparency** 19A

WRITER'S CRAFT
Stage Directions

Display Writing Transparency 19B. Read the directions and work together to create stage directions.

Think Aloud **STAGE DIRECTIONS** Tomorrow we will be writing a TV script. I will include stage directions so that the reader can imagine the characters' actions and emotions. If one character asks, "How are you?" and another character says, "Fine," you might not know how to read the conversation. But if I add stage directions, such as (putting a hand on her shoulder) and (fighting back tears), the meaning becomes clear.

GUIDED WRITING Some students may need more help with stage directions. Refer back to the selection about Elizabeth Blackwell and show students how stage directions set the scene and advance the action.

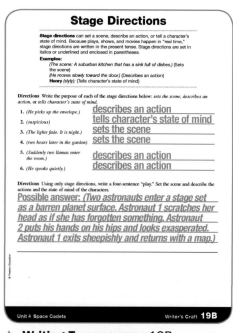

▲ **Writing Transparency** 19B

DAY 3 Prewrite and Draft

READ THE WRITING PROMPT
on page 495 in the Student Edition.

Space Cadets *is written as a drama for the stage.*

Think about a story that you have read recently.

Now rewrite part of the story as a TV script with dialogue and stage directions.

Writing Test Tips

- Replace long descriptions with dialogue.
- Make sure your characters speak and act naturally.
- Short stage directions can connect to the dialogue. Put longer directions, such as the setting, in their own paragraphs.

GETTING STARTED Students can do any of the following:

- Work with a group to dramatize a story. Discuss how the selection could be rewritten as a script.
- Watch a video recording of a short TV segment, and write a script for the segment.
- Imagine a scene in your mind, and then write what the characters say.

DAY 4 Draft and Revise

EDITING/REVISING CHECKLIST

☑ Do my stage directions establish character and setting?

☑ Does my dialogue sound natural?

☑ Do I use indefinite and reflexive pronouns correctly?

☑ Are related words spelled correctly?

See *The Grammar and Writing Book,* pp. 158–163.

Revising Tips

Organization/ Paragraphs

- Make sure each line of dialogue for a speaker has its own paragraph.
- Show stage directions by putting them in parentheses. Underline them if you are writing by hand. Italicize them if you are typing.
- Give longer stage directions their own paragraphs.

PUBLISHING Students can perform their scripts for the class. Some students may wish to revise their work later.

ASSESSMENT Use the scoring rubric to evaluate students' work.

DAY 5 Connect to Unit Writing

	Story
Week 1	News Story 429g–429h
Week 2	Story About an Animal 455g–455h
Week 3	Setting 477g–477h
Week 4	TV Script 499g–499h
Week 5	Summary 527g–527h

PREVIEW THE UNIT PROMPT

Write a story about an adventure, a discovery, or something that happened to you for the first time. Use some of these literary devices: foreshadowing, tension, suspense, conflict, humor.

APPLY

- A story has a beginning, middle, and end and focuses on one incident or event.
- Using dialogue in a story makes characters more realistic and helps readers understand them.

Writing Trait Rubric

	4	3	2	1
Organization/ Paragraphs	Events told in sequence; uses stage directions	Events in logical order; some stage directions	Events in scene lacking sequence; few stage directions	Lacking sequence of events; no stage directions
	TV script format correct	TV script format mostly correct	TV script format attempted	TV script lacking format

Spelling & Phonics **Related Words 1**

DAY 1 Pretest and Sort

DAY 2 Think and Practice

OBJECTIVE

● Spell related words.

Generalization

Connect to Phonics Related words often have parts that are spelled the same but pronounced differently: **po̲e̲m**, **po̲e̲tic**.

Spelling Words

1. poem	11. critic
2. poetic	12. criticize
3. direct	13. history
4. direction	14. historic
5. origin	15. academy*
6. original	16. academic
7. combine	17. inspire
8. combination	18. inspiration
9. repeat	19. depart
10. repetition	20. departure

Challenge Words

21. erode	24. maintenance
22. erosion	25. confiscate
23. maintain	26. confiscation

*Word from the selection

ELL

Spelling/Phonics Support See the ELL and Transition Handbook for spelling support.

PRETEST

Use the Dictation Sentences from Day 5 to administer the pretest. Read the word, read the sentence, and then read the word again. Guide students in self-correcting their pretests and correcting any misspellings.

Monitor Progress

Spelling

If...	then...
If... students misspell more than 5 pretest words,	then... use words 1–10 for Strategic Intervention.
If... students misspell 1–5 pretest words,	then... use words 1–20 for On-Level practice.
If... students correctly spell all pretest words,	then... use words 1–26 for Advanced Learners.

HOMEWORK Spelling Practice Book, p. 73.

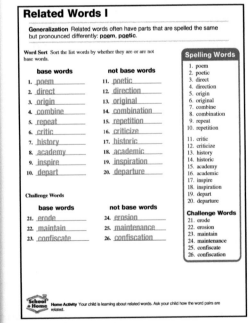

▲ **Spelling Practice Book** p. 73

TEACH

Some words have the same root and similar spelling, but their pronunciations are different. Demonstrate this by writing each spelling word on the board. Have students spell and say each word aloud and explain the different pronunciations of each pair of words.

> repeat
> repetition

FIND THE PATTERN Ask students to group the pairs of spelling words that are related.

HOMEWORK Spelling Practice Book, p. 74.

▲ **Spelling Practice Book** p.74

DAY 3 Connect to Writing

WRITE A NEWS ARTICLE

Have students write a news article, using at least five spelling words. Have students read their articles aloud, or publish them in a class newspaper.

Frequently Misspelled Words

always   myself

These words are difficult for some sixth-graders to spell. Point out that there is only one *l* in *always*. Alert students to these frequently misspelled words and encourage them to think carefully before spelling them.

HOMEWORK Spelling Practice Book, p. 75.

Related Words I

Proofread a Script Circle six spelling errors in the script. Write the words correctly. Find a sentence in the script with a punctuation error. Write it correctly.

Spelling Words: poem, poetic, direct, direction, origin, original, combine, combination, repeat, repetition, critic, criticize, history, historic, academy, academic, inspire, inspiration, depart, departure

Time Out
(Nico is in his room, working on a school project Eric enters.)
Nico: (sighing with frustration) I don't mean to criticize but you're always tardy, Eric.
Eric: (taking off his jacket) Yeah, I'm sorry. I just wanted to finish watching my favorite TV program.
Nico: If you repete this pattern, we'll never finish this history project, or I'll end up doing most of the work myself. It's supposed to be a combenation of our work.
Eric: (shrugging with resignation) I said I was sorry. It seems like time just flies by.
Nico: I know. But it's important that you be here on time. If we miss the deadline we'll be the laughing stock of the acadimy I'll let you borrow my watch until this project is finished if you promise me you'll be prompt from now on. Is that a deal?
Eric: (breaking into a broad grin) Sure. I'll try to be more ackadimic
Nico: Okay then. Now let's get to work.

Frequently Misspelled Words: always, myself

1. criticize   2. repeat
3. history   4. combination
5. academy   6. academic
7. Nico is in his room, working on a school project.

Proofread Words Circle the word that is spelled correctly. Write it on the line.

8. origin   8. origin
9. origenal (original)   9. original
10. cumbine (combine)   10. combine

Home Activity Your child identified misspelled words. Ask your child to identify the words that are most difficult for him or her to spell.

▲ **Spelling Practice Book** p. 75

DAY 4 Review

REVIEW RELATED WORDS

Have students work individually or in pairs to create word-search puzzles. Then have students exchange puzzles and try to solve them.

Spelling Strategy
Related Words

Even though they have different sounds, related words include similar letter combinations, which can make spelling them easier. Have students consider the parts of the words that are similar in spelling.

HOMEWORK Spelling Practice Book, p. 76.

Related Words I

Spelling Words:
poem	poetic	direct	direction	origin
original	combine	combination	repeat	repetition
critic	criticize	history	historic	academy
academic	inspire	inspiration	depart	departure

Related Words Write a related list word for each word below.

1. criticize   1. critical
2. origin   2. original
3. depart   3. departure
4. history   4. historic
5. direct   5. direction
6. academy   6. academic
7. poem   7. poetic
8. inspire   8. inspiration
9. repeat   9. repetition
10. combine   10. combination

Word Search Find and circle ten list words in the word search. Write the words on the lines.

11. academic
12. combination
13. criticize
14. departure
15. direction
16. historic
17. inspiration
18. original
19. poetic
20. repetition

Home Activity Your child has learned to spell related words. Ask your child to pick a list word from Exercises 1-10 and tell how the spelling of the base word changed when the ending was added.

▲ **Spelling Practice Book** p. 76

DAY 5 Posttest

DICTATION SENTENCES

1. She wrote a <u>poem</u> for her mother.
2. Her words were quite <u>poetic</u>.
3. Would you like to <u>direct</u> the play?
4. What is the first <u>direction</u> to take?
5. I don't know the <u>origin</u> of her fear of snakes.
6. This is an <u>original</u> song.
7. Will you <u>combine</u> all the ingredients?
8. I forgot the <u>combination</u> to my lock.
9. Please <u>repeat</u> after me.
10. Sometimes <u>repetition</u> can help you learn.
11. The <u>critic</u> did not like the show.
12. Why do you always <u>criticize</u> me?
13. Her favorite subject is <u>history</u>.
14. This is an <u>historic</u> event.
15. He went to a military <u>academy</u>.
16. She is good at <u>academic</u> subjects.
17. Let the music <u>inspire</u> you.
18. What is the <u>inspiration</u> for his poem?
19. We will <u>depart</u> at nine.
20. Our <u>departure</u> was late.

CHALLENGE

21. The cliff will <u>erode</u> in the rain.
22. We studied <u>erosion</u> in school.
23. You must <u>maintain</u> your home.
24. Who does the <u>maintenance</u> work?
25. Dad will <u>confiscate</u> the candy.
26. The <u>confiscation</u> of the game was punishment for playing in class.

OBJECTIVES

- Formulate an inquiry question that is connected to this week's lesson focus.
- Effectively and efficiently find, evaluate, and communicate information related to an inquiry question using electronic sources.

New Literacies	
Day 1	**Identify Questions**
Day 2	**Navigate/Search**
Day 3	**Analyze**
Day 4	**Synthesize**
Day 5	**Communicate**

NEW LITERACIES

Internet Inquiry Activity

EXPLORE LIFE ON OTHER PLANETS

Use the following 5-day plan to help students conduct this week's Internet inquiry activity on life on other planets. Remind students to follow classroom rules when using the Internet.

DAY 1

Identify Questions Discuss the lesson focus question: *How can we be open to new understandings?* Brainstorm ideas for specific inquiry questions about the possibilities of life on other planets. Have students work individually, in pairs, or in small groups to write an inquiry question they would like answered.

DAY 2

Navigate/Search Explain how to begin a simple Internet search using a student-friendly search engine. Point out that a search engine does not search the Internet directly, but examines a database of Web pages compiled by computer robot programs, called *spiders.* Have students determine keywords related to their inquiry questions. Then have them identify specific Web sites they want to visit.

DAY 3

Analyze Have students explore the Web sites they identified on Day 2. Tell them to scan each site and determine if it provides reliable information. They should ask themselves: Who is the author writing or organization sponsoring this Web site? Are they objective in their viewpoint and what is their relationship to the topic? When was the site last updated? Students can print out and highlight relevant information or take notes.

DAY 4

Synthesize Have students synthesize information from Day 3. Remind them that when they synthesize, they combine relevant ideas and information from different sources in their own words to develop an answer to their inquiry question.

DAY 5

Communicate Have students share their inquiry results. They can use a word-processing program to create a short informational news article on the possibility of life on other planets.

Follow and Clarify Directions

OBJECTIVES

- Review terms to name parts of a set of directions.
- Use directions to complete a task or make something.

TEACH

Ask students what kind of information they might need to make a model of an alien creature. Students may need prompting before they mention directions. Show a set of directions for making a recipe or a model and define these features.

- The **steps** or **instructions** in a set of directions are usually numbered and ordered in a logical sequence.

- **Illustrations** are pictures that accompany directions and help people to visualize what to do in each step.

- **Diagrams** are drawings that show how something is put together. They are visual aids that make directions easier to follow. The parts of a diagram are usually labeled.

Have students work in small groups, and give each group a set of directions. Each group identifies the steps of the directions and any illustrations and diagrams. Then, discuss these questions:

1. **How would you proceed to use the directions?** *(I would follow one step after another in sequence.)*

2. **What kind of illustration might you find in these directions?** *(Possible response: a picture of the finished product.)*

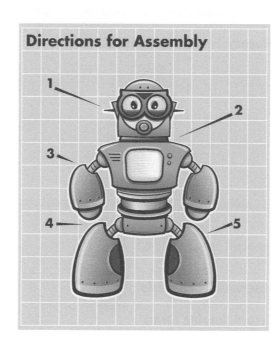

Directions for Assembly

Follow and Clarify Directions

- *Following directions* involves doing or making something. *Clarifying directions* means writing clear directions for others to use.
- Directions usually are numbered. The numbers tell you the sequence of the steps. Read all directions before starting to act on the first direction given. Visualize the purpose or the end result of the directions while reading.

Directions Read the following set of directions.

How to Make a Papier-Mâché Planet

1. Gather the following items: all-purpose flour; water; balloon; old newspapers; large mixing bowl; measuring cups; mixing spoon; old newspapers; paint brush.

2. In a large mixing bowl, combine three cups of water to one cup of flour. Stir together until you have a smooth mixture. (You may double or triple this recipe depending upon size and number of your papier mâché planets.)

3. Cut the old newspapers into two-inch-wide strips. Cover designated work space with the rest of the newspaper.

4. Blow up your balloon to the desired size of your planet. Tie a knot at the bottom of it.

5. Place strips of paper into the mixing bowl. Use a paintbrush or your hands to wet the strips with the mixture. Place the strips of paper onto your balloon. Try to crisscross the strips of paper (or overlap them to form X's) as you add them to the balloon. Cover the entire balloon.

6. Allow the balloon to dry thoroughly before advancing on to the next step.

7. Gather the following items: clean paintbrush; paints of desired colors; paper towels; water; small bowl.

8. Choose the appropriate colors to paint your planet. You may want to consult an encyclopedia or another reference book with pictures or illustrations of the planets to get a good idea of what they look like. Paint your planet accordingly. Make sure to rinse your paintbrush in the small bowl of water between colors. Use the paper towels to wipe off your paintbrushes after painting.

9. Let the balloon dry completely. Cut a small slit into your papier-mâché surface. Insert a needle to pop the balloon. Pull the popped balloon out of the papier-mâché mold.

10. Display your planet for all to see and admire.

▲ **Practice Book** p. 189

Directions Use the directions to answer the following questions.

1. If you were actually going to make a papier-mâché planet what is the first thing you need to do?
   Read all the directions.

2. In what step do you blow up the balloon?
   step 4

3. How could popping the balloon too early change your end result?
   You may end up with a misshapen planet.

4. How could the directions in step 6 be clarified?
   The directions could include how long it should dry.

5. Why do you think the directions include two steps in which you gather materials?
   The papier mâché must dry before you start decorating. The first set of materials also needs to be cleaned up before decorating.

6. How could the directions in step 3 be clarified?
   It could tell you how long to cut the strips of paper, instead of only how wide.

7. Will this project always take the same amount of time to complete?
   No, because it depends on the size of your planets as well as how many you are making.

8. How does visualizing help you to follow directions?
   You can see the product in your head, so you have an idea about how it is supposed to look when it is finished.

9. Is there any way the steps in this process could be changed while getting the same final product?
   Possible answer: Yes, steps 2 and 3 could be switched, and you would still get the same product.

10. Add a direction to the end of this set that explains how to display the papier-mâché planet.
    Students' directions should offer interesting ways to display the planet.

School + Home Home Activity Your child answered questions about a set of directions. Have your child write a set of directions to perform a task that he or she knows well. Help your child to write as clear and accurate directions as possible.

▲ **Practice Book** p. 190

ASSESS

As students work with directions, check that they can identify numbered steps, illustrations, and diagrams. Suggest that students read all the directions first before starting on the first step.

For more practice or to assess students, use Practice Book pp. 189–190.

AFTER READING

Assessment Checkpoints *for the Week*

Selection Assessment

Use pp. 73–76 of Selection Tests to check:

 Selection Understanding

 Comprehension Skill *Draw Conclusions*

 Selection Vocabulary

aliens	ore
barge	refrain
hospitable	universal
molten	version

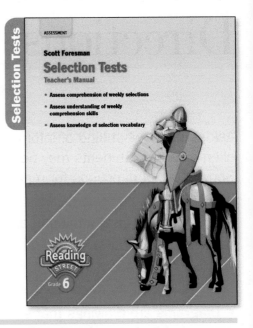

Leveled Assessment

On-Level

Strategic Intervention

Advanced

Use pp. 109–114 of Fresh Reads for Differentiated Test Practice to check:

 Comprehension Skill *Draw Conclusions*

 REVIEW **Comprehension Skill** *Sequence*

 Fluency *Words Correct Per Minute*

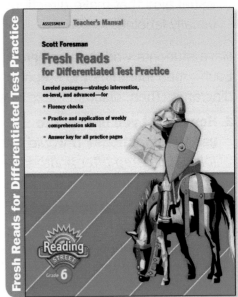

Managing Assessment

Use Assessment Handbook for:

 Observation Checklists

 Record-Keeping Forms

 Portfolio Assessment

Unit 4
Explorers, Pioneers, and Discoverers

Week 5

EXPAND THE CONCEPT
How do inventions happen?

CONCEPT QUESTION

How have those who've gone first influenced others who've gone after?

Week 1

What drives people to explore harsh climates and dangerous places?

Week 2

Why is it important to study animals responsibly?

Week 3

What does it mean to be a pioneer?

Week 4

How can we be open to new understandings?

Week 5

How do inventions happen?

CONNECT THE CONCEPT

▶ **Build Background**
contemplated, invaluable, model

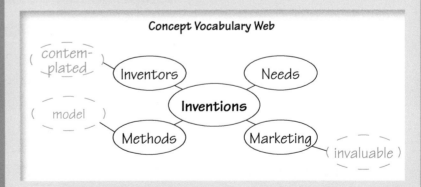

Concept Vocabulary Web

contemplated · Inventors · Needs · Inventions · model · Methods · Marketing · invaluable

▶ **Science Content**
Scientific Inquiry, Phonographs and Music, Scientific Careers, Traffic Signals

▶ **Writing**
Summary

▶ **Internet Inquiry**
Inventions

Preview Your Week

How do inventions happen?

Inventing the Future
A Photobiography of Thomas Alva Edison

by Marfé Ferguson Delano

Genre A **biography** is the story of a real person's life written by another person. Before you read, think about what you may already know about Thomas Edison.

504

Why are Thomas Edison's inventions so important to us today?

Student Edition pages 504–521

Audio CD

Genre	Biography
Vocabulary Strategy	Word Structure
Comprehension Skill	Author's Purpose
Comprehension Strategy	Monitor and Fix Up

Paired Selection

Reading Across Texts
Compare Thomas Edison and Garrett Morgan

Genre
Biography

Text Features
Section Headings
Active Portrayal of Subject

Social Studies in Reading

Biography

Genre
- Biography is nonfiction centered on someone's life but written by another person.
- Biographies are usually organized according to time—the sequence in which events happened in the person's life.

Text Features
- The author uses section headings to separate topics within Garrett Morgan's life to help the reader more easily organize the concepts.
- The author writes about Garrett Morgan doing things. This shows that Garrett Morgan controlled his life and behavior rather than passively letting the things happen. As you read, look for words that show Garrett Morgan taking active control.

Link to Social Studies
Biographies describe events in the lives of important people. Write a short biography of someone important in your life.

Garrett Augustus Morgan

Garrett Augustus Morgan was an African American businessman and inventor whose curiosity and innovation led to the development of many useful and helpful products. A practical man of humble beginnings, Morgan devoted his life to creating things that made the lives of other people safer and more convenient.

Among his inventions was an early traffic signal that greatly improved safety on America's streets and roadways. Indeed, Morgan's technology was the basis for modern traffic signal systems and was an early example of what we know today as Intelligent Transportation Systems.

The Inventor's Early Life

The son of former slaves, Garrett A. Morgan was born in Paris, Kentucky, on March 4, 1877. His early childhood was spent attending school and working on the family farm with his brothers and sisters. While still a teenager, he left Kentucky and moved north to Cincinnati, Ohio, in search of opportunity.

Although Morgan's formal education never took him beyond elementary school, he hired a tutor while living in Cincinnati and continued his studies in English grammar.

In 1895, Morgan moved to Cleveland, Ohio, where he went to work as a sewing machine repairman for a clothing manufacturer. News of his proficiency for fixing things and experimenting traveled fast and led to numerous job offers from various manufacturing firms in the Cleveland area.

In 1907, Morgan opened his own sewing equipment and repair shop. It was the first of several businesses he would establish. In 1909, he expanded the enterprise to include a tailoring shop that employed 32 employees. The new company turned out coats, suits, and dresses, all sewn with equipment that Morgan himself had made.

In 1920, Morgan moved into the newspaper business when he established the *Cleveland Call*. As the years went on, he became a prosperous and widely respected business-man, and he was able to purchase a home and an automobile. Indeed it was Morgan's experience while driving along the streets of Cleveland that led to the invention of the nation's first patented traffic signal.

A sewing machine from the early 1900s

Monitor & Fix-Up How could you keep track of all these dates?

524

Student Edition pages 524–527

Audio CD

Leveled Readers

🔵 **Skill** Author's Purpose

🔵 **Strategy** Monitor and Fix Up

Lesson Vocabulary

Below-Level

On-Level

Advanced

ELL Reader

· Concept Vocabulary
· Text Support
· Language Enrichment

Integrate Science Standards

• Inventions
• Technology and Society

✓ Read

Inventing the Future,
pp. 504–521

"Garrett Augustus Morgan,"
pp. 524–527

Leveled Readers

Below-Level · Support Concepts

On-Level · Develop Concepts

Advanced · Extend Concepts
· Science Extension Activity

ELL Reader

✓ Build

Concept Vocabulary

Inventions, pp. 500l–500m

✓ Teach

Science Concepts

Scientific Inquiry, p. 511
Phonographs, p. 515
Scientific Careers, p. 519
Traffic Signals, p. 525

✓ Explore

Science Center

Design an Invention, p. 500k

Weekly Plan

READING

45–90 minutes

TARGET SKILLS OF THE WEEK

Comprehension Skill
Author's Purpose

Comprehension Strategy
Monitor and Fix Up

Vocabulary Strategy
Word Structure

DAY 1
PAGES 500l–502b, 527a, 527e–527k

Oral Language

QUESTION OF THE WEEK *How do inventions happen?*

Read Aloud: "Inventing the Stethoscope," 500m
Build Concepts, 500l

Comprehension/Vocabulary

Comprehension Skill/Strategy Lesson, 500–501
- Author's Purpose **T**
- Monitor and Fix Up

Build Background, 502a

Introduce Lesson Vocabulary, 502b

converts, devise, efficiency, generated, percentage, proclaimed, reproduce, transmitted **T**

Read Leveled Readers

Grouping Options 500f–500g

Fluency

Model Punctuation Clues, 500l–500m, 527a

DAY 2
PAGES 502–513, 527a, 527e–527k

Oral Language

QUESTION OF THE DAY *What do you think motivated Edison to work so hard?*

Comprehension/Vocabulary

Vocabulary Strategy Lesson, 502–503
- Word Structure **T**

Read *Inventing the Future: A Photobiography of Thomas Alva Edison,* 504–513

Grouping Options 500f–500g

- Author's Purpose **T**
- Monitor and Fix Up
- **REVIEW** Cause and Effect **T**
  Develop Vocabulary

Fluency

Echo Reading, 527a

LANGUAGE ARTS

30–60 minutes

Trait of the Week

Focus/Ideas

Grammar, 527e
Introduce Using *Who* and *Whom* **T**

Writing Workshop, 527g
Introduce Summary
Model the Trait of the Week: Focus/Ideas

Spelling, 527i
Pretest for Word Endings *–ty, –ity, –tion*

Internet Inquiry, 527k
Identify Questions

Grammar, 527e
Develop Using *Who* and *Whom* **T**

Writing workshop, 527g
Improve Writing with Know Your Purpose

Spelling, 527i
Teach the Generalization

Internet Inquiry, 527k
Navigate/Search

DAILY WRITING ACTIVITIES

Day 1 Write to Read, 500	Day 2 Words to Write, 503 Strategy Response Log, 504, 513

DAILY SCIENCE CONNECTIONS

Day 1 Inventions Concept Web, 500l	Day 2 Time for Science: Scientific Inquiry, 511 Revisit the Inventions Concept Web, 513

DAILY SUCCESS PREDICTORS
for Adequate Yearly Progress

Monitor Progress and Corrective Feedback

Vocabulary

Check Vocabulary, *500l*

RESOURCES FOR THE WEEK

- Practice Book, *pp. 191–200*
- Word Study and Spelling Practice Book, *pp. 77–80*
- Grammar and Writing Practice Book, *pp. 77–80*

- Selection Test, *pp. 77–80*
- Fresh Reads for Differentiated Test Practice, *pp. 115–120*
- The Grammar and Writing Book, *pp. 164–169*

Grouping Options for Differentiated Instruction

Turn the page for the small group lesson plan.

DAY 3 PAGES 514–523, 527a, 527e–527k

Oral Language

QUESTION OF THE DAY *What factor do you think was most responsible for Edison's success as an inventor? Why?*

Comprehension/Vocabulary

Read *Inventing the Future: A Photobiography of Thomas Alva Edison, 514–522*

Grouping Options
500f–500g

- Author's Purpose **T**
- Monitor and Fix Up
- Word Structure **T**
- **REVIEW** Cause and Effect **T**

Develop Vocabulary

Reader Response
Selection Test

Fluency

Model Punctuation Clues, 527a

Grammar, 527f
Apply Using *Who* and *Whom* in Writing **T**

Writing Workshop, 523, 527h
Write Now
Prewrite and Draft

Spelling, 527j
Connect Spelling to Writing

Internet Inquiry, 527k
Analyze Sources

Day 3 Strategy Response Log, 520
Look Back and Write, 522

Day 3 Time for Science: Phonographs and Music, 515;
Scientific Careers in Electricity, 519
Revisit the Inventions Concept Web, 521

DAY 4 PAGES 524–527a, 527e–527k

Oral Language

QUESTION OF THE DAY *What qualities make a person a successful inventor?*

Comprehension/Vocabulary

Read "Garret Augustus Morgan," 524–527

Grouping Options
500f–500g

Biography

Reading Across Texts

Content-Area Vocabulary

Fluency

Partner Reading, 527a

Grammar, 527f
Practice Using *Who* and *Whom* for Standardized Tests **T**

Writing Workshop, 527h
Draft, Revise, and Publish

Spelling, 527j
Provide a Strategy

Internet Inquiry, 527k
Synthesize Information

Day 4 Writing Across Texts, 527

Day 4 Time for Science: History of Traffic Signals, 525

DAY 5 PAGES 527a–527l

Oral Language

QUESTION OF THE WEEK *To wrap up the week, revisit the Day 1 question.*
Build Concept Vocabulary, 527c

Fluency

Read Leveled Readers

Grouping Options 500f–500g

Assess Reading Rate, 527a

Comprehension/Vocabulary

- Reteach Author's Purpose, 527b **T**
- Steps in a Process, 527b
- Review Word Structure, 527c **T**

Speaking and Viewing, 527d
Advertisement
Analyze a Photo

Grammar, 527f
Cumulative Review

Writing Workshop, 527h
Connect to Unit Writing

Spelling, 527j
Posttest for Word Endings *–ty, -ity, -tion*

Internet Inquiry, 527k
Communicate Results

Research/Study Skills, 527l
Advertisements

Day 5 Steps in a Process, 527b

Day 5 Revisit the Inventions Concept Web, 527c

KEY = Target Skill **T** = Tested Skill

Comprehension Check Retelling, *522*

Fluency Check Fluency WCPM, *527a*

Vocabulary Check Vocabulary, *527c*

SUCCESS PREDICTOR

Small Group Plan *for Differentiated Instruction*

Daily Plan
AT A GLANCE

Reading
Whole Group
- Oral Language
- Comprehension/Vocabulary

Group Time
Differentiated Instruction

Meet with small groups to provide:
- Skill Support
- Reading Support
- Fluency Practice

Read

This week's lessons for daily group time can be found behind the Differentiated Instruction (DI) tab on pp. DI·42–DI·51.

Whole Group
- Fluency

Language Arts
- Grammar
- Writing
- Spelling
- Research/Inquiry
- Speaking/Listening/Viewing

DAY 1

On-Level	Strategic Intervention	Advanced
Teacher-Led *Page DI · 43*	**Teacher-Led** *Page DI · 42*	**Teacher-Led** *Page DI · 43*
• Develop Concept Vocabulary • **Read** On-Level Reader *Inventors at Work*	• Reinforce Concepts • **Read** Below-Level Reader *Electricity*	• **Read** Advanced Reader *It's About Time!* • Independent Extension Activity

ⓘ Independent Activities
While you meet with small groups, have the rest of the class...

- Visit the Reading/Library Center
- Listen to the Background Building Audio
- Finish Write to Read, p. 500
- Complete Practice Book pp. 193–194
- Visit Cross-Curricular Centers

DAY 2

On-Level	Strategic Intervention	Advanced
Teacher-Led *Pages 506–513*	**Teacher-Led** *Page DI · 44*	**Teacher-Led** *Page DI · 45*
• **Read** *Inventing the Future*	• Practice Lesson Vocabulary • Read Multisyllabic Words • **Read** or Listen to *Inventing the Future*	• Extend Vocabulary • **Read** *Inventing the Future*

ⓘ Independent Activities
While you meet with small groups, have the rest of the class...

- Visit the Reading/Library Center
- Listen to AudioText for *Inventing the Future*
- Finish Words to Write, p. 503
- Complete Practice Book pp. 195–196
- Write in their Strategy Response Logs, pp. 504, 513
- Visit Cross-Curricular Centers
- Work on inquiry projects

DAY 3

On-Level	Strategic Intervention	Advanced
Teacher-Led *Pages 514–521*	**Teacher-Led** *Page DI · 46*	**Teacher-Led** *Page DI · 47*
• **Read** *Inventing the Future*	• Practice Author's Purpose and Monitor and Fix Up • **Read** or Listen to *Inventing the Future*	• Extend Author's Purpose and Monitor and Fix Up • **Read** *Inventing the Future*

ⓘ Independent Activities
While you meet with small groups, have the rest of the class...

- Visit the Reading/Library Center
- Listen to the AudioText for *Inventing the Future*
- Write in their Strategy Response Logs, p. 520
- Finish Look Back and Write, p. 522
- Complete Practice Book p. 197
- Visit Cross-Curricular Centers
- Work on inquiry projects

---

① Begin with whole class skill and strategy instruction.

② Meet with small groups to provide differentiated instruction.

③ Gather the whole class back together for fluency and language arts.

DAY 4

On-Level	Strategic Intervention	Advanced
Teacher-Led *Pages 524–527*	**Teacher-Led** *Page DI·48*	**Teacher-Led** *Page DI·49*
• **Read** "Garrett Augustus Morgan"	• **Read** or Listen to "Garrett Augustus Morgan"	• **Read** "Garrett Augustus Morgan" • Genre Study

ⓘ Independent Activities

While you meet with small groups, have the rest of the class...

• Visit the Reading/Library Center
• Listen to the AudioText for "Garrett Augustus Morgan"
• Visit the Writing/Vocabulary Center

• Finish Writing Across Texts, p. 527
• Visit Cross-Curricular Centers
• Work on inquiry projects

DAY 5

On-Level	Strategic Intervention	Advanced
Teacher-Led *Page DI·51*	**Teacher-Led** *Page DI·50*	**Teacher-Led** *Page DI·51*
• **Reread** Leveled Reader *Inventors at Work* • Retell *Inventors at Work*	• **Reread** Leveled Reader *Electricity* • Retell *Electricity*	• **Reread** Leveled Reader *It's About Time!* • Share Extension Activity

ⓘ Independent Activities

While you meet with small groups, have the rest of the class...

• Visit the Reading/Library Center
• Complete Practice Book pp. 198–200

• Visit Cross-Curricular Centers
• Work on inquiry projects

Grouping Place English language learners in the groups that correspond to their reading abilities in English.

Use the appropriate Leveled Reader or other text at students' instructional level.

TiP Send home the appropriate Multilingual Summary of the main selection on Day 1.

Take It to the NET
ONLINE
PearsonSuccessNet.com

Sharon Vaughn
For ideas on professional development, see the article "The Role of Mentoring . . . " by Scott Foresman authors S. Vaughn and M. Coleman.

TEACHER TALK

An **idiom** is a phrase that cannot be understood from the ordinary meaning of the words that form it, such as "hold your tongue." Idioms are especially difficult for English language learners.

Be sure to schedule time for students to work on the unit inquiry project "Going First." This week students produce posters showing information about the groups they researched.

Looking Ahead

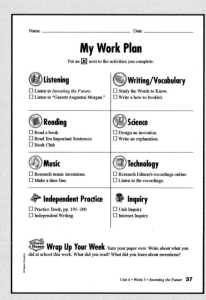

▲ **Group-Time Survival Guide**
p. 37, Weekly Contract

☑ Customize Your Plan *by Strand*

ORAL LANGUAGE

Science

Concept Development

How do inventions happen?

CONCEPT VOCABULARY
contemplated   invaluable   model

BUILD

☐ **Question of the Week** Introduce and discuss the question of the week. This week students will read a variety of texts and work on projects related to the concept *inventions*. Post the question for students to refer to throughout the week. DAY 1 *500d*

☐ **Read Aloud** Read aloud "Inventing the Stethoscope." Then begin a web to build concepts and concept vocabulary related to this week's lesson and the unit theme, Explorers, Pioneers, and Discoverers. Introduce the concept words *contemplated*, *invaluable*, and *model* and have students place them on the web. Display the web for use throughout the week. DAY 1 *500l–500m*

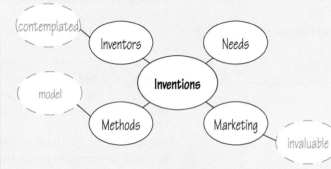

DEVELOP

☐ **Question of the Day** Use the prompts from the Weekly Plan to engage students in conversations related to this week's reading and the unit theme. **EVERY DAY** *500d–500e*

☐ **Concept Vocabulary Web** Revisit the Inventions Concept Web and encourage students to add concept words from their reading and life experiences. DAY 2 *513*, DAY 3 *521*

CONNECT

☐ **Looking Back** Revisit the Inventions Concept Web and discuss how it relates to this week's lesson and the unit theme. DAY 5 *527c*

CHECK

☐ **Concept Vocabulary Web** Use the Inventions Concept Web to check students' understanding of the concept vocabulary words *contemplated*, *invaluable*, and *model*. DAY 1 *500l*, DAY 5 *527c*

VOCABULARY

STRATEGY WORD STRUCTURE
Word structure is the way parts of a word are put together, or arranged. Many words have prefixes that may help you figure out the meaning of a word you don't know. When you come across an unfamiliar word with a prefix, first see if you can identify the base word; if necessary, look for context clues. Then add the meaning of the prefix: *re-* means "again;" *pro-* means "to remove" or "the opposite of;" and *trans-* means "across," "beyond," or "through."

LESSON VOCABULARY
converts	percentage
devise	proclaimed
efficiency	reproduce
generated	transmitted

TEACH

☐ **Words to Know** Give students the opportunity to tell what they already know about this week's lesson vocabulary words. Then discuss word meaning. DAY 1 *502b*

☐ **Vocabulary Strategy Lesson** Use the vocabulary strategy lesson in the Student Edition to introduce and model this week's strategy, *word structure*. DAY 2 *502–503*

Vocabulary Strategy Lesson

PRACTICE/APPLY

☐ **Leveled Text** Read the lesson vocabulary in the context of leveled text. DAY 1 *LR37–LR45*

☐ **Words in Context** Read the lesson vocabulary and apply *word structure* in the context of *Inventing the Future*. DAY 2 *504–513*, DAY 3 *514–522*

Leveled Readers

☐ **Writing/Vocabulary Center** Write a set of instructions for being a successful inventor. **ANY DAY** *500k*

☐ **Homework** Practice Book pp. 194–195. DAY 1 *502b*, DAY 2 *503*

Main Selection—Drama

☐ **Word Play** Have students work with partners to list 5 to 10 words associated with a new technology of their choice, then define the words. **ANY DAY** *527c*

ASSESS

☐ **Selection Test** Use the Selection Test to determine students' understanding of the lesson vocabulary words. DAY 3

RETEACH/REVIEW

☐ **Reteach Lesson** If necessary, use this lesson to reteach and review *word structure*. DAY 5 *527c*

Use assessment data to determine your instructional focus.

Preview this week's instruction by strand.

Choose instructional activities that meet the needs of your classroom.

COMPREHENSION

SKILL AUTHOR'S PURPOSE An author's purpose is the reason that an author writes. Authors write to persuade, inform, express ideas or feelings, or entertain. Preview the title, headings, and pictures to help predict the author's purpose, then adjust your reading speed.

STRATEGY MONITOR AND FIX UP When you monitor and fix up, you stop occasionally in your reading to check that you understand what you're reading. If you're confused, you do something to help you understand, such as rereading or reading more slowly.

TEACH

❑ **Skill/Strategy Lesson** Use the skill/strategy lesson in the Student Edition to introduce and model *author's purpose* and *monitor and fix up*. DAY 1 *500-501*

❑ **Extend Skills** Teach steps in a process. **ANY DAY** *527b*

Skill/Strategy Lesson

PRACTICE/APPLY

❑ **Leveled Text** Apply *author's purpose* and *monitor and fix up* to read leveled text. DAY 1 *LR37-LR45*

Leveled Readers

❑ **Skills and Strategies in Context** Read *Inventing the Future*, using the Guiding Comprehension questions to apply *author's purpose* and *monitor and fix up*. DAY 2 *504-513*, DAY 3 *514-522*

Main Selection—Drama

❑ **Skills and Strategies in Context** Read " Garrett Augustus Morgan," guiding students as they apply *author's purpose* and *monitor and fix up*. Then have students discuss and write across texts. DAY 4 *524-527*

❑ **Homework** Practice Book pp. 193, 197, 198. DAY 1 *501*, DAY 3 *521*, DAY 5 *527b*

Paired Selection—Nonfiction

❑ **Fresh Reads for Differentiated Test Practice** Have students practice *author's purpose* with a new passage. DAY 3

ASSESS

❑ **Selection Test** Determine students' understanding of the selection and their use of *author's purpose*. DAY 3

❑ **Retell** Have students retell *Inventing the Future*. DAY 3 *522-523*

RETEACH/REVIEW

❑ **Reteach Lesson** If necessary, reteach and review *author's purpose*. DAY 5 *527b*

FLUENCY

SKILL PUNCTUATION CLUES Punctuation clues are punctuation marks such as commas, dashes, semicolons, colons, and periods that tell you to pause or stop at appropriate points. Punctuation marks such as the exclamation point and question mark also tell you that the characters are feeling some kind of emotion.

TEACH

❑ **Read Aloud** Model fluent reading by rereading "Inventing the Stethoscope." Focus on this week's fluency skill, punctuation clues. DAY 1 *500l-500m, 527a*

PRACTICE/APPLY

❑ **Echo Reading** Read aloud selected paragraphs from *Inventing the Future*, having students notice how you pause and chunk together the words set apart by commas or dashes. Then practice as a class by doing three echo readings of the paragraphs. DAY 2 *527a*, DAY 3 *527a*

❑ **Partner Reading** Partners practice reading aloud, using punctuation to guide their phrasing and offering each other feedback. As students reread, monitor their progress toward their individual fluency goals. DAY 4 *527a*

❑ **Listening Center** Have students follow along with the AudioText for this week's selections. **ANY DAY** *500j*

❑ **Reading/Library Center** Have students reread a selection of their choice. **ANY DAY** *500j*

❑ **Fluency Coach** Have students use Fluency Coach to listen to fluent readings or practice reading on their own. **ANY DAY**

ASSESS

❑ **Check Fluency** WCPM Do a one-minute timed reading, paying special attention to this week's skill—punctuation clues. Provide feedback for each student. DAY 5 *527a*

GRAMMAR

SKILL **USING *WHO* AND *WHOM*** *Who* is a pronoun that is used as a subject. *Whom* is a pronoun that is used as a direct object and the object of a preposition. Most often, *whom* will be a direct object in a question.

TEACH

☐ **Grammar Transparency 20** Use Grammar Transparency 20 to teach using who and whom. **DAY 1** *527e*

Grammar Transparency 20

PRACTICE/APPLY

☐ **Develop the Concept** Review the concept of using who and whom and provide guided practice. **DAY 2** *527e*

☐ **Apply to Writing** Have students review something they have written and apply using who and whom. **DAY 3** *527f*

☐ **Test Preparation** Examine common errors in using who and whom to prepare for standardized tests. **DAY 4** *527f*

☐ **Homework** Grammar and Writing Practice Book pp. 77–79. **DAY 2** *527e*, **DAY 3** *527f*, **DAY 4** *527f*

ASSESS

☐ **Cumulative Review** Use Grammar and Writing Practice Book p. 80. **DAY 5** *527f*

RETEACH/REVIEW

☐ **Daily Fix-It** Have students find and correct errors in grammar, spelling, and punctuation. **EVERY DAY** *527e–527f*

☐ **The Grammar and Writing Book** Use pp. 164–167 of The Grammar and Writing Book to extend instruction for using who and whom. **ANY DAY**

The Grammar and Writing Book

WRITING

Trait of the Week

FOCUS/IDEAS Good writers focus on a main idea and develop this idea with strong, supporting details. In addition, they know their purpose for writing. This purpose may be to persuade, to inform, to describe, or to entertain. The purpose is important because it helps focus the main idea. For example, when you write a summary, your purpose is to inform. Your writing must be brief and focused on only the most important information.

TEACH

☐ **Writing Transparency 20A** Use the model to introduce and discuss the Trait of the Week. **DAY 1** *527g*

☐ **Writing Transparency 20B** Use the transparency to show students how knowing their purpose can improve their writing. **DAY 2** *527g*

Writing Transparency 20A   **Writing Transparency 20B**

PRACTICE/APPLY

☐ **Write Now** Examine the model on Student Edition p. 523. Then have students write their own summaries. **DAY 3** *523, 527h*, **DAY 4** *527h*

> **Prompt** *Inventing the Future* provides information about Edison's groundbreaking discoveries. Think about an interesting article or story that you have read recently. Now write a summary explaining what the article or story is about.

Write Now p. 523

☐ **Writing/Vocabulary Center** Write a set of instructions for being a successful inventor. **ANY DAY** *500k*

ASSESS

☐ **Writing Trait Rubric** Use the rubric to evaluate students' writing. **DAY 4** *527h*

RETEACH/REVIEW

☐ **The Grammar and Writing Book** Use pp. 164–169 of The Grammar and Writing Book to extend instruction for using who and whom, know your purpose, and summaries. **ANY DAY**

The Grammar and Writing Book

Use assessment data to determine your instructional focus.

Preview this week's instruction by strand.

Choose instructional activities that meet the needs of your classroom.

SPELLING

GENERALIZATION WORD ENDINGS -ty, -ity, -tion When -ty, -ity, and -tion are added to some words, one or more letters may change: social, society. The new word has a different pronunciation from the base word.

TEACH

❑ **Pretest** Give the pretest for words ending in -ty, -ity, -tion. Guide students in self-correcting their pretests and correcting any misspellings. DAY 1 527i

❑ **Think and Practice** Connect spelling to the phonics generalization for words ending in -ty, -ity, -tion. DAY 2 527i

PRACTICE/APPLY

❑ **Connect to Writing** Have students use spelling words to write a journal entry. Then review frequently misspelled words: *finally, really*. DAY 3 527j

❑ **Homework** Phonics and Spelling Practice Book pp. 77–80. EVERY DAY

RETEACH/REVIEW

❑ **Review** Review spelling words to prepare for the posttest. Then provide students with a spelling strategy—problem parts. DAY 4 527j

ASSESS

❑ **Posttest** Use dictation sentences to give the posttest for words ending in -ty, -ity, -ion. DAY 5 527j

Spelling Words

1. electricity*
2. equality
3. society
4. specialty*
5. celebrity*
6. recognition
7. description
8. reduction
9. tradition
10. loyalty
11. security
12. clarity
13. popularity
14. certainty
15. cruelty
16. subscription
17. reputation*
18. intention
19. deception
20. penalty

Challenge Words

21. pronunciation
22. hospitality
23. subtlety
24. technicality
25. demonstration

*Word from the selection

RESEARCH AND INQUIRY

❑ **Internet Inquiry** Have students conduct an Internet inquiry on inventions. EVERY DAY 527k

❑ **Advertisements** Review the parts of a print advertisement, such as product shot, headline, body copy, and signature. Have small groups of students find advertisements and identify the parts and persuasive techniques. DAY 5 527l

❑ **Unit Inquiry** Allow time for students to produce posters showing information about the groups they researched. ANY DAY 407

SPEAKING AND VIEWING

❑ **Advertisement** Have students choose one of Edison's inventions and prepare an oral advertisement that might have been given at a public event in Edison's time. DAY 5 527d

❑ **Analyze a Photo** Have students look closely at the photograph at the top of p. 516, then answer questions orally or in writing. DAY 5 527d

Resources for
Differentiated Instruction

LEVELED READERS

▶ **Comprehension**
- **Skill** Author's Purpose
- **Strategy** Monitor and Fix Up

▶ **Lesson Vocabulary**
- **Word Structure**

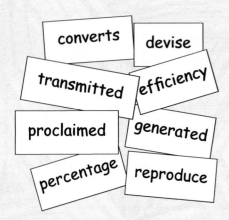

converts · devise · transmitted · efficiency · proclaimed · generated · percentage · reproduce

▶ **Science Standards**
- Inventions
- Technology and Society

Leveled Reader Database ONLINE

PearsonSuccessNet.com

Use the Online Database of over 600 books to

- Download and print additional copies of this week's leveled readers.
- Listen to the readers being read online.
- Search for more titles focused on this week's skills, topic, and content.

On-Level Reader

Author's Purpose

- The **author's purpose** is the reason or reasons an author has for writing.
- An author may have one or more reasons for writing. He or she may want to **inform, persuade, entertain,** or **express** a mood or feeling.

Directions Read the sentences below and write the author's purpose on the line.

1. The strange noises in the night gave him a chill. __express or entertain__
2. There is a growing problem with pollution in this area. __inform__
3. Detective Spade knew she was getting close when she heard a tiny knocking sound. __entertain__
4. Everyone should go out and show our school spirit! __persuade__
5. Scientists have come up with a better way to cure infections. __inform__
6. A dog in New Zealand had a record number of 24 puppies in one litter! __inform__
7. She was dressed in a beautiful, red, sparkling dress. __express__
8. We must vote to make a difference. __persuade__
9. Write a sentence that persuades.
   __Sentences will vary.__
10. Write a sentence that entertains.

On-Level Practice TE p. LR41

Vocabulary
Directions Choose a word from the box that matches each definition.

Check the Words You Know
___converts ___devise ___efficiency ___generated
___percentage ___proclaimed ___reproduce ___transmitted

1. __proclaimed__ made known publicly
2. __efficiency__ the act of doing something without wasting time
3. __transmitted__ sent along

Directions Choose a word from the box that matches each synonym.

4. __converts__ changes
5. __percentage__ part
6. __devise__ invent
7. __reproduce__ copy
8. __generated__ created

Directions Write three sentences using a vocabulary word from the box.
9. __Sentences will vary.__
10.
11.

On-Level Practice TE p. LR42

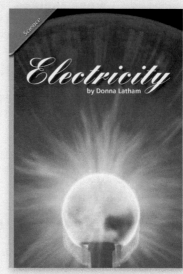

Below-Level Reader

Author's Purpose

- The **author's purpose** is the reason or reasons an author has for writing.
- An author may have one or more reasons for writing. He or she may want to **inform, persuade, entertain,** or **express** a mood or feeling.

Directions Write a letter to a friend to persuade him to join the soccer team. Then write a letter to inform him of the team and sport.

Persuade
__Responses will vary.__

Inform
__Responses will vary.__

Below-Level Practice TE p. LR38

Vocabulary
Directions Choose a word from the box that matches each definition.

Check the Words You Know
___convert ___devise ___efficiency ___generate ___percentage ___proclaim ___reproduce ___transmitted

1. __transmitted__ sent along
2. __proclaim__ to make known publicly
3. __efficiency__ to do something without wasting time
4. __devise__ to invent
5. __reproduce__ to copy

Directions Choose a word from the box that means the opposite of each word.

6. __generate__ destroy
7. __convert__ keep the same
8. __percentage__ whole

Directions Choose four words from the box and write sentences about electricity.
9. __Sentences will vary.__
10.
11.
12.

Below-Level Practice TE p. LR39

Advanced

Advanced Reader

Author's Purpose

An **author's purpose** is his or her reason for writing. There are four main reasons for writing: to **persuade, inform, entertain,** and **express.**

Directions Answer the questions below.   Possible responses are given.

1. What is the author's purpose for starting *It's About Time* with a question?
   To grab the reader's attention; to make the reader think.

2. Why did the author write *It's About Time?*
   To inform

3. Did the author succeed in meeting her purpose?
   Responses will vary.

4. In what ways did the author succeed in her purpose?
   Responses will vary.

5. What was the author's purpose for using photographs, charts, and diagrams?
   To help the reader better understand the text

Advanced Practice TE p. LR44

Vocabulary

Directions Use the vocabulary words in the box to fill in the blanks in the sentences below.

Check the Words You Know			
__analog	__chronometer	__digital	__elusive
__latitude	__longitude	__meridian	__millennium

1. The longitude lines are imaginary lines extending from north to south.
2. Some younger kids may not be familiar with analog clocks.
3. Measuring time accurately is a more elusive problem than many realize.
4. Computer clocks are set in a digital format.

Directions Write the word that belongs with each group.

5. time-keeping instrument, clock, chronometer
6. horizontal "lines" circling Earth, measures north and south of equator, latitude
7. starting "line" for telling time, meridian
8. ten centuries, a thousand years, millennium

Directions Write four sentences about time using a vocabulary word.

9. Sentences will vary.

10. _____
11. _____
12. _____

Advanced Practice TE p. LR45

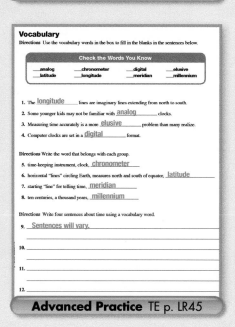

ELL

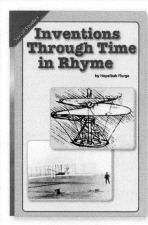

ELL Reader

ELL Poster 20

Teacher's Edition Notes

ELL notes throughout this lesson support instruction and reference additional resources at point of use.

Teaching Guide pp. 134–140, 250–251
- Multilingual summaries of the main selection
- Comprehension lesson
- Vocabulary strategies and word cards
- ELL Reader 6.4.5 lesson

ELL and Transition Handbook

Ten Important Sentences
- Key ideas from every selection in the Student Edition
- Activities to build sentence power

More Reading

Readers' Theater Anthology
- Fluency practice
- Five scripts to build fluency
- Poetry for oral interpretation

Leveled Trade Books

- Extended reading tied to the unit concept
- Lessons in the Trade Book Library Teaching Guide

School + Home

Homework
- Family Times Newsletter
- ELL Multilingual Selection Summaries

Take-Home Books
- Leveled Readers

Cross-Curricular Centers

Listening

Listen to the Selections

MATERIALS　　`SINGLES`
CD player, headphones, AudioText CD, student book

LISTEN TO LITERATURE Listen to *Inventing the Future* and "Garrett Augustus Morgan" as you follow or read along in your book. Listen to identify the author's purpose.

If there is anything you don't understand, you can listen again to any section.

Audio CD

Reading/ Library

Read It Again!

MATERIALS　　`SINGLES`
Collection of books for self-selected reading, reading logs, student book　`PAIRS`　`GROUPS`

Select a book you have already read. Record the title of the book in your reading log. You may want to read with a partner.

Choose from the following:

- Leveled Readers
- ELL Readers
- Stories Written by Classmates
- Books from the Library
- *Inventing the Future*

TEN IMPORTANT SENTENCES Read the Ten Important Sentences from *Inventing the Future*. Then locate the sentences in the student book.

BOOK CLUB Look at "Meet Authors" on p. 788 of the student book to help you set up an author study of Marfé Ferguson Delano.

Music

Create a Time Line

MATERIALS　　`SINGLES`
Writing and art materials, books about music, Internet access　`PAIRS`

Create a time line that shows developments in music-related technology over time.

1. Use library and Internet resources to gather information on important inventions in music. Begin with Edison's invention of the phonograph in 1877.
2. Make a time line showing the inventions you learned about and the dates they were invented.

EARLY FINISHERS Illustrate your time line with pictures of each of the inventions.

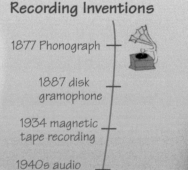

Recording Inventions

1877 Phonograph

1887 disk gramophone

1934 magnetic tape recording

1940s audio tape recording

1962 audio-cassette

Scott Foresman Reading Street Centers Survival Kit

Use the *Inventing the Future* materials from the Reading Street
Centers Survival Kit to organize this week's centers.

Writing/ Vocabulary

Science

Technology

Write a
How-to Booklet

MATERIALS
Writing and drawing materials

`PAIRS`
`GROUPS`

Use details from the selection to write a set of instructions for being a successful inventor.

1. The author of *Inventing the Future* describes Thomas Edison's process for creating and testing various inventions. Use details from the selection to write a "How-to" booklet with the title "How to be a Successful Inventor."

2. Include step-by-step instructions describing the method of team inventing that Edison used, along with any other details or tips.

EARLY FINISHERS Illustrate your booklet.

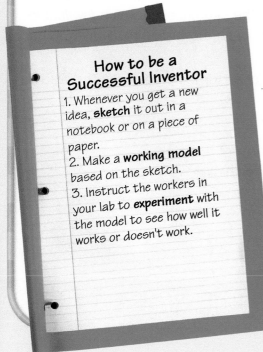

How to be a
Successful Inventor
1. Whenever you get a new idea, **sketch** it out in a notebook or on a piece of paper.
2. Make a **working model** based on the sketch.
3. Instruct the workers in your lab to **experiment** with the model to see how well it works or doesn't work.

Design an
Invention

MATERIALSS,
Writing and drawing materials

`SINGLES`
`PAIRS`
`GROUPS`

Design an invention that makes an everyday task easier or faster to complete.

1. Draw and label a design for an invention that would make an everyday task easier or faster to complete.

2. Write a short, descriptive paragraph explaining how your invention works.

EARLY FINISHERS Write and illustrate an advertisement for your invention.

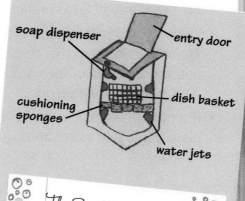

soap dispenser — entry door
cushioning sponges — dish basket
water jets

The Sparkle Dish Washer
This amazing machine washes all of your dishes, glasses, utensils, pots and pans. All you have to do is load them in the top like clothes into a washing machine.

Listen to
Recordings

MATERIALS
Internet access

`SINGLES`
`PAIRS`

Listen to early phonograph recordings made by Edison.

1. Use a student-friendly search engine to find some of Edison's early phonograph recordings, including his first recording, "Mary Had a Little Lamb."

2. Listen to the recordings you find.

3. Follow classroom rules when using the Internet.

EARLY FINISHERS Write a brief paragraph comparing the sound quality of Edison's early recordings with modern CD recordings.

Search Engine
Edison phonograph

`ALL CENTERS`

OBJECTIVES

- Build vocabulary by finding words related to the lesson concept.
- Listen to determine the author's purpose.

Concept Vocabulary

contemplated thought about for a long time

invaluable having great value

model a small copy

Monitor Progress

Check Vocabulary

If... students are unable to place words on the Web,	then... review the lesson concept. Place the words on the Web and provide additional words for practice, such as *experiment* and *computer*.

SUCCESS PREDICTOR

DAY 1 Grouping Options

Reading
Whole Group
Introduce and discuss the Question of the Week. Then use pp. 500l–502b.

Small Group
Differentiated Instruction
Read this week's Leveled Readers. See pp. 500f–500g for the small group lesson plan.

Whole Group
Use p. 527a..

Language Arts
Use pp. 527e–527k.

Build Concepts

FLUENCY

MODEL PUNCTUATION CLUES As you read "Inventing the Stethoscope," use the punctuation marks as clues for when to chunk groups of words together and when to pause.

LISTENING COMPREHENSION

After reading "Inventing the Stethoscope," use the following questions to assess listening comprehension.

1. **What is the author's purpose in writing this article?** *(to inform readers about the process by which the stethoscope was invented)* **Author's Purpose**

2. **Do you think the author met his purpose? Why or why not?** *(Possible response: Yes, because he explained the process in a clear and interesting way.)* **Author's Purpose**

BUILD CONCEPT VOCABULARY

Start a web to build concepts and vocabulary related to this week's lesson and the unit theme.

- Draw the Inventions Concept Vocabulary Web.

- Read the sentence with the word *contemplated* again. Ask students to pronounce *contemplated* and discuss its meaning.

- Place *contemplated* in an oval attached to Inventors. Explain that *contemplated* is related to this concept. Read the sentences in which *invaluable* and *model* appear. Have students pronounce the words, place them on the Web, and provide reasons.

- Brainstorm additional words and categories for the Web. Keep the Web on display and add words throughout the week.

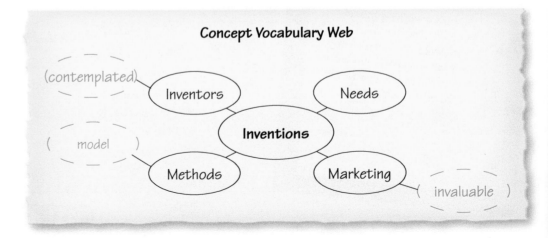

Concept Vocabulary Web

Inventing the Stethoscope

by Edward F. Dolan

In 1816, Paris, France, Doctor René Laënnec (lay NEK) was frustrated as he contemplated a way to help a patient who he knew was suffering from heart trouble. If only he could hear her heart...

As he walked toward the hospital, his hands were locked behind his back. His mind was still struggling for an answer of how to hear the woman's heart. Laënnec's path took him through a garden. All about were sounds—clatter of horses on the street, the talking of people, the laughter of children.

Slowly, that laughter broke through Laënnec's thoughts. He looked up to see a group of children gathered about a long board on the grass. He smiled at the sight of them. All but one, a young boy, were gathered about one end of the board. They were kneeling with their heads lowered right down to the wood. At the other end, the boy was kneeling beside the board, tapping it with a stick. The children laughed with delight at the sounds which met their ears. The sounds traveled down the board from the boy's stick. They were loud—much louder than if they were heard while the boys were standing.

Suddenly the distant smile faded from Dr. Laënnec's face. A look of sharp thought replaced it.

He slapped his hands together. He knew what every school child in France knew: that sound moves through something solid better than through the air. Why hadn't he thought of that before, he wondered. It was so simple. Here, after the long and restless night, was the answer to his problem.

Dr. Laënnec hurried to the hospital. He went right away to his office. There he took a sheet of stiff paper from his desk. He rolled the paper into a tube and put a band around it. Then in an instant, he was standing beside his patient's bed. He placed one end of the tube against her chest. He placed his ear against the other end. He listened for just a few seconds. Then a smile broke over his narrow face.

He could hear her unhealthy heart beating. He could hear it better than he had ever heard any patient's heart in all his life.

Able to hear the heartbeat, Dr. Laënnec could tell what was wrong with his patient. And he knew that he had found an invaluable tool for medicine.

Laënnec's new tool made him one of the leading doctors in his time for diseases of the chest. All during his life, Laënnec worked on making the stethoscope better and better. His final model was made of wood and looked different than those used today. However, it worked in the same way stethoscopes do now.

 SKILLS ⬌ STRATEGIES IN CONTEXT

Author's Purpose
Monitor/Fix Up

OBJECTIVES

⊙ Determine author's purpose.

⊙ Use fix-up strategies to help determine and evaluate the author's purpose.

Skills Trace
⊙ Author's Purpose

Introduce/Teach	TE: 6.4 430–431, 500–501; 6.6 652–653
Practice	Practice Book: 163, 167, 168, 193, 197, 198, 253, 257, 258
Reteach/Review	TE: 6.1 125; 6.4 455b, 465, 527b, DI·53, DI·56; 6.6 733, 671b, DI·52
Test	Selection Test: 65–68, 77–80, 101–104; Benchmark Test: Unit 4

INTRODUCE

Write this summary: *A newspaper columnist writes a humorous account of an attempt to walk his dog after an ice storm.* Ask what the author's likely purpose is. *(to entertain)*

Have students read the information on p. 500. Explain the following:

• Remind students that authors often have more than one purpose in writing.

• Students can use several fix-up strategies to improve their comprehension of difficult passages, such as reread, take notes, or make a graphic organizer.

Use Skill Transparency 20 to teach author's purpose and fix-up strategies.

Inventing the Future

Comprehension

Skill
Author's Purpose

Strategy
Monitor and Fix Up

 # Author's Purpose

• Authors may write to persuade, inform, express, or entertain. Preview the title, headings, and pictures to help predict the author's purpose. Set your reading speed.

• As you read, you may need to adjust your ideas about the author's purpose. If so, you may need to read more slowly or more quickly.

• When you finish, ask yourself, "How did the language or style help meet the purpose?"

Before Reading
Preview to decide purpose. Set reading pace.

↓

During Reading
Look for clues to purpose. Adjust pace if needed.

↓

After Reading
Ask if purpose was met and how.

⊙ Strategy: Monitor and Fix Up

Good readers make sure they understand what they are reading. If you do not understand, use a fix-up strategy. For example, as you read, you may discover the author is giving you brand-new information using difficult words. You might slow down so that you make sure you understand.

Write to Read

1. Read "The Age of Inventions." Make a graphic organizer like the one above in order to determine the author's main purpose.

2. Make notes about what you didn't understand in "The Age of Inventions." Write about what you might do to help you better understand what you read.

500

Strategic Intervention

⊙ **Author's Purpose** Share with students the kinds of questions they should ask themselves to monitor their comprehension as they read nonfiction: What is the author trying to tell me? What does this sentence mean? Does this passage make sense to me? Do I understand this passage?

ELL

Access Content

Beginning/Intermediate For a Picture It! lesson on author's purpose, see the ELL Teaching Guide, pp. 134–135.

Advanced Before reading the "The Age of Inventions," ask a volunteer to explain what an invention is and have students name important inventions.

The Age of Inventions

The period from the mid-1800s to the early 1900s was one of great significance in human history. Many of the machines invented during this time changed the world.

First, new ways to power machines were developed. Inventors learned to generate and use electricity, leading to the widespread use of electric lights and trains. The first gasoline-fueled engine was perfected in 1859, and these engines were soon used in many factories.

Second, transportation changed dramatically. The first motorcycles and motorcars were introduced in 1885. The first large iron ships were constructed during this time as well and soon replaced ships powered by sails. The Wright brothers piloted the first plane flight in 1903.

Third, people were able to communicate in more sophisticated ways. For example, the telephone, which was made in 1876, and the wireless telegraph, invented in 1895, let people converse across long distances. The radio was invented in 1901.

The world changed in so many ways from the mid-1800s to the early 1900s. Was it a better place because of all these inventions? Many people would say yes. However, some might disagree. Transportation and communication were speedier, but noise, pollution, and a faster pace of life also resulted.

1 **Skill** What do you predict the main purpose of the article is?

(a) to inform you which machines were invented during this time period

(b) to entertain you by joking about inventions of the 1800s

(c) to persuade you that this time was very important

2 **Strategy** Are you understanding the author's purpose and the information he is giving you? Do you need to change your reading speed?

3 **Strategy** What could you do here if you had trouble understanding this paragraph?

kill What does the purpose this final paragraph seem be — to inform, to entertain, to express ideas?

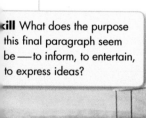

501

Available as **Skill Transparency** 20

TEACH

1 **SKILL** Use the first paragraph to model how to predict the author's main purpose.

Think Aloud **MODEL** The two sentences in this paragraph focus on the significance of this period in history. I would predict that the author's main purpose is either to inform or to persuade. Therefore, Choices *a* and *c* may be correct.

2 **STRATEGY** Discuss fix-up strategies to improve comprehension.

Think Aloud **MODEL** The author is packing a lot of information in this paragraph, which makes it harder to process. I need to slow down and possibly reread the paragraph to make sure I understand it.

PRACTICE AND ASSESS

3 **STRATEGY** Possible responses: reread, take notes, make a time line

4 **SKILL** To express ideas

WRITE Have students complete steps 1 and 2 of the Write to Read activity. You might consider using this as a whole-class activity.

Monitor Progress	
🎯 **Author's Purpose**	
If... students are unable to complete **Write to Read** on p. 500,	**then...** use Practice Book p. 193 to provide additional practice.

Author's Purpose

- The **author's purpose** is the reason or reasons the author has for writing.
- An author may write to persuade, to inform, to entertain, or to express ideas and feelings. An author may have more than one reason for writing.

Directions Read the following passage. Then complete the diagram.

One very cool invention is the refrigerator. Before refrigeration, it was difficult to store and ship fresh food. In the early twentieth century, food was kept cold with a block of ice in a cabinet called an "icebox." The cooling process used in today's refrigerators dates back to Michael Faraday's experiments in the eighteenth century with liquefying ammonia. The first refrigeration machine was designed in 1805 by the American inventor Oliver Evans. Other inventors improved on this device. The first commercial home refrigerator was sold in 1911 by General Electric. Today, homes all over the world have refrigerators.

Possible answers 2–5.

Author's Purpose

1. The author's purpose is to inform.

Details

2. food was once kept cold in a cabinet called an "icebox"

3. first refrigeration machine designed in 1805

4. first commercial home refrigerator sold in 1911

5. How did the author's language or style help meet the purpose?
The author used simple, clear language and presented many facts.

Home Activity Your child identified the author's purpose and cited details to support this analysis. Work with your child to identify the author's purpose and supporting details of individual paragraphs in a magazine article about an innovation. Challenge your child to set his or her reading pace to match the purpose of the article.

Practice Book p. 193

ONLINE

Students can use the keyword *important inventions* in a student-friendly search engine to explore major inventions and their social impacts.

Build Background Use ELL Poster 20 to build background and vocabulary for the lesson concept of how inventions happen.

▲ ELL Poster 20

Build Background

ACTIVATE PRIOR KNOWLEDGE

BEGIN A CAUSE-EFFECT DIAGRAM about a major invention and its social effects.

- Give students two to three minutes to identify as many major inventions as they can. Have the class choose the invention they consider most important and record it in the *Cause* box of the diagram.

- Ask students to think about the invention's social effects. How did it change people's lives? Note students' answers in the *Effect* box.

- Tell students that they should look for the effects of the inventions they will be reading about.

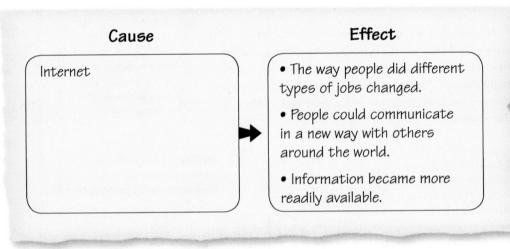

Cause	Effect
Internet	• The way people did different types of jobs changed. • People could communicate in a new way with others around the world. • Information became more readily available.

▲ Graphic Organizer 20

BACKGROUND BUILDING AUDIO This week's audio explores the patent industry. After students listen, discuss what they learned.

Background Building Audio

Introduce Vocabulary

DISCUSS THE VOCABULARY

Share the Words to Know and their definitions with students. Then ask questions that include the new vocabulary, such as the following:

- What kinds of things can you *reproduce?*
- If I *proclaimed* that tomorrow would be a school holiday, would you be happy or sad? Why?
- About what *percentage* of this class are girls?
- A futon *converts* into what?
- What are some examples of situations in which you expect or appreciate *efficiency?*
- Through what kinds of things can information be *transmitted?*
- What product would you like to *devise?*

Activate Prior Knowledge

Have students share where they may have seen some of these words. Point out that many of this week's words are used when talking about electricity (transmitted, converts, generated, efficiency). ***Technical Words***

By the end of the week, students should know the lesson vocabulary words. To demonstrate their knowledge, have students write an appropriate sentence for each word.

Use Multisyllabic Word Routine on p. DI·1 to help students read multisyllabic words.

Lesson Vocabulary

WORDS TO KNOW

T **converts** changes

T **devise** invent

T **efficiency** ability to produce the effect wanted without waste of time or energy

T **generated** produced

T **percentage** allowance figured by percent

T **proclaimed** declared publicly

T **reproduce** to make a copy of

T **transmitted** sent out signals by means of electromagnetic waves or by wire

MORE WORDS TO KNOW

dictation words said or read aloud to another person who writes them down or to a machine that records them

exclusive not divided or shared with others; single; sole

persistence act of refusing to stop, change, or give up

T = Tested Word

Vocabulary

Directions Choose the word from the box that best matches each definition. Write the word on the line.

devise _____ 1. to invent

percentage _____ 2. allowance, figured by percent

generated _____ 3. produced

transmitted _____ 4. sent out signals by means of electromagnetic waves or by wire

reproduce _____ 5. to make a copy of

Check the Words You Know
___converts
___devise
___efficiency
___generated
___percentage
___proclaimed
___reproduce
___transmitted

Directions Choose the word from the box that best completes each sentence below. Write the word on the line shown to the left.

proclaimed _____ 6. The inventor ____ that he had a great invention.

transmitted _____ 7. He claimed that his machine ____ food from one place to another, electronically.

converts _____ 8. "It ____ food into electrical pulses," he declared.

efficiency _____ 9. If it worked, it could result in more ____ by saving time.

generated _____ 10. Although the idea ____ much interest, it turned out to be a fake.

Write a News Report
On a separate sheet of paper, write a news report you might make after observing a new invention. Use as many vocabulary words as you can.

News reports should include words from the vocabulary list and details about the new invention.

Home Activity Your child identified and used vocabulary words from *Inventing the Future*. Have a conversation about useful inventions. Why are they useful? What do they do? Use the vocabulary words from the selection while conversing.

▲ **Practice Book** p. 194

Vocabulary Strategy

OBJECTIVE

⊙ Examine word structure to determine how prefixes affect the meaning of words.

INTRODUCE

Discuss the strategy for word structure using the steps on p. 502.

TEACH

- Have students read "Hats Off to Inventors," paying attention to how vocabulary is used.
- Model using word structure to determine the meaning of the word *transmitted*.

Think Aloud **MODEL** The base word *mit* comes from a Latin word that means "send." The prefix *trans-* means "across." *Transmitted* is in the past tense and means "sent across."

Words to Know

- devise
- transmitted
- efficiency
- converts
- reproduce
- generated
- percentage
- proclaimed

Remember

Try the strategy. Then, if you need more help, use your glossary or a dictionary.

Vocabulary Strategy
for Prefixes

Word Structure A prefix is a word part that is added at the beginning of a base word. The prefix changes the base word's meaning. When you come across an unknown word, check to see if it has a prefix. Knowing the meaning of the prefix may help you figure out the meaning of the word. For example, the prefix *re-* means "again"; *pro-* means "forth" or "forward"; and *trans-* means "across," "beyond," or "through."

1. Look at an unfamiliar word to see if it has a base word you know.

2. Check to see if the prefix *re-*, *pro-*, or *trans-* has been added to the base word.

3. Think about what meaning the prefix adds to the meaning of the base word.

4. Try the meaning in the sentence.

As you read "Hats Off to Inventors," look for words that have prefixes. Use the prefixes to help you figure out the meaning of the words.

ALEXANDER GRAHAM BELL, c. 1915, inventor of the telephone.

502

DAY 2 Grouping Options

Reading
Whole Group Discuss the Question of the Day. Then use pp. 502–505.

Small Group Differentiated Instruction
Read *Inventing the Future*. See pp. 500f–500g for the small group lesson plan.

Whole Group Use p. 527a.

Language Arts
Use pp. 527e–527k.

Strategic Intervention

⊙ **Word Structure** Share with students other words that have prefixes as clues to meaning, such as *promote* and *transplant*.

ELL

Access Content Use ELL Poster 20 to preteach vocabulary. Choose from the following to meet language proficiency levels.

Beginning Use the Multilingual Lesson Vocabulary list in the ELL Teaching Guide and other home-language resources to provide translations of the tested words.

Intermediate After reading, students can choose one of the tested words to use to complete a vocabulary frame.

Advanced Teach the lesson on pp. 502–503. Have students find home-language terms for some of the tested words.

Resources for home-language words may include parents, bilingual staff members, bilingual dictionaries, or online translation sources.

Hats Off to Inventors

We owe the comfort and convenience of our lives to inventors. These creative geniuses devise better ways to do or make something. Sometimes this means coming up with a whole new invention, such as the telephone. Thanks to this machine, sound is transmitted over great distances. At other times, inventors have just improved the efficiency of a machine that already exists. The radial tire, for example, meant that cars would get better gas mileage. Even simple inventions can make a big difference. For example, the sticky note converts paper into a message that can be placed right where you want it. The inventor is a practical dreamer. He or she wants to make a product that is easy to reproduce and useful, so the public will buy it.

Inventors have been around for thousands of years, but in the last 150 years they have generated by far the greatest percentage of new gadgets ever invented. In many ways, their work has made life better for us all. Don't you think a special Inventors Day should be proclaimed?

THOMAS EDISON

Words to Write

Choose an invention you think is important. Write about how it has changed people's lives. Use as many words from the Words to Know list as you can.

503

Connect to Phonics

Word Study/Decoding Point out that a prefix changes the meaning of the root word. Model identifying the prefix and root word using *reproduce* on p. 503, paragraph 1. Have students suggest other words they know with *re-* and *in-*. Have students identify the prefix and root in each word. Then have them identify the meaning of each word with and without the prefix.

PRACTICE AND ASSESS

- Have students determine the meanings of the remaining words and explain the strategy they used.
- Point out that the words *reproduce* and *proclaimed* contain prefixes that students know.
- Have students complete Practice Book p. 195.

WRITE Writing should include at least three of the vocabulary words listed on p. 502.

Monitor Progress
Word Structure

If...	then...
If... students need more practice with the lesson vocabulary,	then... use Tested Vocabulary Cards.

Vocabulary · Word Structure

- If you see an unfamiliar word while you are reading, use word parts to figure out its meaning. **Prefixes** are word parts with their own meanings that are added to base words. They change the meanings of base words.
- The prefix *re-* means "again;" *pro-* means "before;" *trans-* means "over;" and *con-* means "together."

Directions Read the following article. Then answer the questions below.

Who deserves to be recalled as the inventor of the telephone? The principle behind the telephone is that it converts sound waves to electrical impulses that are then transmitted through a wire to reproduce the sound. Although Alexander Graham Bell claimed to be the inventor of the telephone, a little-known inventor named Elisha Gray also devised a telephone. Both men raced to the patent office to apply for a patent, and Bell beat Gray by only hours. Alexander Graham Bell will always be remembered, but not Elisha Gray. If Gray had arrived at the patent office a little bit earlier, he would be the famous one.

1. In the word *converts* how does the prefix *con-*, combined with the Latin root *vertere* for "turn," help you to determine the meaning of the word?
   Con- combines with the root to suggest "turns together," leading to the meaning "changes for a different purpose."

2. What does *transmitted* mean? How does the prefix contribute to the meaning?
   "sent out signals"; *Trans-*, meaning "across," shows the signals are sent across waves or wires.

3. How does the prefix in *reproduce* help you to determine the meaning of the word?
   Re- means "again," which conveys "to produce again."

4. How would the prefix help you to determine the meaning of *proclaimed*?
   Pro- means "before," suggesting news claimed before a group.

5. What are two other words in the article that use the prefix *trans-, con-, re-,* or *pro-*?
   Recalled and *remembered* both use the prefix *re-*.

Home Activity Your child identified and used prefixes to understand new words of a passage. Work with your child to identify unfamiliar words in another article. Then see if he or she can find prefixes to help with the understanding of the new words. Confirm the meanings with your child.

▲ **Practice Book** p. 195

Prereading Strategies

GENRE STUDY

Biography

Inventing the Future is a biography. Explain that a biography is the story of a real person's life written by another person.

PREVIEW AND PREDICT

Have students preview the title, callout quotes, photographs, and other graphic sources, and discuss what they think the phrase "inventing the future" means. Encourage students to use lesson vocabulary words as they talk about what they expect to learn.

Ask Questions Have students write two questions they have about Thomas Edison in their strategy response logs. Students will try to answer their questions in the Strategy Response Log activity on p. 513.

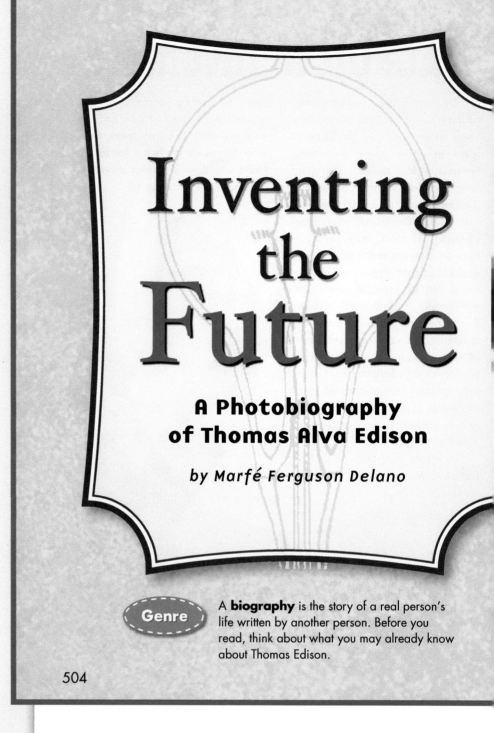

Inventing the Future

A Photobiography of Thomas Alva Edison

by Marfé Ferguson Delano

Genre A **biography** is the story of a real person's life written by another person. Before you read, think about what you may already know about Thomas Edison.

504

ELL

Access Content Preview the selection by looking at all the illustrations and reading the captions. Invite students to share what they already know about any of these inventions. Ask students what they would like to know more about. Consider having students read the selection summary in English or in students' home languages. See the Multilingual Summaries in the ELL Teaching Guide, pp. 138–140.

Why are Thomas Edison's inventions so important to us today?

505

SET PURPOSE

Ask students to tell what they hope to find out as they read, based on the title of the selection.

Remind students to identify the author's purpose as they read.

STRATEGY RECALL

Students have now used these before-reading strategies:

- preview the selection to be aware of its genre, features, and possible content;
- activate prior knowledge about that content and what to expect of that genre;
- make predictions;
- set a purpose for reading.

Remind students to be aware of and flexibly use the during-reading strategies they have learned:

- link prior knowledge to new information;
- summarize text they have read so far;
- ask clarifying questions;
- answer questions they or others pose;
- check their predictions and either refine them or make new predictions;
- recognize the text structure the author is using, and use that knowledge to make predictions and increase comprehension;
- visualize what the author is describing;
- monitor their comprehension and use fix-up strategies.

After reading, students will use these strategies:

- summarize or retell the text;
- answer questions they or others pose;
- reflect to make new information become part of their prior knowledge.

Audio CD AudioText

Guiding Comprehension

1 Foreshadowing • Inferential

How do you think the lesson Edison learned about inventing from his vote recorder foreshadowed the rest of his career?

He most likely began to invent things that people wanted to buy.

2 Author's Purpose • Critical

From your preview and your reading of pp. 506–507, why do you think Delano wrote _Inventing the Future?_

She wrote to inform readers about the life and inventions of Thomas Edison.

Monitor Progress

Author's Purpose

If... students are unable to identify the author's purpose,	then... use the skill and strategy instruction on p. 507.

Tech Files
ONLINE

Students can find more information about the life and work of Thomas Edison by using a student friendly search engine and the keywords _Thomas Edison._ Be sure to follow classroom rules for Internet use.

Pictured here during his "tramp telegrapher" days, Edison preferred to work night jobs, which he said gave him "more leisure to experiment."

In 1868, Thomas Edison took a job in the Western Union telegraph office in Boston. He found the city an exciting place. Not only did it have a large telegraphic community, it was filled with inventors. One of them was Alexander Graham Bell, who in 1876 would invent the telephone. Edison worked nights as a press operator and spent his days exploring the shops where telegraphs and other electrical devices were designed and made. Inspired by all the activity he found, Edison soon quit his job to focus full time on bringing out inventions. He met with people who had money to invest and persuaded them to provide the funds he needed to develop his ideas and have his inventions made. He specialized in telegraphic devices, but he also worked on other inventions.

When he was 22 years old, Edison received his first patent. It was for an electric vote recorder. A patent is an official document issued by the government that gives a person or company the sole right to make or sell an invention. Edison hoped the device would be used by state legislatures, but lawmakers were not interested in buying it. The experience taught him a valuable lesson: Never again would he invent something that people didn't want to buy.

In 1869, Edison moved to New York City. Many telegraph companies, including Western Union, had their headquarters in the city, which brimmed with business opportunities for an ambitious young inventor. Edison worked for a while for the Laws Gold Indicator Company, where he repaired and improved the company's stock printers. Also called stock tickers because of the noise they made, stock printers were a kind of telegraph that sent minute-by-minute reports of the changing price of gold to stockbrokers' offices.

506

Context Clues Remind students that unfamiliar terms are often defined within the context of a selection. Point out that the term _stock printer_ on p. 506 is defined in the sentence that follows it ("stock printers were a kind of telegraph that sent minute-by-minute reports of the changing price of gold to the stockbrokers' offices").

"Anything that won't sell, I don't want to invent. Its sale is proof of utility, and utility is success."

That fall, Edison started a business called Pope, Edison and Company with a fellow inventor named Franklin Pope. They advertised themselves as electrical engineers who could "devise electrical instruments and solve problems to order." The company offered a variety of services having to do with telegraph technology and was also committed to bringing out new devices—Edison's specialty. He patented a number of telegraphic improvements that were eagerly bought by the telegraph industry. Finally he was inventing what people wanted and were willing to pay for.

By the age of 23, Edison had earned a reputation as one of the best electrical inventors in the country, which helped him attract more financial backers. In 1870, his partnership with Pope broke up, and Edison opened his very own manufacturing company and laboratory in Newark, New Jersey.

Edison hired more than 50 employees to make and sell his stock printers and other equipment and to assist with his many experiments. Among the skilled machinists and clockmakers he hired were Charles Batchelor and John Kruesi. A British-born machinist and draftsman, Batchelor soon became Edison's right-hand man as well as his friend. They worked closely together for nearly 25 years. Kruesi, born in Switzerland and trained as a clockmaker, worked with Edison for 20-some years.

Manufactured at his Newark factory and embellished with his name, Edison's Universal Printer, a stock ticker, was among his first commercially successful inventions.

In the fall of 1871, 24-year-old Edison started his own news service, the News Reporting Telegraph Company. Among the company's employees was a pretty 16-year-old clerk named Mary Stilwell, a Newark girl whose father worked in a sawmill. Edison set his sights on Mary, and after a brief courtship, they married on Christmas Day, 1871. When the couple's first child was born, a daughter named Marion, Edison **2**

507

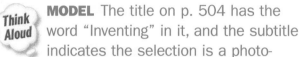
SKILLS ↔ STRATEGIES IN CONTEXT

Author's Purpose

TEACH

- Remind students that the author may write to persuade, inform, express, or entertain.
- Model identifying the author's purpose from previewing the selection and reading pp. 506–507.

Think Aloud **MODEL** The title on p. 504 has the word "Inventing" in it, and the subtitle indicates the selection is a photo-biography of Thomas Edison. When I look through the pages, I see the photographs span his life and focus on his inventions. I can infer that the author wrote this selection to inform readers about Thomas Edison's life and his inventions.

PRACTICE AND ASSESS

Ask students to explain how the quote at the top of p. 507 helps to inform the reader about Edison's life. *(The quote expresses the driving force behind Edison's work and his desire to invent new things.)*

Guiding Comprehension

3 Cause and Effect • Literal

What effects did Edison's devotion to his work have on his family life?

He was frequently at his lab for days and had little time for his family.

Monitor Progress

REVIEW Cause and Effect

If... students have difficulty recognizing causes and effects,	then... use the skill and strategy instruction on p. 509.

4 Paraphrase • Inferential

Describe Edison's method of inventing.

Edison developed a method of team inventing. He would sketch an idea, and his assistants would make a working model. Lab workers then tested the model to see if it would work. If it didn't work, Edison and his crew would keep trying.

EXTEND SKILLS

Idiom

Explain that an idiom is a phrase or expression whose meaning cannot be understood from the ordinary meaning of the words that form it. Point out that the phrase *played second fiddle* on p. 508, paragraph 1, is an idiom that means "was less important." Ask students why the idiom is appropriate here. (*It's appropriate because Edison's wife learns that she is less important to her husband than his work.*)

Mary Stilwell (top) married Edison on Christmas Day, 1871. The couple had three children: Marion (middle), Thomas Alva, Jr., (bottom right), and William (bottom left).

nicknamed her "Dot," after the telegraph signal. Their second child, Thomas Alva, Jr., was dubbed "Dash," of course. The Edisons' third child was named—and called—William.

Soon after their marriage, Mary discovered that she played second fiddle to her husband's true love—inventing. He often spent several days straight at the lab, working through the nights and catching naps on a workbench or desktop when exhaustion overwhelmed him. Whenever Edison was involved with a project, he became totally wrapped up in it. And since he almost always had dozens of inventions going at once, he had little time for anything else.

In Newark, Edison first developed the method of team inventing that would characterize the rest of his career. Whenever a new idea for an invention inspired him, he sketched it out in a notebook and then shared the drawing with Batchelor and Kruesi or other trusted assistants. Their job was to take the sketch and see that it was made into a working model. Lab workers then experimented with the model to see how the invention worked—or did not work, which was often the case. Edison was not discouraged when things went wrong. He and his workers would just keep trying until they found out what did work.

Edison's workers tended to be very loyal to "the old man," as they called their young boss. They admired and respected him for the way he worked alongside them, plunging into the dirtiest jobs with enthusiasm and putting in longer hours than anyone else. Moreover, Edison could be generous. He often gave assistants who worked closely with him on an invention a percentage of the profits it made.

508

Understanding Idioms Help students use context to understand the idiom "totally wrapped up" on p. 508. Ask students to reread the paragraph containing the idiom and describe Edison's behavior. Explain that when someone is "totally wrapped up" in something, they are completely focused on something with no time for anything else.

"Negative results are just what I want. They're just as valuable to me as positive results. I can never find the thing that does a job the best until I find the ones that don't do."

Although Edison's Newark laboratory focused mainly on devices that improved the speed and efficiency of the telegraph, other electrical inventions were also under development. One of these was the electric pen, which could create multiple copies of a handwritten document. Business owners, from lawyers to mapmakers, immediately saw the value of the device, and it sold well. Although Edison manufactured and sold many of his inventions, he also sold the patents for many others. This gave the buyer the exclusive right to make and sell a device. Despite the income this generated, Edison was usually short of cash. That's because he tended to spend most of what he earned from one invention on the next.

In 1876, Edison sold his Newark business. He moved his family and about 20 of his best workers—including Batchelor and Kruesi—

The electric pen was among the inventions Edison developed and manufactured at his Newark facility. An advertisement for the device claimed that it could produce "5,000 copies from a single writing."

509

Cause and Effect REVIEW

TEACH

- Remind students that an effect is something that happens and a cause is what makes it happen.

- Note that sometimes there are no clue words to help readers understand what happened and why. In these cases, a reader has to infer the cause-and-effect relationships.

 Think Aloud **MODEL** The first full paragraph on p. 508 says that Edison's wife came second in his life, after inventing. He would work through the night at the lab and had little time for anything else. So I can conclude that an effect of his devotion to his work was his tremendous productivity in the lab and his many inventions.

PRACTICE AND ASSESS

- Ask students to read p. 509, paragraph 1, and tell why Edison usually had little money available. *(He would spend most of what he earned on one invention to develop the next.)*

- To assess, use Practice Book p. 196.

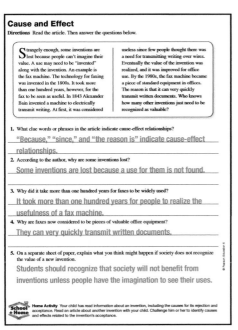

▲ **Practice Book** p. 196

Guiding Comprehension

5 **Compare and Contrast • Inferential**

How was Edison's laboratory at Menlo Park different from most other labs of the time?

Edison's laboratory was devoted exclusively to research and development. Most other labs combined inventing with manufacturing.

6 **Author's Purpose • Critical**

How does the information on p. 511 help serve the author's purpose?

It clearly explains how Edison helped improve the telephone, informing the reader of his achievement.

Monitor Progress	
Author's Purpose	
If... students are unable to identify details that serve the author's purpose,	**then...** use the skill and strategy instruction on p. 511.

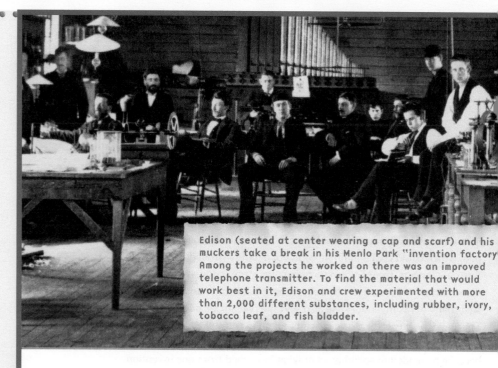

Edison (seated at center wearing a cap and scarf) and his muckers take a break in his Menlo Park "invention factory" Among the projects he worked on there was an improved telephone transmitter. To find the material that would work best in it, Edison and crew experimented with more than 2,000 different substances, including rubber, ivory, tobacco leaf, and fish bladder.

to a small farming village in New Jersey called Menlo Park, located about 20 miles from New York City. There he had a two-story laboratory built to his design. Unlike most other labs of the time, which combined inventing with manufacturing, Edison's new laboratory was devoted exclusively to researching and developing his ideas. It contained well-equipped chemistry and electrical labs and a machine shop for making models of his inventions. Edison often referred to the place as his "invention factory." He bragged that it would turn out "a minor invention every ten days and a big thing every six months or so."

Edison and his "muckers," as he fondly called his crew of fellow experimenters, lived up to the boast. Known as the "Chief Mucker," Edison patented 75 different inventions in the first two years at Menlo Park. Among them was an improved version of Alexander Graham Bell's telephone.

"Genius is 1 percent inspiration and 99 percent perspiration."

510

Extend Language Explain that the term *"muckers"* comes from the word "muck" or dirt and the verb "to muck about" which means to get dirty. Ask students why they think Edison "fondly" called his assistants *"muckers."*

The biggest problem with Bell's telephone was that the sound it transmitted, or sent, was weak. A caller had to shout into it in order to be heard on the other end of the line. Edison felt sure he could not only find a way to make the telephone sound louder and clearer, he also could make it send messages over longer distances. Eager to gain the advantage in the budding telephone industry, Western Union hired him to do just that.

Edison knew that improving the transmitter—the device that converts the sound of a speaker's voice into electrical signals—was the key to better quality sound. The challenge was to find the material that would work best in it.

In 1877, less than a year after Bell's invention of the telephone, Edison discovered that tiny pieces of carbon encased in a small container, or button, gave the best results. Called the carbon button transmitter, the invention not only produced excellent sound, but greatly increased the range of the telephone. A version of it is still used in most **6** telephones today.

Paying customers listen through earphones to a recording in a "phonograph parlor" in Salina, Kansas, in the 1890s. Edison manufactured phonographs with a special coin-in-slot device for use in saloons and other places of entertainment.

511

Scientific Inquiry

TIME FOR Science

Edison's method of inventing involved making observations, collecting relevant evidence, developing explanations, and testing ideas. His method of scientific inquiry required both logical reasoning and imagination.

SKILLS ↔ STRATEGIES IN CONTEXT

Author's Purpose

TEACH

Remind students that the author's purpose in this selection is to inform readers about Thomas Edison's inventions. Model evaluating how the information on p. 511 contributes to this purpose.

Think Aloud **MODEL** In these three paragraphs, the author describes a major problem with Bell's telephone and tells how Edison identified a solution to the problem. This was obviously an important invention of Edison's, as it is still in use today. This information contributes to the author's purpose because it focuses on a specific invention of Edison's.

PRACTICE AND ASSESS

Ask students to evaluate how the photographs, captions, and quotations on pp. 510–511 help serve the author's purpose. *(They help readers visualize what Edison's laboratory was like and how one of his inventions was used at the time.)*

Guiding Comprehension

"I had the faculty of sleeping in a chair anytime for a few minutes at a time."

7 **Cause and Effect • Inferential**

Why did Edison need to take catnaps at work?

Edison catnapped because he often worked around the clock.

8 **Compare and Contrast • Inferential**

Text to Text **Have you seen Edison's method of experimentation described in other books? How was it similar to Edison's?**

Students' responses will vary, but should mention science textbooks they have read.

512

Extend Language Define *catnap* from the caption on p. 513 as a short nap, like the naps cats take.

A taker of catnaps since his days as a young telegrapher, Edison wasn't picky about where he nodded off. Here he snoozes atop a lab table in his West Orange laboratory in 1911.

 8

513

Develop Vocabulary

PRACTICE LESSON VOCABULARY

Use these prompts to give students practice with the lesson vocabulary.

1. What can be *generated*? *(electricity, ideas, power)*

2. What does a computer *convert* electrical signals into? *(images, words, and sounds)*

3. Name a *mechanism* in a kitchen that can increase the *efficiency* of a cook. *(microwave oven)*

BUILD CONCEPT VOCABULARY

Review previous concept words with students. Ask if students have come across any words today in their reading or elsewhere that they would like to add to the Inventions Concept Web, such as *model* and *genius*.

 STRATEGY SELF-CHECK

Monitor and Fix Up

Have students stop and assess whether they need to adjust their rate of reading. This will help them better evaluate what they are reading.

To assess how well students understand the text, students should summarize what they learned so far. Then have students determine how well the author achieves her purpose based on this information.

SELF-CHECK

Students can ask themselves these questions to assess their ability to use the skill and strategy.

- Do I understand the information that the author is trying to convey?
- How does this information serve the author's purpose?
- Do I need to adjust my reading pace because of the number of difficult words and the amount of new information in the text?

Monitor Progress	
Author's Purpose	
If... students have difficulty using fix-up strategies and understanding what the author is trying to convey,	**then...** review the skill lesson on pp. 500–501.

 Strategy Response Log

Answer Questions Have students see if they can answer any of the questions they asked before they started reading the selection. (See p. 504.) Have them write a new question for the rest of the selection.

If you want to teach this selection in two sessions, stop here.

Guiding Comprehension

If you are teaching the selection in two sessions, discuss the author's purpose for writing and review the lesson vocabulary.

9 **Vocabulary • Word Structure**

The prefix *re-* means "again" in the word *rewound*. In which of these words are the letters *re* a prefix meaning "again"?

reasoned, record, reciting, reproduce, replace

The words *reproduce* and *replace* have the prefix *re-* that means "again."

Monitor Progress

Word Structure

If... students are unable to use the meaning of the prefix to determine the meaning a word,	then... use the skill and strategy instruction on p. 515.

10 Draw Conclusions • Inferential

How important was the phonograph to people at the time of its invention?

The phonograph was important, based on people's reactions to it. People felt it was a miracle.

DAY 3 Grouping Options

Reading
Whole Group Discuss the Question of the Day.

Small Group Differentiated Instruction
Read *Inventing the Future*. See pp. 500f–500g for the small group lesson plan.

Whole Group Discuss the Reader Response questions on p. 522. Then use p. 527a.

Language Arts
Use pp. 527e–527k.

While he was working on the telephone, another sound-related idea occurred to Edison. If the human voice could travel over wires, he reasoned, then there should be a way to record the sound so that it could be listened to later. In November 1877, Edison gave a sketch of an invention he called the phonograph to John Kruesi and asked him to build it. A few days later, Kruesi had a model ready for testing. A simple machine, it consisted of a hand-cranked cylinder covered in tinfoil, a mouthpiece with a metal disk called a diaphragm, and a needle.

With his muckers gathered around him, Edison turned the handle of the machine while he shouted a nursery rhyme into the mouthpiece. As the sound waves of his voice vibrated the diaphragm, the attached needle scratched grooves in the foil. When he finished reciting, he **9** rewound the cylinder, put the needle into the tracks it had made, and cranked the handle again. To everyone's surprise, the machine worked the very first time! Out of the phonograph came Edison's voice, faint but clear: "Mary had a little lamb, its fleece was white as snow, and everywhere that Mary went, the lamb was sure to go." The excited experimenters stayed up all night recording themselves with the invention, which was the ancestor of modern CD players.

10 The next morning Edison took his brand-new "baby" to New York City and dazzled the editors of *Scientific American* magazine with a demonstration. Word of the amazing invention spread rapidly, and Edison became a celebrity overnight. The phonograph's ability to reproduce human speech seemed like a miracle. Newspaper headlines proclaimed him the "Inventor of the Age" and the "Wizard of Menlo Park."

Edison, who enjoyed the attention the phonograph attracted, envisioned a variety of commercial uses for the device, including toys and dictation machines. He soon set it aside, however, to concentrate on the greatest challenge of his career—the development of an electric lighting system that could be used in homes and businesses.

Electric lighting was not a new idea. Brightly burning lamps called arc lights (which glowed when a current of electricity jumped between two carbon rods) had already replaced gas street lamps in some large cities by the 1870s. But they were not suitable for home use. Not only

514

ELL

Fluency Use the first two paragraphs of p. 514 for fluency practice with your students. First, model reading with expression and correct phrasing. Then have students work in pairs and practice reading to each other.

"This [the phonograph] is my baby and I expect it to grow up to be a big feller and support me in my old age."

In 1878, Edison demonstrated his phonograph at the National Academy of Sciences in Washington, D.C. While there, he posed with his invention for this photograph taken by famed Civil War photographer Mathew Brady.

515

VOCABULARY STRATEGY

Word Structure

TEACH

Remind students that paying attention to prefixes can sometimes help them determine the meaning of an unknown word. Model how to determine which words contain the prefix *re-*, meaning "again."

Think Aloud **MODEL** First, I need to figure out which words do not contain the prefix *re-*. Looking at the words in the list, I can see that *reasoned, reciting,* and *record* do not contain a prefix. In those words, the letters *re* are part of the base word, and are not prefixes. So the only words with the prefix *re-* are *reproduce* and *replace.*

PRACTICE AND ASSESS

Tell students that the prefix *en-* means "to make or become." Ask how knowing the meaning of the prefix would help them to determine the meaning of the word *envisioned* on p. 514, paragraph 4. *(The root* vis *means "visible," so* envisioned *means "made visible" or "saw.")*

Phonographs and Music

In the decades following Edison's invention of the phonograph, the music recording industry rapidly developed in the United States and Europe. For the first time, the performances of great musical artists could be preserved. In the early 1900s, as classical and jazz recordings became more widely available, the phonograph brought music to a mass audience. It remained in common use until the 1980s, when audio compact discs were introduced.

Guiding Comprehension

11 Judgments • Critical

What do you think of Edison's "gamble"? Was it deceptive or smart?

Students should support their judgments with reasons.

12 Author's Purpose • Critical

What details about Edison's character do you learn on pp. 516–517? How do these details serve the author's purpose?

The author details Edison's intelligence, cleverness, perseverance, and drive. These details serve the author's purpose because they provide important information about Edison and the way in which he conducted business.

Monitor Progress
Author's Purpose

If... students are unable to determine how details serve the author's purpose,	then... use the skill and strategy instruction on p. 517.

EXTEND SKILLS

Invented Words

Point out that the word *phonograph* (p. 514) is an invented word formed from the roots *phono* (meaning "sound") and *graph* (meaning "to write"). A phonograph machine literally wrote with sounds. Have students identify other invented words in the selection and determine their meanings based on word structure. (*Examples include* telegraph, telephone, *and* kinetescope.)

Over the years, Edison produced a variety of phonographs for home use. The records he made to play on them were delivered to homes and could also be bought in stores.

was their glare too intense for indoors, they were also smelly. So people still used candles, oil lamps, or gas lamps to light their homes after dark.

Aware that other inventors were racing toward the same goal as he, Edison vowed to get there first. To gain the financial support he needed, he took a gamble. In September 1878, he announced to reporters that he was very close to developing a practical incandescent lamp, or light bulb. Not only that, he said he expected to have a safe, affordable electric lighting system ready to go in just six weeks. He was exaggerating his progress greatly, but so strong was his reputation at the time that few questioned his claim. Confident of Edison's genius, several rich investors established the Edison Electric Light Company to cover his expenses.

11 Edison's gamble paid off. It was time for the real work to begin.

The groundwork for the incandescent light bulb had been laid many years earlier by an English chemist named Sir Humphry Davy. In 1802, Davy discovered that by passing an electric current through strips of metal, he could make them hot enough to glow brightly, or incandesce, for a few seconds before they burned up.

516

Context Clues Help students use context clues to determine the meaning of the term *gamble* on p. 516. Have students look at the phrase, "he announced to reporters that he was very close to developing a practical incandescent lamp, or light bulb. Then point out the phrase, "He was exaggerating his progress greatly." Define *gamble* as a risk or chance.

The Menlo Park lab hummed with round-the-clock activity as Edison and his muckers—including several newly hired electrical experts—tackled the problem of the light bulb. Edison set some of his associates the task of finding a way to get all the air out of the glass bulb, so that the material giving off the light, called the filament, would not burn up too quickly. Other workers tested more than 1,600 materials—including horsehair, coconut fibers, fish line, spider webs, and even the hair from John Kruesi's beard—to find the best filament.

Finally his persistence was rewarded. In the fall of 1879, Edison and his muckers tested a piece of cotton sewing thread. First they carbonized it by baking it until it charred and turned into carbon. Then they inserted the carbonized thread into the glass bulb, forced out the air with a special vacuum pump, and sealed the glass. When connected to an

The front page of *The Daily Graphic* from July 9, 1879, (top) pictures Edison in sorcerer's garb, a reference to his nickname, the "Wizard of Menlo Park." The cartoon below it illustrates the fear electrical wiring inspired in some people in the 1880s.

This portrait of Edison associate Charles Batchelor is the first photograph ever taken by electric light. Edison sketched hundreds of different designs and tested more than 1,600 different materials in his quest to invent a practical, long-burning light bulb.

517

Author's Purpose Monitor/Fix Up

TEACH

Model the use of the fix-up strategy of re-reading the details on pp. 516–517 in order to determine how they serve the author's purpose.

Think Aloud **MODEL** What traits of Edison has the author focused on so far? I can look back at what I've read on pp. 516–517 to review the information presented by the author. In all the descriptions of Edison at his work, he comes across as an intelligent, hard-working, persistent, clever, and determined man. These details serve the author's purpose by providing important information about Edison.

PRACTICE AND ASSESS

To practice and assess the skill and strategy, ask students to review the selection so far and evaluate how well the author has informed them about Edison's inventions.

EXTEND SKILLS

Editorial Cartoons

Point out that cartoons like the one above express an opinion that is meant to inform and amuse. Editorial cartoons are a form of communication made up of two key elements: caricature and allusion. A caricature is an exaggerated or distorted portrait of an individual or group. An allusion is a reference to an issue or current event. Editorial cartoons are usually one-panel drawings that appear in a newspaper's editorial section. In 1754, Benjamin Franklin was the first person in this country to draw an editorial cartoon. Have students look for editorial cartoons in their local newspaper and discuss the caricature and alussion being portayed.

Guiding Comprehension

13 **Visualize • Critical**

Which details in p. 519, paragraph 1, help the reader visualize the scene being described?

Possible response: Details such as the astounded visitors, the brightly shining lamps, and the "brilliantly illuminated" lab all help the reader visualize the scene.

14 **Cause and Effect • Inferential**

How do you think the invention of the light bulb affected people's lives?

Possible response: The light bulb made it possible for more people to work and play at night.

Monitor Progress	
REVIEW **Cause and Effect**	
If... students have difficulty identifying the effect,	**then...** use the skill and strategy instruction on p. 519.

The inventor mixes chemicals in his West Orange laboratory.

518

Build Background Point out unfamiliar terms related to light and electricity on p. 519. A *generator* is a machine that produces electricity. A *socket* is where you plug in an electrical cord. A *switch* turns the light (or electrical product) on and off. A *safety fuse* is a wire or piece of metal used to break the connection in an electirc circuit in case of overheating. *Current* is the tem used to describe electricity flowing through a wire.

electric current, the bulb glowed steadily for more than 13 hours! Within a few weeks, the lab had produced an improved bulb that burned many hours longer.

In late December 1879, Edison invited the public to Menlo Park to see his marvelous new invention. As visitors got off the train in the evening, they were astounded by the brightly shining electric street lamps lighting their way. Even more impressive was the laboratory, which one newspaper article described as "brilliantly illuminated with twenty-five lamps."

This lab sketch from 1879 expresses the jubilation felt by Edison and his Menlo Park muckers at finally producing a long-burning light bulb.

Over the next two years, Edison and his crew worked feverishly to invent the many other devices besides the light bulb that were needed to get a full lighting system up and running. At the top of the list was an efficient generator, or dynamo, to produce the electricity from the generators, which would be housed in central power stations, to streets and buildings. Sockets, switches, safety fuses, and lamp fixtures also had to be designed. Ever practical, Edison didn't forget to **devise a** meter to measure the amount of electricity that customers used, so they could be charged accordingly. His lighting would be cheap, yes, but not free!

By 1882, Edison had set up the world's first commercially successful electric power station, on Pearl Street in New York City. He and his family had moved to the city sometime earlier, so that he could personally supervise the installation of his lighting system. On September 4 of that year, he was finally ready to deliver what he had promised four years earlier. Standing in the office of millionaire businessman J. P. Morgan—one of his investors—Edison flicked a switch and current from the Pearl Street station lit the office lamps.

By nightfall, some two dozen buildings in the city's financial district glowed with Edison's electric lights. As crowds gathered in the streets to

519

Scientific Careers in Electricity

TIME FOR Science

The uses of electricity have expanded since Edison's time. Today, scientists and engineers in the field of electricity and electronics conduct research and develop products in a wide variety of areas—from the global positioning system (GPS) and industrial robotics to communication systems.

SKILLS ⟷ STRATEGIES IN CONTEXT

Cause and Effect REVIEW

TEACH

Read p. 519, paragraph 2, aloud and then model identifying the effect of the invention of the improved light bulb on cities and towns.

Think Aloud **MODEL** To answer the question, I can think about how life might have been different without the light bulb. For example, without light at night, there would have been many things people could not do. So one of the effects of the invention of the improved light bulb is that people would be able to work and do other important activities at night.

PRACTICE AND ASSESS

Ask students to identify the effect of metering the amount of electricity used. *(Customers could be charged.)*

Guiding Comprehension

15 ⟳ **Author's Purpose • Critical**

How well does the author achieve her purpose for writing? Support your answer.

Possible response: The author does a good job of achieving her purpose because she provides a lot of interesting information about how Edison worked and the many important products he invented.

16 Summarize • Critical

Text to Self **Make a list of four products that Edison invented and identify a product you use in your everyday life that developed from each one.**

Possible responses: carbon button telephone transmitter—cell phone; phonograph—CD player; practical light bulb—reading lamp; kinetoscope—DVD

Strategy Response Log

Summarize When students finish reading the selection, provide this prompt: Imagine that a friend has asked you what Thomas Edison's most important inventions were. In four or five sentences, describe three of his inventions.

Edison's earliest movies were filmed in West Orange. They were viewed through a peephole machine called a kinetoscope (above).

marvel at the latest magic from the Wizard of Menlo Park, his fame soared even higher.

Edison devoted the next few years to improving his electrical system and spreading it around the country and the world. He set up numerous companies to handle the manufacturing and installation of his products and made millions of dollars.

In 1887, Edison built the laboratory of his dreams. Located about a mile from Glenmont, it was the largest, best-equipped research facility in the world. Ten times bigger than Menlo Park, the main lab was three stories high and 250 feet long. Housed in separate buildings were a physics lab, a chemistry lab, and a metallurgical lab. In his new laboratory, Edison continued to improve his lighting system.

Edison's West Orange lab also contributed to the birth of the motion picture industry. Around 1889, Edison and a team of muckers led by William K. L. Dickson started work on "an instrument which does for the Eye what the phonograph does for the Ear."

In a few years, they had invented a movie camera, called a kinetograph, and a peep-hole machine, called a kinetoscope, for watching the movies. To make films for the kinetoscopes, Edison opened the world's first motion picture studio in West Orange in 1893. Only 20 to 30 seconds long, these early movies featured a variety of subjects, from acrobats to boxers to ballet dancers.

Edison also returned to his "baby," the phonograph, in West Orange. While Edison had been working on electric lights, inventors Chichester Bell (a cousin of Alexander Graham Bell) and Charles Tainter had created

TIME LINE OF EDISON'S INVENTIONS

		1877—Tinfoil phonograph	
	1875—Electric pen	1877—Carbon-button	
1869—Electric vote recorder	1875—Quadruplex telegraph	telephone transmitter	1879—First prac light bulb

520

Ⓔ Ⓛ Ⓛ

Extend Language Help students to understand the expression "spurred by the competition" by defining *spurred* as "urged" or "encouraged to proceed."

As part of the 1929 Jubilee, Edison (seated) reenacts the lighting of his famous bulb 50 years earlier. Looking on are Henry Ford (standing, left) and former Edison employee Francis Jehl.

their own, improved version of the machine, which used wax cylinders rather than tinfoil for recording. Spurred by the competition, Edison developed an even better wax-cylinder phonograph. Although he originally envisioned the device as a business machine for taking dictation, people were eager to purchase it for home entertainment. Edison was happy to satisfy them. Not only did he produce a variety of phonographs for home use over the next 40 years, he also made prerecorded cylinders, or records, of popular tunes to play on them. In the process, he helped to create what we now call the recording industry.

15
16

Edison phonograph from 1911

1888—'Perfected' phonograph	1893—System for making and showing motion pictures	1909—Storage battery

521

Develop Vocabulary

PRACTICE LESSON VOCABULARY

As a class, complete the following sentences orally.

1. **A machine that can** *reproduce* **text is known as a** *(copier)*.
2. **The muckers helped Edison** *devise* **an instrument that** *transmitted* *(sound, light,* or *pictures)*.
3. **Newspapers** *proclaimed* **that Edison was a** *(genius)*.

BUILD CONCEPT VOCABULARY

Review previous concept words with students. Ask if students have come across any words today in their reading or elsewhere that they would like to add to the Inventions Concept Web, such as *invaluable* and *envisioned*.

STRATEGY SELF-CHECK

Monitor and Fix Up

Ask students to demonstrate how well they understood the information the author is trying to convey by summarizing Edison's career. Have them use the time line on pp. 520–521 as a basis for their summary. Use Practice Book p. 198.

SELF-CHECK

Students can ask themselves these questions to assess their ability to use the skill and strategy.

- Did I understand the information the author is trying to convey?
- Did I adjust my reading rate to improve my comprehension?
- Did I summarize to organize and understand ideas?

Monitor Progress

Author's Purpose

If... students have difficulty monitoring their comprehension and using a fix-up strategy,	then... use the Reteach lesson on p. 527b.

Author's Purpose

- The **author's purpose** is the reason or reasons the author has for writing.
- An author may write to persuade, to inform, to entertain, or to express ideas and feelings. An author may have more than one reason for writing.

Directions: Read the following passage. Then answer the questions below.

One summer day a walk through the woods led to a clever invention. George de Mestral was hiking the mountain paths of his native Switzerland with his dog in 1948. After he got home, he noticed burrs clinging to his pants and his dog's fur. Burrs are the prickly seed cases of certain plants. As he removed these burrs, he observed how their many curved arms stuck to fabric and fur.

Studying them under the microscope gave him an idea for a new type of closure. He experimented with different materials and formats. Eventually, he invented a fabric covered with tiny hooks. This fabric sticks tight to any fabric with a fuzzy surface. His invention is manufactured to hold pockets, shoes, and clothing closed or to attach one thing to another. People should be glad de Mestral and his dog took a walk that day.

Possible answers given for 2–4.
1. What was the author's main purpose for writing this passage?
   The author's main purpose is to inform.
2. What is one important detail that shows the author's purpose?
   In 1948, George de Mestral found burrs in his dog's fur.
3. What is another important detail that shows the author's purpose?
   de Mestral studied the burrs and invented a new fabric.
4. How well do you think the author met his main purpose for writing? Explain.
   The author does a good job of providing informative facts and details that explain de Mestral's invention.
5. To monitor your comprehension, take notes on the purpose of each sentence. Which sentence in the article has a different purpose from the main purpose of the passage? Explain.
   The purpose of the last sentence is to persuade. It uses the word *should* to persuade readers of the value of the invention.

School + Home Home Activity Your child identified the author's purposes in a nonfiction passage. Read a magazine article about a different invention with your child. Work together to identify the author's main purpose in the article. Talk about secondary purposes too. Challenge your child to monitor his or her comprehension and use fix-up strategies in order to understand the information in the article.

▲ **Practice Book** p. 197

Reader Response

Open for Discussion Personal Response

 MODEL I'd start by asking Edison what else he liked to do besides inventing.

Comprehension Check Critical Response

1. I would remember dates more easily in chronological order, but it may not force me to read more elsewhere. **Author's Purpose**

2. Another purpose is to persuade the reader that Edison was an admirable person with many accomplishments and a likeable personality. **Author's Purpose**

3. Possible responses: Edison's telephone produced better sound and range; his light bulb burned longer. **Monitor and Fix Up**

4. Responses will vary, but should include an understanding of the word *reproduce*. **Vocabulary**

Look Back and Write For test practice, assign a 10–15 minute time limit. For assessment, see the Scoring Rubric at the right.

Retell

Have students retell *Inventing the Future*.

Monitor Progress
Check Retelling ④③②①

If... students have difficulty retelling the selection,	then... use the Retelling Cards and the Scoring Rubric for Retelling on p. 523 to assist fluent retelling.

SUCCESS PREDICTOR

Check Retelling Have students use the selection photographs, illustrations, and captions to guide their retellings. You may need to overlook mistakes in English, such as inconsistent verb tenses, in the retellings. See the ELL and Transition Handbook.

Reader Response

Open for Discussion Suppose that you are a talk show host. Thomas Alva Edison is to be your next guest. You want your audience to learn more about him than a list of his inventions. What are some questions you will ask him?

1. The biographer organizes this article by time. She lists a date followed by Edison's accomplishments during that time, then moves on to another date and another set of accomplishments. How would this way of organizing help you if you were studying to remember the information? How well does it encourage you to find out more about this subject? **Think Like an Author**

2. The author's purpose for writing *Inventing the Future* was to inform you about Thomas Alva Edison's inventions. What is another purpose the author had for writing this piece? Why do you think this? **Author's Purpose**

3. Some of Edison's inventions were improvements of other people's inventions. Create a T-Chart. Write *telephone* on the top left and *light bulb* on the top right. Under each head, record the ways in which Thomas Edison improved upon each of these inventions. **Monitor and Fix Up**

4. What might Thomas Edison tell prospective investors to get them to offer money for his work on the phonograph? Use words from the selection and the Words to Know list in your answer. **Vocabulary**

 Look Back and Write Look back at page 508 to review the steps involved in team inventing. Then write the steps in your own words, placing them in order and numbering them. In one sentence, tell how these steps might help future inventors.

Meet author Marfé Ferguson Delano on page 788.

522

Scoring Rubric — Look Back and Write

Top-Score Response A top-score response will use information from page 508 to list the steps involved in team inventing, and describe how these steps might help future inventors.

Example of a Top-Score Response (1) Sketch out the idea. (2) Share it with others. (3) Create a working model. (4) Experiment with the model to see if it works. (5) Rework model if necessary. These steps might help future inventors by reminding them that the inventions that don't work can teach us just as much as those that do.

For additional rubrics, see p. WA10.

Write Now

Summary

Prompt

Inventing the Future provides information about Edison's groundbreaking discoveries. Think about an interesting article or story that you have read recently.
Now write a summary explaining what the article or story is about.

Student Model

Opening **focuses** the reader on the subject. Topic sentences give the main idea of each paragraph.

Writer chooses key words to summarize big ideas.

The Chimpanzees I Love provides a great deal of fascinating information about chimpanzees. The first section discusses the mind of the chimpanzee. Scientists once thought that only humans could think. Now they are researching how chimps **communicate, learn, and remember.** The second section talks about chimps in captivity and its negative consequences. Many chimps were taken from their homes for research or to perform in circuses. They lived in **prison-like cages.** The final section provides information on challenges facing chimpanzees today. As the trees in African forests are cut down, chimps are **losing their habitats.** People are working to solve these problems.

Use the model to help you write your own summary.

523

Write Now

Look at the Prompt
Explain that each sentence in the prompt has a purpose.

- Sentence 1 presents a topic.
- Sentence 2 suggests students think about the topic.
- Sentence 3 tells what to write—a summary.

Strategies to Develop Focus/Ideas
Have students

- take out details that don't focus on the highlights of the article or story.
- focus each paragraph on one section of the story or article.
- anticipate and answer questions the reader might have.
- eliminate wordiness that detracts from the main ideas.

For additional suggestions and rubric, see pp. 527g–527h.

Writer's Checklist

- ☑ **Focus** Do sentences stick to the summary?
- ☑ **Organization** Are ideas in order?
- ☑ **Support** Do details elaborate key ideas?
- ☑ **Conventions** Are punctuation and spelling correct?

Scoring Rubric Expository Retelling

Rubric 4 3 2 1	4	3	2	1
Connections	Makes connections and generalizes beyond the text	Makes connections to other events, texts, or experiences	Makes a limited connection to another event, text, or experience	Makes no connection to another event, text, or experience
Author's Purpose	Elaborates on author's purpose	Tells author's purpose with some clarity	Makes some connection to author's purpose	Makes no connection to author's purpose
Topic	Describes the main topic	Identifies the main topic with some details early in retelling	Identifies the main topic	Retelling has no sense of topic
Important Ideas	Gives accurate information about events, steps, and ideas using details and key vocabulary	Gives accurate information about events, steps, and ideas with some detail and key vocabulary	Gives limited or inaccurate information about events, steps, and ideas	Gives no information about events, steps, and ideas
Conclusions	Draws conclusions and makes inferences to generalize beyond the text	Draws conclusions about the text	Is able to tell some learnings about the text	Is unable to draw conclusions or make inferences about the text

Retelling Plan

- ☑ **Week 1** Assess Strategic Intervention students.
- ☑ **Week 2** Assess Advanced students.
- ☑ **Week 3** Assess Strategic Intervention students.
- ☑ **Week 4** Assess On-Level students.
- ☑ **This week assess any students you have not yet checked during this unit.**

Use the Retelling Chart on p. TR17 to record retelling.

Selection Test To assess with *Inventing the Future*, use Selection Tests, pp. 77–80.

Fresh Reads for Differentiated Test Practice For weekly leveled practice, use pp. 115–120.

SUCCESS PREDICTOR

Social Studies in Reading

Social Studies in Reading

OBJECTIVES

- Examine features of a biography.
- Practice a test-taking strategy.
- Compare and contrast across texts.

PREVIEW/USE TEXT FEATURES

As students preview "Garrett Augustus Morgan," have them look at the article's section headings and graphic sources. After they preview, ask:

- **How can the subheads or section headings help readers quickly locate specific information about Morgan's life?** *(The subheads indicate what aspect of Morgan's life the text covers.)*

- **How do the graphic sources add to the reader's understanding of Morgan's life?** *(They help the reader connect to the time period in which Morgan lived and worked.)*

Link to Social Studies

Once students have chosen someone, tell them to use a time line or chart to list the most important events in the person's life.

DAY 4 Grouping Options

Reading
Whole Group Discuss the Question of the Day.

Small Group Differentiated Instruction
Read "Garrett Augustus Morgan." See pp. 500f–500g for the small group lesson plan.

Whole Group Use p. 527a.

Language Arts
Use pp. 527e–527k.

Biography

Genre
- Biography is nonfiction centered on someone's life but written by another person.
- Biographies are usually organized according to time—the sequence in which events happened in the person's life.

Text Features
- The author uses section headings to separate topics within Garrett Morgan's life to help the reader more easily organize the concepts.
- The author writes about Garrett Morgan doing things. This shows that Garrett Morgan controlled his life and behavior rather than passively letting the things happen. As you read, look for words that show Garrett Morgan taking active control.

Link to Social Studies
Biographies describe events in the lives of important people. Write a short biography of someone important in your life.

524

Garrett Augustus ～ Morgan ～

Garrett Augustus Morgan was an African American businessman and inventor whose curiosity and innovation led to the development of many useful and helpful products. A practical man of humble beginnings, Morgan devoted his life to creating things that made the lives of other people safer and more convenient.

Among his inventions was an early traffic signal that greatly improved safety on America's streets and roadways. Indeed, Morgan's technology was the basis for modern traffic signal systems and was an early example of what we know today as Intelligent Transportation Systems.

Content-Area Vocabulary — Social Studies

enterprise	an undertaking or project
innovation	bringing in new things or new ways of doing things
pedestrians	people who walk
proficiency	skill

Access Content Preview the text, reading each subhead aloud and verifying student's understanding. Review the content-area vocabulary with students to improve comprehension as they read.

The Inventor's Early Life

The son of former slaves, Garrett A. Morgan was born in Paris, Kentucky, on March 4, 1877. His early childhood was spent attending school and working on the family farm with his brothers and sisters. While still a teenager, he left Kentucky and moved north to Cincinnati, Ohio, in search of opportunity.

Although Morgan's formal education never took him beyond elementary school, he hired a tutor while living in Cincinnati and continued his studies in English grammar.

In 1895, Morgan moved to Cleveland, Ohio, where he went to work as a sewing machine repairman for a clothing manufacturer. News of his proficiency for fixing things and experimenting traveled fast and led to numerous job offers from various manufacturing firms in the Cleveland area.

In 1907, Morgan opened his own sewing equipment and repair shop. It was the first of several businesses he would establish. In 1909, he expanded the enterprise to include a tailoring shop that employed 32 employees. The new company turned out coats, suits, and dresses, all sewn with equipment that Morgan himself had made.

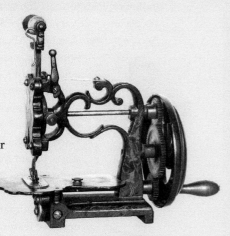

In 1920, Morgan moved into the newspaper business when he established the *Cleveland Call*. As the years went on, he became a prosperous and widely respected businessman, and he was able to purchase a home and an automobile. Indeed it was Morgan's experience while driving along the streets of Cleveland that led to the invention of the nation's first patented traffic signal.

A sewing machine from the early 1900s

Monitor & Fix-Up How could you keep track of all these dates?

525

History of Traffic Signals

No one knows who invented or used the first traffic control device. However, even roads in ancient Rome had traffic signs. The first recorded use of electric traffic signals with red and green lights on streets occurred in Cleveland in 1914. In 1920, Detroit introduced a yellow light to warn traffic of a change to red or green. Since then, traffic signals have been developed to automatically respond to changing traffic demands, but in most areas, signals are timed to change automatically.

BIOGRAPHY

Use the sidebar on p. 524 to guide discussion.

- Explain to students that a biography is the story of a real person's life, written by another person.
- Tell students that a biography may cover a person's whole life or focus on an important part of it. Have students use the subheads to identify what parts of Morgan's life this biography covers.
- Discuss with students the main points the graphic sources illustrate.

Audio CD AudioText

Monitor & Fix Up

Students could make a time line to keep track of the important dates in Morgan's life.

TEST PRACTICE

Strategies for Nonfiction

USE SUBHEADS Remind students that subheads let readers know what topics they are about to read. When a biography like "Garrett Augustus Morgan" has subheads, a reader can use them to locate information to answer test questions. Provide the following strategy.

Use the Strategy

1. Read the test question and identify what is being asked.
2. Find the subhead that focuses on this time period or topic.
3. Read the text following the subhead to find information to help answer the test question.

GUIDED PRACTICE Have students discuss how they would use the strategy to answer the following question.

How did Garrett Morgan demonstrate his ambition while he was still a teenager?

INDEPENDENT PRACTICE After students answer the following test question, discuss the process they used to find information.

What was it like on American roads and streets before traffic signals became common?

The Garrett Morgan Traffic Signal

The first American-made automobiles were introduced to U.S. consumers shortly before the turn of the century. The Ford Motor Company was founded in 1903 and with it American consumers began to discover the adventures of the open road.

In the early years of the 20th century, it was not uncommon for bicycles, animal-powered wagons, and new gasoline-powered motor vehicles to share the same streets and roadways with pedestrians. Accidents were frequent. After

Before the invention of the traffic signal, road intersections were often chaotic and dangerous

witnessing a collision between an automobile and a horse-drawn carriage, Morgan was convinced that something should be done to improve traffic safety.

While other inventors are reported to have experimented with and even marketed traffic signals, Garrett A. Morgan was the first to apply for and acquire a U.S. patent for such a device. The patent was granted on November 20, 1923. Morgan later had the technology patented in Great Britain and Canada as well.

The Morgan traffic signal was a T-shaped pole unit that featured three positions: Stop, Go, and an all-directional stop position. This "third position" halted traffic in all directions to allow pedestrians to cross streets more safely.

Morgan's traffic management device was used throughout North America until it was replaced by

526

ELL

Test Practice Write the Guided Practice test question on the board. Work with students to underline the words that should guide their answer search. Explain that the words *while he was still a teenager* indicate that the question focuses on Morgan's early life.

the red-, yellow-, and green-light traffic signals currently used around the world. The inventor sold the rights to his traffic signals to the General Electric Corporation for $40,000. Shortly before his death, in 1963, Morgan was awarded a citation for his traffic signal by the United States government.

Other Morgan Inventions

Garrett Morgan was constantly experimenting to develop new concepts. Though the traffic signal came at the height of his career and became one of his most renowned inventions, it was just one of several innovations he developed, manufactured, and sold over the years.

Morgan invented a zig-zag stitching attachment for manually operated sewing machines. He also founded a company that made personal grooming products, such as hair dying ointments and the curved-tooth pressing comb.

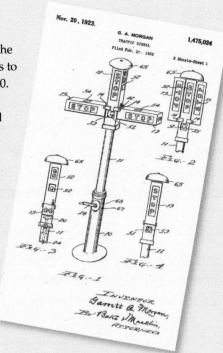

Morgan's sketch of his invention as submitted to the U.S. Patent Office

Reading Across Texts

How were the two inventors, Thomas Edison and Garrett Morgan, alike and different?

Writing Across Texts Write at least two similarities and two differences between Edison and Morgan.

Author's Purpose Why did the author write this article?

527

CONNECT TEXT TO TEXT

Reading Across Texts

Guide students in brainstorming some adjectives that describe both Edison and Morgan. Have students provide examples of behavior to support the adjectives they suggest. Then help students think of ways the two inventors were alike and how they differed, perhaps focusing on the way they worked, the things they invented, and how famous they were.

Writing Across Texts Students can use the class discussion as a starting point to identify the two similarities and two differences they wish to focus on. Suggest that students write two paragraphs, one describing the similarities and one describing the differences.

Author's Purpose

The author wrote this article to inform readers about Garrett Morgan's life and inventions.

Fluency Assessment Plan

☑ **Week 1** Assess Advanced students.

☑ **Week 2** Assess Strategic Intervention students.

☑ **Week 3** Assess On-Level students.

☑ **Week 4** Assess Strategic Intervention students.

☑ **This week assess any students you have not yet checked during this unit.**

Set individual goals for students to enable them to reach the year-end goal.

• Current Goal: 130–138 wcpm
• Year-End Goal: 150 wcpm

Build students' fluency by encouraging them to repeatedly read aloud passages from familiar and favorite selections, including books that reflect their cultures.

Fluency Coach CD To develop fluent readers, use Fluency Coach.

DAY 5 Grouping Options

Reading

Whole Group
Revisit the Question of the Week.

Small Group
Differentiated Instruction
Reread this week's Leveled Readers. See pp. 500f–500g for the small group lesson plan.

Whole Group
Use pp. 527b–527c.

Language Arts
Use pp. 527d–527l.

PUNCTUATION CLUES

Fluency

DAY 1

Model Reread "Inventing the Stethoscope" on p. 500m. Explain that you will use the punctuation marks in the text as clues for grouping words together and for pauses. Model for students as you read.

DAY 2

Echo Reading Read aloud p. 511. Have students notice how you pause and chunk together the words set apart by commas or dashes. Have students practice as a class doing three echo readings of p. 511.

DAY 3

Model Read aloud the first paragraph on p. 517. Have students notice how you pause in the last sentence between words in a series that are set off by commas. Practice as a class by doing three echo readings.

DAY 4

Partner Reading Partners practice reading aloud the first paragraph on p. 517 three times. Students should use punctuation to guide their phrasing and offer each other feedback.

Monitor Progress | Check Fluency WCPM

As students reread, monitor their progress toward their individual fluency goals. Current Goal: 130–138 words correct per minute. End-of-Year Goal: 150 words correct per minute.

If... students cannot read fluently at a rate of 130–138 words correct per minute,
then... make sure students practice with text at their independent level. Provide additional fluency practice, pairing nonfluent readers with fluent readers.

If... students already read at 150 words correct per minute,
then... they do not need to reread three to four times.

SUCCESS PREDICTOR

DAY 5

Assessment
Individual Reading Rate Use the Fluency Assessment Plan and do a one-minute timed reading of either selection from this week to assess students in Week 5. Pay special attention to this week's skill, punctuation clues. Provide corrective feedback for each student.

RETEACH

Author's Purpose

TEACH

Remind students that authors often have more than one reason for writing. After students finish reading a selection, they should think about whether the author met his or her purpose in writing and why the author was or was not successful. Students can complete Practice Book p. 198 on their own, or you can complete it as a class.

ASSESS

Divide students into small groups and have them answer these questions about *Inventing the Future,* pp. 504–521:

1. Do you think the author met her purposes in writing? Why or why not?

2. How did the author make the writing interesting? Give examples.

If you had the same reasons for writing as the author, how would you have written the selection?

For additional instruction of author's purpose, see DI·56.

EXTEND SKILLS

Steps in a Process

TEACH

Identifying the steps in a process involves recognizing and retelling the order of steps taken to complete an action. Setting up a science experiment, solving a math problem, playing a new game, and sending e-mail are all actions that involve steps. Visualizing steps as you read them may help you retell them in the correct order.

Have partners identify and list the steps in operating Edison's first phonograph, described on p. 514, paragraph 2.

ASSESS

Have students list the steps in testing Edison's light bulb, described on pp. 517–518, paragraph 2.

AFTER READING

OBJECTIVES

- Evaluate the author's purpose.
- Identify and retell steps in a process.

Skills Trace

Author's Purpose

Introduce/Teach	TE: 6.4 430–431, 500–501; 6.6 652–653
Practice	Practice Book: 163, 167, 168, 193, 197, 198, 253, 257, 258
Reteach/Review	**TE: 6.1 125; 6.4 455b, 465, 527b, DI•53, DI•56; 6.6 733, 671b, DI•52**
Test	Selection Test: 65–68, 77–80, 101–104; Benchmark Test: Unit 4

Access Content Reteach the skill by reviewing the Picture It! lesson on author's purpose in the ELL Teaching Guide, pp. 134–135.

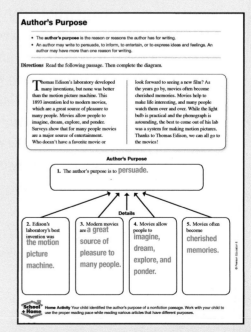

▲ **Practice Book** p. 198

Words Correct Per Minute

SUCCESS PREDICTOR

Vocabulary and Word Study

Word Structure

PREFIXES Review the meaning of the prefixes *re-* (again), *pro-* (forth, forward), and *trans-* (across, beyond, through). Have students identify the prefix, the base word, and the meaning of each word in the chart.

Word	Prefix	Base word	Meaning
reinvent	re-	invent	to invent again
transplant			
protrude			
transform			

Inventions

LOOKING BACK Remind students of the unit theme of explorers, pioneers, and discoverers. Discuss the Unit Focus question: How have those who've gone first influenced those who've gone after? Ask students how the Concept Vocabulary from each week of this unit relates to the unit theme and the unit focus question. Ask students if they have any words or categories to add. If time permits, create a Unit Concept Web.

Technology

New inventions sometimes spark a whole new vocabulary. Think of all the words and acronyms that came into being or acquired new meaning with the advent of the Internet: e-mail, Web site, "surfing" the Net, instant messaging ROM. Have students work with a partner and make a list of 5 to 10 words or acronyms associated with a new technology of their choice. Then have them define the words.

Term	Meaning
LCD	Liquid crystal display screen
voicemail	
RAM	
pixel	

Monitor Progress

Check Vocabulary

If... students suggest words or categories that are not related to the concept,	then... review the words and categories on the Concept Web and discuss how they relate to the lesson concept.

SUCCESS PREDICTOR

Speaking and Viewing

SPEAKING

Advertisement

SET-UP Have students choose one of Edison's inventions and prepare an oral advertisement that might have been given at a public event in Edison's time. In the advertisement, students should describe the invention and tell how it will improve people's lives.

VISUAL AIDS Suggest that students use a visual aid to enhance their advertisement. They might use a photograph from the selection, a photograph or illustration from another book, or an illustration they create themselves.

SPACE Advise students to consider the distance to the last row of seats and adjust how loudly they speak accordingly. Tell students to keep that distance in mind when they practice their advertisements before a family member or friend.

Listening Tips
- Look at the speaker and the speaker's visual aids.
- Show courteous, enthusiastic attention.
- Listen for persuasive appeals.
- Evaluate the speaker's message. Decide whether or not you find the message convincing.

Support Vocabulary Use the following to review and extend vocabulary and to explore lesson concepts further:
- ELL Poster 20, Days 3–5 instruction
- Vocabulary Activities and Word Cards in ELL Teaching Guide, pp. 136–137

Assessment For information on assessing students' speaking, listening, and viewing, see the ELL and Transition Handbook.

VIEWING

Analyze a Photo

Direct students to look closely at the photograph of a home delivery of Edison's records at the top of p. 516. Have students work with partners to answer these questions orally or in writing.

1. **What does the photograph show?** (A man arriving in a neighborhood in a horse-drawn wagon to make a home delivery of Edison's records. Four young children have come to watch the man.)

2. **Based on the photograph, what inferences can you make about people's reactions to Edison's phonograph and records?** (Edison's phonograph and records attracted attention and curiosity.)

3. **What can you tell about the transportation of that time?** (There were no cars, or perhaps cars were not common. Horse-drawn wagons were in use.)

4. **How were records from that time period shaped and packaged?** (They were cylindrical, like soup cans. They were packaged in boxes that held 30 records.)

Over the years, Edison produced a variety of phonographs for home use. The records he made to play on them were delivered to homes and could also be bought in stores.

was their glare too intense for indoors, they were also smelly. So people still used candles, oil lamps, or gas lamps to light their homes after dark.

Aware that other inventors were racing toward the same goal as he, Edison vowed to get there first. To gain the financial support he needed, he took a gamble. In September 1878, he announced to reporters that he was very close to developing a practical incandescent lamp, or light bulb. Not only that, he said he expected to have a safe, affordable electric lighting system ready to go in just six weeks. He was exaggerating his progress greatly, but so strong was his reputation at the time that few questioned his claim. Confident of Edison's genius, several rich investors established the Edison Electric Light Company to cover his expenses.

Edison's gamble paid off. It was time for the real work to begin.

The groundwork for the incandescent light bulb had been laid many years earlier by an English chemist named Sir Humphry Davy. In 1802, Davy discovered that by passing an electric current through strips of metal, he could make them hot enough to glow brightly, or incandesce, for a few seconds before they burned up.

516

SUCCESS PREDICTOR

Grammar Using *Who* and *Whom*

OBJECTIVES

- Identify and define the proper use of the pronouns *who* and *whom*.
- Use *who* and *whom* correctly in writing.
- Become familiar with the correct use of *who* and *whom* on high-stakes tests.

Monitor Progress

Grammar

If... students	then...
have difficulty identifying how to use the pronouns *who* and *whom*,	provide additional instruction and practice in The Grammar and Writing Book pp. 164-167.

DAILY FIX-IT

This week use Daily Fix-It Transparency 20.

Spiral REVIEW

Support Grammar See the Grammar Transition lessons in the ELL and Transition Handbook.

▲ **The Grammar and Writing Book** For more instruction and practice, use pp. 164–167.

DAY 1   Teach and Model

DAILY FIX-IT

1. Thomas Edison needed electricety in their lab. (*electricity; his*)

2. Thomas Edison were the man who invented the electric pen. (*A; was*)

READING-GRAMMAR CONNECTION

Write this sentence from *Inventing the Future* on the board:

> He often gave assistants <u>who</u> worked closely with him on an invention a percentage of the profits it made.

Explain that the underlined pronoun *who* acts as the subject of a dependent clause *(who worked closely with him . . .)* in this complex sentence.

Display Grammar Transparency 20. Read aloud the definitions and sample sentences. Work through the items.

Using *Who* and *Whom*

The pronoun *who* is used as a subject.
Who called my brother? (*Who* is the subject of the sentence.)
My brother asked me who had called him. (*Who* is the subject of the clause *who had called him.*)
The pronoun *whom* is used as the object of a preposition, such as *to, for,* and *from,* and as a direct object. Most often, *whom* will be a direct object in questions.
To whom did you give the assignment? (*Whom* is the object of the preposition *to.*)
This was an assistant whom he trusted. (*Whom* is the direct object of the verb *trusted* in the clause *whom he trusted.*)
Whom did you tell? (*Whom* is a direct object.)
You can check if *who* should be used as a direct object. Change the word order so that the subject comes first. (Whom did you tell? You did tell whom?)

Directions Circle the pronoun in ( ) that correctly completes each sentence.

1. (Who) Whom) was investing in Edison Electric Light Company?
2. With (who, (whom) did Edison work when he had an idea for an invention?
3. (Who) Whom) gave us the most valuable inventions?
4. The committee decided on (who, (whom) they would award the Nobel Prize.
5. With (who, (whom) did J. P. Morgan invest money?
6. The helper (who) whom) worked the hardest became the top assistant.
7. Sir Humphry Davy was uncertain about (who, (whom) he would see.
8. Dot and Dash played with their father, (who) whom) loved them very much.

Directions Write *who* or *whom* to complete each sentence correctly.

9. To **whom** was Edison speaking when he recorded the nursery rhyme?
10. **Who** ran the show at the lab in Menlo Park?
11. He was the man **who** took Thomas Edison's job at the telegraph company after he left.
12. The boss is the one to **whom** the records were sent.

Unit 4 Inventing the Future   Grammar 20

▲ **Grammar Transparency** 20

DAY 2   Develop the Concept

DAILY FIX-IT

3. Edison was a celebraty whom patented 75 inventions in two years. (*celebrity; who*)

4. As the "Chief Mucker," Edison deserved reconition for his work? (*recognition; work.*)

GUIDED PRACTICE

Review the concept of when to use the pronouns *who* and *whom*.

- Use *who* as a subject.
- Use *whom* as the object of a preposition, such as *to, for*, or *from*.
- Use *whom* as a direct object in formal writing. Most often, *whom* will be a direct object in questions.

HOMEWORK Grammar and Writing Practice Book p. 77. Work through the first two items with the class.

Using *Who* and *Whom*

The pronoun *who* is used as a subject.
Who planted the garden? (*Who* is the subject of the sentence.)
My sister is the only one who likes roses. (*Who* is the subject of the clause *who likes roses.*)
The pronoun *whom* is used as the object of a preposition, such as *to, for,* and *from,* and as a direct object. Most often, *whom* will be a direct object in questions.
To whom did you send the flowers? (*Whom* is the object of the preposition *to.*)
This is a man whom I admire. (*Whom* is the direct object of the verb *admire* in the clause whom I admire.)
Whom did you invite? (*Whom* is a direct object.)
You can check if *whom* should be used as a direct object. Change the word order so that the subject comes first. (Whom did you invite? You did invite whom?)

Directions Circle the pronoun in ( ) that correctly completes each sentence.

1. These are the inventors (who, (whom) you should acknowledge.
2. Mr. Edison, (who) whom) was a fond father, nicknamed his children Dot and Dash.
3. Edison was the inventor (who, (whom) wealthy investors supported.
4. The lab assistants were the ones (who) whom) built Edison's prototypes.
5. Edison worked with the assistants (who) whom) were best suited for the positions.
6. He is one of the people (who, (whom) history honors as a brilliant inventor and scientist.
7. Give the data to the woman (who) whom) calls for it.
8. People (who) whom) own CD players can thank Edison for his inventions.

Directions Write *who* or *whom* to complete each sentence correctly.

9. Batchelor and Kruesi were two assistants to **whom** Edison entrusted his work.
10. Edison believed negative results were valuable to a scientist **who** wanted to learn.
11. **Who** stole Edison's heart and married him?
12. To **whom** shall we award the patent for this clever invention?

Home Activity Your child learned about using who and whom. Have your child look through a magazine, point out the pronouns who and whom, and explain why each pronoun is used.

▲ **Grammar and Writing Practice Book** p. 77

DAY 3 — Apply to Writing

D A I L Y   F I X - I T

5. Pope and Edison was engineers with a specialtey in electricity. (*were; specialty*)

6. If you're interest is technology, get a subscribtion to a science magazine. (*your; subscription*)

USE *WHO* AND *WHOM* CORRECTLY

When a clause makes the choice of *who* and *whom* difficult, think about the sentence without the clause.

Example: Edison is the man (who, whom) many Americans believe was the greatest inventor of the century.

Think: Edison is the man (who, whom) ~~many Americans believe~~ was the greatest inventor of the century.

Correct: Edison is the man who many Americans believe was the greatest inventor of the century.

HOMEWORK Grammar and Writing Practice Book p. 78.

Using *Who* and *Whom*

Directions Choose *who* or *whom* to correctly complete each sentence. Then write this sentence and answer or explain it with another sentence or two. **Possible answers:**

1. A person who/whom I admire is _____.
   A person whom I admire is my father. He works hard, and he always does what is right.

2. To who/whom do I go for advice?
   To whom do I go for advice? I usually go to my mother. She always listens, and she gives advice that works.

3. A person who/whom works hard is _____.
   A person who works hard is Aunt Sophie. She has two jobs, she volunteers at the hospital, and she takes classes on the weekends.

4. Who/Whom is a person from history I'd like to meet?
   Who is a person from history I'd like to meet? I'd like to meet Ben Franklin. He invented so many different things. I'd like to know how he did that.

Directions Write two sentences about inventions you use every day. Use *who* or *whom* in each sentence. **Possible answers:**

5. I received my assignments from my teachers, who sent them by e-mail.

6. Dad, with whom I ride to school, drives a hybrid car.

Home Activity Your child learned how to use who and whom in writing. Ask your child to tell about the device in your home that he or she thinks is the most important invention. Ask your child to use who and whom at least once.

▲ **Grammar and Writing Practice Book** p. 78

DAY 4 — Test Preparation

D A I L Y   F I X - I T

7. In many families, the tradishon are to give children nicknames. (*tradition is*)

8. Of all Edison's employees, Batchelor was the more valuable (*most valuable.*)

STANDARDIZED TEST PREP

Test Tip

If you are confused about whether to use *who* or *whom* in a question, make the question into a statement and try substituting *he* or *him*. If *he* sounds correct, use *who*. If *him* sounds correct, use *whom*.

Example: From (who, whom) did you receive the news? (You received the news from <u>he</u>. You received the news from <u>him</u>. The second sentence sounds correct.)

HOMEWORK Grammar and Writing Practice Book p. 79.

Using *Who* and *Whom*

Directions Mark the letter of the pronoun that correctly completes the sentence.

1. Edison sold patents to those _____ wanted exclusive manufacturing rights.
   A Whose
   B which
   C what
   D who

2. In 1876, Edison moved with his wife, _____ he married in 1871, to New York City.
   A whom
   B who
   C that
   D which

3. The investors knew _____ they would blame for the failure of the business.
   A him
   B them
   C whom
   D who

4. _____ thought up the idea for the telephone?
   A Whose
   B Which
   C Who
   D Whom

5. Alexander Graham Bell is the inventor _____ I admire the most.
   A whom
   B who
   C whose
   D which

6. _____ should I thank for inventing the electric light bulb?
   A Who
   B Whom
   C Whose
   D Why

7. Edison sold the electric pen to mapmakers _____ saw value in the device.
   A whose
   B what
   C whom
   D who

8. To _____ did Edison sell his Newark-based business?
   A whom
   B who
   C them
   D that

9. Edison was a man _____ loved catnaps.
   A whom
   B which
   C who
   D what

10. To _____ do we give credit for the invention of the incandescent bulb?
    A who
    B what
    C that
    D whom

Home Activity Your child prepared for taking tests on using who and whom. Have your child write a paragraph about inventions. Ask him or her to use the pronouns who and whom at least once.

▲ **Grammar and Writing Practice Book** p. 79

DAY 5 — Cumulative Review

D A I L Y   F I X - I T

9. When Edison was 22 he patented a electric vote recorder. (*22, he; an*)

10. It was Edisons intention to call his children dot and Dash. (*Edison's; Dot*)

ADDITIONAL PRACTICE

Assign pp. 164–167 in The Grammar and Writing Book.

EXTRA PRACTICE Grammar and Writing Practice Book p. 141.

TEST PREPARATION Grammar and Writing Practice Book pp. 155–156.

ASSESSMENT

CUMULATIVE REVIEW Grammar and Writing Practice Book p. 80.

Using *Who* and *Whom*

Directions Circle the pronoun in ( ) that correctly completes each sentence.

1. Edison bragged about his "mockers" (**who**, whom) turned out inventions.

2. To (who, **whom**) did Edison give blueprints?

3. (**Who**, Whom) was known as the "Wizard of Menlo Park"?

4. Batchelor was the assistant (**who**, whom) posed in a photo taken with electric light.

5. (Who, **Whom**) did *Scientific American* interview about the phonograph?

Directions Write *who* or *whom* to complete each sentence correctly.

6. The inventor ____who____ improved the telephone also invented the phonograph.

7. Edison thought of ____whom____ he could trust.

8. The scientist to ____whom____ Bill was assigned was a brilliant statistician.

9. ____Who____ is responsible for inventing the television?

10. ____Who____ was present when the telephone transmitted Edison's faint voice?

11. The neighbor ____who____ lives down the street is an inventor.

12. Edison spoke to Batchelor, with ____whom____ he had worked for many years.

13. I work with scientists, for ____whom____ I have great respect.

14. Edison met a 16-year-old girl named Mary Stilwell ____who____ worked as a clerk.

15. At 23, Edison was a promising scientist ____who____ had a reputation as an electrical inventor.

Home Activity Your child reviewed using who and whom. Ask your child to say a sentence using who and another sentence using whom and to tell why these words are correctly used.

▲ **Grammar and Writing Practice Book** p. 80

AFTER READING

Writing for Tests Summary

OBJECTIVES

- Write a summary for a test.
- Identify key words in a prompt.
- Focus on focus/ideas.
- Use a rubric.

Genre Summary
Writer's Craft Know Your Purpose
Writing Trait Focus/Ideas

ELL

Focus/Ideas Talk with English learners about what they plan to write. Record ideas and help them generate language for support. Help them narrow their focus by eliminating unrelated details. See more writing support in the ELL and Transition Handbook.

Writing Traits

FOCUS/IDEAS The summary is clear and focused and holds the reader's attention throughout.

ORGANIZATION/PARAGRAPHS The writer organizes the summary by scenes so that it is easy to follow.

VOICE The writing is engaging and lively. The writer shows authority on the subject.

WORD CHOICE Specific words, such as *spoof* and *bluster,* make the summary lively.

SENTENCES Sentence structure is varied, lending interest to the summary.

CONVENTIONS There is excellent control, including punctuation of quotations.

DAY 1 Model the Trait

READING-WRITING CONNECTION

- When you write a response for tests, keep your ideas focused on your purpose to make your writing strong and engaging.
- Think about how *Inventing the Future* is focused on the life and work of Thomas Edison. The selection's purpose is to inform.

MODEL FOCUS/IDEAS Discuss Writing Transparency 20A. Then discuss the model and the writing trait of focus/ideas.

Think Aloud This summary is clearly focused on the drama *Space Cadets.* The first paragraph identifies and describes the work that is going to be summarized. The following paragraphs each focus on one scene from the play. The summary succinctly tells me what happened in the play without any unnecessary or unrelated details.

Writing for Tests

Prompt Write a summary of *Inventing the Future* or another selection that you have read recently. Begin with a topic sentence that explains what the selection is about. Then include only the most important details.

***Space Cadets:* A Summary**

Summary starts with topic sentence.

Space Cadets is a humorous play about a spaceship crew that encounters life on a new planet.

Events are explained in sequence.

In Scene 1, we meet the Captain, First Officer, and Ensign in a spoof of TV science-fiction shows. The Captain is full of bluster, and the Ensign is eager. They and most of the crew are not very bright. Soon the ship arrives at an alien world. The Captain appoints an away team—the First Officer and two space cadets, Tom and Harold.

Writer uses own words or uses quotation marks if words are copied from text.

In Scene 2, team members arrive on the planet's surface where they try to talk to a "space cow." They ignore Mog and Og, two aliens who look "like space dogs." Eventually, the humans get scared and dash back to their ship. Og and Mog, who turn out to be intelligent life forms, are left behind, saying, "There is no intelligent life out there."

Unit 4 Inventing the Future Writing Model 20A

▲ **Writing Transparency** 20A

DAY 2 Improve Writing

WRITER'S CRAFT
Know Your Purpose

Display Writing Transparency 20B. Read the directions and work together to identify different purposes for writing.

Think Aloud **KNOW YOUR PURPOSE** Tomorrow we will be writing a plot summary of a favorite selection. I will summarize *Black Frontiers.* It is important that I know my purpose when writing. For example, is my summary *to inform,* to *persuade,* or to *entertain*? In summarizing *Black Frontiers,* my purpose will be to *inform* you about this historical work.

GUIDED WRITING Students may need help knowing their purpose in writing.

Choose a nonfiction selection and a fiction selection that students have already read. Discuss the differences in style and subject matter.

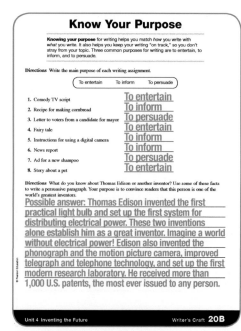

Know Your Purpose

Knowing your purpose for writing helps you match *how* you write with *what* you write. It also helps you keep your writing "on track," so you don't stray from your topic. Three common purposes for writing are to entertain, to inform, and to persuade.

Directions Write the main purpose of each writing assignment.

To entertain To inform To persuade

1. Comedy TV script To entertain
2. Recipe for making cornbread To inform
3. Letter to voters from a candidate for mayor To persuade
4. Fairy tale To entertain
5. Instructions for using a digital camera To inform
6. News report To inform
7. Ad for a new shampoo To persuade
8. Story about a pet To entertain

Directions What do you know about Thomas Edison or another inventor? Use some of these facts to write a persuasive paragraph. Your purpose is to convince readers that this person is one of the world's greatest inventors.

Possible answer: Thomas Edison invented the first practical light bulb and set up the first system for distributing electrical power. These two inventions alone establish him as a great inventor. Imagine a world without electrical power! Edison also invented the phonograph and the motion picture camera, improved telegraph and telephone technology, and set up the first modern research laboratory. He received more than 1,000 U.S. patents, the most ever issued to any person.

Unit 4 Inventing the Future Writer's Craft 20B

▲ **Writing Transparency** 20B

DAY 3 Prewrite and Draft

READ THE WRITING PROMPT

On page 523 of the Student Edition *Inventing the Future provides information about Edison's groundbreaking discoveries.*

Think about an interesting article or story that you have read recently.

Now write a summary explaining what the article or story is about.

Writing Test Tips

1. **Read the prompt carefully.**
 • Find key words.
 • Consider your purpose and audience.
2. **Develop a plan.** Think of what you want to say before writing. Use a graphic organizer. For example, fill out a T-chart or a Venn diagram.
3. **Support your ideas.** Use facts, examples, and details to strengthen your response.
4. **Use a variety of sentence structures.** Include complex, compound, and varied sentence beginnings.
5. **Choose clear, precise words.** Use words that create pictures and help readers understand what you mean.
6. **Check your writing.** You may not have time to recopy your work. However, you can neatly add, delete, or change words and make corrections in spelling, punctuation, or grammar. Make sure your handwriting is legible. Read your work again before handing it in.

DAY 4 Draft and Revise

EDITING/REVISING CHECKLIST

☑ **Focus** Do sentences stick to the topic of the story being summarized?

☑ **Organization** Is the summary developed in a logical, sequential order?

☑ **Support** Do specific words make the summary informative? Is the voice appropriate to the purpose?

☑ **Conventions** Have I indented correctly to make my organization clear? Have I used correct punctuation and capitalization to make the summary easy to follow?

Revising Tips

Focus/Ideas

• Remember to begin with a clear topic sentence. This will help your readers know what to expect.
• Delete any sentences that don't focus on the main idea or important details.
• Rearrange sentences in the summary to follow the sequence of the selection.

ASSESSMENT Use the scoring rubric to evaluate students' work.

DAY 5 Connect to Unit Writing

Story	
Week 1	News Story 429g–429h
Week 2	Story About an Animal 455g–455h
Week 3	Setting 477g–477h
Week 4	TV Script 499g–499h
Week 5	Summary 527g–527h

PREVIEW THE UNIT PROMPT

Write a story about an adventure, a discovery, or something that happened to you for the first time. Use some of these literary devices: foreshadowing, tension, suspense, conflict, humor.

APPLY

• A story has a beginning, middle, and end and focuses on one incident or event.
• In general, the purpose of writing a story is to entertain. Keep this purpose in mind when you are writing.

Writing Trait Rubric

	4	3	2	1
Focus/Ideas	Ideas clear and focused	Ideas generally clear with good details	Weak focus	Lack of focus
	Summary holds reader's attention	Summary generally holds reader's attention	Summary vague or unclear	Summary lacking in details and development

Spelling & Phonics   Word Endings -ty, -ity, -tion

OBJECTIVE

● Spell words ending in -ty, -ity, -tion.

Generalization

Connect to Phonics When -ty, -ity, and -tion are added to some words, one or more letters may change: *social, society*. The new word has a different pronunciation from the base word.

Spelling Words

1. electricity*	11. security
2. equality	12. clarity
3. society	13. popularity
4. specialty*	14. certainty
5. celebrity*	15. cruelty
6. recognition	16. subscription
7. description	17. reputation*
8. reduction	18. intention
9. tradition	19. deception
10. loyalty	20. penalty

Challenge Words

21. pronunciation	24. technicality
22. hospitality	25. demonstration
23. subtlety	

*Words from the selection

ELL

Spelling/Phonics Support See the ELL and Transition Handbook for spelling support.

DAY 1   Pretest and Sort

PRETEST

Use the Dictation Sentences from Day 5 to administer the pretest. Read the word, read the sentence, and then read the word again. Guide students in self-correcting their pretests and correcting any misspellings.

Monitor Progress

Spelling

If...	then...
If... students misspell more than 5 pretest words,	then... use words 1–10 for Strategic Intervention.
If... students misspell 1–5 pretest words,	then... use words 1–20 for On-Level practice.
If... students correctly spell all pretest words,	then... use words 1–25 for Advanced Learners.

HOMEWORK Spelling Practice Book, p. 77.

Word Endings -ty, -ity, -tion

Generalization When -ty, -ity, and -tion are added to some words, one or more letters may change: **social, society.**

Word Sort Sort the list words by their endings.

-ty	-tion
1. society	13. recognition
2. specialty	14. description
3. loyalty	15. reduction
4. certainty	16. tradition
5. cruelty	17. subscription
6. penalty	18. reputation
-ity	19. intention
7. electricity	20. deception
8. equality	
9. celebrity	
10. security	
11. clarity	
12. popularity	

Spelling Words
1. electricity
2. equality
3. society
4. specialty
5. celebrity
6. recognition
7. description
8. reduction
9. tradition
10. loyalty
11. security
12. clarity
13. popularity
14. certainty
15. cruelty
16. subscription
17. reputation
18. intention
19. deception
20. penalty

Challenge Words

-ty	-tion
21. subtlety	24. pronunciation
-ity	25. demonstration
22. hospitality	
23. technicality	

Challenge Words
21. pronunciation
22. hospitality
23. subtlety
24. technicality
25. demonstration

School + Home Home Activity Your child is learning about word endings -ty, -ity, and -tion. Ask your child to say each word and spell it aloud.

▲ **Spelling Practice Book** p. 77

DAY 2   Think and Practice

TEACH

Some base words stay the same when adding -ty, -ity, and -tion, but some base words change their spelling. Demonstrate this by writing each spelling word on the board and having students identify the base word. Guide students to explain if the base word changes, and how it changes.

reduce + tion = reduction

FIND THE PATTERN Have students group the spelling words by which base words change their spelling and which base words do not.

HOMEWORK Spelling Practice Book, p. 78.

Word Endings -ty, -ity, -tion

Spelling Words

electricity	equality	society	specialty	celebrity
recognition	description	reduction	tradition	loyalty
security	clarity	popularity	certainty	cruelty
subscription	reputation	intention	deception	penalty

Definitions Write a list word that fits each definition.

1. faithfulness to a cause, ideal, or custom — 1. loyalty
2. freedom from danger, fear, or anxiety — 2. security
3. the passing of information and beliefs from one generation to the next — 3. tradition
4. the quality of being clear — 4. clarity
5. reduced in number or size — 5. reduction
6. condition of being liked by most people — 6. popularity
7. an account in words — 7. description
8. condition of being free from doubt — 8. certainty
9. the condition of realizing someone or something is previously known — 9. recognition
10. readiness to give pain to others — 10. cruelty

Words in Context Write a list word to finish each statement below.

11. It's time for me to renew my ___ to my local newspaper. — 11. subscription
12. I can't believe I actually got an autograph from my favorite ___. — 12. celebrity
13. That company has a ___ for fine work. — 13. reputation
14. I have many hobbies, but collecting baseball cards is my ___. — 14. specialty
15. It was not my ___ to hurt your feelings. — 15. intention
16. I am glad that we live in a free and open ___. — 16. society
17. I don't believe that you should live your life based on lies and ___. — 17. deception
18. The ___ of the two teams makes the game more interesting. — 18. equality
19. The ___ went off during that big storm last night. — 19. electricity
20. I spent some time in the ___ box during today's hockey game. — 20. penalty

School + Home Home Activity Your child spelled words that end in -ty, -ity, and -tion. Ask your child to choose five list words, say them, and then spell them.

▲ **Spelling Practice Book** p.78

DAY 3 Connect to Writing

WRITE A JOURNAL ENTRY

Have students write a journal entry describing something that happened in their lives. Their entry should use at least four spelling words. Have students read their entries aloud, or post them on the bulletin board for everyone to see.

Frequently Misspelled Words

finally   really

Students often misspell these words because they forget to double the final consonant of the base word before adding -y. Alert students to these frequently misspelled words and encourage them to picture the word in their minds before spelling it.

HOMEWORK Spelling Practice Book, p. 79.

▲ **Spelling Practice Book** p. 79

DAY 4 Review

REVIEW WORD ENDINGS

-ty, -ity, -tion

Have students work in pairs to create word scrambles featuring the spelling words. Students can exchange their puzzles with other groups to solve each puzzle.

Spelling Strategy
Problem Parts

We all have words that are hard for us to spell.

Step 1: Ask yourself: Which part of the word gives me a problem?

Step 2: Underline your problem part.

Step 3: Picture the word. Focus on the problem part.

HOMEWORK Spelling Practice Book, p. 80.

▲ **Spelling Practice Book** p. 80

DAY 5 Posttest

DICTATION SENTENCES

1. The car runs on electricity.
2. They hoped for equality for all.
3. People live together in society.
4. Brownies are Mom's specialty.
5. Who is your favorite celebrity?
6. He deserves recognition for his work.
7. She wrote a good description of the event.
8. There was a reduction in the number of tests.
9. What is your favorite holiday tradition?
10. The students have loyalty to their team.
11. She works as a security guard.
12. Please write with more clarity.
13. Do you think popularity is important?
14. The coming of winter is a certainty.
15. He acted with great cruelty.
16. I bought Bob a subscription to that magazine.
17. That store has a good reputation.
18. What was your intention?
19. Her deception surprised everyone.
20. He had to sit in the penalty box.

CHALLENGE

21. Do you know the pronunciation of that word?
22. Her hospitality was wonderful.
23. The poem was full of subtlety.
24. Please explain the technicality.
25. We enjoyed the cooking demonstration.

OBJECTIVES

- Formulate an inquiry question that is connected to this week's lesson focus.
- Effectively and efficiently find, evaluate, and communicate information related to an inquiry question using electronic sources.

New Literacies

Day 1	Identify Questions
Day 2	Navigate/Search
Day 3	Analyze
Day 4	Synthesize
Day 5	Communicate

NEW LITERACIES

Internet Inquiry Activity

EXPLORE INVENTIONS

Use the following 5-day plan to help students conduct this week's Internet inquiry activity on inventions. Remind students to follow classroom rules when using the Internet.

DAY 1

Identify Questions Discuss the lesson focus question: *How do inventions happen?* Help students brainstorm ideas for specific inquiry questions about inventions. For example, students might want to find out how something as complex as a computer or as simple as a zipper was invented. Have students work individually, in pairs, or in small groups to write an inquiry question they would like answered.

DAY 2

Navigate/Search Tell students to choose a student-friendly search engine to conduct an Internet search on their subject and to create a list of useful Web sites to visit. Advise students to use the brief descriptions that appear with search results to identify potentially useful sites.

DAY 3

Analyze Direct students to examine the Web sites they identified on Day 2 to find information that will help answer their inquiry questions. Tell students that they may need to change their inquiry question if they cannot find information to answer it. Students can formulate a new question based on a site that provides the kind of information they need. Students can then take notes on relevant information, or print out and highlight important facts.

DAY 4

Synthesize Tell students to synthesize information from Day 3 by combining useful information from different sources and forming an answer to their inquiry question. Remind students to avoid plagiarism—using someone else's writing—by restating the information in their own words. Advise students that they cannot change just a few words in sentences; they must reword entire sentences.

DAY 5

Communicate Have students share their inquiry results by developing a poster using graphics and captions to explain the evolution of their chosen invention.

RESEARCH/STUDY SKILLS
Advertisements

TEACH

Ask students what the purpose of an advertisement is. *(to sell a product or service)* Show students a print advertisement, and point out these four parts:

- A **product shot**, or **photo**, shows what is being sold in an appealing setting.
- A **headline,** written in large type, "yells" the most important idea about the product.
- A **body copy** provides information about why someone should buy the product.
- A **signature**, or product trademark, identifies who makes the product.

Have students form small groups and find print advertisements in magazines. Direct the groups to identify all the parts of each advertisement. Then discuss these questions:

1. **How do advertisers make their products appealing to readers?** *(Sample response: by showing attractive or famous people enjoying the products and/or by placing the products in an attractive setting)*
2. **What kinds of words are frequently used in advertisements?** *(words that grab your attention or affect your emotions)*

ASSESS

As students examine print advertisements, check that they can identify the different parts and the persuasive techniques used.

For more practice or to assess students, use Practice Book pp. 199–200.

OBJECTIVES
- Review the parts of a print advertisement.
- Identify the parts and persuasive techniques of a print advertisement.

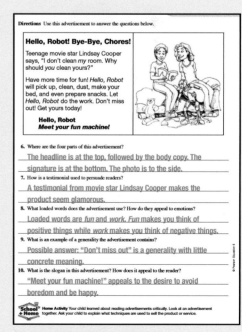

▲ **Practice Book** p. 199

▲ **Practice Book** p. 200

Assessment Checkpoints *for the Week*

Selection Assessment

Use pp. 77–80 of Selection Tests **to check:**

 Selection Understanding

 Comprehension Skill *Author's Purpose*

 Selection Vocabulary

converts	proclaimed
devise	reproduce
efficiency	transmitted
generated	
percentage	

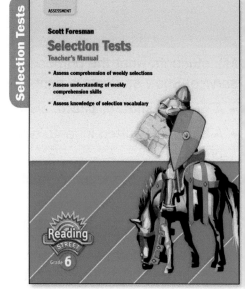

ASSESSMENT
Scott Foresman
Selection Tests
Teacher's Manual
• Assess comprehension of weekly selections
• Assess understanding of weekly comprehension skills
• Assess knowledge of selection vocabulary

Selection Tests

Reading STREET Grade 6

Leveled Assessment

- On-Level
- Strategic Intervention
- Advanced

Use pp. 115–120 of Fresh Reads for Differentiated Test Practice **to check:**

  Comprehension Skill *Author's Purpose*

  REVIEW **Comprehension Skill**
Cause and Effect

 Fluency *Words Correct Per Minute*

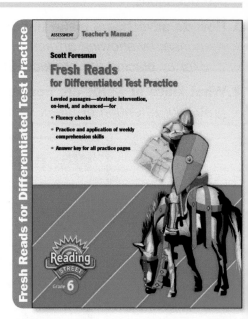

ASSESSMENT   Teacher's Manual
Scott Foresman
Fresh Reads
for Differentiated Test Practice
Leveled passages—strategic intervention, on-level, and advanced—for
• Fluency checks
• Practice and application of weekly comprehension skills
• Answer key for all practice pages

Fresh Reads for Differentiated Test Practice

Reading STREET Grade 6

Managing Assessment

Use Assessment Handbook **for:**

 Observation Checklists

 Record-Keeping Forms

 Portfolio Assessment

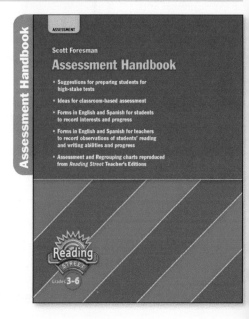

ASSESSMENT
Scott Foresman
Assessment Handbook
• Suggestions for preparing students for high-stake tests
• Ideas for classroom-based assessment
• Forms in English and Spanish for students to record interests and progress
• Forms in English and Spanish for teachers to record observations of students' reading and writing abilities and progress
• Assessment and Regrouping charts reproduced from *Reading Street* Teacher's Editions

Assessment Handbook

Reading STREET Grades 3–6

Unit 4
Concept Wrap-Up

CONCEPT QUESTION

How have those who've gone first influenced others who've gone after?

Students are ready to express their understanding of the unit concept question through discussion and wrap-up activities and to take the Unit 4 Benchmark Test.

Unit Poetry

Use the poetry on pp. 528–531 to help students appreciate poetry and further explore their understanding of the unit theme. It is suggested that you

- **read the poems aloud**
- **discuss and interpret the poems with students**
- **have students read the poems for fluency practice**
- **have students write interpretative responses**

Unit Wrap-Up

Use the Unit Wrap-Up on pp. 532–533 to discuss the unit theme, Explorers, Pioneers, and Discoverers, and to have students show their understanding of the theme through cross-curricular activities.

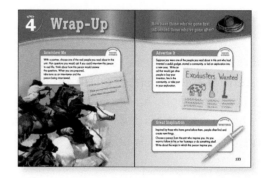

Unit Project

On p. 407, you assigned students a unit-long inquiry project, a poster about a group and what they accomplished. Students have investigated, analyzed, and synthesized information during the course of the unit as they prepared their posters. Schedule time for students to present their projects. The project rubric can be found to the right.

Unit Inquiry Project Rubric

4	3	2	1
• Research is focused, accurate, and very detailed. Sources are reliable and relevant.	• Research is generally focused, accurate, and detailed. Most sources are reliable and relevant.	• Research is somewhat focused, but includes inaccuracies or irrelevant information. Some sources are unreliable.	• Research is unfocused, inaccurate, or irrelevant. Most sources are unreliable.
• Poster is informative and well designed. Text and visuals work well together.	• Poster is informative, but includes some distracting elements, such as too much text or unclear visuals.	• Poster is somewhat informative, but some parts are poorly designed.	• Poster provides little or no information about the group. It is poorly designed.

Unit 4
Reading Poetry

OBJECTIVES

- Listen and respond to poems.
- Identify how meaning is conveyed through word choice.
- Read poetry fluently.
- Connect ideas and themes across texts.

Model Fluent Reading

Read "The Explorers" aloud. Tell students to listen for the cadence, or rhythmic pattern, of the language. Ask students to think about what effect the poet's choice of words has on the meaning of this poem.

Discuss the Poem

1 Draw Conclusions • Critical

What details does the poet give about the explorers' lives? How can you tell the poet admires what these people have done?

Possible responses: The poet writes of explorers basking in sunsets, hiking to hidden springs, and camping on cliffs. She says they were "bound for glory" and seems to think their lives are exciting.

2 Compare and Contrast • Inferential

How is Jemison different from the other explorers in the poem?

Jemison explored space, while the others explored places on Earth.

The Explorers

by Carole Boston Weatherford

Esteban set out to search for gold.
Henson braved ice to find the Pole.
Beckwourth trekked beyond the bounds,
and du Sable settled Chicago town.
They basked in sunsets few had seen
and hiked where hidden springs ran clean.
They forded rivers, bathed in creeks,
camped on cliffs and climbed high peaks.
Bound for glory, compass in hand,
1 they boldly conquered newfound lands.
Some sailed seas and some rode west,
but one went farther than the rest.
2 Mae Jemison gazed at this earthly sphere,
rocketed through the space frontier.

528

Practice Fluent Reading

Have partners take turns reading "The Explorers" aloud. Explain that they do not need to pause at the end of every line. Instead, tell students to let the punctuation guide them. You may wish to have students listen to the AudioText of the poem and compare their readings of the poem with the CD recording.

Audio CD **AudioText**

Bronze Cowboys

by Carole Boston Weatherford

When bison roamed the wild, wild West
dark riders rode the Pony Express
over the mountains, across the plains,
past coyotes, bobcats and wagon trains.
Bronze cowboys rode in cattle drives
where deserts met the turquoise skies.
They busted broncos and bulldogged steer,
made peace with the Indians and showed no fear.
A mail carrier named Stagecoach Mary
fought off wolves on the lonesome prairie.
Nat Love was the surest shot in the land.
Bill Pickett was known as a mean cowhand. **1**
Around the campfire, they strummed guitars,
imagined they could lasso stars. **2**

529

Model Fluent Reading

Read "Bronze Cowboys" aloud twice to students—once stressing the last word of each line and once using meaning to determine which words to stress. Ask students to decide which reading better conveys the sense of the poem.

Discuss the Poem

1 **Character • Inferential**
What qualities do the characters in the poem have in common?

The characters in the poem seem fearless, heroic, and adventurous. They confront danger and travel great distances.

2 **Draw Conclusions • Critical**
What do you think the poet means when she writes that the characters "imagined they could lasso stars"?

Possible response: The poet seems to believe that the bronze cowboys thought that they could do anything, even the impossible.

WRITING POETRY

Have groups of students write a collaborative poem about an explorer or adventurer they admire. Tell students to create poems with end rhymes. Have one member of each group read their poems to the class.

EXTEND SKILLS

End Rhyme

Explain that end rhyme is the rhyming of words at the ends of lines of poetry. "Explorers" and "Bronze Cowboys" both contain end rhymes. Point out that end rhymes do not need to be stressed when reading since the repetition of their sounds emphasizes the words automatically.

Unit 4
Reading Poetry

Model Fluent Reading

Read "Seeds" aloud slowly. Tell students that the poem is one of reflection and hope, so it should be read at a slow rate to reflect its meaning.

Discuss the Poem

1 Draw Conclusions • Critical

What does Gran give the speaker the night before he or she leaves the farm? Why are these gifts important?

Possible responses: Gran gives the speaker a good meal and a sack full of peach pits. These gifts give the speaker warm memories and hope for the future.

2 Imagery • Inferential

What images does the poet create? To which senses does she appeal?

Possible responses: The poet creates images that appeal to the sense of taste (*the dust...in my mouth* and *the taste of pork* and *a taste of our old farm*) and sight (*dried brown hearts*; *black sweet soil*; and *catch the light*).

Seeds

by Ann Turner

When the dust gets in my mouth
I remember the taste of pork
roasted over hickory wood
the night before we left
and how Gran filled a sack
with peach pits,
1 like dried brown hearts to carry west.
Someday I'll dig some black sweet soil,
2 set each seed to catch the light,
and one day I'll watch those peaches ripen.
Each bite
will be a taste of our old farm.

530

Practice Fluent Reading

Have partners take turns reading "Seeds" aloud. Tell students to read the poem slowly, with a serious but personal tone. You may wish to have students contrast readings using different rates. Ask: *How does the mood of the poem change with a faster rate?*

AudioText

Science Fair Project

by Carol Diggory Shields

PURPOSE:
The purpose of my project this year
Is to make my brother disappear.

HYPOTHESIS:
The world would be a better place
If my brother vanished without a trace. ①

MATERIALS:
3 erasers
White-out
Disappearing ink
1 younger brother
1 kitchen sink

PROCEDURE:
Chop up the erasers.
Add the white-out and the ink.
Rub it on the brother
While he's standing in the sink.

RESULTS:
The kid was disappearing!
I had almost proved my theorem!
When all at once my mom came home
And made me re-appear him.

CONCLUSION:
Experiment a failure. ②
My brother is still here.
But I'm already planning
For the science fair *next* year.

531

WRITING POETRY

Have students write a poem about a precious gift they have received
that has had an impact on them. The gift does not need to be
expensive; it can be something like the gift the grandmother gives in
"Seeds."

Model Fluent Reading

Read "Science Fair Project" aloud, using a high pitch and fast rate to convey excitement, particularly the stanza titled *Results*, and a slower rate and lower pitch in the last stanza to convey disappointment. Point out that a reader can use his or her voice to convey emotion.

Discuss the Poem

① Draw Conclusions • Critical
Why might the speaker want his brother to disappear?

Possible response: Perhaps the speaker finds his brother annoying. He says that "the world would be a better place" without his brother.

② Jargon • Inferential
What words relating to scientific experiments does the poet use?

Possible responses: She uses the words *purpose, project, materials, hypothesis, procedure, results, theorem, conclusion,* and *experiment.*

Connect Ideas and Themes

Remind students that this unit is about how those who have gone first influenced others who have gone after. Have students discuss what the individuals in each poem accomplished and how they might have affected others.

Unit 4
Wrap-Up

EXPLORERS, PIONEERS, AND DISCOVERERS

Discuss the Big Idea

How have those who've gone first influenced those who've gone after?

Write the unit theme and Big Idea question on the board. Ask students to think about the selections they have read in the unit. Discuss how each selection and lesson concept can help them answer the Big Idea question from this unit.

Model this for students by choosing a selection and explaining how the selection and lesson concept address the Big Idea.

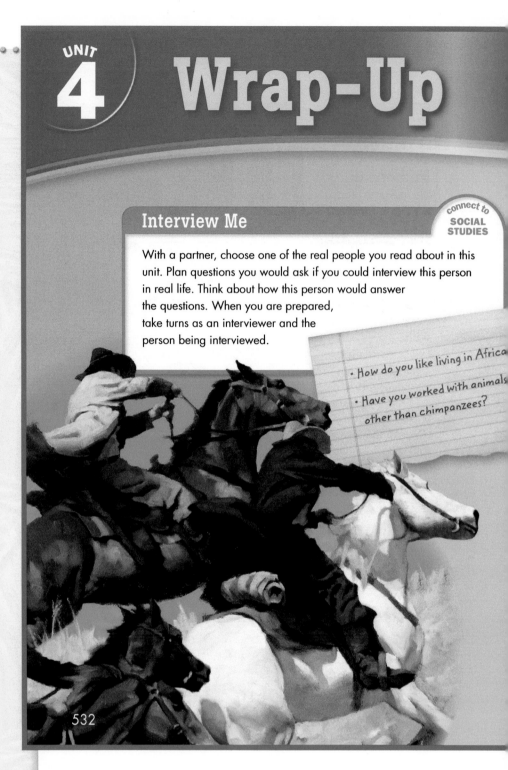

UNIT
4 **Wrap-Up**

Interview Me

connect to
SOCIAL
STUDIES

With a partner, choose one of the real people you read about in this unit. Plan questions you would ask if you could interview this person in real life. Think about how this person would answer the questions. When you are prepared, take turns as an interviewer and the person being interviewed.

- How do you like living in Africa
- Have you worked with animals other than chimpanzees?

532

How have those who've gone first influenced those who've gone after?

Advertise It

connect to SOCIAL STUDIES

Suppose you were one of the people you read about in this unit who had invented a useful gadget, started a community, or led an exploration into a new area. Write an ad that would get other people to buy your invention, live in the community, or take part in your exploration.

Exodusters Wanted

Great Inspiration

connect to WRITING

Inspired by those who have gone before them, people often find and create new things.

Choose a person from the unit who inspires you. Do you want to follow in his or her footsteps or do something else? Write about the ways in which this person inspires you.

533

ACTIVITIES

Interview Me

Conduct an Interview Model the activity by playing the role of a person depicted in the unit. Choose two or three volunteers to ask the person you are portraying a few questions and respond as that person. Then have pairs plan and conduct their own interviews. Remind them to ask open-ended questions that require more than a *yes* or *no* response and to answer questions as they think the person would.

Advertise It

Create an Advertisement Remind students that advertisements are a form of persuasive writing. Students should create a catchy title, write a few lines of text that will make their audience want to buy or do something, and choose appealing images.

Great Inspiration

Write About an Inspirational Person Point out that people can be inspirational for different reasons. For example, students might admire an explorer's courage, determination, and curiosity, even if they do not want to become explorers.

Glossary

How to Use This Glossary

This glossary can help you understand and pronounce some of the words in this book. The entries in this glossary are in alphabetical order. There are guide words at the top of each page to show you the first and last words on the page. A pronunciation key is at the bottom of every other page. Remember, if you can't find the word you are looking for, ask for help or check a dictionary.

The entry word is in dark type. It shows how the word is spelled and how the word is divided into syllables.

The pronunciation is in parentheses. It also shows which syllables are stressed.

Part-of-speech labels show the function or functions of an entry word and any listed form of that word.

con•quer (kong′kər), *V.* to overcome; get the better of: *conquer a bad habit.* ❑ *V.* **con•quered, con•quer•ing, con•querors.**

Sometimes, irregular and other special forms will be shown to help you use the word correctly.

The definition and example sentence show you what the word means and how it is used.

792

absurd•application

Aa

ab•surd (ab sėrd′), *ADJ.* plainly not true or sensible; foolish; ridiculous: *The idea that the number 13 brings bad luck is absurd.*

a•bun•dant (ə bun′dənt), *ADJ.* more than enough; very plentiful: *an abundant supply of food.*

ac•cess (ak′ses), **1.** *N.* right to approach, enter, or use; admittance: *All students have access to the library during the afternoon.* **2.** *V.* to make information available by putting into or retrieving from a computer memory: *access a list of names.* ❑ *V.* **ac•cessed, ac•ces•sing.**

ac•cus•tomed (ə kus′təmd), **1.** *ADJ.* usual; customary: *By Monday I was well again and was back in my accustomed seat in class.* **2.** *ADJ.* accustomed to; used to; in the habit of: *I am accustomed to getting up early.*

a•drift (ə drift′), *ADJ.* floating without being guided; drifting: *During the storm, our boat was adrift on the lake.*

ag•gres•sive (ə gres′iv), *ADJ.* taking the first step in an attack or a quarrel; ready to attack others: *a warlike and aggressive nation.*

al•ien (ā′lyən), **1.** *N.* person who is not a citizen of the country in which he or she lives. **2.** *N.* an imaginary creature from outer space. ❑ *N. PL.* **al•iens.**

aliens

ap•par•ent•ly (ə par′ənt lē), *ADV.* seemingly; with the appearance of.

ap•pli•ca•tion (ap′lə kā′shən), *N.* a request for something, such as employment, an award, a loan, etc.: *I filled out an application for a job at the supermarket.*

architecture•campaign

ar•chi•tec•ture (är′kə tek′chər), *N.* style or special manner of building: *Greek architecture made much use of columns.*

ar•ti•fact (är′tə fakt), *N.* anything made by human skill or work, especially a tool or weapon. ❑ *N. PL.* **ar•ti•facts.** (*Artifact* comes from two Latin words, *artem* meaning "art" and *factum* meaning "made.")

as•tron•o•mer (ə stron′ə mər), *N.* an expert in astronomy, the science that deals with the sun, moon, planets, stars, etc. ❑ *N. PL.* **as•tron•o•mers.** (*Astronomer* comes from the Greek root *astr* meaning "star.")

at•tire (ə tīr′), *V.* to clothe or dress; array: *The king was attired in a robe trimmed with ermine.* ❑ *V.* **at•tired, at•tir•ing.**

au•thor•i•ty (ə thôr′ə tē), *N.* power to enforce obedience; right to command or act: *Parents have authority over their children.*

Bb

barge (bärj), *N.* **1.** a large, strongly built vehicle or flat-bottomed boat for carrying freight: *a grain barge.* **2.** *N.* a large boat used for excursions, pageants, and special occasions.

ba•sin (bā′sn), *N.* all the land drained by a river and the streams that flow into it: *The Mississippi basin extends from the Appalachians to the Rockies.*

bea•con (bē′kən), *N.* fire or light used as a signal to guide or warn.

be•half (bi haf′), *N.* side, interest, or favor: *I acted on her behalf.*

ben•e•fit (ben′ə fit), **1.** *N.* anything which is for the good of someone or something; advantage: *Good roads are of great benefit to travelers.* **2.** *V.* to do good to; be good for: *Rest will benefit a sick person.* ❑ *V.* **ben•e•fits, ben•e•fit•ed, ben•e•fit•ing.**

bi•o•di•ver•si•ty (bī′ō di vėr′sə tē), *N.* a wide variety of different species living together in one place.

birth•right (bėrth′rīt′), *N.* right or privilege that someone is entitled to by birth.

bond•age (bon′dij), *N.* condition of being held against your will under the control or influence of some person or thing; lack of freedom; slavery.

bug (bug), **1.** *N.* a crawling insect with a pointed beak for piercing and sucking. **2.** *N.* a disease germ. **3.** *N.* a very small microphone hidden in a room and used to overhear conversations.

bur•den (bėrd′n), *N.* something carried; load of things, care, work, duty, or sorrow: *Everyone in my family shares the burden of housework.*

Cc

ca•coph•o•ny (kə kof′ə nē), *N.* series of harsh, clashing sounds; discord.

cal•a•bash (kal′ə bash), *N.* gourd or gourdlike fruit whose dried shell is used to make bottles, bowls, drums, pipes, etc. ❑ *N. PL.* **cal•a•bash•es.**

cam•paign (kam pān′), **1.** *N.* in a war, a series of related military operations which are aimed at some special purpose: *In order to capture the enemy's most important city, the general planned one of the largest campaigns of the war.* **2.** *N.* series of connected activities to do or get something: *Our town had a campaign to raise money for a new hospital.* ❑ *N. PL.* **cam•paigns.**

a	in hat	ō	in open	sh	in she
ā	in age	ȯ	in all	th	in thin
â	in care	ô	in order	ᴛʜ	in then
ä	in far	oi	in oil	zh	in measure
e	in let	ou	in out	ə	= a in about
ē	in equal	u	in cup	ə	= e in taken
ėr	in term	u̇	in put	ə	= i in pencil
i	in it	ü	in rule	ə	= o in lemon
ī	in ice	ch	in child	ə	= u in circus
o	in hot	ng	in long		

793

candidate•convert

can•di•date (kan′də dāt), *N.* person who seeks, or is suggested by others for some office, honor, or acceptance: *There is only one candidate for president of the club.*

cap•tive (kap′tiv), *ADJ.* kept in confinement: *captive animals.*

car•a•van (kar′ə van), *N.* group of merchants, pilgrims, etc., traveling together for safety through difficult or dangerous country. ❑ *N. PL.* **car•a•vans.**

car•bon di•ox•ide (kär′bən di ok′sīd), *N.* a colorless, odorless gas, present in the atmosphere and formed when any fuel containing carbon is burned. The air that is breathed out of an animal's lungs contains carbon dioxide. Plants absorb it from the air and use it to make plant tissue. Carbon dioxide is a greenhouse gas.

car•da•mom (kär′ də məm), *N.* a spicy seed used as seasoning and in medicine.

chap•ar•ral (shap′ə ral′), *N.* dense, often thorny thicket of low bushes.

char•ac•ter•is•tic (kar′ik tə ris′tik), *ADJ.* distinguishing one person or thing from others; special: *Bananas have their own characteristic smell.*

char•i•ty (char′ə tē), *N.* fund or organization for helping the sick, the poor, the helpless, or the environment: *She gives money regularly to the Red Cross and to other charities.* ❑ *N. PL.* **char•i•ties.**

clois•ter (kloi′stər), *N.* place of religious retirement; convent or monastery. ❑ *N. PL.* **clois•ters.**

col•lapse (kə laps′), *V.* to fold or push together: *The card table would collapse so that it could be stored easily.* ❑ *V.* **col•lapsed, col•laps•ing.**

col•lide (kə līd′), *V.* to hit or strike violently together; crash: *Two ships collided in the harbor and sank.* ❑ *V.* **col•lid•ed, col•lid•ing.**

com•bus•tion (kəm bus′chən), *N.* act or process of burning. Many houses are heated by the rapid combustion of coal, oil, or gas.

com•mis•sioned (kə mish′ənd), *ADJ.* holding the rank of second lieutenant or above in the U.S. Army, Air Force, or Marine Corps, or of ensign or above in the U.S. Navy.

com•pact (kom′pakt), *ADJ.* firmly packed together; closely joined: *Cabbage leaves are shaped into a compact head.*

com•pan•ion•ship (kəm pan′yən ship), *N.* friendly feeling among companions; fellowship.

com•pas•sion•ate (kəm pash′ə nit), *ADJ.* wishing to help those who suffer; sympathetic; pitying.

com•rade (kom′rad), **1.** *N.* a close companion and friend. **2.** *N.* fellow worker; partner. ❑ *N. PL.* **com•rades.**

con•fi•dent•ly (kon′fə dənt lē), *ADV.* certainly; surely; with firm belief.

con•form (kən fôrm′), *V.* to agree; be the same as. ❑ *V.* **con•formed, con•form•ing.**

con•quer (kong′kər), *V.* to overcome; get the better of: *conquer a bad habit.* ❑ *V.* **con•quered, con•quer•ing.**

con•sump•tion (kən sump′shən), *N.* act or process of using up; use: *We took along some food for consumption on our trip.*

con•ven•tion•al (kən ven′shə nəl), *ADJ.* of the usual type or design; commonly used or seen: *conventional furniture.*

con•vert (kən vėrt′), *V.* to turn to another for a particular use or purpose; change: *The generators at the dam convert water power into electricity.* ❑ *V.* **con•verts, con•vert•ed, con•vert•ing.**

794

coordinate•desolate

co•or•di•nate (kō ôrd′n āt), *V.* to work or cause to work together in the proper way; fit together: *I have difficulty trying to coordinate the movements of my arms and legs in ballet class.* ❑ *V.* **co•or•di•nat•ed, co•or•di•nat•ing.**

cor•ri•dor (kôr′ə dər), *N.* a long hallway; passage in a large building into which rooms open: *There are many corridors leading from the school's front entrance to the numerous classrooms.* ❑ *N. PL.* **cor•ri•dors.**

cor•rode (kə rōd′), *V.* to wear or eat away gradually: *Acid caused the pipes to corrode.* ❑ *V.* **cor•rod•ed, cor•rod•ing.**

cor•sage (kôr säzh′), *N.* a small bouquet of flowers to be worn on the shoulder of a woman's clothes or on her wrist. ❑ *N.* **cor•sages.**

cos•mic (koz′mik), *ADJ.* having to do with the whole universe: *Cosmic forces produce galaxies.*

coun•sel•or (koun′sə lər), *N.* person who gives advice; adviser.

cus•tom•ar•y (kus′tə mer′ē), *ADJ.* according to custom; usual: *Ten o'clock is her customary bedtime.*

Dd

dean (dēn), *N.* head of a division or school in a college or university: *the dean of the law school.*

de•cline (di klīn′), *N.* process of losing power, strength, wealth, beauty, etc.; growing worse: *Lack of money led to a decline in the condition of the school.*

de•cree (di krē′), *N.* something ordered by authority; official decision; law: *The new state holiday was one of three new decrees by the governor.* ❑ *N. PL.* **de•crees.**

de•lir•i•ous (di lir′ē əs), *ADJ.* wildly excited: *The students were delirious with joy when their team won the tournament.*

de•moc•ra•cy (di mok′rə sē), *N.* government that is run by the people who live under it. In a democracy, the people rule either directly through meetings that all may attend, such as the town meetings in New England, or indirectly through the election of representatives to attend to the business of government.

dense (dens), *ADJ.* closely packed together; thick: *In the densest fog it is difficult to see your hand held out in front of your face.* ❑ *ADJ.* **dens•er, dens•est.**

de•prive (di prīv′), *V.* to keep from having or doing: *Crash diets can deprive the dieter of proper nutrition.* ❑ *V.* **de•prived, de•priv•ing.**

des•o•late (des′ə lit), *ADJ.* not lived in; deserted: *a desolate house.*

desolate

a	in hat	ō	in open	sh	in she
ā	in age	ȯ	in all	th	in thin
â	in care	ô	in order	ᴛʜ	in then
ä	in far	oi	in oil	zh	in measure
e	in let	ou	in out	ə	= a in about
ē	in equal	u	in cup	ə	= e in taken
ėr	in term	u̇	in put	ə	= i in pencil
i	in it	ü	in rule	ə	= o in lemon
ī	in ice	ch	in child	ə	= u in circus
o	in hot	ng	in long		

795

destination•efficiency

des·ti·na·tion (des/tə nā/shən), *N.* place to which someone or something is going or is being sent.

des·ti·ny (des/tə nē), *N.* what becomes of someone or something; your fate or fortune: *It was young Washington's destiny to become the first President of the United States.*

de·tect (di tekt/), *V.* to find out; discover; catch: *Can you detect any odor in the room?* □ *V.* **de·tec·ted, de·tec·ting.**

de·vise (di vīz/), *V.* to think out; plan or contrive; invent: *She needed to devise a way of raising boards up to her tree house.* □ *V.* **de·vised, dev·is·ing.**

dic·ta·tion (dik tā/shən), *N.* words said or read aloud to another person who writes them down or to a machine that records them: *The secretary took the dictation in shorthand and typed it out later.*

dil·i·gent·ly (dil/ə jənt lē), *ADV.* carefully; steadily.

din·gy (din/jē), *ADJ.* lacking brightness or freshness; dirty-looking; dull: *Dingy curtains covered the windows of the dusty room.*

di·plo·ma (də plō/mə), *N.* a written or printed paper given by a school, college, or university, which states that someone has completed a certain course of study or has graduated after a certain amount of work.

dis·grace (dis grās/), *V.* to cause loss of honor or respect; to bring shame upon: *The embezzler disgraced her family.* □ *V.* **dis·graced, dis·grac·ing.**

dis·mount (dis mount/), *V.* to get off something, such as a horse or bicycle: *The riders dismounted and led their horses across the stream.* □ *V.* **dis·mount·ed, dis·mount·ing.**

dis·tress (dis tres/), *V.* to cause great pain or sorrow to; to make unhappy: *Her tears distressed me.* □ *V.* **dis·tressed, dis·tress·ing.**

doc·u·men·ta·tion (dok/yə men tā/shən), *N.* proof or support of a claim or opinion by documentary evidence: *Your essay provides good and proper documentation.*

dom·i·nate (dom/ə nāt), *V.* to control or rule by strength or power: *She has the authority needed to dominate the meeting.* □ *V.* **dom·i·nat·ed, dom·i·nat·ing.**

dra·mat·ic (drə mat/ik), *ADJ.* like a drama; of or about plays: *a dramatic actor.*

du·bi·ous·ly (dü/bē əs lē), *ADV.* doubtfully; uncertainly.

Ee

earth·en (ėr/thən), *ADJ.* made of ground, soil, or earth.

an earthen house

eave (ēv), *N.* the projecting lower level. □ *N. PL.* **eaves.**

ed·i·fice (ed/ə fis), *N.* a building, especially a large one.

ef·fi·cien·cy (ə fish/ən sē), *N.* ability to produce the effect wanted without waste of time, energy, etc.: *The skilled carpenter worked with great efficiency.*

elude•exclusive

e·lude (i lüd/), *V.* to avoid or escape by cleverness or quickness; slip away from: *The fox could always elude the hunting dogs.* □ *V.* **e·lud·ed, e·lud·ing.**

em·pha·size (em/fə sīz), *V.* to stress; call attention to: *The number of car accidents emphasized the need for careful driving.* □ *V.* **em·pha·sized, em·pha·siz·ing.**

em·pire (em/pīr), *N.* group of countries or states under one ruler or government: *The Roman Empire consisted of many separate territories and different peoples.*

en·coun·ter (en koun/tər), *v.* to meet as an enemy; meet in a fight or battle: *He knew he would encounter the enemy in direct combat.* □ *V.* **en·coun·tered, en·coun·ter·ing.**

en·gulf (en gulf/), *V.* to swallow up; overwhelm: *A wave engulfed the small boat.* □ *V.* **en·gulfed, en·gulf·ing.**

en·rage (en rāj/), *V.* to make very angry; make furious: *The dog was enraged by the teasing.* □ *V.* **en·raged, en·rag·ing.**

en·rich (en rich/), *V.* to make rich or richer: *Some companies add vitamins or minerals to enrich their food products.* □ *V.* **en·riched, en·rich·ing.**

en·roll·ment (en rōl/mənt), *N.* number who are members, who are registered: *The school has an enrollment of 200 students.*

en·thu·si·as·ti·cal·ly (en thü/zē as/tik lē), *ADV.* with great and eager interest: *The audience applauded enthusiastically.*

e·qua·tor (i kwā/tər), *N.* an imaginary circle around the middle of Earth, halfway between the North Pole and the South Pole. The equator divides the earth into the Northern Hemisphere and the Southern Hemisphere.

e·ro·sion (i rō/zhən), *N.* the process of gradually eating or wearing away by rain, glaciers, running water, waves, or wind: *Trees help prevent the erosion of soil.*

e·ter·ni·ty (i tėr/nə tē), *N.* the endless time period after death.

eth·ics (eth/iks), *N. SING.* the study of standards of right and wrong; the part of philosophy dealing with moral conduct, duty, and judgment.

et·i·quette (et/ə ket), *N.* the customary rules for behavior in polite society: *Etiquette requires that we eat peas with a fork, not a knife.*

e·vap·o·rate (i vap/ə rāt/), *V.* to change from a liquid into a gas: *Boiling water evaporates rapidly.* □ *V.* **e·vap·o·rates, e·vap·o·rat·ed, e·vap·o·rat·ing.**

ex·as·pe·ra·tion (eg zas/pə rā/shən), *N.* extreme annoyance; irritation; anger.

ex·ca·va·tion (ek/skə vā/shən), *N.* the act of or process of uncovering by digging: *The excavation revealed an ancient, buried city.*

ex·clu·sive (ek sklü/siv), *ADJ.* not divided or shared with others; single; sole: *exclusive rights to sell a product.*

a in hat	ò in open	sh in she
ā in age	ò in all	th in thin
â in care	ô in order	ᴛʜ in then
ä in far	oi in oil	zh in measure
e in let	ou in out	ə = a in about
ē in equal	u in cup	ə = e in taken
ėr in term	ù in put	ə = i in pencil
i in it	ü in rule	ə = o in lemon
ī in ice	ch in child	ə = u in circus
o in hot	ng in long	

existence•fresco

ex·ist·ence (eg zis/təns), *N.* condition of being: *Dinosaurs disappeared from existence millions of years ago.*

ex·o·dus (ek/sə dəs), *N.* act of going out; departure: *Every June, there is an exodus of students from the college.*

ex·panse (ek spans/), *N.* open or unbroken stretch; wide, spreading surface: *The Pacific Ocean is a vast expanse of water.*

ex·pe·di·tion (ek/spə dish/ən), *N.* journey for some special purpose, such as exploration, scientific study, or military purposes.

ex·ploit (ek sploit/), *V.* to make use of: *The men wanted to exploit the mine for its minerals.* □ *V.* **ex·ploit·ed, ex·ploit·ing.**

ex·port (ek spôrt/), *V.* to send goods out of one country for sale and use in another: *The United States has exported corn for many years.* □ *V.* **ex·port·ed, ex·port·ing.**

ex·tract (ek strakt/), *V.* to pull out or draw out, usually with some effort: *extract iron from the earth.* □ *V.* **ex·tract·ed, ex·tract·ing.**

Ff

fes·tive (fes/tiv), *ADJ.* of or suitable for a feast, festival, or holiday; merry: *A birthday is a festive occasion.*

fix·ture (fiks/chər), *N.* thing put in place to stay: *a bathroom fixture, light fixtures.* □ *N. PL.* **fix·tures.**

flam·ma·ble (flam/ə bəl), *ADJ.* easily set on fire; inflammable: *Paper is flammable.*

flim·sy (flim/zē), *ADJ.* easily torn or broken; not strongly made: *I accidentally tore the flimsy paper.*

flour·ish (flėr/ish), *V.* to grow or develop well; thrive: *His radishes flourish with the right conditions.* □ *V.* **flour·ished, flour·ish·ing.**

fo·reign·er (fôr/ə nər), *N.* person from another country; alien. □ *N. PL.* **fo·reign·ers.**

for·mal (fôr/məl), **1.** *ADJ.* according to set customs or rules: *The ambassador paid a formal call on the prime minister.* **2.** *ADJ.* done with or having authority; official: *A written contract is a formal agreement to do something.*

for·mer (fôr/mər), *ADJ.* earlier; past: *In former times, cooking was done in fireplaces instead of stoves.*

for·ti·tude (fôr/tə tüd), *N.* courage in facing pain, danger, or trouble; firmness of spirit.

frag·ile (fraj/əl), *ADJ.* easily broken, damaged, or destroyed; delicate; frail: *Be careful; that thin glass is fragile.*

fran·tic (fran/tik), *ADJ.* very much excited; wild with rage, fear, pain, or grief: *The trapped animal made frantic efforts to escape.*

fres·co (fres/kō), *N.* picture or design created by painting with water colors on clean, fresh plaster. □ *N. PL.* **fres·coes.**

fresco

frustration•ignite

frus·tra·tion (fru strā/shən), *N.* a feeling of anger and helplessness, caused by bad luck, failure, or defeat.

ful·fill (fùl fil/), *V.* to perform or do a duty, command, etc.: *She felt she was able to fulfill all the teacher's requests.* □ *V.* **ful·filled, ful·fill·ing.**

Gg

gal·ax·y (gal/ək sē), *N.* group of billions of stars forming one system. Earth and the sun are in the Milky Way galaxy. Many galaxies outside our own can be seen with a telescope. (Galaxy comes from the Greek word *galaktos* meaning "milk.")

gen·er·ate (jen/ə rāt/), *V.* to cause to be; bring into being; produce: *The politician generated a great deal of enthusiasm among voters.* □ *V.* **gen·er·at·ed, gen·er·at·ing.**

ge·ol·o·gist (jē ol/ə jist), *N.* scientist who studies the composition of the earth or of other solid heavenly bodies, the processes that have formed them, and their history. □ *N. PL.* **ge·ol·o·gists.**

gloat (glōt), *V.* to think about or gaze at with great satisfaction: *She gloated over her success.* □ *V.* **gloat·ed, gloat·ing.**

grope (grōp), *V.* to feel about with the hands: *He was groping in the dark for a flashlight after the lights went out.* □ *V.* **groped, grop·ing.**

Hh

has·sle (has/əl), *N.* bother; trouble: *the hassle of fixing a broken bicycle.*

hatch·et (hach/it), *N.* a small ax with a short handle, for use with one hand.

heart·sick (härt/ sik/), *ADJ.* sick at heart; very depressed; very unhappy.

hoard (hôrd), *N.* what is saved and stored away; things stored: *They have a hoard of candy.*

home·stead·er (hōm/sted/ər), *N.* a person who owns and lives on land granted by the U.S. government. □ *N. PL.* **home·stead·ers.**

hos·pi·ta·ble (ho spit/ə bəl), *ADJ.* friendly; receptive.

hov·er (hov/ər), *V.* to stay in or near one place; wait nearby: *My mother tells me not to hover by the kitchen door before dinner.* □ *V.* **hov·ers, hov·ered, hov·er·ing.**

hu·mil·i·ty (hyü mil/ə tē), *N.* humbleness of mind; lack of pride; meekness.

Ii

i·de·al (ī dē/əl), *ADJ.* just as you would wish; perfect: *A warm, sunny day is ideal for a picnic.*

i·den·ti·ty (ī den/tə tē), *N.* who or what you are: *The writer concealed her identity by signing her stories with a pen name.*

ig·nite (ig nīt/), *V.* to set on fire: *A spark from a campfire can ignite dry grass.* □ *V.* **ig·nit·ed, ig·nit·ing.**

a in hat	ò in open	sh in she
ā in age	ò in all	th in thin
â in care	ô in order	ᴛʜ in then
ä in far	oi in oil	zh in measure
e in let	ou in out	ə = a in about
ē in equal	u in cup	ə = e in taken
ėr in term	ù in put	ə = i in pencil
i in it	ü in rule	ə = o in lemon
ī in ice	ch in child	ə = u in circus
o in hot	ng in long	

Glossary

im·bed (im bed′), *V.* to enclose in a surrounding mass; fasten or fix firmly: *Precious stones are often found imbedded in rock.* ◻ *V.* **im·bed·ded, im·bed·ding.**

im·mor·tal (i môr′tl), *ADJ.* living forever; never dying; everlasting: *Most religions teach that the soul is immortal.* (*Immortal* comes from the Latin word *mort* meaning "death.")

im·po·lite (im′pə līt′), *ADJ.* not polite; having or showing bad manners; rude; discourteous.

im·print (im print′), *V.* to fix firmly in the mind: *His boyhood home was imprinted in his memory.* ◻ *V.* **im·print·ed, im·print·ing.**

in·ci·dent (in′sə dənt), *N.* something that happens; event: *an exciting incident.* (*Incident* comes from the Latin word *incidentem* meaning "happening, befalling.")

in·dus·tri·al (in dus′trē əl), *ADJ.* engaged in or connected with business, trade, or manufacture: *industrial worker, industrial development.*

in·fin·i·ty (in fin′ə tē), *N.* condition of having no limits; endlessness: *the infinity of space.*

in·laid (in lād′), *ADJ.* set in the surface as a decoration or design.

in·su·late (in′sə lāt), *V.* to keep something from losing electricity, heat, or sound by lining or surrounding it with a material that does not conduct the kind of energy involved: *Telephone wires are often insulated by a covering of rubber.* ◻ *V.* **in·su·lat·ed, in·su·lat·ing.**

in·vad·er (in vād′ər), *N.* person who enters with force or as an enemy: *The invaders conquered the country.* ◻ *N. PL.* **in·vad·ers.**

i·so·la·tion (ī′sə lā shən), *N.* the state of being separated from others, of being alone.

Ll

lance (lans), *N.* a long, wooden spear with a sharp iron or steel head: *The knight carried a lance as he rode into battle.*

leg·a·cy (leg′ə sē), *N.* something handed down from an ancestor or predecessor; heritage.

lei·sure (lē′zhər or lezh′ər), *ADJ.* free; not busy: *leisure hours.*

lunge (lunj), *V.* to move suddenly forward; thrust: *The dog is always lunging at strangers.* ◻ *V.* **lunged, lung·ing.**

lush (lush), *ADJ.* having thick growth; covered with growing things: *The hillside was lush with spring flowers.*

lush

Mm

main·te·nance (mān′tə nəns), *N.* act or process of keeping in good repair.

mal·nour·ished (mal nér′isht), *ADJ.* improperly nourished: *The stray cat looked malnourished.*

800

man·u·script (man′yə skript), *N.* a handwritten or keyboarded book or article. Manuscripts are sent to publishers to be made into printed books, magazine articles, and the like. ◻ *N. PL.* **man·u·scripts.**

ma·te·ri·al·ize (mə tir′ē ə līz), *V.* to appear or cause to appear suddenly in material or bodily form: *A woman would materialize from the smoke of the magician's fire.* ◻ *V.* **ma·te·ri·al·ized, mat·er·i·al·iz·ing.**

me·an·der (mē an′dər), *V.* to follow a winding course: *The hikers meandered through the woods.* ◻ *V.* **me·an·dered, me·an·der·ing.**

me·di·e·val (mē dē′val or med ē′val), *ADJ.* of or belonging to the Middle Ages (the years from about A.D. 500 to about 1450).

men·ac·ing (men′is ing), *ADJ.* threatening: *The dog had a menacing growl.*

mi·gra·tion (mī grā′shən), **1.** *N.* the act of going from one region to another with the change in the seasons. **2.** *N.* the act of moving from one place to settle in another.

mis·for·tune (mis fôr′chən), *N.* bad luck: *She had the misfortune to break her arm.*

mois·ture (mois′chər), *N.* slight wetness; water or other liquid suspended in very small drops in the air or spread on a surface. Dew is moisture that collects at night on the grass.

mol·ten (mōlt′n), *ADJ.* made liquid by heat; melted: *molten steel.*

mo·men·tous (mō men′təs), *ADJ.* very important: *Choosing between peace and war is a momentous decision.*

mon·grel (mong′grəl), *N.* animal or plant of mixed breed, especially a dog.

my·thol·o·gy (mi thol′ə jē), *N.* a group of legends or stories about a particular country or person: *Greek mythology.*

Nn

nav·i·ga·tor (nav′ə gā′tər), *N.* person in charge of finding the position and course of a ship, aircraft, or expedition.

ne·go·ti·ate (ni gō′shē āt), *V.* to talk over and arrange terms; confer; consult: *The two countries came together to negotiate for peace.* ◻ *V.* **ne·go·ti·at·ed, ne·go·ti·at·ing.**

no·ble·man (nō′bəl mən), *N.* man of noble rank, title, or birth. ◻ *N. PL.* **no·ble·men.**

non·vi·o·lence (non vī′ə ləns), *N.* belief in the use of peaceful methods to achieve any goal; opposition to any form of violence.

nub (nub), *N.* lump or small piece.

Oo

o·be·di·ent (ō bē′dē ənt), *ADJ.* doing what you are told; willing to obey: *The obedient dog came at its owner's whistle.*

ob·serv·a·to·ry (əb zėr′və tôr′ē), *N.* building equipped with telescopes and other devices for watching and studying astronomical objects.

ob·sta·cle (ob′stə kəl), *N.* something that prevents or stops progress; hindrance: *The fallen tree was an obstacle to traffic.*

a	in hat	ō	in open	sh	in she
ā	in age	ò	in all	th	in thin
â	in care	ô	in order	ᴛʜ	in then
ä	in far	oi	in oil	zh	in measure
e	in let	ou	in out	ə	= a in about
ē	in equal	u	in cup	ə	= e in taken
ėr	in term	ù	in put	ə	= i in pencil
i	in it	ü	in rule	ə	= o in lemon
ī	in ice	ch	in child	ə	= u in circus
o	in hot	ng	in long		

801

op·er·a (op′ər ə), *N.* a play in which music is an essential and prominent part, featuring arias, choruses, etc., with orchestral accompaniment.

op·ti·mis·tic (op′tə mis′tik), *ADJ.* hoping for the best: *I am optimistic about the chance of continued good weather.*

or·deal (ôr dēl′), *N.* a severe test or experience: *I dreaded the ordeal of going to the dentist.*

ore (ôr), *N.* rock containing enough of a metal or metals to make mining profitable. After it is mined, ore must be treated to extract the metal.

out·burst (out′bėrst′), *N.* act of bursting forth. ◻ *N. PL.* **out·bursts.**

Pp

pack·ing·house (pak′ing hous′), *N.* place where foods are prepared and packed to be sold.

pains·tak·ing (pānz′tā′king), *ADJ.* very careful; particular; diligent: *a painstaking painter.*

pa·le·on·tol·o·gist (pā′lē on tol′ə jist), *N.* a scientist who studies the forms of life existing in prehistoric time, as represented by fossil animals and plants. ◻ *N. PL.* **pa·le·on·tol·o·gists.**

pa·py·rus (pə pī′rəs), *N.* a tall water plant from which the ancient Egyptians, Greeks, and Romans made a material upon which to write.

par·ti·cle (pär′tə kəl), *N.* a very little bit: *I got a particle of dust in my eye.* ◻ *N. PL.* **par·ti·cles.** (*Particle* comes from the Latin word *partem* meaning "part.")

pa·trol·man (pə trōl′ mən), *N.* a policeman or policewoman who keeps watch over a particular area in order to protect life and property.

pa·tron (pā′trən), *N.* person who gives approval and support to some person, art, cause, or undertaking: *A well-known patron of art, she helped several young painters.*

per·cent·age (pər sen′tij), *N.* allowance, commission, discount, etc., figured by percent.

per·mis·sion (pər mish′ən), *N.* consent; leave: *My sister gave me permission to use her camera.*

per·sist (pər sist′), *V.* to keep on; refuse to stop or be changed: *Though we've asked her not to, she persisted in reading at the table.* ◻ *V.* **per·sist·ed, per·sist·ing.**

per·sist·ence (pər sis′təns), *N.* act of refusing to stop or be changed: *Her persistence in practicing led to her making the team.*

phys·i·cal (fiz′ə kəl), *ADJ.* of or for the body: *physical exercise, physical strength, physical work.*

plea (plē), *N.* request or appeal; an asking: *The firefighters heard many pleas for help.* ◻ *N. PL.* **pleas.**

poi·son·ous (poi′zn əs), *ADJ.* containing dangerous substance; very harmful to life and health: *The rattlesnake's bite is poisonous.*

poul·tice (pōl′tis), *N.* a soft, moist mass of mustard, herbs, etc., applied to the body to reduce pain or swelling.

prej·u·dice (prej′ə dis), *N.* unreasonable dislike of an idea, group of people, etc.

pres·ence (prez′ns), *N.* condition of being present in a place: *I just learned of her presence in the city.*

prey (prā), *N. SING.* or *PL.* animal or animals hunted and killed for food by another animal: *Mice and birds are the prey of cats.*

prim·i·tive (prim′ə tiv), *ADJ.* very simple, such as people had early in history: *A primitive way of making fire is by rubbing two sticks together.*

priv·i·leged (priv′ə lijd), *ADJ.* having some special rights, advantage, or favor: *The nobility of Europe was a privileged class.*

802

pro·claim (prə klām′), *V.* to make known publicly and officially; declare publicly: *The congresswoman proclaimed that she would run for reelection.* ◻ *V.* **pro·claimed, pro·claim·ing.**

pro·gress (prog′res), *N.* an advance or growth; development; improvement: *the progress of science, showing rapid progress in your studies.*

pro·mote (prə mōt′), **1.** *V.* to raise in rank, condition, or importance: *Pupils who pass the test will be promoted to the next higher grade.* **2.** *V.* to further the sale of something by advertising. ◻ *V.* **pro·mot·ed, pro·mot·ing.**

pro·vi·sions (prə vizh′ons), *N. PL.* a supply of food and drinks: *After a long winter, the settlers were low on provisions.*

Qq

quest (kwest), *N.* expedition by knights in search of something: *There are many stories about the quests of King Arthur's knights.* ◻ *N. PL.* **quests.**

quill (kwil), *N.* a stiff, sharp hair or spine like the pointed end of a feather. A porcupine has quills on its back.

quills

Rr

rab·bi (rab′i), *N.* teacher of the Jewish law and religion; leader of a Jewish congregation.

re·cede (ri sēd′), *V.* to go backward; move backward; withdraw: *When the tide receded, we dug for clams.* ◻ *V.* **re·ced·ed, re·ced·ing.**

re·cit·al (ri sī′tl), *N.* a musical entertainment, given usually by a single performer. ◻ *N. PL.* **re·cit·als.**

re·cy·cle (rē sī′kəl), *V.* to process or treat something so that it can be used again. ◻ *V.* **re·cy·cled, re·cy·cling.**

re·frain¹ (ri frān′) *V.* to keep yourself from doing something: *refrain from wrongdoing.* ◻ *V.* **re·frained, re·frain·ing.**

re·frain² (ri frān′) *N.* phrase or verse repeated regularly in a song or poem. In "The Star-Spangled Banner," the refrain is "O'er the land of the free and the home of the brave."

reg·is·ter (rej′ə stər), *V.* to have some effect, to make an impression. ◻ *V.* **reg·is·tered, reg·is·ter·ing.**

reign (rān), *V.* to rule: *The king and queen reigned over the kingdom.* ◻ *V.* **reigned, reign·ing.**

a	in hat	ō	in open	sh	in she
ā	in age	ò	in all	th	in thin
â	in care	ô	in order	ᴛʜ	in then
ä	in far	oi	in oil	zh	in measure
e	in let	ou	in out	ə	= a in about
ē	in equal	u	in cup	ə	= e in taken
ėr	in term	ù	in put	ə	= i in pencil
i	in it	ü	in rule	ə	= o in lemon
ī	in ice	ch	in child	ə	= u in circus
o	in hot	ng	in long		

803

Page 804

re·ject (ri jekt′), *V.* to refuse to take; turn down: *The army will reject any applicants under the age of eighteen.* □ *V.* **re·ject·ed, re·ject·ing.**

rel·ish (rel′ish), **1.** *N.* a pleasant taste; good flavor: *Hunger gives relish to simple food.* **2.** *N.* a side dish to add flavor to food: *Olives and pickles are relishes.*

re·new (ri nü′), *V.* make like new; restore: *The rain renewed the greenness of the fields.* □ *V.* **re·newed, re·new·ing.**

re·nowned (ri nound′), *ADJ.* famous: *a renowned scientist.*

re·pay (ri pā′), *V.* to do something in return for something received: *No thanks can repay such kindness.* □ *V.* **re·paid, re·pay·ing.**

re·pro·duce (rē′prə düs′), *V.* to make a copy of: *to reproduce a photograph.* □ *V.* **re·pro·duced, re·pro·duc·ing.**

re·pul·sive (ri pul′siv), *ADJ.* causing strong dislike or aversion: *the repulsive smell of a skunk.*

re·sound (ri zound′), *V.* be much talked about: *They knew that the fame of the first flight across the Atlantic would resound all over the world.* □ *V.* **re·sound·ed, re·sound·ing.**

re·treat (ri trēt′), **1.** *N.* act of moving back or withdrawing: *The army's retreat was orderly.* **2.** *N.* a retirement or period of retirement by a group of people for religious exercises, meditation, etc.: *The monks conducted a retreat.*

re·volt·ing (ri vōl′ting), *ADJ.* disgusting; repulsive: *a revolting odor.*

riv·et (riv′it), *N.* a metal bolt with a head at one end, the other end being hammered into a head after insertion: *The rugged blue jeans had a rivet on each corner of the pockets.*

romp (romp), *V.* to play in a rough, boisterous way; rush and tumble. □ *V.* **romped, romp·ing.**

row·dy (rou′dē), *ADJ.* rough; disorderly; quarrelsome: *The gym was full of rowdy kids.*

rur·al (rür′əl), *ADJ.* in the country; belonging to the country; like that of the country: *a rural school, rural roads.*

rural

Ss

sanc·tu·ar·y (sangk′chü er′ē), *N.* place of refuge or protection: *Wildlife sanctuaries help ensure animals' safety.* □ *N. PL.* **sanc·tu·ar·ies.**

se·cre·tive (sī′krē tiv), *ADJ.* having the habit of secrecy; not frank and open.

seg·re·gate (seg′rə gāt), *V.* to separate people of different races by having separate schools, restaurants, etc. □ *V.* **seg·re·gat·ed, seg·re·gat·ing.**

set·tle·ment (set′l mənt), *N.* group of buildings and the people living in them: *The prairie settlement was a day's ride from the next town.*

share·crop·per (shâr′krop′ər), *N.* person who farms land for the owner in return for part of the crops. □ *N. PL.* **share·crop·pers.**

Page 805

sling (sling), *V.* to throw; cast; hurl; fling: *I slung the bag of oats into the truck.* □ *V.* **slung, sling·ing.**

slug·gish (slug′ish), *ADJ.* slow-moving; not active; lacking energy or vigor: *When I stay up too late, I am often sluggish the next day.*

smol·der (smōl′dər), *V.* to burn and smoke without flame: *The campfire smoldered for hours after the blaze died down.* □ *V.* **smol·dered, smol·der·ing.**

smug·gle (smug′əl), *V.* to bring something into or take something out of a country secretly and unlawfully, especially without payment of legal duties. □ *V.* **smug·gled, smug·gling.**

sol·vent (sol′vənt), *N.* substance, usually a liquid, that can dissolve other substances: *Water is a solvent of sugar and salt.* □ *N. PL.* **sol·vents.**

spa·cious (spā′shəs), *ADJ.* containing much space; with plenty of room; vast: *The rooms were bright and spacious.*

spec·i·men (spes′ə mən), *N.* one of a group or class taken to show what the others are like; sample: *He collects specimens of all kinds of rocks and minerals. The two statues were fine specimens of Greek sculpture.* *N. PL.* **spec·i·mens.**

speck·led (spek′əld), *ADJ.* marked with many small spots: *A speckled bird flew out of the bush.*

squawl (skwôl), *V.* to cry; bawl. □ *V.* **squawl·ed, squawl·ing.**

squire (skwīr), *N.* attendant.

stif·fen (stif′ən), *V.* to make or become rigid, fixed: *Her muscles stiffened in the cold wind.* □ *V.* **stif·fened, stif·fen·ing.**

stim·u·lat·ing (stim′yə lāt ing), *ADJ.* lively; engaging. *The stimulating conversation made the party interesting.*

stun (stun), *V.* to daze; bewilder; shock; overwhelm: *She was stunned by the news of her friend's injury.* □ *V.* **stunned, stun·ning.**

sub·scribe (səb skrīb′), *V.* to give your consent or approval; agree: *She does not subscribe to my opinion.* □ *V.* **sub·scribed, sub·scrib·ing.** (*Subscribe* comes from two Latin words, *sub* meaning "under" and *scribe* meaning "to write.")

suf·fi·cient (sə fish′ənt), *ADJ.* as much as is needed; enough: *sufficient proof.*

su·per·sti·tious (sü′pər stish′əs), *ADJ.* having belief or practice based on ignorant fear or mistaken reverence.

sur·plus (sér′pləs or sér′plus), *N.* amount over and above what is needed; extra quantity left over; excess: *The bank keeps a large surplus of money in reserve.*

sur·vive (sər viv′), *V.* to continue to exist; remain; to continue to live: *No one thought the old, bent tree would survive being hit by lightning.* □ *V.* **sur·vived, sur·viv·ing.**

Tt

tech·nol·o·gy (tek nol′ə jē), *N.* the use of scientific knowledge to control physical objects and forces: *overcome problems by technology.*

tol·e·rate (tol′ə rāt′), *V.* to allow or permit: *Gum chewing in the classroom was not tolerated.* □ *V.* **tol·e·rat·ed, tol·e·rat·ing.**

a in hat	ō in open	sh in she
ā in age	ò in all	th in thin
â in care	ô in order	ᴛʜ in then
ä in far	oi in oil	zh in measure
e in let	ou in out	ə = a in about
ē in equal	u in cup	ə = e in taken
ėr in term	ù in put	ə = i in pencil
i in it	ü in rule	ə = o in lemon
ī in ice	ch in child	ə = u in circus
o in hot	ng in long	

Page 806

toll¹ (tōl), **1.** *V.* to sound with single strokes that are slowly and regularly repeated. **2.** *N.* something paid, lost, suffered, etc.: *Accidents take a heavy toll of human lives.* □ *V.* **tolled, toll·ing.**

toll² (tōl), *N.* tax or fee paid from some right or privilege. We pay a toll when we use the bridge.

tor·ment (tôr′ment), *N.* a cause of very great pain: *A bad burn can be a torment.*

tour·ism (tür′iz′əm), *N.* the business of serving people who are traveling for pleasure.

tou·sle (tou′zəl), *V.* to put into disorder; make untidy; muss: *tousled hair.* □ *V.* **tou·sled, tou·sling.**

trades·man (trādz′mən), *N.* storekeeper; shopkeeper.

trans·mit (tran smit′ *or* tranz mit′), *V.* to send out signals by means of electromagnetic waves or by wire: *Some station is transmitting every hour of the day.* □ *V.* **trans·mit·ted, trans·mit·ting.**

trav·erse (trav′ərs), *V.* to pass across, over, or through: *Explorers traversed the desert by truck.* □ *V.* **tra·versed, tra·vers·ing.**

treach·er·ous (trech′ər əs), *ADJ.* having a false appearance of strength, security, etc.; not reliable; deceiving: *Thin ice is treacherous.*

tread (tred), **1.** *V.* to set a foot down; walk; step: *Don't tread on the flower beds.* **2.** *V.* tread water; to keep the body straight in the water with the head above the surface by moving the arms and legs. □ *V.* **trod, tread·ed, tread·ing.**

trop·ics (trop′iks), *N. PL.* the regions between the equator and imaginary circles 23.45 degrees north and south of the equator. The hottest part of the Earth is in the tropics.

tropics

tu·i·tion (tü ish′ən), *N.* money paid for instruction: *a $300 increase in college tuition.*

tur·bu·lent (tér′byə lənt), *ADJ.* stormy; tempestuous: *turbulent weather.*

Uu

un·ac·com·pa·nied (un′ə kum′pə nēd), *ADJ.* not accompanied; alone.

un·can·ny (un kan′ē), *ADJ.* strange and mysterious; weird: *The trees took uncanny shapes in the mist.*

un·con·ven·tion·al (un′kən ven′shə nəl), *ADJ.* not bound by or conforming to convention, rule, or precedent; free from conventionality.

u·ni·son (yü′nə sən), *N.* agreement: *The marchers' feet moved in unison. We spoke in unison.*

Page 807

u·ni·ver·sal (yü′nə vér′səl), **1.** *ADJ.* of or belonging to all; concerning all: *Food is a universal need.* **2.** *ADJ.* existing everywhere: *The law of gravity is universal.*

un·la·dy·like (un lā′dē lik′), *ADJ.* impolite; not like a lady; not well-bred.

ur·ban (ér′bən), *ADJ.* typical of cities: *urban life.*

urban

Vv

ven·ture (ven′chər), *V.* to dare to come or go: *We ventured out on the thin ice and fell through.* □ *V.* **ven·tured, ven·tur·ing.**

ver·i·fy (ver′ə fi), *V.* to prove to be true; confirm: *The witness's account of the accident would verify the driver's report.* □ *V.* **ver·i·fied, ver·i·fy·ing.**

ver·sion (vér′zhən), **1.** *N.* one particular statement, account, or description: *Each of the three boys gave his own version of the quarrel.* **2.** *N.* a special form or variant of something: *I liked the movie version better than the book.*

vig·or·ous·ly (vig′ər əs lē), *ADV.* strongly; actively; energetically.

vis·ta (vis′tə), *N.* opening or passage through or from which you see a wide view.

vol·can·ic (vol kan′ik), *ADJ.* of or caused by a volcano; about volcanoes: *a volcanic eruption.*

Ww

waft (wäft), **1.** *V.* to carry over water or through air: *A breeze wafted the aroma of fresh bread to me.* □ *V.* **waft·ed, waft·ing. 2.** *N.* a breath or puff of air, wind, scent, etc.: *A waft of fresh air came through the window.*

wane (wān), *V.* to go through the moon's regular reduction in the amount of its visible portion. The moon wanes when the side facing the Earth moves gradually out of the sun's light. □ *V.* **waned, wan·ing.**

wel·fare (wel′fâr′), *N.* health, happiness, and prosperity; condition of being or doing well: *My uncle asked about the welfare of everyone in our family.*

wilt (wilt), *V.* to become limp and bend down; wither: *Flowers wilt when they don't get enough water.* □ *V.* **wilt·ed, wilt·ing.**

Zz

ze·nith (zē′nith), *N.* the highest point: *the zenith of a ferris wheel.*

a in hat	ō in open	sh in she
ā in age	ò in all	th in thin
â in care	ô in order	ᴛʜ in then
ä in far	oi in oil	zh in measure
e in let	ou in out	ə = a in about
ē in equal	u in cup	ə = e in taken
ėr in term	ù in put	ə = i in pencil
i in it	ü in rule	ə = o in lemon
ī in ice	ch in child	ə = u in circus
o in hot	ng in long	

English/Spanish Selection Vocabulary List

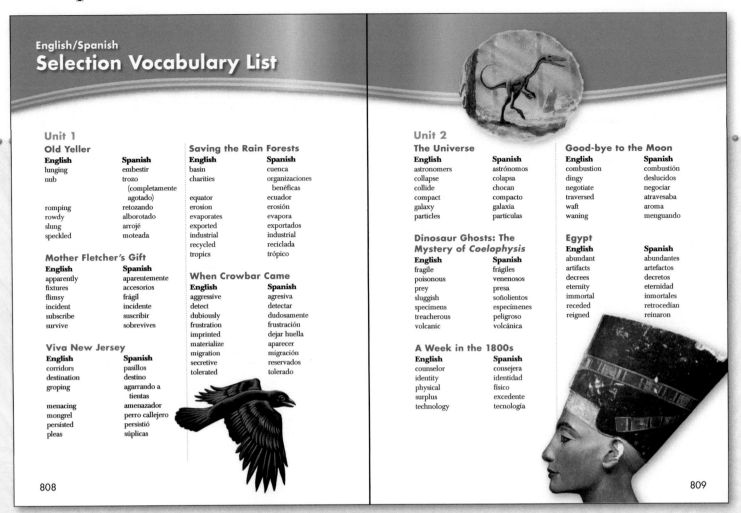

English/Spanish
Selection Vocabulary List

Unit 1

Old Yeller

English	Spanish
lunging	embestir
nub	trozo (completamente agotado)
romping	retozando
rowdy	alborotado
slung	arrojé
speckled	moteada

Mother Fletcher's Gift

English	Spanish
apparently	aparentemente
fixtures	accesorios
flimsy	frágil
incident	incidente
subscribe	suscribir
survive	sobrevives

Viva New Jersey

English	Spanish
corridors	pasillos
destination	destino
groping	agarrando a tientas
menacing	amenazador
mongrel	perro callejero
persisted	persistió
pleas	súplicas

Saving the Rain Forests

English	Spanish
basin	cuenca
charities	organizaciones benéficas
equator	ecuador
erosion	erosión
evaporates	evapora
exported	exportados
industrial	industrial
recycled	reciclada
tropics	trópico

When Crowbar Came

English	Spanish
aggressive	agresiva
detect	detectar
dubiously	dudosamente
frustration	frustración
imprinted	dejar huella
materialize	aparecer
migration	migración
secretive	reservados
tolerated	tolerado

Unit 2

The Universe

English	Spanish
astronomers	astrónomos
collapse	colapsa
collide	chocan
compact	compacto
galaxy	galaxia
particles	partículas

Dinosaur Ghosts: The Mystery of *Coelophysis*

English	Spanish
fragile	frágiles
poisonous	venenosos
prey	presa
sluggish	soñolientos
specimens	especímenes
treacherous	peligroso
volcanic	volcánica

A Week in the 1800s

English	Spanish
counselor	consejera
identity	identidad
physical	físico
surplus	excedente
technology	tecnología

Good-bye to the Moon

English	Spanish
combustion	combustión
dingy	deslucidos
negotiate	negociar
traversed	atravesaba
waft	aroma
waning	menguando

Egypt

English	Spanish
abundant	abundantes
artifacts	artefactos
decrees	decretos
eternity	eternidad
immortal	inmortales
receded	retrocedían
reigned	reinaron

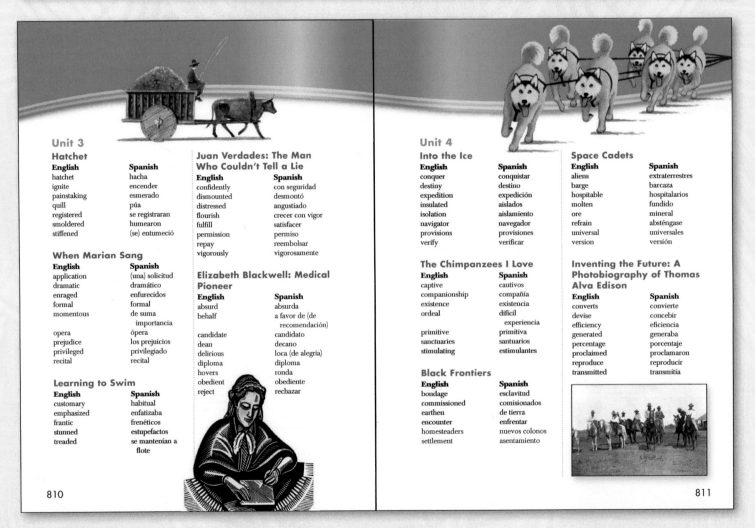

Unit 3

Hatchet

English	Spanish
hatchet	hacha
ignite	encender
painstaking	esmerado
quill	púa
registered	se registraran
smoldered	humearon
stiffened	(se) entumeció

When Marian Sang

English	Spanish
application	(una) solicitud
dramatic	dramático
enraged	enfurecidos
formal	formal
momentous	de suma importancia
opera	ópera
prejudice	los prejuicios
privileged	privilegiado
recital	recital

Learning to Swim

English	Spanish
customary	habitual
emphasized	enfatizaba
frantic	frenéticos
stunned	estupefactos
treaded	se mantenían a flote

Juan Verdades: The Man Who Couldn't Tell a Lie

English	Spanish
confidently	con seguridad
dismounted	desmontó
distressed	angustiado
flourish	crecer con vigor
fulfill	satisfacer
permission	permiso
repay	reembolsar
vigorously	vigorosamente

Elizabeth Blackwell: Medical Pioneer

English	Spanish
absurd	absurda
behalf	a favor de (de recomendación)
candidate	candidato
dean	decano
delirious	loca (de alegría)
diploma	diploma
hovers	ronda
obedient	obediente
reject	rechazar

Unit 4

Into the Ice

English	Spanish
conquer	conquistar
destiny	destino
expedition	expedición
insulated	aislados
isolation	aislamiento
navigator	navegador
provisions	provisiones
verify	verificar

The Chimpanzees I Love

English	Spanish
captive	cautivos
companionship	compañía
existence	existencia
ordeal	difícil experiencia
primitive	primitiva
sanctuaries	santuarios
stimulating	estimulantes

Black Frontiers

English	Spanish
bondage	esclavitud
commissioned	comisionados
earthen	de tierra
encounter	enfrentar
homesteaders	nuevos colonos
settlement	asentamiento

Space Cadets

English	Spanish
aliens	extraterrestres
barge	barcaza
hospitable	hospitalarios
molten	fundido
ore	mineral
refrain	absténgase
universal	universales
version	versión

Inventing the Future: A Photobiography of Thomas Alva Edison

English	Spanish
converts	convierte
devise	concebir
efficiency	eficiencia
generated	generaba
percentage	porcentaje
proclaimed	proclamaron
reproduce	reproducir
transmitted	transmitía

English/Spanish Selection Vocabulary List

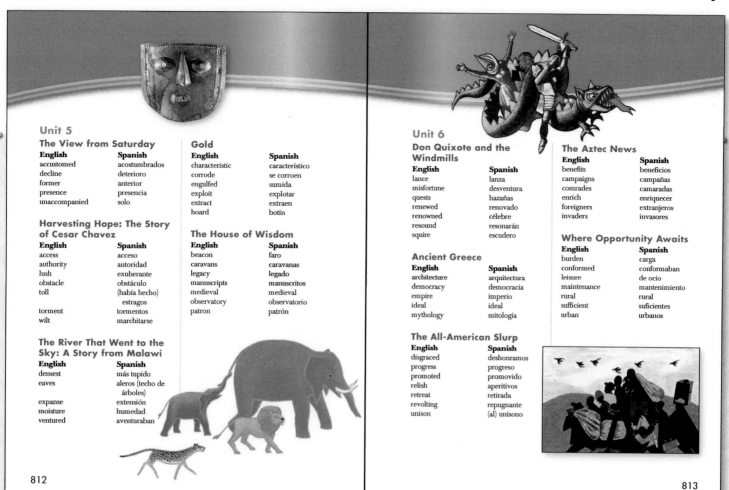

Unit 5

The View from Saturday

English	Spanish
accustomed	acostumbrados
decline	deterioro
former	anterior
presence	presencia
unaccompanied	solo

Harvesting Hope: The Story of Cesar Chavez

English	Spanish
access	acceso
authority	autoridad
lush	exuberante
obstacle	obstáculo
toll	(había hecho) estragos
torment	tormentos
wilt	marchitarse

The River That Went to the Sky: A Story from Malawi

English	Spanish
densest	más tupido
eaves	aleros (techo de árboles)
expanse	extensión
moisture	humedad
ventured	aventuraban

Gold

English	Spanish
characteristic	característico
corrode	se corroen
engulfed	sumida
exploit	explotar
extract	extraen
hoard	botín

The House of Wisdom

English	Spanish
beacon	faro
caravans	caravanas
legacy	legado
manuscripts	manuscritos
medieval	medieval
observatory	observatorio
patron	patrón

Unit 6

Don Quixote and the Windmills

English	Spanish
lance	lanza
misfortune	desventura
quests	hazañas
renewed	renovado
renowned	célebre
resound	resonarán
squire	escudero

Ancient Greece

English	Spanish
architecture	arquitectura
democracy	democracia
empire	imperio
ideal	ideal
mythology	mitología

The All-American Slurp

English	Spanish
disgraced	deshonramos
progress	progreso
promoted	promovido
relish	aperitivos
retreat	retirada
revolting	repugnante
unison	(al) unísono

The Aztec News

English	Spanish
benefits	beneficios
campaigns	campañas
comrades	camaradas
enrich	enriquecer
foreigners	extranjeros
invaders	invasores

Where Opportunity Awaits

English	Spanish
burden	carga
conformed	conformaban
leisure	de ocio
maintenance	mantenimiento
rural	rural
sufficient	suficientes
urban	urbanos

812

813

Acknowledgments

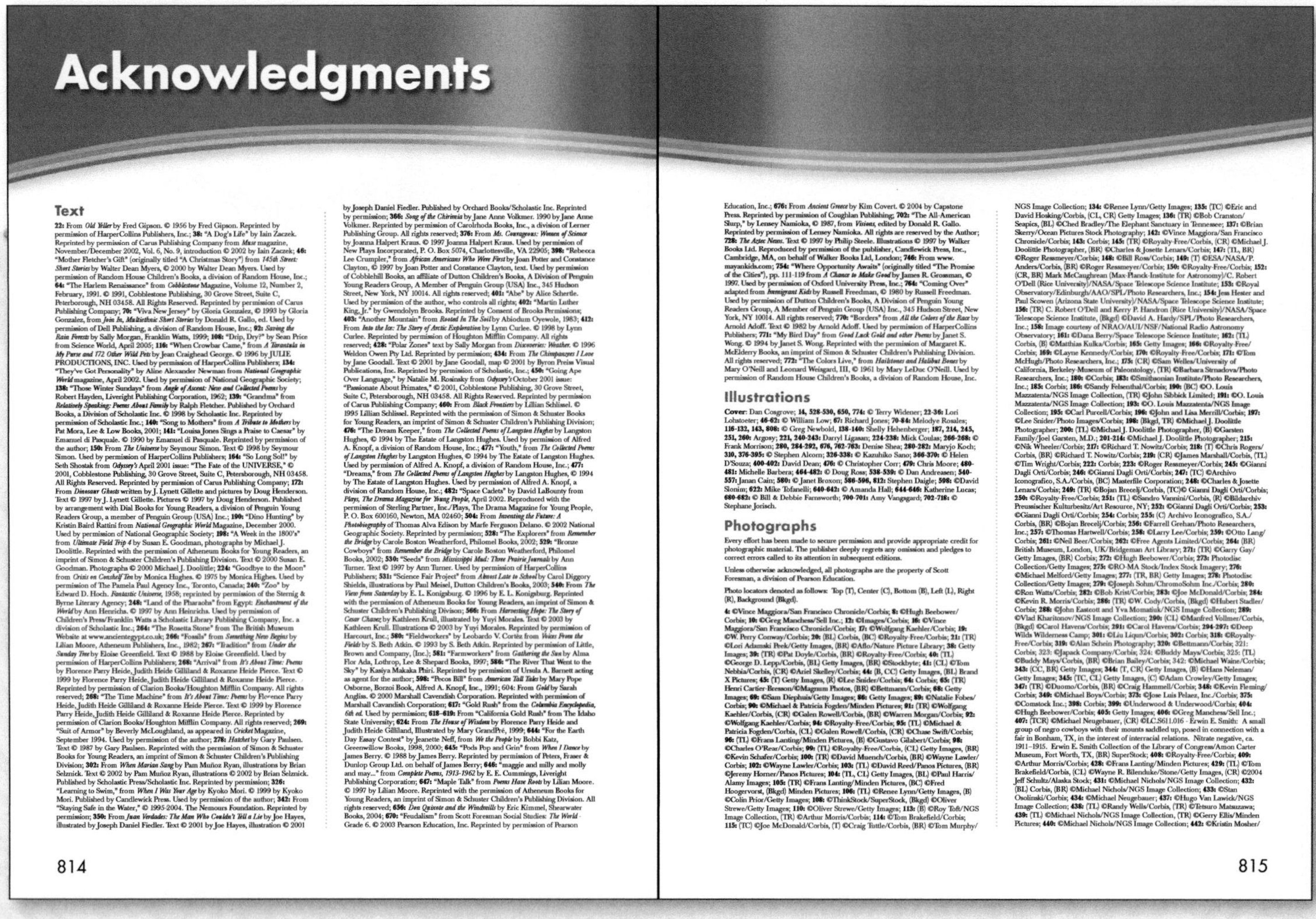

Acknowledgments

Text

2b From *Old Yeller* by Fred Gipson. © 1956 by Fred Gipson. Reprinted by permission of HarperCollins Publishers, Inc. [...] Text © 2001 by Joe Hayes, illustration © 2001

[credits continue]

814

[second column continues]

by Joseph Daniel Fiedler. Published by Orchard Books/Scholastic Inc. Reprinted by permission; [...] Grade 6. © 2003 Pearson Education, Inc. Reprinted by permission of Pearson

Illustrations

Cover: Dan Cosgrove; [...] Stephane Jorisch.

Photographs

Every effort has been made to secure permission and provide appropriate credit for photographic material. The publisher deeply regrets any omission and pledges to correct errors called to its attention in subsequent editions.

Unless otherwise acknowledged, all photographs are the property of Scott Foresman, a division of Pearson Education.

Photo locators denoted as follows: Top (T), Center (C), Bottom (B), Left (L), Right (R), Background (Bkgd).

[credits continue]

815

[page 816]

[credits continue]

Glossary

The contents of this glossary have been adapted from *Thorndike Barnhart Intermediate Dictionary* and *Thorndike Advanced Dictionary*. Copyright © 1997, Pearson Education, Inc.

795 The National Park Service; 796 Corbis; 798 Kosmos, Corbis; [...] 806 SuperStock

816

Rubric
| 4 | 3 | 2 | 1 |

Focus/Ideas

Organization/ Paragraphs

Voice

Word Choice

Sentences

Conventions

Writing Traits

Focus/Ideas refers to the main purpose for writing and the details that make the subject clear and interesting. It includes development of ideas through support and elaboration.

Organization/Paragraphs refers to the overall structure of a piece of writing that guides readers. Within that structure, transitions show how ideas, sentences, and paragraphs are connected.

Voice shows the writer's unique personality and establishes a connection between writer and reader. Voice, which contributes to style, should be suited to the audience and the purpose for writing.

Word Choice is the use of precise, vivid words to communicate effectively and naturally. It helps create style through the use of specific nouns, lively verbs and adjectives, and accurate, well-placed modifiers.

Sentences covers strong, well-built sentences that vary in length and type. Skillfully written sentences have pleasing rhythms and flow fluently.

Conventions refers to mechanical correctness and includes grammar, usage, spelling, punctuation, capitalization, and paragraphing.

Writing Workshop

Story

OBJECTIVES

- Develop an understanding of a story.
- Use vivid words to create interest for readers.
- Use literary elements such as suspense, foreshadowing, tension, and humor.
- Establish criteria for evaluating a story.

Key Features

Story

In a story, a writer narrates a series of related events featuring specific characters in a specific setting.

- Has a beginning, middle, and end
- Focuses on one incident or event
- Uses time-order words to show the sequence of events
- Has characters, plot, and a setting

Connect to Weekly Writing

Week 1	News Story 429g–429h
Week 2	Story About an Animal 455g–455h
Week 3	Describe a Setting 477g–477h
Week 4	TV Script 499g–499h
Week 5	Summary 527g–527h

Strategic Intervention

See Differentiated Instruction p. WA8.

Advanced

See Differentiated Instruction p. WA9.

ELL

See Differentiated Instruction p. WA9.

Additional Resources for Writing
Writing Rubrics and Anchor Papers, pp. 56–62

Writing Prompt: Explorers, Pioneers, and Discoverers
Write a story about an adventure, a discovery, or something that happened to you for the first time. Use some of these literary devices: foreshadowing, tension, suspense, conflict, humor.
Purpose: Tell an interesting story about a fictional or real event
Audience: Readers of adventure and discovery stories

READ LIKE A WRITER

Look back at *Into the Ice*. Remind students that although this is a nonfiction account, it is a narrative that has characters, a plot, and a setting—all elements of a story. Tell students that they will use these elements when they write a **story.**

EXAMINE THE MODEL AND RUBRIC

GUIDED WRITING Read the model aloud. Ask students how the first paragraph creates interest. Discuss how the model reflects traits of good writing.

Trip to Planet X

   Suddenly the satellite's signal disappeared from the screen. We had followed satellite GX17 since it was knocked out of its orbit by a meteoroid. The satellite carried valuable instruments and data, and we needed to find it. It couldn't have just disappeared. Jackson and I had to find out what really happened to GX17.

   We flew toward where we had last seen the satellite's signal. After many hours, an orange mass came into view. It appeared to be a very small planet. Had the satellite hit the planet? We didn't know. But exploring this mysterious place was an opportunity Jackson and I couldn't pass up.

   We were trembling with anticipation as we stepped out onto the planet. All around us were deep orange craters and wide valleys. The sky was a pale yellow without a single cloud. We spotted part of the satellite 100 yards away and hiked toward it.

   The satellite was in pieces. Luckily, the recording equipment was unharmed. We took photos of the planet with the satellite's camera and collected a soil sample. We needed proof to take home. Our suits were running low on oxygen; it was time to head back to the ship.

   On the way home, Jackson and I could not keep the smiles off our faces. Not only did we find the satellite, but we had discovered something extraordinary—an unknown planet.

Traits of a Good Story

Focus/Ideas	Story is focused on the quest to find the lost satellite.
Organization/ Paragraphs	The story has a beginning, middle, and end. Paragraphs are smoothly connected.
Voice	Writer uses literary elements such as foreshadowing, tension, suspense, and conflict to make the story exciting.
Word Choice	Specific words and vivid imagery keep the reader interested. *(orange craters and wide valleys)*
Sentences	Varied sentence lengths and structures create a rhythm that fits the action in the story.
Conventions	Writer has excellent control of grammar, capitalization, spelling, and punctuation.

▲ **Writing Transparency** WP22   ▲ **Writing Transparency** WP23

FINDING A TOPIC

- Have students brainstorm people they know or have read about who have explored or discovered something. Write a list on the board.
- Have students collaborate on investigating an exciting discovery or exploration.
- Suggest students list experiences they have had exploring new places or things and how they felt about them.

NARROW A TOPIC

An adventure at sea   Not specific enough

Planning a birthday party   Not exciting enough

A mysterious barn and a discovery   This would make a suspenseful story.

PREWRITING STRATEGY

GUIDED WRITING Display Writing Transparency WP24. Model how to complete a story chart.

 Think Aloud

MODEL The student has chosen an interesting event to write about and has mapped out the title, setting, characters, events, and solution. Now the student can write a draft using vivid language to expand each part of the story.

PREWRITING ACTIVITIES

- Have students use Grammar and Writing Practice Book p. 172 to map out the characters, setting, events, and solution for their story.
- Students can freewrite about their story topic for 10 to 15 minutes, writing without worrying about grammar or organization.

Freewriting

Barn is old, dusty and kids have never been inside cause Grandma keeps it locked. Kids are scared, but they break in and find car.

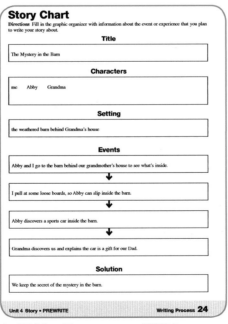

Story Chart

Directions Fill in the graphic organizer with information about the event or experience that you plan to write your story about.

Title

The Mystery in the Barn

Characters

me   Abby   Grandma

Setting

the weathered barn behind Grandma's house

Events

Abby and I go to the barn behind our grandmother's house to see what's inside.

↓

I pull at some loose boards, so Abby can slip inside the barn.

↓

Abby discovers a sports car inside the barn.

↓

Grandma discovers us and explains the car is a gift for our Dad.

Solution

We keep the secret of the mystery in the barn.

Unit 4 Story • PREWRITE   Writing Process **24**

▲ **Writing Transparency** WP24

Monitor Progress

Differentiated Instruction

If... students have trouble choosing a story topic,	then... suggest that they answer these questions: *What is an event I can clearly imagine? What is an event that would hold readers' interest?*

Story Chart

Directions Fill in the graphic organizer with information about your story.

Title

Characters

Answers should include details about each part of student's story.

Setting

Events

↓

↓

Solution

▲ **Grammar and Writing Practice Book** p. 172

Writing Workshop

Think Like a Writer

Organize Your Story Before writing your story, decide on the order of the events. You will most likely tell the story in time order, beginning with the first thing that happened and ending with the last. However, you may want to begin with an event in the middle before relating the events that happened first. You may also flashback to a past event to create suspense.

Support Writing Help students make lists of specific language for their stories:
- Precise nouns and strong verbs for good beginnings
- Adjectives and adverbs for vivid details

Good Beginnings

Directions Below are some different ways to begin a story. Write an opening sentence or sentences using each idea. You can use one of your beginnings in your story.

Ask a Question (*Example:* Have you ever done something that you almost instantly regretted doing? That's how I felt when I accepted this job.)
Answers should be based on the provided ideas and should be complete sentences with appropriate capitalization and punctuation.

Use a Sound Word or an Exclamation (*Example:* Watch out! The loose rocks slid out from under my feet, and I almost slipped over the edge.)

Set the Scene (*Example:* It was a bitterly cold December day. My surroundings looked more like an Arctic wasteland than a Midwestern suburb.)

Use Humor (*Example:* I looked ridiculous in the chicken costume. It was so big that the head covered most of my body, and I could barely walk.)

Use Foreshadowing (*Example:* I thought nothing would keep me from going to Antarctica. I guess I was wrong.)

▲ **Grammar and Writing Practice Book** p. 173

WRITING THE FIRST DRAFT

GUIDED WRITING Use Writing Transparency WP25 to practice writing good beginnings.

- Discuss why a good beginning is essential to a story. Have students read the ways to begin a story.

- Read the first set of sentences aloud and discuss with students which kind of beginning the writer used.

Think Aloud **MODEL** After I read the first set of opening sentences, I ask myself, "What is the writer doing here? How is the writer trying to grab my attention?" The writer is hinting about something that will happen later in the story. This is using foreshadowing. Let's read the other beginnings. You might choose one of these ways when writing the beginning of your own story.

Good Beginnings

The beginning sentences of your story should grab readers' attention and make them want to read on. Here are some ways to begin a story.

Ways to Begin a Story
Ask a question.
Use a sound word or an exclamation.
Set the scene.
Use humor.
Use foreshadowing.

Directions Identify which kind of beginning is used in each sentence below.

1. Crumbling walls and sludge. The townspeople said that's all we would find in the ruins of the lost city. Apparently they hadn't looked closely.
   Use foreshadowing.

2. Why was I here? I was only a beginning skier, and the sight of the gigantic mountain looming in front of me made my stomach hurt.
   Ask a question.

3. Whump! Kurt's body hit the floor after he tripped, once again, over an untied shoelace. As he picked himself up, he saw something shiny under the dresser.
   Use a sound word or an exclamation.

4. Amelia lay quietly on the sidewalk. Perhaps if she stayed still, no one would notice that she had slipped and fallen flat on the ice in front of the entire school population.
   Use humor.

5. The night was warm and humid. Wet grass slapped against their legs as they walked toward the river. In a nearby tree they heard an owl hooting.
   Set the scene.

Unit 4 Story • DRAFT   Writing Process **25**

▲ **Writing Transparency** WP25

WRITER'S CRAFT Use Vivid Words

Here are some ways writers use vivid words in their stories.
- Replace words that are dull, vague, or overused (*stuff, things, get, a lot of*) with precise, colorful words.
- Use words that paint a clear picture of a character or setting.
- Look for forms of the verb *to be* that could be changed to active verbs. (*I shivered* instead of *I was cold*)

DRAFTING STRATEGIES

- Have students review their story chart before they write.
- Students should write an attention-grabbing beginning.
- Remind students to keep their audience and purpose in mind.
- Students should reread their stories to see where they might add vivid words.
- Have students use Grammar and Writing Practice Book p. 173 to write a good beginning for their stories.

WRITER'S CRAFT Elaboration

WHO AND WHOM Explain that one way to elaborate is to add details to sentences using clauses that begin with *who* or *whom*.

General   Christopher Columbus is honored every October.

Improved   Christopher Columbus, who was the first European to travel to the Americas, is honored every October.

Use Grammar and Writing Practice Book p. 174 to practice elaboration by adding clauses with *who* or *whom*.

REVISING STRATEGIES

GUIDED WRITING Use Writing Transparency WP26 to model revising. Point out the Revising Marks, which students should use when they revise their work.

Think Aloud

MODEL This is part of the story "The Mystery in the Barn." In the first sentence, the writer eliminated wordiness by replacing *were getting close to* with one strong verb, *approached*. Also, to create a more vivid description of the narrator's feelings, the writer replaced *I suddenly felt scared* with *chills ran up my spine*. In the second sentence, the writer added *old weathered* to describe the barn. The next sentence uses too many words to describe a feeling that can be described with one strong verb: *feared*. In the last sentence, the writer added the adverbs *always* and *tightly* to paint a more specific picture.

PEER REVISION Write the Revising Checklist on the board or make copies to distribute. Students can use this checklist to revise their stories. Have partners read each other's first drafts. Remind them to be courteous and specific with suggestions.

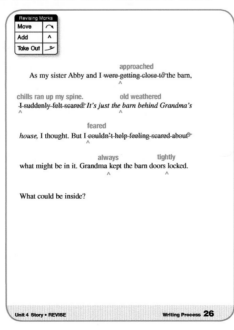

▲ **Writing Transparency** WP26

Elaboration
Using *Who* and *Whom*

You can use clauses beginning with *who* and *whom* to add specific details to sentences. You can also use these clauses to combine short, related sentences. Remember to use *who* as a subject in a clause and *whom* as a direct object or the object of a preposition.

General   I talked with the man.
Specific   I talked with the man who explored the South Pole.
Choppy   The man has written a book. I traveled with him.
Smooth   The man with whom I traveled has written a book.

Directions Combine each pair of sentences. Make the second sentence into a clause beginning with *who* or *whom* and add it to the first sentence. Write the new sentence. **Possible answers:**

1. Explorers began sailing around the world in the 1400s. They had a spirit of adventure.
   <u>Explorers who had a spirit of adventure began sailing around the world in the 1400s.</u>

2. The two women set out to explore the Grand Canyon. They were experienced hikers.
   <u>The two women who were experienced hikers set out to explore the Grand Canyon.</u>

3. The man has traveled to many islands in the South Pacific. I admire him.
   <u>The man whom I admire has traveled to many islands in the South Pacific.</u>

4. The divers have often viewed the ocean floor. We spoke with them.
   <u>The divers whom we spoke with have often viewed the ocean floor.</u>

5. The pilot has been around the world many times. She has been flying for 20 years.
   <u>The pilot who has been flying for 20 years has been around the world many times.</u>

▲ **Grammar and Writing Practice Book** p. 174

Writing Workshop

1 PREWRITE 2 DRAFT 3 REVISE 4 EDIT 5 PUBLISH

Monitor Progress

Differentiated Instruction

If... students are having difficulty with pronouns and antecedents,	then... review the grammar lesson on pp. 455e–455f.

Editing Checklist

✔ Did I spell complex words correctly?

✔ Did I use *who* or *whom* correctly?

✔ Did I use commas to set off clauses?

✔ Did I use pronouns that agree with their antecedents?

Support Writing Invite students to read their drafts aloud to you. Observe whether they seem to note any spelling or grammatical errors by stumbling or self-correcting. Return to those errors and show students how to correct them. Use the appropriate Grammar Transition Lessons in the ELL and Transition Handbook to explicitly teach the English spelling and grammar conventions.

EDITING STRATEGY

SENTENCE BY SENTENCE Suggest that students check their work sentence by sentence. Have them look first at the sentence's structure and then at specific features such as spelling, punctuation, and capitalization.

GUIDED WRITING Use Writing Transparency WP27 to model the process of editing sentence by sentence. Indicate the Proofreading Marks, which students should use when they edit their work. Write the Editing Checklist on the board or make copies to distribute. Students can use this checklist to edit their work.

MODEL Proofreading sentence by sentence helps you systematically edit your writing. In the first sentence, the writer added commas after *Grandma* and *casserole* to set off a dependent clause. The writer recognized that *whom* was incorrect and changed it to *who*. In the next sentence, the writer changed the misspelled word to *intention* and replaced *our grandmother* with the pronoun *her* to avoid repetition. In the third sentence, the writer added a comma after *barn* because this is a compound sentence.

▲ **Writing Transparency** WP27

OFFLINE

USING TECHNOLOGY Students who have written or revised their stories on computers should keep these points in mind as they edit:

- If your program has a spell checker, use it to check your spelling, but do not rely on this feature exclusively. A good dictionary is the best source.
- Use the Format menu to make sure your paragraphs are correctly indented.

SELF-EVALUATION

Prepare students to fill out a Self-Evaluation Guide. Display Writing Transparency WP28 to model the self-evaluation process.

Think Aloud **MODEL** I would give the story a *4*.

Focus/Ideas This story focuses on a discovery and builds suspense about the outcome.

Organization/Paragraphs Events are described in time order.

Voice The narrative voice is clear and engaging.

Word Choice The writer uses vivid words and time-order words.

Sentences The kinds and lengths of sentences are varied.

Conventions Grammar, capitalization, and spelling are excellent.

EVALUATION Assign Grammar and Writing Practice Book p. 175. Tell students that when they evaluate their own stories, assigning a score of 3, 2, or even 1 does not necessarily indicate a bad paper. The ability to identify areas for improvement in future writing is a valuable skill.

The Mystery in the Barn

As my sister Abby and I approached the barn, chills ran up my spine. *It's just the old weathered barn behind Grandma's house,* I thought. But I feared what might be in it. Grandma always kept the barn doors tightly locked. What could be inside?

Grandma, who was making tuna casserole, would be wondering where we were. It was never our intention to worry her, so we had to hurry. I quickly yanked a loose board on the side of the barn, and Abby wiggled inside. At first, Abby was silent. Then she yelled, "Whoa!" I helped her squeeze back through the boards.

"What did you see?" I asked excitedly.

"You know that car you and Dad are always talking about? The red convertible? Well, it's in there under a dusty tarp." I couldn't believe it! Grandma had been keeping a sports car in her barn?

Just then we heard footsteps. Abby and I tried to run and hide, but Grandma had seen us. "Isn't it a sensational gift?" she said. *A gift for whom?* I wondered. It turned out that the car had been Grandpa's. It had fallen into disrepair. Grandma had it restored as a birthday surprise for our dad. Abby and I would keep her secret. I couldn't wait for Dad to discover the mystery inside the barn for himself.

Unit 4 Story • PUBLISH   Writing Process **28**

▲ **Writing Transparency** WP28

For 6-, 5-, and 3-point Scoring Rubrics, see pp. WA11-WA14.

Ideas for Publishing

Illustrated Books Students can make their stories into books with construction paper and illustrations. Books can be displayed in the classroom.

Partner Readings Students can share their stories with a partner. Partners can comment and ask questions.

Self-Evaluation Guide
Story

Directions Think about the final draft of your story. Then rate yourself on a scale from 4 to 1 (4 is the highest) on each writing trait. After you fill out the chart, answer the questions.

Writing Traits	4	3	2	1
Focus/Ideas				
Organization/Paragraphs				
Voice				
Word Choice				
Sentences				
Conventions				

1. What is the best part of your story?
   Answers should show that students have thought carefully about the details and techniques used in their stories.

2. Write one thing you would change about this story if you had the chance to write it again.

▲ **Grammar and Writing Practice Book** p. 175

Scoring Rubric — Story

Rubric 4 3 2 1	4	3	2	1
Focus/Ideas	Story focused on one event; many strong details	Story generally focused with good details	Story often off topic; lacks good details	Story with no focus or insufficient details
Organization/ Paragraphs	Clear beginning, middle, and end	Reasonably clear beginning, middle, and end	Unclear beginning, middle, and end	No attempt at beginning, middle, or end
Voice	Engaging and unique voice	Pleasant voice but not compelling or unique	No clear, original voice	Uninvolved or indifferent
Word Choice	Vivid; creates humor, suspense, or tension	Some vivid words that convey a certain feeling	Few vivid words; little emotional connection	No attempt to use vivid words
Sentences	Clear sentences; variety of sentences	Mostly clear sentences with some variety	Some sentences unclear; little or no variety	Incoherent sentences, or short, choppy sentences
Conventions	Few, if any, errors	Several minor errors	Frequent errors that detract from writing	Many errors that seriously detract from writing

Writing Workshop

Story Differentiated Instruction

WRITING PROMPT: Explorers, Pioneers, and Discoverers

Write a story about an adventure, a discovery, or something that happened to you for the first time. Use some of these literary devices: foreshadowing, tension, suspense, conflict, humor.

Purpose: Tell an interesting story about a fictional or real event

Audience: Readers of adventure and discovery

MODIFY INSTRUCTION

ALTERNATIVE PROMPTS

Pick One

ALTERNATIVE PROMPTS: Narrative Writing

Strategic Intervention Write an adventure story that a reader four or five years old would enjoy. In three paragraphs, tell what happens in the beginning, middle, and end of the adventure.

On-Level You are writing a story for an adventure magazine for young people. Imagine an adventure you would like to experience, such as mountain climbing or deep-sea diving. Build a story with a beginning, middle, and end around the adventure.

Advanced Write a story about an adventure or discovery with an unusual setting that is vividly described. You may want to research the setting before describing it. Include several instances of foreshadowing. Plan beforehand where you will place hints to the reader about what will happen next.

Strategic Intervention

MODIFY THE PROMPT

Pair emerging writers with more able writers. Partners can collaborate and brainstorm to find a suitable topic. At the drafting stage, they can talk through their story before beginning to write. Able writers can guide emerging writers through the revising and editing stages.

PREWRITING SUPPORT

• Share stories of real explorers, discoverers, and pioneers with students. Have them comment on how these people risked their lives to do something great.

• Read an adventure story aloud to students. Point out how the beginning engages readers and how the writer uses suspense, tension, foreshadowing, or humor in the story. Discuss the sequence of events. Write the order of events on a time line on the board.

• In a class discussion, ask volunteers to describe the event or incident they have chosen as their topic. Discuss ways in which students might flesh out their setting and characters as well as the main events of the story.

OPTIONS

• Give students the option of writing a group story under your supervision.

CHECK PROGRESS Segment the assignment into manageable pieces. Check work at intervals, such as graphic organizers and first drafts, to make sure writing is on track.

MODIFY THE PROMPT

Expect advanced writers to produce stories with several literary elements, such as foreshadowing, tension, suspense, or humor. Students should use words that evoke their chosen mood and tone. They should also decide whether a first-person or third-person narrator would tell their story most effectively.

APPLY SKILLS

- As students revise their work, have them consider some ways to improve it.

  Begin with a strong opening that makes readers want to continue reading.

  Add vivid words that help readers see, hear, touch, taste, and smell what is being described.

  Use foreshadowing to create suspense.

  Add dialogue to reveal the characters and advance the plot.

OPTIONS

- Students can follow these steps to create their own class rubrics.

  1. Read examples of class stories and rank them 1–4, with 4 the highest.

  2. Discuss how they arrived at each rank.

  3. Isolate the six traits and make a rubric based on them.

CHECK PROGRESS Discuss students' Self-Evaluation Guides. Work with students to monitor their growth and identify their strengths and weaknesses as writers.

MODIFY THE PROMPT

Have beginning speakers list the main events they want to include in their stories. Help them write about the events in complete sentences that show action. Show how they can integrate these sentences into their stories. Suggest details they might add to support the main events.

BUILD BACKGROUND

- Explain that a story has a beginning, middle, and end. Discuss familiar folk tales and have students point out the beginning, middle, and end. Make sure students understand that the writer needs to add details to these story parts to keep the reader's interest. Discuss the list of Key Features of a story that appears in the left column of p. WA2.

OPTIONS

- As students write their stories, guide them toward books, magazines, or Web sites that provide comprehension support through features such as the following:

  stories with photographs and other illustrations

  accounts of adventure or discovery

  text in the home-language

- For more suggestions on scaffolding the Writing Workshop, see the ELL and Transition Handbook.

CHECK PROGRESS You may need to explain certain traits and help students fill out their Self-Evaluation Guides. Downplay conventions and focus more on ideas. Recognize examples of vocabulary growth and efforts to use language in more complex ways.

Scoring Rubric | Look Back and Write

2 points The response indicates that the student has a complete understanding of the reading concept embodied in the task. The response is accurate, complete, and fulfills all the requirements of the task. Necessary support and/or examples are included, and the information given is clearly text-based.

1 point The response indicates that the student has a partial understanding of the reading concept embodied in the task. The response includes information that is essentially correct and text-based, but the information is too general or too simplistic. Some of the support and/or examples may be incomplete or omitted.

0 points The response indicates that the student does not demonstrate an understanding of the reading concept embodied in the task. The student has either failed to respond or has provided a response that is inaccurate or has insufficient information.

Scoring Rubric | Look Back and Write

4 points The response indicates that the student has a thorough understanding of the reading concept embodied in the task. The response is accurate, complete, and fulfills all the requirements of the task. Necessary support and/or examples are included, and the information is clearly text-based.

3 points The response indicates that the student has an understanding of the reading concept embodied in the task. The response is accurate and fulfills all the requirements of the task, but the required support and/or details are not complete or clearly text-based.

2 points The response indicates that the student has a partial understanding of the reading concept embodied in the task. The response that includes information is essentially correct and text-based, but the information is too general or too simplistic. Some of the support and/or examples and requirements of the task may be incomplete or omitted.

1 point The response indicates that the student has a very limited understanding of the reading concept embodied in the task. The response is incomplete, may exhibit many flaws, and may not address all requirements of the task.

0 points The response indicates that the student does not demonstrate an understanding of the reading concept embodied in the task. The student has either failed to respond or has provided a response that is inaccurate or has insufficient information.

Scoring Rubric — Narrative Writing

Rubric 4 3 2 1	6	5	4	3	2	1
Focus/Ideas	Excellent, focused narrative; well elaborated with quality details	Good, focused narrative; elaborated with telling details	Narrative focused; adequate elaboration	Generally focused narrative; some supporting details	Sometimes unfocused narrative; needs more supporting details	Rambling narrative; lacks development and detail
Organization/ Paragraphs	Strong beginning, middle, and end; appropriate order words	Coherent beginning, middle, and end; some order words	Beginning, middle, and end easily identifiable	Recognizable beginning, middle, and end; some order words	Little direction from beginning to end; few order words	Lacks beginning, middle, end; incorrect or no order words
Voice	Writer closely involved; engaging personality	Reveals personality	Pleasant but not compelling voice	Sincere voice but not fully engaged	Little writer involvement, personality	Careless writing with no feeling
Word Choice	Vivid, precise words that bring story to life	Clear words to bring story to life	Some specific word pictures	Language adequate but lacks color	Generally limited or redundant language	Vague, dull, or misused words
Sentences	Excellent variety of sentences; natural rhythm	Varied lengths, styles; generally smooth	Correct sentences with some variations in style	Correctly constructed sentences; some variety	May have simple, awkward, or wordy sentences; little variety	Choppy; many incomplete or run-on sentences
Conventions	Excellent control; few or no errors	No serious errors to affect understanding	General mastery of conventions but some errors	Reasonable control; few distracting errors	Weak control; enough errors to affect understanding	Many errors that prevent understanding

Scoring Rubric — Narrative Writing

Rubric 4 3 2 1	5	4	3	2	1
Focus/Ideas	Excellent, focused narrative; well elaborated with quality details	Good, focused narrative; elaborated with telling details	Generally focused narrative; some supporting details	Sometimes unfocused narrative; needs more supporting details	Rambling narrative; lacks development and detail
Organization/ Paragraphs	Strong beginning, middle, and end; appropriate order words	Coherent beginning, middle, and end; some order words	Recognizable beginning, middle, and end; some order words	Little direction from beginning to end; few order words	Lacks beginning, middle, end; incorrect or no order words
Voice	Writer closely involved; engaging personality	Reveals personality	Sincere voice but not fully engaged	Little writer involvement, personality	Careless writing with no feeling
Word Choice	Vivid, precise words that bring story to life	Clear words to bring story to life	Language adequate but lacks color	Generally limited or redundant language	Vague, dull, or misused words
Sentences	Excellent variety of sentences; natural rhythm	Varied lengths, styles; generally smooth	Correctly constructed sentences; some variety	May have simple, awkward, or wordy sentences; little variety	Choppy; many incomplete or run-on sentences
Conventions	Excellent control; few or no errors	No serious errors to affect understanding	Reasonable control; few distracting errors	Weak control; enough errors to affect understanding	Many errors that prevent understanding

Scoring Rubric — Narrative Writing

Rubric 4 3 2 1	3	2	1
Focus/Ideas	Excellent, focused narrative; well elaborated with quality details	Generally focused narrative; some supporting details	Rambling narrative; lacks development and detail
Organization/ Paragraphs	Strong beginning, middle, and end; appropriate order words	Recognizable beginning, middle, and end; some order words	Lacks beginning, middle, end; incorrect or no order words
Voice	Writer closely involved; engaging personality	Sincere voice but not fully engaged	Careless writing with no feeling
Word Choice	Vivid, precise words that bring story to life	Language adequate but lacks color	Vague, dull, or misused words
Sentences	Excellent variety of sentences; natural rhythm	Correctly constructed sentences; some variety	Choppy; many incomplete or run-on sentences
Conventions	Excellent control; few or no errors	Reasonable control; few distracting errors	Many errors that prevent understanding

Scoring Rubric — Descriptive Writing

Rubric 4 3 2 1	6	5	4	3	2	1
Focus/Ideas	Excellent, focused description; well elaborated with quality details	Good, focused description; elaborated with telling details	Description focused; good elaboration	Generally focused description; some supporting details	Sometimes unfocused description; needs more supporting details	Rambling description; lacks development and detail
Organization/ Paragraphs	Compelling ideas enhanced by order, structure, and transitions	Appealing order, structure, and transitions	Structure identifiable and suitable; transitions used	Adequate order, structure, and some transitions to guide reader	Little direction from beginning to end; few transitions	Lacks direction and identifiable structure; no transitions
Voice	Writer closely involved; engaging personality	Reveals personality	Pleasant but not compelling voice	Sincere voice but not fully engaged	Little writer involvement, personality	Careless writing with no feeling
Word Choice	Vivid, precise words that create memorable pictures	Clear, interesting words to bring description to life	Some specific word pictures	Language adequate; appeals to senses	Generally limited or redundant language	Vague, dull, or misused words
Sentences	Excellent variety of sentences; natural rhythm	Varied lengths, styles; generally smooth	Correct sentences with variations in style	Correctly constructed sentences; some variety	May have simple, awkward, or wordy sentences; little variety	Choppy; many incomplete run-on sentences
Conventions	Excellent control; few or no errors	No serious errors to affect understanding	General mastery of conventions but some errors	Reasonable control; few distracting errors	Weak control; enough errors to affect understanding	Many errors that prevent understanding

Scoring Rubric — Descriptive Writing

Rubric 4 3 2 1	5	4	3	2	1
Focus/Ideas	Excellent, focused description; well elaborated with quality details	Good, focused description; elaborated with telling details	Generally focused description; some supporting details	Sometimes unfocused description; needs more supporting details	Rambling description; lacks development and detail
Organization/ Paragraphs	Compelling ideas enhanced by order, structure, and transitions	Appealing order, structure, and transitions	Adequate order, structure, and some transitions to guide reader	Little direction from beginning to end; few transitions	Lacks direction and identifiable structure; no transitions
Voice	Writer closely involved; engaging personality	Reveals personality	Sincere voice but not fully engaged	Little writer involvement, personality	Careless writing with no feeling
Word Choice	Vivid, precise words that create memorable pictures	Clear, interesting words to bring description to life	Language adequate; appeals to senses	Generally limited or redundant language	Vague, dull, or misused words
Sentences	Excellent variety of sentences; natural rhythm	Varied lengths, styles; generally smooth	Correctly constructed sentences; some variety	May have simple, awkward, or wordy sentences; little variety	Choppy; many incomplete or run-on sentences
Conventions	Excellent control; few or no errors	No serious errors to affect understanding	Reasonable control; few distracting errors	Weak control; enough errors to affect understanding	Many errors that prevent understanding

Scoring Rubric — Descriptive Writing

Rubric 4 3 2 1	3	2	1
Focus/Ideas	Excellent, focused description; well elaborated with quality details	Generally focused description; some supporting details	Rambling description; lacks development and detail
Organization/ Paragraphs	Compelling ideas enhanced by order, structure, and transitions	Adequate order, structure, and some transitions to guide reader	Lacks direction and identifiable structure; no transitions
Voice	Writer closely involved; engaging personality	Sincere voice but not fully engaged	Careless writing with no feeling
Word Choice	Vivid, precise words that create memorable pictures	Language adequate; appeals to senses	Vague, dull, or misused words
Sentences	Excellent variety of sentences; natural rhythm	Correctly constructed sentences; some variety	Choppy; many incomplete or run-on sentences
Conventions	Excellent control; few or no errors	Reasonable control; few distracting errors	Many errors that prevent understanding

Scoring Rubric — Persuasive Writing

Rubric 4 3 2 1

	6	5	4	3	2	1
Focus/Ideas	Persuasive argument carefully built with quality details	Persuasive argument well supported with details	Persuasive argument focused; good elaboration	Persuasive argument with one or two convincing details	Persuasive piece sometimes unfocused; needs more support	Rambling persuasive argument; lacks development and detail
Organization/Paragraphs	Information chosen and arranged for maximum effect	Evident progression of persuasive ideas	Progression and structure evident	Information arranged in a logical way with some lapses	Little structure or direction	No identifiable structure
Voice	Writer closely involved; persuasive but not overbearing	Maintains persuasive tone	Persuasive but not compelling voice	Sometimes uses persuasive voice	Little writer involvement, personality	Shows little conviction
Word Choice	Persuasive words carefully chosen for impact	Argument supported by persuasive language	Uses some persuasive words	Occasional persuasive language	Generally limited or redundant language	Vague, dull, or misused words; no persuasive words
Sentences	Excellent variety of sentences; natural rhythm	Varied lengths, styles; generally smooth	Correct sentences with variations in style	Carefully constructed sentences; some variety	Simple, awkward, or wordy sentences; little variety	Choppy; many incomplete or run-on sentences
Conventions	Excellent control; few or no errors	No serious errors to affect understanding	General mastery of conventions but some errors	Reasonable control; few distracting errors	Weak control; enough errors to affect understanding	Many errors that prevent understanding

Scoring Rubric — Persuasive Writing

Rubric 4 3 2 1

	5	4	3	2	1
Focus/Ideas	Persuasive argument carefully built with quality details	Persuasive argument well supported with details	Persuasive argument with one or two convincing details	Persuasive piece sometimes unfocused; needs more support	Rambling persuasive argument; lacks development and detail
Organization/Paragraphs	Information chosen and arranged for maximum effect	Evident progression of persuasive ideas	Information arranged in a logical way with some lapses	Little structure or direction	No identifiable structure
Voice	Writer closely involved; persuasive but not overbearing	Maintains persuasive tone	Sometimes uses persuasive voice	Little writer involvement, personality	Shows little conviction
Word Choice	Persuasive words carefully chosen for impact	Argument supported by persuasive language	Occasional persuasive language	Generally limited or redundant language	Vague, dull, or misused words; no persuasive words
Sentences	Excellent variety of sentences; natural rhythm	Varied lengths, styles; generally smooth	Carefully constructed sentences; some variety	Simple, awkward, or wordy sentences; little variety	Choppy; many incomplete or run-on sentences
Conventions	Excellent control; few or no errors	No serious errors to affect understanding	Reasonable control; few distracting errors	Weak control; enough errors to affect understanding	Many errors that prevent understanding

Scoring Rubric — Persuasive Writing

Rubric 4 3 2 1

	3	2	1
Focus/Ideas	Persuasive argument carefully built with quality details	Persuasive argument with one or two convincing details	Rambling persuasive argument; lacks development and detail
Organization/Paragraphs	Information chosen and arranged for maximum effect	Information arranged in a logical way with some lapses	No identifiable structure
Voice	Writer closely involved; persuasive but not overbearing	Sometimes uses persuasive voice	Shows little conviction
Word Choice	Persuasive words carefully chosen for impact	Occasional persuasive language	Vague, dull, or misused words; no persuasive words
Sentences	Excellent variety of sentences; natural rhythm	Carefully constructed sentences; some variety	Choppy; many incomplete or run-on sentences
Conventions	Excellent control; few or no errors	Reasonable control; few distracting errors	Many errors that prevent understanding

Scoring Rubric — Expository Writing

Rubric 4 3 2 1	6	5	4	3	2	1
Focus/Ideas	Insightful, focused exposition; well elaborated with quality details	Informed, focused exposition; elaborated with telling details	Exposition focused, good elaboration	Generally focused exposition; some supporting details	Sometimes unfocused exposition needs more supporting details	Rambling exposition; lacks development and detail
Organization/ Paragraphs	Logical, consistent flow of ideas; good transitions	Logical sequencing of ideas; uses transitions	Ideas sequenced with some transitions	Sequenced ideas with some transitions	Little direction from beginning to end; few order words	Lacks structure and transitions
Voice	Writer closely involved; informative voice well suited to topic	Reveals personality; voice suited to topic	Pleasant but not compelling voice	Sincere voice suited to topic	Little writer involvement, personality	Careless writing with no feeling
Word Choice	Vivid, precise words to express ideas	Clear words to express ideas	Words correct and adequate	Language adequate but may lack precision	Generally limited or redundant language	Vague, dull, or misused words
Sentences	Strong topic sentence; fluent, varied structures	Good topic sentence; smooth sentence structure	Correct sentences that are sometimes fluent	Topic sentence correctly constructed; some sentence variety	Topic sentence unclear or missing; wordy, awkward sentences	No topic sentence; many incomplete or run-on sentences
Conventions	Excellent control; few or no errors	No serious errors to affect understanding	General mastery of conventions but some errors	Reasonable control; few distracting errors	Weak control; enough errors to affect understanding	Many errors that prevent understanding

Scoring Rubric — Expository Writing

Rubric 4 3 2 1	5	4	3	2	1
Focus/Ideas	Insightful, focused exposition; well elaborated with quality details	Informed, focused exposition; elaborated with telling details	Generally focused exposition; some supporting details	Sometimes unfocused exposition needs more supporting details	Rambling exposition; lacks development and detail
Organization/ Paragraphs	Logical, consistent flow of ideas; good transitions	Logical sequencing of ideas; uses transitions	Sequenced ideas with some transitions	Little direction from beginning to end; few order words	Lacks structure and transitions
Voice	Writer closely involved; informative voice well suited to topic	Reveals personality; voice suited to topic	Language adequate but may lack precision	Little writer involvement, personality	Careless writing with no feeling
Word Choice	Vivid, precise words to express ideas	Clear words to express ideas	Topic sentence correctly constructed; some sentence variety	Generally limited or redundant language	Vague, dull, or misused words
Sentences	Strong topic sentence; fluent, varied structures	Good topic sentence; smooth sentence structure	Sincere voice suited to topic	Topic sentence unclear or missing; wordy, awkward sentences	No topic sentence; many incomplete or run-on sentences
Conventions	Excellent control; few or no errors	No serious errors to affect understanding	Reasonable control; few distracting errors	Weak control; enough errors to affect understanding	Many errors that prevent understanding

Scoring Rubric — Expository Writing

Rubric 4 3 2 1	3	2	1
Focus/Ideas	Insightful, focused exposition; well elaborated with quality details	Generally focused exposition; some supporting details	Rambling exposition; lacks development and detail
Organization/ Paragraphs	Logical, consistent flow of ideas; good transitions	Sequenced ideas with some transitions	Lacks structure and transitions
Voice	Writer closely involved; informative voice well suited to topic	Sincere voice suited to topic	Careless writing with no feeling
Word Choice	Vivid, precise words to express ideas	Language adequate but may lack precision	Vague, dull, or misused words
Sentences	Strong topic sentence; fluent, varied structures	Topic sentence correctly constructed; some sentence variety	No topic sentence; many incomplete or run-on sentences
Conventions	Excellent control; few or no errors	Reasonable control; few distracting errors	Many errors that prevent understanding

Unit 4
Monitoring Fluency

Ongoing assessment of student reading fluency is one of the most valuable measures we have of students' reading skills. One of the most effective ways to assess fluency is taking timed samples of students' oral reading and measuring the number of words correct per minute (WCPM).

How to Measure Words Correct Per Minute—WCPM

Choose a Text
Start by choosing a text for the student to read. The text should be:
• narrative
• unfamiliar
• on grade level

Make a copy of the text for yourself and have one for the student.

Timed Reading of the Text
Tell the student: As you read this aloud, I want you to do your best reading and to read as quickly as you can. That doesn't mean it's a race. Just do your best, fast reading. When I say *begin*, start reading. As the student reads, follow along in your copy. Mark words that are read incorrectly.

Incorrect	Correct
• omissions	• self-corrections within 3 seconds
• substitutions	• repeated words
• mispronunciations	
• reversals	

After One Minute
At the end of one minute, draw a line after the last word that was read. Have the student finish reading but don't count any words beyond one minute. Arrive at the words correct per minute—WCPM—by counting the total number of words that the student read correctly in one minute.

Fluency Goals
Grade 6 End-of-Year Goal = 150 WCPM

Target goals by unit

Unit 1 115 to 120 WCPM	**Unit 4** 130 to 138 WCPM
Unit 2 120 to 126 WCPM	**Unit 5** 135 to 144 WCPM
Unit 3 125 to 132 WCPM	**Unit 6** 140 to 150 WCPM

More Frequent Monitoring
You may want to monitor some students more frequently because they are falling far below grade-level benchmarks or they have a result that doesn't seem to align with their previous performance. Follow the same steps above, but choose 2 or 3 additional texts.

Fluency Progress Chart Copy the chart on the next page. Use it to record each student's progress across the year.

WCPM

	85	90	95	100	105	110	115	120	125	130	135	140	145	150	155	160	165	170	175	180
1																				
2																				
3																				
4																				
5																				
6																				
7																				
8																				
9																				
10																				
11																				
12																				
13																				
14																				
15																				
16																				
17																				
18																				
19																				
20																				
21																				
22																				
23																				
24																				
25																				
26																				
27																				
28																				
29																				
30																				

Timed Reading

Name _____   Date _____

Assessment and Regrouping Chart   Unit 4

Day 3 Retelling Assessment			Day 5 Fluency Assessment			Reteach	Teacher's Comments	Grouping
The assessed group is highlighted for each week.	Benchmark Score	Actual Score	The assessed group is highlighted for each week.	Benchmark WCPM	Actual Score	✓		
WEEK 1 *Into the Ice* Cause/Effect								
Strategic	1–2		Strategic	Less than 130				
On-Level	3		On-Level	130–138				
Advanced	4		Advanced*	130–138				
WEEK 2 *The Chimpanzees I Love* Author's Purpose								
Strategic	1–2		Strategic	Less than 130				
On-Level	3		On-Level	130–138				
Advanced	4		Advanced*	130–138				
WEEK 3 *Black Frontiers* Cause/Effect								
Strategic	1–2		Strategic	Less than 130				
On-Level	3		On-Level	130–138				
Advanced	4		Advanced*	130–138				
WEEK 4 *Space Cadets* Draw Conclusions								
Strategic	1–2		Strategic	Less than 130				
On-Level	3		On-Level	130–138				
Advanced	4		Advanced*	130–138				
WEEK 5 *Inventing the Future* Author's Purpose								
Strategic	1–2		Strategic	Less than 130				
On-Level	3		On-Level	130–138				
Advanced	4		Advanced*	130–138				
Unit 4 Benchmark Test Score								

- **RECORD SCORES** Use this chart to record scores for the Day 3 Retelling, Day 5 Fluency, and Unit 4 Benchmark Test Assessments.

  *Students in the advanced group should read above-grade-level materials.

- **REGROUPING** Compare the student's actual score to the benchmark score for each group level and review the *Questions to Consider*. Students may move to a higher or lower group level, or they may remain in the same group.

- **RETEACH** If a student is unable to complete any part of the assessment process, use the weekly Reteach lessons for additional support. Record the lesson information in the space provided on the chart. After reteaching, you may want to reassess using the Unit Benchmark Test.

Unit 4
Assess and Regroup

FYI In Grade 6 there are opportunities for regrouping every six weeks—at the end of Units 2, 3, 4, and 5. These options offer sensitivity to each student's progress although some teachers may prefer to regroup less frequently.

Regroup for Unit 5

To make regrouping decisions at the end of Unit 4, consider student's end-of-unit scores for

- Unit 4 Retelling
- Fluency (WCPM)
- Unit 4 Benchmark Test

Group Time

On-Level	Strategic Intervention	Advanced
To continue On-Level or to move into the On-Level group, students should	**Students would benefit from Strategic Intervention if they**	**To move to the Advanced group, students should**
• score 3 or better on their cumulative unit rubric scores for Retelling	• score 2 or lower on their cumulative unit rubric scores for Retelling	• score 4 on their cumulative unit rubric scores for Retelling and demonstrate expansive vocabulary and ease of language in their retellings
• meet the current benchmark for fluency (130–138 WCPM), reading On-Level text such as Student Edition selections	• do not meet the current benchmark for fluency (130–138 WCPM)	• score 95% on the Unit 4 Benchmark Test
• score 80% or better on the Unit 4 Benchmark Tests	• score below 60% on the Unit 4 Benchmark Tests	• read above-grade-level material fluently (130–138 WCPM)
• be capable of working in the On-Level group based on teacher judgment	• are struggling to keep up with the On-Level group based on teacher judgment	• be capable of handling the problem solving and investigative work of the Advanced group based on teacher judgment

QUESTIONS TO CONSIDER

- What types of test questions did the student miss? Are they specific to a particular skill or strategy?
- Does the student have adequate background knowledge to understand the test passages or selections for retelling?
- Does the student read for enjoyment, different purposes, and varied interests?

- Has the student's performance met expectations for daily lessons and assessments with little or no reteaching?
- Is the student performing more like students in another group?

Benchmark Fluency Scores

Current Goal: **130–138** WCPM

End-of-Year Goal: **150** WCPM

Life in the Arctic

Unit 4 Week 1

◎ **CAUSE AND EFFECT**

◎ **SUMMARIZE**

LESSON VOCABULARY conquer, destiny, expedition, insulated, isolation, navigator, provisions, verify

SUMMARY This nonfiction book introduces the reader to many of the land and sea creatures that make their homes in the Arctic and the adaptations that allow these animals to make their homes there.

INTRODUCE THE BOOK

BUILD BACKGROUND Put the word *Arctic* at the center of a concept web on the board. Have students brainstorm all the words and ideas that come to mind when they think of the word *Arctic*.

PREVIEW/USE TEXT FEATURES Have students turn to pages 4 and 5. Point out the location of the Arctic Circle and the countries whose territories lie in the region. Then have students flip through the book. Have them discuss the types of creatures featured in the selection and the animals that are unfamiliar.

TEACH/REVIEW VOCABULARY Point out the location in the text where each vocabulary word is found. Have students write a predicted definition for each word based on the context. Then have students check the definitions against the glossary.

TARGET SKILL AND STRATEGY

◎ **CAUSE AND EFFECT** Review with students that a *cause* is why something happens and an *effect* is what happens. Point out that sometimes authors use clue words to show causes—*because, since, reason*—and effects—*as a result, therefore, consequently.* Have students read the selection looking for cause-and-effect indicaters.

ELL Have ELL students use cause-and-effect charts for the Target Skill activity.

◎ **SUMMARIZE** Remind students that when they *summarize*, they are giving a brief statement that tells the main ideas of a book or part of a book. Suggest that they think about one statement that would summarize the main ideas about the Arctic animals.

READ THE BOOK

Use the following questions to support comprehension.

PAGE 3 Summarize the environment in the Arctic. *(The Arctic is freezing cold and covered with ice in the winter and covered with grass and moss in the summer.)*

PAGE 10-11 How do the graphic sources on these pages help you understand this animal? *(Shown are the different types of coats the fox has depending on the season.)*

PAGE 14 What causes the snowy owl to build its nest out of dry grass and move slowly when returning to the nest with food? *(The arctic fox often hunts snowy owl eggs.)*

TALK ABOUT THE BOOK

READER RESPONSE
1. Possible response: thick fur and blubber protect them from the extreme cold; they would not survive
2. Possible response: Some of the survival skills of arctic animals include changing the color of their fur, growing claws, and hibernating.
3. Possible response: *to navigate*: guide or lead; *to isolate*: keep something or someone away from others
4. Possible response: The polar bear is a strong, able predator. Its white fur camouflages it.

RESPONSE OPTIONS

VIEWING Show students a film about the Arctic Circle. Have them write brief paragraphs in which they explain what new information they learned from the film or how the movie helped them better understand concepts presented in *Life in the Arctic*.

CONTENT CONNECTIONS

SCIENCE Have students research plants, animals, or fish that are not mentioned in the the selection. Their reports should focus on the adaptations, or special characteristics, of the species that help it survive in the Arctic Circle.

TIME FOR Science

Cause and Effect

- A **cause** is *why* something happens. An **effect** is *what* happens.
- Sometimes there is more than one cause of an effect, and sometimes there are multiple effects of a cause.

Directions Several animals from *Life in the Arctic* are listed below. For each animal, elements of the Arctic environment have caused the animal to have special traits or effects. Write the effect of each cause.

Polar Bear

Cause	Effect
1. Polar bears' white fur coat	
2. Very cold environment	
3. Polar bears hunt seals and wait for them to come up for air	

Arctic Fox

Cause	Effect
4. Color of its fur changes with the seasons	
5. The ground is frozen	
6. Small ears and muzzles	

Walruses

Cause	Effect
7. Have long, sharp tusks	
8. Filling up the air sacs in their necks	

© Pearson Education 6

74

Name_____

Vocabulary

Directions Choose the word from the box that best matches each definition below. Write the word on the line.

Check the Words You Know

___conquer
___destiny
___expedition
___insulated
___isolation
___navigator
___provisions
___verify

1. a state of being alone _____

2. to overcome _____

3. to show that something is true _____

4. an adventure _____

5. a guide _____

6. fate _____

7. kept warm _____

8. supplies _____

Directions For each of the following words, write your own synonym. Then use a dictionary or thesaurus to write another synonym.

Vocabulary Word	Your Synonym	Synonym from a Dictionary or Thesaurus
verify		
conquer		
insulated		

75

Life Inside the Arctic Circle

Life Inside the Arctic Circle by Sam Brelsford

CAUSE AND EFFECT

SUMMARIZE

LESSON VOCABULARY conquer, destiny, expedition, insulate, isolation, navigator, provisions, verify

SUMMARY This selection describes the many plants, animals, and peoples that make their home in the Arctic Circle, despite its harsh conditions.

INTRODUCE THE BOOK

BUILD BACKGROUND Locate the Arctic Circle on a map and ask students what they already know about this region or what images come to mind from books or movies they may have read or seen.

ELL Invite students to share home-language words related to the Arctic circle, such as words for *frozen* or *North Pole*.

PREVIEW/USE TEXT FEATURES Have students read the title and skim through the book, looking at the headings, pictures, maps, and captions. Ask: Based on these features, what do you expect to learn about the Arctic Circle?

TEACH/REVIEW VOCABULARY Assign vocabulary words to groups of students. Have groups find their words in the selection and use context clues to come up with their own definitions. Then, as a class, have groups share their definitions and check them against the glossary.

TARGET SKILL AND STRATEGY

CAUSE AND EFFECT Review with students that a *cause* is why an event happens and an *effect* is what happens because of the event. Then read question 1 in the Reader Response section at the back of the book. Ask students what causes they are looking for in the selection and what effects they should find.

SUMMARIZE Tell students that understanding cause and effect in a book can help them *summarize* the main ideas. Have students jot down some of the main ideas in the book as they read and think about cause and effect.

READ THE BOOK

Use the following questions to support comprehension.

PAGES 6–7 Name three characteristics of the environment in the Arctic Circle. *(Possible responses: winters are frigid and long; permafrost covers the ground; the Sun does not set during a long period in some areas during the summer months.)*

PAGES 13–15 What is one survival skill that the Aleuts, some Chukchi, and the Athapaska have in common? *(They all fish.)*

PAGE 17 Why are most of today's Nenets unable to migrate with their reindeer? *(Industries have made reindeer herding more difficult.)*

TALK ABOUT THE BOOK

READER RESPONSE

1. Possible response: Causes: frigid weather, few plants, abundant animals and fish; Effects: using fur, feathers, and skins to make warm clothing; hunting animals and fishing; building houses with bones

2. Possible response: The people of the Arctic have learned to adapt to their environment, as well as to modern technology. They will probably be able to adapt to changes in the future too.

3. Stories will vary, but should include words from the glossary.

4. Possible response: I can learn what countries are close to the Arctic Circle.

RESPONSE OPTIONS

WRITING Ask students to suppose that they are members of one of the Inuit groups that live in the Arctic Circle. Have each student write a diary entry that describes a day in his or her life.

CONTENT CONNECTIONS

SCIENCE Have students choose the environment of one of the Inuit groups from the selection and diagram the ecosystems of the group's habitat.

Cause and Effect

- A **cause** is *why* something happens. An **effect** is *what* happens.
- Sometimes there is more than one cause of an effect, and sometimes there are multiple effects of a cause.

Directions Skim through the following sections of *Life Inside the Arctic Circle*. For each section, write one effect or trait that is unique to the people or animals of the Arctic. Then write the element of the Arctic environment that is the cause of this effect or trait.

The Environment

Effect:	Cause:
1.	2.

The Arctic Tundra

Effect:	Cause:
3.	4.

Chukchi

Effect:	Cause:
5.	6.

Science and Research

Effect:	Cause:
7.	8.

74

Vocabulary

Directions For each of the following vocabulary words, use a dictionary to find the base word and its definition. Then write the suffix of the vocabulary word.

Check the Words You Know

___conquer   ___destiny
___expedition   ___insulate
___isolation   ___navigator
___provisions   ___verify

Vocabulary Word	Base and Definition	Suffix
1. expedition		
2. isolation		
3. destiny		
4. navigator		

Directions Answer the following questions based on the table above.

5. Think about the definitions of *expedition* and *isolation* and the definitions of their base words. What do you think the suffixes *-tion* or *-sion* mean?

_____

6. Look at the definitions of *navigator* and its base word. What do you think the suffix *-or* means?

_____

7. What do you think the word *conqueror* means?

_____

8. What do you think the word *destination* means?

_____

9. What do you think the word *navigation* means?

_____

10. Another spelling of the suffix *-or* is *-er*. What do you think an *expediter* is?

_____

75

The Race to the South Pole

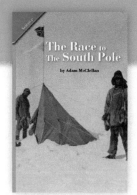

Unit 4 Week 1

🔊 **CAUSE AND EFFECT**

🔊 **SUMMARIZE**

LESSON VOCABULARY depots, din, expedition, gangrene, man hauling, rash, remote, scurvy, trek, turbulent

---

SUMMARY This nonfiction selection tells the exciting story of two competing expeditions to the South Pole and their vastly different fates.

INTRODUCE THE BOOK

BUILD BACKGROUND Locate the South Pole on a map. Point out other locations from the selection: Great Britain, Norway, Australia, and Antarctica. Ask students what they already know about the South Pole.

PREVIEW/USE TEXT FEATURES Have students read the title and skim the headings, pictures, and captions. Discuss with students what clues these features give about the selection's main concepts.

TEACH/REVIEW VOCABULARY. Have groups find vocabulary words in the selection and use context clues to come up with their own definitions. As a class, have groups share their definitions.

ELL Reinforce the meaning by having students sort vocabulary words by parts of speech.

TARGET SKILL AND STRATEGY

🔊 **CAUSE AND EFFECT** Review with students that a *cause* is why an event happens and an *effect* is what happens because of the event. Ask students to look for clue words for causes and effects as they read. Remind them that authors do not always use clue words to show cause and effect.

🔊 **SUMMARIZE** Tell students that understanding cause and effect can help them *summarize* main ideas. Have students read question 2 in the Reader Response section. Ask them to pay attention to the events in this section of the story.

READ THE BOOK

Use the following questions to support comprehension.

PAGES 6–7 Name a difference between Scott's and Amundsen's expeditions. (*Possible response: Scott left with thousands watching; Amundsen in secret*)

PAGE 10 Why did some of Scott's men risk their lives to collect penguin eggs? (*They wanted the eggs for scientific research.*)

PAGE 19 What earlier decisions caused problems for Scott and his men as they left the Pole? (*He had left only one flag to mark depots; he had taken too many men for the food supplies; and the sled dogs had been sent home.*)

TALK ABOUT THE BOOK

READER RESPONSE
1. Possible response: Amundsen planted many supply depots and marked them well, skied, and used sled dogs. As a result, his travel was quick and well supplied. Scott planted fewer depots and didn't mark them well, used ponies and motor sledges and man hauling. As a result, his travel was slow and poorly supplied.
2. Possible response: Amundsen's group was well prepared, and it reached the South Pole first and returned without serious problems. Scott's group was ill prepared; after reaching the Pole second, everyone died. Answers on improving summaries will vary.
3. Possible response: crowds cheering, blowing whistles, and sirens blowing, means *din* is a loud noise
4. They indicate the information to be discussed.

RESPONSE OPTIONS

WRITING Ask students to imagine that they are members of either Scott's or Amundsen's expedition. Have each student write a letter home describing a day with the expedition.

CONTENT CONNECTIONS

SCIENCE Invite students to use the Internet to research and report on what scientists are currently studying at the South Pole.

Name_____

Cause and Effect

- A **cause** is *why* something happens. An **effect** is *what* happens.
- Sometimes there is more than one cause of an effect, and sometimes there are multiple effects of a cause.

Directions Use the reader *The Race to the South Pole* to answer the following questions.

1. In 1909, Ernest Shackleton attempted to reach the South Pole and came within 100 miles. What effect did his expedition have on the explorer Robert Falcon Scott?

_____

_____

2. What caused thousands of people to make offers to Robert Scott and thousands more to cheer as Scott sailed from London?

_____

_____

3. What were the effects of Robert Scott's decision to spend time in Australia and New Zealand?

_____

_____

4. Look again at the timing of Roald Amundsen's expedition, on pages 6 and 9 of the reader. What was another effect of Robert Scott's decision to spend a long time in Australia and New Zealand?

_____

_____

5. What caused Roald Amundsen to leave flags at the South Pole, and letters to Scott and the King of Norway? Remember, there may be more than one cause for these actions.

_____

_____

6. Look through the book again, paying close attention to the activities of the men on Scott's expedition. What factors caused Scott and four of his men to lose their lives?

_____

_____

74

Name_____

Vocabulary

Directions Read each of the following sentences. Select the word from the box that best completes each sentence and write it on the line.

Check the Words You Know

____depots
____din
____expedition
____gangrene
____man hauling
____rash
____remote
____scurvy
____trek
____turbulent

1. When going on a _____, it is important to make careful plans in advance for supplies, housing, and transportation.

2. The whistles of the boats in the harbor could be heard above the _____ of the crowd.

3. Antarctica is surrounded by _____ seas, which makes approaching the continent extremely difficult.

4. The South Pole is one of the most _____ locations in the world.

5. On treacherous expeditions like the one to the South Pole, it's wise not to make any _____ decisions that might put people into trouble.

6. Amundsen was able to get supplies at _____ on the first leg of his trip.

Directions Write a paragraph about Robert Falcon Scott's fateful expedition to the South Pole. Use the words *gangrene, man hauling, scurvy,* and *expedition* in your paragraph.

_____

_____

_____

_____

_____

_____

_____

© Pearson Education 6

75

AUTHOR'S PURPOSE

ANSWER QUESTIONS

LESSON VOCABULARY captive, companionship, existence, ordeals, primitive, sanctuaries, stimulating

Great Apes

SUMMARY There are four types of great apes: orangutans, gorillas, chimpanzees, and bonobos. This book tells about each type of ape's behavior and life. It compares and contrasts the different apes to show a more in-depth view of their world.

INTRODUCE THE BOOK

BUILD BACKGROUND Discuss what students know about apes. If they have seen apes at a zoo or on television, have them talk about the experience. Prompt them to discuss ape behaviors and habitats.

PREVIEW/USE TEXT FEATURES As students preview the book, suggest that they notice the different types of apes photographed. Review photographs on page 3 and compare the different apes.

TEACH/REVIEW VOCABULARY Review vocabulary words and their definitions with students. Divide students into small groups. Assign each group a vocabulary word and have the group come up with two sentences using the word. Ask a member from each group to write their sentences on the board.

ELL Have students write each vocabulary word and definition on a sheet of paper. Then have them look up the root of words with suffixes. Prompt them to explain how the root word's meaning changes when a suffix is added.

TARGET SKILL AND STRATEGY

AUTHOR'S PURPOSE Remind students that an *author's purpose* is the reason for writing. Remind them that the four main reasons for writing are to persuade, to inform, to entertain, and to express. As they read, have students ask themselves this question: Why might the author have written this book? Have them write the question and answer on a sheet of paper.

ANSWER QUESTIONS Tell students that *answering questions* is the ability to provide complete, accurate, and focused responses to questions. Remind them

that they can often find an answer to a question about a text in four ways: in one sentence in the text, in several different sentences in the text, using the text plus what they already know about a subject, and when the answer is not in the text, they can use what they already know about a subject.

READ THE BOOK

Use the following questions to support comprehension.

PAGE 4 What is the author's purpose? *(To inform the reader what different types of apes have in common)*

PAGE 11 Describe some features of gorillas. (*Largest primates, can weigh up to 600 pounds, usually black, walk on knuckles, no two noses are alike*)

PAGE 14 In what ways do gorillas communicate? *(Sounds, facial expressions)*

READER RESPONSE
1. Possible response: to inform and to persuade
2. Possible response: I would like to know how to help protect great apes. I could go onto the Internet and search for information.
3. Sentences will vary.
4. Possible response: They are peaceful animals and very intelligent. Some can communicate using sign language.

RESPONSE OPTIONS

WRITING Tell students that they are on an assignment to study gorilla behaviors in Africa. Have them write a journal describing their observations.

CONTENT CONNECTIONS

SCIENCE Students can learn more about apes by researching them on the Internet or in the library. Suggest that they choose their favorite type of ape and find out a little known or interesting fact about it.

TIME FOR Science

Author's Purpose

An **author's purpose** is his or her reason for writing. There are four main reasons for writing: to **persuade, inform, entertain,** and **express.**

Directions Reread the following text from *Great Apes*.

> Another great ape is the gorilla. Gorillas were often misunderstood by humans before they were closely studied. Some people thought they were aggressive and vicious. Now we know this is not true. Gorillas are actually peaceful primates who do not attack unless they are provoked or startled. They spend most of their time eating, resting, and sleeping in the mountains and lowlands of Africa.

1. Why might the author have included this in the book?

_____

_____

2. Did the author succeed in her purpose? Why or why not?

_____

_____

Directions Answer the following questions.

1. What was the author's purpose for writing this book?

_____

_____

2. What was the author's purpose for using photographs in this book?

_____

_____

3. In what ways did the author succeed in her purpose?

_____

_____

78

Vocabulary

Directions Write the vocabulary word that means the same as the words below.

1. hardships _____

2. being _____

3. confined _____

4. ancient _____

5. exciting _____

6. company _____

7. refuges _____

Directions Write the vocabulary word that means the opposite as the words below.

1. alone _____

2. boring _____

3. free _____

4. modern _____

5. easy solutions _____

6. dangerous places _____

7. extinction _____

Directions Fill in the blanks with vocabulary words from the box.

The animal _____ came into _____ to give animals _____ and freedom.

How Animals Change

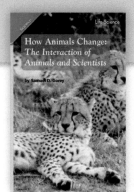

Unit 4 Week 2

🔘 **AUTHOR'S PURPOSE**

🔘 **ANSWER QUESTIONS**

LESSON VOCABULARY captive, companionship, existence, ordeal, primitive, sanctuary, stimulating

SUMMARY This book explores some of the ways that wild animals' lives change when researchers study them. It discusses the effects of using radio tracking collars, tiny video cameras, photo surveys, and other methods.

INTRODUCE THE BOOK

BUILD BACKGROUND Discuss what students know about how scientists study animal behavior. If they have seen shows about animal behavior, have them talk about what they learned. Prompt students to discuss how studying animals may affect the animals.

PREVIEW/USE TEXT FEATURES As students preview the book, suggest that they notice the different animals in their habitats. Review the photographs on pages 4 and 16 and ask how these photographs were obtained.

TEACH/REVIEW VOCABULARY Divide students into small groups. Have each group choose a vocabulary word and write a sentence using that word. Then have each group write their sentence on the board, leaving a blank where the vocabulary word should go. Have other groups guess which vocabulary word fits based on the sentences.

ELL Have students list vocabulary words and their definitions on note cards to study.

TARGET SKILL AND STRATEGY

🔘 **AUTHOR'S PURPOSE** Remind students that an *author's purpose* is the reason for writing. Remind them that the four main reasons for writing are to persuade, to inform, to entertain, and to express. As they read, have students write down the author's purpose.

🔘 **ANSWER QUESTIONS** Tell students that they can often find an answer to a question about a text in four ways: in one sentence in the text, in several sentences in the text, using the text plus what they already know about a subject, and relying only on what they already know about a subject. As students read, have them answer these questions: In what ways do scientists study animals? How does each method affect the animals?

READ THE BOOK

Use the following questions to support comprehension.

PAGE 3 What is the author's purpose? *(To inform the reader about ways animals are affected by researchers' studies)*

PAGE 14 What is a panda's main diet? *(bamboo)*

PAGE 18 Why did Pavlov's dogs salivate? *(They thought they were about to be fed.)*

READER RESPONSE

1. Responses will vary but can include: to explain the effects of scientific study of animals; to demonstrate the pros and cons of observing animal behavior.
2. Responses will vary.
3. A stimulus is something that incites activity. A consequence is something produced by a set of conditions. Sentences will vary.
4. A positive reinforcer is the reward that an animal receives for performing the correct behavior during operant conditioning. Positive reinforcers for dolphins include food like fish; touching; rub-downs; being squirted with water; ice; and floating toys.

RESPONSE OPTIONS

WRITING Ask students to imagine that they are a scientist interested in observing Australia's wallabies. Ask them to think about how they would go about studying this animal's behavior. Have them write a checklist of items and equipment they will need for their trip.

CONTENT CONNECTIONS

SCIENCE Students can learn more about ways that scientists study animals by researching it on the Internet or in the library. Suggest that they pick one animal that interests them and read about ways in which this animal is studied.

TIME FOR Science

Author's Purpose

An **author's purpose** is his or her reason for writing. There are four main reasons for writing: to **persuade, inform, entertain,** and **express** a mood or feeling.

Directions Answer the questions below about the author's purpose.

1. Why might the author have written this book?

_____

_____

2. What was the author's purpose for using photographs?

_____

3. In what ways did the author succeed in her purpose?

_____

_____

Directions Read the following sentences from *How Animals Change: The Interaction of Animals and Scientists* and write the author's purpose.

1. Using a Global Positioning System, or GPS, the collar can pinpoint an animal's exact longitude and latitude at any time, day or night for researchers. _____

2. Worst of all, ducks could get so frightened by the dragging operation that they give up on nesting altogether. _____

3. For instance, researchers seeking an effective way of drawing cheetahs to camera traps in the wild recently stumbled across a strange fact. _____

4. As we move into the future, we must listen to scientists' recommendations about animals and the environment. _____

5. The main idea behind operant conditioning is that if an animal performs a behavior, and if the consequences of that behavior are pleasing to the animal, then the animal will probably repeat the behavior. _____

© Pearson Education 6

78

Name _____

Vocabulary

Directions Use the vocabulary words in the box to fill in the blanks in the sentences below.

> ### Check the Words You Know
>
> ___captive   ___companionship
> ___existence   ___ordeal
> ___primitive   ___sanctuary
> ___stimulating

1. There are many kinds of bears in _____ today.

2. _____ people had to hunt animals to survive.

3. Animals are happier when there are other animals around for _____.

4. Exercise is _____ for zoo animals.

5. It is an _____ to keep track of all the wild buffalo.

6. _____ animals are not free to roam.

7. A _____ keeps animals safe and protected.

Directions Write a synonym for each vocabulary word below.

1. stimulating _____

2. existence _____

3. sanctuary _____

4. companionship _____

5. captive _____

6. ordeal _____

7. primitive _____

Directions Write a sentence using any three vocabulary words from the box.

_____

_____

79

Captive or Free: Zoos in Debate

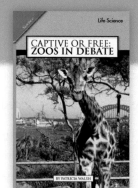

Life Science

CAPTIVE OR FREE: ZOOS IN DEBATE

BY PATRICIA WALSH

Unit 4 Week 2

AUTHOR'S PURPOSE

ANSWER QUESTIONS

LESSON VOCABULARY activists, confinement, controversial, exotic, moats, realistic, species, zoological

SUMMARY This book discusses the pros and cons of keeping animals in zoos from the animals' point of view. It gives clear reasons why people support zoos and reasons why people are opposed to them.

INTRODUCE THE BOOK

BUILD BACKGROUND Discuss what students know about zoos and how the animals are treated. If they have visited a zoo, have them discuss their observations about the environment in which the animals live. Ask them whether they think the animals at zoos are happy.

PREVIEW/USE TEXT FEATURES As students preview the book, have them look at the photographs and read the chapter titles. Ask them what type of information they think this book will provide. Review the photographs on pages 13 and 15 and ask them why they think the author chose to include these photographs.

TEACH/REVIEW VOCABULARY Review vocabulary words and their definitions with students. Have volunteers come up with a sentence using a vocabulary word and read it aloud. Repeat this with all the vocabulary words.

ELL Have students list vocabulary words and their definitions on a sheet of paper. Ask them to write sentences of their own, using each vocabulary word.

TARGET SKILL AND STRATEGY

AUTHOR'S PURPOSE Remind students that an *author's purpose* is the reason for writing. Remind them that the four main reasons for writing are to persuade, to inform, to entertain, and to express. As they read, have students write down the author's purpose and facts to back up this purpose.

ANSWER QUESTIONS Tell students that *answering questions* is the ability to provide complete, accurate, and focused responses to questions. As students read, have them use a graphic organizer to answer the following questions: What are the pros and cons of keeping animals in a zoo?

READ THE BOOK

Use the following questions to support comprehension.

PAGE 5 What is the author's purpose? *(To tell about the benefits and drawbacks of keeping animals in a zoo)*

PAGE 8 Why is Carl Hagenbeck important? *(He built the first zoo that allowed animals access to the outside.)*

PAGE 15 What reasons do activists give for their disapproval of animal treatment in zoos? *(Clipping birds' wings, herd animals living alone, not giving animals enough water)*

READER RESPONSE

1. The author's purpose in writing this book is to inform by presenting the pros and cons of keeping animals in zoos. Examples will vary.

2. Responses will vary: Questions and responses might address the kinds of animals they design areas for and what kinds of things they need to think of when designing a zoo.

3. Responses will vary but should show that students understand how to use this word in different ways.

4. Possible response: I can see where the different animals are located.

RESPONSE OPTIONS

WRITING Have students think about what they learned about keeping animals in zoos. Then have them make a list of these pros and cons, expressing their own opinions of keeping animals in zoos. Remind them to give valid reasons to support their position.

CONTENT CONNECTIONS

SCIENCE Students can learn more about the benefits and drawbacks of keeping animals in zoos by researching it on the Internet or in the library. Suggest that they choose one side of the argument for or against zoos and find out more information about it.

TIME FOR Science

Author's Purpose

An **author's purpose** is his or her reason for writing. There are four main reasons for writing: to **persuade, inform, entertain,** and **express** a mood or feeling.

Directions Answer the questions below about the author's purpose.

1. Why might the author have written this book?

_____

_____

2. What was the author's purpose for using photographs?

_____

3. In what ways did the author succeed in her purpose?

_____

_____

Directions Write whether each statement's purpose is to persuade, inform, entertain, or express.

1. The blue water was so clear that you could almost see to the bottom of the ocean. _____

2. It's up to you to save those precious birds from extinction. _____

3. The animals finally broke free and raided the ice cream truck. _____

4. There are over 1,000 kinds of fish in the ocean. _____

5. Anyone who donates money will get a free zoo pass. _____

6. The kangaroo, koala bear, and wallaby are all natives of Australia. _____

7. It was quiet and still, except for the gentle breeze blowing through the trees. _____

8. You must see this great movie about the wilderness! _____

9. The elephant is the largest zoo animal, weighing about 12,000 pounds. _____

10. The man was startled by a low growl behind him. _____

© Pearson Education 6

78

Vocabulary

Directions Write a definition for each vocabulary word below.

1. realistic _____

2. exotic _____

3. zoological _____

4. activists _____

5. confinement _____

6. moats _____

7. species _____

8. controversial _____

Directions Fill in the blanks with vocabulary words from the box.

1. Professor Talbot consulted a _____ expert for our class project on mammals.

2. The hundreds of _____ demanded that labs stop killing rabbits.

3. The Supreme Court has made some _____ rulings.

4. That movie set was very _____.

5. It was common for kings and queens to construct palaces with _____.

6. Some new _____ are still being discovered.

7. Many _____ environments exist close to the equator.

8. For certain animals, _____ seems like abuse.

Directions Write a sentence below using any two vocabulary words.

_____

_____

79

A Very Special Gift

A VERY SPECIAL GIFT
by Natalie Anagusta

Illustrated by Cynthia Sears

🔾 **CAUSE AND EFFECT**

🔾 **PRIOR KNOWLEDGE**

LESSON VOCABULARY bondage, commissioned, earthen, encounter, homesteaders, settlement

SUMMARY Thirteen-year-old James and his family are African Americans who leave Tennessee and slavery to set out for Kansas where they plan to become homesteaders.

INTRODUCE THE BOOK

BUILD BACKGROUND Invite students to say what they know about the period after the Civil War. Ask them if they know what it means to be a homesteader.

PREVIEW/USE TEXT FEATURES Have students preview the book by first looking at the illustrations. Have them note the art of the commemorative postage stamp on page 7. Ask: how do these text features give you an idea of what the book will be about?

TEACH/REVIEW VOCABULARY To help them understand the contextual meaning of the word *bondage,* have students read the fourth paragraph on page 3. Ask them what other words help them understand the meaning of bondage. Continue in a similar fashion with the other vocabulary words.

🄴🄻🄻 Invite students to write a sentence for each vocabulary word, leaving out one or two words. Have them exchange their sentences with a partner and then fill in the missing words.

TARGET SKILL AND STRATEGY

🔾 **CAUSE AND EFFECT** Remind students that an *effect* is something that happens. A *cause* is why something happens. Invite students to look for cause-and-effect relationships between events as they read.

🔾 **PRIOR KNOWLEDGE** Remind students that *prior knowledge* is what a reader already knows about a given topic from reading and personal experience. Remind them that good readers connect their prior knowledge to text to help them comprehend it. Invite students to use a 3-column chart to list everything they know about African American homesteaders, cowboys, and soldiers in the period after the Civil War, before they read.

READ THE BOOK

Use the following questions to support comprehension.

PAGE 6 What was the Homestead Act? *(Passed by Lincoln, it gave any citizen over twenty-one the right to claim 160 acres of frontier land if he or she promised to work it for five years.)*

PAGE 7 How did the prairie setting affect the Johnsons? *(Yellow dust from prairie grass got in their eyes, powdered their hair, and made their teeth gritty, making them grateful to find water)*

PAGE 9 According to the African American cowboy, why were there many jobs in Texas? *(many people needed to drive cattle to the railroad because of a big need for beef out East)*

REVISIT THE BOOK

READER RESPONSE
1. The homesteading life was very hard; she hated the sound of rattlesnakes; they ran out of meat.
2. Students should explain what they knew and if this knowledge helped them understand the story better.
3. clay, village, pioneer, to meet, lawfully given, captivity
4. Students should talk about the many obstacles the family faced.

RESPONSE OPTIONS

WRITING Invite students to write a journal entry from the point of view of one of the characters in the story. They should include details about the setting and how it affects the character.

CONTENT CONNECTIONS

SOCIAL STUDIES Students can learn more about African American cowboys and soldiers, and the homesteaders of Nicodemus, Kansas, by going to the library or using the Internet and tell the class their findings.

Time for SOCIAL STUDIES

Name _____

Cause and Effect

- A **cause** is "why something happened." An **effect** is "what happened."

Directions Fill in the graphic organizer below.

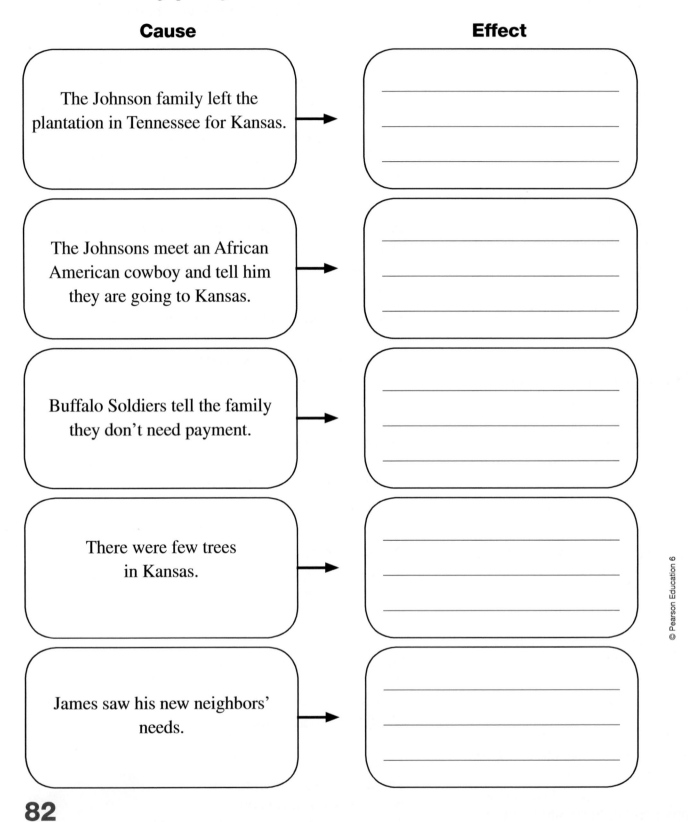

Cause

Effect

The Johnson family left the plantation in Tennessee for Kansas.

The Johnsons meet an African American cowboy and tell him they are going to Kansas.

Buffalo Soldiers tell the family they don't need payment.

There were few trees in Kansas.

James saw his new neighbors' needs.

82

Name _____

Vocabulary

Directions Write the word from the box that matches each definition.

Check the Words You Know

___bondage   ___commissioned   ___earthen
___encounter   ___homesteaders   ___settlement

1. _____ made of clay

2. _____ people who work on a piece of land to improve it, so that they may eventually own it

3. _____ a grouping of homes, a small village or town

4. _____ meet or become acquainted with

5. _____ slavery or captivity

6. _____ paid to do something

Directions Imagine you are a member of the Johnson family in *A Very Special Gift*. Write a brief journal entry from the point of view of one of the characters in the story. Use as many vocabulary words as you can.

_____

_____

_____

_____

_____

_____

_____

83

Homesteaders in Nebraska

Homesteaders in Nebraska
by Horatio Treemont

Unit 4 Week 3

CAUSE AND EFFECT

PRIOR KNOWLEDGE

LESSON VOCABULARY bondage, commissioned, earthen, encounter, homesteaders, settlement

SUMMARY When Timothy and his family move from Philadelphia to Nebraska, they have no idea of the difficulties in store for them. As homesteaders, they must build their own house, raise their own food, and make new friends.

INTRODUCE THE BOOK

BUILD BACKGROUND Invite students to say what they know about homesteaders in Nebraska in the 19th century. Ask them to say why they think immigrant families from Eastern cities might have wanted to try their luck at homesteading in Nebraska.

PREVIEW/USE TEXT FEATURES Have students preview the book by looking at the illustrations and note the map on page 7. Have them tell how these text features help give them an idea what the book will be about.

TEACH/REVIEW VOCABULARY To help students better remember the meaning of the word *bondage,* have them look it up in the dictionary. Have them identify any prefixes or suffixes that are part of the word. Ask them what the suffix signifies (noun). Continue in a similar fashion with the other vocabulary words.

TARGET SKILL AND STRATEGY

CAUSE AND EFFECT Remind students that an *effect* is something that happens. A *cause* is why something happens. Challenge them, as they read, to look for events that happen and for explanations of why they happened. Have them record their findings.

PRIOR KNOWLEDGE Remind students that *prior knowledge* is what a reader knows about a given topic, gathered from reading and personal experience. Challenge them to think about events that happen in the story and similar events from their own lives.

ELL Invite students to conduct interviews with each other telling about times they had to move to new places with their families. Help them develop their questions and answers.

READ THE BOOK

Use the following questions to support comprehension.

PAGE 5 What two reasons does Timothy's father give to explain why the government wants people to move out West? *(There is overcrowding in the cities in the East, and land is going to waste out West.)*

PAGE 16 How was the school in Nebraska different from the school in Philadelphia? *(Nebraska: one room; 50 students ranging from 5 to 18 years old, one teacher, off dirt road on empty prairie; Philadelphia: many corridors, classrooms, big red brick building on busy city block)*

PAGE 22 How did moving to Nebraska change Scarlet? *(She no longer whined, and she seemed to sense that they each had a job to do.)*

TALK ABOUT THE BOOK

READER RESPONSE
1. Snakes fell through the roof and scared Timothy's mom and sister. The heavy rains soaked the sod roof, forcing the snakes to come out.
2. Students should tell what they know and how this knowledge helped them understand the story.
3. *encounter*: unexpected meeting; *commissioned*: to give authority to. Sentences will vary.
4. The clean snow represented a fresh beginning.

RESPONSE OPTIONS

WRITING Invite students to write two paragraphs about a time they had to adjust to changes like the family in the story. Challenge them to say what happened and explain why it happened.

CONTENT CONNECTIONS:

SOCIAL STUDIES By going to the library or using the Internet, students can learn about Willa Cather, who moved to Red Cloud, Nebraska, with her family in 1883 when she was ten. Invite students to tell their findings to the class.

Time for SOCIAL STUDIES

Name _____

Cause and Effect

- A **cause** is "why something happened."
- An **effect** is "what happened."

Directions Draw a line to match each cause with its effect.

Cause

1. The government wanted to encourage people to move West.

2. Timothy's father cannot find work.

3. There is little timber in Nebraska.

4. The children pitched in and worked until their arms and legs ached.

5. There is little water in Nebraska.

6. Mrs. Apple introduces Timothy in the one-room schoolhouse.

7. A huge snowfall covers the prairie landscape.

Effect

The children begin to feel like real pioneers.

Timothy wishes he could become invisible.

Timothy learns to love the Nebraska prairie.

The family decides to move to Nebraska.

The government passed the Homestead Act.

Homesteaders build their homes out of sod.

Sod has a root network that branches out through every inch of soil.

Cause: A government agent comes to inspect the improvements the O'Hare family have made to their land.

Effect: _____

_____

© Pearson Education 6

82

Name _____

Vocabulary

Directions Write the word from the box that belongs in each group.

Check the Words You Know
___bondage   ___commissioned   ___earthen ___encounter   ___homesteaders   ___settlement

1. village, town _____

2. greet, meet _____

3. slavery, captivity _____

4. clay, sod _____

5. registered, paid _____

6. homebuilders, pioneers _____

Directions Write a brief paragraph about *Homesteaders in Nebraska.* Use as many vocabulary words as you can.

_____

_____

_____

_____

_____

_____

_____

_____

83

Grizzled Bill Turns . . .

Unit 4 Week 3

🔾 **CAUSE AND EFFECT**

🔾 **PRIOR KNOWLEDGE**

LESSON VOCABULARY arrogant, cattle barons, feat, profitable, suspicious, treasury

SUMMARY A young ranch hand meets a grizzled outlaw on the open range of Texas in 1865. The encounter changes them both. Sam Granite helps the outlaw reform. Grizzled Bill finds he can help people without breaking the law.

INTRODUCE THE BOOK

BUILD BACKGROUND Invite students to say what they know about the life of cowboys in the 1800s. Ask them what they know about the kind of work they did and their living conditions.

PREVIEW/USE TEXT FEATURES Have students preview the book by looking at the illustrations and the chapter titles. Ask them to say how these text features help give them an idea of what the book will be about.

TEACH/PREVIEW VOCABULARY To help students better remember the contextual meaning of the word *treasury,* have them read the fourth paragraph on page 14. Ask: What words help you understand the meaning of *treasury?* Continue with the other vocabulary words.

TARGET SKILL AND STRATEGY

🔾 **CAUSE AND EFFECT** Remind students that an *effect* is something that happens. A *cause* is why something happens. Explain that clue words are not always present in text to point out causes and effects. As they read, students should try to identify causes and effects by asking: "What happened?" And "Why did it happen?"

ELL Invite pairs of students to page through the selection and take turns asking: "What happened?" and "Why did it happen?" If they have trouble understanding cause-effect relationships, pair less language-proficient peers with more language-proficient peers.

🔾 **PRIOR KNOWLEDGE** Remind students that *prior knowledge* is what a reader knows about a given topic, gathered from reading and personal experience. Challenge them to think about text-to-world connections and text-to-text connections.

READ THE BOOK

Use the following questions to support comprehension.

PAGE 4–5 What is the setting? How does it affect common people? How does it affect Grizzled Bill? *(Texas cattle country in 1865; life is not easy; Bill helps poor people against the rich.)*

PAGE 16 What is Sam's argument for trying to get Grizzled Bill to change his ways? *(You don't need to steal to help people; crime is crime, regardless of why you're committing it.)*

PAGE 26 How does Grizzled Bill use his new position to help people at the end of the story? *(He fines Wilkinson for underpaying and overworking his men.)*

TALK ABOUT THE BOOK

READER RESPONSE

1. Possible responses: Grizzled Bill stops the most dangerous thief in Oklahoma. Yes, Bill becomes sheriff after Abernathy retires.

2. 1st question: What I Know: Robin Hood stole from the rich; gave to the poor. Answer: Grizzled Bill is a cowboy who stole from the rich and gave to the poor. 2nd question: What I Know: People are judged by their appearances. Answer: Grizzled Bill did not want to look like an outlaw.

3. Possible response: captivity

Responses will vary.

RESPONSE OPTIONS

WRITING Invite students to make up their own story about an outlaw who decides to change his ways. Have them show how and why the outlaw decides to change.

CONTENT CONNECTIONS

SOCIAL STUDIES Have students research how a cowboy's life has changed from the 1800s to today and report their findings to the class.

Name _____

Cause and Effect

- A **cause** is "why something happened."
- An **effect** is "what happened."

Directions Read the following sentences. Write a cause or an effect on the lines below.

1. **Cause:** Sam Granite is educated, but from a poor family.

   Effect: _____

   _____

2. **Cause:** _____

   _____

   Effect: Sam blurts out his feelings about working for Curtis Clay Wilkinson.

3. **Cause:** The outlaw tells Sam his name.

   Effect: _____

4. **Cause:** _____

   _____

   Effect: Grizzled Bill gets a haircut and trims his gray beard, wears nice clothes, and has cleaned his hat.

5. **Cause:** Bill admits he's robbed plenty of general stores.

   Effect: _____

   _____

Directions On the lines below, write a brief paragraph about the effects of the events that happen, and what causes them to happen, starting with Chapter 4 of the story.

_____

_____

_____

_____

82

Vocabulary

Directions Write the word from the box that belongs in each sentence.

Check the Words You Know
___arrogant ___cattle barons ___feat
___profitable ___suspicious ___treasury

1. Normally, not much happened to the _____ in Texas.

2. Some new ranchers moved here to build their _____ businesses.

3. It was as if we were to do whatever Mr. Wilkinson wanted and help him add to his

   _____.

4. That's why I was surprised, one day, when a wild-looking outlaw offered me a cool drink of water. I thought he would be _____.

5. It was quite a _____ to go from outlaw to sheriff, but Grizzled Bill did it.

6. You could have knocked me over with a feather when the sheriff asked Grizzled Bill to be his deputy; I thought for sure he would be _____.

Directions On the lines below, write a brief tale about a do-good outlaw in the Wild West. Use as many of the vocabulary words as you can.

_____

_____

_____

_____

_____

_____

83

The Solar System and Beyond

Space and Technology
The Solar System and Beyond
by Jen Coates-Conroy

Unit 4 Week 4

⊙ **DRAW CONCLUSIONS**

⊙ **VISUALIZE**

LESSON VOCABULARY alien, barge, hospitable, molten, ore, refrain, universal, version

SUMMARY This book describes the wonders of our solar system and beyond, exploring planetary moons, comets, asteroids, and the search for alien life. It discusses recent space activities, including the International Space Station and plans for Starship 2040.

INTRODUCE THE BOOK

BUILD BACKGROUND Invite students to discuss what they know about our solar system. Ask students whether they'd like to become astronauts. Encourage a discussion of current NASA activities, such as the space shuttle or the International Space Station.

PREVIEW/USE TEXT FEATURES Have students preview the book by looking at the photographs and captions, the time line on pages 4 and 5, and the diagram of the solar system on pages 12 and 13. Ask students what they expect to learn from this book.

ELL Invite English language learners to share the names of the planets and other space terms in their native language.

TEACH/REVIEW VOCABULARY Write the vocabulary words on the board. Ask students to define words they know and use them in a sentence. Use the glossary to explain words that are unfamiliar. Have students practice using the words in oral sentences.

TARGET SKILL AND STRATEGY

⊙ **DRAW CONCLUSIONS** Remind students that to *draw a conclusion*, or to make inferences, is a sensible decision reached after thinking about details or facts in what they've read. Remind students that they should always be able to back up their conclusions with information from the text.

⊙ **VISUALIZE** Remind students that to *visualize* means to create a picture or pictures in your mind as you read. As they read, encourage students to look for words that can help them to visualize and form mental pictures.

READ THE BOOK

Use the following questions to support comprehension.

PAGE 4 Name several Soviet space accomplishments in the late 1950s and early 1960s. *(Launch of Sputnik 1; Luna 1 becomes first craft to escape Earth's gravity; first human ventures into space.)*

PAGE 13 How do planets stay in orbit? *(Gravity holds them in place around the sun.)*

PAGES 16–17 What can you conclude about life in the universe outside Earth? *(So far, no evidence has proven there is life beyond Earth.)*

TALK ABOUT THE BOOK

READER RESPONSE

1. Responses will vary but should include possibility of traveling in cruise liners and living aboard craft like Starship 2040.
2. Responses should reflect a planet that has features like those on Earth, such as sunlight and oxygen.
3. *Barge* means "a large vehicle" or "to move clumsily"; *refrain* means "to keep yourself from doing something" or "a section of music."
4. June 18, 1983; twenty-two years; answers will vary.

RESPONSE OPTIONS

WRITING Have students write a brief description of what they imagine life to be like aboard a spacecraft. Encourage the students to base their description on factual information learned from the text or from other reliable sources.

CONTENT CONNECTIONS

SCIENCE Find diagrams of spacecraft, including the space shuttle and the International Space Station to share in class. Have students work in groups to investigate one of the planets and report back to the class.

TIME FOR Science

Drawing Conclusions

- A **conclusion** is a sensible decision you reach after you think about facts and details in what you read.
- **Drawing conclusions** means to make sensible decisions or form reasonable opinions after thinking about those facts and details.
- A **conclusion** may be stated at the beginning or end of a passage. Or you may need to reach your own conclusion after reading.

Directions Read the following passage.

> What would we be without the Sun? The Sun is the most prominent feature in our solar system. It is the largest object and contains approximately 98 percent of the total solar system mass. One hundred and nine Earths would be required to fit across the Sun's face, and its interior could hold over 1.3 million Earths. The Sun's outer visible layer is called the photosphere and has a temperature of more than 9,930 degrees Fahrenheit. This layer has a rough appearance due to the turbulent eruptions of energy at the surface. Even though Earth is about 93 million miles from the Sun, the rays that hit the planet are still very powerful. Astronomers study the Sun by using special telescopes.

Directions Use the graphic organizer below. First, find a conclusion in the passage above, or draw a conclusion on your own. Write the conclusion in the center circle labeled *Conclusion*. In the small circles around the main circle, write facts or details that helped you or the author reach that conclusion.

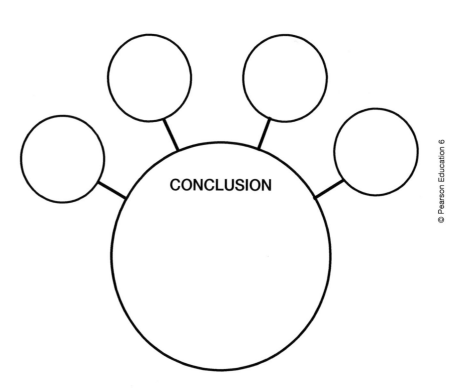

© Pearson Education 6

86

Vocabulary

Directions Choose the word from the box that best matches each definition. Write the word on the line.

> ## Check the Words You Know
>
> ___alien   ___barge
> ___hospitable   ___molten
> ___ore   ___refrain
> ___universal   ___version

1. _____ one particular statement, account, or description

2. _____ friendly; receptive

3. _____ made liquid by heat; melted

4. _____ an imaginary creature from outer space

5. _____ rock containing metals extracted after mining

6. _____ large, strongly built vehicle or flat-bottomed boat for carrying freight

7. _____ of or belonging to all; concerning all

8. _____ to keep yourself from doing something

Directions For each word below, write a meaning different from the ones above.

9. barge

_____

10. refrain

_____

87

United States and Russian Space . . .

Space and Technology
THE UNITED STATES AND RUSSIAN
SPACE RACE
SPAC
BY KATHLEEN COX

⊚ **DRAW CONCLUSIONS**

⊚ **VISUALIZE**

LESSON VOCABULARY alien, barge, hospitable, molten, ore, refrain, universal, version

SUMMARY For nearly 25 years, following the end of World War II, the United States and Soviet Union/Russia were locked in a space race to send men into orbit around the Earth and to land a man on the moon. This book gives the details and reasons for this tense battle and how it has eased in recent years.

INTRODUCE THE BOOK

BUILD BACKGROUND Invite students to discuss what they know about current and past explorations of space by the U.S. and Russia/Soviet Union, as well as what they know about the life and training of astronauts.

PREVIEW/USE TEXT FEATURES Have students preview the book by looking at the photographs and captions as well as the diagram on page 6. Ask students to describe what they expect to learn from this book.

ⒺⓁⓁ To help English language learners with the many events in this selection, encourage them to create a three-column graphic organizer. In the middle row of the organizer, from top to bottom, students can write the years, from 1958 to 1975. In the left column, they will write events that the U.S. achieved. In the right column, they write events that the Soviets achieved.

TEACH/REVIEW VOCABULARY Write the vocabulary words on the board. Ask students to define words they know and use them in a sentence. Explain unfamiliar words. Have students practice using the words in sentences.

TARGET SKILL AND STRATEGY

⊚ **DRAW CONCLUSIONS** Remind students that to *draw a conclusion* is a sensible decision reached after thinking about details or facts in a text. As they read, encourage students to think about the facts in the text and to ask themselves questions about the facts to draw conclusions. Remind students that they should always be able to back up their conclusions with information.

⊚ **VISUALIZE** Remind students that to *visualize* means to create a picture in your mind as you read.

READ THE BOOK

Use the following questions to support comprehension.

PAGE 3 What conclusion can you draw about why explorers sought to land on the Moon? *(Possible response: They had conquered terrain and oceans on Earth and sought a new challenge.*

PAGE 16 What goal did President Kennedy lay out in 1961? *(Land a man on the moon and bring him safely back within a decade.)*

PAGE 19 How did the moon-bound spacecraft work? *(Sections were discarded as they performed their tasks, but the lunar module would land on the moon, and the command module would orbit the moon, waiting to bring the astronauts back to Earth.)*

TALK ABOUT THE BOOK

READER RESPONSE

1. They would benefit by working together.
2. Responses will vary.
3. Possible responses: *lunar* for *moon; flying machine, rocket,* or *spaceship* for *spacecraft; imagined* for *envisioned;* and *circled* for *orbited.*
4. Jupiter. The Inner Planets are much closer to Earth compared to the Outer Planets.

RESPONSE OPTIONS

WRITING Have students write a two or three paragraph description of what they imagine life to be like aboard a spacecraft. Students should base their description on factual information learned from the text or from other reliable sources.

CONTENT CONNECTIONS

SCIENCE Have students work in groups to investigate one mission in the Apollo space program and report back to the class.

Name_____

Draw Conclusions

- A conclusion is a sensible decision reached after thinking about details or facts.
- Drawing conclusions, or making inferences, is the process of making those decisions.
- You should always be able to back up your conclusions with information from the text.

Directions Read the paragraph below, then answer the questions that follow.

> During the late 1950s, the Soviets and Americans were locked in a space race. On October 4, 1957, the Soviets launched *Sputnik,* the world's first man-made satellite. *Sputnik* traveled about 400 miles above the Earth at a speed of 18,000 miles per hour and took about 96 minutes to circle the planet. About a month later, the Soviet Union launched *Sputnik II.* This second satellite was much heavier than the original *Sputnik.* It also had a passenger: a dog named Laika, the world's first Earthling in space. After the launch of *Sputnik II,* U.S. President Dwight D. Eisenhower tried to restore the confidence of the American people in the U.S. space program. And on December 6, 1957, American scientists launched a rocket called the *Vanguard.* It carried a satellite intended to orbit the Earth. But the rocket went up four feet, then fell to the ground. People called it "kaputnik." Americans did succeed in launching a rocket in January 1958, but just three months later, the Soviets successfully launched *Sputnik III.* This third Russian satellite weighed more than a ton. It was hard to believe at the time that the Americans would beat the Russians in landing a man on the moon.

1. What conclusion can you reach about the success of the Soviet space program in the late 1950s?

_____

2–3. What are two facts or examples that support your conclusion?

_____

_____

_____

4. What can you infer about why President Eisenhower tried to restore the confidence of the American people?

_____

_____

5. What can you infer from the last sentence in this paragraph?

_____

_____

_____

86

© Pearson Education 6

Vocabulary

Directions Choose the word from the box that best matches each definition. Write the word on the line.

> ### Check the Words You Know
>
> ___alien   ___barge
> ___hospitable   ___molten
> ___ore   ___refrain
> ___universal   ___version

1. _____ one particular statement, account, or description

2. _____ friendly; receptive

3. _____ made liquid by heat; melted

4. _____ an imaginary creature from outer space

5. _____ rock containing metals to make mining profitable. After it is mined, it must be treated to extract the metal.

6. _____ large, strongly built vehicle or flat-bottomed boat for carrying freight

7. _____ of or belonging to all; concerning all

8. _____ to keep yourself from doing something

Directions Write a paragraph about the space race using as many vocabulary words as possible.

_____

_____

_____

_____

_____

_____

© Pearson Education 6

87

Destination: Mars

Destination: MARS
by Scott Gillam

DRAW CONCLUSIONS

VISUALIZE

LESSON VOCABULARY axis, durable, infrared, interaction, Martian, panoramic, robotic, routine

SUMMARY Since 1976, when the U.S. landed Viking spacecraft on Mars, scientists have been learning vast amounts about the "red planet" in hopes of discovering whether Mars once harbored, or could support, life. This text imagines that students have been chosen for the first manned flight to Mars.

INTRODUCE THE BOOK

BUILD BACKGROUND Invite students to discuss what they know about Mars and the missions to the Red Planet.

PREVIEW/USE TEXT FEATURES Have students preview the book by looking at the photographs, charts, and diagrams. Ask students to describe what they expect to learn from this book.

TEACH/REVIEW VOCABULARY Write the vocabulary words on the board. Ask students to use the glossary or a dictionary to define words. Have volunteers use the words in oral sentences to show meaning.

TARGET SKILL AND STRATEGY

DRAW CONCLUSIONS Remind students that *drawing a conclusion* is a sensible decision reached after thinking about details or facts in a text. Remind students that they should always be able to back up their conclusions with text information.

VISUALIZE Remind students that to *visualize* means to create a picture or pictures in your mind as you read.

READ THE BOOK

Use the following questions to support comprehension.

PAGE 10 What conclusions have been drawn about Mars since the 1960s? (*Mars's magnetic field is weak; atmosphere is thin and has very little oxygen.*)

PAGES 16-18 Describe some differences between *Pathfinder* and *Exploration* rovers. (*Pathfinder's rover was smaller, lighter and couldn't travel as far. Explorer's rovers carried all the mission's scientific instruments.*)

PAGE 20 For humans to work on Mars, what precautions must be taken? (*Protection against cold, dust storms, lack of oxygen, and sudden weather changes*)

ELL Invite students to share information about how the "red planet" is perceived in their native cultures. To keep track of information in the text, encourage them to keep a graphic organizer detailing the findings from each Mars mission.

TALK ABOUT THE BOOK

READER RESPONSE

1. Responses will vary. Photos showed volcanoes, plains, highlands, and canyons. No signs of life. Temperatures vary from –107 deg. F to 7 deg. F.

2. Sample response: A typical piece of Martian land would show dusty red soil with rocks of all shapes and sizes on a mostly flat surface. You might see mountains or craters formed by meteors.

3. Possible responses: *robotic:* robot; *Martian:* Mars; *panoramic: panorama*.

4. MER was protected by its heat shield. Parachute protected it from heat and a hard landing. Airbags cushioned its final impact and petals protected the fragile solar panels inside them.

RESPONSE OPTIONS

WRITING Have students imagine they are Space Explorers visiting Mars for two weeks. Have them write a two or three paragraph description of what their trip will be like and what tasks they hope to accomplish.

CONTENT CONNECTIONS

SCIENCE Have students work in groups to prepare reports on each of the major Mars exploratory trips, describing length and purpose of mission; hardware used; information learned; and so forth. Presentations can be made on posterboard, including photos and diagrams pulled from library books or the Internet.

TIME FOR Science

Draw Conclusions

- **A conclusion** is a sensible decision reached after thinking about details or facts.
- **Drawing conclusions,** or making inferences, is the process of making those decisions.
- You should always be able to back up your **conclusions** with information from the text.

Directions Read the paragraph below, then answer the questions that follow.

> Recent trips to Mars have turned up how different Mars is from Earth. Mars Global Surveyor, launched in 1996, revealed a surface made up of dust at least three feet thick caused by millions of years of meteoroid impacts, and an atmosphere made up of 95 percent carbon dioxide and only about .1 percent oxygen. The elevation of Mars' polar ice cap was found to be between 6,600 and 7,900 feet higher than the surrounding terrain. MGS also found canyons and troughs as deep as 3,600 feet in the frozen water and carbon dioxide in Mars' polar ice cap. Additional explorations have found that the deepest canyon on Mars is six times deeper than the Grand Canyon and as long as the United States from the West to the East Coast. The highest mountain on Mars covers an area that is the size of the entire state of Arizona. In addition, Mars has a much thinner atmosphere than Earth and much higher radiation levels. In fact, Mars' radiation is about two to three times higher than the radiation around Earth.

1. What conclusion can you reach about how easily humans could survive on Mars?

_____

2–3. Give at least two facts or examples that support your conclusion.

_____

_____

4. What can you infer about differences between the environments of Mars compared to Earth?

_____

5. What can you infer about differences between the physical terrains of Mars and Earth?

_____

_____

6. What facts help you support this conclusion?

_____

_____

86

© Pearson Education 6

Vocabulary

Directions Choose the word from the box that best completes each sentence. Write the word on the line.

```
         Check the Words You Know

        ___axis              ___durable
        ___infrared          ___interaction
        ___Martian           ___panoramic
        ___robotic           ___routine
```

1. The technicians designed the _____ parts to withstand extreme temperatures.

2. One of the _____ arms would have to be fixed.

3. The satellite launch was planned around the _____ of the "red planet."

4. Astronauts are less protected from _____ radiation while traveling in space.

5. Is it possible that someday we will have _____ with other intelligent life forms?

6. The _____ environment continues to be an interesting mystery.

7. Earth displays its natural beauty when seen from space in a _____ view.

8. Sending orbiters and rovers to other planets has become more _____ since the 1960s.

Directions For each word below, write a sentence that highlights its meaning.

9. axis

_____

10. routine

_____

87

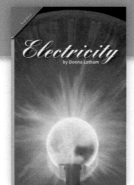

Electricity

AUTHOR'S PURPOSE

MONITOR AND FIX UP

LESSON VOCABULARY convert, devise, efficiency, generate, percentage, proclaim, reproduce, transmitted

SUMMARY This book will cover the invention of electricity and how it has changed people's lives.

INTRODUCE THE BOOK

BUILD BACKGROUND Ask students to name things they use every day that run on electricity. Generate discussion about what people did or ways in which they lived before electricity was invented.

PREVIEW/USE TEXT FEATURES As students preview the book, draw their attention to the table of contents. Ask them what they think this book will teach them based on the information here.

TEACH/REVIEW VOCABULARY Divide students into small groups. Have each group find the base word of each vocabulary word and use it in a sentence. Allow them to use the glossary or a dictionary. Have volunteers tell how the affix changes the meaning of the word.

ELL Have students look up vocabulary words in the glossary or a dictionary. Then have them use the word in a sentence to show meaning.

TARGET SKILL AND STRATEGY

AUTHOR'S PURPOSE Remind students that an *author's purpose* is his or her reason for writing. Remind them that the four main reasons for writing are to persuade, to inform, to entertain, and to express. As they read, ask students to keep the author's purpose in mind.

MONITOR AND FIX UP Remind students that good readers know if they understand the text and if it makes sense to them. As students read, have them write the important points using a graphic organizer, read on, reread, or generate questions to help them understand the text.

READ THE BOOK

Use the following questions to support comprehension.

PAGE 4 What is the author's purpose in Chapter 1? *(To inform and to explain what electricity is and does)*

PAGES 12–13 How does this diagram help me understand how electricity travels? *(It shows where it starts and its path.)*

PAGE 19 How much does it cost to use a dishwasher per year? *(About $45)*

TALK ABOUT THE BOOK

READER RESPONSE
1. To inform readers about electricity, its early experiments, and ways we use it
2. Sample responses: Main Idea: We depend on convenience of electricity. Details: In the home, for transportation, for communication
3. Possible answer: From power plant, voltage is generated at 25,000 volts. Voltage has to be increased to be transmitted over long distances and converted to lower voltage use at home.
4. Possible responses: Refrigerators, light, and heat are necessary; pool pumps and waterbed heaters are not.

RESPONSE OPTIONS

WRITING Ask students to describe a day at school before electricity was invented. Prompt them to talk about not having electric lights or computers.

CONTENT CONNECTIONS

SCIENCE Students can learn more about electricity by researching it on the internet or in the library. Prompt them to search for new ways in which electricity has helped our lives.

TIME FOR Science

Author's Purpose

- The **author's purpose** is the reason or reasons an author has for writing.

- An author may have one or more reasons for writing. He or she may want to **inform, persuade, entertain,** or **express** a mood or feeling.

Directions Write a letter to a friend to persuade him to join the soccer team. Then write a letter to inform him of the team and sport.

Persuade

_____

_____

_____

_____

_____

Inform

_____

_____

_____

_____

_____

_____

90

Vocabulary

Directions Choose a word from the box that matches each definition.

1. _____ sent along

2. _____ to make known publicly

3. _____ to do something without wasting time

4. _____ to invent

5. _____ to copy

Check the Words You Know

___convert
___devise
___efficiency
___generate
___percentage
___proclaim
___reproduce
___transmitted

Directions Choose a word from the box that means the opposite of each word.

6. _____ destroy

7. _____ keep the same

8. _____ whole

Directions Choose four words from the box and write sentences about electricity.

9. _____

_____

10. _____

_____

11. _____

_____

12. _____

_____

91

Inventors at Work

🔊 **AUTHOR'S PURPOSE**

🔊 **MONITOR AND FIX UP**

LESSON VOCABULARY converts, devise, efficiency, generated, percentage, proclaimed, reproduce, transmitted

---

SUMMARY Throughout time, inventors have come up with things that have made our lives better, such as the plane or the telephone. Some inventors were not so successful. This book tells about successful and unsuccessful attempts at inventing things and the steps in the process of invention.

INTRODUCE THE BOOK

BUILD BACKGROUND Ask students to name some popular inventions. Have them name inventions that they use every day, such as a light bulb, a phone, or a computer. Discuss how these inventions have made their lives easier.

PREVIEW/USE TEXT FEATURES As students preview the book, draw their attention to the charts and the time line on pages 18 and 19. Prompt them to discuss how these features might help them better understand what they are reading.

TEACH/REVIEW VOCABULARY Have students work in pairs and write one sentence for each vocabulary word in the form of a question. Then have one person from each pair write one of their sentences on the board, leaving a blank for the vocabulary word. Have the class try to guess which vocabulary word fits into the blanks.

ELL Have students look up vocabulary words in the dictionary or glossary. Then have them divide the vocabulary words into syllables.

TARGET SKILL AND STRATEGY

🔊 **AUTHOR'S PURPOSE** Remind students that an *author's purpose* is his or her reason for writing. Go over the four main reasons for writing: to persuade, to inform, to entertain, and to express. As they read, have students think about the author's purpose and write reasons to support their answer.

🔊 **MONITOR AND FIX UP** Remind students that good readers are aware of their understanding of the text and know if it makes sense to them. As students read, have them answer the following questions on a sheet of paper: What is the author trying to tell me? What details help me understand the author's purpose?

READ THE BOOK

Use the following questions to support comprehension.

PAGES 5 AND 6 What is the author's purpose here? (*To inform and to tell about the steps of inventing*)

PAGES 6 AND 7 How does the chart help you understand the steps in inventing? (Possible responses: *It gives a process. It organizes the steps chronologically.*)

PAGE 20 What other inventions has the invention of the car led to? (*Paved roads, gas stations, traffic lights*)

TALK ABOUT THE BOOK

READER RESPONSE
1. Although the Wrights were the first to fly, many people before them wanted to fly.
2. Possible response: Main idea: Cars have brought changes. Details: Easier to go places, can get to places faster, can travel in comfort, can be fun, new roads, gas causes air pollution
3. /dōv/, past tense of *dive*; context clues on page 9
4. The invention either works or it doesn't.

RESPONSE OPTIONS

WRITING Ask students to think about how their lives would be changed if there were no telephones. On a sheet of paper, have them make a list of these changes.

CONTENT CONNECTIONS

SCIENCE Students can learn more about inventions by researching on the Internet or in the library. Suggest that they choose an invention and find out more about it.

TIME FOR Science

Author's Purpose

- The **author's purpose** is the reason or reasons an author has for writing.
- An author may have one or more reasons for writing. He or she may want to **inform, persuade, entertain,** or **express** a mood or feeling.

Directions Read the sentences below and write the author's purpose on the line.

1. The strange noises in the night gave him a chill. _____

2. There is a growing problem with pollution in this area. _____

3. Detective Spade knew she was getting close when she heard a tiny knocking sound.

   _____

4. Everyone should go out and show our school spirit! _____

5. Scientists have come up with a better way to cure infections. _____

6. A dog in New Zealand had a record number of 24 puppies in one litter! _____

7. She was dressed in a beautiful, red, sparkling dress. _____

8. We must vote to make a difference. _____

9. Write a sentence that persuades.

   _____

   _____

10. Write a sentence that entertains.

   _____

   _____

90

Vocabulary

Directions Choose a word from the box that matches each definition.

Check the Words You Know

___converts   ___devise   ___efficiency   ___generated
___percentage   ___proclaimed   ___reproduce   ___transmitted

1. _____ made known publicly

2. _____ the act of doing something without wasting time

3. _____ sent along

Directions Choose a word from the box that matches each synonym.

4. _____ changes

5. _____ part

6. _____ invent

7. _____ copy

8. _____ created

Directions Write three sentences using a vocabulary word from the box.

9. _____

_____

10. _____

_____

11. _____

_____

© Pearson Education 6

91

Unit 4 Week 5

It's About Time!
by Anne Cambal

It's About Time

🔘 **AUTHOR'S PURPOSE**

🔘 **MONITOR AND FIX UP**

LESSON VOCABULARY analog, chronometer, digital, elusive, latitude, longitude, meridian, millennium

SUMMARY This book presents the many ways time is measured throughout history. It also tells about inventions that help us measure time.

INTRODUCE THE BOOK

BUILD BACKGROUND Ask students how they measure time. Prompt them to think about time not only in terms of hours, but in days, weeks and months as well. Ask students what they use to measure time, such as a clock or a calendar.

PREVIEW/USE TEXT FEATURES As students preview the book, draw their attention to the headings and the pictures. Based on these features, ask students what they think this book will be about.

TEACH/PREVIEW VOCABULARY Have students work in small groups and have each group choose two vocabulary words. Groups can make up a riddle for each word for classmates to guess.

ELL Have students look up vocabulary words in the glossary or a dictionary. Then have each student choose a word, define it in their own words, and use it correctly in a written sentence.

TARGET SKILL AND STRATEGY

🔘 **AUTHOR'S PURPOSE** Remind students that an *author's purpose* is the reason for writing. Review the four main reasons for writing: to persuade, to inform, to entertain, and to express. As they read, ask students to write the author's purpose for writing this book and give examples to back up their answers.

🔘 **MONITOR AND FIX UP** Remind students that good readers are aware of their understanding of the text and know if it makes sense to them. One way to do to this is to write down important details as they read. Have students use or make a graphic organizer such as a web, three or four column chart, or a T-chart to write the important details in each section to monitor their comprehension.

READ THE BOOK

Use the following questions to support comprehension.

PAGE 6 What is the author's purpose here? *(to inform; to tell about the early methods of keeping time)*

PAGE 8 How does this chart help me understand latitude and longitude? (Possible responses: *It shows which direction latitude is and which direction longitude is. It also shows the degrees of latitude and longitude.)*

PAGE 14 What are the four main time zones in the continental United States? *(Eastern Standard, Central Standard, Mountain Standard, and Pacific Standard)*

TALK ABOUT THE BOOK

READER RESPONSE
1. Responses will vary.
2. The friend in New York will not be tired because when it's 9:00 A.M. in California, it's noon in New York.
3. /wīnd/, as in winding a clock. I know this from context clues in the sentence in which *wind* appears.
4. Responses will vary, but students should use military time.

RESPONSE OPTIONS

WRITING Ask students to describe a typical Saturday for them using a diary or journal format. Have them write a time with each new activity, starting with what time they get out of bed.

CONTENT CONNECTIONS

SCIENCE Students can learn more about ancient methods of telling time by researching it on the Internet or in the library. Encourage them to find the most unusual way of keeping time.

Author's Purpose

An **author's purpose** is his or her reason for writing. There are four main reasons for writing: to **persuade, inform, entertain,** and **express**.

Directions Answer the questions below.

1. What is the author's purpose for starting *It's About Time* with a question?

_____

_____

2. Why did the author write *It's About Time*?

_____

3. Did the author succeed in meeting her purpose?

_____

4. In what ways did the author succeed in her purpose?

_____

_____

5. What was the author's purpose for using photographs, charts, and diagrams?

_____

_____

90

Vocabulary

Directions Use the vocabulary words in the box to fill in the blanks in the sentences below.

Check the Words You Know

___analog   ___chronometer   ___digital   ___elusive
___latitude   ___longitude   ___meridian   ___millennium

---

1. The _____ lines are imaginary lines extending from north to south.

2. Some younger kids may not be familiar with _____ clocks.

3. Measuring time accurately is a more _____ problem than many realize.

4. Computer clocks are set in a _____ format.

Directions Write the word that belongs with each group.

5. time-keeping instrument, clock, _____

6. horizontal "lines" circling Earth, measures north and south of equator, _____

7. starting "line" for telling time, _____

8. ten centuries, a thousand years, _____

Directions Write four sentences about time using a vocabulary word.

9. _____

_____

10. _____

_____

11. _____

_____

12. _____

_____

91

Answer Key for Below-Level Reader Practice

Life in the Arctic   LR1

 Cause and Effect, LR2

Possible responses given. **1.** helps disguise them in the snowy landscape, making it easier to prey on animals. **2.** develop thick coats and a layer of blubber **3.** Polar bears wait by breathing holes waiting for seals to surface. **4.** blends in with its surroundings so is less likely to be seen by predators **5.** developed fur on bottom of feet **6.** less skin is exposed so less heat is lost **7.** helps them defend themselves **8.** allows them to float and sleep at same time

Vocabulary, LR3

1. isolation **2.** conquer **3.** verify **4.** expedition **5.** navigator **6.** destiny **7.** insulated **8.** provisions. Possible answers given. Your Synonym: prove, defeat, protected. Synonym from a Dictionary or Thesaurus: confirm, surmount, shielded

Great Apes   LR10

 Author's Purpose, LR11

1. To inform the reader that apes have been misunderstood; to persuade the reader that apes are peaceful. **2.** She succeeded by giving examples of apes being peaceful, such as eating, resting, and sleeping

1. To inform the reader of the differences in apes. **2.** To better express the differences in the apes; to help the reader further understand what she is saying about the apes **3.** She helped me understand the differences in apes by giving facts about them and showing photographs of them.

Vocabulary, LR12

1. ordeals **2.** existence **3.** captive **4.** primitive **5.** stimulating **6.** companionship **7.** sanctuaries

1. companionship **2.** stimulating **3.** captive **4.** primitive **5.** ordeals **6.** sanctuaries **7.** existence. sanctuaries, existence, companionship

A Very Special Gift   LR19

 Cause and Effect, LR20

Freeing of slaves after Civil War, passing of the Homestead Act. Cowboy gives them a cloth sack to open if they need help. Johnsons encounter Buffalo Soldiers who spend the night at their campfire. Homesteaders built their homes out of sod. The Johnsons give the sack to a new homesteading family.

Vocabulary, LR21

1. earthen **2.** homesteaders **3.** settlement **4.** encounter **5.** bondage **6.** commissioned **7–10.** Responses will vary.

The Solar System and Beyond   LR28

Drawing Conclusions, LR 29

Conclusion: Possible responses given. The Sun is the most prominent feature in our solar system. Supporting Facts or Details: **1.** largest object of solar system mass. **2.** 109 Earths could fit on Sun's face **3.** its interior could hold 1.3 million Earths. **4.** The Sun creates very powerful rays that hit Earth.

Vocabulary, LR30

1. version **2.** hospitable **3.** molten **4.** alien **5.** ore **6.** barge **7.** universal **8.** refrain. **9–10.** Responses will vary.

Electricity   LR37

Author's Purpose, LR38
Persuade: Responses will vary. **Inform:** Responses will vary

Vocabulary, LR39

1. transmitted **2.** proclaim **3.** efficiency **4.** devise **5.** reproduce **6.** generate **7.** convert **8.** percentage **9–12.** Sentences will vary.

Answer Key for On-Level Reader Practice

Life Inside the Arctic Circle   LR4

 Cause and Effect, LR5

Possible responses given. **1.** An alarm sounds so schoolchildren know when to go home at night. **2.** The sun stays in the sky all night for six months of the year. **3.** Birds like the willow ptarmigan have thick, downy feathers. **4.** extremely cold climate in the Arctic **5.** One group herds reindeer and the other hunts marine mammals. **6.** People use the different natural resources in the areas where they live. **7.** Scientists have been able to learn a lot about the Earth's history. **8.** The cold has preserved the soil for thousands of years.

Vocabulary, LR6

Possible responses given. **1.** expedite; to speed up or make easy; to send off, -tion **2.** to isolate; to set apart from others; place alone, -tion **3.** destine; to determine beforehand, -tions **4.** navigate; to steer or direct a ship or aircraft, -or **5.** the thing that happens when the action (root verb) takes place **6.** the person who does something **7.** the person who overcomes something or someone **8.** the thing that happens when your destiny occurs **9.** the thing that happens when someone steers **10.** a person who speeds things up or makes them happen more easily

How Animals Change: The Interaction of Animals and Scientists   LR13

 Author's Purpose, LR14

1. To inform people about the effects of scientific study on animals. **2.** To help the reader better understand what she is saying. **3.** She gave facts about how studying animals affects them.
1. inform **2.** inform **3.** entertain **4.** persuade **5.** inform

Vocabulary, LR15

1. existence **2.** Primitive **3.** companionship **4.** stimulating **5.** ordeal **6.** Captive **7.** sanctuary

1. interesting, exciting **2.** survival, life, being **3.** haven, refuge **4.** friendship, company **5.** caged, jailed **6.** trial, test, problem **7.** ancient, prehistoric

Homesteaders in Nebraska   LR22

 Cause and Effect, LR23

1. The government passed the Homestead Act. **2.** The family decides to move to Nebraska. **3.** Homesteaders build their homes out of sod. **4.** The children begin to feel like real pioneers. **5.** Sod has a root network that branches out through every inch of soil. **6.** Timothy wishes he could become invisible. **7.** Timothy learns to love the Nebraska prairie. The O'Hares become the official owners of their land, under the provisions of the Homesteaders Act.

Vocabulary, LR24

1. settlement **2.** encounter **3.** bondage **4.** earthen **5.** commissioned **6.** homesteaders. Responses will vary.

The United States and Russian Space Race   LR31

Draw Conclusions, LR32

Possible responses given. **1.** The Soviets were more successful than the Americans. **2–3.** Soviets launched three rockets with satellites on board; Americans launched one successful rocket and one unsuccessful one. **4.** He wanted Americans to feel that the U.S. would catch up and build the best space program in the world. **5.** Americans will be first to land a man on the moon.

Vocabulary, LR33

1. version **2.** hospitable **3.** molten **4.** alien **5.** ore **6.** barge **7.** universal **8.** refrain Paragraphs will vary.

Inventors at Work   LR40

Author's Purpose, LR41

1. express or entertain **2.** inform **3.** entertain **4.** persuade **5.** inform **6.** inform **7.** express **8.** persuade **9–10.** Answers will vary.

Vocabulary, LR42

1. proclaimed **2.** efficiency **3.** transmitted **4.** converts **5.** percentage **6.** devise **7.** reproduce **8.** generated **9–11.** Sentences will vary.

The Race to the South Pole — LR7

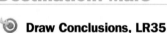 Cause and Effect, LR8

Possible responses given. **1.** It made Scott even more anxious to reach the Pole himself. **2.** Scott had announced that he would lead an expedition to find the South Pole. **3.** Scott raised money and brought on supplies, had another festive send-off, and then ran into a fierce storm and seas thick with ice. **4.** Amundsen was able to make up time against Scott, arriving in Antarctica only nine days after Scott. **5.** Amundsen wanted to prove he had reached the Pole first and wanted Scott to take the news to the world. **6.** Some had been weakened by frostbite during research; the ponies had died, so they had to man haul their heavy supplies; there wasn't enough food; there were blizzards.

Vocabulary, LR9

1. trek **2.** din **3.** turbulent **4.** remote **5.** rash **6.** depots. Responses will vary.

Captive or Free: Zoos in Debate — LR16

 Author's Purpose, LR17

1. To inform the reader about the pros and cons of keeping animals in zoos. **2.** To help the reader better understand what she is saying. **3.** She helped me understand the pros and cons of keeping animals in zoos by giving facts.

1. express **2.** persuade **3.** entertain **4.** inform **5.** persuade **6.** inform **7.** express **8.** persuade **9.** inform **10.** entertain

Vocabulary, LR18

Answers will vary. **1.** actual **2.** rare **3.** animal study **4.** advocates **5.** trapped **6.** waterways used for protection **7.** group with common properties **8.** debatable

1. zoological **2.** activists **3.** controversial **4.** realistic **5.** moats **6.** species **7.** exotic **8.** confinement

Grizzled Bill Turns Over a New Leaf — LR25

Cause and Effect, LR26

1. Sam works at the Triple J, where cowboys get room and board. **2.** Sam encounters an outlaw who asks him if he likes working for Wilkinson. **3.** Sam faints dead away. **4.** Sam meets Bill in Heiferville to help him find a job. **5.** The owner of the Heiferville General Store shows them the door.

Vocabulary, LR27

1. cattle barons **2.** profitable **3.** treasury **4.** arrogant **5.** feat **6.** suspicious

Destination: Mars — LR34

Draw Conclusions, LR35

Possible responses are given. **1.** Humans could not survive on Mars without special protections. **2–3.** Radiation is 2–3 times higher, Mars has a thinner atmosphere, dust on Mars's surface is at least three feet thick. **4.** The atmosphere on Mars has only 0.1 percent oxygen. **5.** Mars's mountains and polar ice caps are much more extreme—larger and colder—than those on Earth. **6.** Mars's polar ice cap is over 6,600 feet higher than the surrounding terrain. Canyons on Mars are 3,600 feet deep.

Vocabulary, LR36

1. durable **2.** robotic **3.** axis **4.** infrared **5.** interaction **6.** Martian **7.** panoramic **8.** routine **9–10.** Answers will vary.

It's About Time! — LR43

Author's Purpose, LR44

Possible responses are given. **1.** To grab the reader's attention; to make the reader think. **2.** To inform **3.** Responses will vary. **4.** Responses will vary. **5.** To help the reader better understand the text.

Vocabulary, LR45

1. longitude **2.** analog **3.** elusive **4.** digital **5.** chronometer **6.** latitude **7.** meridian **8.** millennium **9–12.** Sentences will vary.

Routine Cards

Routine Card

Multisyllabic Word Routine

Teach students this Routine to read long words with meaningful parts.

1 Teach Tell students to look for meaningful parts and to think about the meaning of each part. They should use the parts to read the word and determine meaning.

2 Model Think aloud to analyze a long word for the base word, ending, prefix, and/or suffix and to identify the word and determine its meaning.

3 Guide Practice Provide examples of long words with endings (-ing, -ed, -s), prefixes (un-, re-, dis-, mis-, non-), and/or suffixes (-ly, -ness, -less, -ful, and so on). Help students analyze base words and parts.

4 Provide Feedback Encourage students to circle parts of the words to help identify parts and determine meaning.

Routine Card

Picture Walk Routine

To build concepts and vocabulary, conduct a structured picture walk before reading.

1 Prepare Preview the selection and list key concepts and vocabulary you wish to develop.

2 Discuss As students look at the pages, discuss illustrations, have students point to pictured items, and/or ask questions that target key concepts and vocabulary.

3 Elaborate Elaborate on students' responses to reinforce correct use of the vocabulary and to provide additional exposure to key concepts.

4 Practice For more practice with key concepts, have each student turn to a partner and do the picture walk using the key concept vocabulary.

Routine Card

Multisyllabic Word Routine

Teach students this Routine to chunk words with no recognizable parts.

1 Teach Tell students to look for chunks in words with no meaningful parts. They should say each chunk slowly and then say the chunks fast to make a whole word.

2 Model Think aloud to demonstrate breaking a word into chunks, saying each chunk slowly, and then saying the chunks fast to make a word.

3 Guide Practice Provide examples of long words with no meaningful parts. Help students chunk the words.

4 Provide Feedback If necessary, reteach by modeling how to break words into chunks.

Routine Card

Concept Vocabulary

Use this Routine to teach concept vocabulary.

1 Introduce the Word Relate the word to the week's concept. Supply a student-friendly definition.

2 Demonstrate Provide several familiar examples to demonstrate meaning.

3 Apply Have students demonstrate understanding with a simple activity.

4 Display the Word Relate the word to the concept by displaying it on a concept web. Have students identify word parts and practice reading the word.

5 Use the Word Often Encourage students to use the word often in their writing and speaking. Ask questions that require students to use the word.

Into the Ice

Group Time

DAY
1

ONLINE
PearsonSuccessNet.com

ROUTINE

① Build Background

REINFORCE CONCEPTS Display the Polar Exploration Concept Web. This week's concept is polar exploration. Exploration at the poles of the Earth, the North and South Poles, is just one type of exploration. Discuss the meaning of each word on the web, using the definitions on p. 408l and the Concept Vocabulary Routine on p. DI·1.

CONNECT TO READING This week you will read about some of the most famous polar explorers. The excerpt from *20,000 Leagues Under the Sea* is a fictional story about a visit to Antarctica. Using the information you know about the two regions, explain the ways in which you think the Arctic and Antarctica are similar. *(They are both very cold and covered with ice.)*

② Read Leveled Reader *Life in the Arctic*

BEFORE READING Using the Picture Walk Routine on p. DI·1, guide students through the text focusing on key concepts and vocabulary. Ask questions such as:

pp. 4–5 This selection gives readers information about the Arctic region and the different types of animals that can be found there. What does this map tell you about the Arctic? *(The Arctic region includes parts of three different continents.)*

pp. 6–7 Why do you think that polar bears' fur is white? *(It helps them blend in with their surroundings.)*

DURING READING Read pp. 3–5 aloud, while students track the print. Do a choral reading of pp. 6–9. If students are capable, have them read and discuss the remainder of the book with a partner. Ask: What kinds of animals live in the Arctic? Why is blubber or a thick coat of fur important to these animals' survival?

AFTER READING Encourage pairs of students to discuss how arctic animals might have been important to the explorers who came to the Arctic. We read *Life in the Arctic* to learn more about the animals that live in the Arctic. Understanding the life forms that exist in this cold, barren region will help us better understand the explorers' experiences in *Into the Ice.*

Monitor Progress

Selection Reading and Comprehension

If... students have difficulty reading the selection with a partner,	then... have them follow along as they listen to the Online Leveled Reader Audio.
If... students have trouble understanding where the Arctic is located,	then... look back at pp. 4–5 and discuss the diagram together.

For alternate Leveled Reader lesson plans that teach
🌀**Cause and Effect,** 🌀**Summarize,** and
Lesson Vocabulary, see pp. LR1–LR9.

On-Level

DAY 1

1 Build Background

DEVELOP VOCABULARY Write the word *thermometer,* and ask students to define it in their own words. *(something used to find out a temperature)* When have you seen someone use a thermometer? *(when I had a fever; to find out how cold it was outside)* Repeat this activity with the word *caribou* and other words from the Leveled Reader *Life Inside the Arctic Circle.* Use the Concept Vocabulary Routine on p. DI·1 as needed.

ROUTINE

2 Read Leveled Reader *Life Inside the Arctic Circle*

BEFORE READING Have students create T-charts with the labels Animals and People. As you read, look for information about how animals and people survive and adapt to living in an arctic climate. Note the information you find in the appropriate column of your T-chart.

DURING READING Have students follow along as you read pp. 3–9. Then let them complete the book on their own. Remind students to add facts to their T-charts as they read.

AFTER READING Have students compare the information they recorded on their T-charts. Point out that the information they learned about survival in the Arctic will help them as they read tomorrow's selection *Into the Ice.*

Advanced

DAY 1

1 Leveled Reader *The Race to the South Pole*

ROUTINE

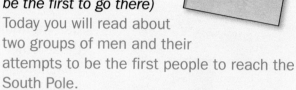

BEFORE READING Recall the Read Aloud story *20,000 Leagues Under the Sea.* What makes people want to explore harsh, unfamiliar places? *(to see it for themselves; to be the first to go there)* Today you will read about two groups of men and their attempts to be the first people to reach the South Pole.

CRITICAL THINKING Have students read the Leveled Reader independently. Encourage them to think critically. For example, ask:

• What do you think was the most difficult part of the Amundsen party's expedition?
• What could Scott's party have done differently to make their expedition successful?

AFTER READING Have students review the selection to find five or more unfamiliar words. Tell them to use context clues to come up with their own definition for each word. Direct students to verify their definitions using a dictionary or glossary and to then write paragraphs that include the correct usage of each word. Encourage students to share their paragraphs with you or with one another.

2 Independent Extension Activity

NOW TRY THIS Assign "Now Try This" on pp. 22–23 of *The Race to the South Pole* for students to work on throughout the week.

Into the Ice
Group Time

DAY 2

Audio CD AudioText

① Word Study/Phonics

LESSON VOCABULARY Use p. 410b to review the meanings of *conquer, destiny, expedition, insulated, isolation, navigator, provisions,* and *verify.* Have individuals practice reading the words from word cards.

DECODING MULTISYLLABIC WORDS Write *penetrating,* saying the word as you write it. Then model how to use meaningful parts to read longer words. First I look for meaningful parts. If I see a part I know, such as *-ing* or *-es,* then I look for a base word. In this word, I see *pen* and *trat,* which probably has a long sound since the *t* is not doubled. I then say the parts of the word: *pen e trat ing.* Then I read the word.

Use the Multisyllabic Word Routine on p. DI·1 to help students read these other words from *Into the Ice: proposal, deliberately, scientific, treacherous, triumphant, unprepared,* and *theoretical.* Be sure students understand the meanings of words such as *treacherous.*

Use *Strategies for Word Analysis,* Lesson 16, with students who have difficulty mastering word analysis and need practice with decodable text.

② Read Leveled Reader *Into the Ice,* pp. 412–421

BEFORE READING *Life in the Arctic* explained where the Arctic is located as well as the types of wildlife that live in its harsh climate. Think about what you've learned about the Arctic as you read *Into the Ice.*

Using the Picture Walk Routine on p. DI·1, guide students through the text asking questions such as those listed below. Read the question on p. 413. Together, set a purpose for reading.

pp. 412–415 What do these illustrations tell you about the landscape of the Arctic? *(It is cold and icy.)*

pp. 416–421 What types of transportation do you see on these pages? *(a sailing ship, a hot air balloon, and a sled pulled by dogs)* What are some other kinds of transportation? Why might they *not* be shown here?

DURING READING Follow the Guiding Comprehension routine on pp. 414–421. Have students read along with you while tracking the print or do a choral reading. Stop every two pages to ask what has happened so far. Prompt as necessary.

- Why did Fridtjof Nansen choose to freeze his ship into the pack ice?
- What did you learn about polar exploration that you didn't already know?

AFTER READING What have you learned so far? What do you think you will learn about next? Reread passages with students for comprehension as needed.

Monitor Progress

Word and Selection Reading

If...	then...
If... students have difficulty reading multisyllabic words in the selection,	**then...** have them look for and read meaningful parts in the words or have them chunk words with no recognizable parts.
If... students need practice reading words fluently,	**then...** use the Fluent Word Reading Routine on the DI tab.
If... students have difficulty reading along with the group,	**then...** have them follow along as they listen to the AudioText.

Advanced

ROUTINE

① Extend Vocabulary

🔊 **CONTEXT CLUES** Choose and read a sentence or passage containing a difficult word, such as this passage from p. 6 of *The Race to the South Pole:* "This had been Amundsen's original plan, but he abandoned it once he learned the North Pole had already been discovered and turned his sights to the South Pole." What does the word *abandoned* mean? *(gave up entirely)* How did you determine the word's meaning? (*I used the context clues* had been his original plan, but, *and* North Pole had already been discovered.) Discuss why the context clues are helpful in determining the meanings of unfamiliar words, and remind students to use the strategy as they read *Into the Ice.*

② Read *Into the Ice,* pp. 412–421

BEFORE READING Today you will read about northern polar explorers. The selection *Into the Ice* will explain the efforts that were taken by various groups in their attempts to be the first to reach the North Pole. As you read, think about the conditions that a polar explorer must endure to reach his or her goal.

Have students create a KWL chart for their Strategy Response Log (p. 412). Encourage them to note on their charts what they have learned as they read.

CRITICAL THINKING Have students read pp. 414–421 independently. Encourage them to think critically. For example, ask:

• Why do you think these men were so determined to reach the North Pole?

AFTER READING Have partners discuss the selection and share their Strategy Response Log entries. Encourage the pairs to take turns discussing what they think they will find out as they read the final segment of the selection. Then have each student write a conclusion to the selection based on his or her prediction.

DAY 2

INTO THE ICE
The Story of Arctic Exploration
by Lynn Curlee

Audio CD   AudioText

Into the Ice
Group Time

DAY 3

Audio CD AudioText

ROUTINE

1 Reinforce Comprehension

⊙ SKILL CAUSE AND EFFECT Have students tell what cause and effect are *(an effect is what happened; a cause is why something happened)* and clue words that often signal causes and effects *(because, so, since)*. If necessary, review the meaning and provide a model. A cause is defined as "why something happened" and an effect is defined as "what happened." *He got a bad grade because he didn't study for his test* shows cause and effect. His getting a bad grade is what happened, or the effect, and "because he didn't study for his test" is why it happened, the cause or reason.

Have students list the events that occurred between Peary and Cook in the order in which they happened. Have them try to identify the cause-and-effect relationships between these events. For instance, Peary refused to allow Cook to publish his article. Then Cook decided to try for the Pole himself. Ask students if they think the first event caused the second. Have them explain their answer.

2 Read *Into the Ice,* pp.422–425

BEFORE READING Have students retell what happened in the selection so far. Ask: What happened to Fridjtof Nansen and Hjalmar Johansen between the time that they reached the island and June of 1896? Reread the last two paragraphs on pp. 416–417 and model how to summarize the events. The two men had made little progress in two weeks. They were running out of food and needed to get to land. They found an island and waited out the winter. In the spring, they were eventually picked up by another expedition. Remind students to summarize as they read the rest of *Into the Ice.* **⊙ STRATEGY Summarize**

DURING READING Follow the Guiding Comprehension routine on pp. 422–425. Have students read along with you while tracking print or do a choral reading. Stop every two pages to ask students what has happened so far. Prompt as necessary.

- When did Robert Peary's group reach the North Pole? Why was that date controversial?
- What was Joseph Fletcher known for?

AFTER READING What have you learned about polar exploration from reading *Into the Ice?* Reread with students for comprehension as needed. Tell them that tomorrow they will read "Polar Zones," which will tell them more about the northern and southern polar regions.

Monitor Progress

Word and Selection Reading

If... students have difficulty reading multisyllabic words in the selection,	then... have them look for and read meaningful parts in the words or have them chunk words with no recognizable parts.
If... students have difficulty reading along with the group,	then... have them follow along as they listen to the AudioText.

Advanced

ROUTINE

1 Extend Comprehension

◉ SKILL CAUSE AND EFFECT Have students think about some causes and effects in their daily lives. Perhaps they woke up in the morning (effect) because their alarm went off (cause). They may have chosen cereal for breakfast (effect) because there was no oatmeal left (cause). Have students make a list of causes and effects that are a part of their daily lives. Then have them explain which are causes, which are effects, and why. Remind students that one cause can have more than one effect, and an effect can be a result of more than one cause.

◉ STRATEGY SUMMARIZE Have volunteers take turns summarizing the events of *Into the Ice.* Have each student reread two or three paragraphs and summarize their contents for the other students. Remind students that summarizing means relaying only the most important information, leaving out details or unimportant information.

2 Read *Into the Ice,* pp. 422–425

DAY 3

AudioText

BEFORE READING Have students recall what has happened in the selection so far. Remind them to look for cause-and-effect relationships as they read the remainder of the selection.

CREATIVE THINKING Have students read pp. 422–425 independently. Encourage them to think critically and creatively. For example, ask:

• How are Nansen and Peary similar and different?

AFTER READING Have students complete the Strategy Response Log activity (p. 424). Then ask students to imagine that they are part of one of the expeditions to the North Pole featured in *Into the Ice.* Have students write a letter home describing a day on the expedition.

Into the Ice

Group Time

Audio CD AudioText

Monitor Progress

Word and Selection Reading

If... students have difficulty reading multisyllabic words in the selection,	then... have them look for and read meaningful parts in the words or have them chunk words with no recognizable parts.
If... students have difficulty reading along with the group,	then... have them follow along as they listen to the AudioText.

Strategic Intervention

ROUTINE

1 Practice Retelling

REVIEW MAIN IDEAS Help students identify the main ideas in *Into the Ice.* List the ideas students mention. Then ask questions to help students differentiate between essential and nonessential information.

RETELL Using the Retelling Cards, have students work with partners to retell *Into the Ice.* Show partners how to summarize in as few words as possible. Monitor retelling and prompt students as needed. For example, ask:

- Tell me the major events in order.
- What did you learn from reading this selection?
- Why do you think the author wrote this selection?

If students struggle, model a fluent retelling.

Grade 6
Retelling Cards

PEARSON
Scott Foresman

2 Read "Polar Zones"

BEFORE READING Read the genre information on p. 428. Recall the Leveled Reader *Life in the Arctic,* and hold up a copy for students to see. *Life in the Arctic* is another example of expository nonfiction. How did it present facts and information about the wildlife of the Arctic? *(It had text as well as graphic elements, such as a diagram, photographs, and captions.)*

Read the remainder of the panel on p. 428. Then have students point out the selection's text features, such as photographs, captions, the sidebar, and the map.

DURING READING Have students read along with you while tracking the print or do a choral reading of the selection. Stop to discuss how to read selections with multiple text features.

AFTER READING Have students share their reactions to the selection. Then guide them through the Reading Across Texts and Writing Across Texts activities, prompting if necessary.

- In what ways are the Arctic and Antarctic regions similar?
- Why might people want to explore such regions?

Advanced

ROUTINE

① Read "Polar Zones"

CREATIVE THINKING Have students read pp. 428–429 independently. Encourage them to think critically. For example, ask:

- In what way does the information in "Polar Zones" add to what you already know about polar regions?
- What do you think would be the most difficult part of living in a polar climate?

AFTER READING Discuss Reading Across Texts. Have students do Writing Across Texts independently.

② Extend Genre Study

RESEARCH Have students find other examples of expository nonfiction in magazines from the school library. Have them make a list of the titles of at least five articles and those text features in each that help them determine that what they've chosen is expository nonfiction.

WRITE Have students choose one of the expository nonfiction articles they've found and write a sidebar to accompany the information in the article. Remind them that the sidebar information must be topically connected and should be interesting to readers.

DAY 4

AudioText

Into the Ice

Group Time

ONLINE

PearsonSuccessNet.com

1 Reread for Fluency

MODEL Read aloud pp. 3–4 of the Leveled Reader *Life in the Arctic,* pausing at appropriate places for commas, periods, and exclamation marks so that listeners can follow what you are saying. Then read p. 5 without pausing at the periods and question marks at the end of the sentences. Have students tell you which model sounded better. Discuss how pausing at appropriate places—using punctuation as a guide—helps listeners follow what you are saying.

PRACTICE Have students reread passages from *Life in the Arctic* with a partner or individually. For optimal fluency, they should reread three or four times. As students read, monitor fluency and provide corrective feedback. Students in this group are assessed in Weeks 2 and 4.

2 Read Retell Leveled Reader *Life in the Arctic*

Model how to skim the book, retelling as you skim. Then ask students to retell the book, presenting first the introductory pages, then each type of arctic animal. Prompt them as needed.

- What do you learn from the first three pages?
- What information does the book give you about polar bears?

Monitor Progress

Fluency

If... students have difficulty reading fluently,	then... provide additional fluency practice by pairing nonfluent readers with fluent ones.

For alternate Leveled Reader lesson plans that teach
⟳ **Cause and Effect,** ⟳ **Summarize,** and
Lesson Vocabulary, see pp. LR1–LR9.

On-Level

1 Reread for Fluency ROUTINE

MODEL Read aloud p. 3 of the Leveled Reader *Life Inside the Arctic Circle,* pausing at appropriate places during and at the end of sentences. Have students pay attention to the way you pause during and after sentences. Discuss how pausing appropriately while reading helps listeners better understand the message you are trying to convey.

PRACTICE Have students reread passages from *Life Inside the Arctic Circle* with a partner or individually. For optimal fluency, they should reread three or four times. As students read, monitor fluency and provide corrective feedback. Students in this group are assessed in Week 3.

2 Read Retell Leveled Reader *Life Inside the Arctic Circle*

BEFORE READING Have students use the subheads and photographs to retell the selection, *Life Inside the Arctic Circle.* Prompt as needed.

- What is this book mostly about?
- What did you learn from reading this section?
- Why do you think the author wrote this selection?

Advanced

1 Reread for Fluency ROUTINE

PRACTICE Have students reread passages from the Leveled Reader *The Race to the South Pole* with a partner or individually. As students read, monitor fluency and provide corrective feedback. If students read fluently on the first reading, they do not need to reread three or four times. Assess the fluency of this group using p. 429a.

2 Revisit Leveled Reader *The Race to the South Pole*

RETELL Have students retell the Leveled Reader *The Race to the South Pole.*

NOW TRY THIS Have students complete their projects. You may wish to review their reports and see whether they need a different type of transport or additional supplies. Have them present their projects.

Group Time

DAY 1

ONLINE

PearsonSuccessNet.com

Strategic Intervention

ROUTINE

1 Build Background

REINFORCE CONCEPTS Display the Animal Research Concept Web. This week's concept is *animal research.* Scientists make important discoveries through animal research. What they learn can benefit both animals and people. Discuss the meaning of each word on the web, using the definitions on p. 430l and the Concept Vocabulary Routine on p. DI·1.

CONNECT TO READING This week you will read about the discoveries people make by studying animals. Many of these discoveries can help us protect animals. Do you think that the research in "Something in the Elephants' Silence" helps protect elephants? Why or why not? *(Yes, because it helps scientists track elephant populations.)*

2 Read Leveled Reader *Great Apes*

BEFORE READING Using the Picture Walk Routine on p. DI·1, guide students through the text focusing on key concepts and vocabulary. Ask questions such as:

pp. 3–4 This selection explains what all great apes have in common. After looking at the photographs, what is one thing that great apes eat? *(plants)*

pp. 5–6 The map on p. 5 shows the area where orangutans can be found. Have students locate Indonesia on a world map. These islands are tropical rain forests. What do you know about the climate of tropical rain forests?

DURING READING Read pp. 3–4 aloud, while students track the print. Do a choral reading of pp. 5–9. If students are capable, have them read and discuss the remainder of the book with a partner. Ask: Why are ape sanctuaries important? Why would researchers want to teach gorillas to communicate with sign language?

AFTER READING Have pairs of students discuss the ways that apes communicate in the wild. We read *Great Apes* to learn about how smart apes really are. Understanding how smart apes are will help us when we read *The Chimpanzees I Love.*

Monitor Progress

Selection Reading and Comprehension

If... students have difficulty reading the selection with a partner,	then... have them follow along as they listen to the Online Leveled Reader Audio.
If... students have trouble understanding how animal research can protect animals,	then... reread p. 23 and discuss animal research together.

For alternate Leveled Reader lesson plans that teach
🔖 **Author's Purpose,** 🔖 **Answer Questions,**
and **Lesson Vocabulary,** see pp. LR10–LR18.

DAY 1

The Chimpanzees I Love

On-Level

1 Build Background

DEVELOP VOCABULARY Write the word *data* and ask students to define it in their own words. *(information or facts gathered from research)* What reasons might scientists have for collecting data? *(to learn about how or why things act as they do)* Repeat this activity with the word *surveys* and other words from the Leveled Reader *How Animals Change: The Interaction of Animals and Scientists.* Use the Concept Vocabulary Routine on p. DI·1 as needed.

2 Read Leveled Reader *How Animals Change: The Interaction of Animals and Scientists*

BEFORE READING Have students create a three-column chart. In the first column, list the ways scientists learn about animals. In the second column, record details about each method. In the last column, students should tell if they feel each method is a responsible form of research. This book talks about the different tools that scientists use to study animals in the wild.

As you read, record on your three-column chart the tools scientists use, the details about each tool, and finally whether you feel the method is a responsible form of research.

DURING READING Have students follow along as you read pp. 3–9. Then let them complete the book on their own. Remind students to add information to their three-column charts as they read.

AFTER READING Have students compare the facts on their three-column charts. Point out that this information will help them as they read tomorrow's selection *The Chimpanzees I Love.*

Advanced

1 Read Leveled Reader *Captive or Free: Zoos in Debate*

BEFORE READING Recall the Read Aloud "Something in the Elephants' Silence." How might this research help elephants in zoos? *(Zoo keepers will understand the behaviors, traits, and emotional needs of captive elephants.)* Today you will read about the pros and cons of keeping animals in zoos.

CRITICAL THINKING Have students read the Leveled Reader independently. Encourage them to think critically. For example, ask:

- How might the information learned from animals in zoos help protect animals in the wild?
- Why are animal rights activists opposed to zoos? What might be some flaws in their thinking?

AFTER READING Have students review the selection to find five or more unfamiliar words and determine their meanings by using context clues or by consulting a dictionary. Then ask them to write statements or questions that both include the words and convey their meanings. Have students meet together or with you to discuss the selection and the statements they wrote.

2 Independent Extension Activity

NOW TRY THIS Assign "Now Try This" on pp. 22–23 of *Captive or Free: Zoos in Debate* for students to work on throughout the week.

The Chimpanzees I Love

Group Time

DAY 2

Audio CD AudioText

Strategic Intervention

ROUTINE

1 Word Study/Phonics

LESSON VOCABULARY Use p. 432b to review the meanings of *captive, companionship, existence, ordeal, primitive, sanctuaries,* and *stimulating.* Have individuals practice reading the words from word cards.

DECODING MULTISYLLABIC WORDS Write the word *intimidate,* saying the word as you write it. Then model how to use meaningful parts. I see a chunk at the beginning of the word: *in.* I see a chunk in the middle too: *tim* and *i.* Finally, I see a chunk at the end of the word: *date.* I say each chunk slowly: *in tim i date.* I say the chunks fast to make a whole word: *intimidate.* Is it a real word? Yes, I know the word *intimidate.*

Use the Multisyllabic Word Routine on DI·1 to help students read these other words from *The Chimpanzees I Love: offspring, endangered, behavior, populations, organizations, solutions, recognize, uncomfortable,* and *memories.* Be sure that students understand the meanings of words such as *endangered* and *offspring.*

Use *Strategies for Word Analysis,* Lesson 17, with students who have difficulty mastering word analysis and need practice with decodable text.

2 Read *The Chimpanzees I Love,* pp. 434–441

BEFORE READING *Great Apes* showed how intelligent apes really are. Think about what apes can do as you read *The Chimpanzees I Love.*

Using the Picture Walk Routine on DI·1, guide students through the text asking questions such as those listed below. Read the question on p. 435. Together, set a purpose for reading.

pp. 434–437 Do these photos show how chimpanzees interact with each other and humans? Do they seem friendly? *(yes, chimpanzees seem to be very social and friendly animals)*

pp. 438–441 What two kinds of environments do you see chimpanzees in? *(they are in cages and in natural settings)* Do you think that zoos should have more natural settings for animals? Why? *(yes, because chimpanzees will be happier if they have lots of room to live)*

DURING READING Follow the Guiding Comprehension routine on pp. 436–441. Have students read along with you while tracking the print or do a choral reading. Stop every two pages to ask what they have learned so far. Prompt as necessary.

• What are two things chimpanzees can do that show us they are smart?
• What is wrong with people buying baby chimpanzees?

AFTER READING What have you learned so far about chimpanzees? What do you think you will learn about tomorrow? Reread passages with students for comprehension as needed.

Monitor Progress

Word and Selection Reading

If...	then...
If... students have difficulty reading multisyllabic words in the selection,	**then...** have them look for and read meaningful parts in the words or have them chunk words with no recognizable parts.
If... students need practice reading words fluently,	**then...** use the Fluent Word Reading Routine on the DI tab.
If... students have difficulty reading along with the group,	**then...** have them follow along as they listen to the AudioText.

Advanced

ROUTINE

1 Extend Vocabulary

🔊 **DICTIONARY/GLOSSARY** Choose and read a sentence or passage containing a difficult word, such as this passage from p. 4 of *Captive or Free: Zoos in Debate:* "The idea of holding animals in zoos has become very controversial in the last century." Use a dictionary to find out what *controversial* means. (*Controversial means something that is marked by controversy or debate.*) Discuss why sometimes a dictionary gives a more helpful definition of the word. Remind students to look up any difficult words as they read *The Chimpanzees I Love.*

2 Read *The Chimpanzees I Love,* pp. 434–441

BEFORE READING Today you will read an expository nonfiction selection about chimpanzees. It describes the struggles of people like Jane Goodall to protect chimpanzee populations around the world. As you read, think about possible solutions for helping to protect chimpanzees.

Have students write three questions on what they want to find out about chimpanzees for the Strategy Response Log (p. 434). Have them check to see if their questions are answered as they read the selection.

CREATIVE THINKING Have students read pp. 434–441 independently. Encourage them to think critically and creatively. For example, ask:

• Why is research with chimpanzees so controversial?

AFTER READING Have partners discuss the selection and share their Strategy Response Log questions. Have students create a discussion panel to brainstorm ideas for ways they and others can help animals be treated responsibly. Have them present their ideas to the class.

DAY 2

The Chimpanzees I Love
Saving Their World and Ours
by Jane Goodall

Audio CD   AudioText

The Chimpanzees I Love
Group Time

DAY 3

Audio CD · AudioText

ROUTINE

1 Reinforce Comprehension

SKILL AUTHOR'S PURPOSE Have students tell what author's purpose is *(it is the author's reasons for writing as he or she has)* and list four common reasons authors have for writing *(to persuade, to inform, to entertain, or to express ideas or feelings).* If necessary, review the meaning and provide a model. Knowing the author's purpose affects the way I read a selection and helps me understand why the author has written it. *Chimps can learn 300 signs or more* tells me that chimpanzees are intelligent animals. The author's purpose is to inform me about what smart animals chimpanzees are.

Ask students to make a statement about animals that reveals their purpose, or have them choose a statement from a group of statements about animals. For example, ask: Which of the following statements reveals that the author's purpose is to inform? *(Dogs have 42 teeth.)*

> **My dog Rex likes to watch cartoons.**
> **Dogs have 42 teeth.**
> **We need to build more animal shelters.**

2 Read *The Chimpanzees I Love,* pp. 442–447

BEFORE READING Have students retell what they have learned so far in the selection. Ask: What are the conditions like for chimpanzees in research labs? Reread the second paragraph on p. 441 and model how to think and search for an answer. In the passage, Jane Goodall says that the chimpanzees had thick steel bars on the sides, floor, and ceiling. Then she says they didn't have any windows in the lab. She also says the chimpanzees are separated from other chimpanzees. Remind students that as they read *The Chimpanzees I Love,* they may have to think and search for answers to questions. **STRATEGY Answer Questions**

DURING READING Follow the Guiding Comprehension routine on pp. 442–447. Have students read along with you while tracking print or do a choral reading. Stop every two pages and ask students what they have learned so far. Prompt as necessary.

• What are some reasons chimpanzees in the wild are disappearing?
• How long will chimpanzees normally live?

AFTER READING How does the selection address the problem of animal research? Reread with students for comprehension as needed. Tell them that tomorrow they will read "'Going Ape' Over Language" about research that is teaching chimpanzees and gorillas sign language.

Monitor Progress

Word and Selection Reading

If... students have difficulty reading multisyllabic words in the selection,	then... have them look for and read meaningful parts in the words or have them chunk words with no recognizable parts.
If... students have difficulty reading along with the group,	then... have them follow along as they listen to the AudioText.

Advanced

1 Extend Comprehension

◎ SKILL AUTHOR'S PURPOSE Have students evaluate the credibility and reliability of the author's information. Have them write a list of questions they can ask themselves to assess the reliability of the information, such as: Does the author use mostly statements of opinion or statements of fact? What is the author's purpose? Does the author list sources for any supporting evidence?

◎ STRATEGY ANSWER QUESTIONS Have a volunteer read the first full paragraph on p. 440 to the top three lines of p. 441 while other students generate a list of questions that could be asked about the text. Have students ask questions such as:

- How can zoos work with research laboratories to care for chimpanzees?
- Why are chimpanzees an important part of research laboratories?

DAY 3

Audio CD   AudioText

2 Read *The Chimpanzees I Love*, pp. 442–447

BEFORE READING Have students recall what information they have learned so far in the selection. Remind them to look for statements of fact and statements of opinion and to generate a list of questions they would like answered as they read the remainder of the selection.

CRITICAL THINKING Have students read pp. 442–447 independently. Encourage them to think critically. For example, ask:

- How can we eliminate our need to use chimpanzees for entertainment purposes?

AFTER READING Have students complete the Strategy Response Log activity (p. 446). Then have them write other questions about chimpanzees they could research, such as recent examples of chimpanzee intelligence, whether their numbers are still declining in the world, how chimpanzees behave in groups, and so on. Students can research to find answers and present their findings to the class. They should be sure to document their sources of information.

The Chimpanzees I Love

Group Time

DAY 4

Audio CD — AudioText

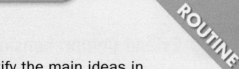

ROUTINE

Strategic Intervention

1 Practice Retelling

REVIEW MAIN IDEAS Help students identify the main ideas in *The Chimpanzees I Love.* List the ideas students mention. Then ask questions to help students differentiate between essential and nonessential information.

RETELL Using the Retelling Cards, have students work with partners to retell the important ideas in *The Chimpanzees I Love.* Show partners how to summarize in as few words as possible. Monitor retelling and prompt students as needed. For example, ask:

- What is this selection mostly about?
- Why do you think the author wrote this selection?

If students struggle, model a fluent retelling.

2 Read "'Going Ape' Over Language"

BEFORE READING Read the genre information on p. 450. Recall the Read Aloud "Something in the Elephants' Silence," rereading portions of the text as needed. *We have read several expository nonfiction selections this week. What did "Something in the Elephants' Silence" tell us about animal research? (that by studying animals we can help protect them)* As we read "'Going Ape' Over Language," think about the information you learn.

Read the rest of the panel on p. 450. Then have students scan the pages looking for quotation marks.

DURING READING Have students read along with you while tracking the print or do a choral reading of the selection. Stop to discuss difficult language, such as proper nouns and terms relating to the study of language.

AFTER READING Have students share their reactions to the selection. Then guide them through the Reading Across Texts and Writing Across Texts activities, prompting if necessary.

- How many spoken words does Koko understand?
- Does Washoe have feelings?

Monitor Progress

Word and Selection Reading

If... students have difficulty reading multisyllabic words in the selection,	**then...** have them look for and read meaningful parts in the words or have them chunk words with no recognizable parts.
If... students have difficulty reading along with the group,	**then...** have them follow along as they listen to the AudioText.

Advanced

ROUTINE

1 Read "'Going Ape' Over Language"

CRITICAL THINKING Have students read pp. 450–455 independently. Encourage them to think critically. For example, ask:

- What do Washoe's responses show about her ability to experience emotion?
- Are the objections to training chimpanzees valid? Why or why not?

AFTER READING Discuss Reading Across Texts. Have students do Writing Across Texts independently.

2 Extend Genre Study

RESEARCH Have students use online or print resources to find other expository nonfiction articles on how captured wild animals have been treated by humans. Have them list the titles, noting the author's purpose and the supporting evidence.

WRITE Have students design and write a pamphlet that would persuade people to support better treatment of chimpanzees.

DAY 4

Audio CD   **AudioText**

The Chimpanzees I Love

Group Time

ONLINE

PearsonSuccessNet.com

DAY 5

Strategic Intervention

ROUTINE

① Reread for Fluency

MODEL Read aloud pp. 3–4 of the Leveled Reader *Great Apes,* emphasizing the rhythmic patterns of language. Have students notice how you pause for commas, dashes, and periods. Discuss how you pause slightly longer at the ends of sentences than for internal punctuation. Then quickly read pp. 5–7 without pausing for commas and periods. Have students tell you which sounded better. Discuss how commas, dashes, and periods create a more pleasing rhythm.

PRACTICE Have students reread passages from *Great Apes* with a partner or individually. For optimal fluency, they should reread three or four times. As students read, monitor fluency and provide corrective feedback. Assess the fluency of students in this group using p. 455a.

② Retell Leveled Reader *Great Apes*

Model how to skim the book, retelling as you skim. Then ask students to retell the book, one section at a time. Prompt them as needed.

- What is the section on gorillas mostly about?
- What did you learn from reading this section?

Monitor Progress

Fluency

| If... students have difficulty reading fluently, | then... provide additional fluency practice by pairing nonfluent readers with fluent ones. |

For alternate Leveled Reader lesson plans that teach
👁 **Author's Purpose,** 👁 **Answer Questions,**
and **Lesson Vocabulary,** see pp. LR10–LR18.

On-Level

1 Reread for Fluency ROUTINE

MODEL Read p. 3 of the Leveled Reader *How Animals Change: The Interaction of Animals and Scientists,* emphasizing the rhythmic patterns of language. Have students notice how you pause for commas, dashes, and periods. Discuss how you pause slightly longer at the ends of sentences than for internal punctuation.

PRACTICE Have students reread passages from *How Animals Change: The Interaction of Animals and Scientists* with a partner or individually. For optimal fluency, they should reread three or four times. As students read, monitor fluency and provide corrective feedback. Students in this group are assessed in Week 3.

2 Retell Leveled Reader *How Animals Change: The Interaction of Animals and Scientists*

Have students use subheads and illustrations as a guide to summarize the important facts they learned from each section of the book. Prompt as needed.

- What did you learn from reading this book?
- What was the author trying to teach us?
- Why do you think the author wrote this book?

Advanced

1 Reread for Fluency ROUTINE

PRACTICE Have students reread passages from the Leveled Reader *Captive or Free: Zoos in Debate* with a partner or individually. As students read, monitor fluency and provide corrective feedback. If students read fluently on the first reading, they do not need to reread three or four times. Students in this group were assessed in Week 1.

2 Revisit Leveled Reader *Captive or Free: Zoos in Debate*

RETELL Have students retell the Leveled Reader *Captive or Free: Zoos in Debate.*

NOW TRY THIS Have students complete their projects. You may wish to review their sources and see whether they need any additional supplies or resources. Have them form pairs and debate each other. You may want to have the whole class listen to some of the debates.

Group Time

ROUTINE

DAY 1

Leveled Reader
Database

ONLINE

PearsonSuccessNet.com

1 Build Background

REINFORCE CONCEPTS Display the American Frontier Concept Web. This week's concept is *the American frontier*. A *frontier* is the farthest point of a settled country. The American frontier was an area of land in the middle and western parts of the United States. People moving from the southern and eastern parts of the United States settled in this area in the late 1800s. Discuss the meaning of each word on the web, using the definitions on p. 456l and the Concept Vocabulary Routine on p. DI·1.

CONNECT TO READING This week you will read about people who settled the American frontier and the difficulties they faced. Davy Crockett, from "Under the Coonskin Cap," was a frontiersman. Why do you think he was so successful at surviving on the frontier? *(He was good at hunting and fishing, and he knew how to survive in nature.)*

2 Read Leveled Reader *A Very Special Gift*

BEFORE READING Using the Picture Walk Routine on p. DI·1, guide students through the text focusing on key concepts and vocabulary. Ask questions such as:

pp. 4–5 This story is about a family that travels to their new home on the frontier. What does the frontier land in the picture look like? Is it hilly or flat? *(flat)* Yes, the land is very flat with no trees or other buildings nearby.

pp. 6–7 The stamp on p. 7 commemorates The Homestead Act of 1862. This law gave citizens 160 acres of land, as long as they worked on the land for five years and built a house. Do you think this was an easy thing to do? Why or why not? *(No, because families had to build their own homes and farm without machines.)* Homesteaders worked very hard to prepare the land and build their sod houses.

DURING READING Read pp. 3–9 aloud, while students track the print. Do a choral reading of pp. 10–13. If students are capable, have them read and discuss the remainder of the book with a partner. Ask: What special gift did the Johnson family receive from the cowboy? How did others help the family survive the journey to a new home on the frontier?

AFTER READING Have pairs of students discuss life on the American frontier. We read A *Very Special Gift* to learn how one African American family found a new home on the American frontier. Understanding this family's experiences will help us as we read *Black Frontiers*.

Monitor Progress

Selection Reading and Comprehension

If... students have difficulty reading the selection with a partner,	then... have them follow along as they listen to the Online Leveled Reader Audio.
If... students have trouble understanding how people helped each other on the American frontier,	then... reread pp. 12–14 and discuss the illustrations together.

For alternate Leveled Reader lesson plans that teach
⟳ **Cause and Effect,** ⟳ **Prior Knowledge,** and
Lesson Vocabulary, see pp. LR19–LR27.

On-Level

ROUTINE

① Build Background

DEVELOP VOCABULARY Write the word *scout* and ask students to think of a synonym for it. *(lookout, spy)* What kinds of things might a scout try to find out? *(how many soldiers are in the enemy army, where they are, what they are planning, and what weapons they have)* Repeat this activity with the word *hardships* and other words from the Leveled Reader *A Very Special Gift.* Use the Concept Vocabulary Routine on p. DI·1 as needed.

② Read Leveled Reader *Homesteaders in Nebraska*

BEFORE READING Have students fill out Venn diagrams to compare and contrast their lives with Timothy, the boy they will read about in the story. Think about how yours and Timothy's lives are alike and different. Record what you learn on your Venn diagram.

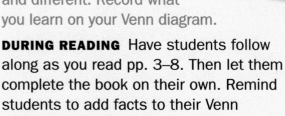

DURING READING Have students follow along as you read pp. 3–8. Then let them complete the book on their own. Remind students to add facts to their Venn diagrams as they read.

AFTER READING Have students compare their Venn diagrams with others. Point out that knowing how people lived on the American frontier will help them as they read tomorrow's story *Black Frontiers.*

Advanced

ROUTINE

① Read Leveled Reader *Grizzled Bill Turns Over a New Leaf*

BEFORE READING Recall the Read Aloud selection "Under the Coonskin Cap." Why do you think Davy Crockett became a legend on the American frontier? *(He entertained others by telling tall tales about himself, and he accomplished a lot, from being a scout in the Creek War to serving in the legislature. He also fought at the Alamo.)*

CRITICAL THINKING Have students read the Leveled Reader independently. Encourage them to think critically. For example, ask:

- What was wrong with the way Grizzled Bill helped poor people?
- Was the justice system on the American frontier different from the way our society deals with criminals today? If so, how?

AFTER READING Have students review the selection to find five or more unfamiliar words and determine their meanings by using context clues or by consulting a dictionary. Then ask them to create a vocabulary activity for a classmate to complete. Students can create fill-in-the-blank sentences, a crossword puzzle, or an activity to match words to definitions. Have students meet together or with you to discuss the selection and complete the activities.

② Independent Extension Activity

KEEP A JOURNAL Have students use print or online resources to find out more about the events that led up to the Battle of the Alamo. Tell students to imagine they are United States settlers that revolt against the Mexican government in Texas in 1835. Tell them to write several journal entries describing these events.

Black Frontiers
Group Time

DAY 2

ROUTINE

1 Word Study/Phonics

LESSON VOCABULARY Use p. 458b to review the meanings of *bondage, commissioned, earthen, encounter, homesteaders,* and *settlement.* Have individuals practice reading the words from word cards.

DECODING MULTISYLLABIC WORDS Write *Israelites,* saying the word as you write it. Then model how to use meaningful parts to read longer words. This is a multisyllabic word formed from the base word *Israel. Israel* was a kingdom long ago that is talked about in the Bible. It is also a country in the Middle East. The suffix *-ite* means "a person from," so *Israelites* are people from Israel. Use the Multisyllabic Word Routine on p. DI·1 to help students read these other words from *Black Frontiers: slithering, migrated, designated, legacy, desolate, courageous,* and *prejudice.* Be sure students understand the meanings of words such as *legacy* and *desolate.*

Use *Strategies for Word Analysis,* Lesson 18, with students who have difficulty mastering word analysis and need practice with decodable text.

2 Read *Black Frontiers,* pp. 460–467

BEFORE READING *A Very Special Gift* described the difficulties one family of homesteaders had on the way to their new home on the frontier. Think about their experiences as you read *Black Frontiers.*

Using the Picture Walk Routine on p. DI·1, guide students through the text asking questions such as those listed below. Read the question on p. 461. Together, set a purpose for reading.

pp. 460–461 Was this picture taken recently or long ago? *(long ago)* We can tell from the old-fashioned clothes, the black-and-white photograph, and the men on horseback that this was taken long ago.

pp. 464–465 What is this house made of? *(sod)* The house was made of sod. Why was it not made of wood or brick? *(Sod was the only material they had.)* The homesteaders knew there were few trees and little clay to use for wood or brick houses.

DURING READING Follow the Guiding Comprehension Routine on pp. 462–467. Have students read along with you while tracking the print or do a choral reading. Stop every two pages to ask what has happened so far. Prompt as necessary.

- Why did many former slaves leave the South after the Civil War?
- Who were the Exodusters?

AFTER READING What have you learned so far in the selection? Where did the people in the selection settle? Reread passages with students for comprehension as needed.

Audio CD AudioText

Monitor Progress

Word and Selection Reading	
If... students have difficulty reading multisyllabic words in the selection,	**then...** have them look for and read meaningful parts in the words or have them chunk words with no recognizable parts.
If... students need practice reading words fluently,	**then...** use the Fluent Word Reading Routine on the DI tab.
If... students have difficulty reading along with the group,	**then...** have them follow along as they listen to the AudioText.

Advanced

1 Extend Vocabulary

CONTEXT CLUES Choose and read a sentence or passage containing a difficult word, such as this passage from p. 10 of *Grizzled Bill Turns Over a New Leaf:* "I always make allowances for idle gossip, rumors, and speculation. When a man is a success, it can cause some tongues to wag." What does the word *speculation* mean? *(the act of guessing about what someone is doing or thinking)* How did you determine the word's meaning? *(I used the context clues* gossip, rumors, *and* cause some tongues to wag*)* Discuss why context clues are helpful, and remind students to use the strategy as they read *Black Frontiers*.

2 Read *Black Frontiers*, pp. 460–467

BEFORE READING Today you will read a nonfiction selection about African Americans who settled on the American frontier. As you read, think about what you have learned about other people's experiences on the frontier.

Have students write what they already know about frontier life in their Strategy Response Logs (p. 460). Have them add what they learn as they read.

CREATIVE THINKING Have students read pp. 460–467 independently. Encourage them to think critically and creatively. For example, ask:

• How did the first black pioneer families make it easier for those who came after?

AFTER READING Have partners discuss the selection and share their Strategy Response Log entries. Encourage them to think about the skills or personal qualities that were needed to be a pioneer. Have students list personal qualities, physical skills, and talents that helped pioneers survive. Then, in pairs, have one student act as a former slave who now lives in Nicodemus and the other interview this student as if for a magazine or television news program.

DAY 2

Audio CD AudioText

Black Frontiers
Group Time

DAY 3

Audio CD AudioText

1 Reinforce Comprehension

SKILL CAUSE AND EFFECT Have students tell what a cause-and-effect relationship is *(the relationship between what happens and why it happens)* and list clue words that often signal cause-and-effect relationships *(so, because, if, then, since)*. If necessary, review the meaning and provide a model. We can better understand what happens in a story by looking for cause-and-effect relationships. An effect is something that happens; a cause is why it happens. In the statement *The U.S. government gave homesteaders 160 acres of land if they stayed on the land for five years*, the cause is *homesteaders stayed for five years* and the effect is *The U.S. government gave them 160 acres of land.*

Ask students to work in pairs to draw a cause-and-effect diagram such as the one on p. 456. After putting "African Americans became homesteaders" in the Effect box, they can add three causes to the diagram using what they have learned about African Americans' motivation to leave the South.

2 Read *Black Frontiers*, pp. 468–473

BEFORE READING Have students retell what has happened in the selection so far. Ask: Why did former slaves travel to the American frontier after the Civil War? Reread the first paragraph on p. 462 and model how to use prior knowledge to understand new information. I know that slavery ended after the North won the Civil War, so the slaves were set free. In the beginning, former slaves would have been free to begin a new life. They would have needed to earn a living. Remind students to use their prior knowledge as they read the rest of *Black Frontiers.* **STRATEGY Prior Knowledge**

DURING READING Follow the Guiding Comprehension Routine on pp. 468–473. Have students read along with you while tracking print or do a choral reading. Stop every two pages to ask students what has happened so far. Prompt as necessary.

- What were Nicodemus and Dunlap?
- How did the Buffalo Soldiers get their name?

AFTER READING Why did African Americans settle on the American frontier? Reread with students for comprehension as needed. Tell them that tomorrow they will read three poems by Langston Hughes about dreams and new experiences.

ROUTINE

1 Extend Comprehension

SKILL CAUSE AND EFFECT What was the effect of the end of the Civil War on people like Benjamin Singleton? Why would he have wanted to build a total community of black families? Have students complete a cause-and-effect chart like the one on p. 456.

STRATEGY PRIOR KNOWLEDGE Using what they already know about the experiences of white pioneers on the American frontier, ask students to list ways the experiences of black pioneers were the same and different. Ask questions such as:

• Do you think working the land or building a home was easier for black or white homesteaders? Give reasons for your answer.

2 Read *Black Frontiers*, pp. 468–473

DAY 3

Audio CD AudioText

BEFORE READING Have students recall what has happened in the selection so far. Remind them to think about events in the selection and why each happened. Tell them to use what they already know to help them understand the people and places in the selection.

CRITICAL THINKING Have students read pp. 468–473 independently. Encourage them to think critically. For example, ask:

• What does it mean to be a pioneer?

AFTER READING Have students complete the Strategy Response Log activity (p. 472). Then have them research other African Americans who settled the American frontier. Students can present their information to the class.

Black Frontiers
Group Time

DAY 4

Audio CD AudioText

Strategic Intervention

ROUTINE

1 Practice Retelling

REVIEW MAIN IDEAS Help students identify the main ideas in *Black Frontiers*. List the ideas students mention. Then ask questions to help students differentiate between essential and nonessential information.

RETELL Using the retelling cards, have students work with partners to retell the important ideas. Show partners how to summarize in as few words as possible. Monitor retelling and prompt students as needed. For example, ask:

- What was this selection mostly about?
- Why do you think the author wrote this selection?
- What was the author trying to teach us?

If students struggle, model a fluent retelling.

2 Read "Poems" by Langston Hughes

BEFORE READING Read the genre information on p. 476. Poets often write about feelings, experiences, and dreams that people everywhere have. As we read three poems by Langston Hughes, think about the feelings and experiences written about in the poems and how you may have felt the same things.

Read the rest of the panel on p. 476. Then point out that the poems "Youth" and "Dreams" are divided into short verses, while "The Dream Keeper" is a single verse.

DURING READING Have students read along with you while tracking the print or do a choral reading of the poems. Stop to discuss difficult language, such as hyphenated terms and the metaphors *Life is a broken-winged bird/That cannot fly* and *Life is a barren field/Frozen with snow.*

AFTER READING Have students share their reactions to the poems. Then guide them through the Reading Across Texts and Writing Across Texts activities, prompting if necessary.

- What are these poems mostly about?
- What problems do you think black settlers faced?
- How might they have felt during the first months in their new homes? How might these poems have encouraged them if they had been written then?

Advanced

1 Read "Poems" by Langston Hughes

CRITICAL THINKING Have students read pp. 476–477 independently. Encourage them to think critically. For example, ask:

- Why would it be important for settlers on the American frontier to "hold fast to their dreams"?
- What might happen to those who gave up on their dreams?

AFTER READING Discuss Reading Across Texts. Have students do Writing Across Texts independently.

2 Extend Genre Study

RESEARCH Have students use online or print resources to find other poems about dreams and dreamers. Then have them choose one or two that could lift the spirits of weary pioneers as they toiled on the American frontier. Have students note the writing styles and rhyme and rhythm of these poems.

WRITE Tell students to use ideas from the poems of Langston Hughes and those they discovered in their research to write an inspirational poem to help pioneers rediscover their dreams.

DAY 4

Audio CD AudioText

Black Frontiers

Group Time

DAY 5

ONLINE
PearsonSuccessNet.com

Strategic Intervention

ROUTINE

1 Reread for Fluency

MODEL Read aloud pp. 3–5 of the Leveled Reader *A Very Special Gift*, emphasizing the changes in your tone of voice as you read dialogue. Model how to read in a higher tone of voice when a child is speaking and a lower tone when an adult is speaking. Point out how your voice goes up at the end of a question. Then read pp. 6–7 in a monotone voice. Have students tell you which sounds more natural. Discuss how changing your tone of voice while reading makes the story more interesting to listeners.

PRACTICE Have students reread passages from *A Very Special Gift* with a partner or individually. For optimal fluency, they should reread three or four times. As students read, monitor fluency and provide corrective feedback. Students in this group are assessed in Weeks 2 and 4.

2 Retell Leveled Reader *A Very Special Gift*

Model how to use illustrations to retell the story. Then ask students to retell the book, using what is pictured. Prompt them as needed.

• What is happening in this picture?
• Who are the people in this picture and what are they doing?

Monitor Progress

Fluency

If... students have difficulty reading fluently,	then... provide additional fluency practice by pairing nonfluent readers with fluent ones.

For alternate Leveled Reader lesson plans that teach
⟳ **Cause and Effect,** ⟳ **Prior Knowledge,** and
Lesson Vocabulary, see pp. LR19–LR27.

On-Level

① Reread for Fluency ROUTINE

MODEL Read aloud p. 3 of the Leveled Reader *Homesteaders in Nebraska,* emphasizing the changes in your tone of voice. Have students notice the rise and fall of your voice as you read dialogue and questions. Discuss how changing your tone of voice makes the story more enjoyable to listeners.

PRACTICE Have students reread passages from *Homesteaders in Nebraska* with a partner or individually. For optimal fluency, they should reread three or four times. As students read, monitor fluency and provide corrective feedback. Assess the fluency of students in this group using p. 477a.

② Retell Leveled Reader *Homesteaders in Nebraska*

Have students use illustrations to retell the plot of the story, chapter by chapter. Prompt as needed.

- Tell me what this story is about in a few sentences.
- What is the character Timothy like in this story?
- Why do you think the author wrote this story?

Advanced

① Reread for Fluency ROUTINE

PRACTICE Have students reread passages from the Leveled Reader *Grizzled Bill Turns Over a New Leaf* with a partner or individually. As students read, monitor fluency and provide corrective feedback. If students read fluently on the first reading, they do not need to reread three or four times. Students in this group were assessed in Week 1.

② Revisit Leveled Reader *Grizzled Bill Turns Over a New Leaf*

RETELL Have students retell the Leveled Reader *Grizzled Bill Turns Over a New Leaf.*

SHARE JOURNALS Have students complete the journals they began on Day 1. You may wish to discuss with them any questions they have about Texas history of the 1800s. Have them present one entry of their journal to their classmates.

Space Cadets
Group Time

ROUTINE

DAY 1

ONLINE

PearsonSuccessNet.com

① Build Background

REINFORCE CONCEPTS Display the Other Worlds Concept Web. This week's concept is *other worlds*. We can see our world around us. We can think about exploring other worlds, such as planets or imaginary planets. Discuss the meaning of each word on the web, using the definitions on p. 478l and the Concept Vocabulary Routine on p. DI·1.

CONNECT TO READING This week you will read about real planets around our sun and an imaginary planet that characters from Earth visit. Is the dog in "MUSH, A Dog from Space" real or imaginary? Why? *(Imaginary; talking dogs and the planet Growf-Woof-Woof are make-believe.)*

② Read Leveled Reader *The Solar System and Beyond*

BEFORE READING Using the Picture Walk Routine on p. DI·1, guide students through the text, focusing on key concepts and vocabulary. Ask questions such as:

pp. 3 and 13 This book tells about the solar system—the sun and its planets. Have any people visited the other planets besides Earth? *(no)*

pp. 8–15 Planets are not the only bodies in the solar system. What kind of "worlds" move around planets? *(moons)* What other kinds of objects do you think move around the solar system? *(asteroids, comets, perhaps other bodies)*

You may want to point out that this Leveled Reader refers to Pluto as the ninth planet, but a group of astronomers has classified it as a *dwarf planet*. In August 2006 the International Astronomical Union reclassified Pluto and several other bodies discovered in the solar system as dwarf planets, leaving eight planets, according to the group of scientists.

DURING READING Read pp. 3–7 aloud, while students track the print. Do a choral reading of pp. 8–11. If students are capable, have them read and discuss the remainder of the book with a partner. Ask: What is the solar system? How do humans learn about objects in space?

AFTER READING Have groups of two or three students discuss how humans have explored other worlds of the solar system and how they may explore more. We have read *The Solar System and Beyond* to learn about real planets. Knowing about these planets will help us enjoy the humor about exploring a planet in *Space Cadets*.

Monitor Progress

Selection Reading and Comprehension

If... students have difficulty reading the selection with a partner,	then... have them follow along as they listen to the Online Leveled Reader Audio.
If... students have trouble distinguishing historic space travel from the unproven claims about seeing space aliens,	then... reread pp. 16–17 and discuss the differences between known history and the movies and claims about aliens.

For alternate Leveled Reader lesson plans that teach
⟳ **Draw Conclusions,** ⟳ **Visualize,** and
Lesson Vocabulary, see pp. LR28–LR36.

On-Level

ROUTINE

❶ Build Background

DEVELOP VOCABULARY Have students write the word *Planets* at the top of a T-chart on their own paper. On the left, they can write similarities of the planets (for example, *round shape, moving through space*). On the right, they can write differences (such as *size, distance from sun*). Repeat this activity with the word *satellite* and other words from the Leveled Reader *The United States and Russian Space Race*. Use the Concept Vocabulary Routine on p. DI·1 as needed.

❷ Read Leveled Reader
The United States and Russian Space Race

BEFORE READING Have students make time lines of the Space Race. This book tells of events in a space race, a competition between nations and their explorers. As you read, make notes, in order by dates, about important events in the space race.

DURING READING Have students follow along as you read pp. 3–10. Then let them complete the book on their own. Remind students to add events to their time lines as they read.

AFTER READING Have students compare the events on their time lines. Point out that information about space travel will help them understand the setting and appreciate the humor as they read tomorrow's play *Space Cadets*.

Advanced

ROUTINE

❶ Read Leveled Reader
Destination: Mars

BEFORE READING Recall the Read Aloud story "MUSH, A Dog from Space." What can be entertaining about stories that include imaginary planets? *(adventure, unusual or extreme settings, interesting characters)* Today you will read about a real world, Mars, and how humans have investigated it and may try to travel there.

CRITICAL THINKING Have students read the Leveled Reader independently. Encourage them to think creatively. For example, ask:

• If astronauts were training to go to Mars in a "Mars camp," what skills and knowledge should they learn?
• If scientists could solve the problems of visiting the environment of Mars, what would you imagine humans doing there on a day of exploration?

AFTER READING Have students review the selection to find five or more words or phrases they can use to write advice to a person who will explore Mars. Then have them write three or more statements of advice. They can present the statements to other students or to you and discuss the selection.

❷ Independent Extension Activity

NOW TRY THIS Assign "Now Try This" on pp. 22–23 of *Destination: Mars* for students to work on throughout the week.

Space Cadets
Group Time

ROUTINE

DAY 2

Audio CD AudioText

Monitor Progress

Word and Selection Reading

If... students have difficulty reading multisyllabic words in the selection,	then... have them look for and read meaningful parts in the words or have them chunk words with no recognizable parts.
If... students need practice reading words fluently,	then... use the Fluent Word Reading Routine on the DI tab.
If... students have difficulty reading along with the group,	then... have them follow along as they listen to the AudioText.

1 Word Study/Phonics

LESSON VOCABULARY Use p. 480b to review the meanings of *aliens, barge, hospitable, molten, ore, refrain, universal,* and *version.* Have individuals practice reading the words from word cards.

DECODING MULTISYLLABIC WORDS Write *timepieces,* saying the word as you write it. Model how to use meaningful parts. First I look for parts I know. I see *time* at the beginning of the word and *pieces* at the end. I know that *time* refers to the minutes and hours of a day and that *pieces* means "parts," such as jigsaw puzzle pieces. I have heard of clocks called *timepieces,* so the meaning "a thing that tells time" makes sense.

Use the Multisyllabic Word Routine on p. DI·1 to help students read these other words from *Space Cadets: spaceship, intently, identical, communication, spacedate, operational, breadcrumbs, stabilizer, sarcastically,* and *disappointed.* Be sure students understand the meaning of words such as *stabilizer* and *sarcastically.*

Use *Strategies for Word Analysis,* Lesson 19, with students who have difficulty mastering word analysis and need practice with decodable text.

2 Read *Space Cadets,* pp. 482–489

BEFORE READING *The Solar System and Beyond* explained the planets that orbit our sun. Think about space travel as you read *Space Cadets.*

Using the Picture Walk Routine on p. DI·1, guide students through the text, asking questions such as those listed below. Read the question on p. 482. Together, set a purpose for reading.

pp. 482–483 Does the shape of the spaceship and how close the planets are in the picture make this look like serious science or an entertaining selection? Why? *(an entertaining selection, because the spaceship looks funny and the art is not realistic)*

pp. 484–489 Names are shown at the beginning of most paragraphs to show who is speaking. What kind of selection is this? *(a play)*

DURING READING Follow the Guiding Comprehension routine on pp. 484–489. Have students read along with you while tracking the print, or do a choral reading. Stop every two pages to ask what has happened so far. Prompt as necessary.

• Who will travel from the ship to the surface of the planet?
• How is the Captain different from most leaders in space adventure dramas?

AFTER READING What has happened in the play so far? What do you think will happen next? Reread passages with students as needed.

Advanced

1 Extend Vocabulary

CONTEXT CLUES Find and read aloud this passage from p. 7 of *Destination: Mars* or another passage containing a multiple-meaning word: "…each of your three fellow astronauts is an expert in some branch of science that you will need to survive…." In that statement, what does the word *branch* mean? *(a part or division of something, such as a part of science)* How did you know that the meaning was not "part of a tree"? *(The context clues* expert in *and* of science *helped me.)* Discuss how context clues help readers understand the appropriate meaning of multiple-meaning words. Remind students to use the strategy as they read *Space Cadets*.

DAY 2

Audio CD   AudioText

2 Read *Space Cadets*, pp. 482–489

BEFORE READING Today you will read a play about characters on a spaceship traveling to another world, a distant planet. As you read, determine whether the selection is as serious as the book *Destination: Mars.*

Have students write a prediction, an "educated guess," for their Strategy Response Log (p. 482). Encourage them to add notes and adjust or evaluate the prediction as they read.

CRITICAL THINKING Have students read pp. 484–489 independently. Encourage them to think critically. For example, ask:

• How would you compare or contrast the Captain and the First Officer?

AFTER READING Have partners discuss Scene 1 and share their Strategy Response Log entries. Encourage them to consider the question "Is there any intelligent life in outer space?" and discuss how this play humorously applies the question to certain characters inside the I.N. Ept starship. Then have students imagine two brief conversations and write dialogue for them: the First Officer answers a command that is communicated by the Commander at Star Base 12, and then the Captain tries to answer a radio communication from the same Commander.

Space Cadets
Group Time

DAY 3

Audio CD — AudioText

❶ Reinforce Comprehension

◎ SKILL DRAW CONCLUSIONS Have students tell what it means to draw conclusions as they read. *(to form opinions that are reasonable about the reading, using one's knowledge)* If necessary, review the meaning and provide a model. To draw conclusions is to form reasonable opinions, opinions that make sense. As I read the play, I draw the conclusion that the Captain is in charge of the starship. In real life, a captain is the commanding officer of a ship or an aircraft. It is reasonable to conclude that the character in this play called Captain is in command.

Ask students to draw a conclusion about space travel or to choose the more reasonable conclusion from a pair of statements. Which of the following is a better conclusion? Why?

> **People traveling in space can visit their home towns often.**
> **People traveling in space are far from their home towns.**

(People in space are far from their home towns; it is more reasonable because space travel covers very long distances.)

❷ Read *Space Cadets*, pp. 490–493

BEFORE READING Have students retell what has happened in the play so far. Ask: What planets or other bodies in space are near the starship? Reread the first three speeches of dialogue near the top of p. 486, beginning with Ensign (EN suhn), and model how to visualize the setting. As I read, I try to picture in my mind where the spaceship is. It is in a solar system with a star and seven planets. It is near— but has not landed on—a planet with an atmosphere that these people can breathe. Remind students to visualize as they read Scene 2 of *Space Cadets*. **◎ STRATEGY Visualize**

DURING READING Follow the Guiding Comprehension routine on pp. 490–493. Have students read along with you while tracking the print, or do a choral reading. Stop every two pages to ask what has happened so far. Prompt as necessary.

- Where are the humans in Scene 2, and who else is there?
- Do the humans learn much about the creatures of the planet? Why or why not?

AFTER READING What have the space travelers learned about this other world? Reread with students for comprehension as needed. Tell them that tomorrow they will read "Exploring Space Travel," a selection about using the Internet to learn about the topic.

Monitor Progress

Word and Selection Reading

If... students have difficulty reading multisyllabic words in the selection,	then... have them look for and read meaningful parts in the words or have them chunk words with no recognizable parts.
If... students have difficulty reading along with the group,	then... have them follow along as they listen to the AudioText.

Advanced

ROUTINE

1 Extend Comprehension

SKILL DRAW CONCLUSIONS Have students imagine that they are helping to stage the play *Space Cadets* for an audience. Have them draw conclusions about how the actors playing First Officer, Tom, Harold, and other roles should look, speak, and move, based on each character's traits.

STRATEGY VISUALIZE Have volunteers pantomime the movements of the space cadets, Tom and Harold, practicing their "space walking" in Scene 1. Then have students draw diagrams showing overhead views of the characters on stage at various points in the play.

2 Read *Space Cadets*, pp. 490–493

BEFORE READING Have students recall what has happened in the play so far. Remind them to visualize and to draw conclusions about the characters as they read Scene 2.

CREATIVE THINKING Have students read pp. 490–493 independently. Encourage them to think creatively. For example, ask:

• Imagine that you are directing the play. How would you direct the actors to stand and move on stage so that the humans can get close to the Space Cow but have no close contact with Mog and Og?

AFTER READING Have students complete the Strategy Response Log activity (p. 492). Then have partners plan a poster that could advertise a stage or video performance of *Space Cadets*. Students can present to you or one another the poster or poster plans reflecting their knowledge and appreciation of the play.

DAY **3**

Audio CD **AudioText**

Space Cadets
Group Time

DAY 4

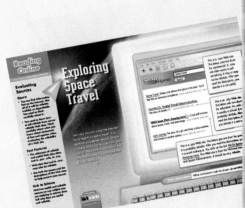

Audio CD AudioText

ROUTINE

1 Practice Retelling

REVIEW ELEMENTS OF A PLAY Help students identify the characters and the setting of *Space Cadets*. Then guide them in using the Retelling Cards to list the play's events in sequence. Prompt students to include important details.

RETELL Using the Retelling Cards, have students work in pairs to retell *Space Cadets*. Monitor retelling, and prompt students as needed. For example, ask:

- Tell me what this play is about in a few sentences.
- What happened at the end of the play?
- Why do you think the author wrote this play?

If students struggle, model a fluent retelling.

Grade 6
Retelling Cards
PEARSON
Scott Foresman

2 Read "Exploring Space Travel"

BEFORE READING Read the genre information on p. 496. Remind students that the Internet is an extremely large computer network. It includes many smaller networks of university, government, business, and personal computers, all linked by telephone lines. It is not easy for a person to know who wrote much of the information on a Web site or how well-informed each writer is. That is why users must judge the value of each Web site and the information on it.

Read the rest of the panel on p. 496, and discuss the text features. Then have students scan the pages to see Web addresses with .edu, .com, .org, and .gov endings.

DURING READING Have students read along with you while tracking the print. If you decide to do any choral reading, guide students to read the boxed text at appropriate points. Stop as needed to discuss technical terms such as "w-w-w dot," "dot e-d-u," and *link*.

AFTER READING Have students share their reactions to the selection. Then guide them through the Reading Across Texts and Writing Across Texts activities, prompting if necessary.

- Does either selection—*Space Cadets* or "Launch a 'Rocket' from a Spinning 'Planet'"—describe a real flight through outer space?
- Which of the two selections teaches serious ideas?

Monitor Progress

Word and Selection Reading

If... students have difficulty reading multisyllabic words in the selection,	**then...** have them look for and read meaningful parts in the words or have them chunk words with no recognizable parts.
If... students have difficulty reading along with the group,	**then...** have them follow along as they listen to the AudioText.

Advanced

ROUTINE

1 Read "Exploring Space Travel"

PROBLEM SOLVING Have students read pp. 496–499 independently. Encourage them to think about problems that they might encounter during Internet research and how to solve them. For example, ask:

- If the description of a Web site on a search engine is hard to understand and your time is limited, what is a useful thing to do?
- If a Web site has not been revised or written recently, how can a person determine whether the information is still valid and useful?

AFTER READING Discuss Reading Across Texts. Have students do Writing Across Texts independently.

2 Extend Genre Study

RESEARCH Have students use a student-friendly search engine, following your school's Internet policies, to explore a particular topic concerning space travel, such as recent scientific discoveries about Mars or another planet. Have them list three or four Web addresses that may be reliable.

WRITE Have students work in pairs to write initial ideas for a new Web page about a planet of their choice. Encourage them to describe the kinds of information and images they think would help students.

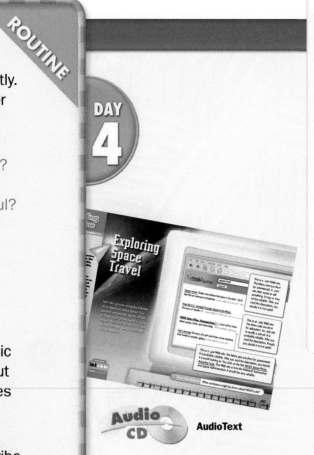

AudioText

DAY 4

DAY 5

Leveled Reader
Database
ONLINE

PearsonSuccessNet.com

Strategic Intervention

ROUTINE

1 Reread for Fluency

MODEL Read aloud pp. 8–9 of the Leveled Reader *The Solar System and Beyond,* demonstrating how the punctuation guides your reading to communicate the ideas clearly. Help students recognize that periods at the end of sentences separate the statements, and commas (minor pauses) can separate parts of a sentence for clarity. Then, in contrast, read a paragraph rapidly with no pauses at periods or commas, and discuss with students whether the effect is clear.

PRACTICE Have students reread passages from *The Solar System and Beyond* with a partner or individually. For optimal fluency, they should reread three or four times. Monitor fluency and provide corrective feedback. Assess the fluency of students in this group using p. 499a.

2 Retell Leveled Reader *The Solar System and Beyond*

Model how to use the headings and pictures on successive pages to retell important ideas from the book. Then ask students to retell several important ideas, using the headings and pictures to recall topics. Prompt them as needed. For example, ask:

- What did you learn about the sun?
- What did you learn about planets' orbits? (pp. 12–13)
- How can people learn about future space travel? (pp. 20–21)

Monitor Progress

Fluency

If... students have difficulty reading fluently,	then... provide additional fluency practice by pairing nonfluent readers with fluent ones.

For alternate Leveled Reader lesson plans that teach 🔄 **Draw Conclusions,** 🔄 **Visualize,** and **Lesson Vocabulary,** see pp. LR28–LR36.

On-Level

ROUTINE

1 Reread for Fluency

MODEL Read aloud p. 3 of the Leveled Reader *The United States and Russian Space Race,* showing how punctuation helps you communicate ideas clearly. Help students recognize the separation between sentences and the comma pauses that enhance clarity. Discuss how punctuation helps readers group words and phrases and separate them meaningfully.

PRACTICE Have students reread passages from *The United States and Russian Space Race* with a partner or individually. For optimal fluency, they should reread three or four times. As students read, monitor fluency and provide corrective feedback. Students in this group were assessed in Week 3.

2 Retell Leveled Reader *The United States and Russian Space Race*

Have students use pictures and captions as a guide to summarize the important facts they learned from this book. Prompt as needed.

• What is this book mostly about?
• Tell me about the major events.
• What was the author trying to teach us?

Advanced

ROUTINE

1 Reread for Fluency

PRACTICE Have students reread passages from the Leveled Reader *Destination: Mars* with a partner or individually. As students read, monitor fluency and provide corrective feedback. If students read fluently on the first reading, they do not need to reread three or four times. Students in this group were assessed in Week 1.

2 Revisit Leveled Reader *Destination: Mars*

RETELL Have students retell what they learned from the Leveled Reader *Destination: Mars.*

NOW TRY THIS Have students complete their Letter to the Editor projects. You may wish to review their outlines and any information sources. Students can present their letters to you and other students. If they plan to send their letters to a newspaper, it is advisable to seek parental permission and follow any school policies on such activities.

Group Time

ONLINE

PearsonSuccessNet.com

DAY 1

Strategic Intervention

ROUTINE

1 Build Background

REINFORCE CONCEPTS Display the Inventions Concept Web. This week's concept is *inventions*. Inventions are new things, such as machines, that are created. Explorers, pioneers, and discoverers create and use inventions. Discuss the meaning of each word on the web, using the definitions on p. 500I and the Concept Vocabulary Routine on p. DI·1.

CONNECT TO READING This week you will read about how important inventions were created and learn about the inventors who created them. What important invention does "Inventing the Stethoscope" tell about? *(the stethoscope)* Why is this invention important? *(It allows doctors to hear their patients' hearts.)*

2 Read Leveled Reader *Electricity*

BEFORE READING Using the Picture Walk Routine on p. DI·1, guide students through the text focusing on key concepts and vocabulary. Ask questions such as:

pp. 4 This selection discusses electricity and how it is used. What kind of a musical instrument that uses electricity is shown here? *(electric guitar)* Yes. It is one of many inventions that uses electricity.

pp. 6–7 Look at the drawing of Benjamin Franklin. He was one of the Founding Fathers of the United States and helped write the Declaration of Independence and the Constitution. He was also a scientist and inventor. What do you know about Benjamin Franklin and what he discovered while flying his kite?

DURING READING Read p. 4 aloud, while students track the print. Do a choral reading of pp. 7–9. If students are capable, have them read and discuss the remainder of the book with a partner. Ask: Why is the word "henry" used as the unit of measurement in electrical currents? Why must electricity move through a circuit, or circle?

AFTER READING Encourage pairs of students to discuss the evolution of and uses for electricity. We read *Electricity* to learn about and appreciate the importance of electricity. This information will help us as we read about Thomas Edison's work in *Inventing the Future*.

For alternate Leveled Reader lesson plans that teach
🔄 **Author's Purpose,** 🔄 **Monitor and Fix Up,**
and **Lesson Vocabulary,** see pp. LR37–LR45.

On-Level

ROUTINE

① Build Background

DEVELOP VOCABULARY Write the word *needs* and ask students to define it in their own words. *(things you must have to live)* What are some human needs? *(food, water, shelter)* Repeat this activity with the word *devise* and other words from the Leveled Reader *Inventors at Work.* Use the Concept Vocabulary Routine on p. DI·1 as needed.

② **Read** Leveled Reader *Inventors at Work*

BEFORE READING Have students create three-column charts with the labels Inventors, Inventions, and Impact. This book tells a lot about inventors, their inventions, and the effect they have had on the world. As you read, look for facts about inventors and their inventions. Record them in your chart.

DURING READING Have students follow along as you read pp. 3–9. Then let them complete the book on their own. Remind students to add facts to their three-column charts as they read.

AFTER READING Have students compare the facts on their three-column charts. Point out that facts about the inventing process will help them as they read tomorrow's selection *Inventing the Future.*

Advanced

ROUTINE

DAY 1

① **Read** Leveled Reader *It's About Time*

BEFORE READING Recall the Read Aloud selection "Inventing the Stethoscope." How can inventions help people? *(They can be used for medical purposes.)* Today you will read about how inventions dealing with time have shaped the way people live.

It's About Time! by Anne Cambal

CRITICAL THINKING Have students read the Leveled Reader independently. Encourage them to think critically. For example, ask:

• How does time affect the way people live?
• What are the advantages and disadvantages of the various methods of tracking time?

AFTER READING Have students review the selection to find five or more unfamiliar words and determine their meanings by looking at word structure, such as base words and prefixes, or by consulting a dictionary. Then ask them to write statements or questions that both include the words and convey their meanings. Encourage students to meet with you to discuss the selection and the statements or questions they wrote.

② Independent Extension Activity

NOW TRY THIS Assign "Now Try This" on pp. 22–23 of *It's About Time!* for students to work on throughout the week.

Inventing the Future
Group Time

DAY 2

Audio CD · AudioText

Monitor Progress

Word and Selection Reading

If...	then...
If... students have difficulty reading multisyllabic words in the selection,	**then...** have them look for and read meaningful parts in the words or have them chunk words with no recognizable parts.
If... students need practice reading words fluently,	**then...** use the Fluent Word Reading Routine on the DI tab.
If... students have difficulty reading along with the group,	**then...** have them follow along as they listen to the AudioText.

1 Word Study/Phonics

LESSON VOCABULARY Use p. 502b to review the meanings of *converts, devise, efficiency, generated, percentage, proclaimed, reproduce,* and *transmitted.* Have individuals practice reading the words from word cards.

DECODING MULTISYLLABIC WORDS Write *laboratory,* saying the word as you write it. Then model how to use meaningful parts to read longer words. *I see a chunk at the beginnng of the word: lab. I see a part in the middle: or and another part: a and another part: tory. I say each chunk slowly: lab or a tory. I say the chunks fast to make a whole word: laboratory. Is it a real word? Yes, I know the word laboratory.*

Use the Multisyllabic Word Routine on p. DI·1 to help students read these other words from *Inventing the Future: telegraphic, exhaustion, plunging, document,* and *celebrity.* Be sure students understand the meaning of words such as *telegraphic* and *plunging.*

Use *Strategies for Word Analysis,* Lesson 20, with students who have difficulty mastering word analysis and need practice with decodable text.

2 Read *Inventing the Future,* pp. 504–513

BEFORE READING *Electricity* explored the invention of electricity and how it has changed people's lives over the years. Think about this information as you read *Inventing the Future.*

Using the Picture Walk Routine on p. DI·1, guide students through the text, asking questions such as those listed below. Read the question on p. 505. Together, set a purpose for reading.

pp. 504–505 What do you think Thomas Edison is holding? *(a light bulb)* Why do you think so? *(It looks like light bulbs we use.)*

pp. 511 What are the women in the photo doing? *(listening to something)* Do you think they can hear what they're listening to well? Why? *(Yes. You can tell from the expressions on their faces.)* Yes. In the late 1800s, paying customers listened through earphones to recordings using Edison's coin-in-slot phonographs.

DURING READING Follow the Guiding Comprehension routine on pp. 506–513. Have students read along with you while tracking the print or do a choral reading. Stop every two pages to ask what has happened so far. Prompt as necessary.

• Why was Edison able to attract financial backers by age 23?
• What was the biggest problem with Bell's telephone?

AFTER READING What has happened in the selection so far? What do you think you will learn about Edison's inventions tomorrow? Reread passages with students for comprehension as needed.

Advanced

ROUTINE

DAY

2

1 **Extend Vocabulary**

🎯 **WORD STRUCTURE** Choose and read a sentence or passage containing a difficult word, such as this sentence from p. 9 of *It's About Time!:* "This was an early step toward such improvements as the addition of the minute and second hands and the internal design features that improved precision." What does the word *precision* mean? *(accuracy or exactness)* How did you determine the word's meaning? *(I used the definition of the base word* precise.*)* Discuss how word structure can help a reader determine the meaning of unfamiliar words, and remind students to use the strategy as they read *Inventing the Future.*

2 **Read** *Inventing the Future*, pp. 504–513

BEFORE READING Today you will read a biography of Thomas Edison. It shows how Edison became one of the greatest inventors in history. As you read, consider the importance of other inventions you have read about.

Before reading, have students develop questions about Thomas Edison and write them in their Strategy Response Logs (p. 504). Encourage them to answer these questions as they read the selection.

CREATIVE THINKING Have students read pp. 504–513 independently. Encourage them to think critically and creatively. For example, ask:

• How would you improve upon one of Edison's inventions?

AFTER READING Have partners discuss the selection and share their Strategy Response Log entries. Have students meet with you to identify three character traits that they think were the most critical to Edison's success. Challenge them to explain the reason for their choices.

Inventing
the
Future
a Photobiography
of Thomas Alva Edison
by Marfé Ferguson Delano

Why are Thomas Edison's
inventions so important
to us today?

Audio CD **AudioText**

Inventing the Future
Group Time

DAY 3

1 Reinforce Comprehension

SKILL AUTHOR'S PURPOSE Have students tell what author's purpose is *(the reason an author has for writing)* and cite various purposes an author may have *(to persuade, inform, express ideas or feelings, entertain)*. If necessary, review the meaning and provide a model. Author's purpose is the reason an author has for writing. If an author writes an article on how to make a bird feeder, the purpose is to inform.

Ask students to identify the purpose—to entertain, to inform, to persuade—of each writing assignment.

Recipe for making pancakes
Letter convincing a parent to raise your allowance
Fairy tale

2 Read *Inventing the Future*, pp. 514–521

BEFORE READING Have students summarize what happened in the selection so far. Ask: Why did Edison improve the telephone? Reread the first paragraph on p. 511 and model the fix-up strategy of summarizing details to understand ideas. This paragraph talks about the weaknesses of Alexander Graham Bell's telephone and that Edison wanted to improve it. It shows Edison as smart and hard-working and highlights another of his inventions. Remind students to use fix-up strategies as needed as they read the rest of *Inventing the Future*. **STRATEGY Monitor and Fix Up**

DURING READING Follow the Guiding Comprehension routine on pp. 514–521. Have students read along with you while tracking print or do a choral reading. Stop every two pages to ask students what has happened so far. Prompt as necessary.

- What other features had to be designed to support the invention of the light bulb?
- Look at the timeline on pp. 520 and 521. Which invention did Edison create first, the tinfoil phonograph or the "perfected" phonograph? How can you determine this from the time line?

AFTER READING How does this selection show Edison as a discoverer? Reread with students for comprehension as needed. Tell them that tomorrow they will read "Garrett Augustus Morgan," a biography of a businessman and inventor who created many useful inventions, such as the traffic signal.

Audio CD AudioText

Monitor Progress

Word and Selection Reading

If... students have difficulty reading multisyllabic words in the selection,	then... have them look for and read meaningful parts in the words or have them chunk words with no recognizable parts.
If... students have difficulty reading along with the group,	then... have them follow along as they listen to the AudioText.

Advanced

1 Extend Comprehension

SKILL AUTHOR'S PURPOSE Review with students the author's purpose in *Inventing the Future. (to inform readers of Edison's life and inventions)* Encourage them to think of other purposes an author could have for writing a biography of Edison.

STRATEGY MONITOR AND FIX UP Have students reread pp. 507–508 independently. Have them summarize the text to determine how well they understood the information presented. Then ask: There are questions you can ask yourself that will help you monitor your comprehension. Did you ask yourself any, such as:

- Did I summarize to organize and understand ideas?
- Did I adjust my reading rate to improve my comprehension?

Audio CD   AudioText

2 Read *Inventing the Future*, pp. 514–521

BEFORE READING Have students recall what has happened in the selection so far. Remind them to look for author's purpose and to monitor their comprehension and use fix-up strategies as they read the remainder of the selection.

CRITICAL THINKING Have students read pp. 514–521 independently. Encourage them to think creatively. For example, ask:

- Why is it important for inventors to be good problem-solvers?

AFTER READING Have students complete the Strategy Response Log Activity (p. 520). Then have them trace the history of related inventions. For example, students can trace the history of musical recording devices, from Edison's early phonograph to today's digital recorders. If possible, have students print or photocopy pictures of related inventions and use them to create an illustrated time line.

Inventing the Future

Group Time

DAY 4

Strategic Intervention

ROUTINE

① Practice Retelling

REVIEW MAIN IDEAS Help students identify the main ideas in *Inventing the Future.* List the ideas students mention. Then ask questions to help them differentiate between essential and nonessential information.

RETELL Using the Retelling Cards, have students work in pairs to retell the important ideas of *Inventing the Future.* Show partners how to summarize in as few words as possible. Monitor retelling, and prompt students as needed. For example, ask:

Grade 6
Retelling Cards

PEARSON
Scott Foresman

- What was this selection mostly about?
- Why do you think the author wrote this selection?

If students struggle, model a fluent retelling.

② Read "Garrett Augustus Morgan"

BEFORE READING Read the genre information on p. 524. Recall the Read Aloud "Inventing the Stethoscope," rereading portions of the text as needed. We have read several biographies this week. What did "Inventing the Stethoscope" tell the story of? *(how the stethoscope was invented)* As we read "Garrett Augustus Morgan," think about how his inventions developed.

Read the rest of the panel on p. 524. Then have students scan the pages, looking at the section headings.

DURING READING Have students read along with you while tracking the print or do a choral reading of the selection. Stop to discuss difficult vocabulary, such as the words *innovation, proficiency,* and *enterprise.*

AFTER READING Have students share their reactions to the selection. Then guide them through the Reading Across Texts and Writing Across Texts activities, prompting as necessary.

- What were Edison's greatest inventions? What were Morgan's greatest inventions?
- Did Edison ever work as anything other than an inventor? Did Morgan have other types of jobs?

Audio CD AudioText

Monitor Progress

Word and Selection Reading

If... students have difficulty reading multisyllabic words in the selection,	then... have them look for and read meaningful parts in the words or have them chunk words with no recognizable parts.
If... students have difficulty reading along with the group,	then... have them follow along as they listen to the AudioText.

ROUTINE

1 Read "Garrett Augustus Morgan"

CRITICAL THINKING Have students read pp. 524–527 independently. Encourage them to think critically and to support their opinions. For example, ask:

- How does the use of graphic sources enhance an author's writing about inventors and inventions?
- Are the graphic sources in the selection effective? Which were especially effective? Which were not helpful? Are there any graphics that should have been included? Why?

AFTER READING Discuss Reading Across texts. Have students do Writing Across texts independently.

2 Extend Genre Study

RESEARCH Have students use online or print resources to find other biographies. Have them make a list of titles, noting the inventions and inventors that each biography features.

WRITE Ask students to research another inventor and something he or she invented. Have them write a biography of this person, including details about his or her life and work. Encourage students to use active words that illustrate the inventor's ingenuity and drive. Remind students to include section headings to separate topics in their biographies.

DAY 4

AudioText

Inventing the Future
Group Time

DAY
5

ONLINE
PearsonSuccessNet.com

ROUTINE

1 Reread for Fluency

MODEL Read aloud pp. 10–11 of the Leveled Reader *Electricity,* emphasizing punctuation marks as cues for grouping words together and for pausing. Have students notice how you pause and chunk words set apart by dashes and commas, including words in a series. Then read pp. 16–17 without pausing for punctuation. Have students tell you which model sounded better. Discuss how pausing for punctuation when reading creates a more pleasing rhythm.

PRACTICE Have students reread passages from *Electricity* with a partner or individually. For optimal fluency, they should reread three or four times. As students read, monitor fluency and provide corrective feedback. Assess any students you have not yet checked during this unit.

2 Retell Leveled Reader *Electricity*

Model how to retell the selection using chapter titles and subheads. Then ask students to retell the selection, one chapter at a time. Prompt them as needed.

- What is this selection mostly about?
- What did you learn from reading this selection?

Monitor Progress

Fluency

If... students have difficulty reading fluently,	then... provide additional fluency practice by pairing nonfluent readers with fluent ones.

For alternate Leveled Reader lesson plans that teach
⟳ **Author's Purpose,** ⟳ **Monitor and Fix Up,**
and **Lesson Vocabulary,** see pp. LR37–LR45.

On-Level

① Reread for Fluency   ROUTINE

MODEL Read aloud p. 9 of the Leveled Reader *Inventors at Work,* emphasizing the rhythmic patterns of language. Have students note how you group words and pause as you read. Discuss how reading with punctuation creates a more pleasing rhythm than without it.

PRACTICE Have students reread passages from *Inventors at Work* with a partner or individually. For optimal fluency, they should reread three or four times. As students read, monitor fluency and provide corrective feedback. Assess any students you have not yet checked during this unit.

② Retell Leveled Reader *Inventors at Work*

BEFORE READING Have students use graphics and art as a guide to summarize the important facts they learned from the book. Prompt as needed.

- What is this selection mostly about?
- What did you learn from reading this selection?
- Why do you think the author wrote this selection?

Advanced

① Reread for Fluency   ROUTINE

PRACTICE Have students reread passages from the Leveled Reader *It's About Time!* with a partner or individually. As students read, monitor fluency and provide corrective feedback. If students read fluently on the first reading, they do not need to reread three or four times. Assess any students you have not yet checked during this unit.

② Revisit Leveled Reader *It's About Time!*

RETELL Have students retell the Leveled Reader *It's About Time!*

NOW TRY THIS Have students complete their projects. You may wish to review their data and see whether they need any additional supplies or resources. Have them present their projects.

Cause and Effect

Students who are able to connect what happens in a selection to the reason why it happens can better understand what they read. In fiction, this skill will help them figure out why characters do what they do. In nonfiction, it will give them a better grasp of factual information. Use the following routine to teach cause and effect.

1 DEMONSTRATE CAUSE AND EFFECT

Remind students that a cause is what makes something happen. An effect is something that happens as the result of a cause. Demonstrate by turning out the lights. Ask:

What is the effect? (It is dark.)

What is the cause? (The light was turned off.)

2 IDENTIFY CAUSE AND EFFECT

Write this sentence on the board: *Because it is raining, I took my umbrella to school.* Explain that sometimes a sentence has a clue word such as *because, so,* or *therefore* that signals a cause-and-effect relationship. Have volunteers circle the cause *(it is raining)* and the effect *(I took my umbrella)* and underline the clue word *(because).*

3 APPLY TO A SELECTION

Read with students a story that has causes and effects. Several causes can lead to one effect: Sunshine <u>and</u> water make flowers grow. One cause can lead to several effects: Leaving a bike in the hallway can cause someone to trip <u>and</u> break an arm.

4 RECORD CAUSES AND EFFECTS

Have students use a cause-effect chart to record the causes and effects in the selection.

Causes	Effects
The expedition's ship was so comfortable that Nansen grew bored and decided to strike out over the ice. **Why did it happen?**	Fridtjof Nansen and Hjalmar Johansen survive sixteen months on their own in the artic, and travel farther north than anyone had before. **What happened?**
Temperature changes caused the balloon to leak its precious gases away, and the team was unprepared to survive the winter on land. **Why did it happen?**	Salomon Andrée and his team perish while trying to reach the North Pole in a balloon. **What happened?**
Cook lacked documentation and witnesses of his achievement, and it was shown that he'd lied once before about another achievement. **Why did it happen?**	Dr. Frederick Cook's claim that he had reached the North Pole was officially rejected. **What happened?**

▲ **Graphic Organizer** 20

Research on Cause and Effect

"A great deal of our thought process has to do with cause and effect. To be fully fluent thinkers, children need to learn the logic of cause and effect."

Stanley Greenspan and Serena Weider,
Learning to Think Abstractly

Greenspan, Stanley, and Serena Welder. "Learning to Think Abstractly." *Scholastic Early Childhood Today* (May/June 1998).

Author's Purpose

Evaluating the author's purpose for writing helps students decide how quickly or slowly and carefully to read. Use this routine to teach author's purpose.

1 DISCUSS AUTHOR'S PURPOSE

Explain that the author's purpose is the author's reason or reasons for writing. Four common reasons for writing are to persuade, to inform, to entertain, or to express ideas or feelings.

2 EXPLAIN ITS USE

Tell students that one reason they need to consider the author's purpose is to adjust their reading rate. If a story is meant to be fun, they may decide to read quickly. If the author wants to explain how something works, they may need to read slowly and carefully.

3 ASK QUESTIONS

Authors don't usually state their purposes for writing, and they often have more than one purpose. Before, during, and after reading a selection, ask questions to help students draw conclusions about the author's purposes: *Why do you think the author wrote this story? What reasons might the author have for writing the story this way? What is the author trying to tell the reader? Why is the author telling readers that?*

4 USE A GRAPHIC ORGANIZER

Have students predict the author's purpose before reading by previewing the title, illustrations, and graphics. During and after reading, students should check and confirm their predictions. Have them record ideas and evidence in a three-column chart.

	Author's Purpose	Why Do You Think So?
Before you read: What do you think it will be?	To show some of the reasons why the author loves chimpanzees	The pictures show the author with the chimpanzees and the chimpanzees communicating with each other or taking care of their babies. The title says that the author loves chimpanzees.
As you read: What do you think it is?	To encourage the reader to sympathize with the chimpanzees	The author gives examples of how human and chimpanzee behavior is similar. She also tells sad stories about chimpanzees in captivity, and why we need to protect them.
After you read: What was it?	To convince the reader of the importance of studying, understanding, and protecting chimpanzees	The author describes how much we can learn from chimpanzees, and how like humans they are. She tells how and why we should protect them, and gives many facts about chimpanzees so we can better understand them.

▲ Graphic Organizer 26

Research on Author's Purpose

"Younger and less proficient readers are unlikely to differentiate between 'study' reading and 'fun' reading."

Ruth Garner,
"Metacognition and Self-Monitoring Strategies"

Garner, Ruth. "Metacognition and Self-Monitoring Strategies." In *What Research Has to Say About Reading Instruction*, edited by S. J. Samuels and A. E. Farstrup. Second Edition. International Reading Association, 1992, p. 238.

Cause and Effect

Students who are able to connect what happens in a selection to the reason why it happens can better understand what they read. In fiction, this skill will help them figure out why characters do what they do. In nonfiction, it will give them a better grasp of factual information. Use the following routine to teach cause and effect.

① DEMONSTRATE CAUSE AND EFFECT

Remind students that a cause is what makes something happen. An effect is something that happens as the result of a cause. A cause is why it happened. Demonstrate by turning out the lights. Ask:

What is the effect? (It is dark.)

What is the cause? (The light was turned off.)

② IDENTIFY CAUSE AND EFFECT

Write this sentence on the board: *Because it is raining, I took my umbrella to school.* Explain that sometimes a sentence has a clue word such as *because, so,* or *therefore* that signals a cause-and-effect relationship. Have volunteers circle the cause (*it is raining*) and the effect (*I took my umbrella*) and underline the clue word (*because*).

③ APPLY TO A SELECTION

Read with students a story that has causes and effects. Several causes can lead to one effect: Sunshine <u>and</u> water make flowers grow. One cause can lead to several effects: Leaving a bike in the hallway can cause someone to trip <u>and</u> break an arm.

④ RECORD CAUSES AND EFFECTS

Have students use a cause-effect chart to record the causes and effects in the selection.

Causes	Effects
Former slaves were expected to pay back a share of everything they raised and were always in debt. **Why did it happen?**	Many black sharecroppers and their families left the South after the Civil War ended. **What happened?**
Black pioneer families stick it out through bad weather, poor harvests, and loneliness. **Why did it happen?**	It became easier after time for black families to become homesteaders. **What happened?**
Fliers promised black settlers their own land, to be paid in installments, as well as the opportunity to be part of new communities. **Why did it happen?**	All-black communities grew in the Midwest after the Civil War. **What happened?**

▲ **Graphic Organizer** 20

Research on Cause and Effect

"A great deal of our thought process has to do with cause and effect. To be fully fluent thinkers, children need to learn the logic of cause and effect."

Stanley Greenspan and Serena Weider,
Learning to Think Abstractly

Greenspan, Stanley, and Serena Welder. "Learning to Think Abstractly." *Scholastic Early Childhood Today* (May/June 1998).

Draw Conclusions

When students move beyond the literal meaning of a text to draw conclusions, they get more ideas from what they read and understand better the points an author is trying to make. Use the following routine to guide students in drawing conclusions.

1 DISCUSS DRAWING CONCLUSIONS

Tell students a conclusion is a sensible decision they reach based on details or facts in a story or an article. Explain when they draw conclusions, they think about information in the text and what they already know.

2 MODEL DRAWING A CONCLUSION

Model using your own experiences to draw a conclusion.

 Think Aloud **MODEL** The smell of peanuts and cotton candy filled the air. I heard clapping, I even heard loud bellows that sounded like elephants. I knew that a circus was nearby.

Discuss how you combined what you already knew with details (smell of peanuts and cotton candy, clapping, loud bellows) to draw a conclusion.

3 ASK QUESTIONS

Read aloud a passage and ask questions that foster drawing conclusions. For example: *What kind of person is the main character? How do you know? Why do you think the character acts this way?*

4 USE A GRAPHIC ORGANIZER

Have partners read both fiction and nonfiction passages. Students can ask each other questions that lead to drawing conclusions. Suggest that they use webs or charts to show the facts or details that support their conclusions.

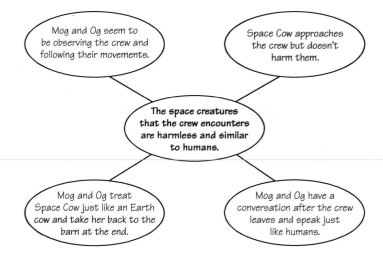

▲ **Graphic Organizer** 15

Research on Drawing Conclusions

"Inference is a mosaic, a dazzling constellation of thinking processes, but the tiles available to form each mosaic are limited, circumscribed. There must be a fusion of words on a page—and constraints of meaning they impose—and the experience and knowledge of the reader."

Ellin Oliver Keene and Susan Zimmerman,
Mosaic of Thought

Keen, Ellin Oliver, and Susan Zimmermann. *Mosaic of Thought: Teaching Comprehension in a Reader's Workshop.* Heinemann, 1997, p. 154.1992, p. 238.

Author's Purpose

Evaluating the author's purpose for writing helps students decide how quickly or slowly and carefully to read. Use this routine to teach author's purpose.

1 DISCUSS AUTHOR'S PURPOSE

Explain that the author's purpose is the author's reason or reasons for writing. Four common reasons for writing are to persuade, to inform, to entertain, or to express ideas or feelings.

2 EXPLAIN ITS USE

Tell students that one reason they need to consider the author's purpose is to adjust their reading rate. If a story is meant to be fun, they may decide to read quickly. If the author wants to explain how something works, they may need to read slowly and carefully.

3 ASK QUESTIONS

Authors don't usually state their purposes for writing, and they often have more than one purpose. Before, during, and after reading a selection, ask questions to help students draw conclusions about the author's purposes: *Why do you think the author wrote this story? What reasons might the author have for writing the story this way? What is the author trying to tell you? Why is the author telling you that?*

4 USE A GRAPHIC ORGANIZER

Have students predict the author's purpose before reading by previewing the title, illustrations, and graphics. During and after reading, students should check and confirm their predictions. Have them record ideas and evidence in a three-column chart.

	Author's Purpose	Why Do You Think So?
Before you read: What do you think it will be?	To tell about Thomas Edison's life and inventions	The pictures show Edison at different ages with his family and his lab. The pictures also show some of his inventions.
As you read: What do you think it is?	To show what a hard worker Thomas Edison was and what methods he used to invent	The author tells how Edison started inventing at a very young age, how he developed his inventing method, and how he worked longer and harder than anyone else.
After you read: What was it?	To paint a detailed picture of Thomas Edison as both an inventor and a man	The author describes Edison's inventions and how he came up with his ideas. The author also tells about Edison's family, his character, and how these factors contributed to his success as an inventor.

▲ **Graphic Organizer** 26

Research on Author's Purpose

"Younger and less proficient readers are unlikely to differentiate between 'study' reading and 'fun' reading."

Ruth Garner,
"Metacognition and Self-Monitoring Strategies"

Garner, Ruth. "Metacognition and Self-Monitoring Strategies." In *What Research Has to Say About Reading Instruction,* edited by S. J. Samuels and A. E. Farstrup. Second Edition. International Reading Association, 1992, p. 238.

Providing students with reading materials they can and want to read is an important step toward developing fluent readers. A running record allows you to determine each student's instructional and independent reading level. Information on how to take a running record is provided on pp. DI•59–DI•60.

Instructional Reading Level

Only approximately 1 in 10 words will be difficult when reading a selection from the Student Edition for students who are at grade level. (A typical sixth-grader reads approximately 130–150 words correct per minute.)

- Students reading at grade level should read regularly from the Student Edition and On-Level Leveled Readers, with teacher support as suggested in the Teacher's Editions.
- Students reading below grade level can read the Strategic Intervention Leveled Readers. Instructional plans can be found in the Teacher's Edition and the Leveled Reader Teaching Guide.
- Students who are reading above grade level can read the Advanced Leveled Readers. Instructional plans can be found in the Teacher's Edition and the Leveled Reader Teaching Guide.

Independent Reading Level

Students should read regularly in independent-level texts in which no more than approximately 1 in 20 words is difficult for the reader. Other factors that make a book easy to read include the student's interest in the topic, the amount of text on a page, how well illustrations support meaning, and the complexity and familiarity of the concepts. Suggested books for self-selected reading are provided for each lesson on p. TR14 in this Teacher's Edition.

Guide students in learning how to self-select books at their independent reading level. As you talk about a book with students, discuss the challenging concepts in it, list new words students find in sampling the book, and ask students about their familiarity with the topic. A blackline master to help students evaluate books for independent reading is provided on p. DI•58.

Self-Selected/Independent Reading

While oral reading allows you to assess students' reading level and fluency, independent reading is of crucial importance to students' futures as readers and learners. Students need to develop their ability to read independently for increasing amounts of time.

- Schedule a regular time for sustained independent reading in your classroom. During the year, gradually increase the amount of time devoted to independent reading.
- Help students track the amount of time they read independently and the number of pages they read in a given amount of time. Tracking will help motivate them to gradually increase their duration and speed. Blackline masters for tracking independent reading are provided on pp. DI•58 and TR15.

Choosing a Book for Independent Reading

When choosing a book, story, or article for independent reading, consider these questions:

_____ 1. Do I know something about this topic?

_____ 2. Am I interested in this topic?

_____ 3. Do I like reading this kind of book (fiction, fantasy, biography, or whatever)?

_____ 4. Have I read other things by this author? Do I like this author?

If you say "yes" to at least one of the questions above, continue:

_____ 5. In reading the first page, was only about 1 of every 20 words hard?

If you say "yes," continue:

_____ 6. Does the number of words on a page look about right to me?

If you say "yes," the book or article is probably at the right level for you.

Silent Reading

Record the date, the title of the book or article you read, the amount of time you spent reading, and the number of pages you read during that time.

Date	Title	Minutes	Pages

Taking a Running Record

A running record is an assessment of a student's oral reading accuracy and oral reading fluency. Reading accuracy is based on the number of words read correctly. Reading fluency is based on the reading rate (the number of words correct per minute) and the degree to which a student reads with a "natural flow."

How to Measure Reading Accuracy

1. Choose a grade-level text of about 80 to 120 words that is unfamiliar to the student.

2. Make a copy of the text for yourself. Make a copy for the student or have the student read aloud from a book.

3. Give the student the text and have the student read aloud. (You may wish to record the student's reading for later evaluation.)

4. On your copy of the text, mark any miscues or errors the student makes while reading. See the running record sample on page DI·60, which shows how to identify and mark miscues.

5. Count the total number of words in the text and the total number of errors made by the student. Note: If a student makes the same error more than once, such as mispronouncing the same word multiple times, count it as one error. Self-corrections do not count as actual errors. Use the following formula to calculate the percentage score, or accuracy rate:

$$\frac{\text{Total Number of Words} - \text{Total Number of Errors}}{\text{Total Number of Words}} \times 100 = \text{percentage score}$$

Interpreting the Results

- A student who reads **95–100%** of the words correctly is reading at an **independent level** and may need more challenging text.

- A student who reads **90–94%** of the words correctly is reading at an **instructional level** and will likely benefit from guided instruction.

- A student who reads **89%** or fewer of the words correctly is reading at a **frustrational level** and may benefit most from targeted instruction with lower-level texts and intervention.

How to Measure Reading Rate (wcpm)

1. Follow Steps 1–3 above.

2. Note the exact times when the student begins and finishes reading.

3. Use the following formula to calculate the number of words correct per minute (wcpm):

$$\frac{\text{Total Number of Words Read Correctly}}{\text{Total Number of Seconds}} \times 60 = \text{words correct per minute}$$

Interpreting the Results

An appropriate reading rate for a sixth-grader is 130–150 (wcpm).

Running Record Sample

Running Record Sample

Symbols

I'm late. I'm late. The words beat in Jenna's head as she rode her bicycle out of Central Park, dismounted, waited *(sc)* impatiently for the light to change, and then fast-walked it across the street. She *H* hurried into her apartment building and onto the elevator. It was six-thirty. She had said she would be back *at* ~~by~~ six.

She'd been with Rosa and Joanne, her best friends from elementary school, *she* and had lost track of time. On Monday, all three would be starting different */sools/* middle schools. They wouldn't see much of each other from then on, and Jenna *(had)* wanted to spend some time with them.

—From *Scatterbrain*
On-Level Reader 6.3.4

Accurate Reading
The student reads the word correctly.

Self-Correction
The student reads a word incorrectly but then corrects the error. Do not count self-corrections as actual errors. However, noting self-corrections will help you identify words the student finds difficult.

Hesitation
The student hesitates over a word, and the teacher provides the word. Wait several seconds before telling the student what the word is.

Substitution
The student substitutes words or parts of words for the words in the text.

Insertion
The student inserts words or parts of words that are not in the text.

Mispronunciation/Misreading
The student pronounces or reads a word incorrectly.

Omission
The student omits words or word parts.

Running Record Results	▶	**Reading Accuracy**	▶	**Reading Rate—**WCPM
Total Number of Words: **107**		$\frac{107-5}{107}$ x 100 = 95.3 = 95%		$\frac{102}{46}$ x 60 = 133.04 = 133 words correct per minute
Number of Errors: **5**				
Reading Time: **46 seconds**		Accuracy Percentage Score: **95%**		Reading Rate: **133** WCPM

Unit 1   Vocabulary Words   Spelling Words

Old Yeller

Vocabulary Words: lunging, nub, romping, rowdy, slung, speckled

Adding -ed and -ing

answered	qualified	omitted	skied
answering	qualifying	omitting	skiing
traveled	panicked	magnified	
traveling	panicking	magnifying	
chopped	interfered	patrolled	
chopping	interfering	patrolling	

Mother Fletcher's Gift

Vocabulary Words: apparently, fixtures, flimsy, incident, subscribe, survive

Short vowels

damage	mustard	glimpse	property
gentle	legend	strict	cannon
injury	clumsy	dungeon	
palace	message	fender	
cottage	modify	fantastic	
honesty	ruffle	dignity	

Viva New Jersey

Vocabulary Words: corridors, destination, groping, menacing, mongrel, persisted, pleas

Vowel sounds with r

porch	worth	attorney	particle
servant	purchase	barge	nervous
shore	kernel	detergent	
disturb	perhaps	corridor	
market	ignore	ornament	
margin	concern	artistic	

Saving the Rain Forests

Vocabulary Words: basin, charities, equator, erosion, evaporates, exported, industrial, recycled, tropics

Difficult spellings

fierce	soldier	deceit	pinnacle
weird	model	perception	preliminary
piece	multiple	vegetable	
perceive	fuel	preferable	
perfume	briefcase	rectangle	
preserve	retrieve	bushel	

When Crowbar Came

Vocabulary Words: aggressive, detect, dubiously, frustration, imprinted, materialize, migration, secretive, tolerated

Plural or possessive

country's	library's	crows
countries'	libraries'	witness's
countries	libraries	witnesses'
its	niece's	witnesses
ours	nieces'	secretary's
theirs	nieces	secretaries'
hers	crow's	

Unit 2

Unit 2	Vocabulary Words		Spelling Words

The Universe

Vocabulary Words: astronomers, collapse, collide, compact, galaxy, particles

Multisyllabic words

possibility	curiosity	correspon-dent	sophisti-cated
linear	organization		satisfac-tory
ridiculous	individual	cauliflower	
artificial	encyclopedia	optimistic	irritable
calculator	peony	enthusiastic	simultane-ously
competitive	tarantula		

Dinosaur Ghosts: The Mystery of Coelophysis

Vocabulary Words: fragile, poisonous, prey, sluggish, specimens, treacherous, volcanic

Latin roots I

suspend	reserve	novelty	induct
pendant	numerous	numerator	innovative
conductor	preserve	reservoir	
novel	pending	conservatory	
productive	pendulum	appendix	
numeral	deduction	impending	

A Week in the 1800s

Vocabulary Words: counselor, identity, physical, surplus, technology

Final syllable patterns

ancestor	encounter	abandon	cinnamon
hospital	shoulder	governor	interior
grumble	skeleton	endeavor	
sponsor	forbidden	outspoken	
superior	appetizer	durable	
escalator	identical	lengthen	

Good-bye to the Moon

Vocabulary Words: combustion, dingy, negotiate, traversed, waft, waning

Schwa

different	material	communi-cate	ingredients
sentence	complete		invitation
American	jewelry	hesitate	discipline
brilliant	dramatic	elementary	lasagna
substitute	instance	vitamin	desperate
opinion			

Egypt

Vocabulary Words: abundant, artifacts, decrees, eternity, immortal, receded, reigned

Suffixes -ian, -ant, -ent, -ist

musician	student	specialist	descen-dent
politician	patient	motorist	
novelist	resident	merchant	chemist
scientist	comedian	participant	
historian	vegetarian	occupant	
tenant	soloist	custodian	

Unit 3   Vocabulary Words   Spelling Words

Hatchet	hatchet ignite painstaking quill	registered smoldered stiffened	**Unusual spellings**	

crescent	parachute	exotic	rhinoceros
language	unique	brochure	bureau
vehicle	conquer	symptom	
exhibit	rhyme	antique	
examine	penguin	exhausted	
Michigan	exertion	heirloom	

When Marian Sang	application dramatic enraged formal momentous	opera prejudice privileged recital	**Multisyllabic words 2**

international	preparation	biodegrad- able	executive
prehistoric	Philadelphia	coordination	companion- ship
untrustworthy	promotional	compassion- ate	unthink- able
constellation	constitution	impossibility	predica- ment
honorary	unbreakable	entirety	
disagreement			

Learning to Swim	customary emphasized frantic	stunned treaded	**Using just enough letters**

nuclear	athletic	lantern	icicles
helicopter	escape	fulfill	escort
anxious	apologize	souvenir	
appreciate	Washington	tragedy	
plastic	pastime	sherbet	
familiar	exquisite	algebra	

Juan Verdades: The Man Who Couldn't Tell a Lie	confidently dismounted distressed flourish	fulfill permission repay vigorously	**Compound words**

field trip	thunder- storm	lightning rod	area code
someone	leftovers	myself	cliffhanger
snowflakes	cell phone	life jacket	wheelchair
polka dot	whitewash	bulldozer	hour hand
roller coaster		masterpiece	rain forest
solar system			

Elizabeth Blackwell: Medical Pioneer	absurd behalf candidate dean delirious	diploma hovers obedient reject	**Homophones**

heel	patients	aisle	bread
heal	patience	isle	bred
symbol	capitol	stationery	
cymbal	capital	stationary	
herd	straight	sheer	
heard	strait	shear	

Unit 4	Vocabulary Words		Spelling Words			
Into the Ice	conquer destiny expedition insulated	isolation navigator provisions verify	**Greek word parts**			
			hydrant chronic archive synonym antonym democracy	hydrogen aristocrat dehydrated chronicle hydroplane chronology	archaic homonym synchronize hydraulic archaeology anarchy	hydroelectric bureaucracy
The Chimpanzees I Love	captive companionship existence ordeal	primitive sanctuaries stimulating	**Prefixes dis-, de-, out-, un-**			
			discontent decline outward dispatch unwavering destruction	disintegrate outstanding uncommon outburst outrageous defensive	unappetizing disillusioned disarray unconscious outskirts unfasten	disenchanted decompose
Black Frontiers	bondage commissioned earthen encounter	homesteaders settlement	**Words with ci and ti**			
			precious commercial especially ancient gracious position	question suggestion friction lotion potion digestion	artificial glacier cautious efficient sensational vicious	official ration
Space Cadets	aliens barge hospitable molten	ore refrain universal version	**Related words I**			
			poem poetic direct direction origin original	combine combination repeat repetition critic criticize	history historic academy academic inspire inspiration	depart departure
Inventing the Future: A Photobiography of Thomas Alva Edison	converts devise efficiency generated	percentage proclaimed reproduce transmitted	**Word endings -ty, -ity, -tion**			
			electricity equality society specialty celebrity recognition	description reduction tradition loyalty security clarity	popularity certainty cruelty subscription reputation intention	deception penalty

Unit 5 — Vocabulary Words — Spelling Words

The View from Saturday

Vocabulary Words: accustomed, decline, former, presence, unaccompanied

Spelling Words — Suffixes -ate, -ive, -ship

activate, negative, friendship, objective, representative, attractive, creative, membership, partnership, compassionate, fortunate, considerate, secretive, scholarship, restrictive, affectionate, cooperative, originate, township, relationship

Harvesting Hope: The Story of Cesar Chavez

Vocabulary Words: access, authority, lush, obstacle, toll, torment, wilt

Spelling Words — Words from many cultures

ivory, cocoa, lilac, gorilla, pretzel, safari, kayak, crocodile, fiesta, dandelion, monsoon, slalom, amateur, boutique, suede, poncho, hammock, bungalow, sequin, yogurt

The River That Went to the Sky: A Story from Malawi

Vocabulary Words: densest, eaves, expanse, moisture, ventured

Spelling Words — Compound words

old-fashioned, daydream, summertime, follow-up, knee-deep, foothills, nevertheless, self-control, themselves, baby-sit, make-believe, sunburn, bloodhound, fine-tune, great-grandmother, roller-skating, folklore, empty-handed, self-esteem, runner-up

Gold

Vocabulary Words: characteristic, corrode, engulfed, exploit, extract, hoard

Spelling Words — Suffixes -ism, -age, -ure

mileage, moisture, heroism, storage, passage, organism, journalism, failure, mixture, postage, luggage, departure, patriotism, optimism, acreage, percentage, enclosure, voltage, temperature, mannerism

The House of Wisdom

Vocabulary Words: beacon, caravans, legacy, manuscripts, medieval, observatory, patron

Spelling Words — Prefixes bi-, tri-, uni-, semi-

bisect, triangle, universal, semicircle, biceps, bilingual, tricycle, university, semifinal, uniform, bifocals, reunion, unison, semicolon, unicorn, semiprivate, triplicate, semisweet, semiannual, biplane

Unit 6	Vocabulary Words		Spelling Words

Don Quixote and the Windmills

Vocabulary Words: lance, misfortune, quests, renewed, renowned, resound, squire

Suffixes -ary, -ery, -ory

bakery	directory	voluntary	secondary
scenery	pottery	honorary	bravery
vocabulary	discovery	satisfactory	
temporary	imaginary	introductory	
surgery	machinery	advisory	
inventory	nursery	bribery	

Ancient Greece

Vocabulary Words: architecture, democracy, empire, ideal, mythology

Related words II

alternate	normal	gene	crime
alternative	normality	genetic	criminal
office	restore	excel	
official	restoration	excellence	
economy	indicate	adapt	
economics	indicative	adaptation	

The All-American Slurp

Vocabulary Words: disgraced, progress, promoted, relish, retreat, revolting, unison

Easily confused words

proceed	further	college	envelope
precede	farther	collage	envelop
advise	personal	descent	
advice	personnel	dissent	
formerly	immigrate	persecution	
formally	emigrate	prosecution	

The Aztec News

Vocabulary Words: benefits, campaigns, comrades, enrich, foreigners, invaders

Word endings -ice, -ise, -ize

memorize	recognize	sympathize	vocalize
advertise	organize	enterprise	compromise
service	civilize	minimize	
realize	apprentice	cowardice	
justice	supervise	improvise	
exercise	sacrifice	paradise	

Where Opportunity Awaits

Vocabulary Words: burden, conformed, leisure, maintenance, rural, sufficient, urban

Latin roots II

vision	current	inspector	donor
suspect	revise	excursion	donation
visible	pardon	spectacle	
donate	prospective	concur	
spectator	provision	recur	
visor	supervisor	visitor	

Grade 5 Vocabulary

Use this list of fifth grade tested vocabulary words for review and leveled activities.

A

abdomen
accomplishments
achieved
acquainted
admiringly
adorn
advice
advised
agreement
algae
appreciate
architect
armor
artificial
assignment
astonished

B

background
barber
bass
behavior
benefactor
bleached
bluish
blunders
branded
bronze

C

cable
cannon
carcasses
cartwheels
caterpillar
cavities
choir
circumstances
civilization
clarinet
cleanse

cocoon
combination
complex
concealed
confidence
conservation
constructed
contribute
cramped
critical
criticizing
cruised

D

daintily
debris
decay
demonstrates
depressed
devastation
diplomat
disrespect
distribution
drenching
driftwood

E

economic
eerie
elbow
emerge
enables
encases
enthusiastic
environment
envy
episode
era
erected
essential
expanded
explosion

explosions
extinct

F

fashioned
fastball
fate
fearless
fidgety
fleeing
focus
forgetful
foundations

G

gait
glimmer
gnawed
gratitude
gravity
guaranteed
gymnastics

H

hammocks
handicapped
headland
hesitation
hideous
hustled
hydrogen

I

immigrants
independence
inspired
interior
intersection
investigation
issue

J

jammed

K

kelp

L

lair
lamented
landscape
lifeless
limelight
lingers
lullaby
luxury

M

magnified
midst
migrant
miniature
mocking
mold
monitors
mucus

N

newcomer
nighttime

O

occasion
ooze
outfield
overrun

P

parasites
peddler
permit

philosopher
pitch
plunged
pondered
precious
prehistoric
procedures
procession
profile
proportion

R

ravine
realm
reassembled
recommend
refugees
released
religious
representatives
reputation
resourceful
rival
robotic
role
rustling

Grade 5 Vocabulary

Use this list of fifth grade tested vocabulary words for review and leveled activities.

S

sacred
scarce
scoundrel
scrawled
scrawny
sea urchins
secondhand
sediment
serpent
severe
shellfish
sinew
sketched
skidded
slavery
somber
somersault
sonar
specialize
specific
spectacles
spoonful
starvation
steed
sterile
sternly
strategy
strict
subject
superiors
suspicions

T

teenager
therapist
thieving
throbbing
tidied
traditions
tundra
tweezers

U

unique
unscrewed

V

vacant
veins
visa

W

weakness
wheelchair
wincing
windup
withered
workshop
worshipped
worthless

Legibility

When handwriting is legible, letters, words, and numbers can be read easily. Handwriting that is not legible can cause problems for the reader and make communication difficult. Legibility can be improved if students are able to identify what is causing legibility problems in their handwriting. Focus instruction on the following five elements of legible handwriting.

Size

Letters need to be a consistent size. Students should focus on three things related to size: letters that reach to the top line, letters that reach halfway between the top and bottom line, and letters that extend below the bottom line. Writing letters the correct size can improve legibility. Often the letters that sit halfway between the top and bottom line cause the most problems. When students are writing on notebook paper, there is no middle line to help them size letters such as *m, a, i,* and *r* correctly. If students are having trouble, have them draw middle lines on their notebook paper.

Shape

Some of the most common handwriting problems are caused by forming letters incorrectly. These are the most common types of handwriting problems:

- Round letters such as *a, o,* and *g* are not closed.
- Looped letters such as *l, e,* and *b* have no loops.
- Letters such as *i, t,* and *d* have loops that shouldn't be there.

Have students examine one another's writing to indicate which words are hard to read, and then discuss which letters aren't formed correctly. They can then practice those particular letters.

Spacing

Letters within words should be evenly spaced. Too much or too little space can make writing difficult to read. A consistent amount of space should also be used between words in a sentence and between sentences. Suggest that students use the tip of their pencil to check the spacing between words and the width of their pencil to check the spacing between sentences.

Slant

Correct writing slant can be to the right or to the left, or there may be no slant at all. Slant becomes a legibility problem when letters are slanted in different directions. Suggest that students use a ruler to draw lines to determine if their slant is consistent.

Smoothness

Written letters should be produced with a line weight that is not too dark and not too light. The line should be smooth without any shaky or jagged edges. If students' writing is too dark, they are pressing too hard. If the writing is too light, they are not pressing hard enough. Usually shaky or jagged lines occur if students are unsure of how to form letters or if they are trying to draw letters rather than using a flowing motion.

D'Nealian™ Cursive Alphabet

a b c d e f g
h i j k l m n
o p q r s t u
v w x y z

A B C D E F G
H I J K L M N
O P Q R S T U
V W X Y Z . , ' ?

1 2 3 4 5 6
7 8 9 10

D'Nealian™ Alphabet

a b c d e f g h i

j k l m n o p q r s t

u v w x y z

A B C D E F G

H I J K L M N O

P Q R S T U V

W X Y Z . , ' ?

1 2 3 4 5 6

7 8 9 10

Manuscript Alphabet

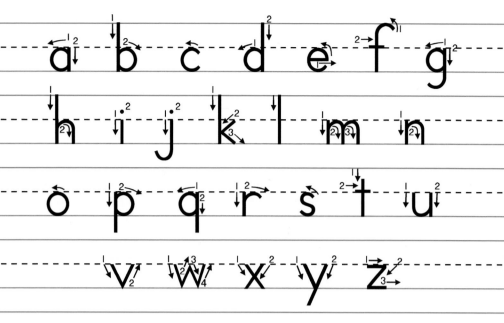

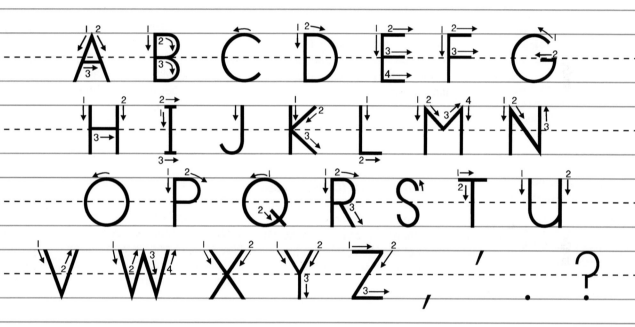

Unit 4 Explorers, Pioneers, and Discoverers

	Below-Level	On-Level	Advanced

Into the Ice

To Read Aloud!
Once Upon Ice: And Other Frozen Poems
by Jane Yolen (Boyds Mills Press, 1997) An intricate collection of winter poetry inspired by beautiful photography of ice formations. The whimsical, descriptive, and story-like quality to each of the poems makes this a wonderful read-aloud book.

Before Columbus: The Leif Eriksson Expedition: A True Adventure
by Elizabeth Cody Kimmel (Random House Books for Young Readers, 2003) A colorful account of Eriksson's life and explorations, including many photographs and lots of interesting information on the Vikings.

The Coast Mappers
by Taylor Morrison (Walter Lorraine Books, 2004) This book follows the trials and tribulations of George Davidson, selected by the U.S. Coast Survey to map America's Pacific Coast in 1850.

From Kansas to Cannibals: The Story of Osa Johnson
by Suzanne Middendorf (Avisson Press, Inc., 2001)
A biography of a fearless woman who explored cannibal headhunters with her husband in the South Seas in the early 20th century.

The Chimpanzees I Love

To Read Aloud!
The World According to Dog: Poems and Teen Voices
by Joyce Sidman (Houghton Mifflin, 2003) Teens speak in honest words about how pointless homework, mixed emotions, and heart-twisting crushes are brought to balance by dogs.

Sea Turtles
by Gail Gibbons (Holiday House, 1995) Bright illustrations and extremely accessible text combine to provide information about the physical characteristics and the life cycle of sea turtles.

Koko's Story: Dr. Francine Patterson
by Francine Patterson (Scholastic, 1987) This is a story about a young gorilla and her incredible relationship with the woman who is teaching her to speak through American Sign Language.

Animal Stories
compiled by Michael Morpurgo (Larousse Kingfisher Chambers, 1999) This collection contains excerpted novel pieces, short stories, and nonfiction.

Black Frontiers

To Read Aloud!
Sweet Words So Brave: The Story of African American Literature
by Barbara K. Curry and James Michael Brodie (Zino, 1996) Told as a grandfather's stories to his granddaughter, the text combines anecdotes from the authors' lives with discussions of their works.

Buffalo Bill Cody
by Charles Shields (Chelsea House Publications, 2001) The biographical account of a man who was instrumental in changing people's views of the West, through his famous stage-show.

Voyagers, Lumberjacks and Farmers: Pioneers of the Midwest
by Kieran Doherty (Oliver Press, 2003) This book includes profiles of eight people who played an important role in settling the Midwestern region of the United States.

The Black Soldier: 1492 to the Present
by Catherine Clinton (Houghton Mifflin, 2000) An historical account of African American participation in America's wars, highlighting the harsh realities and suffering these soldiers faced.

Space Cadets

To Read Aloud!
Do Your Ears Pop in Space? And 500 Other Surprising Questions About Space Travel
by R. Mike Mullane (John Wiley and Sons, 1997) The Space Shuttle astronaut tells readers what space travel is really like, as he talks about the adventures of a real astronaut.

Life on Mars
by David Getz (Henry Holt and Company, 2004) Through beautiful full-color illustrations and interviews with astronauts and NASA officials, David Getz tells a riveting story of the steps necessary to make a trip to Mars.

UFOs and Aliens
by Colin Wilson (DK Publishing, 1997) This book examines different explanations and evidence related to the question of the existence of intelligent life outside of Earth.

Aliens in the Family
by Margaret Mahy (Scholastic, 1988) When Jake Raven and her younger stepsiblings discover an alien boy named Bond, they become involved in a dangerous time and space war in order to help him get back home.

Inventing the Future

To Read Aloud!
Extraordinary Women of Medicine
by Darlene Stille (Children's Press, 1997) Florence Nightengale, Clara Barton, and dozens of other women who have achieved success in the medical field are profiled here.

1000 Inventions and Discoveries
by Roger Bridgman Bridgman highlights 1,000 groundbreaking moments in history, from ancient to modern times. The book gives the whole story behind each invention or discovery.

Girls Think of Everything: Stories of Ingenious Inventions by Women
by Katherine Thimmesh (Houghton Mifflin, 2000) An outstanding biography of women and girls who have changed the course of history with their inventions, including White-Out, the "space bumper," and the Snugli.

Motion Pictures: Making Cinema Magic
by Gina De Angelis (Oliver Press, 2004) A history of the lives and work of eight of the most important innovators in cinema history.

Unit 4 Reading Log

Name _____

Dates Read	Title and Author	What is it about?	How would you rate it?	Explain your rating.
From _____ to _____			Great 5 4 3 2 1 Awful	
From _____ to _____			Great 5 4 3 2 1 Awful	
From _____ to _____			Great 5 4 3 2 1 Awful	
From _____ to _____			Great 5 4 3 2 1 Awful	
From _____ to _____			Great 5 4 3 2 1 Awful	

Unit 4 Narrative Retelling Chart

Selection Title _____   Name _____   Date _____

Retelling Criteria/Teacher Prompt	Teacher-Aided Response	Student-Generated Response	Rubric Score (Circle one.)
Connections			
Has anything like this happened to you?			
How does this story remind you of other stories?			4 3 2 1
Author's Purpose			
Why do you think the author wrote this story?			
What was the author trying to tell us?			4 3 2 1
Characters			
Describe _____ (character's name) at the beginning and end of the story.			4 3 2 1
Setting			
Where and when did the story happen?			4 3 2 1
Plot			
Tell me what the story was about in a few sentences.			4 3 2 1

Summative Retelling Score   4   3   2   1

Comments _____
_____

Unit 4 Expository Retelling Chart

Selection Title ——————— **Name** ——————— **Date** ———————

Retelling Criteria/Teacher Prompt	Teacher-Aided Response	Student-Generated Response	Rubric Score (Circle one.)
Connections Did this selection make you think about something else you have read? What did you learn about as you read this selection?			4 3 2 1
Author's Purpose Why do you think the author wrote this selection?			4 3 2 1
Topic What was the selection mostly about?			4 3 2 1
Important Ideas What is important for me to know about ——— (topic)?			4 3 2 1
Conclusions What did you learn from reading this selection?			4 3 2 1

Summative Retelling Score   4   3   2   1

Comments ———————————————————

———————————————————

Reading

Concepts of Print and Print Awareness

	Pre-K	K	1	2	3	4	5	6
Develop awareness that print represents spoken language and conveys and preserves meaning	•	•	•					
Recognize familiar books by their covers; hold book right side up	•	•						
Identify parts of a book and their functions (front cover, title page/title, back cover, page numbers)	•	•	•					
Understand the concepts of letter, word, sentence, paragraph, and story	•	•	•					
Track print (front to back of book, top to bottom of page, left to right on line, sweep back left for next line)	•	•	•					
Match spoken to printed words	•	•	•					
Know capital and lowercase letter names and match them	•	• T	•					
Know the order of the alphabet		•	•					
Recognize first name in print	•	•	•					
Recognize the uses of capitalization and punctuation		•	•					
Value print as a means of gaining information	•	•	•					

Phonological and Phonemic Awareness

	Pre-K	K	1	2	3	4	5	6
Phonological Awareness								
Recognize and produce rhyming words	•	•	•					
Track and count each word in a spoken sentence and each syllable in a spoken word	•	•	•					
Segment and blend syllables in spoken words			•					
Segment and blend onset and rime in one-syllable words		•	•					
Recognize and produce words beginning with the same sound	•	•	•					
Identify beginning, middle, and/or ending sounds that are the same or different	•	•	•					
Understand that spoken words are made of sequences of sounds	•	•	•					
Phonemic Awareness								
Identify the position of sounds in words		•	•					
Identify and isolate initial, final, and medial sounds in spoken words	•	•	•					
Blend sounds orally to make words or syllables		•	•					
Segment a word or syllable into sounds; count phonemes in spoken words or syllables		•	•					
Manipulate sounds in words (add, delete, and/or substitute phonemes)	•	•	•					

Phonics and Decoding

	Pre-K	K	1	2	3	4	5	6
Phonics								
Understand and apply the **alphabetic principle** that spoken words are composed of sounds that are represented by letters	•	•	•					
Know letter-sound relationships		• T	• T	• T				
Blend sounds of letters to decode		•	• T	• T	• T			
Consonants, consonant blends, and consonant digraphs		•	• T	• T	• T			
Short, long, and r-controlled vowels; vowel digraphs; diphthongs; common vowel patterns			• T	• T	• T			
Phonograms/word families		•	•	•	•			
Word Structure								
Decode words with common word parts		•	• T	• T	• T	•	•	•
Base words and inflected endings			• T	• T	•	•	•	•
Contractions and compound words			• T	• T	• T	•	•	•
Suffixes and prefixes			• T	• T	• T	•	•	•
Greek and Latin roots						•	•	•
Blend syllables to decode words			• T	• T	• T	•	•	•
Decoding Strategies								
Blending strategy: Apply knowledge of letter-sound relationships to decode unfamiliar words		•	•	•	•			
Apply knowledge of word structure to decode unfamiliar words		•	•	•	•	•	•	•
Use context and syntax along with letter-sound relationships and word structure to decode		•	•	•	•	•	•	•
Self-correct			•	•	•	•	•	•

Fluency

	Pre-K	K	1	2	3	4	5	6
Read aloud fluently with accuracy, comprehension, appropriate pace/rate; with expression/intonation (prosody); with attention to punctuation and appropriate phrasing			• T	• T	• T	• T	• T	• T
Practice fluency in a variety of ways, including choral reading, partner/paired reading, Readers' Theater, repeated oral reading, and tape-assisted reading		•	•	•	•	•	•	•

• instructional opportunity   **T** tested in standardized test for

	Pre-K	K	1	2	3	4	5	6
ork toward appropriate fluency goals by the end of each grade			•T	•T	•T	•T	•T	•T
ead regularly in independent-level material			•	•	•	•	•	•
ead silently for increasing periods of time			•	•	•	•	•	•

Vocabulary (Oral and Written)

Word Recognition

	Pre-K	K	1	2	3	4	5	6
ecognize regular and irregular high-frequency words	•	•	•T	•T				
ecognize and understand selection vocabulary		•	•	•T	•	•	•	•
nderstand content-area vocabulary and specialized, technical, or topical words			•	•	•	•	•	•

Word Learning Strategies

	Pre-K	K	1	2	3	4	5	6
evelop vocabulary through direct instruction, concrete experiences, reading, listening to text read aloud	•	•	•	•	•	•	•	•
se knowledge of word structure to figure out meanings of words			•	•T	•T	•T	•T	•T
se context clues for meanings of unfamiliar words, multiple-meaning words, homonyms, homographs			•	•T	•T	•T	•T	•T
se grade-appropriate reference sources to learn word meanings	•	•	•	•	•T	•T	•T	•T
se picture clues to help determine word meanings	•	•	•	•	•			
se new words in a variety of contexts	•	•	•	•	•	•	•	•
xamine word usage and effectiveness		•	•	•	•	•	•	•
reate and use graphic organizers to group, study, and retain vocabulary			•	•	•	•	•	•

Extend Concepts and Word Knowledge

	Pre-K	K	1	2	3	4	5	6
cademic language	•	•	•	•	•	•	•	•
lassify and categorize	•	•	•	•	•	•	•	•
ntonyms and synonyms			•	•T	•T	•T	•T	•T
omographs, homonyms, and homophones			•	•T	•T	•T	•T	•T
ultiple-meaning words			•	•	•T	•T	•T	•T
elated words and derivations					•	•	•	•
nalogies						•	•	
onnotation/denotation						•	•	•
gurative language and idioms				•	•	•	•	•
escriptive words (location, size, color, shape, number, ideas, feelings)	•	•	•	•	•	•	•	•
igh-utility words (shapes, colors, question words, position/directional words, and so on)	•	•	•	•				
me and order words	•	•	•	•	•	•	•	•
ansition words						•	•	•
ord origins: Etymologies/word histories; words from other languages, regions, or cultures					•	•	•	•
hortened forms: abbreviations, acronyms, clipped words			•	•	•	•	•T	

Text Comprehension

Comprehension Strategies

	Pre-K	K	1	2	3	4	5	6
review the text and formulate questions	•	•	•	•	•	•	•	•
et and monitor purpose for reading and listening	•	•	•	•	•	•	•	•
ctivate and use prior knowledge	•	•	•	•	•	•	•	•
ake predictions	•	•	•	•	•	•	•	•
onitor comprehension and use fix-up strategies to resolve difficulties in meaning: adjust reading rate, reread and read on, seek help from reference sources and/or other people, skim and scan, summarize, se text features			•	•	•	•	•	•
reate and use graphic and semantic organizers		•	•	•	•	•	•	•
nswer questions (text explicit, text implicit, scriptal), including *who, what, when, where, why, what if, how*	•	•	•	•	•	•	•	•
Look back in text for answers			•	•	•	•	•	•
Answer test-like questions			•	•	•	•	•	•
enerate clarifying questions, including *who, what, where, when, how, why,* and *what if*	•	•	•	•	•	•	•	•
ecognize text structure: story and informational (cause/effect, chronological, compare/contrast, escription, problem/solution, proposition/support)	•	•	•	•	•	•	•	•
ummarize text		•	•	•	•	•	•	•
Recall and retell stories	•	•	•	•	•	•	•	•
Identify and retell important/main ideas (nonfiction)	•	•	•	•	•	•	•	•
Identify and retell new information			•	•	•	•	•	•
isualize; use mental imagery		•	•	•	•	•	•	•
se strategies flexibly and in combination			•	•	•	•	•	•

Comprehension Skills

	Pre-K	K	1	2	3	4	5	6
Author's purpose			•T	•T	•T	•T	•T	•T
Author's viewpoint/bias/perspective					•	•	•	•T
Categorize and classify	•	•	•	•				
Cause and effect		•	•T	•T	•T	•T	•T	•T
Compare and contrast	•	•	•T	•T	•T	•T	•T	•T
Details and facts		•	•	•	•	•	•	•
Draw conclusions		•	•T	•T	•T	•T	•T	•T
Fact and opinion				•T	•T	•T	•T	•T
Follow directions/steps in a process	•	•	•	•	•	•	•	•
Generalize					•T	•T	•T	•T
Graphic sources		•	•	•		•T	•T	•T
Main idea and supporting details		•T	•T	•T	•T	•T	•T	•T
Paraphrase			•	•	•	•	•	•
Persuasive devices and propaganda			•	•	•	•	•	•
Realism/fantasy	•	•	•T	•T	•T	•	•	
Sequence of events	•	•T	•T	•T	•T	•T	•T	•T

Higher Order Thinking Skills

	Pre-K	K	1	2	3	4	5	6
Analyze				•	•	•	•	•
Describe and connect the essential ideas, arguments, and perspectives of a text			•	•	•	•	•	•
Draw inferences, conclusions, or generalizations, support them with textual evidence and prior knowledge	•	•	•	•	•	•	•	•
Evaluate and critique ideas and text				•	•	•	•	•
Hypothesize							•	•
Make judgments about ideas and text				•	•	•		
Organize and synthesize ideas and information				•			•	•

Literary Analysis, Response, & Appreciation

	Pre-K	K	1	2	3	4	5	6
Genre and Its Characteristics								
Recognize characteristics of a variety of genre	•	•	•	•	•	•	•	•
Distinguish fiction from nonfiction	•	•	•	•	•	•	•	•
Identify characteristics of literary texts, including drama, fantasy, traditional tales		•	•	•	•	•	•	•
Identify characteristics of nonfiction texts, including biography, interviews, newspaper articles		•	•	•	•	•	•	•
Identify characteristics of poetry and song, including nursery rhymes, limericks, blank verse	•	•	•	•	•	•	•	•
Literary Elements and Story Structure								
Character	•	•T	•T	•T	•T	•T	•T	•
Recognize and describe traits, actions, feelings, and motives of characters		•	•	•	•	•	•	•
Analyze characters' relationships, changes, and points of view		•	•	•	•	•	•	•
Analyze characters' conflicts				•		•	•	•
Plot and plot structure	•	•T	•T	•T	•T	•T	•T	•
Beginning, middle, end	•	•	•	•	•			
Goal and outcome or problem and solution/resolution		•	•	•	•	•	•	•
Rising action, climax, and falling action/denouement; setbacks						•	•	•
Setting	•	•T	•T	•T	•T	•T	•	•
Relate setting to problem/solution						•	•	•
Explain ways setting contributes to mood						•	•	•
Theme		•	•T	•T	•	•	•	•
Use Literary Elements and Story Structure	•	•	•	•	•	•	•	•
Analyze and evaluate author's use of setting, plot, character					•	•	•	•
Identify similarities and differences of characters, events, and settings within or across selections/cultures	•	•	•	•	•	•	•	•
Literary Devices								
Allusion								•
Dialect						•	•	•
Dialogue and narration	•	•	•	•	•	•	•	•
Exaggeration/hyperbole						•	•	•
Figurative language: idiom, jargon, metaphor, simile, slang			•	•	•	•	•	•

• instructional opportunity   **T** tested in standardized test for

	Pre-K	K	1	2	3	4	5	6
Flashback						•	•	•
Foreshadowing							•	•
Formal and informal language				•	•	•	•	•
Humor					•	•	•	•
Imagery and sensory words			•	•		•	•	•
Mood				•	•		•	•
Personification				•	•	•	•	•
Point of view (first person, third person, omniscient)					•	•	•	•
Puns and word play				•	•	•	•	•
Sound devices and poetic elements	•	•	•	•	•	•	•	•
Alliteration, assonance, onomatopoeia	•	•	•	•	•	•	•	•
Rhyme, rhythm, repetition, and cadence	•	•	•	•	•	•	•	•
Word choice				•	•	•	•	•
Symbolism				•	•	•	•	•
Theme							•	•

Author's and Illustrator's Craft

	Pre-K	K	1	2	3	4	5	6
Distinguish the roles of author and illustrator	•	•	•	•				
Recognize/analyze author's and illustrator's craft or style			•	•	•	•	•	•

Literary Response

	Pre-K	K	1	2	3	4	5	6
Collect, talk, and write about books	•	•	•	•	•	•	•	•
Reflect on reading and respond (through talk, movement, art, and so on)	•	•	•	•	•	•	•	•
Ask and answer questions about text	•	•	•	•	•	•	•	•
Write about what is read	•	•	•	•	•	•	•	•
Use evidence from the text to support opinions, interpretations, or conclusions			•	•	•	•	•	•
Support ideas through reference to other texts and personal knowledge				•	•	•	•	•
Locate materials on related topic, theme, or idea				•	•	•	•	•
Generate alternative endings to plots and identify the reason for, and the impact of, the alternatives	•	•	•			•	•	•
Synthesize and extend the literary experience through creative responses	•	•	•			•	•	•
Make connections: text to self, text to text, text to world	•	•	•			•	•	•
Evaluate and critique the quality of the literary experience				•	•	•	•	•
Offer observations, react, speculate in response to text				•	•	•	•	•

Literary Appreciation/Motivation

	Pre-K	K	1	2	3	4	5	6
Show an interest in books and reading; engage voluntarily in social interaction about books	•	•	•	•	•	•	•	•
Choose text by drawing on personal interests, relying on knowledge of authors and genres, estimating text difficulty, and using recommendations of others	•	•	•	•	•	•	•	•
Read a variety of grade-level appropriate narrative and expository texts		•	•	•	•	•	•	•
Read from a wide variety of genres for a variety of purposes	•	•	•	•	•	•	•	•
Read independently		•	•	•	•	•	•	•
Establish familiarity with a topic		•	•	•	•	•	•	•

Cultural Awareness

	Pre-K	K	1	2	3	4	5	6
Develop attitudes and abilities to interact with diverse groups and cultures	•	•	•	•	•	•	•	•
Connect experiences and ideas with those from a variety of languages, cultures, customs, perspectives	•	•	•	•	•	•	•	•
Understand how attitudes and values in a culture or during a period in time affect the writing from that culture or time period						•	•	•
Compare language and oral traditions (family stories) that reflect customs, regions, and cultures	•	•	•			•	•	•
Recognize themes that cross cultures and bind them together in their common humanness						•	•	•

Language Arts

Writing	Pre-K	K	1	2	3	4	5	6
Concepts of Print for Writing								
Develop gross and fine motor skills and hand/eye coordination	•	•	•					
Print own name and other important words	•	•	•					
Write using pictures, some letters, and transitional spelling to convey meaning	•	•	•					
Dictate messages or stories for others to write	•	•	•					

	Pre-K	K	1	2	3	4	5	6
Create own written texts for others to read; write left to right on a line and top to bottom on a page	•	•	•					
Participate in shared and interactive writing	•	•	•					

Traits of Writing

Focus/Ideas

	Pre-K	K	1	2	3	4	5	6
Maintain focus and sharpen ideas		•	•	•	•	•	•	•
Use sensory details and concrete examples; elaborate		•	•	•	•	•	•	•
Delete extraneous information			•	•	•	•	•	•
Rearrange words and sentences to improve meaning and focus				•	•	•	•	•
Use strategies, such as tone, style, consistent point of view, to achieve a sense of completeness						•	•	•

Organization/Paragraphs

	Pre-K	K	1	2	3	4	5	6
Use graphic organizers to group ideas		•	•	•	•	•	•	•
Write coherent paragraphs that develop a central idea		•	•	•	•	•	•	•
Use transitions to connect sentences and paragraphs		•	•	•	•	•	•	•
Select an organizational structure based on purpose, audience, length						•	•	•
Organize ideas in a logical progression, such as chronological order or by order of importance	•	•	•	•	•	•	•	•
Write introductory, supporting, and concluding paragraphs						•	•	•
Write a multi-paragraph paper				•	•	•	•	•

Voice

	Pre-K	K	1	2	3	4	5	6
Develop personal, identifiable voice and an individual tone/style		•	•	•	•	•	•	•
Maintain consistent voice and point of view						•	•	•
Use voice appropriate to audience, message, and purpose						•	•	•

Word Choice

	Pre-K	K	1	2	3	4	5	6
Use clear, precise, appropriate language		•	•	•	•	•	•	•
Use figurative language and vivid words				•	•	•	•	•
Select effective vocabulary using word walls, dictionary, or thesaurus		•	•	•	•	•	•	•

Sentences

	Pre-K	K	1	2	3	4	5	6
Combine, elaborate, and vary sentences		•	•	•	•	•	•	•
Write topic sentence, supporting sentences with facts and details, and concluding sentence			•	•	•	•	•	•
Use correct word order				•	•	•	•	•
Use parallel structure in a sentence						•	•	•

Conventions

	Pre-K	K	1	2	3	4	5	6
Use correct spelling and grammar; capitalize and punctuate correctly		•	•	•	•	•	•	•
Correct sentence fragments and run-ons					•	•	•	•
Use correct paragraph indention				•	•	•	•	•

The Writing Process

	Pre-K	K	1	2	3	4	5	6
Prewrite using various strategies	•	•	•	•	•	•	•	•
Develop first drafts of single- and multiple-paragraph compositions		•	•	•	•	•	•	•
Revise drafts for varied purposes, including to clarify and to achieve purpose, sense of audience, precise word choice, vivid images, and elaboration	•	•	•	•	•	•	•	•
Edit and proofread for correct spelling, grammar, usage, and mechanics		•	•	•	•	•	•	•
Publish own work	•	•	•	•	•	•	•	•

Types of Writing

	Pre-K	K	1	2	3	4	5	6
Narrative writing (such as personal narratives, stories, biographies, autobiographies)	•	•	• T	• T	• T	• T	• T	• T
Expository writing (such as essays, directions, explanations, news stories, research reports, summaries)		•	• T	• T	• T	• T	• T	• T
Descriptive writing (such as labels, captions, lists, plays, poems, response logs, songs)	•	•	• T	• T	• T	• T	• T	• T
Persuasive writing (such as ads, editorials, essays, letters to the editor, opinions, posters)		•	• T	• T	• T	• T	• T	• T

Writing Habits and Practices

	Pre-K	K	1	2	3	4	5	6
Write on a daily basis	•	•	•	•	•	•	•	•
Use writing as a tool for learning and self-discovery				•	•	•	•	•
Write independently for extended periods of time			•	•	•	•	•	•

ENGLISH LANGUAGE CONVENTIONS in WRITING and SPEAKING

	Pre-K	K	1	2	3	4	5	6

Grammar and Usage in Speaking and Writing

Sentences

	Pre-K	K	1	2	3	4	5	6
Types (declarative, interrogative, exclamatory, imperative)	•	•	• T	• T	• T	• T	• T	• T
Structure (simple, compound, complex, compound-complex)	•	•	•	•	•	• T	• T	• T

• instructional opportunity   T tested in standardized test for

Skill	Pre-K	K	1	2	3	4	5	6
Parts (subjects/predicates: complete, simple, compound; phrases; clauses)				• T	•	• T	• T	• T
Fragments and run-on sentences		•	•	•	•	•	•	•
Combine sentences, elaborate			•	•	•	•	•	•
arts of speech: nouns, verbs and verb tenses, adjectives, adverbs, pronouns and antecedents, onjunctions, prepositions, interjections		•	• T	• T	• T	• T	• T	• T
sage								
Subject-verb agreement		•	• T	•	•	• T	• T	• T
Pronoun agreement/referents			• T	•	•	• T	• T	• T
Misplaced modifiers						•	• T	• T
Misused words					•	•	•	• T
Negatives; avoid double negatives					•	•	•	•

Mechanics in Writing

Skill	Pre-K	K	1	2	3	4	5	6
apitalization (first word in sentence, proper nouns and adjectives, pronoun *I*, titles, and so on)	•	•	• T	• T	• T	• T	• T	• T
unctuation (apostrophe, comma, period, question mark, exclamation mark, quotation marks, and so on)		•	• T	• T	• T	• T	• T	• T

Spelling

Skill	Pre-K	K	1	2	3	4	5	6
pell independently by using pre-phonetic knowledge, knowledge of letter names, sound-letter knowledge	•	•	•	•	•	•	•	•
se sound-letter knowledge to spell	•	•	•	•	•	•	•	•
Consonants: single, double, blends, digraphs, silent letters, and unusual consonant spellings		•	•	•	•	•	•	•
Vowels: short, long, *r*-controlled, digraphs, diphthongs, less common vowel patterns, schwa		•	•	•	•	•	•	•
se knowledge of word structure to spell			•	•	•	•	•	•
Base words and affixes (inflections, prefixes, suffixes), possessives, contractions and compound words			•	•	•	•	•	•
Greek and Latin roots, syllable patterns, multisyllabic words			•	•	•	•	•	•
pell high-frequency, irregular words		•	•	•	•	•	•	•
pell frequently misspelled words correctly, including homophones or homonyms			•	•	•	•	•	•
se meaning relationships to spell					•	•	•	•

Handwriting

Skill	Pre-K	K	1	2	3	4	5	6
ain increasing control of penmanship, including pencil grip, paper position, posture, stroke	•	•	•	•				
rite legibly, with control over letter size and form; letter slant; and letter, word, and sentence spacing		•	•	•	•	•	•	•
rite lowercase and capital letters	•	•	•	•				
Manuscript	•	•	•	•	•	•	•	•
Cursive				•	•	•	•	•
rite numerals	•	•	•					

istening and Speaking

istening Skills and Strategies

Skill	Pre-K	K	1	2	3	4	5	6
sten to a variety of presentations attentively and politely	•	•	•	•	•	•	•	•
elf-monitor comprehension while listening, using a variety of skills and strategies	•	•	•	•	•	•	•	•
sten for a purpose								
For enjoyment and appreciation	•	•	•	•	•	•	•	•
To expand vocabulary and concepts	•	•	•	•	•	•	•	•
To obtain information and ideas	•	•	•	•	•	•	•	•
To follow oral directions	•	•	•	•	•	•	•	•
To answer questions and solve problems	•	•	•	•	•	•	•	•
To participate in group discussions	•	•	•	•	•	•	•	•
To identify and analyze the musical elements of literary language	•	•	•	•	•	•	•	•
To gain knowledge of one's own culture, the culture of others, and the common elements of cultures	•	•	•	•	•	•	•	•
ecognize formal and informal language			•	•	•	•	•	•
sten critically to distinguish fact from opinion and to analyze and evaluate ideas, information, experiences	•			•	•	•	•	•
valuate a speaker's delivery				•	•	•	•	•
terpret a speaker's purpose, perspective, persuasive techniques, verbal and nonverbal messages, and se of rhetorical devices						•	•	•

peaking Skills and Strategies

Skill	Pre-K	K	1	2	3	4	5	6
peak clearly, accurately, and fluently, using appropriate delivery for a variety of audiences, and purposes	•	•	•	•	•	•	•	•
se proper intonation, volume, pitch, modulation, and phrasing		•	•	•	•	•	•	•
peak with a command of standard English conventions	•	•	•	•	•	•	•	•
se appropriate language for formal and informal settings	•	•	•	•	•	•	•	•

	Pre-K	K	1	2	3	4	5	6
Speak for a purpose								
To ask and answer questions	•	•	•	•	•	•	•	•
To give directions and instructions	•	•	•	•	•	•	•	•
To retell, paraphrase, or explain information		•	•	•	•	•	•	•
To communicate needs and share ideas and experiences	•	•	•		•	•	•	•
To participate in conversations and discussions	•	•	•	•	•	•	•	•
To express an opinion	•	•	•	•	•	•	•	•
To deliver dramatic recitations, interpretations, or performances	•	•	•	•	•	•	•	•
To deliver presentations or oral reports (narrative, descriptive, persuasive, and informational)	•	•	•	•	•	•	•	•
Stay on topic	•	•	•	•	•	•	•	•
Use appropriate verbal and nonverbal elements (such as facial expression, gestures, eye contact, posture)	•	•	•	•	•	•	•	•
Identify and/or demonstrate methods to manage or overcome communication anxiety						•	•	•

Viewing/Media	Pre-K	K	1	2	3	4	5	6
Interact with and respond to a variety of print and non-print media for a range of purposes	•	•	•	•	•	•	•	•
Compare and contrast print, visual, and electronic media					•	•	•	•
Analyze and evaluate media			•	•	•	•	•	•
Recognize purpose, bias, propaganda, and persuasive techniques in media messages			•	•	•	•	•	•

Research and Study Skills

Understand and Use Graphic Sources	Pre-K	K	1	2	3	4	5	6
Advertisement			•	•	•	•	•	•
Chart/table	•	•	•	•	•	•	•	•
Diagram/scale drawing			•	•	•	•	•	•
Graph (bar, circle, line, picture)			•	•	•	•	•	•
Illustration, photograph, caption, label	•	•	•	•	•	•	•	•
Map/globe	•	•	•	•	•	•	•	•
Order form/application						•	•	•
Poster/announcement	•	•	•	•	•	•	•	
Schedule						•	•	•
Sign	•	•	•	•		•		
Time line				•	•	•	•	•

Understand and Use Reference Sources	Pre-K	K	1	2	3	4	5	6
Know and use parts of a book to locate information	•	•	•	•	•	•	•	
Use alphabetical order			•	•	•	•		
Understand purpose, structure, and organization of reference sources (print, electronic, media, Internet)	•	•	•	•	•	•	•	•
Almanac						•	•	•
Atlas		•	•	•	•	•	•	•
Card catalog/library database				•	•	•	•	•
Dictionary/glossary		•	•	•	•T	•T	•T	•T
Encyclopedia			•	•	•	•	•	•
Magazine/periodical				•	•	•	•	•
Newspaper and newsletter			•		•	•	•	•
Readers' Guide to Periodical Literature						•	•	•
Technology (computer and non-computer electronic media)		•	•	•	•	•	•	•
Thesaurus				•	•	•	•	•

Study Skills and Strategies	Pre-K	K	1	2	3	4	5	6
Adjust reading rate			•	•	•	•	•	•
Clarify directions	•	•	•	•	•	•	•	•
Outline				•	•	•	•	•
Skim and scan			•	•	•	•	•	•
SQP3R						•	•	•
Summarize		•	•	•	•	•	•	•
Take notes, paraphrase, and synthesize			•	•	•	•	•	•
Use graphic and semantic organizers to organize information		•	•	•	•	•	•	•

• instructional opportunity   **T** tested in standardized test for

Test-Taking Skills and Strategies	Pre-K	K	1	2	3	4	5	6
Understand the question, the vocabulary of tests, and key words			•	•	•	•	•	•
Answer the question; use information from the text (stated or inferred)		•	•	•	•	•	•	•
Write across texts				•	•	•	•	•
Complete the sentence				•	•	•	•	•

Technology/New Literacies	Pre-K	K	1	2	3	4	5	6
Non-Computer Electronic Media								
Audio tapes/CDs, video tapes/DVDs	•	•	•	•	•	•	•	
Film, television, and radio		•	•	•	•	•	•	•
Computer Programs and Services: Basic Operations and Concepts								
Use accurate computer terminology	•	•	•	•	•	•	•	•
Create, name, locate, open, save, delete, and organize files		•	•	•	•	•	•	•
Use input and output devices (such as mouse, keyboard, monitor, printer, touch screen)	•	•	•	•	•	•	•	•
Use basic keyboarding skills		•	•	•	•	•	•	•
Responsible Use of Technology Systems and Software								
Work cooperatively and collaboratively with others; follow acceptable use policies	•	•	•	•	•	•	•	•
Recognize hazards of Internet searches		•	•	•	•	•	•	•
Respect intellectual property					•	•	•	•
Information and Communication Technologies: Information Acquisition								
Use electronic web (non-linear) navigation, online resources, databases, keyword searches				•	•	•	•	•
Use visual and non-textual features of online resources	•	•	•	•	•	•	•	•
Internet inquiry			•	•	•	•	•	•
Identify questions			•	•	•	•	•	•
Locate, select, and collect information			•	•	•	•	•	•
Analyze information			•	•	•	•	•	•
Evaluate electronic information sources for accuracy, relevance, bias				•	•	•	•	•
Understand bias/subjectivity of electronic content (about this site, author search, date created)					•	•	•	•
Synthesize information					•	•	•	•
Communicate findings			•	•	•	•	•	•
Use fix-up strategies (such as clicking *Back, Forward,* or *Undo;* redoing a search; trimming the URL)			•	•	•	•	•	•
Communication								
Collaborate, publish, present, and interact with others		•	•	•	•	•	•	•
Use online resources (e-mail, bulletin boards, newsgroups)			•	•	•	•	•	•
Use a variety of multimedia formats			•	•	•	•	•	•
Problem Solving								
Select the appropriate software for the task	•	•	•	•	•	•	•	•
Use technology resources for solving problems and making informed decisions			•	•	•	•	•	•
Determine when technology is useful				•	•	•	•	•

The Research Process	Pre-K	K	1	2	3	4	5	6
Choose and narrow the topic; frame and revise questions for inquiry		•	•	•	•	•	•	•
Choose and evaluate appropriate reference sources		•	•	•	•	•	•	•
Locate and collect information	•	•	•	•	•	•	•	•
Take notes/record findings				•	•	•	•	•
Combine and compare information				•	•	•	•	•
Evaluate, interpret, and draw conclusions about key information		•	•	•	•	•	•	•
Summarize information		•	•	•	•	•	•	•
Make an outline				•	•	•	•	•
Organize content systematically		•	•	•	•	•	•	•
Communicate information		•	•	•	•	•	•	•
Write and present a report			•	•	•	•	•	•
Include citations						•	•	•
Respect intellectual property/plagiarism						•	•	•
Select and organize visual aids		•	•	•	•	•	•	•

ACKNOWLEDGMENTS

Teacher's Edition

Text

KWL Strategy: The KWL Interactive Reading Strategy was developed and is used by permission of Donna Ogle, National-Louis University, Evanston, Illinois, co-author of *Reading Today and Tomorrow*, Holt, Rinehart & Winston Publishers, 1988. (See also *The Reading Teacher*, February 1986, pp. 564–570.)

Page 408m: From "The South Pole" from *20,000 Leagues Under the Sea* by Jules Verne. Copyright © 1946 by The World Publishing Company. Reprinted by permission of The World Publishing Company.

Page 430m: From "Something in the Elephants' Silence" from *Secrets of Sound: Studying the Calls and Songs of Whales, Elephants, and Birds* by April Pulley Sayre. Copyright © 2002 by April Pulley Sayre. Reprinted by permission of Houghton Mifflin Company. All rights reserved.

Page 478m: From *Mush, a Dog from Space* by Daniel Pinkwater. Copyright © 1995 by Daniel Pinkwater. Reprinted with the permission of Atheneum Books for Young Readers, an imprint of Simon & Schuster Children's Publishing Division.

Page 500m: From *Inventors for Medicine* by Edward F. Dolan, Crown Publishers, 1969.

Illustration

Cover Dan Cosgrove
356i Joseph Fiedler

Photographs

Every effort has been made to secure permission and provide appropriate credit for photographic material. The publisher deeply regrets any omission and pledges to correct errors called to its attention in subsequent editions.

Unless otherwise acknowledged, all photographs are the property of Scott Foresman, a division of Pearson Education.

Photo locators denoted as follows: Top (T), Center (C), Bottom (B), Left (L), Right (R), Background (Bkgd)

18m Getty Images

42m (Bkgd) Getty Images, (TR) Getty Images, (T) Hemera Technologies

87l (BC) ©Royalty-Free/Corbis, (B) Comstock Images/Getty Images

88m (T) Getty Images, (BR) Digital Vision

112m Brand X Pictures

137n Getty Images

146m Getty Images

148j NASA

220m Brand X Pictures

223n Getty Images

240j Getty Images

322m Getty Images

346m Getty Images

408m Getty Images

430m Getty Images

456m Getty Images

536m Hemera Technologies

582m Getty Images

600m ©Dover Publications

643m (TC) Brand X Pictures, (Bkgd) Getty Images

700m (C) ©Dover Publications, (Bkgd) Getty Images

724m ©Dover Publications

TEACHER NOTES